SIXTH EDITION

SECURITY ANALYSIS AND PORTFOLIO MANAGEMENT

Donald E. Fischer

Professor of Finance
University of Texas—Tyler

Ronald J. Jordan

President
Financial Resources Management Corporation
Hartford, Connecticut

Prentice Hall, Englewood Cliffs, New Jersey 07632

Library of Congress Cataloging-in-Publication Data

Fischer, Donald E.
    Security analysis and portfolio management / Donald E. Fischer,
Ronald J. Jordan. — 6th ed.
        p.   cm.
    Includes bibliographical references and index.
    ISBN 0-13-157256-3
    1. Investment analysis.   2. Portfolio management.   I. Jordan,
Ronald J.   II. Title.
HG4529.F57   1995
332.63′2—dc20   94-19435
                                                                  CIP

To our parents,
to Mary,
to Sheryl,
and Noah, Joshua,
and Geremy

Acquisitions editor: Leah Jewell
Assistant editor: Teresa Cohan
Project manager: Robert C. Walters, PMI
Interior design: Suzanne Behnke
Design director: Linda Fiordilino
Cover design: Linda Fiordilino/Maria Lange
Cover illustration: Tom Bookwalter
Production coordinator: Patrice Fraccio

© 1995, 1991, 1987, 1983, 1979, 1975 by Prentice-Hall, Inc.
A Simon & Schuster Company
Englewood Cliffs, New Jersey 07632

Printed in the United States of America
10 9 8 7 6 5 4 3 2 1

ISBN 0-13-157256-3

Prentice-Hall International (UK) Limited, *London*
Prentice-Hall of Australia Pty. Limited, *Sydney*
Prentice-Hall Canada, Inc., *Toronto*
Prentice-Hall Hispanoamericana, S.A., *Mexico*
Prentice-Hall of India Private Limited, *New Delhi*
Prentice-Hall of Japan, Inc., *Tokyo*
Simon & Schuster Asia Pte. Ltd., *Singapore*
Editora Prentice-Hall do Brasil, Ltda., *Rio de Janeiro*

CONTENTS

15 TECHNICAL ANALYSIS   510

16 EFFICIENT-MARKET THEORY   538

17 PORTFOLIO ANALYSIS   559

18 PORTFOLIO SELECTION   590

19 CAPITAL MARKET THEORY   636

20 MANAGED PORTFOLIOS AND PERFORMANCE MEASUREMENTS   651

PREFACE

This book celebrates its twentieth anniversary with the publication of this edition. The longevity of the text can be attributed to an expansive list of loyal academics and professionals both here and abroad who have found it readable, real world, and rational in its approach.

This text is about investing in securities. It is aimed at providing a comprehensive introduction to the areas of security analysis and portfolio management. The text emphasizes the "how-to" aspects of the subject by using detailed real world examples throughout. Above all we have tried to make the contents as readable, understandable, and nonmathematical as possible. Only simple algebra and some elementary statistics are used in the book. For those who dread mathematics, even the algebra and the statistics are explained in lay terms.

In the past several decades the fields of security analysis and portfolio management have changed from a completely descriptive institutional body of literature to a highly formalized quantitative area of study. We have attempted to blend the best and most relevant pieces from the evolving field of endeavor into a meaningful, cohesive framework of analysis that would be of interest to the student of business and finance, the practitioner in the field, and the informed investor.

The text starts with the premise that the reader has no knowledge of investments but some knowledge of economics and accounting. As such, it should serve for an introductory course in investment analysis at either the undergraduate or graduate level. The material builds in difficulty as the chapters progress. The text is designed to be followed as presented; however, some users will prefer to cover Chapters 16 to 20 early in the course. This can be done without loss in continuity. All chapters end with comprehensive questions and problems that apply to the material presented in the chapter. Many chapters have short cases for those interested in testing the application of knowledge beyond short problem exercises.

This edition continues an innovation pioneered in this work. This innovation involves the inclusion of a comprehensive, continuing illustration of the application of the techniques of security analysis and portfolio management to a real company and a real portfolio. Each chapter that presents tools of analysis includes an application of the tools to McDonald's Corporation. This approach permits the reader to see the transference of explicated theory to a tangible real-life situation.

The book is divided into seven parts. Part I, The Investment Environment, contains two chapters. Chapter 1 surveys alternative investment vehicles and their more salient attributes. The functioning of major securities markets, or how an investor goes about buying and selling particular security types, is also examined in Chapter 2.

In Part II, Framework of Risk and Return, Chapter 3, sets forth in detail the theoretical tenets and practical dimensions of the two major elements of any investment that investors must be mindful of, risk and return. Return is what investors seek most of all. Equally important, however, is the notion of risk, and what creates it. Both return and risk are characterized in explicit quantitative terms.

In Part III, Common-Stock Analysis, a detailed systematic approach to estimating future dividends and prices for common stocks is developed. The framework for the approach is an economic-industry-company analysis. The strong link between economic activity and security prices requires that the investor forecast the direction and degree of change in economic activity (Chapter 4). Key sectors of overall economic activity influence particular industries in different ways; the investor must link forecasts of economic activity to the prediction of relative movements in specific industries and analysis of selected industries (Chapter 5). From the industry level to the level of individual companies, the investor must examine and analyze factors that influence earnings, dividends, and stock prices of companies (Chapters 6-8).

Part IV, Bond Analysis, discusses bonds and preferred stocks, which represent less exciting, but, nonetheless, important alternatives to common-stock investing. The systematic sources of risk affecting bonds, particularly inflation, and changes in the level and structure of interest rates are the key areas in bond analysis that are examined first (Chapter 9). In addition, unsystematic risk and other nonrisk factors that influence required yields on bonds are explored in depth (Chapter 10). The final chapter in Part IV, Chapter 11, probes specific passive and active strategies used to manage bond portfolios.

The Chapters (12-14) in Part V, Options and Futures, examine various forms of security options and futures that might be purchased or sold. These options and futures represent rights to underlying common shares as well as fixed-income securities.

The approach detailed in Parts III and IV is best described as fundamental analysis. Considerations of economic-industry-company analysis are linked in order to reach considered estimates of return and risk on individual securities. In Part VI, Technical Analysis and the Efficient Market Theory, we also develop the rationale and explore the methods employed by so-called technical analysis (Chapter 15). This approach concentrates on supply and demand relationships in the market and on historical price and volume relationships to predict the movement of the market as well as the movement of prices of individual securities. The last segment of Part VI is devoted to the idea of efficient markets and the theory of random walk. The efficient markets notion questions the validity of technical analysis and also raises some questions about fundamental analysis (Chapter 16).

The risk-return output of security analysis is the raw material for portfolio management. Part VII, Portfolio Analysis, Selection, and Management, deals systematically with the procedures involved in portfolio management. Using modern methods for analyzing portfolios and packaging securities in such a way as to achieve diversification of risk is the first task to be accomplished (Chapter 17). The selection of the one best portfolio from those available to the investor is stage two of portfolio management (Chapter 18). Chapter 19 introduces capital market theory. The final chapter in the text (Chapter 20) explores the ways in which an investor might place his or her funds in the hands of professionals for management, and how portfolios managed personally, or by others, might be evaluated for performance over time.

This edition represents a significant revision of the text. Items worth noting include:

1. A new chapter on risk and return that integrates concepts that were spread throughout several chapters in the previous edition of the book.

2. New detailed material on the varied segments of the bond market.

3. Integration of international investing materials into specific chapters on equities, bonds, and derivatives. The previous edition included a free-standing chapter on this important subject.

4. A complete update of materials relating to the food services industry and McDonald's Corp.

5. Updated information on the latest developments in taxation and accounting that are relevant to securities analysis and investing.

6. New and visually improved boxed inserts that draw contemporary real world examples into the text from popular financial publications.

7. Revised and expanded cases placed throughout the text. These cases integrate two-to-three chapters and can be assigned to help students deal with real world situations.

8. Greatly expanded end of chapter questions and problems. The stock of questions and problems has been increased over forty percent from the fifth edition.

9. Expanded materials on derivatives to include newer option forms and discussion of the general subject of financial engineering.

Many people have given us advise and counsel in this undertaking. Dr. Richard McEnally, University of North Carolina-Chapel Hill, has been a source of continuing encouragement since the first edition of this book. His suggestions have been enormously helpful. A number of investment professionals have provided especially useful information and suggestions. David Marks, CFA, President, Allianz Investment Corporation, Thomas Hylinski, CFA, Senior Vice President, Peoples Bank, and Douglas DeSilva, Bloomberg Financial Markets gave without stint of their enormous store of on-line experience in investment management. We are indebted to the Association of Investment Management and Research [AIMR] for permission to use certain questions and problems appearing as part of the annual Chartered Financial Analyst (CFA) examinations.

Special thanks are due to Dr. Tony Wingler, University of North Carolina at Greensboro, who did a first rate job in preparing the instructor's manual. His high level of professional competence and his thoroughness are in evidence throughout our supplementary materials. The following individuals guided us with skill and dedication in reviewing the manuscript and offering invaluable suggestions for changes: Tony R. Wingler, University of North Carolina, Greensboro, Frederick P. Schadler, East Carolina University, Allen S. Anderson, University of Akron, and Elizabeth Strock Bagnani, Boston College.

Finally, we are indebted to the Prentice Hall staff, principally to Leah Jewel, Acquisitions Editor and Bob Walters, Project Manager, for their special efforts in preparing the manuscript for publication.

Donald E. Fischer
Ronald J. Jordan

CHAPTER 1

INTRODUCTION TO SECURITIES

This book is about investing in securities. Unfortunately, however, we cannot provide the toll for the easy road to riches. Security analysis and portfolio management are hard work, requiring discipline and patience, and the work is not always rewarded by exceptional returns.

None can deny that handsome returns have been reaped in the market by a variety of methods ranging from sheer genius to the occult. The unfortunate thing about most of these techniques is that they are difficult to duplicate consistently by everyone. Often they just cannot be verbalized in a way that permits systematizing.

Our approach is straightforward and consistent within a well-developed framework for decision making. We propose that investors are interested primarily in eventually selling a security for more than they paid for it. Including the receipt of interest or dividends during the time the security is held, the investor hopes to achieve a higher reward than would have been possible by simply placing the same amount of money in a savings account. This reward, or *return,* must be measured and estimated for each security being considered, with appropriate adjustments for decision-making costs.

But in seeking rewards that exceed those available on savings accounts, every investor, consciously or not, faces the very real risk that his hoped-for return will fall short of his expectations. *Risk* means the uncertainty in the probability distribution of returns. This aspect of investing in securities must also be measurable and estimated for each security being considered. The entire process of estimating return and risk for individual securities is known as *security analysis.*

This has not always been the function of security analysis in practice. Traditionally, analysts have attempted to identify undervalued securities to buy, and overvalued securities to sell. Modern-day thinking, strongly influenced by the efficient-markets hypothesis—sometimes popularly called the random-walk theory—questions the validity of or benefit to be derived from traditional security analysis. In fact, the efficient-markets hypothesis sees only indirect benefits emanating from the analyst's risk-return calculations.

Briefly stated, the concept of market efficiency means that stock prices nearly always fully reflect *all* available information. If this is so, it would be exceedingly difficult for the average investor or analyst to earn exceptional returns—particularly on a consistent basis. In fact, the only way for the analyst in such a market to achieve superior performance is by having (1) access to "secret" or "inside" information, (2) superior analytical tools, or (3) superior forecasting abilities. This last item can include everything from being able to forecast earnings per share for some future period to being able to assess the impact of technological and economic developments on the firm's future. We hope that this book will aid the reader in developing analytical ability and useful tools of analysis. For if the domestic stock markets are efficient, only through unique insights can the investor achieve unusually high returns—and then, perhaps only rarely.

Securities that have return and risk characteristics of their own, in combination, make up a *portfolio*. Portfolios may or may not take on the aggregate characteristics of their individual parts. *Portfolio analysis* thus takes the ingredients of risk and return for individual securities and considers the blending or interactive effects of combining securities. *Portfolio selection* entails choosing the one best portfolio to suit the risk-return preferences of the investor. *Portfolio management* is the dynamic function of evaluating and revising the portfolio in terms of stated investor objectives.

INVESTMENT VERSUS SPECULATION

Because this text deals with investments, we will begin our venture with a clear understanding of just what an investment is and what the investment process entails.

An *investment* is a commitment of funds made in the expectation of some positive rate of return. If the investment is properly undertaken, the return will be commensurate with the risk the investor assumes.

Generally, investment is distinguished from speculation by the time horizon of the investor and often by the risk-return characteristics of the investment. The true investor is interested in a *good* rate of return, earned on a rather consistent basis for a relatively long period of time. The speculator seeks opportunities promising *very large* returns, earned rather quickly. The speculator is less interested in consistent performance than is the investor and is more interested in the abnormal, extremely high rate of return than the normal, more moderate rate. Furthermore, the speculator wants to get these high returns in a short time and then seek greener pastures in other investment outlets. In this text the emphasis will be on investments and investment analysis, although speculative situations will also be considered.

The same stock can be purchased as a speculation or an investment, depending on the motivation of the purchaser. For example, AT&T—American Telephone and Telegraph—is generally considered an investment-grade security. That is, it represents a basic service in our economy, and therefore the firm and the price of its shares should grow pretty much with the economy on average over time. However, if a student of the stock market feels that AT&T, selling at $50 a share, is

underpriced and is likely to rise to the mid-50s very quickly, he[1] might buy it as a speculation. He is unconcerned with AT&T's dividend or long-term growth prospects. His only concern is with its potential short-term price appreciation.

Consider another example to differentiate between investment and speculation. A friend calls you to tell you about Zippy Mining Corp. selling at $.10 per share. He says Zippy is mining for gold in Western Canada and has just hit a major find. He says when this news is confirmed and circulated the stock will fly to between $3 and $5 per share. If you buy based on this, it would be speculation. The purchase is motivated by greed and a fast buck. Investment is concerned with purchasing something of value that will appreciate at a "fair" rate of return commensurate with the risk assumed over a long period of time.

Despite his motivations, the speculator adds to the market's liquidity and depth, for he is frequently "turning over" (changing) his portfolio. Thus, his presence provides a market for securities (depth) and a wider distribution of ownership of securities (breadth), and enhances the capital markets.

Investment in securities in the *capital markets* (markets for securities with maturities over one year) is a key factor in the U.S. economy. If the economic environment is ripe and corporate management expectations are optimistic, a firm normally wishes to expand. This expansion can take the form of an enlarged physical facility, an increased sales force, or any one of a number of such factors. If conditions are appropriate, all this will eventually lead to higher earnings and higher prices for the firm's outstanding securities. Financing this expansion often comes about by gaining access to the capital markets—namely, through the sale of stocks and bonds. Investors who have earned profits, called *capital gains,* on previous investments in securities or have observed others doing this will be standing ready to finance expansions by providing funds. Thus firms grow, jobs are provided, families prosper, and the economy grows.[2]

THE INVESTMENT PROCESS

Now that we have distinguished between investment and speculation and extolled some of the virtues of the capital markets, it becomes necessary to see how one goes about entering the investment arena.

Security Analysis

Traditional investment analysis, when applied to securities, emphasizes the projection of prices and dividends. That is, the potential price of a firm's common stock and the future dividend stream are forecast, then discounted back to the present.

---

[1]The use of *he, his,* and so on, is only for the purpose of simplifying the exposition, and should be understood as including both sexes.

[2]Obviously, the presence of organized secondary markets, where already-issued securities are traded, facilitates and boosts investor participation because these markets provide liquidity for the investor. These issues will be discussed in Chapter 2.

This *intrinsic value* is then compared with the security's current market price (after adjusting for commissions). If the current market price is below the intrinsic value, a purchase is recommended. Conversely, if the current market price is above this intrinsic value, a sale is recommended.

Although modern security analysis is deeply rooted in the fundamental concepts just outlined, the emphasis has shifted. The more modern approach to common-stock analysis emphasizes risk-and-return estimates rather than mere price and dividend estimates. The return-and-risk estimates, of course, are dependent on the share price and the accompanying dividend stream. Chapters 3 and 4 will establish the framework of analysis for risk and return that we will be using throughout the text.

Any forecast of securities must necessarily consider the prospects of the economy. As we shall see in Chapter 5, the economic setting greatly influences the prospects of certain industries, as well as the psychological outlook of the investment public. Among industries the impact of the economy will differ, and thus it is incumbent on the analyst to be thoroughly informed about any industry peculiarities. This industry analysis will be the subject of Chapter 6. Even within industries, the outlook for specific firms will differ. A company's outlook will be related to such things as product line, production efficiency, marketing force, finances, and management capability. A recommended procedure for screening firms and their securities will be presented in Chapters 7 through 12; the analysis in these chapters will provide estimates of risk and return.

The Computer and Investment Analysis

Most of the techniques of security analysis can be applied manually by a limited number of personnel using desk calculators, but this process is feasible only for analyzing a small number of securities. For a large number, the use of a computer becomes a necessity. However, today investors can make use of home computers or microcomputers for limited numbers of securities.

Computers can absorb many thousands of pieces of information and can make use of them as the computer program instructs. The analyst informs a programmer as to the given inputs, the required operations, and the desired format of the output. The required calculations, which might take days to perform manually, can be done by the computer in seconds. This kind of quick turnaround is invaluable to the analyst.

The computer also assists in other valuable ways. First, the analyst can vary his assumptions, resubmit the data, and observe what differences arise as a result of the changed assumptions. Second, alternative constructs can be tested on data of various companies merely by applying "canned" (already-existing) programs to data that have been collected and are stored at the computer center.[3] The results of these various constructs can be compared—often within minutes after they have

[3]Services exist that provide pertinent balance-sheet, income-statement, stock-price, trading-volume, and other data on magnetic tape to subscribers. The data are regularly updated.

been conceived. This allows the analyst to follow through immediately with various thought processes without interrupting them for several days while the data are being compiled and processed.

These advantages are realized not only by the largest research organization; individuals can lease limited amounts of time on computers, and various data banks as well, for a reasonable cost. The implication is not that all small investors can (or should) run out and lease computer time for mere pennies a day. It does mean, however, that an individual investor with the necessary know-how and a portfolio of above-average size can avail himself of more sophisticated research techniques and systems.

From time to time throughout the text, we will point out areas where computer applications are both efficient and necessary.[4]

Portfolio Management

We have already seen that modern security analysis differs in emphasis from traditional security analysis. The former emphasizes risk-and-return estimates; the latter emphasizes the calculation of an intrinsic value. Portfolio management is also characterized by an old and a new way of solving the portfolio problem.

Portfolios are combinations of assets. In this text, portfolios will consist of collections of securities. Traditional portfolio planning called for the selection of those securities that best fit the personal needs and desires of the investor. For example, a young, aggressive, single adult would be advised to buy stocks in newer, dynamic, rapidly growing firms. A retired widow would be advised to purchase stocks and bonds in old-line, established, stable companies, such as utilities.

Modern portfolio theory suggests that the traditional approach to portfolio analysis, selection, and management may well yield less than optimum results—that a more scientific approach is needed, based on estimates of risk and return of the portfolio and the attitudes of the investor toward a risk-return trade-off stemming from the analysis of the individual securities.

The return of the portfolio, as we shall see in Chapter 20, is nothing more than the weighted average of the returns of the individual stocks. The weights are based on the percentage composition of the portfolio. (A stock representing 10 percent of the portfolio receives a weight of .10). The total risk of the portfolio is more complex. Here we need only point out that securities when combined may have a greater or lesser risk than the sum of their component risks. This fact arises from the degree to which the returns of individual securities move together or interact. Modern portfolio management techniques will be discussed in Chapters 21–23.

---

[4]Before turning to portfolio analysis in Chapter 20, we will examine two alternative explanations for the behavior of stock prices. Chapter 18 will present the essentials of technical analysis—a set of techniques based on a study of the patterns of share prices. Chapter 19 will discuss the theory of random walk, which denies the existence of such patterns.

INVESTMENT CATEGORIES

Investments generally involve *real assets* or *financial assets*. Real assets are tangible, material things such as buildings, automobiles, and textbooks. Financial assets are pieces of paper representing an indirect claim to real assets held by someone else. These pieces of paper represent debt or equity commitments in the form of IOUs or stock certificates.

Among the many properties that distinguish real from financial assets, one of special interest to investors is *liquidity*. Liquidity refers to the ease of converting an asset into money quickly, conveniently, and at little exchange cost. Real assets are generally less liquid than financial assets, largely because real assets are more heterogeneous, often peculiarly adapted to a specific use, and yield benefits only in cooperation with other productive factors. In addition, returns on real assets are frequently more difficult to measure accurately, owing to the absence of broad, ready, and active markets. Many of the concepts, techniques, and decision rules applicable to financial assets are applicable to real assets, but our principal concern in this book is with financial assets.

Financial assets can be categorized in a variety of ways. We will examine them according to their source of issuance (public or private) and the nature of the buyer's commitment (creditor or owner).

Debt Instruments

Financial assets often take the form of IOUs, issued by governments, corporations, and individuals. They call for fixed periodic payments, called *interest*, and eventual repayment of the amount borrowed, called the *principal*. Debt instruments provide interest in either of two ways. Interest is paid periodically (for example, every six months), or the securities are sold to the investor on a discount-price basis. In the latter type, the instrument is sold at a price below the eventual redemption price, and the difference between the sale price and redemption value constitutes interest. Thus, 6 percent interest is received from a debt security due in one year and redeemable for $100 by either (a) paying $100 at the start and receiving $6 interest payments or (b) paying $94.30 at the outset and receiving $100 at redemption.[5] The redemption amount is referred to as the *face, par,* or *maturity value*. The interest payment in dollars, stated as a percentage of the face, par, or maturity value, is referred to as the *nominal* or *coupon rate*. The repayment of principal is either on demand or at some future time. When the principal is paid in the future, it can be in one lump-sum payment or piecemeal payments spread over time. In all cases it is important to remember that debt instruments represent money loaned rather than ownership to the investor.

---

[5]The $5.70 difference ($100 – $94.30) is 6 percent of $94.30.

INSTITUTIONAL DEPOSITS AND CONTRACTS

Money and checking and savings accounts all represent fixed-dollar commitments that are debtlike in character. Currency is in reality a government IOU. Checking and savings accounts, referred to as *demand* and *time deposits,* are loans to banks and other financial institutions. Demand deposits bear no interest and are redeemable upon demand. Savings accounts, or time deposits, technically cannot be withdrawn without notice, although institutions normally provide this privilege. Savings accounts draw interest, and some forms, called *certificates of deposit* (CDs), have specified maturities (such as one, two, four, or six years). CDs pay higher interest than do normal savings accounts, and penalties are exacted (e.g., loss of interest) if withdrawal is made before the maturity date.

Certain types of life insurance policies build up what is called *cash surrender value.* This reserve accumulates primarily because premiums paid by policyholders normally exceed death benefits in early years. This difference is placed in reserve for later years, when death benefits exceed premiums paid. A policyholder's share of the reserve is similar to a savings account. A policy can be turned in for its cash surrender value, or money may be borrowed from the insurance company against it.

Employees who contribute to pension funds in anticipation of retirement can usually withdraw their own contributions if they leave the company before that time. Normally, during the years of employment, both the employer and the employee will contribute to the pension fund. Upon retirement, the employee receives a pension supported partly by his own and his employer's contributions. Leaving the company before retirement does not usually entitle the employee to the share contributed by his employer.

Thus cash, demand and savings accounts, and reserves built up in insurance policies and pension funds all represent fixed-dollar commitments. Some bear interest, others do not. Maturities may run from demand to several years' duration. In all cases, however, these "investments" originate with some institution (bank, savings and loan association, insurance company, or other corporation) and are transferable to or redeemed only by the issuer. They may not have title transferred to a third party.

GOVERNMENT DEBT SECURITIES[6]

Debt securities are issued by federal, state, and local governments. They differ in quality (risk), yield, and maturity. U.S. government securities (USGs) are among the safest and most liquid securities available anywhere. Securities of states and municipalities vary substantially in quality.

SHORT-TERM.   Short-term USGs have maturities of one year or less and include Treasury bills offered weekly at a discount, with maturities of ninety-one days up to one year. Government agencies, such as Federal Home Loan Banks and the

[6]See, in particular, First Boston Corp., *Handbook of Securities of the United States Government and Federal Agencies,* 35th ed. (New York: First Boston Corp., 1990).

Federal National Mortgage Association, frequently sell short-term, interest-bearing obligations.[7] State and local governments frequently sell short-term notes in advance of receipts from taxes and bond issues. These instruments are called *tax* or *bond anticipation notes.*

LONG-TERM.   The U.S. government issues Treasury notes (one- to ten-year maturities) and Treasury bonds (maturities of ten to thirty years), which bear interest. More than 60 percent of the USGs held by individuals represent savings bonds. These securities are sold at a discounted price and can be acquired via payroll deductions through employers. Federal agencies also sell long-term issues. States and municipalities sell long-term debt of two types: *general obligations* and *revenue obligations.* General obligations are backed by the taxing powers of the issuer, whereas revenue bonds pay interest and principal from a special revenue source. In the latter case, a toll-road bond would pay interest and principal from toll receipts. It is easy to see that revenue bonds can represent high risks if the revenue source does not meet expectations.

PRIVATE ISSUES

Private debt issues are offered by corporations engaged in mining, manufacturing, merchandising, and financing activities. As a unit, private issues run the spectrum in quality (risk) and yield, from the high quality of AT&T bonds to the defaulted securities of the Washington Public Power Supply.

SHORT-TERM.   The most common short-term privately issued debt securities are *commercial paper.* Commercial paper is unsecured promissory notes of from 30 to 270 days' maturity. These securities are issued to supplement bank credit and are sold by companies of prime credit standing. *Banker's acceptances* are issued in international trade. They are of high quality, because they carry bank guarantees, and have maturities of from ninety days to one year. Large corporate time deposits in commercial banks are often of certain minimum amounts for a specified time period. Unlike time deposits of individuals, these CDs are negotiable; that is, they can be sold to and redeemed by third parties.

LONG-TERM.   There is a great variety of subclassifications in long-term corporate or private bonds. It may be well to remember that these subclasses merely represent modifications of the two basic promises in a debt contract: (1) to pay regular interest, and (2) to redeem the principal at maturity.

Interest is usually paid on bonds every six months. Failure to make such payments constitutes an act of default, and bondholders may seek relief from default in the courts. All interest on bonds, current and accumulated, must be paid before any dividends are distributed to shareholders. The only exception to this rule is with the *income bond,* on which interest is paid only if earnings are sufficient to

---

[7]USGs are technically not guaranteed by the full faith and taxing powers of the U.S. government.

permit it. These bonds often result from reorganizations and are infrequently sold to raise new capital because of the residual nature of interest payments.

We normally associate bonds with the fixed return from interest that gives them their basic appeal to investors seeking safety and regular income. However, the *convertible bond* provides the holder with an option to exchange his bond for a predetermined number of common shares at any time prior to maturity. As the cost of this option, convertible bonds usually provide lower interest (yield) than straight bonds do because at some future time, if converted into shares, the bond might provide more current income; and/or there may be a handsome capital gain as the bond price moves up with the value of the underlying shares. Obviously, the underlying shares can prove a disappointment both in dividends and in price movement.

The promise to redeem bonds at maturity can be altered or modified by what is termed a *call feature,* provided for the benefit of the issuer (borrower). If interest rates decline after the sale of a bond issue, the borrower would want the option to accelerate the maturity (call the bonds) and replace them at a lower interest cost. Issuers are normally required to pay a penalty (premium) of one year's interest for the call privilege. Quite frequently, call privileges are given but deferred (inoperative) for a period of years.

A special form of call feature, called a *sinking fund,* is often found in bond issues for the benefit of investors. Under a sinking fund, bonds are redeemed piecemeal over the nominal maturity, very much as monthly payments amortize a home mortgage. Such payments give the investor peace of mind that the principal will be repaid, an assurance that is not inherent in the promise of a single lump-sum payment at a distant maturity date. Bonds are retired for sinking-fund purposes at a price not greater than par (plus accrued interest). Bonds are retired in the open market if market prices are below par. If market prices exceed par, bonds are redeemed by random lot. An alternative strategy to sinking-fund bonds is the *serial bond.* Serial issues are really several small bond issues carrying many maturity dates rather than a single one. Each series is redeemed as it comes due, usually at par. Rather than a single bond issue with a thirty-year maturity, we might have thirty subissues due one year apart for from one to thirty years.

To protect the return of principal and any unpaid interest if adversity occurs, bond investors often seek a lien against specific assets of the issuer. The advantage is that during liquidation, creditors with specific liens receive proceeds from the sale of those assets, up to a limit of the debt and interest owed. Otherwise, in the absence of any specific asset claim, bondholders become general or unsecured creditors sharing equally in asset distributions (after creditors with liens or secured creditors). The names attached to bonds often indicate the existence of the security and the type. Unsecured bonds are normally referred to as *debentures.* Bonds secured by real property are known as *mortgage bonds,* with first lienholders called *first-mortgage bondholders,* and so on. Personal property usually stands behind *collateral trust bonds* (bonds and stocks of other companies) and *equipment trust certificates* (railroad rolling stock, airplanes).

The types and variations of bonds available are substantial. Every investor should study the *indenture,* or bond contract, which spells out all the details behind

the issue. Most investors do not examine the actual indenture, but more likely an abbreviated version found in the offering *prospectus* available for all new issues of securities sold publicly. A prospectus is a document required by law that is issued for the purpose of describing a new security issue.

Short-term or long-term loans to government and business can be bought from or sold to other investors, often via middlemen or "brokers." Thus, unlike the case with savings accounts and contract reserves, investors in these debt securities need not deal exclusively with the original issuer of the claim. This swapping of debt securities for cash and vice versa takes place through well-established markets, or exchanges.

INTERNATIONAL BOND INVESTING

More than one-half of all fixed-income securities are from countries outside the United States. These bonds can be distinguished basically by whether interest and principal are payable in U.S. dollars or other currencies. International domestic bonds are sold by an issuer within the country of issue in that country's currency—such as a bond sold by Sony in Tokyo and yen-denominated. Some foreign bonds are issued in the currency of the country where they are sold but sold by a borrower of a different nationality. A dollar-denominated bond sold in New York by Sony is called a *Yankee bond.* A yen-denominated bond sold in Tokyo by IBM is referred to as a *Samuarai bond.* The purchase of any fixed-income security subjects the investor to the risk that interest rates will change. Dollar-denominated bonds respond to interest rates in the United States. Foreign-currency-denominated bonds respond to interest rates in the country where they are denominated. Moreover, the investor faces currency-exchange risk, such as converting interest payments in yen to dollars, for example.

Equities

We have just discussed investment media that represent a debtor position—that is, in which the investor in bonds or in other debt instruments is a creditor of the party issuing the debt. In this section we will discuss investment media that represent an ownership position—that is, in which the investor in stocks or certain options is an owner of the firm and is thus entitled to a residual share of profits.[8] We will divide equity ownership into two main categories, one representing indirect equity investment through institutions and the other representing direct equity investment through the capital markets.

EQUITY INVESTMENT VIA INSTITUTIONS

Several vehicles permit an equity investment that requires less supervision than does a direct investment in common or preferred stocks. These investments involve a commitment of funds to an institution of some sort that in return manages the in-

[8]Admittedly, the holder of an option is often not an owner of the firm until he exercises his option and acquires stock.

vestment for the investor. The most common vehicle is shares of an investment company, but we will defer our discussion of this form of professionally managed portfolio to a later chapter. Several other important institutional outlets for investment dollars should be noted.

VARIABLE ANNUITIES.   Under current federal tax laws, certain taxpayers are permitted to have certain portions of their salaries withheld by their employers for investment in a variable annuity. The great advantage of this scheme is that the amount invested in the variable annuity is not taxable to the investor until it (along with accumulated earnings on it) is withdrawn from the plan. Generally, this is during retirement, when the taxpayer is in a lower tax bracket. Quite simply, then, the *tax-sheltered variable annuity* is a device for deferring the payment of federal income taxes. Although variable annuities are not always of the tax-sheltered variety (the setup is the same in all cases, though), this is the form usually thought of in discussions of variable annuities.

The equity characteristic is that the organization managing the annuity typically invests the proceeds of all the participants in the plan in a portfolio. It is called *variable* because the amount of the monthly annuity payment can vary, depending on the success of the portfolio's investments, which are mainly equities. Thus this form of planning for retirement is not only tax-sheltered but also quite aggressive.

INSURANCE POLICIES.   Purchasing a life insurance policy could well be considered an investment. In fact, if the policy is purchased from a mutual insurance company, the insured becomes an owner of the company. The discussion of adequate life insurance coverage is a specialized area, and we recommend that the interested reader consult any basic life insurance text for further information. In this book we will assume that the investor has already made proper provisions for life insurance, savings accounts, a home, automobile, and other necessities and is contemplating an investment with other available funds.

DIRECT EQUITY INVESTMENTS

The two main direct equity investments are common stock and preferred stocks. In addition, several options exist that, when exercised, permit the purchase of one of these types of stocks.

COMMON STOCK.   Common stock represents an ownership position. The holders of common stock are the owners of the firm, have the voting power that, among other things, elects the board of directors, and have a right to the earnings of the firm after all expenses and obligations have been paid; but they also run the risk of receiving nothing if earnings are insufficient to cover all obligations.

Common-stock holders hope to receive a return based on two sources—dividends and capital gains. Dividends are received only if the company earns sufficient money *and* the board of directors deems it proper to declare a dividend. Capital gains arise from an advance in the market price of the common stock, which is generally associated with a growth in per-share earnings. Because earn-

ings often do not grow smoothly over time, stock prices historically have been quite volatile over time. This fact points out the need for careful analysis in the selection of securities for purchase and sale, as well as in the timing of these investment decisions, for common stock has no maturity date at which a fixed value will be realized. We advocate the use of fundamental analysis, as outlined in later chapters.

STOCK SPLITS.   Often one reads of a firm declaring a stock split. When this occurs, the company ends up with more shares outstanding, which sell at a lower price and have a lower par value than the outstanding shares did before the split. Stock splits are frequently prompted when the company's stock price has risen to a level that corporate management feels is out of the "popular trading range." If this is so, trading volume in the shares will decrease and investor interest may subside. To overcome this, management may declare a stock split.[9]

For example, suppose ABC Corp. has 1 million shares of common outstanding. The par value is $2 per share and the current market price is $100 per share. Management may rightfully believe that the average investor wishes to deal in lots of 100 shares—round lots—and would like to buy 100 shares of ABC but cannot afford to invest $10,000 at one time. Therefore, management decides to declare a 2-for-1 split.[10] Then there will be 2 million shares outstanding, with a par value of $1 per share and a theoretical market price of $50 per share. Thus it would require only $5,000 (ignoring commissions) to purchase 100 shares of ABC for cash. Of course, earnings per share would be proportionately reduced (by half, in this case) because of the split. Splits can occur at any ratio of new-to-old shares. Several popular ratios are 2-for-1, 3-for-2, and 5-for-4.

STOCK DIVIDENDS.   Instead of (and sometimes in addition to) cash dividends, investors can receive dividends in the form of stock. The result to the investor is the same as from a stock split: He receives more shares. Stock dividends are typically stated in percentage terms—such as 20 percent stock dividend, meaning a 20 percent increase in the number of shares outstanding.[11] The investor previously owning 100 shares of common would own 120 shares after the stock dividend has been paid. Instead of reducing the par value of the stock on the corporate books, as in the stock-split case, the firm in this case transfers amounts from retained earnings to the capital-stock account for par value of the newly issued stock in the case of a

---

[9]Sometimes the price of a firm's stock is very low, and management wishes to raise the prestige of the stock. One way to do this is to declare a π *reverse split*. This has the opposite effect of a stock split. Fewer shares will be outstanding, but each will sell at a higher price.

[10]In conjunction with management's desire to bring the price of the stock into a more popular trading range is its desire to improve the stock's liquidity. Because more shares are outstanding after a stock split, more shares are available for trading, and a wider distribution of ownership (more stockholders) is quite likely. These events aid in providing a fluid market in the shares of the firm. In addition, certain findings indicate that an increase in price may be associated with some stock splits.

[11]A 20 percent stock dividend is equivalent to a 6-for-5 split.

large stock dividend (generally more than 25 percent), and transfers the market value of the shares from retained earnings to the common-stock and paid-in-capital accounts in the case of a small stock dividend. Frequently, firms will have to account for stock splits as large stock dividends. These seemingly arbitrary rules have been set up by the accounting profession.

Let us suppose that our firm, with its 1 million shares of $2-par common, declares a 3-for-2 stock split. But its accountants rule that the announced split does not meet the American Institute of Certified Public Accountants (AICPA) definition of a stock split. Therefore, the firm must account for the split as a large stock dividend (because a 3-for-2 stock split is equivalent to a 50 percent stock dividend, and 50 percent is greater than 25 percent). The only effect on the balance sheet of the firm is that the retained-earnings account is reduced by $1 million (500,000 shares $\times$ $2 par) and the common-stock account is increased by a like amount. Because dividends, both cash and stock, can be paid only out of retained earnings, the payment of a stock dividend reduces the firm's ability to pay future dividends by the amount of par value issued. Stock splits do not have this implication.

As in the stock-split case, earnings, dividends, and theoretical share prices are proportionately reduced by the stock dividend. A 100 percent stock dividend has the same theoretical effect on these values as a 2-for-1 stock split.

PREFERRED STOCK.   Preferred stock is said to be a "hybrid" security because it has features of both common stock and bonds. Preferred stock is preferred with respect to assets and dividends. In the event of liquidation, preferred-stock holders have a claim on available assets before the common-stock holders. Furthermore, preferred-stock holders get their stated dividends before common-stock holders can receive any dividends. Preferred dividends are stated in either percentage-of-par or dollar terms. Thus the issue might be known as a $6 preferred or a 6 percent preferred. If the preferred had a $100 par value, this would mean that a 6 percent preferred paid $6 per share per annum in dividends.

Thus, the dividends are fixed for preferred stocks; however, they must be declared before a legal obligation exists to pay them. The fixed characteristic is akin to that of bond interest; the declaration feature is similar to that of common-stock dividends.

Frequently, preferreds are said to be *cumulative* with respect to dividends. This means that if a quarterly dividend is passed (that is, not declared), *all* preferred dividend arrearages must be paid before *any* dividends can be paid to common-stock holders. Most companies provide that if a certain number of preferred dividend payments are missed, the preferred-stock holders may elect representatives to the board of directors in the hope that the new directors will reinstate the dividends. In addition, preferred stock sometimes, although rarely, is *participating*. This means that it can sometimes receive a double dividend—the stated dividend plus an extra dividend bonus after the common has received a dividend. Of course, as in the case of common stock, preferred stock has no maturity date.

INTERNATIONAL EQUITIES

Foreign stocks are attractive because many international companies afford investors superior return potential. Foreign stocks also offer diversification possibilities, because the correlation between rates of return on foreign and U.S. stocks is much lower than it is among alternative U.S. stocks. Foreign shares can be acquired directly at foreign stock exchanges by purchase of American Depository Receipts (ADRs) or by acquiring international mutual funds. ADRs are trust receipts evidencing ownership of underlying shares in safekeeping by a bank for convenience in transfer. International equities face the same currency risks previously noted for foreign bonds.

Real Estate

Real estate investments have had a checkered history. One can participate in real estate as a creditor or an owner. Debt participation is afforded by the direct acquisition of mortgages or the indirect purchase of mortgage-backed securities.

The most common direct equity ownership of real estate is purchasing a home. Real estate partnerships permit shared equity ownership in various properties from raw land to apartments. Real estate pools that are similar to mutual funds are called real estate investment trusts (REITs). They are available for diversified debt and equity ownership in pools of property of various types.

Options and Futures

Some investments are available that derive their value from an underlying security (stock, bond, or "basket" of securities). These so-called derivatives include options and financial futures. An *option agreement* is a contract in which the writer of the option grants the buyer of the option the right to purchase from or sell to the writer a designated instrument at a specified price (or receive a cash settlement) within a specified period of time. Call options are options to buy. Puts are options to sell.

Financial futures represent a firm legal commitment between a buyer and seller, where they agree to exchange something at a specified price at the end of a designated period of time. The buyer agrees to take delivery and the seller agrees to make delivery. Futures are available on baskets of stocks (e.g., S&P 500 Stock Index) and are referred to as *stock index futures.* Futures on fixed-income securities (e.g., Treasury bonds) are called *interest-rate futures.*

SUMMARY

This chapter provided a broad overview of the nature of security analysis and portfolio management. It was noted that the measurement of return and risk are the main focus of the job of the security analyst and the portfolio manager.

We explored the primary categories of securities—debt and equity instruments. We learned that debt and equity securities include a wide array of variations on the central themes of creditor and ownership interests.

QUESTIONS

1. Distinguish carefully between *investing* and *speculating.* Is it possible to incorporate investment and speculation within the same security? Explain.

2. Compare briefly the traditional and modern approaches to security analysis; to portfolio management.

3. What is liquidity, and why is it so important to the efficient operation of securities markets?

4. What are the two basic promises embodied in debt contracts? Indicate examples of how each of these promises is often modified.

5. Archway, Inc. stock is selling for $100 per share. Currently, the company pays $2 per year in cash dividends. At the most recent meeting of the board of directors, it was decided that (1) three new shares would be issued for each two shares currently outstanding, and (2) a quarterly dividend of $.48 on new shares would be declared.

    a. Is the 3-for-2 a stock split or a stock dividend? Does it make a difference what we call it?

    b. What should happen to the price per share after the 3-for-2 split, assuming that the dividend was advanced to $1.33 per year?

    c. After the 3-for-2 split and the new $.48 quarterly dividend, what is the effective percentage increase in the dividend?

6. Why do you suppose so many types of equity securities exist?

7. Why do you suppose so many types of debt securities exist?

8. Recently many specialized types of mutual funds have appeared. They invest in many companies in the same industry. Some invest in the same types of securities of many different forms in different industries. Why do you suppose this has happened?

9. Why would U.S. investors have any interest in investing in international equities? Should they? Why or why not?

REFERENCES

FABOZZI, F., and I. M. POLLACK, eds. *The Handbook of Fixed Income Securities.* 2d ed. Homewood, Ill.: Dow Jones-Irwin, 1987.

FEDERAL RESERVE BANK OF RICHMOND. *Instruments of the Money Market.* 8th ed. Richmond: Federal Reserve Bank of Richmond, 1990.

FIRST BOSTON CORP. *Handbook of Securities of the United States Government and Federal Agencies.* 35th ed. New York: First Boston Corp., 1990.

LOGUE, D. E., ed. *Handbook of Modern Finance.* 2d ed. Boston: Warren, Gorham and Lamont, 1989.

CHAPTER 2

MARKETS
FOR SECURITIES
AND TAXES

We have examined the broad universe of investment vehicles that are available. Now we are ready to focus on the mechanism through which securities can be bought and sold.

Securities markets is a broad term embracing a number of markets in which securities are bought and sold. In this chapter the function, structure, and operations of major types of markets will be discussed, including how an individual investor goes about the business of placing any order to buy or sell, how the order is executed, the process of settling the payment and transfer costs, and—one hopes—the payment of federal personal income taxes on the profits from the transaction.

MARKETS AND THEIR FUNCTIONS

One way in which securities markets may be classified is by the types of securities bought and sold there. The broadest classification is based upon whether the securities are new issues or are already outstanding and owned by investors. New issues are made available in the *primary markets;* securities that are already outstanding and owned by investors are usually bought and sold through the *secondary markets.* Another classification is by maturity: Securities with maturities of one year or less normally trade in the *money market;* those with maturities of more than one year are bought and sold in the *capital market.* Needless to say, the classification system has many variations.

The existence of markets for securities is of advantage to both issuers and investors. As to their benefit to issuers, securities markets assist business and government in raising funds. In a society with private ownership of the means of production and distribution of goods and services, savings must be directed toward investment in industries where capital is most productive. Governments must also be able to borrow for public improvements. Market mechanisms make possible the transfer of funds from surplus to deficit sectors, efficiently and at low cost.

Investors also benefit from market mechanisms. If investors could not resell securities readily, they would be hesitant to acquire them, and such reluctance would reduce the total quantity of funds available to finance industry and government. Those who own securities must be assured of a fast, fair, orderly, and open system of purchase and sale at known prices.

The classification of markets we are most interested in is the one that differentiates between new and old securities—the primary and secondary markets. In recent years the secondary markets have been further fragmented, creating "third" and "fourth" markets. We will discuss each of these markets in turn. First, let us look at some factors to consider in choosing a broker.

Selecting a Broker

The investor's first step in establishing a satisfactory relationship with a broker is to choose a firm that is suitable for his needs and to select a representative of the firm with whom he can work. In practice separating the two choices is hard, for if one has chosen a satisfactory firm but is unhappy with the representative, it is embarrassing to shift one's account to another representative within the same firm. The brokerage firm should be a well-known and long-established institution. In selecting a firm an investor can ask for recommendations from his bank or from friends whose opinions he trusts.

Brokerage houses differ enormously in the type of clientele they attempt to attract. Some try to develop a large business with investors of modest means who are primarily interested in buying and selling odd lots; others seek wealthier customers; and still others are interested primarily in soliciting institutional business. These differences are apparent in the public advertising of brokerage firms.

The research reports of certain houses are obviously written for general public reading, while other houses turn out detailed and sophisticated evaluations aimed primarily at analysts for large institutions. Some houses emphasize mutual funds and advertise the New York Stock Exchange's monthly investment plan.

In short, while almost all brokerage firms welcome all types of investors, some houses are keyed to a particular type. In choosing a brokerage firm that will serve his needs best, an investor should try to judge the type of clientele sought by the firm in relation to the type of investor he is.

At first glance most brokers appear to offer about the same services. To the average investor, all firms appear equally efficient in executing orders. Differences among firms relate more to the availability of a special service that an investor may or may not want.

Most brokerage firms have research departments. The staff in these departments varies from large groups of full-time, highly competent analysts to relatively uninformed persons who process the analytical work of others and in effect turn out "secondhand" analyses. The measure of professional competence in the security analysis field is the designation chartered financial analyst (CFA). Holders of

the CFA have passed a series of three rigorous examinations on investment management decision making, and they must have had a minimum of three years' experience as a financial analyst and must possess a bachelor's degree from an accredited academic institution or the equivalent in training. An investor selecting a brokerage firm on the basis of its research department should know the size of the department and the number of CFAs on the staff. Also he should read some of their reports and compare them with similar ones published by other brokerage houses.

Many firms combine their regular brokerage business with a volume of activity as underwriters of new corporate securities. (This activity will be discussed shortly in the investment banking section of this chapter.) For an investor who is interested in purchasing new issues, such a house is desirable.

Many brokerage offices maintain a research library in which their customers can check on companies that interest them. If such facilities are important to an investor, he should certainly investigate their availability.

The person within the brokerage office with whom an investor will have the most contact is the *registered representative.* One can evaluate a representative by inquiring into his business and educational background and his investment philosophies and goals. An investor should also determine whether the representative is available at all times during business hours and should make sure that this individual is not so overburdened with other accounts that he will be unable to give the investor sufficient attention. The representative should be able to furnish the investor at all times, on reasonable notice, information on any specific company's securities.

The representative should not be the type who is always trying to sell the investor something. On the other hand, he should be aware of the securities held by the investor and should inform him of any news that is relevant to these holdings. Basically, the representative should give service and information to the investor so that the latter can make investment decisions and can have them executed properly and swiftly. A share of the responsibility for a mutually satisfactory business relationship between the two lies with the investor, for he must make his own investing philosophies and goals quite clear so that the representative will be able to offer the type of service desired.

Primary Markets

Securities available for the first time are offered through the primary securities markets. The issuer may be a brand-new company or one that has been in business for many, many years. The securities offered may be a new type for the issuer or additional amounts of a security used frequently in the past. The key is that these securities absorb new funds for the coffers of the issuer, whereas in the secondary markets, existing securities are simply being transferred between parties, and the issuer is not receiving new funds. After their purchase in the primary market, securities are traded subsequently in the secondary markets.

ROLE OF INVESTMENT BANKERS

Billions of dollars worth of new securities reach the market each year. The traditional middleman in the primary markets is called an *investment banker*. The investment banker's principal activity is to bring sellers and buyers together, thus creating a market. He normally buys the new issue from the issuer at an agreed-upon price and hopes to resell it to the investing public at a higher price. In this capacity, investment bankers are said to *underwrite*, or guarantee, an issue. Usually, a group of investment bankers joins to underwrite a security offering and form what is called an *underwriting syndicate*. The commission received by the investment banker in this case is the *differential*, or *spread*, between his purchase and resale prices. The risk to the underwriter is that the issue may not attract buyers at a positive differential.

Sales through investment bankers can take the form of a *best-efforts*, or agency, arrangement. In such a case the investment banker does not underwrite the issue but merely uses his best efforts to sell it. Any unsold securities are returned to the issuer. This best-efforts activity is mainly employed in the sale of securities of two types of issuers. New, small companies may represent too much risk for an investment banker to underwrite their securities, so he takes them only on a best-efforts basis. At the other end of the spectrum, many established and popular companies feel that their new issues will be enthusiastically received, so it would be less expensive to use a best-efforts arrangement rather than a more costly, and unnecessary, full underwriting.

Not all new issues are underwritten. Many issuers make direct sales to investor groups, with only some investment-banking services provided. For example, securities are often sold directly to institutions. This is referred to as a *private placement*. The investment banker may act only as a finder; that is, he locates the institutional buyer for a fee. Such private placements are normally restricted to bond and preferred-stock issues. Common-stock issues are frequently offered directly to existing shareholders, with the investment banker standing ready to sell any shares not taken by the existing shareholders. This is called a *standby* underwriting.

Thus, the investment banker is a middleman. He is paid a fee commensurate with services performed. These services can range from serving merely as a finder to assuming full market risk for the successful sale of an issue (underwriting). As a true intermediary, the investment banker brings buyer and seller together, thus creating a market.

BUYING NEW ISSUES

In marketing goods, we traditionally think of the marketing channel comprising the manufacturer, wholesaler, and retailer. In the primary markets for securities, the issuer can be thought of as the manufacturer. The investment banker serves the wholesaling function in the channel of distribution. He will locate and do business with buyers through retail outlets. These retail outlets are what we know as brokerage firms. Many investment bankers also serve as brokers and dealers; that is, they both underwrite and distribute shares to ultimate buyers.

Investors are informed of new issues in a formal way through a *prospectus,* a summary of important facts relative to the company and the securities being offered. The document is intended to ensure that potential investors are fully apprised of all important facts that may bear upon the value of the securities. In an informal sense, new issues are available only through those firms that are a part of the retail distribution group.[1]

Local brokerage firms will have "allotments" of new issues, depending upon, among other things, the size of the total issue, number of retail distributors, and degree of regional or local interest. For example, issues that are awaited with high enthusiasm are widely distributed, and one may find a participating broker in a given town with only several hundred shares available. To obtain part of a new issue locally, an investor may locate the name of the underwriter and then ascertain from him which brokers are retail distributors of that issue. The alternative means is to request that your broker keep you apprised of any new issues his firm participates in selling.

Issues that are in short supply relative to apparent demand have to be rationed by brokers. Suppose that a firm has 1,000 shares of a new issue in its office in Portland, Oregon, and customers place orders for 20,000 shares. Something has to give. Quite often another office in, say, Seattle has an allotment of 5,000 shares and orders for only 1,000. The Portland office may request the excess. Commonly, when the demand exceeds available supply, brokers will fill the requests of their best customers first. (A "best" customer is one who provides generous annual commissions.)

ATTRACTION OF NEW ISSUES

New stock issues of companies whose shares are already publicly traded are normally offered at prices very near those of the companies' existing shares. The area of the new-issues market that generates the most excitement and publicity concerns companies coming to the public market for the first time. Because these companies do not have publicly traded shares, investors and speculators are keen to test their assessment of the value of the new shares against the offering price.

The record is replete with stories of spectacular success, as well as of horror. We hear of the new issue of a fledgling computer equipment firm that is offered at $10 a share on Monday. By Wednesday it is at $20. Within six months it has rocketed to $65. Similarly, periods of speculative excess in the new-issues market have seen the same kind of stock, having risen to $65, fall to $1 almost overnight. The 1969–70 period saw examples of collapse in new issues; many feel that small investors who lost money then may never emotionally recover from that blow.

New issues are attractive to many because no brokerage commissions are charged to investors when these shares are purchased. The brokerage fees consist of the spread between the price paid the issuer by the investment banker and the

---

[1]*Barron's* publishes a list of new securities planned for future offering as well as those being offered, by day, for a week ahead. The name of the principal underwriter is provided. The *New Issues Digest* deals with the new-issues market in depth.

resale price to the public. Regular commissions, however, are paid upon the sale of these shares.

Secondary Markets: The Organized Exchanges

Once new issues have been purchased by investors, they change hands in the secondary markets. There are actually two broad segments of the secondary markets: the organized exchanges and the over-the-counter (OTC) market.

The primary middlemen in the secondary markets are *brokers* and *dealers.* The distinction between the two is important. The technical difference rests upon whether the person acts as an agent (broker) or as a principal (dealer) in a transaction.

Organized exchanges are physical marketplaces where the agents of buyers and sellers operate through the auction process. There are a number of organized exchanges. Two are truly national marketplaces, and the others are regional or local.

The largest and best-known national exchange is the *New York Stock Exchange* (NYSE). It accounts for about 85 percent of the share volume on all organized exchanges. The *American Stock Exchange* (AMEX) accounts for another 3 percent of all exchange volume. Regional exchanges, located in major areas, include the Pacific, Midwest, and Philadelphia-Baltimore-Washington, and local exchanges are found in Boston and Cincinnati. Collectively they account for about 12 percent of all exchange volume. These exchanges generally concentrate their efforts on securities of regional or local interest.[2]

The membership, listing activities, and functioning of organized exchanges are somewhat similar. We will focus on the NYSE because of its impact and degree of development.

WHAT SHARES ARE TRADED?

Each exchange lists certain stocks for trading. On the national exchanges, only these shares are traded. The NYSE has long enjoyed a reputation as the place where large, seasoned companies are listed for trading. Its sister exchange, the AMEX, is identified with listing smaller and younger companies than those that qualify for the NYSE, or "Big Board."

Certain strict standards must be met and fees paid for initial and continued listing. The initial listing requirements concentrate on minimum demonstrated earnings, asset size, number of shares outstanding, and number of shareholders. Continued listing is dependent upon number of holders, number of public holders, and aggregate market value of shares.

Not all companies qualify for listing on the NYSE. Some qualify but do not wish to be listed—perhaps because they do not want wider distribution of their

---

[2]Many also list some NYSE and/or AMEX shares. This practice is referred to as *dual,* or *multiple, listing.* In addition, many NYSE and AMEX issues are traded but not listed on local exchanges.

shares or do not want to meet the requirements concerning disclosure of their affairs.

In any event, listing brings certain advantages to companies as well as their shareholders. Investors get reasonably full and timely information on the company, constant price quotations, and all the benefits and safeguards built into exchange requirements for continued listings. And the prestige and publicity associated with listing will have an influence on the company's future financing and its products.

MEMBERSHIP ON THE EXCHANGE

Only members of the exchange may participate in trading its listed securities on the floor of the exchange. Since 1953 the NYSE has consisted of 1,366 members who own seats. Being a member is often referred to as having a *seat* on the exchange. Seats, or memberships, are bought and sold each year, and the board of governors of the exchange must approve all such transfers of exchange membership. Over the years, seats have sold for amounts from as low as $17,000 to more than $1 million. Recently, access to the NYSE floor has been broadened by allowing brokerage firms to rent the right to electronic access to the floor (channel orders via existing computer communications equipment). Electronic access, however, does not confer the right to physical access.

Members perform various functions. According to these functions, they are classified as commission brokers, floor brokers, odd-lot dealers, registered traders, specialists, and bond brokers.

COMMISSION BROKERS.   About one-half the members of the NYSE are commission brokers, primarily concerned with executing customer orders to buy and sell on the exchange. They receive commissions for such executions. Prominent commission brokers include such firms as Merrill Lynch, Pierce, Fenner & Smith; Smith Barney Shearson; and Prudential-Bache. Many firms have more than one membership.

FLOOR BROKERS.   When a commission broker has orders that he cannot execute personally because of their number or because of the activity of the market, he engages the services of a floor broker. These floor brokers were once referred to as $2 brokers, because at one time they charged a fee of $2 per transaction; today this fee is considerably higher. Commissions are shared on these orders. It is easy to see that smaller commission brokers are especially prone to being swamped by an influx of orders. The floor broker, as a freelance operator, provides a vital function in ensuring that the exchange's business is conducted rapidly and efficiently.

ODD-LOT DEALERS.   Trading on the floor of the exchange is conducted in round, or full, lots of 100 shares. Many investors and speculators buy and sell in lots of less than 100 shares, called *odd lots*. Odd-lot trades must be executed through an odd-lot dealer who supplies commission brokers, or buys from them, any number of shares less than a round lot. Odd-lot orders account for more than one-third of all orders.

REGISTERED TRADERS.   Some thirty members of the exchange trade for themselves; they do not engage in business for the public or for other members. These registered traders roam the floor of the exchange in search of buying and selling opportunities. One moment they may buy a stock, only to sell it shortly thereafter. A trader's profits depend upon the size and rapidity of his turnover of stock and on the accuracy of his estimate of future price movements. Traders pay no commissions and can afford to take narrower margins than others do. They are subject to myriad rules and regulations governing their activities, owing to their special status.[3]

SPECIALISTS.   One-fourth of the membership of the exchange function as specialists. Specialists now also handle odd-lot orders. Their key role in the market mechanism will be discussed at length later in this chapter.

BOND BROKERS.   Bond brokers handle trades in the bond issues traded on the exchange.

LISTED STOCK TABLES

The regular source of reference for basic stock price and volume information is the stock tables appearing in major newspapers throughout the country. The style and statistical information table used for stocks listed on the NYSE are provided by the Associated Press. The format is, therefore, uniform throughout the country. Issues that have traded each day are recorded in alphabetical order and appear as shown in Figure 2–1. From this portion of the tables, let us isolate the facts for McDonald's Corp. to explain their meaning (highlighted in Figure 2–1):

(1)		(2)	(3)	(4)	(5)	(6)	(7)	(8)	(9)	(10)	(11)
52 WEEKS					YLD.	P/E	VOL				NET
HIGH	LOW	STOCK	SYM	DIV.	%	RATIO	100S	HIGH	LO	CLOSE	CHG.
57⅞	45½	McDonald's	McD	.43	.8	20	6474	56¼	54¾	55⅝	−⅞

1. The first columns indicate both the highest and lowest closing prices at which this issue traded in the last fifty-two weeks.

2. This column briefly identifies the issue, citing its full name or abbreviated title (e.g., McDonDoug is McDonnell Douglas). If it is one of several preferred stocks issued by that company, some means of distinguishing this item from the others also appears. It may be a designation of "A," "B," or "C" preferred or, if the issues carry different dividend rates, that associated rate may be used instead.

---

[3]In 1964 new rules and regulations were instituted to correct certain practices of traders that had come under criticism. Prior to that time, a trader could buy 100 shares of a $25 stock and sell it the same day at a profit if it rose as much as 8 cents a share. To do as well, the public would require a price rise of 68 cents. See *Report of the Special Study of the Securities Markets of the Securities and Exchange Commission, Parts I and II,* 88th Cong., 1st sess., House Document No. 95 (Washington, D.C.: U.S. Government Printing Office, 1963).

	52 Weeks Hi	52 Weeks Lo	Stock	Sym	Div	Yld %	PE	Vol 100s	Hi	Lo	Close	Net Chg
	10⅞	9¼	MFS Charter	MCR	.94e	9.8	...	2366	9¾	9½	9⅝	– ⅛
	8	6⅞	MFS GvMkTr	MGF	.66e	9.4	...	2572	7¼	7	7	– ¼
	8	7	MFS Intermd	MIN	.67e	9.1	...	4981	7½	7¼	7⅜	...
	8	7	MFS MultInco	MMT	.71e	10.1	...	3904	7⅛	7	7	...
	10	8⅜	MFS MuniTr	MFM	.70	7.3	...	205	9¾	9⅝	9⅝	– ⅛
	17½	14⅝	MFS SpcVal	MFV	1.65	9.7	...	100	17⅛	16⅞	17	+ ⅛
	71⅜	45½	MGIC Inv	MTG	.32	.5	14	3189	60⅞	58¼	58½	–2⅜
	16½	11	MGI Prop	MGI	.84	6.3	27	547	13⅝	12⅞	13¼	– ⅜
	49¾	18⅛	MGMGrand	MGG		...	dd	948	38⅝	36⅞	37½	–1⅜
s	11½	5	MHI Gp	MH■		...	12	31	10	9⅞	10	...
n▼	14⅞	13⅝	MI SchottHm	MHO		...	...	687	13¾	13	13⅛	– ½
	20⅛	11¾	MacFrugals	MFI		...	42	539	16⅞	16¼	16½	+ ⅛
n	22¼	15	Madeco	MAD		...	...	127	21¾	21¼	21¼	– ¼
n	21	14⅞	MaderasSintet	MYS	.20e	1.0	...	224	20¼	19¾	19¾	– ⅜
	18⅝	8¾	MagmaCopper	MCU		...	23	1624	11⅝	11½	11⅝	...
nx	55½	45¾	MagmaCopper pfD		2.81	5.5	...	211	51⅛	50¾	50⅞	– ⅜
	11⅝	3⅞	MagmaCopper wt			...	...	46	6	5¾	5¾	– ¼
	45⅝	22⅝	MagnaInt g	MGA	.60	...	...	872	43¼	41¾	41¾	–2⅛
	25½	12¼	MagneTek	MAG		...	17	1005	14⅝	14⅜	14½	– ¼
	25	14¾	MalaysaFd	MF		...	...	744	21¼	21⅛	21¼	– ⅛
n	12⅝	11¾	MngdHghInc	MHY	1.15	9.5	...	684	12¼	12	12⅛	...
	13⅛	11⅜	ManagdMuni	MMU	6.12	50.0	...	795	12½	12¼	12¼	– ⅛
	13⅛	11¼	ManagdMuni II	MTU	7.08	57.2	...	122	12⅝	12⅜	12⅜	– ⅛
	33¼	24½	Manitowc	MTW	1.00	3.2	45	335	31	30¾	31	...
	26⅝	17½	ManorCare	MNR	.09	.4	19	1582	22	21½	21½	– ¾
	17⅞	13½	Manpower	MAN		...	dd	456	16⅛	15⅜	15⅜	– ¾
n	48¼	27½	MfrdHome	MHC	2.12f	5.3	...	500	40⅞	40	40	– ⅞
	10⅛	6½	Manville	MVL	2.08e	25.6	16	1040	8⅛	8	8⅛	...
	24¾	18⅝	Manville pf			...	...	8	24½	24½	24½	– ⅛
	2½	1	Manville wt			...	...	94	1¾	1⅝	1¾	...
	65⅜	48¾	MAPCO	MDA	1.00	1.7	17	265	60⅝	60⅜	60⅜	– ¼
	19¾	12¾	MargFnl	MRG	.16	1.1	cc	344	14¼	14	14	– ½
n▼	25	23¾	MargFnl dep pfA		.53p	2.2	...	47	23¾	23⅝	23¾	...
	48½	39¼	MarineMid pf		3.00	6.5	...	8	46½	46	46½	– ½
	27⅝	16¼	MarionMDow	MKC	1.00	5.0	14	2825	20⅛	19⅝	19⅞	– ⅛
	4¼	2	Maritrans	TUG		...	5	519	3¾	3⅝	3⅝	– ⅛
n▼	20⅜	15⅛	MarkCtrsTr	MCT	.47e	3.2	...	221	15	14¾	14¾	– ½
	25⅞	14⅛	MarkIV	IV	.10b	.5	18	297	21⅞	21⅜	21½	– ⅛
n▼	27⅜	23¼	MarriottInt	MAR	.28	1.2	...	2546	23⅜	22¾	23	– ½
▼	97⅝	79	MarshMcL	MMC	2.70	3.4	18	866	80	78¾	79⅛	– ⅞
	50⅛	33⅞	Marshl Ind	MI		...	15	145	45	44½	44½	– ⅞
	12⅜	3½	Martech	MUS		...	15	155	3⅞	3⅝	3¾	...
	1¾	½	MLawrencEds	MLE		...	dd	176	¾	⅝	11/16	+ 1/16
s	46⅝	28¾	MartinMar	ML	.90	2.2	10	2002	41	40⅝	40⅞	– ⅛
s	**35¾**	**8½**	**MarvelEntn**	**MRV**		**...**	**52**	**6617**	**28½**	**26⅜**	**26¾**	**–3¼**
	35¼	25⅛	Masco	MAS	.68f	2.0	25	4303	34½	34	34½	– ⅜
	22⅝	8⅜	Mascotech	MSX	.04e	.2	25	1095	22	21⅜	21⅝	...
n	21¾	19	Mascotech pf		.27p	1.3	...	850	20¾	20¾	20¾	...
	31¼	25¼	MassMuInv	MCI	2.80	9.4	...	83	30⅛	29¾	29¾	– ¼
	8¾	7⅛	MassMuPrtInv	MPV	.68	8.2	...	115	8½	8¼	8¼	– ⅛
	26	12	MaterlSci	MSC		...	22	203	22¼	21⅞	21⅞	– ⅛
	141½	84¾	MatsuElec	MC	1.10e	.9	...	4	128	127¾	128	–3⅞
	30¾	20½	Mattel	MAT	.24	.8	17	3548	29	28¼	28⅝	– ¼
	6⅜	3⅞	MaunaLoa	NUT	.40	9.4	28	117	4¼	4⅛	4¼	+ ⅛
	10⅜	5¾	MaxusEngy	MXS		...	12	3579	6	5⅞	5⅞	– ⅛
▼	49⅞	41	MaxusEngy pf		4.00	9.5	...	135	42⅛	40¼	42⅛	– ⅜
s	46½	33⅜	MayDeptStrs	MA	.92	2.2	16	9119	43¼	41¾	42	– ⅞
n	31	16¾	Maybelline	MAY	.12e	.5	...	262	23⅞	23⅜	23½	...
	17¾	13	Maytag	MYG	.50	3.1	37	1826	16⅜	15⅞	15⅞	– ½
n▼	26⅝	23½	McArthurGln	MCG		...	...	540	23½	22⅝	22⅝	–1
	23½	18⅛	McClatchy A	MNI	.29f	1.3	22	6	23	22⅞	22⅞	...
	32⅞	20⅛	McDermInt	MDR	1.00	3.7	14	924	27¼	27	27⅛	...
	35⅞	28¾	McDermInt pfA		2.20	6.5	...	31	33¾	33¾	33¾	– ¼
s	16	9⅝	McDnInvst	MDD	.30	2.1	7	40	14⅝	14½	14½	– ⅛
	57⅞	45½	McDonalds	MCD	.43	.8	20	6474	56¼	54¾	55⅝	– ⅞
n	28	24⅛	McDonalds dep pf		1.93	7.3	...	242	26⅜	26	26⅜	...
	107¾	42⅞	McDonDoug	MD	1.40	1.4	3	1760	106¾	103	103	–4
	75¼	55¼	McGrawH	MHP	2.28	3.3	cc	1311	70	68¼	69	+ ½
	57⅛	38⅝	McKesson	MCK	1.68	3.0	16	963	56½	55¾	56	– ¼
	48½	37½	Mead	MEA	1.00	2.4	21	1266	41⅝	41⅛	41½	– ⅛

	52 Weeks Hi	52 Weeks Lo	Stock	Sym	Div	Yld %	PE	Vol 100s	Hi	Lo	Close	Net Chg
	58¼	42	NACCO	NC	.66	1.5	29	95	45	43½	45	+1¼
	37⅞	30¼	Nalco	NLC	.90	2.4	19	1390	37½	36⅞	37½	...
	31¾	24¼	Nashua	NSH	.72	2.7	13	126	27¼	27	27⅛	– ¼
	43⅛	23⅞	NtlAustrlBk	NAB	1.60e	4.0	...	281	40⅝	40	40½	–1⅜
s	28⅛	23⅛	NtlCity	NCC	1.08	4.6	10	2875	23⅞	23⅛	23¼	– ⅜
	74½	64	NtlCity pf		4.00	6.2	...	45	65⅛	64¼	64¼	–1
	19½	11½	NtlDataCp	NDC	.44	2.7	21	64	16⅜	16	16⅛	– ⅛
	8⅛	5	NtlEducat	NEC		...	dd	400	6¼	6	6	– ¼
	½	7/64	NtlEnt	NEI		...	...	9	5/32	9/64	9/64	– 1/64
	36⅞	27⅜	NtlFuelG	NFG	1.54	4.7	15	550	33¼	32⅝	32¾	– ⅜
n	21⅜	17½	NtlGolfProp	TEE	.16p	.9	...	241	18¼	17¾	17⅞	– ⅜
	29⅝	21½	NtlHlthInv	NHI	2.13e	7.5	16	179	28¾	28¼	28½	– ¼
	25⅛	12	NtlHlthLab	NH	.32	2.5	20	5979	13¼	12¾	12¾	– ½
	15⅞	12¼	NtlIntgp	NII		...	dd	626	14⅜	13⅝	14¼	+ ¼
n▼	33¼	32	NtlIntgp pfA			...	...	209	31⅞	31½	31⅝	– ⅜
	52	49¾	NtlIntgp pf		5.00	10.1	...	11	50	49¾	49¾	– ¼
	12¾	**4⅝**	**NtlMedia**	**NM**		**...**	**20**	**564**	**6¼**	**5⅝**	**5⅞**	**– ⅜**
	13¼	6½	NtlMedEnt	NME	.36j	...	cc	3419	11⅛	10¾	11	– ⅛
	60⅛	48¾	NtlPresto	NPK	1.80a	3.4	11	38	53	52¼	52⅜	– ⅝
	39⅝	27	NatlRe	NRE	.12	.4	10	239	32	31¾	31¾	– ⅜
	21¾	10⅛	NtlSemi	NSM		...	14	4158	16½	16	16⅜	+ ⅜
	72	47½	NtlSemi pf		4.00	6.8	...	8	59¾	59	59	– ⅜
	27⅞	23⅛	NtlSvcInd	NSI	1.04	4.3	16	784	24⅜	23¾	24	– ⅜
	10	2½	NtlStand	NSD		...	dd	137	8	7⅝	8	– ⅛
n	20⅝	10⅜	NtlSteel B	NS		...	...	233	11¼	11	11⅛	– ¼
	52	35	NtlWestmin	NW	2.00e	4.1	...	14	49	48¾	48¾	–1
n	25⅞	24	NtlWestmin B		.78e	3.1	...	214	25⅛	24¾	25	...
	28⅞	25⅜	NtlWestmin A		2.66	9.3	...	727	28¾	28⅝	28⅝	...
nx	10⅜	8⅝	NationGovInc	NGI	.09p	.9	...	91	9⅞	9¾	9¾	+ ⅛
	58	44½	NationsBank	NB	1.68	3.6	10	6788	47⅛	46¼	46⅜	– ¾
	42½	30	NatwdHlth	NHP	2.43e	6.3	17	324	38¾	37⅝	38½	– ½
n	25	13	NatuzziInd	NTZ		...	...	77	24½	24	24⅛	– ⅜
s	33¾	18¾	Navistar	NAV		...	dd	1132	25⅜	25	25⅛	– ⅜
	61	26	Navistar pfG		6.00e	10.0	...	908	60¼	60	60	– ⅛
	11/16	1/128	Navistar wtA			...	...	1092	5/256	3/256	3/256	+ 1/256
	19⅞	13⅛	NeimanMarc	NMG	.20	1.1	39	305	17⅞	17¾	17⅞	– ⅛
	11½	5⅜	NetwkEqpt	NWK		...	dd	517	10	9⅝	10	– ⅛
	26¾	22⅜	NevPwr	NVP	1.60	7.0	13	590	23⅛	22⅝	23	...
n▼	16⅛	14⅝	NewAgeMedia	NAF		...	...	512	14⅝	14⅜	14⅜	– ¼
	5⅛	3⅞	NewAmFd	HYB	.48	9.8	...	829	4⅞	4¾	4⅞	...
	43⅜	36¼	NewEngElec	NES	2.24	6.0	14	218	37⅝	37⅜	37⅜	– ¼
	23⅞	13⅜	NewEngInv	NEW	1.60	7.4	14	31	22	21½	21½	– ½
	29½	22½	NewJerRes	NJR	1.52	5.8	15	115	26¼	25⅞	26⅛	– ⅛
	26⅜	21½	NewPinRlty	NPR	1.29e	5.8	25	1376	22⅜	22	22¼	+ ¼
	36½	28¾	NYSE&G	NGE	2.20	7.5	15	670	29⅝	29¼	29½	– ⅛
	26⅜	24¾	NYSE&G pfA		1.88	7.3	...	3	25¾	25¾	25¾	– ⅛
	107¾	100	NYSE&G pfB		8.80	8.5	...	z10	104	104	104	– ½
	28½	25½	NYSE&G pfC		2.12	8.0	...	42	27⅛	26½	26½	– ½
	43⅝	30¾	Newell	NWL	.72	1.8	19	2099	41⅜	40⅞	41	...
n	18½	16½	NewfieldExpl	NFX		...	...	365	17¼	16¾	17⅛	+ ⅝
	17½	12	NewhallLd	NHL	.40	2.7	70	22	15	14⅝	14⅝	– ⅜
	51⅝	27⅞	NewmtGold	NGC	.05	.1	45	613	45¾	44¾	45¼	+ ⅝
	58⅞	36½	NewmtMin	NEM	.60	1.1	55	2397	56	55	55	– ¼
	63¼	36	NewsCorp	NWS	.16e	.3	...	7785	51⅝	49⅜	49¾	–2½
n	26½	24⅜	Newscorp A		.37p	1.5	...	100	24⅝	24⅜	24⅜	– ¼
	25½	18¾	NiaMoPwr	NMK	1.00	5.0	11	3598	20⅛	19¾	20	...
	26¾	23½	NiaMoPwr pf		1.63	6.5	...	5	25	24¾	25	...
	50½	41½	NiaMoPwr pfA		3.40	7.7	...	4	45	44¼	44¼	–2¼
	57	48¼	NiaMoPwr pfC		3.90	7.2	...	1	54½	54½	54½	...
	88	73½	NiaMoPwr pfH		6.10	7.5	...	z70	81¾	81¾	81¾	– ¼
s	31⅝	23⅜	NICOR	GAS	1.22	4.5	13	556	27⅛	26⅞	27	...
	90¼	44	Nike B	NKE	.80	1.6	11	2195	50⅝	50⅛	50½	– ⅛
n	35	17¾	NineWest	NIN		...	...	180	31⅞	30⅞	30⅞	– ⅞
	31	15⅛	NobleAffil	NBL	.16	.6	28	497	27	26⅜	26⅜	– ⅜
	7½	4	NordRes	NRD		...	dd	1158	5¼	4⅞	5⅛	+ ⅛
	69⅞	58½	NorflkSo	NSC	1.92	2.8	18	1612	67⅞	66¾	67⅜	+ ¼
	43	37½	NSoRlwy pf		2.60	6.4	...	5	40½	40½	40½	– ½
	30⅜	19⅞	Norsk	NHY	.42e	1.4	...	397	29⅞	29¾	29⅞	...
	8	4¼	Nortek	NTK		...	dd	81	7¾	7⅝	7⅝	– ¼
	34¾	14⅞	NoAmerMtg	NAC	.24f	1.0	8	2337	24¾	22	24⅜	+ ⅜

Figure 2–1 NYSE Composite Transactions (Tuesday, November 23, 1993) (*Source:* Reprinted by permission of *The Wall Street Journal*, © Dow Jones & Company, 1985. All rights reserved worldwide.)

3. This column identifies the ticker symbol of the issue.

4. If the company makes a *dividend* distribution to its stockholders, that information appears next to the corporate title or abbreviation. Thus, McDonald's has established a policy of paying a $.43 per share dividend *annually*. Because of the unique character of some distributions, they appear with a footnote designation.

5. The *yield* is the indicated dividend (column 3) divided by the closing price of the stock. For McDonald's that yield is .8 percent (.43 ÷ 55⅝).

6. The *P/E ratio,* meaning price-earnings ratio, is used by some investors to gauge the relative value of a particular security. It compares the current market price of an issue to the latest twelve-month earnings announcement on a per-share basis. Thus, because the number 20 appears in this column and the stock is selling at about $56, simple arithmetic advises that twelve-month earnings were approximately $2.80 per share (56 ÷ 20). No figure appears in this column if the issue is a preferred stock or if the company had no earnings or deficit income to report. Negative P/E ratios are meaningless.

7. Daily quantity figures are recorded only in terms of the number of round lots traded. Because the typical trading unit is 100 shares, the actual share volume is derived by adding two zeros to the number of round lots shown. Thus, the figure 6474 actually means that 647,400 shares changed hands this day. One important exception to this statement concerns ten-share trading unit stocks. The quantity figure for these issues is always stated in full and is recognizable by the letter "z" preceding the volume. Sales indicated as "z100" mean, in fact, that a total of 100 shares traded today. The "x" preceding the volume figure signifies that this issue began trading ex-dividend today.

8. *High* refers to the highest-priced transaction for that issue this day.

9. *Low* refers to the lowest-priced transaction for that issue this day. Both these columns are included for the benefit of readers interested in determining the extent of the security's daily fluctuation. Note: The letter "d" next to a price is a new low for the year. If the stock had traded at a yearly high price, the letter "u" would appear next to that price in the column labeled "high."

10. *Close* is the final sale price of that security on the exchange today.

11. *Net change* (Net Chg.) is the difference between *yesterday's closing price and today's closing price.* It is an indicator of daily price trend, and it enables you to determine a monetary result of trading activity on an issue you particularly favor.

Secondary Markets: The Over-the-Counter Market

The OTC market is not a central physical marketplace but a collection of broker-dealers scattered across the country. This market is more a way of doing business than a place. Buying and selling interest in unlisted stocks are matched not through

the auction process on the floor of an exchange but through *negotiated bidding,* over a massive network of telephone and Teletype wires that link thousands of securities firms here and abroad.

Scope of Market

The OTC market encompasses all securities not traded on national organized exchanges.[4] It is really a group of markets, each tending to specialize in certain securities. The first of these markets deals in the securities of the U.S. Treasury and government agencies. The second encompasses the trading in municipal bonds. The third is not as clear-cut but deals in listed and unlisted corporate bonds, in many preferred stocks, and in bank and insurance stocks. The fourth major market deals in unlisted stocks of manufacturing, merchandising, and miscellaneous companies. The quality of issues traded in these heterogeneous and diffuse markets ranges all the way from the highest (U.S. governments) to the lowest (small, highly speculative stocks).

Many more securities are traded OTC than on the organized exchanges. Perhaps 50,000 securities, of which one-third are actively traded, are traded in the OTC market. However, the volume of activity in the OTC market is such that only about one-third of all stock trading activity in the United States takes place there. The OTC market remains dominant in number of issues traded and dollar volume of bonds.

Participants

OTC activity is both wholesale and retail in character. The participants are broker-dealers. A wholesale dealer buys and sells for his own account and from or to professionals. These dealers "make markets" by standing ready to buy or sell securities. They maintain an inventory position in many securities and are actively engaged as principals in buying and selling those in which they are interested. The market here is an interdealer market because the business transacted is only with other securities firms.

Larger OTC firms are linked by private telephone and Teletype. These means of communication serve as the vehicles for buying and selling. Traders quote buy and sell prices to other dealers who call, usually without knowing whether the caller wants to buy or sell.

Individual investors deal with retail firms. For example, if you wish to buy an OTC stock, your brokerage firm might buy the stock from a wholesale dealer for its own account and resell it to you at a slightly higher price. In this case, your firm is functioning as a dealer. The other way your firm could have handled the deal would be to act as your agent in buying the stock from a wholesaler, and it would charge you a commission for its services.

---

[4]Some listed stocks are also traded OTC.

PRICES AND QUOTATIONS

Buyers and sellers of listed stocks meet through brokers on the floor of an exchange and arrive at prices by the *auction* method. OTC transactions are effected within or between the offices of securities houses, prices being arrived at by *negotiation*.

Answering an inquiry as to the market on a particular security, a dealer may quote "20 bid, offered at 21." The prices quoted are "inside," or wholesale, prices at which dealers will sell to each other. The bid is the highest price the dealer will pay for the stock, and the lowest price he will sell it for (offer it) is 21.

The caller frequently asks about the size of the dealer's market. The reply indicates the number of shares the dealer is willing to buy or sell at the quoted prices. Suppose that the response is "300 shares either way" (buy or sell). The next move is up to the caller. He has instructions from his customer as to price limits. If the customer wanted 100 shares at a limit of $20.75, the broker may tell the dealer, "I will pay 20½ for 100 shares." He is *negotiating* for the best price for his customer by bidding away from the offering price (21) and below his customer's limit (20¾). The dealer may or may not be willing to make a concession from his offering price of 21. Perhaps he will counter by paring his offering price somewhat, but not all the way to the broker's offer to buy. The dealer may counter with, "I will sell 100 at 20⅝." The broker may accept this or negotiate further. If he accepts the price of 20⅝, he has been able to obtain the stock for his customer below the limit and dealer's first quote.

The ultimate price to the customer will exceed 20⅝ by the charges he must pay. If his firm acts as his agent (broker), he will pay the 20⅝ plus the regular commission. In other cases, his firm might sell from its own inventory at a "net" price, at which a markup is involved but buried in the price. In our example above, if the shares came from the firm's inventory rather than purchase from a wholesaler, the net price might still be 20⅝; however, it would be difficult to ascertain how much the firm marked up its own stock.[5]

NATIONAL ASSOCIATION OF SECURITIES DEALERS AUTOMATED QUOTATIONS (NASDAQ).   In 1971 a computerized communications network called NASDAQ came into being to provide automated quotations for OTC securities. Securities salespeople can get up-to-date bid and asked prices on OTC securities from a small console that is electronically connected to the NASDAQ computer. They can then contact dealers offering the best prices and negotiate a trade. This rapid centralizing of bid-asked quotes replaced a long-archaic system of "shopping around" by brokers. Under the old system an investor had no assurance that he was receiving the best price available.

Not all OTC stocks are active enough to be included in the NASDAQ system. At the end of 1988, more than 5,000 issues having a market value of $350 billion were listed solely on NASDAQ. Of those in the system, the more widely held and

---

[5]The National Association of Securities Dealers, which supervises activities of OTC broker-dealers, suggests that a 5 percent markup is reasonable under normal conditions.

traded are quoted in *The Wall Street Journal* according to the bid-ask prices and volume of trading. The latter information was unavailable under the old system.

NASDAQ is a dealer market made by approximately 600 dealers who stand ready to buy and sell the securities in the system. Each stock has at least two dealers. In 1988, the average number of dealers per stock was 9.4, with a number of stocks having more than 20 dealers. Individual dealers may make markets in as many as 300 to 400 stocks. Access to NASDAQ occurs at various levels. Possession of a level 1 terminal allows a broker to determine the inside quote—the highest bid price of any dealer and the lowest ask price of any dealer. A terminal with level 2 capability allows a broker to determine the bid-ask prices of each dealer in a stock. Dealers in NASDAQ possess terminals with level 3 capability, which in addition to allowing level 1 and level 2 capability, also permit the dealers to enter price quotations for the stocks in which they make a market.

The trading information provided on NASDAQ depends on the security. For most securities NASDAQ provides bid and ask quotations on a real-time basis and summary information on the volume of trading in the security for each day. Transaction data are not currently available for most NASDAQ securities. In 1982 NASDAQ began providing transaction data for selected stocks, termed *national market securities,* which are comparable to that provided for listed stocks.

THE BOND MARKET

About 2,200 bond issues are on the NYSE, representing the debt of U.S. and foreign corporations, the U.S. government, New York City, international banks, foreign governments, and so forth. Because bonds are traded in large amounts and have special characteristics, the rules of the NYSE ordinarily permit transactions to be executed off the floor even though the issue is listed. Accordingly, bonds are handled primarily in the OTC market.

The actual buying and selling of securities is carried on by traders associated with dealer firms or with large institutions. An institutional trader becomes familiar with the dealers who make markets in the securities in which the institution is interested. By keeping close ties, the institutional trader can gauge whether the dealer is long or short, and the side of the market in which the dealer is likely to be aggressive.

An institution may have direct communications lines to the active dealers; the number of lines depends on its size. On the other hand, individual investors place orders with brokers, who transmit them to their traders for execution. The trader will probably explore the market and obtain several quotations before actually effecting a purchase or sale.

Dealer banks play an important role in the market for bonds in the U.S. government and federal agencies and for general obligations of state and local governments. In the case of U.S. government bonds, the Federal Reserve Bank of New York, which is the fiscal agent for the U.S. government and the Federal Reserve System, recognizes certain "primary dealers." By agreeing to abide by certain rules, such a dealer becomes entitled to a private line between the reserve bank's trading desk and its own. Without this direct line, which may be with-

drawn if its performance is considered unsatisfactory, a dealer would be severely handicapped.

TYPES OF MARKET TRANSACTIONS

One prerequisite to successful investing in stocks is a basic understanding of the operational mechanics of the secondary securities markets. Before a security is purchased or sold, the investor must instruct his broker about the order. This means clearly specifying how the order is to be placed. Much confusion and ill will can be avoided if proper jargon, which has a widely accepted usage, is utilized.

Investors should be concerned that they get the best "execution" in market transactions. This means the best price on the buy or sell. The adroit handling of orders to buy or sell can have an appreciable effect on the rate of return that an investor realizes from the holding of a security.

Basically, two types of stock transactions exist—buy orders and sell orders. Sell orders can be further classified as either selling long or selling short.

BUY ORDERS.   Buy orders, obviously, are used when the investor anticipates a rise in prices. When he deems the time appropriate for the stock purchase, the investor enters a buy order. As will be seen shortly, the investor must make several other determinations besides just instructing his broker to buy XYZ common.

SELL-LONG ORDERS.   When the investor determines that a stock he already owns (long position) is going to experience a decline in price, he may decide to dispose of it. To do this, he enters a sell-long order (generally just called a sell order). Here also, other determinations must be made to accompany the sell order.

SELL-SHORT ORDERS.   Short selling, or "going short," is a special and quite speculative variety of selling. Basically, it involves selling shares of a stock that are not owned but borrowed, in anticipation of a price decline. When and if the price declines, the executor of the short sale buys the equivalent number of shares of the same stock at the lower price and returns to the lender the stock he borrowed. On a per-share basis, the short seller profits by the difference between the sale price and the purchase price (minus taxes and commissions).

The procedure just outlined, carried out in the hope of a stock price decline, is probably the most widely used form of short selling. Furthermore, this speculative form of short selling is the stereotype of a sell-short order in the eyes of the general public. Various other uses of short selling, as well as a discussion of its technical aspects, will be presented later in this chapter.

SIZE OF ORDER

All trading in NYSE stocks occurs as either a round-lot order or an odd-lot order.

ROUND LOTS.   When an order is considered a round lot, it is for the proper unit of trading for the particular stock, or some multiple of that unit. For most NYSE se-

curities, the unit of trading is 100 shares.[6] Therefore, orders for 100 shares or multiples thereof, such as 300, 500, or 1,000, are considered round-lot orders.

ODD LOTS.   An order for less than the unit of trading is considered an odd-lot order. Thus, an order for one, fifty, or ninety-nine shares is an odd-lot order. An order for, say, 132 shares is treated as both types of orders; the 100 shares is treated as a round lot and the 32 shares as an odd lot. Odd-lot orders carry somewhat higher costs than round lots, as we shall see in the following chapter.

PRICE LIMIT OF ORDERS

An investor can have his order executed either at the best prevailing price on the exchange or at a price he determines.

MARKET ORDERS.   Market orders are executed as fast as possible at the best prevailing price on the exchange. They account for 75 to 80 percent of all transactions. In the case of a buy order, the best price is the lowest obtainable price; in the case of a sell order, the highest obtainable price. When such an order is desired, the investor merely tells his broker to "buy 100 PQR at the market."

The obvious advantage of a market order is the speed with which it is executed. The disadvantage is that the investor does not know the exact execution price until after the fact, when his broker receives confirmation of the order execution. This disadvantage is potentially most troublesome when dealing in either very inactive or very volatile securities.

LIMIT ORDERS.   Limit orders overcome the disadvantage of the market order—namely, not knowing in advance the price at which the transaction will take place. Thus, limit orders aid in setting the boundaries of dollar risk the investor wishes to assume. When using a limit order, the investor specifies in advance the limit price at which he wants the transaction carried out. It is always understood that the price limitation includes an "or better" instruction. In the case of a limit order to buy, the investor specifies the maximum price he will pay for the stock; the order can be carried out only at the limit price or lower. In the case of a limit order to sell, the investor specifies the minimum price he will accept for the stock; the order can be carried out only at the limit price or higher.

Assume that McDonald's Corp. (symbol MCD) is currently trading at $29 per share. You want to buy the stock soon, but you want to be certain to obtain shares not much higher than the current price. You might place a limit order to buy at 29½. This order will be executed only at 29½ or less. In this fashion you have stated the maximum price ($29.50) you are willing to pay and thus have limited your dollar risk. Conversely, if you wanted to sell MCD or go short, you might desire to specify the minimum sale price you will accept. Therefore, your order might be

---

[6]Some relatively inactive or high-priced stocks and many preferred stocks have units of trading of 10 shares.

"Sell MCD 28 limit." This order will be carried out only if $28 or more per share can be obtained. Thus, you would not sell at 27¾, but you would at 28¼.

Generally, limit orders are placed "away from the market." This means the limit price is somewhat removed from the prevailing price (generally, above the prevailing price in the case of a limit order to sell, and below the prevailing price in the case of a limit order to buy). Obviously, the investor operating in this manner believes that his limit price will be reached and executed in a reasonable period of time. Therein, however, lies the chief disadvantage of a limit order—that it may never be executed at all. If the limit price is set very close to the prevailing price, there is little advantage over the market order. Furthermore, if the stock is moving sharply upward or downward, to place a limit order very close to the market and risk not getting the trade-off is sheer folly. On the other hand, if the limit is considerably removed from the market, the price may never reach the limit—even because of a fractional difference. And because limit orders are filled on a first-come, first-served basis as trading permits, it is also possible that so many of them are in ahead of the investor's limit at a given price that his order will never be executed. Thus, selecting a proper limit price is a delicate maneuver.

The nonexecution risk of limit orders must be balanced against the potential gain from achieving a more attractive price. If an imminent development is expected to affect the price, the limit might be set close to the current price. For example, heavy selling often occurs near the end of the year for tax loss purposes. This activity might only temporarily depress the stock price. If there are no known imminent developments, the limit price might be set near a forthcoming low (high) for a buy (sell). It is useful to check past trading ranges as a high-low guide.

Many have noted that orders tend to cluster around certain prices. For example, a whole number, say, 23, is more popular than prices in halves (23½). Prices in eighths are even less popular among investors (e.g., 23⅛, 23⅞, etc.). Suppose a stock has just moved down from 23¼ to 23. There could be a heavy list of buyers at 23, some of whom may end up paying more than 23 because trades are executed on a first-come, first-served basis. Suppose you wanted to buy the stock. You may achieve more likely execution if you set a buy limit at 23⅛ than at 23 where congestion is more likely.

TIME LIMIT OF ORDERS

Thus far we have classified orders by type of transaction (buy or sell), by size (round lot or odd lot), and by price (market or limit). Now we examine differences stemming from the time limit placed on the order. Orders can be for either a day, a week, a month, or until canceled.

DAY ORDERS.   A day order is one that remains active only for the trading day during which it was entered. Unless otherwise requested by the customer, brokers enter all orders as day orders. Market orders are almost always day orders because they do not specify a particular price. One key rationale for the day order is that market, economic, industry, and firm conditions might change markedly overnight,

and thus a seemingly good investment move one day might seem considerably less desirable the following day.

WEEK ORDERS AND MONTH ORDERS.   Week orders expire at the end of the calendar week during which they were entered—generally, at the close of Friday's trading session. Month orders expire at the end of the last trading session during the calendar month. As the longevity of the order increases, it approaches an open order.

OPEN ORDERS.   Open orders remain in effect until they are either executed or canceled. Thus they are often referred to as GTC (good-till-canceled) orders. Frequently, open orders are used in conjunction with limit orders. When using an open or GTC order, the investor is implying that he understands the supply and demand conditions of the stock in question, and therefore feels sufficiently confident that, given enough time, his order will be executed on his terms. Open orders are regularly (monthly or quarterly) confirmed by the broker with the investor to ensure that he is aware of their continued existence.

Several very similar types of risks are associated with open orders. First is the substantial risk the situation surrounding the proposed transaction has changed markedly so that the contemplated action is no longer advisable. For example, some very bullish information may be boosting the stock's price so that a limit sell order is reached. However, circumstances may have changed, and a sell order may be inappropriate and unwanted, but the investor may not have time to cancel the open order. Conversely, some very bearish news may have depressed the stock so that an open limit order to buy is activated. However, the buy may have meanwhile become completely unwarranted. Yet because of the open order and an inability to cancel it in time, the new unwanted purchase may be made. A related risk is that the investor may just forget about the open order because considerable time has passed since it was confirmed by the broker. When this occurs, the investor may (1) not want the transaction any more or (2) be unable to pay for the stock in the event of an open order to buy. Finally, the open order may be at a limit price just below (in the case of a buy order) or just above (in the case of a sell order) the price the stock reaches before a major move. In this event, a desired transaction is not consummated because of a fraction of a point differential. Under such circumstances, the open order is indeed penny-wise and pound-foolish.

SPECIAL TYPES OF ORDERS

In this section, several key varieties of orders will be discussed and several situations in which these orders may be desired will be outlined. The discussion will represent a number of possible situations and is not meant to be exhaustive. The appendix at the end of this chapter lists and describes an array of types of orders available to stock traders.

STOP ORDERS.   A stop order may be used to protect a profit or limit a loss. In effect, a stop order is a special type of limit order but with very important differences

in intent and applications. A stop order to sell is treated as a market order when the stop price or a price below it is "touched" (reached); a stop order to buy is treated as a market order when the stop price or a price above it is reached. Thus, a stop order to sell is set at a price below the current market price, and a stop order to buy is set at a price above the current market price. A few examples will help clarify the rationale of the stop order.

Suppose that you bought 100 shares of a stock at 20 and it is currently selling at 40. Thus, on paper (excluding taxes and commissions) you have a 20-point, or $2,000, profit, which you wish to protect as much as possible; however, if the stock's price continues upward, you wish to maintain your long position. One way of achieving this profit protection is to enter a sell stop order at a price below 40—say, 38. Now if the price falls to 38 or below, your stop order becomes a market order, and your position will be sold out in the area of $38 per share at the best obtainable price. Let's say that you are "stopped out" at 38. In this case you would realize an 18-point, or $1,800, profit (ignoring taxes and commissions). On the other hand, if the price declines to 39, then turns around and continues upward, your long position will be maintained.[7] Thus, a certain level of profit is maintained. Such profit protection can also be obtained in a short sale, as you can see by thinking through the procedure for protecting a short-sale profit.

Next let us see how a short-position loss can be minimized through the judicious use of a stop order. Suppose that you shorted 100 shares of a stock at 50. However, you are a bit leery about your position; you wish to minimize a possible loss resulting from an upward movement in price, but at the same time, if the stock's price moves downward, you wish to maintain your short position. This can be achieved by entering a buy stop order at a price above the current 50 (where you went short)—say, at 52. Now if the price rises to 52 or above, your stop becomes a market order, and your short will be covered at the best obtainable price, say, 52. Then your loss will be two points, or $200, rather than considerably more. On the other hand, if the price goes to 51 and then goes down, or just declines from 50, your short position will remain intact.

Several possible dangers are inherent when using stops. First, if the stop is placed too close to the market, the investor might have his position closed out because of a minor price fluctuation, even though his idea will prove correct in the long run. On the other hand, if the stop is too far away from the market, the stop order serves no purpose. Second, because stop orders become market orders only after the proper price level has been reached, the actual transaction could take place some distance away from the price the investor had in mind when he placed the order. (One reason may be a prior accumulation of orders.) In summary, then, stop orders may be useful if used wisely by a generally knowledgeable investor; however, they cannot rectify basically bad investment decisions, and, poorly placed, they can close out good investment positions.

STOP-LIMIT ORDERS.   The stop-limit order is a device to overcome the uncertainty connected with a stop order—namely, that of not knowing what the execu-

---

[7]In such a situation, you might raise your stop to "lock in" a larger profit.

tion price will be after the order becomes a market order. The stop-limit order gives the investor the advantage of specifying the limit price: the maximum price he will pay in the case of a stop limit to buy, or the minimum price he will accept in the case of a stop limit to sell. Therefore, a stop-limit order to buy is activated as soon as the stop price or higher is reached, and then an attempt is made to buy at the limit price or lower. Conversely, a stop-limit order to sell is activated as soon as the stop price or lower is reached, and then an attempt is made to sell at the limit price or higher. For example, suppose that you are long 100 shares of a stock at 40 and wish to protect most of a profit you currently have. You could enter a stop limit to sell at 38. If and when the stock reaches 38 or below, your order is activated, and an attempt is made to sell at 38 or above. But nothing below 38 will be accepted.[8]

The obvious danger is that the order may not be executed in a down market because you have quibbled about a small amount, and the result may well be a substantially greater loss. Thus, the investor using stop-limit orders must exercise even greater caution than the investor utilizing stop orders. However, if things work out as planned, the stop-limit order to sell will be very effective. The reader should work through the mechanics of a stop-limit order to buy. See the accompanying box on page 36 for a discussion of stop-loss orders.

DISCRETIONARY ORDERS.   As the name implies, the discretionary order permits the broker leeway in the filling of a customer's order. This leeway can be complete, in which case the broker decides everything from the security to the price to the direction of the order—that is, buy or sell. In the case of a limited discretion account, the broker decides only the timing and price of the transaction. This type of order is frequently used when the investor goes on vacation and does not want to follow and worry about his investments. Obviously, an investor giving his broker any type of discretion must have great faith in the broker's ability, his judgment, and the time at his disposal.

ORDER EXECUTION

Once the investor instructs his broker about his order, a chain of events is set off. Without going into complete detail on every step, let us trace the process. In the discussion, the reader should note the key role played by the specialist in the proper functioning of the NYSE.

First, let us trace how a round-lot order to buy 800 shares of McDonald's Corp. was handled until 1984. The investor called his broker to determine the current price of McDonald's stock. In addition, he wanted to know the high and low prices for the day and the price on the last trade. The broker would also give the bid and asked prices. The bid represents the highest offer to buy that the specialist has received, and the asked represents the lowest offer to sell.

---

[8]The stop and limit may be placed at different prices. In our example, you could specify 38 stop, 37 limit. This means you will sell at 37 or above.

A COSTLY MYTH: THE CASE AGAINST STOP-LOSS ORDERS

JERRY HELZNER

The smug little world of investors who depend on stop-loss orders to guard their portfolios against steep declines in individual stocks was at least temporarily shaken on the evening of Nov. 7, when the New York Stock Exchange summarily cancelled all stop-loss orders on ICN Pharmaceuticals. ICN, a small drug company, had been the object of frenzied speculative interest, and its stock price had nearly tripled in the preceding month. In implementing the ban, the exchange reasoned that, if wave after wave of the existing stop orders in ICN were somehow triggered, the shares would suffer a sharp drop.

On Nov. 8, with news of the exchange's action made public, ICN shares suffered a sharp drop anyway. They shed more than 25% of their value, sliding from 16½ to 12⅛.

Two weeks later, the American Stock Exchange imposed a similar ban on stop-loss orders (also known as stop-limit or stop orders) for U.S. Bioscience, again out of fear that they could touch off a domino effect on the downside, if any negative news about the company developed. The stock has been one of Wall Street's hottest performers of late.

While both the ICN and U.S. Bioscience incidents were isolated actions, they illustrate a larger fact about the supposed wisdom of using stop-loss orders. In reality, the stop loss is an appealing delusion. It offers about the same amount of protection as a bad deodorant does on a scorching day: not much. Investors would be much better served if they relied less on stop-loss orders and thought more about the quality of the stocks they purchase.

The stop-loss myth has wide credence. It is a trading tactic that has been almost universally praised by the most respected and experienced students of the market. Almost every book on investing advises novices to use stop-loss orders as a means of avoiding serious hits on individual stocks. And while the conventional wisdom of "cut your losses—let your profits run" sounds great in theory, it doesn't work very well in the rough-and-tumble world of 1991 investing.

Stop-loss orders are rather simple. If you own a stock listed on the New York or American exchange, you pick a price—usually 10%–15% below the current one—and enter an order to automatically sell your shares if the stock falls to that price. (You also can enter a stop-loss on an OTC stock, if your broker will accept one on an issue not traded on the Big Board or Amex.)

Ideally, if your stock takes a sudden drop, you are "stopped out" and your loss is limited. You have preserved most of your capital and you're ready to try again on another day. Or you might have used the stop order to protect an existing gain. This concept appeals to all the right psychological instincts—it's conservative, it's a kind of insurance, it's a form of controlling your own destiny.

How could anyone quarrel with this?

To my thinking, any strategy that sounds so wise, so wholesome, so mature—and is so widely recommended—has to be wrong. And this one is.

I'm sure there was a time back in the 'Seventies—when stocks didn't swing so wildly and specialists actually had an interest in keeping markets orderly—that stop-loss orders were mildly useful.

But those days are gone. This is the era of the gap opening, the 100-point freefall and the out-to-lunch specialist. A stop-loss order isn't going to help you very much when

your Bio-Immunogeneran fails to win FDA approval for its new wonder drug one after-noon and opens down 15 points the next morning. Oh, you had a stop-loss in at 55? Sorry, the best price you can get is 42.

The supposed "protection" offered by a stop-loss order actually encourages small investors to dabble in fad stocks. Investors wrongly believe they can't lose much if they use a stop loss.

Most people would be far better off if they limited their trading activities to stocks that can be purchased on a value basis. They should steer clear of "performance" stocks that move up fast and go down faster.

I consider myself a fairly successful trader, and I have never considered using stop-loss orders. If your stock selection techniques are fundamentally sound—and emphasize value—you don't need the "protection" of the stop loss. After all, you can always sell if you think a stock is turning into a disappointment. Why take the chance of getting stopped out of a good stock just because of some Russian coup attempt or credit-card interest rate fiasco that turns the market into Silly Putty for a day or two?

History tells us to buy good stocks when they're cheap. Stop-loss strategy encourages investors to *get rid of stocks* when they're inexpensive. Therefore, it's time for the so-called experts to stop promoting this highly dubious strategy. Too often, the only thing halted by a stop-loss order is an investor's chance of making nice profits.

Source: Barron's, December 9, 1991, p. 22.

The broker checked his stock-quote machine, and he reported back that MCD is quoted at "60 to a quarter." This means that the investor would probably pay 60 if he put in a market order immediately. If this seemed appropriate, the market order was placed. The written order was then wired to the New York office of the brokerage firm.[9] From there it was phoned to a clerk of the firm on the floor of the NYSE. The clerk notified a member partner of the firm (only members—those having seats—are entitled to execute orders) via an annunciator board system—huge boards on which each member can be paged via his assigned number. The member then returned to his clerk (or if he was too busy, he sent an exchange employee) to pick up the orders. Next he went to the location on the floor at which MCD is traded. (Each stock is assigned to a specialist at a particular U-shaped trading post.) There he checked with the specialist to ascertain the current bid and asked prices of MCD, and he executed the buy order at the best obtainable price. This frequently occurred through face-to-face contact with another member partner representing another investor. They "auctioned" with each other through offers to buy and sell and reached a mutually satisfactory transaction price. This is called a *double-auction process*. It should be observed that buyer bought from seller. One party dealt with another party. The NYSE provided a place and apparatus that allowed agents of buyers and sellers to meet and transact business.

After the trade was consummated, the brokers noted the transaction and with whom it was made, an exchange reporter noted the transaction for reporting on the

---

[9]This procedure would be followed regardless of where the investor was located.

ticker, and the phone clerks reversed the order-placing process so that the investor is notified how his buy of 800 shares of MCD at the market was executed. This entire process (including the appearance of the trade on the ticker) occurred within minutes of the initial phone call by the investor to his broker. Today, member firms can transmit market and limit orders directly to the appropriate trading post electronically.

ROLE OF THE SPECIALIST

The most attractive and important feature of a stock exchange listing is marketability at fair and reasonable prices. Toward this objective, one category of members has been delegated with responsibility for ensuring that each listed stock experiences an "orderly succession of prices." These members are known as *specialists*. Each stock issue traded on an exchange is assigned a specialist to supervise and conduct an equitable market for that security. To perform this function, a specialist is obliged to act in a dual capacity—as agent and as principal.

Today each specialist firm controls all the trading in one or more stocks or options. There is ordinarily only one specialist firm to a stock. There are about 400 specialists on the NYSE and about 225 specialists on the AMEX. When new stocks are listed, specialists apply for them, and an allocation committee makes the assignments based upon the grading of the specialist firms by the brokerage houses. The names of specialist firms are not as well known to the general public as the brokerage firms (such as Smith Barney Shearson and Merrill Lynch). For example, the specialist in IBM is deCordova, Cooper & Co., and Stokes, Hoyt & Co. handles General Electric.

The specialist in a particular security normally receives orders to buy or sell when a firm's commission house or $2 brokers are unable to execute them immediately. Usually, this means that the specialist receives orders away from the current price levels of that issue. Such orders include limit orders to buy and stop orders to sell at prices below the prevailing market level, as well as limit orders to sell and stop orders to buy at prices above the prevailing market level. The specialist then enters them in a book maintained as a constant reminder to satisfy these instructions if and when market conditions favor their execution. When able to execute an order, the specialist may charge and receive a floor brokerage fee for this service, as can any $2 broker. The brokerage fee is negotiated between the specialist and the firm for whom that order was executed.

Many specialists in stocks that are popular with the public earn a substantial portion of their income acting in this riskless agency capacity. However, there is no assurance that

1. the customers' instructions can ever be satisfied,
2. these orders will not be canceled just prior to execution, or
3. sufficient quantities of customers' orders will be given to the specialist for execution.

In fact, the specialist's book is often empty of customer orders on the side of the quotation or at the time when they are needed most to maintain depth and

price continuity. It is especially important at this time for the specialist to act as a dealer.

The specialist is encouraged to buy and sell for a personal account and risk in order to maintain marketability and an orderly succession of prices. The specialist is expected personally to bid or offer when the public is reluctant to do so and thus provide continuous two-sided markets in all quotations.

The exchanges do not expect the specialist to act as a barrier in a rising market or as a support in a falling market. The specialist must merely try to keep these rises and declines equitable and consistent. Because of the variable facts influencing supply and demand for individual stocks, a specific formula for an orderly market cannot be defined.

To maintain the market a specialist usually purchases stock at a higher price than anyone else is willing to pay. For example, let us assume that a stock has just sold at 55. The highest price anyone is willing to pay is 54¼ (the best bid), and the lowest price at which anyone is willing to sell is 55¼ (the best offer). The specialist, acting as a dealer for his own account, may now decide to bid 54¾ for 600 shares, making the quotation 54¾–55¼, which narrows the spread between the bid and offer prices to ½ point. Now, if a prospective seller wishes to sell 600 shares at the price of the best bid, the specialist will purchase his stock at 54¾. By doing this, the specialist not only provides the seller with a better price, but also maintains better price continuity, since the variation from the last sale is ¼ of a point.

Here, on the other hand, is an example of how the specialist may sell stock for his own account to maintain a market. Let us assume that with the last sale in a stock at 62¼ the best bid is 62 and the best offer 63, the specialist offers 600 shares at 62½ for his own account, changing the quotation to 62–62½. A buyer enters the market and buys the stock from the specialist. Thus, the buyer purchased the stock ½ point cheaper than would have been the case without the specialist's offer, and again, better price continuity and depth have been maintained.

In his efforts to maintain an orderly market, a specialist sometimes makes both the best bid and best offer in a stock for his own account. Many times, when the specialist does not have sufficient stock in his inventory, he will sell "short" to maintain a market. In doing this, he must observe all the rules and regulations governing short selling.

Obviously, a single, specific formula cannot be applied to markets in individual stocks to determine whether they are fair and orderly. What is considered fair and orderly in one stock may be regarded as completely inadequate in another. It depends on such things as market conditions, price level of the stock, normal volume of transactions, number of outstanding shares, and how widely the stock is distributed. This can prove to be an expensive public service. If only sell orders prevail, and the specialist continually bids for stock, albeit at consecutively lower prices, there is no way for him to deal profitably. However, professional traders, including specialists, realize that prices do not fall continuously, even in bear markets, nor, on the other hand, do they rise continuously in bull markets. Prices of securities do, in fact, fluctuate as speculators, traders, and investors attempt to gain advantage of what they consider to be attractive values. This fluctuation enables specialists to trade out of their positions as they satisfy both supply and demand in

a market-making capacity. They do not always have an opportunity to trade profitably. They often incur losses to keep their stock positions at manageable levels and still provide equitable prices for the public.

As a legally recognized market-maker, a specialist enjoys certain financing and tax advantages not available to most investors. The specialist is privileged to maintain both a specialty (trading) account and an investment account for each assigned stock. By keeping these positions physically separate and distinct, the specialist can

1. take advantage of favorable long-term capital gains rates for profits established in an investment account, and
2. arrange financing for securities in the specialty account exempted from the restrictive provisions of the Federal Reserve Board's Regulation U. Generally, this means that the specialist can obtain credit in amounts up to 90 percent of the market value of the security pledged.

A specialist may also repurchase stocks sold at a loss within the past thirty days and still be able to use that loss to offset profits in calculating taxable income. That privilege, known as a *wash sale*, is denied to most investors under the Internal Revenue Code.

On the other hand, the government does not grant specialists any privileges to provide a tactical advantage over competing brokers in the trading crowd. Specialists must observe the unique rules about executing short sales for themselves or for customers in the same manner as do all other members. This means that when selling short, they too must sell shares short at least $\frac{1}{8}$ point above the previous different-priced transaction. Just like everyone else, a specialist cannot depress the price of a stock when selling it short.

The NYSE realizes that the specialist's vantage point in the marketplace provides information that could prove to be personally profitable if the specialist were permitted to use it. Because the contents of his book are generally unavailable to anyone else except NYSE officials, the specialist alone knows how many orders and shares are entered at prices just away from the prevailing quotation—orders that may serve as support or resistance levels. The specialist alone knows of the presence of stop orders and their memorandum price levels—orders that may accentuate price volatility if activated. Consequently, although the NYSE urges specialists to maintain personal trading relative to total volume in each assigned security, it must be done under restrictive regulations to avoid prejudicing the public interest.

Because of their key function in maintaining fair and orderly markets, specialists are required to submit to the exchange—about eight times a year—details of their dealings for unannounced one-week periods selected at random by the exchange. These figures and studies of price continuity, spreads in quotations, and depth are examined carefully by the exchange to determine the specialist's effectiveness in maintaining fair and orderly markets.

In addition, the exchange maintains an on-line price surveillance program based on trading data obtained from the exchange's computers, which run the

stock ticker. This program monitors all trades reported on the ticker throughout the market session. When the price movement of a stock exceeds preset standards, the computer prints the symbol, time, and price of the transaction on a Teletype machine in the exchange's surveillance section. The surveillance section retrieves from the computer's memory bank the chronological sequence of sales, which is then carefully examined.

If no apparent cause is found for the fluctuation, the surveillance section alerts a trading floor official in the area where the stock is traded. The official will then speak to the specialist to determine if a problem exists.

Short Selling

Technical Aspects of a Sell-Short Order.   Most neophytes involved in the stock market tend to think that the only way to make money is to buy a stock that is subsequently expected to rise in price. In other words, if stocks in general are expected to decline in price the best way to behave is to stay out of the market. However, astute speculators use the technique of *short selling* to capitalize on *downward* movement in stock prices. The Federal Reserve Board requires short-selling customers to deposit 50 percent of the net proceeds of such sales with the brokerage firm effecting those transactions. It is from this deposit that all marks to the market, cash dividends, interest obligations, and so on are deducted.

This relationship for a short sale in which the net proceeds amount to $10,000 is shown in Figure 2–2.

Note that the short-selling broker-dealer organization has use of the $5,000 cash deposit from its customer. It may use this deposit to finance other customers' debit balances in their margin accounts or segregate it in a special bank reserve account. In effect, whenever any customer sells short, the broker-dealer organization enjoys somewhat of a financial advantage as a result. Fundamentally, a short sale is the sale of a security that is not owned at the time of the transaction. The short sale necessitates the purchase of the security by the seller some time in the future to eliminate the deficiency.

Obviously, people sell short to make money. They hope that their purchase expense will be lower than their sale proceeds; thus, the difference becomes their

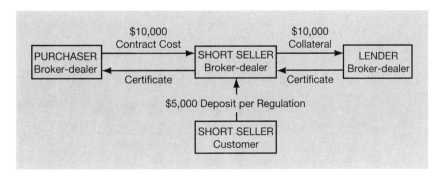

Figure 2–2   Short Sale with Net Proceeds of $10,000

profit. If expenses are greater than proceeds, the difference represents their loss. A short sale is really not an unusual investment practice in today's markets. Typically, investors buy a security first and subsequently sell it. What is so strange if they merely reverse this procedure to take advantage of market conditions?

Selling short is sometimes maligned because of its implication of illegality (selling something not owned) or even failed patriotism ("Don't sell America short"). However, this is a basic premise of business not confined solely to the securities industry. Any time a manufacturer is awarded a contract for merchandise that is not immediately available, to be delivered on a future date at a fixed price, that concern is selling the merchandise short. It is speculating that it will be able to produce those goods for less money than the contract price of sale.

People selling short in the securities market are, to be sure, creating an artificial supply. But at the same time, they are also satisfying an aggressive demand and thereby moderating the otherwise violent effect that demand would have upon price.

The short sellers' usefulness is best demonstrated when they are needed most. During periods of falling prices, when there is a scarcity of ordinary demand, the people who are already short represent a built-in buying interest because they must eventually cover (purchase) their short position. This demand serves to cushion the depression of a bear market just as the original sale cushioned the optimism of a bull market.

One key requirement in executing a short sale is worthy of note for those who sense that short sellers can drive down the price of the stock through successive short sales (which thereby increases the supply of stock). The Securities Exchange Act of 1934 requires that the short sale occur at a price higher than the preceding sale, or at the same price as the preceding sale if that took place at a higher price than a preceding *different* trade price. For example, if the seller wants to go short at 42 and the preceding trade was at 41¾, there is no problem. However, if he wants to go short at 42 and the preceding trade took place at 42, he can do so only if the last preceding *different* trade price before a 42 trade was below 42, such as 41⅛. Thus, the 42 trade was an *uptick*. If the previous different price was above 42, such as 42⅛, no short sale can take place, because the 42 trade was a *downtick*. Thus, we say that a short can take place only on either an "uptick" or a *zero tick* (no price change) that follows an *uptick*.[10] This is called a *zero plus tick* or *zero uptick*. This regulation militates against successively lower prices instigated by a series of shorts.

EXAMPLE.   Assume that the following are successive prices involving a specific stock. The time sequence is numbered 1–12:

(1)	(2)	(3)	(4)	(5)	(6)	(7)	(8)	(9)	(10)	(11)	(12)
50	50½	51	51	51	48	49	49½	51	50	50	51½

---

[10] If a zero tick follows a series of zero ticks, the records must be traced back to determine if a previous trade at a different price was an uptick or a downtick. An uptick is required to execute a short sale.

Legitimate short sales may take place at time sequence points (2), (3), (7), (8), and (9) following the uptick rule and at points (4), (5), and (12) under the zero plus tick rule. We cannot tell about price (1) because no prior prices are given. Shorting OTC stocks is quite popular. Among other reasons, the uptick and zero tick rules do not apply because of the nonauction character of the market.

Short-sale transactions are ever mindful of protecting the lender's rights and privileges. First, the lender is entitled to cash collateral, equivalent at all times to the market value of the shares loaned. For example, suppose that 100 shares of a stock were sold short at $50. The lender is entitled to receive the $5,000 in proceeds as collateral for the loan. Moreover, as the price of the shares rises or falls subsequent to the short sale, this collateral must be adjusted. If the shares rise from $50 to $52, say, the borrower must advance an additional $200 to the account of the lender. Similarly, if the stock falls from $50 to $48, the lender must remit $200 to the borrower. This process is referred to as *marking-to-the-market*. The lender always has a 100 percent collateralized loan.

If the lender decides to sell his shares, another lender must be found if the short seller intends to maintain his short position. This is frequently a simple book-keeping transfer. Thus, shares can be borrowed with no time limit. The lenders simply change.

The lender is entitled to all the privileges of ownership even though physical possession of certificates has been surrendered. The short seller is ultimately responsible also for protection of the lender's interest in the receipt of interest or divident payments as well as voting rights. The borrower must send the lender a check in the amount of any interest or dividends paid by the issuing corporation because such payments are now being made directly to a new holder of record (the party buying the shares from the short seller).

Short selling cannot create more votes than actually exist. If the lender insists on casting a proxy, the seller's broker merely allows the use of another, more disinterested customer's right.

Short selling is risky. It should be noted that the most that can be lost (ignoring taxes and commissions) on a buy (going long) is the sum paid. The loss is limited to 100 percent of the investment. However, no such finite limit on the loss can be sustained on a short sale, for theoretically, the stock's price can continue to rise indefinitely. As a practical matter, an investor can prevent this occurrence by the judicious use of stop orders. This also points out the very speculative nature of this form of short-sell order, and why it is recommended for use only by more sophisticated investors.

OTHER MAJOR USES OF SELL-SHORT ORDERS.   Several uses of sell-short orders have come to be called short sales "against the box." These are situations in which the investor going short already has a long position in the same stock. The "box" in the expression refers to the fact that the stock certificate is, so to speak, in his safe deposit box.

Shorting against the box can be used for tax purposes, for hedging or insurance purposes, and for convenience in delivery of the actual shares. In the first in-

stance, the investor may want to avoid earning any more capital gains in a given tax year. By shorting against the box, he can guarantee a certain profit and postpone taxes for a year. For example, assume that you own 100 shares of JKL with a December market price of $30 per share. Your cost was $20 per share; thus your profit (ignoring taxes and commissions) is $1,000. However, you would rather earn the $1,000, and be taxed on it, in the following year. So you go short JKL at $30 in December. The following year, perhaps in January, you deliver the JKL shares you own long and close out the short position. Thus both positions (short and long) are closed, the $1,000 profit is retained, and the taxes are deferred to the next year.

Suppose that you have a $1,000 profit from a long position in 100 shares of MNO; however, it is December, and for tax reasons you do not wish to take your profit in this calendar year. Assume that MNO is now trading at 60. You can short 100 MNO against the box. If MNO rises to 70 next year, you will profit an additional $1,000 on the long position. Conversely, if MNO drops to 50, your $1,000 profit on the short position will be offset by a loss of the same amount in the original long position (again ignoring transaction costs). The merit of this technique is simply that your $1,000 profit has remained intact and yet has been transferred into a more favorable tax year. Bear in mind, however, that this technique does not allow you to extend a short-term gain into a long-term gain.

This technique can also be used to hedge or ensure a position about which the investor is unsure and insecure. Suppose that you own MNO but feel it may decline from its current level. On the other hand, for some reason you do not want to sell out your position. One way of handling this dilemma is to short the security against the box. If the stock's price declines, as was thought possible, the profit on the short position will exactly offset the loss on the long position (ignoring commission and taxes). Thus you have ensured or hedged yourself against the decline. Conversely, if the stock's price rises, the gain on the long position will be offset exactly by the loss on the short (again ignoring commission and taxes). Obviously, if you knew what was going to happen and had no qualms about closing out your position, this technique would not be necessary, for in both cases profits would have been greater without the short. In the former case, an outright sale followed by a new long position at a lower price would have increased profits, and in the latter case, merely maintaining the long position would have increased profits.

Finally, shorting against the box can be used to facilitate delivery of securities.[11] For example, you are out of town on a business trip or vacation and wish to dispose of one of your holdings, but you will be unable to get the stock certificate to your broker within the allotted time. You can call your broker, sell the stock against the box at the current price, thus ensuring the desired sale price, and deliver your stock (held long in your safe deposit box) upon return from your trip.

---

[11]This feature can also be used in conjunction with a highly specialized variety of arbitraging; that is, simultaneously carrying on transactions in the same security in different markets.

Margin Trading

Securities purchased can be paid for in cash, or a mix of cash and some borrowed funds. Conservative investors use borrowed funds sparingly, often as a convenience. For example, an investor might wish to buy securities before his tax refund or other cash arrives to pay for them, or he may simply want to avoid taking money out of the bank for a while. Buying with borrowed funds permits him to buy at a good price at a good time. Most users of borrowed funds in the securities markets, however, are more interested in stretching their buying power and getting more "bang for the buck."

Borrowing money from a bank or a broker to execute a securities transaction is referred to as using *margin*. When an investor buys on margin, he simply borrows money from his broker to buy securities. When he sells short on margin, he borrows the money to guarantee that he will be able to buy back the securities that he also borrowed and sold. The amount that an investor can borrow is determined by Regulation T of the Federal Reserve Board. Regulation T permits brokers to lend up to 50 percent of the value of stocks or convertible bonds acquired or sold short by customers, 70 percent for corporate bonds, and about 90 percent for U.S. government securities. In stock market parlance, the cash paid by the customer is the customer's margin. Thus, if an investor buys shares worth $10,000 and puts up $7,000 in cash, his margin is $7,000, or 70 percent of the value of the shares acquired. At all times the customer's margin can be calculated as:

$$\text{Margin (\%)} = \frac{\text{Customer's equity}}{\text{Market value of securities}}$$

Again, when we indicated the permissible limits on borrowing for bonds, we could have said that the margin requirement was 30 percent for corporate bonds and 10 percent for U.S. government bonds.

After the initial transaction takes place, the Federal Reserve Board no longer concerns itself with the investor's margin. The effect of fluctuating market prices on the customer's margin is largely regulated by stock exchanges and the generally more restrictive policies of brokerage firms themselves. The NYSE requires that the customer maintain an equity of 25 percent of the market value of all securities in the account, although most brokers actually require equity of 30 percent. *Equity* is simply the market value of the customer's portfolio less margin debt, or the market value of any securities that were sold short. The Federal Reserve requirements are referred to as the initial margin requirement and the exchange and/or brokers' guidelines are called *maintenance requirements*. Now that we know most of the nomenclature and the rules, let's see how it all works.

Assume, for example, that you buy 1,000 shares of a $20 stock (net cost $20,000) and you deposit $10,000 (50 percent of $20,000) to meet the initial requirement. At this point your margin account shows a market value of $20,000 and a loan balance (called a *debit balance*) of $10,000. The equity in the account stands at $10,000. With a $20,000 market value, the exchange requires that equity must be at least $5,000, or 25 percent of $20,000. So far, so good; the account more than conforms to the minimum maintenance rule (25 percent).

Customer's Account

Stock $20,000 Debt $10,000
                Equity   10,000

$$\text{Margin} = \frac{10,000}{20,000} = 50\%$$

Now suppose that the stock falls. Gradually, it moves down to $17. Where are we now?

Stock $17,000 Debt $10,000
                Equity   7,000

$$\text{Margin} = \frac{7,000}{20,000} = 41.2\%$$

Note that all the shock of the falling price must be absorbed by the customer's equity because the debt has not been repaid. Also, the lender's (broker's) stake is rising because the borrowed funds represent a larger part of the total value of the shares. The broker's risk is rising.

The maintenance margin of 30 percent will be reached under the following conditions:[12]

$$\text{Market value of securities} = \frac{\text{Loan (\$)}}{1 - \text{Maintenance margin (\%)}}$$

$$= \frac{(\$10,000)}{(1 - .30)}$$

$$= \$14,286, \text{ or } \$14.28/\text{share}$$

Another way of saying the same thing is to note that the maintenance margin is reached when the market value of the stock is equal to 1.4286 times the amount of the loan. So, at a price per share of $14.28 we have

Stock $14,286 Debt $10,000
                Equity   3,000

$$\text{Margin} = \frac{4,286}{14,286} = 30\%$$

If the maintenance margin falls below 30 percent, the broker will send a maintenance margin call (*margin call*) requiring that the customer supply additional funds in cash or securities in two to five days. Otherwise, the securities in his account will be sold and cash used to repay the outstanding margin loan.

[12]For short sales the maintenance margin is reached when

$$\text{Market value of securities} = \frac{\text{Initial proceeds} + \text{Initial margin (\$)}}{1 + \text{Maintenance margin (\%)}}$$

Suppose that the stock hits $13. Then we have

$$\text{Stock} \quad \$13,000 \quad \begin{array}{ll} \text{Debt} & \$10,000 \\ \text{Equity} & 3,000 \end{array}$$

$$\text{Margin} = \frac{3,000}{13,000} = 23\%$$

To lift the margin to the 30 percent maintenance level requires equity of 30 percent of $13,000, or $3,900. This means that an additional $900 in cash and/or securities must be advanced ($3,900 – $3,000).

It is important to remember that the maintenance requirement applies to the market value of all securities in a customer's account. You could buy shares that would plummet into worthlessness without receiving a single margin call. How so? As long as cash and securities are kept in the account equal to 1.4286 times the amount of the loan, you are okay.

Margin calls represent instances in which the investor has already lost 60 percent of his equity. The reason such calls are feared is that borrowing has been done heavily on losing stocks. Frequently, the investor lacks backup resources because he may be at the limit. His equity melts away.

The other side of the coin is simple enough. Suppose that the stock rises. Let's say that it moves from $20 to $25.

$$\text{Stock} \quad \$25,000 \quad \begin{array}{ll} \text{Debt} & \$10,000 \\ \text{Equity} & 15,000 \end{array}$$

$$\text{Margin} = \frac{15,000}{25,000} = 60\%$$

What happens? First, equity has risen from $10,000 to $15,000 or 50 percent against a mere 25 percent increase in the price of the stock. This is the magic lure of using margin in the first place. Moreover, the investor now has additional borrowing power. He can borrow another $5,000 to buy stock without depositing another dime of his own. This brings the situation to the following:

$$\text{Stock} \quad \$30,000 \quad \begin{array}{ll} \text{Debt} & \$15,000 \\ \text{Equity} & 15,000 \end{array}$$

His equity is now at the required 50 percent under Regulation T.

Note in Table 2–1 the equity and margin position of the investor at varied stock prices. For example, if the stock rise to $25, the market value is $25,000, and because $10,000 was borrowed initially, the investor's equity is now $15,000 ($25,000 – $10,000). Because only $12,500 in equity is required to support a 50 percent margin ($25,000 × .5), the investor has excess equity of $2,500 ($15,000 actual – $12,500 required). The actual margin at a price of $25 is 60 percent ($15,000 equity/$25,000 market value).

TABLE 2–1

Excess Equity and Margin at Various Stock Prices

STOCK PRICE (1)	MARKET VALUE ($) (2)	EQUITY ($) (3)	EXCESS EQUITY ($) (4)	MARGIN (%) (5) = (3)/(2)
$26	26,000	16,000	3,000	61.54
$25	25,000	15,000	2,500	60.00
$24	24,000	14,000	2,000	58.33
$23	23,000	13,000	1,500	56.52
$22	22,000	12,000	1,000	54.55
$21	21,000	11,000	500	52.38
$20	20,000	10,000	0	50.00
$19	19,000	9,000	0	47.37
$18	18,000	8,000	0	44.44
$17	17,000	7,000	0	41.18
$16	16,000	6,000	0	37.50
$15	15,000	5,000	0	33.33
$14	14,000	4,000	0	28.57
$13	13,000	3,000	0	23.08
$12	12,000	2,000	0	16.67

	NO MARGIN		
	PRICE = $15	PRICE = $23	PRICE = $25
Proceeds	$15,000	$23,000	$25,000
Cost	−20,000	−20,000	−20,000
Net proceeds	(5,000)	3,000	5,000
Equity	20,000	20,000	20,000
Return on equity	(25%)	15%	25%

	50% MARGIN		
	PRICE = $15	PRICE = $23	PRICE = $25
Proceeds	$15,000	$23,000	$25,000
Cost	−20,000	−20,000	−20,000
Interest	−1,500	−1,500	−1,500
Net proceeds	(6,500)	1,500	3,500
Equity	10,000	10,000	10,000
Return on equity	(65%)	15%	35%

Risk is attached to any kind of speculative borrowing designed to enhance the borrower's return significantly. To appreciate this risk-return relationship, let us assume the original parameters of our example: 1,000 shares purchased at $20 using 50 percent margin. Let us add a hypothetical cost of borrowing at 15 percent on margin loans. What are the results of using margin versus not using margin at some assumed price levels? Taxes and commissions are ignored to simplify matters.

The message is clear. As long as the stock rises at least 15 percent (the cost of the borrowing) or above $23 the returns are enhanced by using margin. The returns

at $25 are 25 percent without and 35 percent with margin. But look out! You will lose 25 percent of your money if the stock falls to $15, without the help of margin. Borrowing 50 percent of the money at 15 percent causes you to lose almost half your funds (43 percent). There can be more "bang for the buck" with margin . . . provided that things work out.

The extent of the magnification of profits and losses can be quantified. The magnification factor is the reciprocal of the margin, or 1/margin (%):

MARGIN (%)	MAGNIFICATION FACTOR
100	1.00
80	1.25
75	1.33
60	1.67
55	1.82
50	2.00
40	2.50
33	3.00
25	4.00

An investor needs to adjust his portfolio to obtain the return-risk combination he deems appropriate and acceptable. He can accomplish this in two basic ways. He varies the proportions of available securities and security-types he holds in his portfolio. Also, he can use short-selling and margin trading to vary the risk-return characteristics of his portfolio. With these techniques, he can adjust risks and return combinations of over those possible from available securities alone.

Clearing Process

After a trade has been executed, securities and money must change hands within five business days of the trade date, on what is called the settlement date (Saturdays, Sundays, and holidays are excluded). For example, a trade on a Wednesday is settled the following Wednesday. Basically, two tasks are carried out in the clearing process: trade comparison and settlement. Trade comparisons are made through the facilities of a clearing corporation that receives reports of each transaction from the brokers participating in the transaction. The largest clearing corporation is the National Securities Clearing Corporation (NSCC).

The first four days of the clearing period are devoted to the trade comparison process and to resolving any discrepancies in the transaction information provided by parties to a transaction. Unmatched trades are flagged, and advisory notices are sent to participants who fail to report a transaction reported by the contraside. Much of this process is automated.

The second step in the clearing process—the final settlement—is also auto-

mated and usually carried out through computer book entries. The key change permitting the use of book entries has been the immobilization of securities certificates, which has been made possible by the increased willingness of brokers and financial institutions to forgo physical delivery of certificates. Instead, certificates are immobilized at a securities depository. The principal depository is the Depository Trust Co. (DTC), owned jointly by the NYSE, AMEX, National Association of Securities Dealers (NASD), and its major participants (brokers and banks). The DTC is regulated by the Securities and Exchange Commission (SEC) and the Federal Reserve System as a limited trust company.

Federal Personal Income Taxes

Interest

Interest received on municipal bonds is free of federal income taxes and is, therefore, not included in gross income. Thus, many wealthy individuals invest in municipal bonds, receive regular interest payments, and pay no federal income taxes on them. However, some states levy state income taxes on interest earned on certain municipal bonds.

U.S. government Series E and EE bonds are sold on a discounted basis. These bonds earn interest while they are being held by the investors and mature at their face value. The difference between the purchase price and the face value is interest earned. Normally, individual taxpayers report their income on a cash basis; that is, income is reported for tax purposes as it is received. But taxpayers investing in U.S. government bonds of Series E and EE have an option in reporting the interest earned on these bonds. They can elect to wait until they cash in the bond, or maturity, and then report the entire increase in value to that point as interest income; or, they can elect to report each year's increase in value—that is, the interest for that year—as it is earned. Electing one method or the other depends upon the expected future tax bracket the investor will be in in the various years under consideration.

Series HH bonds are current-income bonds; the interest is paid to the investor semiannually by check, rather than accumulated. Income tax must be paid by the individual on this interest as it is received. Therefore, the Series E and EE bonds have an advantage over Series H and HH bonds from a tax viewpoint.

Capital Gains and Losses on Common Stock

Generally, capital gains stem from the increased value of capital assets. In the context of this text, we are talking about the increase in value of a security from the time it is purchased to the time it is sold. Under current tax laws the results of transactions from the sale of securities are classified as either long-term or short-term. Let's assume the investor had a gain from the transaction. The transaction would be considered a long-term capital gain if the security were held for at least twelve months. If the security were held for less than a year, the gain would be considered short-term. The current tax rate for federal income tax on ordinary income can

range up to 39.6 percent for individuals. However, net capital gains are taxed at a maximum rate of 28 percent. Thus, with a possible 11.6 percent differential in rates for high-income individuals, taxes can be a factor on investment decisions. If the investor has a net capital loss from securities transactions, the deduction is limited to $3,000 per year. Any unused losses may be carried forward to future years, and the nature of the loss—that is, short-term or long-term—retains its original character. To calculate capital gain or loss, the investor generally takes the sales price less brokerage commissions and other transfer taxes and from this number subtracts the adjusted basis in the asset, which again is generally his cost plus brokerage commissions paid on purchase. The net gain is taxed at ordinary income tax rates.

INDIVIDUAL RETIREMENT ACCOUNTS

Individual retirement accounts (IRAs) are a mechanism that provide some build-up in savings on a tax-deferred basis. Individuals can invest up to $2,000 per year ($2,250 if the spouse is nonworking). This $2,000 can be excluded from taxable income under certain specified conditions. If these conditions are not met, only a partial exclusion (or perhaps no exclusion at all) from taxable income will be allowed. The interest dividends and capital gains earned on the investment while it is held in an IRA are not taxed until withdrawn. Withdrawals may not be made without penalty until the taxpayer attains age 59½. Thus, the sums invested in an IRA accumulate interest, dividends, and so on on a tax-free basis.

INSTITUTIONAL INVESTORS AND CHANGING MARKETS

Need for Changes

The growth in size and activity of institutional investors has produced increasing pressures on the securities markets. The commission structure, membership requirements, and auction process of the organized exchanges have shown great incompatibility with the nature and needs of institutional investors.

The fact remains that organized exchanges account for two-thirds of all stock-trading activity. Moreover, the NYSE accounts for two-thirds of all exchange share volume. The impact of the NYSE is even more substantial when one considers that the kinds of stocks that are of interest to institutional investors are virtually monopolized by the NYSE.

The growing size and needs of institutional investors have increasingly come up against exchange rules, regulations, and other rigidities. The result has been the effort of institutional investors to circumvent the floor of the NYSE, primarily to avoid paying the normal commissions.

For many, many years, NYSE commission rates were fixed. Volume discounts were not allowed. The commission on a 5,000-share order was fifty times that of a 100-share order. Institutions bought and sold most stocks they held in large blocks and thus paid high commissions. To overcome these constraints, certain institutional investors employed several strategies. First, because NYSE mem-

ber firms were prohibited from trading or executing orders off the floor of the exchange except with special permission, institutions began to buy and sell through nonmembers who made markets in listed shares at markups below the NYSE commission schedule. The nonmember firms would accommodate institutions either as dealer-wholesalers or as agents, matching buys and sells between institutions off the floor in much the same way specialists do on the floor. These dealers traded only with big institutions, not with the public. This activity became known as the *"third" market.*

The need for a third market has essentially disappeared because of two events. First, in 1975 the SEC required that all commissions be negotiated. This brought volume discounts into full bloom. Second, in 1979 the SEC established a rule that any stock not already being traded on an exchange can be traded off board as well as on the floor by member firms.

The second strategy was for many institutions to try to obtain seats on the NYSE and other exchanges, thus eliminating commissions. Some sought and obtained seats on regional exchanges, but the NYSE forbids institutional membership. Attempts at mergers with member firms were similarly thwarted.

A third strategy developed whereby institutions bought and sold directly with each other, completely bypassing the exchange and broker-dealer services. This is known as *"fourth"-market* activity. Several privately owned fourth-market organizations have developed, each operating differently, in which block traders deal with each other through varied communications networks.

The key is to find one institution to trade with another. The Instinet System, developed by International Networks Corp., allows subscribers to trade in any listed stock via a terminal display that is connected with a central computer. Subscribers submit limit buy and sell orders for any stock in the system. Orders are thus accessible to all subscribers. The system permits subscribers to communicate anonymously in haggling over price or quantity. Commissions, charged only if a transaction is consummated, average about 30 percent of typical exchange rates.[13] This is but one example of private fourth-market activity (see the boxed article on page 53).

INSTITUTIONALIZATION OF THE MARKET

Possibly the most important development in the postwar period has been the gradual domination of the stock market by institutions.

The expanding role of institutions in the securities markets has had several important consequences, including a shift in the site of much trading from the floor of the exchange to the third market and the regional exchanges, the erosion of the minimum commission rate system, and the development of special trading patterns.

---

[13]R. R. West, "Institutional Trading and the Changing Stock Market," *Financial Analysts Journal* (May–June 1971), pp. 22–23.

BYPASSING THE BROKERS

RICHARD BEHAR

Gary Ciuffetelli once scraped out a living in a machine shop, but now he's getting ready to "ride a wave," as they say at All-Tech Investment Group in Suffern, New York. Dressed in shorts and a T shirt, the 33-year-old trader stares at a computer screen linked to the National Association of Securities Dealers Automated Quotation System (NASDAQ), the world's second largest stock market after the New York Stock Exchange. Sensing that Lotus stock is starting to climb, Ciuffetelli tells an All-Tech clerk to buy 1,000 shares. The clerk presses a few buttons on his keyboard, and the deal is automatically made for $32 a share. Minutes later, the ex-machinist sells. "Hallelujah, I made an eighth of a point!" shouts Ciuffetelli. By day's end, 58 trades later and $900 richer, he is ready to return to his family's trailer home.

For Ciuffetelli and his fellow small traders, who hope to parlay tiny price fluctuations into handsome profits, All-Tech and dozens of similar firms have become Wall Street's version of off-track betting parlors. Visitors to the Suffern office find plumbers, bartenders, retirees and out-of-work lawyers crammed elbow to elbow in nine rooms filled with clerks, computer screens and high hopes. The screens show the various "bid" and "asked" prices offered by dozens of marketmakers—firms such as Goldman Sachs and Morgan Stanley that deal in specific stocks.

While the quoted prices appear to move in concert, a few sometimes lag behind, creating brief price differentials that clients spot and pounce on. Customers who correctly predict the direction of a stock can reap $250 (less commissions) for each quarter-point gain on a 1,000-share bet. But "riding a wave" is not so easy: a stock can blip upward, enticing a small trader to buy it, and then come tumbling down. "Oh my God!" cries a forty-something beautician as she loses $250 in a split-second transaction involving Genzyme, a biotechnology firm. "This has been the longest trade of my life."

At a time when stockbrokers garner about as much trust as politicians and journalists, All-Tech's do-it-yourself trading generates an astonishing total of nearly 2% of the national over-the-counter market's $5.2 billion of daily volume. Founded in 1988, the firm now includes thriving branches in Dallas and Minneapolis. This week All-Tech is opening its first New York City office. "We're turning people away every day because we don't have enough terminals," boasts chief executive Harvey Houtkin. "We could be the largest brokerage in the country in a year."

Not if the National Association of Securities Dealers can help it. The trade group, which represents 470 marketmakers, has fired off repeated barrages of new rules aimed at crippling Houtkin's business. The association even threatens to cut him off by scrapping the order-execution capability of its advanced computer system, which it touts in TV ads as "the stock market for the next hundred years." Why the hysteria? Houtkin's clients stir up "waves of orders that increase short-term volatility," charges Richard Ketchum, chief operating officer of the dealers' group. "This substantially increases the risk for marketmakers, which winds up costing the individual investor more money."

Houtkin says he is merely using technology to give the little guy an even break. Under the small-order system, each marketmaker must trade at the displayed quote price with no chance to adjust to whatever other firms are doing. The system simply assigns the

transaction to the marketmaker with the highest bid or lowest offer at the time. Result: if a Merrill Lynch specialist happens to be away from his desk when a stock starts moving, a savvy bartender could swiftly pinch $250 from his hide for every quarter-point change in price. Without the automated system, Houtkin's clients would have to call brokers and have them place orders with a marketmaker. By the time all that was done, the price gap would probably have vanished.

The roots of the feud between Houtkin and the dealers go back to 1975, when Congress first nudged regulators to have marketmakers install computerized order systems to make stock trading more efficient. Congress said the firms should be encouraged to do so even if it meant that orders could be "executed without the participation of a dealer." The securities group unveiled its small-order system with great fanfare a decade later. But it was not until many marketmakers failed to honor their quoted prices in the Crash of 1987 that the group ordered all members to use the automated system.

The association now says it never intended the system to be used for rapid-fire trading, particularly at the expense of its own marketmakers. Fighting back, the group has limited the shares traded on the system to no more than 1,000 per transaction, and has restricted the number of trades for each account to just 10 a day. But All-Tech customers simply—and legally—open numerous accounts under different names. Meanwhile, Houtkin has sued the Securities and Exchange Commission in federal court to overturn the rules.

Defenders of Houtkin say the burden of proof is on dealers to show that small-order players really are harming the market. After all, these supporters contend, no marketmaker has bailed out of the dealers' association, and many Wall Street firms enjoyed record profits in the first quarter of this year. In response, the association sent the SEC a study last month that purports to show that traders using the system drove down the price of nine stocks, mostly health-care firms, during two weeks in February and March.

Other market watchers blame the drops on factors ranging from disappointing corporate announcements to investor fears about President Clinton's health reforms. "The NASD study is a pile of crap," says Morris Mendelson, a professor of finance at the University of Pennsylvania. "Dammit, these are retail customers at All-Tech! Just because they happen to be more interested in the market than the average investor, that's no reason to keep them out." That view is echoed by Edward Fleischman, a former SEC commissioner, who wonders, "How can the SEC justify approving any rule that takes liquidity out of the market? Once you've given people the capability of direct trading, you can't take it away."

While the sides battle it out in court, Houtkin plans to keep his revolution moving ahead, opening new branches and even placing computers in customers' homes so they can ride waves without getting dressed. "This is exhilarating," says 56-year-old Don Traponese, a high school dropout who earns $18,000 a year cutting hair. "I wish I could go to the races and be as successful as I am here." While Traponese has good days and bad days at All-Tech, he estimates that his part-time trading brings in about $12,000 a year. "Brokers over the phone will quote me higher prices than what I can see for myself is available on the screens," he says. "I think the powers that be are trying to keep us little guys down."

Source: Reprinted with permission, *Time,* June 7, 1993, pp. 42–43.

Fragmentation of the Market

The relatively liberal rules of the regional exchanges and the latitude permitted third-market dealers have attracted institutional business. As a result, the exchange market has been fragmented. The efficiency of the auction system is impaired by the dissipation of orders to different channels.

Fragmentation not only means less business to the NYSE but also causes the floor to become a poorer market. There was and is a real possibility that this deterioration will accelerate. Worsening of the floor as a market and the improvement of other markets would give institutions more reason to execute orders elsewhere. To avert this possibility, the NYSE has sought legislative or SEC sanction to require securities that meet specified standards to trade on the floor. Such a provision is bitterly opposed by the third-market firms because it would mean the end of their activities.

New Trading Patterns

While the NYSE developed substantially to meet the needs of individual investors, other sectors of the market, especially the block positioners, thrived by responding to the needs of institutional trading. This type of business requires a considerable amount of capital and a willingness to risk it. That willingness, in turn, depends on the ability of the trader to determine what other blocks of a given stock might appear on the market and who might be interested in accumulating a position.

Some specialists are capable of handling large orders as well as a block positioner can. Others are less proficient, either because their capital is inadequate or because they are reluctant to commit their capital to risky positions. Institutional traders soon learned that using these less-qualified specialists meant poor executions, and they arranged their transactions off the floor even if the block finally crossed on the floor. Sometimes, to avoid the participation of a specialist, the block was brought to a regional exchange. As a result of the inroads of block positioners, even able specialists found that they were not seeing all the orders, and they began to fear that the appearance of an unexpected block would depress the price of the stock in which they had a position. This situation added to the difficulty of making a good market.

Institutional Membership

The minimum-commission-rate system contributed to the fragmentation of the markets and to the drive for a central market. It also abetted institutional interest in stock exchange membership. In part, this interest arose because of the desire of the financial institutions and brokerage firms to diversify. By acquiring a broker-dealer affiliate that did a public business, for example, an insurance company or investment adviser would not only broaden its own activity but also provide a new source of capital to the broker-dealer.

In part, also, the interest reflected a desire to reduce the costs of brokerage. Thus the institution might acquire a *shell broker*—that is, a broker who became a member of a regional exchange solely to get back some of the brokerage commissions paid by the parent to other brokers. At times, this recapture was effected through a circuitous route whereby the affiliate referred its parent's order to a dual member who executed the transaction on the NYSE, then directed a predetermined amount of commissions on unrelated transactions to the affiliate, which finally rebated part or all of the commissions to the parent.

Efforts toward a Central Market

Because of the problems that the securities markets encountered in recent years, a general agreement arose that change was necessary. The SEC was concerned that trading barriers prevented the markets from serving the best interests of the investor; the NYSE saw fragmentation as a threat to its dominance; the regional exchanges wanted freedom to build local impact; and third-market dealers complained about rules that limited their ability to trade with NYSE members. Eventually, these conflicting views came together under the concept of a *central market*.

The term *central market system* refers to a system of communications by which the various elements of the marketplace, be they exchanges or OTC markets, are tied together. It also includes a set of rules governing the relationships that will prevail among market participants.

The central market is intended to allow investors to buy or sell shares at the then-best-possible price wherever a stock may be traded. The heart of the system is a set of communications linkages consisting of a computer-reporting mechanism, a composite quotation arrangement for displaying the bids and offers of all qualified market-makers in listed securities, and a central repository for limit orders. Progress has been slow because of disputes among the interested parties and because of uncertainty regarding the specifics of the new rules.

Tying the several stock markets together into a national market is a matter of establishing mechanisms that will allow a participant in one market to gain access to the facilities of another market. Those facilities include order price and quantity information, order routing, execution, reporting, and clearing and settlement. The separate markets currently limit access to one another's facilities, but some links are in place, and more appear to be in the offing. And the feasibility of linking the markets increases as each becomes more completely automated internally.

Consolidated Information

The best-known vehicle for providing market information probably is the NYSE ticker. But today's consolidated tape is a far cry from the old ticker. The Big Board's full consolidated tape immediately prints all trades of its listed stocks on participating markets—these being the two exchanges in New York (NYSE and AMEX) and the four regionals (Boston, Midwest, Pacific, and Philadelphia), along with the Cincinnati Stock Exchange, NASD, and Instinet. Trades of stocks listed

on other exchanges also are reported promptly and automatically, and OTC transactions are reported through NASDAQ.

Information on the latest trade, however, is only one part of the picture. For trading purposes the really vital information is in the quotes. The trader has to know at what prices a quantity of stock is being bid or offered. In the past, up-to-date bid and offer information would be available only from the local exchange specialist for listed stocks, and only for one exchange. In 1978, however, with the advent of the consolidated quotation service, bid and offer prices from the various registered exchanges were brought together for display on a single screen. The specialist or broker could look at this screen to see where the best price was to be had and, if the best price was in another market, he could communicate with that market. Since 1979, NASD OTC quotes have been listed in the consolidated service along with the exchanges quoted.

ORDER ROUTING AND EXECUTION

The reason for consolidating information is to make trading in other markets not only possible but as easy as possible. It is a way of reducing the information cost of getting the best trade. But some of that gain may be lost if market participants are not able to route their orders to the preferred market and get them executed efficiently.

At the NYSE, the Designated Order Turnaround (DOT) system, inaugurated in 1976, allows a firm to transmit smaller routing orders directly to the specialist at his trading post on the floor, bypassing the floor booth. Upon execution, the specialist sends confirmation of the trade back to the member firm office over the same data link that brought it in. DOT orders now participate in about 45 percent of all Big Board trades, and that percentage is expected to rise. At the AMEX, a similar but less comprehensive system—Post Execution Reporting (PER)—handles routing of market orders and odd lots (less than 100 shares). These routing systems represent a considerable saving in floor brokerage.

The NYSE and AMEX routing systems are just that—internal routing systems. The Philadelphia Stock Exchange and the Pacific Stock Exchange both use systems that not only route but also execute orders. The Philadelphia Automated Communication and Execution (PACE) system, which handles about 20 percent of Philadelphia's total equity share volume, automatically executes orders under 400 shares at the better of the prices available in Philadelphia and on the Big Board, and it does so without levying a floor brokerage fee or a specialist fee on any order. Although some market observers fear that regional automated execution systems may introduce a certain amount of fragmentation and keep some bids and offers from meeting, the users apparently find them to be highly cost-effective.

INTERMARKET TRADES

For years the industry heard a great deal of discussion about what form the national market should take—whether it should build on then-current organizations or start over from scratch. But even while that discussion was going on, the exchanges were working at a trading system that would help to reduce regional frag-

mentation. Extension of this system to NASDAQ subscribers and others is highly likely.

One prototype is the Intermarket Trading System (ITS). This system provides brokers and market-makers with an electronic link for transmitting buy or sell orders from one exchange to another after seeing the bids and offers in all markets. So, for example, a floor broker at the NYSE who takes an order to a trading post can look at the ITS television monitor mounted over the post and see the last trade price, the local bid and offer spread, and the best prices available in all the other markets. And if the price displayed on the Midwest or Pacific exchange, say, is better than the Big Board price, he can communicate across country and make a trade. Further, ITS trades require no extra clearing and settlement procedures. In short, ITS allows market centers to compete in certain stocks, regardless of location, by using a central computer to store bid and offer prices.

The second possible form is an electronic system similar to the Cincinnati Stock Exchange. Unlike the traditional face-to-face trading on other exchanges, in the Cincinnati Stock Exchange all buying and selling is done through the computer. Brokers simply enter their orders through terminals located in their offices, and then trades are automatically confirmed. In place of the specialist system, the Cincinnati computer automatically logs limit orders and executes them when prices hit the predetermined level.

Critics of the ITS have noted that the system does not guarantee that orders are routed to the market with the best price. Many times NYSE brokers ignore, as they have the right to do, better quotes elsewhere. Also, time delays occur with the ITS that are due to its separation from the composite quotation system. Consequently, during times of heavy trading, brokers avoid using ITS. Supporters of the Cincinnati's electronic exchange believe that elimination of exchange floors and manual trading methods can provide substantial savings to investors. Furthermore, the Cincinnati system automatically executes limit orders, which would save brokers the fees now paid to specialists. Nevertheless, only forty-six securities now trade on the Cincinnati system. With the exception of Merrill Lynch, which accounts for more than half of Cincinnati's trading, many brokers are reluctant to trade on the Cincinnati system due to its low volume. However, a proposed linkage of the Cincinnati Exchange to the ITS could dramatically improve its acceptance.

National limit order protection has encountered the least amount of progress. The SEC proposed a system that would electronically pool and display limit orders from all markets. This central file would provide nationwide limit order protection by treating all limit orders on a simple time and price priority basis, regardless of where the limit orders were placed. An example of such a system, known as a *central limit order book* (CLOB), is the Cincinnati Stock Exchange. However, a nationwide CLOB does not exist. There now is no assurance that a customer's limit order on one exchange will be executed when the specified price is reached on another exchange. The composite quotation system only provides the highest bid and the lowest ask prices from each of the exchanges. Furthermore, the existing ITS system does not store or execute limit orders.

The CLOB has several advantages. First, the system could easily and automatically impose execution priorities according to price and time. The computer

would provide a clear record for regulating the participating dealers. Second, the CLOB encourages effective competition by allowing any qualified dealer to submit price quotes. Third, investors' transaction costs would be reduced by eliminating fees and physical inefficiencies associated with manually operating the book on exchange floors.

FUTURE DEVELOPMENTS AND INTERNATIONAL INVESTING

In the longer run, the exact shape of the future market remains far from certain. Nevertheless, the trend of recent developments has outlined the general shape of the market during the 1980s and beyond.

The growing trading volume of the 1980s has demanded more automation. The once mythical 100-million-share day is already a reality. The Securities Industry Automation Corp. (SIAC), a subsidiary of the NYSE and AMEX, is an industry resource to provide key systems support to the NYSE, AMEX, NSCC, and the securities industry in general. The SIAC, among other things, manages automated information handling in communication systems for the aforementioned arms of the securities industry. In 1968 daily trading volume on the NYSE averaged 13 million shares. During that year the biggest trading day was 21 million shares. During 1987 the daily share volume averaged almost 189 million shares. And during one week in October trading volume totaled more than 2 billion shares. This volume was nearly equal to the entire trading volume for 1968. Through the efforts of the SIAC, this hugely expanded trading volume was handled very efficiently. The SIAC is continuing to expand its level of technological support in order to handle the ever-increasing expected daily volume. With the widely expanded use of computers, many of the previous paperwork styles that developed, particularly during busy trading days, will disappear.[14]

As part of the trend to reduce the costs of paperwork, stock certificates will be eliminated. An electronic funds transfer system will automate the settlement mechanism. A majority of the brokerage business will be concentrated among a few large, full-service firms. Mergers of brokerage firms have signaled a more capital-intensive industry. Capital is needed for the new dealer opportunities in a national market system environment.

Eventually, a twenty-four-hour global market will emerge. The large, multinational firms such as IBM, Sperry Rand, and General Motors are each listed on more than ten exchanges around the world. Ultimately, a single universal financial marketplace that trades stocks, options, bonds, futures, and commodities might emerge.

With the advance of economic standards worldwide and with the advance in telecommunication capabilities, savvy U.S. investors must now consider worldwide investment opportunities. Historically, international markets have delivered higher returns than the U.S. market. This is caused in part because of the evolution of other countries' economic sophistication. The United States started at a much higher level and therefore sustaining high levels of growth when the base is clearly

---

[14]Information in this paragraph was drawn heavily from the 1987 annual report of the SIAC.

very large and impressive is difficult. Twenty years ago, the United States accounted for more than two-thirds of worldwide market capitalization. Currently, the United States accounts for less than one-third of the market capitalization. The rest of the world is maturing, and as their economies expand, increasing opportunities exist for high growth rates. Some stock markets around the world do not move in the same direction at the same time. Not only can returns be increased by including international securities on a portfolio, volatility or risk in a portfolio may be lowered through international diversification. We will discuss international mutual funds later in Chapter 20.

The National Market System is no longer a vague, abstract concept. Key elements have already been established, providing benefits to investors. The record of progress includes lower brokerage commission rates; increasing automation of trading, which provides the ability to handle more trading volume; intense cost-consciousness and cost-effectiveness among brokerage firms; and new technologies that eliminate many barriers to competition. Given the conflict of interests among different market participants, the optimal rate of change is debatable. But above all the discussion of the ultimate trading mechanism, the essential characteristic of the National Market System is a system based on equitable principles of trade that will reduce costs of transacting for investors.

SUMMARY

In this chapter we have explored the securities markets, both their nature and mode of operation. We reviewed the distinction between primary and secondary markets and discussed in some depth the inner workings of the main secondary market, the NYSE, as well as the OTC markets. In the process, we explored the various types of orders available to an investor and their advantages and disadvantages, as well as the mechanics of paying for and receiving stocks, and federal income tax considerations.

QUESTIONS AND PROBLEMS

1. Why is maintaining a liquid secondary market in securities in the United States necessary?

2. Discuss the functions of commission brokers, floor brokers, and odd-lot dealers.

3. The NYSE is often used as an example of a competitive market because of the direct confrontation of buyers and sellers. Discuss this statement.

4. How does the OTC market differ from the organized exchanges?

5. It has been said that short selling is an uncomfortable maneuver for most investors, whereas they are quite comfortable going long. Why should this be so?

6. Under what circumstances would you be inclined to place a limit order to buy?

7. What are some possible disadvantages of limit orders?

8. Assume you have a friend who says that when he finds a stock he would like to buy, he selects an appropriate price and places an open or GTC order. What advice, if any, would you give him?

9. Suppose that you are generally bearish on the market. In particular you feel that the craze over home insulation (due to rising energy costs) has caused the price of Sterling Fiberglas to move ahead too far to $60.

   a. If you shorted 100 shares of Sterling, what sort of order(s) might it be appropriate to use? Why?

   b. Suppose that you shorted 100 shares of Sterling in March at $60 using the margin limit (cost of borrowing, 10 percent):

   (i)   Would your order be executed if the immediate last price of the stock was $60? Why?

   (ii) At what price on the stock would a 25 percent maintenance margin be reached if the initial margin was 50 percent?

   (iii) If you repurchased the stock four months later at $51, how much better (worse) would you do being on 50 percent margin as opposed to 100 percent margin?

   c. Suppose that you owned 100 shares of the stock "long" at a cost of $55. What are two reasons why you might go "short" at $60?

10. The following represents a consecutive series of prices (hypothetical) during part of a trading day in IBM shares:

A	B	C	D	E	F	G	H	I	J	K	L
125	125.5	126	126	125	124	125	125.5	126	125	125	126

   a. Indicate by letter reference those prices at which short sales would be permitted (ignore "A").

   b. Why would someone "long" 100 shares of IBM consider shorting 100 shares at, say, $125?

11. What are three possible uses of shorting against the box?

12. Answer each of the following questions, given the following information: You have $100,000 to invest in a single stock. The initial margin limit is 40 percent. The maintenance margin is set at 25 percent. Funds can be borrowed from your broker at 10 percent per annum (ignore commissions and taxes).

   a. How many dollars in securities could you buy if margined to the limit?

   b. Suppose that you bought $20,000 of Disney stock, borrowing the maximum from your broker. You sell Disney at the end of six months for $22,000. What is the annual rate of return on your equity?

13. How is a stop order different from a limit order?

14. How can an investor use a stop order to protect a short-sale profit?

15. Because each stock is assigned to only one specialist on the NYSE, the specialist has a monopoly; therefore, the specialist function as it currently exists cannot be efficient. Do you agree?

16. How does the operation of the OTC differ from the operation of the NYSE with respect to order execution?

17. Is trading on margin a good idea? Explain.

18. If margin requirements are 40 percent and an investor has $6,000 on deposit with his broker, how much stock can he purchase?

19. Suppose that you used $10,000 to purchase $15,000 in stocks (nondividend payers). The $5,000 needed is borrowed from a broker at 10 percent. Six months later you sell out at $20,000 (debt has not been reduced). Demonstrate the effect of margining on your rate of return.

20. Because many brokerage firms have research departments housed with analysts with similar backgrounds, why do you suppose some analysts are writing positive reports on some companies while analysts at other firms are writing negative reports on the same companies at the same time?

21. If you were a stockbroker, how would you allocate shares to customers of a "hot" new issue?

22. How would the taxation of capital gains affect people's interest in investing in securities?

23. Assume that an investor is in the 28 percent marginal tax bracket. If corporate bonds offer 6 percent yield, what is the after-tax yield to the investor? What is the after-tax (federal) yield to an investor on a 5 percent municipal?

24. What is the equivalent yield on a municipal of a corporate bond yielding 5 percent if the investor's relevant tax bracket is:

  a. 15 percent?

  b. 28 percent?

  c. 30 percent?

APPENDIX

∎

Types of Orders

All-or-none order. A market or limited price order that is to be executed in its entirety or not at all.

Alternative, or either/or, order. An order to do either of two alternatives; e.g., sell (buy) at a limit price or sell (buy) on stop.

At-the-close order. A market order to be executed at or as near the close as practicable.

At the opening order. A market or limited price order to be executed at the opening of the stock or not at all.

Buy "minus" order. A market or limited price order to buy a stated amount of a stock provided that the price is not higher than the last sale if the last sale was a "minus" or "zero minus" tick, and is not higher than the last sale minus the minimum fractional change in the stock if the last sale was a "plus" or "zero plus" tick.

Day order. An order to buy or sell that, if not executed, expires at the end of the trading day on which it was entered.

Do not reduce (DNR) order. A limited order to buy or a stop limit order to sell a round lot or odd lot, or a stop order to sell an odd lot that may not be reduced by the amount of an ordinary cash dividend on the ex-dividend date.

Fill or kill order. A market or limited price order to be executed in its entirety as soon as it is represented in the crowd and if not so executed is to be treated as canceled.

Good-till-canceled (GTC) or open order. An order to buy or sell that remains in effect until executed or canceled.

Immediate, or cancel, order. A market or limited price order to be executed in whole or in part as soon as such order is represented in the trading crowd; the portion not executed is to be treated as canceled.

Limit, limited, or limited price order. An order to buy or sell a stated amount of a security at a specified price, or at a better price, if obtainable after the order is represented in the trading crowd.

Market order. An order to buy or sell at the most advantageous price obtainable after the order is represented in the trading crowd.

Not held order. A market or limited price order marked "not held," "disregard tape," "take time," or any such qualifying notation.

Order good until a specified time. A market or limited price order to be represented in the trading crowd until a specified time, after which such order or any portion not executed is to be canceled.

Percentage order. A market or limited price order to buy (sell) a stated amount of a specified stock after a fixed number of shares in that stock have traded.

Scale order. An order to buy (sell) a security specifying the total amount to be bought (sold) and the amount to be bought (sold) at specified price variations.

Sell "plus" order. A market or limited price order to sell a stated amount of a stock provided that the price is not lower than the last sale if the last sale was a "plus" or "zero plus" tick, and is not lower than the last sale plus the minimum fractional change in the stock if the last sale was a "minus" or "zero minus" tick.

Stop order (odd lots only). An order to buy (sell) that becomes a market order when a transaction in the security occurs at or above (below) the stop price after the order is represented in the trading crowd.

Stop-limit order. A buy (sell) order executable at the limit price or better when a transaction in the security occurs at or above (below) the stop price after the order is represented in the trading crowd.

Switch, or contingent, order. An order for the purchase (sale) of one stock and the sale (purchase) of another stock at a stipulated price difference.

Time order. An order that will become a market or limited price order at a specified time.

CHAPTER 3

RISK
AND RETURN

People have many motives for investing. Some people invest in order to gain a sense of power or prestige. Often the control of corporate empires is a driving motive. For most investors, however, their interest in investments is largely pecuniary—to earn a return on their money. However, selecting stocks exclusively on the basis of maximization of return is not enough.

The fact that most investors do not place available funds into the one, two, or even three stocks promising the greatest returns suggests that other factors must be considered besides return in the selection process. Investors not only like return, they dislike risk. Their holding of an assortment of securities attests to that fact.

To say that investors like return and dislike risk is, however, simplistic. To facilitate our job of analyzing securities and portfolios within a return-risk context, we must begin with a clear understanding of what risk and return are, what creates them, and how they should be measured.

The ultimate decisions to be made in investments are (1) what securities should be held, and (2) how many dollars should be allocated to each. These decisions are normally made in two steps. First, estimates are prepared of the return and risk associated with available securities over a forward holding period. This step is known as *security analysis*. Second, return-risk estimates must be compared in order to decide how to allocate available funds among these securities on a continuing basis. This step comprises *portfolio analysis, selection,* and *management.* In effect, security analysis provides the necessary inputs for analyzing and selecting portfolios. Parts II through IV of this text cover security analysis, and Part VIII examines portfolios.

Security analysis is built around the idea that *investors are concerned with two principal properties inherent in securities: the return that can be expected from holding a security, and the risk that the return that is achieved will be less than the return that was expected.* The primary purpose of this chapter is to focus upon return and risk and how they are measured.

SECURITY RETURNS

Investors want to maximize expected returns subject to their tolerance for risk. Return is the motivating force and the principal reward in the investment process, and it is the key method available to investors in comparing alternative investments. Measuring historical returns allows investors to assess how well they have done, and it plays a part in the estimation of future, unknown returns.

We need to distinguish between two terms often used in the language of investments: *realized return* and *expected return*. *Realized return* is after the fact return—return that was earned (or could have been earned). *Realized return* is history.

A deposit of $10,000 in the Second National Bank on January 1 in a certificate of deposit at a stated annual interest rate of 5 percent will be worth $10,500 one year later. The realized return for the year is $500/$10,000, or 5 percent. The total annual return on the S&P 500 Stock Index for 1992 was 7.62 percent. This was the realized return if an investor bought the 500 shares in the index on January 1, 1992, and sold them on December 31, 1992.

Expected return is the return from an asset that investors anticipate they will earn over some future period. It is a predicted return. It may or may not occur. Investors should be willing to purchase a particular asset if the expected return is adequate, but they must understand that their expectation may not materialize.

Elements in Return

Return on a typical investment consists of two components. The basic component is the periodic cash receipts (or income) on the investment, either in the form of interest or dividends. The second component is the change in the price of the asset—commonly called the capital gain or loss. This element of return is the difference between the purchase price and the price at which the asset can be or is sold; therefore, it can be a gain or a loss.

The income from an investment consists of one or more cash payments paid at specified intervals of time. Interest payments on most bonds are paid semiannually, whereas dividends on common stocks are usually paid quarterly. The distinguishing feature of these payments is that they are paid in cash by the issuer to the holder of the asset.

The term *yield* is often used in connection with this component of return. *Yield* refers to the income component in relation to some price for a security. For our purposes, the price that is relevant is the purchase price of the security. The yield on a $1,000 par value, 6 percent coupon bond purchased for $950 is 6.31 percent ($60/$950). The yield on a common stock paying $2 in dividends per year and purchased for $50 per share is 4 percent. One must remember that yield is not, for most purposes, the proper measure of return from a security. The capital gain or loss must also be considered.

$$\text{Total return} = \text{Income} + \text{Price change} (+/-) \qquad \textbf{(3.1)}$$

Equation 3.1 is a conceptual statement for total return. The important point is that a security's total return consists of the sum of two components, income and price change. Note that either component can be zero for a given security over any given time period. A bond purchased at par and held to maturity provides a stream of income in the form of interest payments. A bond purchased for $800 and held to maturity provides both income and a price change. The purchase of a nondividend-paying stock that is sold six months later produces either a capital gain or a capital loss, but no income.

Return Measurement

The correct measurement must incorporate both income and price change into a total return. Returns across time or from different securities can be measured and compared using the total return concept. The total return for a given holding period relates all the cash flows received by an investor during any designated time period to the amount of money invested in the asset. It is defined as

$$\text{Total return} = \frac{\text{Cash payments received} + \text{Price change over the period}}{\text{Purchase price of the asset}}$$

The price change over the period, is the difference between the beginning (or purchase) price and the ending (or sales) price. This number can be either positive (sales price exceeds purchase price) or negative (purchase price exceeds sales price).

Return Applications

As an illustration of the calculation and use of total returns, consider Table 3–1, which shows the S&P 500 Stock Index average for 1960–89. Included in the table are year-end values for the index and dividends on the index, which permit calculating capital gains and losses, and dividends on the index permit determination of the income component of total return. The total returns for each year can be calculated as shown at the bottom of the table. In 1981 the S&P had a total return of −4.85 percent. In 1989, in contrast, the same market index showed a total return of 31.23 percent.

The total return is an acceptable measure of return for a specified period of time. But we also need statistics to describe a series of returns. For example, investing in a particular stock for ten years or a different stock in each of ten years could result in 10 total returns, which must be described mathematically.

TABLE 3–1

S&P 500 Composite Index Total Returns and
Dividends in Index Form, 1960–89

YEAR	INDEX* [YEAR-END]	DIVIDEND	TOTAL RETURN (%)[†]
1960	58.11	1.95	28.40
1961	71.55	2.02	26.60
1962	63.10	2.13	–8.83
1963	75.02	2.28	22.50
1964	84.75	2.50	16.30
1965	92.43	2.72	12.27
1966	80.33	2.87	–9.99
1967	96.47	2.92	23.73
1968	103.86	3.07	10.84
1969	92.06	3.16	–8.32
1970	92.15	3.14	3.51
1971	102.09	3.07	14.12
1972	118.05	3.15	18.72
1973	97.55	3.38	–14.50
1974	68.56	3.60	–26.03
1975	90.19	3.68	36.92
1976	107.46	4.05	23.64
1977	95.10	4.67	–7.16
1978	96.11	5.07	6.39
1979	107.94	5.70	18.24
1980	135.76	6.16	31.48
1981	122.55	6.63	–4.85
1982	140.64	6.87	20.37
1983	164.93	7.09	22.31
1984	167.24	7.53	5.97
1985	211.28	7.90	31.06
1986	242.17	8.28	18.54
1987	247.08	8.81	5.67
1988	277.72	9.73	16.34
1989	353.40	11.05	31.23

*$1941 - 43 = 10$

[†]1966: $\dfrac{(80.33 - 92.43) + 2.87}{92.43} = -9.99\%$

Arithmetic and Geometric Return

The statistic familiar to most people is the arithmetic average. The *arithmetic average,* customarily designated by the symbol $\overline{X}$ (*X*-bar), is:

$$\overline{X} = \frac{\Sigma x}{n},$$

or the sum of each the values being considered divided by the total number of values.

Using data from Table 3–1 for the ten years ending in 1989 (1980-1989), the arithmetic average is calculated as

$$= [31.48 - 4.847 + 20.367 + \ldots 31.23]/10$$

$$= 178.1/10$$

$$= 17.8\%$$

The arithmetic average return is appropriate as a measure of the central tendency of a number of returns calculated for a particular time, such as a year. However, when percentage changes in value over time are involved, the arithmetic mean of these changes can be misleading. For example, suppose an investor purchased a stock in Year 1 for $50 and it rose to $100 by year-end. This is a 100 percent return [(100−50)/50]. Then the stock went from $100 at the start of Year 2 to $50 at the end of that year. The return for Year 2 is −50 percent [(50–100)/100)]. The arithmetic average return is 25 percent [(+100−50)/2)]. But, realistically, if an investor bought a stock for $50 and held it two years and it was still at $50, clearly there is no return at all.

A different average is needed to describe accurately the true rate of return over multiple periods. The geometric average return measures compound, cumulative returns over time. It is used in investments to reflect the realized change in wealth over multiple periods.

The *geometric average* is defined as the nth root of the product resulting from multiplying a series of returns together, as in Equation 3.2

$$G = [(1 + R_1)(1 + R_2) \ldots (1 + R_n)]^{\frac{1}{n}} - 1 \tag{3.2}$$

where:

R = total return
n = number of periods

Note that adding 1.0 to each return (R) produces what we call a *return relative*. If the return for a period is 10 percent (.10), then the return relative is 1.10. The investor has received $1.10 relative to each $1 invested. If the return for a period is −15 percent (−.15) then the return relative is .85 (1−.15). Return relatives are used in calculating geometric average returns because negative total returns cannot be used in the math.

For our stock that started at $50, rose to $100, and then dropped to $50 over a two-year period, the geometric return would be calculated as follows:

$$\text{Return relative, Year 1} = 1.00 + 1.00 = 2.00$$
$$\text{Year 2} = -.50 + 1.00 = \ \ .50$$

and

$$G = [(2.0)*(.5))]^{1/2} - 1$$
$$= [1.0]^{1/2} - 1$$
$$= .00$$

Refer to Table 3–1. For the period 1980–89, the geometric average return for the S&P 500 would be calculated as:

$$G = [(1.3148)(.9515)(1.2037)\ldots(1.3123)]^{1/10} - 1$$
$$= 1.1720 - 1$$
$$= 0.1720, \text{ or } 17.20\%$$

The geometric average reflects compound, cumulative returns over time. Thus, $1 invested in the S&P 500 would have compounded at an average annual rate of 17.2 percent over 1980–89. Notice that this geometric average rate of return is lower than the arithmetic average rate of return of 17.8 percent because it reflects compounding rather than simple averaging.

RISK IN A TRADITIONAL SENSE

Risk in holding securities is generally associated with the possibility that realized returns will be less than the returns that were expected. The source of such disappointment is the failure of dividends (interest) and/or the security's price to materialize as expected.[1]

Forces that contribute to variations in return—price or dividend (interest)—constitute elements of risk. Some influences are external to the firm, cannot be controlled, and affect large numbers of securities. Other influences are internal to the firm and are controllable to a large degree. In investments, those forces that are uncontrollable, external, and broad in their effect are called *sources of systematic risk*. Conversely, controllable, internal factors somewhat peculiar to industries and/or firms are referred to as *sources of unsystematic risk*.

Systematic risk refers to that portion of total variability in return caused by factors affecting the prices of all securities. Economic, political, and sociological changes are sources of systematic risk. Their effect is to cause prices of nearly all individual common stocks and/or all individual bonds to move together in the same manner. For example, if the economy is moving toward a recession and corporate profits shift downward, stock prices may decline across a broad front. Nearly all stocks listed on the New York Stock Exchange (NYSE) move in the same direction

[1]The words *risk* and *uncertainty* are used interchangeably. Technically, their meanings are different. Risk suggests that a decision maker knows the possible consequences of a decision and their relative likelihoods at the time he makes that decision. Uncertainty, on the other hand, involves a situation about which the likelihood of the possible outcomes is not known.

PROFILE OF THE S&P 500 STOCK PRICE INDEX

The Standard & Poor's stock price index was introduced in 1917 and has steadily gained popularity as a measure of market performance. From 200 issues, the list was expanded to 500 in 1957.

Today, individual investors are becoming increasingly aware that the S&P 500 best combines the breadth, weighting and statistical integrity needed to accurately portray the stock market's pattern of movement.

Professional investors generally use the "500" as the yardstick against which to measure their own performances. And, in recognition of its position as the premier stock market indicator, the S&P index is one of the U.S. Commerce Department's 12 leading economic indicators.

The "500" is made up of 400 Industrial, 40 Financial and 20 Transportation companies, and 40 Public Utilities. So that the index will have broad representation, it includes some of the most prominent companies from the American Stock Exchange and Over-the-Counter market. However, the great majority of the stocks in the index are traded on the New York Stock Exchange. These issues represent about 75% of the market value of all issues traded on the NYSE.

The "500" has a number of features that set it apart from other market indicators and one of them is unique. The stocks in the index represent more than 90 industry sub-groups that range, alphabetically, from Aerospace to Truckers. Thus, investors are able to focus on the often disparate performances of the diverse segments of the market.

Another salient feature of the "500" is that it is *market value* weighted rather than *price* weighted. This means that the price of each stock is multiplied by the number of outstanding shares, with the result that each issue influences the index in proportion to its true significance in the stock market. The Dow Jones Industrial average, on the other hand, is price weighted, so that a one-point change in a $20 stock with 10 million shares outstanding exercises as great an influence as a one-point change in a $60 stock with a capitalization of 100 million shares.

The composition of the "500" is continuously monitored by a committee of S&P executives who consult regularly with our sizable department of industry and stock analysts. The objective of this ongoing effort is to keep the index representative and up-to-date, but always with due regard for the principle of avoiding excessive turnover of the issues comprising the index.

Calculations are performed continuously during the trading session for each of the 500 stocks in the index. The index, itself, is available minute-by-minute on quote machines worldwide.

Source: Standard & Poor's Corp., *The Outlook*, October 15, 1988.

---

as the NYSE Index. On the average, 50 percent of the variation in a stock's price can be explained by variation in the market index.[2] In other words, about one-half the total risk in an average common stock is systematic risk.[3]

---

[2]B. F. King, "Market and Industry Factors in Stock Price Behavior," *Journal of Business* (January 1966), pp. 139–90. Since King's study, other researchers have found that the market effect has declined in importance. However, King's work did pick up this approaching trend.
[3]Systematic risk/Total risk = Systematic risk (%).

Unsystematic risk is the portion of total risk that is unique to a firm or industry. Factors such as management capability, consumer preferences, and labor strikes cause systematic variability of returns in a firm. Unsystematic factors are largely independent of factors affecting securities markets in general. Because these factors affect one firm, they must be examined for each firm.

SYSTEMATIC RISK

Market Risk

Finding stock prices falling from time to time while a company's earnings are rising, and vice versa, is not uncommon. The price of a stock may fluctuate widely within a short span of time even though earnings remain unchanged. The causes of this phenomenon are varied, but it is mainly due to a change in investors' attitudes toward equities in general, or toward certain types or groups of securities in particular. Variability in return on most common stocks that is due to basic sweeping changes in investor expectations is referred to as *market risk*.

Market risk is caused by investor reaction to tangible as well as intangible events. Expectations of lower corporate profits in general may cause the larger body of common stocks to fall in price. Investors are expressing their judgment that too much is being paid for earnings in the light of anticipated events. The basis for the reaction is a set of real, tangible events—political, social, or economic.

Intangible events are related to market psychology. Market risk is usually touched off by a reaction to real events, but the emotional instability of investors acting collectively leads to a snowballing overreaction. The initial decline in the market can cause the fear of loss to grip investors, and a kind of herd instinct builds as all investors make for the exit. These reactions to reactions frequently culminate in excessive selling, pushing prices down far out of line with fundamental value. With a trigger mechanism such as the assassination of a politician, the threat of war, or an oil shortage, virtually all stocks are adversely affected. Likewise, stocks in a particular industry group can be hard hit when the industry goes "out of fashion."

This discussion of market risk has emphasized adverse reactions. Certainly, buying panics also occur as reactions to real events, however, investors are not likely to think of sharp price advances as risk.

Two other factors, interest rates and inflation, are an integral part of the real forces behind market risk and are part of the larger category of systematic or uncontrollable influences. Let us turn our attention to interest rates. This risk factor has its most direct effect on bond investments.

Interest-Rate Risk

Interest-rate risk refers to the uncertainty of future market values and of the size of future income, caused by fluctuations in the general level of interest rates.

The root cause of interest-rate risk lies in the fact that, as the rate of interest paid on U.S. government securities (USGs) rises or falls, the rates of return demanded on alternative investment vehicles, such as stocks and bonds issued in the private sector, rise or fall. In other words, as the cost of money changes for nearly risk-free securities (USGs), the cost of money to more risk-prone issuers (private sector) will also change.

Investors normally regard USGs as coming closest to being risk-free. The interest rates demanded on USGs are thought to approximate the "pure" rate of interest, or the cost of hiring money at no risk. Changes in rates of interest demanded on USGs will permeate the system of available securities, from corporate bonds down to the riskiest common stocks.

Interest rates on USGs shift with changes in the supply and demand for government securities. For example, a large operating deficit experienced by the U.S. government will require financing. Issuance of added amounts of USGs will increase the available supply. Potential buyers of this new supply may be induced to buy only if interest rates are somewhat higher than those currently prevailing on outstanding issues. If rates on USGs advance from, say, 9 percent to 9¼ percent, investors holding outstanding issues that yield 9 percent will notice a decline in the price of their securities. Because the 9 percent rate is fixed by contract on these "old" USGs, a potential buyer would be able to realize the competitive 9¼ percent rate only if the current holder "marked down" the price. As the rate on USGs advances, they become relatively more attractive and other securities become less attractive. Consequently, bond purchasers will buy governments instead of corporates. This will cause the price of corporates to fall and the rate on corporates to rise. Rising corporate bond rates will eventually cause preferred- and common-stock prices to adjust downward as the chain reaction is felt throughout the system of security yields. (The exact nature and extent of this markdown process and the relationships between rates, prices, and maturity will be explored in Chapter 9.)

Thus, a rational, highly interconnected structure of security yields exists. Shifts in the "pure" cost of money will ripple through the structure. The direct effect of increases in the level of interest rates is to cause security prices to fall across a wide span of investment vehicles. Similarly, falling interest rates precipitate price markups on outstanding securities.

In addition to the direct, systematic effect on bonds, there are indirect effects on common stocks. First, lower or higher interest rates make the purchase of stocks on margin (using borrowed funds) more or less attractive. Higher interest rates, for example, may lead to lower stock prices because of a diminished demand for equities by speculators who use margin. Ebullient stock markets are at times propelled to some excesses by margin buying when interest rates are relatively low.

Second, many firms such as public utilities finance their operations quite heavily with borrowed funds. Others, such as financial institutions, are principally in the business of lending money. As interest rates advance, firms with heavy doses of borrowed capital find that more of their income goes toward paying interest on borrowed money. This may lead to lower earnings, dividends, and share prices. Advancing interest rates can bring higher earnings to lending institutions whose

principal revenue source is interest received on loans. For these firms, higher earnings could lead to increased dividends and stock prices.

Purchasing-Power Risk

Market risk and interest-rate risk can be defined in terms of uncertainties as to the amount of current dollars to be received by an investor. *Purchasing-power risk* is the uncertainty of the purchasing power of the amounts to be received. In more everyday terms, purchasing-power risk refers to the impact of inflation or deflation on an investment.

If we think of investment as the postponement of consumption, we can see that when a person purchases a stock, he has foregone the opportunity to buy some good or service for as long as he owns the stock. If, during the holding period, prices on desired goods and services rise, the investor actually loses purchasing power. Rising prices on goods and services are normally associated with what is referred to as *inflation*. Falling prices on goods and services are termed *deflation*. Both inflation and deflation are covered in the all-encompassing term *purchasing-power risk*. Generally, purchasing-power risk has come to be identified with inflation (rising prices); the incidence of declining prices in most countries has been slight.

Rational investors should include in their estimate of expected return an allowance for purchasing-power risk, in the form of an expected annual percentage change in prices. If a cost-of-living index begins the year at 100 and ends at 103, we say that the rate of increase (inflation) is 3 percent [(103–100)/100]. If from the second to the third year, the index changes from 103 to 109, the rate is about 5.8 percent [(109–103)/103].

Just as changes in interest rates have a systematic influence on the prices of all securities, both bonds and stocks, so too do anticipated purchasing-power changes manifest themselves. If annual changes in the consumer price index or other measure of purchasing power have been averaging steadily around 3.5 percent, and prices will apparently spurt ahead by 4.5 percent over the next year, required rates of return will adjust upward. This process will affect government and corporate bonds as well as common stocks.

Market, purchasing-power, and interest-rate risk are the principle sources of systematic risk in securities; but we should also consider another important category of security risks—unsystematic risks.

UNSYSTEMATIC RISK

Unsystematic risk is that portion of total risk that is unique or peculiar to a firm or an industry, above and beyond that affecting securities markets in general. Factors such as management capability, consumer preferences, and labor strikes can cause unsystematic variability of returns for a company's stock. Because these factors

affect one industry and/or one firm, they must be examined separately for each company.

The uncertainty surrounding the ability of the issuer to make payments on securities stems from two sources: (1) the operating environment of the business, and (2) the financing of the firm. These risks are referred to as business risk and financial risk, respectively. They are strictly a function of the operating conditions of the firm and the way in which it chooses to finance its operations. Our intention here will be directed to the broad aspects and implications of business and financial risk. In-depth treatment will be the principal goal of later chapters on analysis of the economy, the industry, and the firm.

Business Risk

Business risk is a function of the operating conditions faced by a firm and the variability these conditions inject into operating income and expected dividends. In other words, if operating earnings are expected to increase 10 percent per year over the foreseeable future, business risk would be higher if operating earnings could grow as much as 14 percent or as little as 6 percent than if the range were from a high of 11 percent to a low of 9 percent. The degree of variation from the expected trend would measure business risk.

Business risk can be divided into two broad categories: external and internal. *Internal business risk* is largely associated with the efficiency with which a firm conducts its operations within the broader operating environment imposed upon it. Each firm has its own set of internal risks, and the degree to which it is successful in coping with them is reflected in operating efficiency.[4]

To a large extent, *external business risk* is the result of operating conditions imposes upon the firm by circumstances beyond its control. Each firm also faces its own set of external risks, depending upon the specific operating environmental factors with which it must deal. The external factors, from cost of money to defense-budget cuts to higher tariffs to a downswing in the business cycle, are far too numerous to list in detail, but the most pervasive external risk factor is probably the business cycle. The sales of some industries (steel, autos) tend to move in tandem with the business cycle, while the sales of others move countercyclically (housing). Demographic considerations can also influence revenues through changes in the birthrate or the geographical distribution of the population by age, group, race, and so on. Political policies are a part of external business risk; government policies with regard to monetary and fiscal matters can affect revenues through the effect on the cost and availability of funds. If money is more expensive, consumers who buy on credit may postpone purchases, and municipal governments may not sell bonds to finance a water-treatment plant. The impact upon retail stores, television manufacturers, and producers of water-purification systems is clear.

---

[4]For more on business risk, see J. F. Weston and T. E. Copeland, *Managerial Finance,* 8th ed. (Hinsdale, Ill.: Dryden Press, 1986)

Financial Risk

Financial risk is associated with the way in which a company finances its activities. We usually gauge financial risk by looking at the capital structure of a firm. The presence of borrowed money or debt in the capital structure creates fixed payments in the form of interest that must be sustained by the firm. The presence of these interest commitments—fixed-interest payments due to debt or fixed-dividend payments on preferred stock—causes the amount of residual earnings available for common-stock dividends to be more variable than if no interest payments were required. Financial risk is avoidable risk to the extent that managements have the freedom to decide to borrow or not to borrow funds. A firm with no debt financing has no financial risk.[5]

By engaging in debt financing, the firm changes the characteristics of the earnings stream available to the common-stock holders. Specifically, the reliance on debt financing, called *financial leverage,* has at least three important effects on common-stock holders.[6] Debt financing (1) increases the variability of their returns, (2) affects their expectations concerning their returns, and (3) increases their risk of being ruined.

Assigning Risk Allowances (Premiums)

One way of quantifying risk and building a required rate of return (r), would be to express the required rate as comprising a riskless rate plus compensation for individual risk factors previously enunciated, or as:

$$r = i + p + b + f + m + o$$

where:

i = real interest rate (riskless rate)
p = purchasing-power-risk allowance
b = business-risk allowance
f = financial-risk allowance
m = market-risk allowance
o = allowance for "other" risks

The first step would be to determine a suitable riskless rate of interest. Unfortunately, no investment is risk-free. The return on U.S. Treasury bills or an insured savings account, whichever is relevant to an individual investor, can be used as an approximate riskless rate. Savings accounts possess purchasing-power risk and are

---

[5]For a discussion of financial leverage, see E. F. Brigham, *Financial Management: Theory and Practice,* 7th ed. (Hinsdale, Ill.: Dryden Press, 1994).

[6]Debt financing is also referred to as *trading on the equity,* because by its use the company is able to acquire a larger amount of assets than with equity contributed by owners.

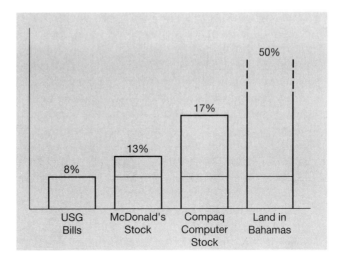

FIGURE 3–1   Building a Required Rate of Return

subject to interest-rate risk of income but not principal. U.S. government bills are subject to interest-rate risk of principal. The riskless rate might by 8 percent.

Using the rate on U.S. government bills and assuming that interest-rate-and-risk compensation is already included in the U.S. government bill rate, we see in Figure 3–1 the process of building required rate of return for alternative investments.

To quantify the separate effects of each type of systematic and unsystematic risk is difficult because of overlapping effects and the sheer complexity involved. In the remainder of the chapter, we will examine some proxies for packaging into a single measure of risk all those qualitative risk factors taken together that perhaps cannot be measured separately.

Stating Predictions "Scientifically"

Security analysts cannot be expected to predict with certainty whether a stock's price will increase or decrease or by how much. The amount of dividend income may be subject to more or less uncertainty than price in the estimating process. The reasons are simple enough. Analysts cannot understand political and socioeconomic forces completely enough to permit predictions that are beyond doubt or error.

This existence of uncertainty does not mean that security analysis is valueless. It does mean that analysts must strive to provide not only careful and reasonable estimates of return but also some measure of the degree of uncertainty associated with these estimates of return. Most important, the analyst must be prepared to quantify the risk that a given stock will fail to realize its expected return.

The quantification of risk is necessary to ensure uniform interpretation and comparison. Verbal definitions simply do not lend themselves to analysis. A deci-

sion on whether to buy stock A or stock B, both of which are expected to return 10 percent, is not made easy by the mere statement that only a "slight" or "minimal" likelihood exists that the return on either will be less than 10 percent. This sort of vagueness should be avoided. Although whatever quantitative measure of risk is used will be at most only a proxy for true risk, such a measure provides analysts with a description that facilitates uniform communication, analysis, and ranking.

Pressed on what he meant when he said that stock A would have a return of 10 percent over some holding period, an analyst might suggest that 10 percent is, in a sense, a "middling" estimate or a "best guess." In other words, the return could be above, below, or equal to 10 percent. He might express the degree of confidence he has in his estimate by saying that the return is "very likely" to be between 9 and 11 percent, or perhaps between 6 and 14 percent.

A more precise measurement of uncertainty about these predictions would be to gauge the extent to which actual return is likely to differ from predicted return—that is, the dispersion around the expected return. Suppose that stock A, in the opinion of the analyst, could provide returns as follows:

RETURN (%)	LIKELIHOOD
7	1 chance in 20
8	2 chances in 20
9	4 chances in 20
10	6 chances in 20
11	4 chances in 20
12	2 chances in 20
13	1 chance in 20

This is similar to weather forecasting. We have all heard the phrase "a 2-in-10 chance of rain." This likelihood of outcome can be stated in fractional or decimal terms. Such a figure is referred to as a probability. Thus, a 2-in-10 chance is equal to 2/10, or .10. A likelihood of four chances in twenty is 4/20, or .20. When individual events in a group of events are assigned probabilities, we have a probability distribution. The total of the probabilities assigned to individual events in a group of events must always equal 1.00 (or 10/10, 20/20, and so on). A sum less than 1.00 indicates that events have been left out. A sum in excess of 1.00 implies incorrect assignment of weights or the inclusion of events that could not occur. Let us recast our "likelihoods" into "probabilities."

RETURN (%)	PROBABILITY
7	.05
8	.10
9	.20
10	.30
11	.20
12	.10
13	.05
	1.00

Based upon his analysis of economic, industry, and company factors, the analyst assigns probabilities subjectively. The number of different holding-period returns to be considered is a matter of his choice. In this case, the return of 7 percent could mean "between 6.5 and 7.5 percent." Alternatively, the analyst could have specified 6.5 to 7 percent and 7 to 7.5 percent as two outcomes, rather than just 7 percent. This fine tuning provides greater detail in prediction.

Security analysts use the probability distribution of return to specify expected return as well as risk. The expected return is the weighted average of the returns. That is, if we multiply each return by its associated probability and add the results together, we get a weighted-average return or what we call the expected average return.

(1) RETURN (%)	(2) PROBABILITY	(1) × (2)
7	.05	.35
8	.10	.80
9	.20	1.80
10	.30	3.00
11	.20	2.20
12	.10	1.20
13	.05	.65
	1.00	10.00%

The expected average return is 10 percent. The expected return lies at the center of the distribution. Most of the possible outcomes lie either above or below it. The "spread" of possible returns about the expected return can be used to give us a proxy of risk. Two stocks can have identical expected returns but quite different spreads, or dispersions, and thus different risks. Consider stock B:

(1) RETURN (%)	(2) PROBABILITY	(1) × (2)
9	.30	2.7
10	.40	4.0
11	.30	3.3
	1.00	10.0%

Stocks A and B have identical expected average returns of 10 percent. But the spreads for stocks A and B are not the same. For one thing, the rage of outcomes from high to low return is wider for stock A (7 to 13). For stock B, the range is only 9 to 11. However, a wider range of outcomes does not necessarily imply greater risk; the range as a measure of dispersion ignores the relative probabilities of each of the outcomes.

The spread or dispersion of the probability distribution can also be measured by the degree of variation around the expected return. The deviation of any outcome from the expected return is:

$$\text{Outcome} - \text{Expected return}$$

Because outcomes do not have equal probabilities of occurrence, we must weight each difference by its probability:

$$\text{Probability} \times (\text{Outcome} - \text{Expected return})$$

For purposes of computing a *variance,* we will square the deviations or differences before multiplying them by the relative probabilities:

$$\text{Probability} \times (\text{Outcome} - \text{Expected return})^2$$

The value of the squaring can be seen in a simple example. Assume three returns—9, 10, and 11 percent—each equally likely to occur. The expected return is thus $(9\%)\ .33 + (10\%)\ .33 = .10$. Because 10 percent is the expected return, the other values must lie equally above and below it. If we took an average of the deviations from 10 percent, we would get:

$$\text{Weighted deviation} = .33 \times (9 - 10) = -.33$$
$$.33 * (10 - 10)$$
$$= .33 \times (11 - 10) = +.33$$

The sum of the deviations or differences, multiplied by their respective probabilities, equals $+.33 + (-.33)$, or zero. Squaring the differences eliminates the plus and minus signs to give us a better feel for the deviation. The *variance* is the weighted average of the squared deviations, with each weighted by its probability.

Table 3–2 shows the calculation of the variance for stocks A and B. The larger variation about the expected return for stock A is indicated in its variance

TABLE 3–2

Calculation of Variance and Standard Deviation for Two Stocks, A and B

STOCK A				STOCK B			
(1)	(2)	(3)	(4)	(5)	(6)	(7)	(8)
RETURN MINUS EXPECTED RETURN	DIFFER- ENCE SQUARED	PROB- ABILITY	(2) × (3)	RETURN MINUS EXPECTED RETURN	DIFFER- ENCE SQUARED	PROB- ABILITY	(6) × (7)
7 − 10 = −3	9	.05	.45				
8 − 10 = −2	4	.10	.40				
9 − 10 = −1	1	.20	.20	9 − 10 = −1	1	.30	.30
10 − 10 = 0	0	.30	.00	10 − 10 = 0	0	.40	.00
11 − 10 = +1	1	.20	.20	11 − 10 = +1	1	.30	.30
12 − 10 = +2	4	.10	.40				
13 − 10 = +3	9	.05	.45				
		1.00	2.10			1.00	.60
Variance			2.10				.60
Standard deviation			1.45				.77

relative to stock B (2.1 versus .6). Also shown is the *standard deviation*, the square root of the variance. Its usefulness will be examined shortly.

In general, the expected return, variance, and standard deviation of outcomes can be shown as:

$$R = \sum_{i=1}^{n} P_i O_i \tag{3.3}$$

$$\sigma^2 = \sum_{i=1}^{n} P_i (O_i - R)^2$$

$$\sigma = \sqrt{\sigma^2}$$

where:

R = expected return
σ^2 = variance of expected return
σ = standard deviation of expected return
P = probability
O = outcome
n = total number of different outcomes

The variability of return around the expected average is thus a quantitative description of risk. Moreover, this measure of risk is simply a proxy or surrogate for risk because other measures could be used. The total variance is the rate of return on a stock around the expected average that includes both systematic and unsystematic risk.

RISK IN A CONTEMPORARY MODE

Much time and effort has been expended on developing a measure of risk and a system for using this measure in assessing returns. The two key components of that have emerged from this theoretical effort are *beta*, which is a statistical measure of risk, and the *capital asset pricing model* (CAPM), which links risk (beta) to the level of required return.[7]

The total risk of an investment consists of two components: diversifiable and nondiversifiable risk. *Diversifiable,* or *unsystematic,* risk represents the portion of an investment's risk that can be eliminated by holding enough stocks. This risk results from uncontrollable or even random events that tend to be unique to an industry and/or a company such as management changes, labor changes, labor strikes, lawsuits, and regulatory actions. *Nondiversifiable,* or *systematic,* risk is external to an industry and/or business and is attributed to broad forces, such as war, inflation, and political and even sociological events. Such forces impact all invest-

---

[7]The underpinnings of CAPM are discussed in greater detail in Chapter 19.

ments and are therefore not unique to a given vehicle. The relationship between total risk, diversifiable risk, and nondiversifiable risk is given by the equation:

$$\text{Total risk} = \text{Diversifiable risk} + \text{Nondiversifiable risk}$$

Because any knowledgeable investor can eliminate diversifiable risk by holding a large enough portfolio of securities, the only relevant risk to be concerned about is nondiversifiable risk. Studies have shown that by carefully selecting as few as fifteen securities for a portfolio, diversifiable risk can be almost entirely eliminated. Nondiversifiable risk is unavoidable, and each security possesses its own level of nondiversifiable risk, measured using the beta coefficient.

What Beta Means

Beta measures nondiversifiable risk. Beta shows how the price of a security responds to market forces. In effect, the more responsive the price of a security is to changes in the market, the higher will be its beta. Beta is calculated by relating the returns on a security with the returns for the market. Market return is measured by the average return of a large sample of stocks, such as the S&P 500 Stock Index. The beta for the overall market is equal to 1.00 and other betas are viewed in relation to this value.

Betas can be positive or negative. However, nearly all betas are positive and most betas lie somewhere between .4 and 1.9. Listed in Table 3–3 are the betas for some stocks, as reported by *Value Line* in late 1993.

TABLE 3–3

Beta Coefficients on Selected Stocks

COMPANY	BETA	COMPANY	BETA
Avon Products	1.40	Kellogg	1.10
Bausch & Lomb	1.25	LaQuinta Inns	0.80
Benguet Corp.	0.15	Mattel	1.45
Black & Decker	1.65	McDonald's	0.86
California Water	0.50	Merrill Lynch	1.75
Campbell Soup	1.00	Newmont Mining	0.35
Chrysler Corp.	1.25	PepsiCo	1.15
Club Med	1.05	Peidmont Natural Gas	0.60
Coca-Cola	1.15	Quaker State Corp.	0.90
Compaq Computer	1.45	Reebok, Intl.	1.60
Delta Air Lines	1.15	Smucker, J. M.	0.90
Disney	1.25	Texaco	0.60
Goodyear Tire	1.05	Tootsie Roll	0.80
Hecla Mining	0.35	Toys 'R' Us	1.45
Idaho Power	0.60	Wendy's Intl.	1.10
IBM	0.95		

Many large brokerage firms (such as Merrill Lynch) as well as subscription services (such as *Value Line*) publish betas for a large number of stocks.

Investors will find beta helpful in assessing systematic risk and understanding the impact market movements can have on the return expected from a share of stock. For example, if the market is expected to provide a 10 percent rate of return over the next year, a stock having a beta of 1.80 would be expected to experience an increase in return of approximately 18 percent (1.80 × 10%) over the same period. This particular stock is much more volatile than the market as a whole.

Decreases in market returns are translated into decreasing security returns—and this is where the risk lies. In the preceding example, if the market is expected to experience a negative return 10 percent, then the stock with a beta of 1.8 should experience a 18 percent decrease in its return [1.8 times −10]. Stocks having betas of less than 1 will, of course, be less responsive to changing returns in the market, and therefore are considered less risky.

Calculating Beta

The appropriate numbers and formulas that we must have for calculating beta is illustrated in Table 3–3 using McDonald's Corp. and recent monthly data. The line that goes through the middle of the points in the graphic space ("splits" the data) is called the *characteristic line*. This line could be eyeballed by minimizing the spread of the data points above and below the line. Use the proper math for describing the line is more accurate. The equation for the line is:

$$R_s = a + B_s R_m \qquad \qquad \textbf{(3.3A)}$$

where:

R_s = estimated return on the stock
a = estimated return when the market return is zero
B_s = measure of stock's sensitivity to the market index
R_m = return on the market index

USING BETA TO ESTIMATE RETURN

CAPM uses beta to link formally the notions of risk and return. CAPM was developed to provide a system whereby investors are able to assess the impact of an investment in a proposed security on the risk and return of their portfolio. We can use CAPM to understand the basic risk-return tradeoffs involved in various types of investment decisions. CAPM can be viewed both as a mathematical equation and, graphically, as the security market line (SML).

Capital Asset Pricing Model

Using beta as the measure of nondiversifiable risk, the capital asset pricing model (CAPM) is used to define the required return on a security according to the following equation:

$$R_s = R_f + B_s(R_m - R_f) \qquad \textbf{(3.4)}$$

where:

R_s = the return required on the investment
R_f = the return that can be earned on a risk-free investment (e.g., U.S. Treasury bill)
R_m = the average return on all securities (e.g., S&P 500 Stock Index)
B_s = the security's beta (systematic) risk

It is easy to see that the required return for a given security increases with increases in its beta.

Application of the CAPM can be demonstrated. Assume a security with a beta of 1.2 is being considered at a time when the risk-free rate is 4 percent and the market return is expected to be 12 percent. Substituting these data into the CAPM equation, we get

$$R_s = 4\% + [1.20 \times (12\% - 4\%)]$$
$$= 4\% + [1.20 \times 8\%]$$
$$= 4\% + 9.6\% = 13.6\%$$

The investor should therefore require an 13.6 percent return on this investment as compensation for the nondiversifiable risk assumed, given the security's beta of 1.2. If the beta were lower, say 1.00, the required return would be 12 percent [4% + [1.00 × (12% − 4%)]]; and if the beta had been higher, say 1.50, the required return would be 16 percent [4% + [1.50 × (12% − 4%)]]. CAPM reflects a positive mathematical relationship between risk and return, since the higher the risk (beta) the higher the required return.

The Security Market Line

When the capital asset pricing model (CAPM) is depicted graphically, it is called the Security Market Line (SML) (see Figure 3–2). Plotting CAPM, we would find that the SML is a straight line. It tells us the required return an investor should earn in the marketplace for any level of unsystematic (beta) risk. The CAPM can be plotted by using Equation 3.3A. Make beta zero and the required return is 4 percent [4 + 0 (12% − 4%)]. As we saw above, using a 4 percent risk-free rate and a 12 percent market return, the required return is 13.6 percent when beta is 1.2. Increase the beta to 2.0, and the required return equals 22 percent [6% + [2.0 × (12% − 4%)]]. And

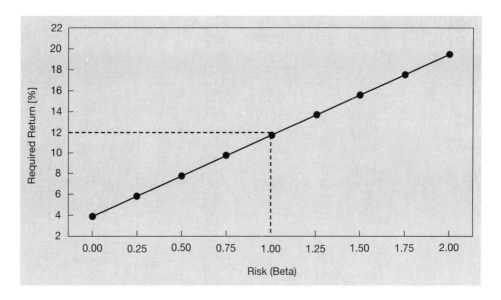

FIGURE 3–2   Security Market Line

so on. We end up with the combinations of risk (beta) and required return. Plotting these values on a graph (with beta on the horizontal axis and required returns on the vertical axis), we would have a straight line such as the one in Figure 3–2. The SML clearly indicates that as risk (beta) increases so does the required return and vice versa.

Evaluating Risk

In the end investors must somehow relate the risk perceived in a given security not only to return but also to their own attitudes toward risk. Thus, the evaluation process is not one in which we simply calculate risk and compare it to a maximum risk level associated with an investment offering a given return. The individual investor typically tends to want to know if the amount of perceived risk is worth taking in order to get the expected return and whether a higher return is possible for the same level of risk (or a lower risk is possible for the same level of return).

Because of differing investor preferences, specifying a general acceptable level of risk is impossible. However, most investors are assumed to be risk-averse. For the risk-averse investor, the required return increases for an increase in risk. Conversely the risk-taking investor the required return decreases for an increase in risk. Of course, the amount of return required by each investor for a given increase in risk will differ depending upon how the investor trades risk for return—a kind of degree of risk aversion. Although in theory the risk disposition of each investor can be measured, in practice individual investors tend to accept only those risks with which they feel comfortable.

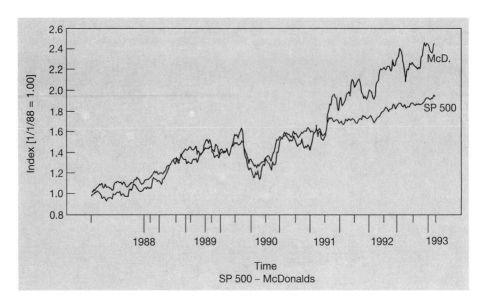

FIGURE 3–3   McDonald's and S&P 500 Stock Index, Weekly (1988–93)

In the decision process investors evaluate the risk-return behavior of each alternative investment to ensure that the return expected is "reasonable" given its level of risk. If other vehicles with lower levels of risk provide greater returns, the investment would not be deemed acceptable. An investor would select the opportunities that offer the highest returns associated with the level of risk they are willing to take. If most investors were risk-averse they would acquire lower-risk vehicles, thereby receiving lower investment returns. As long as investors get the highest return for the acceptable level of risk, they have made a good choice.

PICTURING RISK AND RETURN

Figure 3–3 compares the progression of the weekly stock price of McDonald's Corp. and the S&P 500 Stock Index for 1988–93. The graph assumes a $1 invest-ment in each at the beginning of 1988. It is obvious that McDonald's outdistanced the S&P 500 (the "market"). One dollar invested in McDonald's stock at the begin-ning of 1988 was worth more than $2.50 by October 1993, one-third more than what $1 invested in the market yielded.

Figure 3–4 displays the weekly variation (volatility) in the rate of return on McDonald's stock. It looks to the naked eye like random "noise," similar to the tracings produced by an EKG machine recording heart activity. It is difficult to see any pattern(s) clearly. Figure 3–5 displays the weekly returns in histogram form. That is, it shows the relative frequency (number of weeks) when specific weekly rates of return are experienced. For example, a weekly return of .5 percent (.005) was experienced about ten times. Notice that this representation displays some-

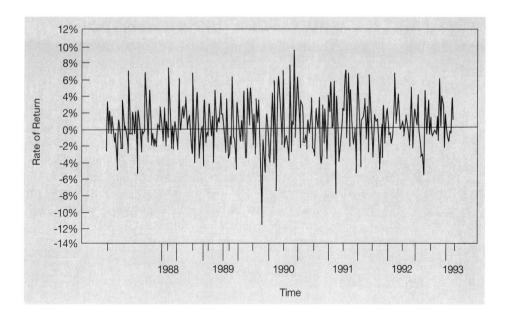

FIGURE 3–4   McDonald's Corp. Weekly Stock Returns (1988–93)

what of a bell-shaped, or normal, distribution. The distribution would probably have displayed even a more pronounced bell-shaped character if we had used daily returns. The average weekly return over this time period was .34 percent, with a standard deviation of 3.05 percent. Does it look like 99 percent of the returns lie between plus or minus three standard deviations?

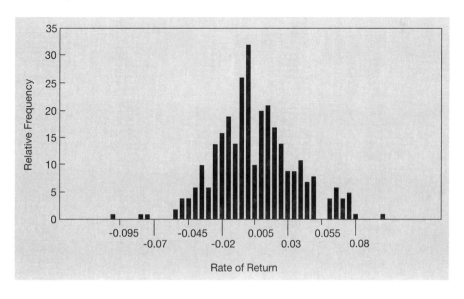

FIGURE 3–5   McDonald's Corp. Weekly Stock Returns (1988–93)

CALCULATING EXPECTED RETURN AND RISK: MCDONALD'S CORP.

The appropriate numbers and formulas that we must have to calculate return and risk on a stock, and the relationship of the stock's return with the market, are illustrated in Table 3–4 for McDonald's Corp. using recent monthly data.

The data for McDonald's are monthly in format. Therefore, the alpha of .328 suggests that McDonald's should have a return of about .328 percent per month if the market is "flat" (neither going up nor going down). The beta of .86 suggests that the stock is less volatile than the market (market = 1.0). Combining the alpha and the beta we can predict the return on McDonald's stock if the market moves up or down. Suppose the market were expected to produce an expected annual rate of return of 13 percent (.25 percent weekly). The expected weekly return on McDonald's stock using Equation 3.4 would be:

$$R_s = \alpha + \beta_s(R_m)$$

$$= .328 + .86(.25)$$

$$= .543 \text{ percent}$$

The characteristic line for McDonald's using the recent monthly data is shown in Figure 3–6.

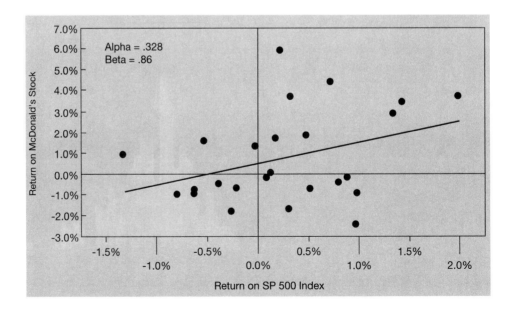

FIGURE 3–6 McDonald's Characteristic Line, Monthly Returns vs. S&P 500
(May 3–October 25, 1993)

TABLE 3–4

Beta Calculation McDonald's Corp. Weekly Returns vs. S&P 500 Stock Index
May 3 – October 25, 1993

(1) YEAR MONTH/DAY		(2) STOCK PRICE	(3) S&P 500 PRICE	(4) STOCK RETURN (Y)	(5) MARKET RETURN (X)	(6) (X)*(Y)	(7) X^2	(8) Y^2
5	3	48.13	440.19					
	10	49.00	442.31	1.81	0.48	0.87	0.23	3.27
	17	48.63	439.56	–0.76	–0.62	0.47	0.39	0.57
	24	50.25	445.84	3.33	1.43	4.76	2.04	11.10
	31	49.75	450.19	–1.00	0.98	–0.97	0.95	0.99
6	7	50.38	450.06	1.27	–0.03	–0.04	0.00	1.60
	14	50.00	447.26	–0.75	–0.62	0.47	0.39	0.57
	21	49.50	443.68	–1.00	–0.80	0.80	0.64	1.00
	28	49.38	447.60	–0.24	0.88	–0.21	0.78	0.06
7	5	49.13	445.84	–0.51	–0.39	0.20	0.15	0.26
	12	48.75	448.13	–0.77	0.51	–0.40	0.26	0.60
	19	49.50	445.75	1.54	–0.53	–0.82	0.28	2.37
	26	48.63	447.10	–1.76	0.30	–0.53	0.09	3.09
8	2	51.50	448.13	5.90	0.23	1.36	0.05	34.83
	9	51.50	448.68	0.00	0.12	0.00	0.02	0.00
	16	53.38	450.14	3.65	0.33	1.19	0.11	13.33
	23	54.88	456.16	2.81	1.34	3.76	1.79	7.90
	30	53.50	460.54	–2.51	0.96	–2.41	0.92	6.32
9	6	54.38	461.34	1.64	0.17	0.29	0.03	2.71
	13	54.25	461.72	–0.24	0.08	–0.02	0.01	0.06
	20	53.75	458.83	–0.92	–0.63	0.58	0.39	0.85
	27	52.75	457.63	–1.86	–0.26	0.49	0.07	3.46
10	4	52.50	461.29	–0.47	0.80	–0.38	0.64	0.22
	11	52.13	460.31	–0.70	–0.21	0.15	0.05	0.50
	18	54.00	469.50	3.59	2.00	7.16	3.99	12.87
	25	54.50	463.27	0.93	–1.33	–1.23	1.76	0.86
Sum				12.97	5.19	15.52	16.03	109.36
Average				0.50	0.20			
Observations [n] = 25								

Formulas:

$$\text{BETA} = \frac{n\Sigma xy - (\Sigma x)(\Sigma y)}{n\Sigma x^2 - (\Sigma x)^2}$$

$$= \frac{(25)(15.52) - (5.19)(12.97)}{(25)(16.03) - (5.19)^2}$$

$$= .86$$

$$\text{ALPHA} = \bar{y} - \beta\bar{x}$$

$$= .50 - (.86)(.2)$$

$$= .328$$

HISTORICAL RISK AND RETURN
ON ASSET CLASSES

The risks and rewards available from holding various classes of assets for 1945–91 have been measured. Table 3–5 shows returns and standard deviations of returns on assets from stocks to silver. During the period 1945–91 we can note that high returns are generally associated with high risk (standard deviation) just as theory and common sense suggest. There are some notable exceptions, especially the relatively low risk on farmland compared to its return and the opposite characteristics for gold and silver. During 1945–91 S&P 500 stocks beat inflation (consumer price index) by 7.3 points while corporate and U.S. government bonds just squeeked by inflation. U.S. stocks (S&P 500) earned an impressive 11.8 percent per year over this nearly one-half century since World War II. While Japanese stocks outdistanced U.S. stocks, they did so with greater associated risk.

TABLE 3–5

Annual Rates of Return and Risk,
Selected Asset Categories

ASSET CATEGORY	1945–91		1982–91		1987–91	
	ANNUAL RETURN	STANDARD DEVIATION	ANNUAL RETURN	STANDARD DEVIATION	ANNUAL RETURN	STANDARD DEVIATION
Venture capital	18.0	35.8	15.8	29.2	2.3	33.2
Japanese stocks	17.4	28.9	18.9	21.3	6.5	28.2
Emerging growth stocks	14.9	29.2	12.3	18.5	12.8	22.8
Small stocks	13.3	26.0	12.0	20.7	6.9	23.4
S&P 500 stocks (big stocks)	11.8	16.6	17.6	11.5	15.4	13.7
U.S. farmland	10.0	7.5	3.3	5.9	7.6	1.1
Art	8.5	15.0	12.4	16.6	16.4	22.1
Commercial real estate	7.5	5.2	6.9	4.6	4.5	3.4
U.S. gross domestic product	7.4	3.5	6.4	2.1	5.9	1.7
Residential housing	7.4	4.0	4.2	1.4	8.9	1.8
Corporate bonds	5.4	9.9	16.3	12.3	10.4	7.1
Gold	5.1	26.2	–1.3	14.7	–2.1	13.5
U.S. Treasury bills	4.9	3.3	7.7	1.7	6.7	1.1
U.S. Treasury bonds	4.8	9.8	15.6	12.8	9.8	8.1
Consumer price index	4.5	3.9	3.9	1.2	4.6	1.1
Silver	4.4	56.8	–7.3	18.3	–6.4	15.5
Foreign bonds	n.a.	n.a.	14.2	15.0	12.5	13.9
Foreign stocks	n.a	n.a.	18.0	24.1	8.7	17.9

Source: *Barron's*, March 23, 1992.

RISK AND TIME

It was Archimedes, the Greek philosopher, who said, "Give me a lever long enough, and I can move the Earth." In investing, that lever is time.

Looking at the returns on common stocks each year from 1926 through 1987 would show that if we are investing on a one-year basis, you should expect the return to be almost random, from a high of 54% to a low of –43% (ouch!).

However, when we extend the holding period, we get a different picture of volatility, or risk, in holding common stocks. A glance at the accompanying table will show that in no twenty-year holding period have stocks lost money. This is astonishing, considering that this history includes the Depression years. Moreover, the probability of beating inflation increases with the length of the holding period.

Are stocks too volatile? No—as long as you have a reasonable time horizon for capturing their premium returns!

Common Stocks Compound Annual Return Data Various Holding Periods* (1926–87)

HOLDING PERIOD (YEARS)	NUMBER OF PERIODS	NUMBER OF NEGATIVE RETURNS	PERCENT OF PERIODS BEATING INFLATION
1	62	19	65%
5	58	7	75
10	53	2	85
20	43	0	100

*Rolling holding periods (e.g., five years: 1926–30, 1927–31, etc.).

SUMMARY

Investors want to maximize expected return subject to their tolerance for risk. Such returns take the form of dividend and/or interest income and appreciation in the price of the asset held.

The risk associated with holding common stocks is really the likelihood that expected returns will not materialize. If dividends or price appreciation fall short of expectations, the nvestor is disappointed. The principal sources behind dividend and price-appreciation uncertainties are forces and factors that are either controllable or not subject to control by the firm.

Uncontrollable forces, called sources of systematic risk, include market, interest-rate, and purchasing-power risks. Market risk reflects changes in investor attitudes toward equities in general that stem from tangible and intangible events. Tangible events might include expectations of lower corporate profits; intangible events might be overreaction to lower expected profits and the resultant panic selling. Interest-rate risk and purchasing-power risk are associated with changes in the price of money and other goods and services. Increases in interest rates (the price of money) cause the prices of all types of securities to be

marked down. Rising prices of goods and services (inflation or purchasing-power changes) have an adverse effect on security prices because the postponement of consumption through any form of investment means less "real" buying power in the future.

The principal sources of unsystematic risk affecting the holding of common stocks are business risk and financial risk. Business risk refers to changes in the operating environment of the firm and how the firm adapts to them. Financial risk is related to the debt-and-equity mix of financing in the firm. Operating profits can be magnified up or down, depending upon the extent to which debt financing is employed and under what terms.

The various sources of risk in holding common stocks must be quantified so that the analyst can examine risk in relationship to measures of return employed in Chapter 3. A reasonable surrogate of risk is the variability of return. This proxy measure in statistics is commonly the variance or standard deviation of the returns on a stock around the expected return. In reality, the variation in return *below* what is expected is the best measure of risk, but we saw that because the distribution of returns on stocks is nearly normal in a statistical sense, the semideviation or semivariance below the expected value need not be calculated.

Total risk of an investment can be thought of as consisting of two components: diversifiable and nondiversifiable risk. The former risk can be almost entirely by holding a large enough mix of carefully selected securities. The only risk an investor is compensated for taking is thus nondiversifiable risk. Beta measures this risk and can be used to determine the appropriate required return on a security.

QUESTIONS

1. Identify the risks normally associated with the following terms:
   a. investor panic,
   b. cost of living,
   c. labor strikes,
   d. increased debt-to-equity ratios, and
   e. product obsolescence.

2. Of those risks normally associated with the holding of securities,
   a. what three risks are commonly classified as systematic in nature?
   b. what risks are most prevalent in holding common stocks?

3. What is the probability of drawing the following from a single deck of playing cards:
   a. a heart?
   b. an ace?
   c. an ace of hearts?

4. Show in tabular form a frequency distribution of the sums obtained by tossing a pair of dice.

5. Show a simple example using probabilities where two securities have equal expected returns but unequal variances or risk in returns.

6. Cite recent examples of political, social, or economic events (market risk) that have excited
   a. the stock market, and
   b. stocks in a specific industry, to surge ahead or plummet sharply.

7. Chin Corp. has been distributing national brands of swimming pools for many years. Recently the owner's son has been encouraging his father to increase the size of the business by 50 percent through distributing a complete line of ski equipment and accessories. In what ways would the expansion alter the business risk associated with the operation of Chin Corp. as merely a swimming-pool distributor?

8. What is the significance of a characteristic line that has a negative slope?

9. Electric power companies are often cited for the fact that they typically have betas well below 1.0. Similarly, manufacturers of recreational vehicles (e.g., cross-country campers) have betas close to 2.0. What is it about the operating characteristics (products, financing) of these two industries that might intuitively explain the wide differences in their betas?

PROBLEMS

1. The shares of Barker Ltd. were purchased for $50 on January 1. The stock paid dividends totalling $2 during ensuing year. At year-end, the stock was sold for $45. What was the total return on Barker stock for the year?

2. Dunaway, Inc., stock had the following rates of return for 1991–95: .20, .13, –.09, .05, –.11. What is the arithmetic average rate of return on Dunaway's stock over this period? The geometric average? Why are these returns different?

3. Consult *Value Line,* Moody's, Standard & Poor's or other investment services to determine price and dividend data for PepsiCo and Tootsie Roll Industries. If you had purchased each stock at the average of its high and low prices in 1990 and sold each stock at the average of its high and low prices in 1994, what rate of return would you have earned on each stock (before transaction costs and taxes)? Assume that dividends paid each year are collected in one payment at the end of the year.

4. A stock costing $100 pays no dividends. The possible prices that the stock might sell for at year-end and the probability of each are:

YEAR-END PRICE	PROBABILITY
$90	.1
95	.2
100	.4
110	.2
115	.1

a. What is the expected return on the stock?

b. What is the standard deviation of the expected return?

5. Mr. Mulloy has analyzed a stock for a one-year holding period. The stock is currently selling for $10 but pays no dividends, and there is a fifty-fifty chance that the stock will sell for either $10 or $12 by year-end. What is the expected return and risk if 250 shares are acquired with 80 percent margin? Assume the cost of borrowed funds is 10 percent. (Ignore commissions and taxes.)

6. Stocks Q and R do not pay dividends. Stock Q currently sells for $50 and R for $100. At the end of the year ahead there is a fifty-fifty chance that Q will sell for either $61 or $57 and R for either $117 or $113. Which stock, Q or R, would you prefer to purchase now? Why?

7. Determine dividends paid and the high and low prices on shares of IBM from *Value Line,* Moody's, or other sources. Assuming the IBM was bought and sold each year from 1985 through 1990 at the average of the high-low price and that dividends for the year were collected in a single sum at the end of the year, calculate, for 1985–90,

a. the average annual holding-period yield, and

b. the standard deviation of the annual returns.

8. Financial risk or leverage in the case of individuals is normally associated with margin trading, or increasing one's ability to purchase securities by borrowing money. Investor A has analyzed a stock for a one-year holding period. There is a fifty-fifty chance that the stock, currently selling at $10, will sell for $9 or $12 by year-end. The investor can borrow on 50 percent margin from his bank at 9 percent per annum. (Ignore taxes and transaction costs.)

a. What are the investor's expected holding-period yield and risk if he buys 100 shares and does not borrow from his bank?

b. What are expected yield and risk if he buys 200 shares, paying half the cost with borrowed funds at 9 percent per annum?

9. The following statistics result from correlating the rates of return on PepsiCo stock and the rates of return on the S&P 500 Stock Index:

	PEPSICO	S&P 500
Average return	9.80%	3.53%
Total variance	127.32	42.26
Alpha	5.87	
Beta	1.11	
Correlation with SP 500	.62	

   a. What rate of return is expected on PepsiCo stock if the S&P 500 Stock Index has an expected return of 15 percent?

   b. How closely does the rate of return on PepsiCo correlate with the rate of return on the S&P 500 Stock Index?

10. Compute the expected return for each of the following stocks when the risk-free rate is .08 and the expected return on the market is .15:

STOCK	BETA
Green	1.72
Blue	1.14
Black	0.76
Brown	0.44
Orange	0.03
Red	–0.79

11. The following historical rate of return information is provided for Funky Software Co. and the stock market:

YEAR	FUNKY	MARKET
1990	12	15
1991	9	13
1992	–11	14
1993	8	–9
1994	11	12
1995	4	9

   a. What are the arithetic and geometric average rates of return on the market for the period 1990–95?

   b. What is Funky's beta?

   c. What is the equation for Funky's characteristic line?

C A S E

Nike, Inc.

Diana Boyd had recently been hired by Dean Witter Reynolds as an account executive and was participating along with other new brokers in a company training program, the objectives of which were to familiarize the participants with the pro-

EXHIBIT 1

Weekly Stock Prices: S&P 500 Stock Index vs. Nike, Inc. (September 1992–February 1993)

MONTH	DAY	S&P 500 INDEX	NIKE PRICE
9/92	7	417.08	72.00
	14	419.58	74.88
	21	422.93	75.63
	28	414.35	76.75
10	5	410.47	77.87
	12	402.66	77.63
	19	411.73	77.63
	26	414.10	77.50
11	2	418.68	77.88
	9	417.58	83.50
	16	422.43	85.50
	23	426.65	87.88
	30	430.16	87.63
12	7	432.06	84.25
	14	433.73	87.25
	21	441.28	88.38
	28	439.77	84.75
1/93	4	435.71	83.00
	11	429.05	80.00
	18	437.15	85.13
	25	436.11	82.50
2	1	438.78	81.63
	8	448.93	85.00
	15	444.58	82.13

cedures of the brokerage house, develop selling skills, prepare account executives for the NYSE registration examination, and provide an introduction to investment analysis and management.

Before joining the firm, Diana had been successful in sales with a large Los Angeles retail chain. She was a history major at Stanford University and had taken no business courses. Because of her lack of business background, Diana was particularly interested in the investment-training sessions. At the first meeting on investment analysis and management, the session leader dealt with the importance of diversification. He felt that account executives spent entirely too much time selling individual securities.

Diana had been able to grasp the general points brought out in the initial session but felt she had missed much of the detail. The session leader had used terms unfamiliar to her, such as *beta, systematic* and *unsystematic risk,* and the *coefficient of correlation.* At the end of the lecture, Diana asked the instructor if he would provide her with some materials to help her with the terminology. The instructor provided Diana some reading material as well as a short exercise and examples to

EXHIBIT 2

Nike, Inc., Financial Data

($ IN MILLIONS)	1992	1991	1990	1989	1988	1987
Income Data						
Revenue	$3,402	3,004	2,235	1,711	1,203	877
Operating income	$593	516	407	291	164	87
Net income (NI)	$329	287	243	167	102	36
NI revenue (%)	9.7	9.6	10.9	9.8	8.5	4.1
Cash flow	$377	321	260	182	116	48
Balance Sheet Ratios						
Current ratio	3.3	2.0	3.1	3.0	2.2	3.6
Return on assets (%)	18.4	20.4	25.3	21.7	16.8	7.2
Debt to capital (%)	5.0	2.8	3.2	5.7	6.8	9.3
Return on equity (%)	27.8	31.5	36.0	34.2	27.4	10.9
Market Data						
Earnings per share	4.30	3.77	3.21	2.23	1.35	.47
Dividends per share	0.58	0.48	0.35	0.25	0.20	0.15
Price Range (High-Low)	75/35	48/24	35/13	17/9	12/6	10/5
P/E Ratio (Range)	18-8	13-6	11-4	8-4	9-4	22-11

help familiarize her with risk-return concepts. Later that week the instructor provided some selected readings from the *Journal of Portfolio Management* dealing with investment management issues. He also gave her some monthly prices for the common stock of the Nike, Inc., and the S&P composite average of 500 stocks (see Exhibit 1). He suggested that examining Nike stock in terms of its volatility both absolutely and relative to the market (S&P 500) was possible. In the latter case, one could also calculate an expected return for Nike stock given a conditional return for the market. This expected return could further be predicted with a certain degree of confidence in a statistical sense.

Nike is one of the world's largest suppliers of high-quality athletic footware. The company also produces sports apparel. Nike's earnings have grown substantially in recent years on strong domestic and international sales. International sales are approaching 50 percent of total sales. Some relevant financial data is shown in Exhibit 2. During the training sessions, the participants examined historical risk-and-return information and interrelationships between assets available in the world equity markets. Data provided in Exhibits 3 and 4 depict historical risk-and-return information for a number of foreign stock markets.

Exhibit 3 shows annual returns and risk (standard deviation of returns) for foreign stock markets for 1980–92. Exhibit 4 is a correlation matrix using codes for the markets in Exhibit 3. For example, Amsterdam is "ANP," Paris is "PSE," and so on. It can be interpreted as follows: for example, the correlation between U.S.

EXHIBIT 3

Annual Returns and Risk

ASSET CODE	NAME OF MARKET	RETURN (%)	STANDARD DEVIATION
SPC	S&P 500 Composite (USA)	15.61	14.12
ANP	Amsterdam	14.99	21.08
AAO	Australia	6.65	22.72
FSE	Frankfurt	8.70	21.24
HSE	Hong Kong	15.38	29.08
LSE	London	13.74	12.92
MSE	Madrid	16.22	25.60
MSI	Milan	14.88	34.39
PSE	Paris	14.81	23.39
SGE	Singapore	10.46	24.70
SSE	Switz.	8.76	15.38
TOS	Tokyo	8.00	21.88
TSE	Toronto	4.31	18.74

---

stocks (SPC) and Japanese stocks (TOS) is .35 (see number within the box). This suggests that the returns of these two series move together, but weakly. Correlation coefficients have a range of +1.0 (move up and down together in perfect synchronization) to −1.0 (move exactly in opposite directions). A correlation of zero would mean that two series are unrelated. None of these markets are negatively correlated, but they vary in strength of positive comovement.

EXHIBIT 4

Correlation Matrix

ASSET CODE	ANP	AAO	FSE	HSE	LSE	MSE	MSI	PSE	SPC	SGE	SSE
ANP	1.00	0.50	0.85	0.11	0.51	0.25	0.60	0.78	0.60	0.09	0.78
AAO	0.50	1.00	0.48	0.52	0.72	0.58	0.54	0.59	0.73	0.48	0.62
FSE	0.85	0.48	1.00	0.17	0.47	0.25	0.60	0.75	0.51	0.02	0.82
HSE	0.11	0.52	0.17	1.00	0.41	0.37	0.47	0.20	0.33	0.36	0.25
LSE	0.51	0.72	0.47	0.41	1.00	0.42	0.43	0.50	0.70	0.41	0.56
MSE	0.25	0.58	0.25	0.37	0.42	1.00	0.57	0.42	0.29	0.10	0.20
MSI	0.60	0.54	0.60	0.47	0.43	0.57	1.00	0.48	0.51	0.18	0.46
PSE	0.78	0.59	0.75	0.20	0.50	0.42	0.48	1.00	0.52	0.16	0.74
SPC	0.60	0.73	0.51	0.33	0.70	0.29	0.51	0.52	1.00	0.51	0.68
SGE	0.09	0.48	0.02	0.36	0.41	0.10	0.18	0.16	0.51	1.00	0.18
SSE	0.78	0.62	0.82	0.25	0.56	0.20	0.46	0.74	0.68	0.18	1.00
TOS	0.25	0.61	0.16	0.12	0.49	0.72	0.36	0.33	0.35	0.25	0.18
TSE	0.53	0.79	0.44	0.29	0.61	0.28	0.44	0.41	0.89	0.52	0.65

QUESTIONS

1. Calculate the ingredients of the characteristic line (alpha and beta) for Nike stock for the period September 7, 1992, through February 15, 1993. Interpret the meaning of these ingredients individually and in combination.

2. How would you characterize the behavior of this stock during the period (e.g., aggressive, neutral, defensive, etc.) relative to the market? State why in terms of
   a. underlying statistical relationships, and
   b. company basics (e.g., products, services, operations, financing).

3. Suppose the S&P 500 Stock Index was expected to move up .3 percent in a week. How much of a return would you expect from Nike stock?

4. Look at Exhibit 3. Which market afforded the highest return between 1980 and 1992? Where was the greatest risk? Using the notion of risk per unit of return (standard deviation/return), rank these markets from best to worst.

5. The correlation matrix in Exhibit 4 compares the comovement of the various markets. The closer the correlation is to 1.0 the more two markets are almost carbon copies of each other in terms of return variation.
   a. What is the correlation between the following markets: Switzerland (SSE) and Frankfurt (FSE); London (LSE) and Hong Kong (HSE); Singapore (SGE) and Amsterdam (ANP); Toronto (TSE) and New York (SPC)?
   b. Locate the highest correlations. What can be said to explain the underlying economic/political reasons that might explain this strength of correlation? What about the weak correlations?

REFERENCES

BREALEY, R. A. *An Introduction to Risk and Return on Common Stocks.* Cambridge, Mass.: M.I.T. Press, 1969.

BROWN, R. "Risk and Return in the Emerging Markets." *Investing* (Spring 1991).

HARRINGTON, D. R. *Modern Portfolio Theory, The Capital Asset Pricing Model and Arbitrage Pricing Theory: A User's Guide.* 2d ed. Englewood Cliffs, N.J.: Prentice Hall, 1987.

IBBOTSON, R. G., and R. A. SINQUEFIELD. *Stocks, Bonds, Bills and Inflation: Historical Returns* (1926–1987). Charolttesville, Va.: Research Foundation of the Institute of Chartered Financial Analysts, 1989.

IBBOTSON ASSOCIATES. *Stocks, Bonds, Bills and Inflation: Yearbook.* Annual. Chicago: Ibbotson Associates.

KOSMICKE, R. "The Limited Relevance of Volatility to Risk." *Journal of Portfolio Management* (Fall 1986).

LLOYD, W. P., and N. K. MODANI. "Stocks, Bonds, Bills, and Time Diversification." *Journal of Portfolio Management* (Spring 1983).

ROSENBERG, B. "Prediction of Common Stock Betas." *Journal of Portfolio Management* (Winter 1985).

SOLDOFSKY, R. M., and D. F. MAX. *Holding Period Yields and Risk—Premium Curves for Long-Term Marketable Securities: 1910–1976.* New York University, 1978.

WIGGINS, JAMES B. "Betas in Up and Down Markets." *Financial Review* (February 1992).

ECONOMIC
ANALYSIS

ANALYTICAL FRAMEWORK FOR COMMON STOCKS

The primary motive for buying a stock is to sell it subsequently at a higher price. In many cases, dividends will be expected also. Dividends and price changes are the principal ingredients in what investors regard as return or yield.

If an investor had impeccable information and insight about dividends and stock prices over subsequent periods, he would be well on his way to great riches. But the real world of investing is full of political, economic, social, and other forces that we do not understand sufficiently to permit us to predict anything with absolute certainty. Forces intermix and flow at crosscurrents. Nothing is static.

For the security analyst, what primary influences will determine the dividends to be paid on a stock in the future and what the stock price will be in the future are the ultimate questions to be answered. A logical systematic approach to estimating future dividends and stock price is indispensable.

The framework we will be using is the economic-industry-company approach, or the E-I-C framework. This approach is sometimes referred to as a "top-down" method of analysis.

ECONOMIC AND INDUSTRY ANALYSIS

King observed that, on the average, over half the variation in a stock's price could be attributed to a market influence that affects all stock-market indexes, such as the Dow Jones Industrial Average or the S&P 500 Stock Index.[1] But stocks are also subject to an industry influence, over and above the influence common to all stocks. King noted that this industry influence explained, on the average, about 13 percent of the variation in a stock's price. In sum, about two-thirds of the variation

---

[1] B. F. King, "Market and Industry Factors in Stock Price Behavior," *Journal of Business,* 39 (January 1966), 139–90. Subsequent studies confirm the importance of macro factors although the degree of influence might be somewhat less than King found.

in the prices of stocks observed in King's study was the result of market and industry influences or factors. King actually examined only about sixty companies, so it is dangerous to extrapolate from this small sample to a generalization about *all* stocks. However, although the amount of variation in a stock's price attributable to the market may be more or less than the percentage observed by King, the impact of a common market influence is obviously something to contend with.

The significance of these conclusions seems to be that in order to estimate stock price changes, an analyst must spend more than a little time probing the forces operating in the overall economy, as well as influences peculiar to industries he is concerned with. A failure to examine overall economic and industry influences is a naive error, that of assuming that individual companies follow their own private paths in a vacuum.

It is important to predict the course of the national economy because economic activity affects corporate profits, investor attitudes and expectations, and ultimately security prices. An outlook of sagging economic growth can lead to lower corporate profits, a prospect that can engender investor pessimism and lower security prices. Some industries might be expected to hold up better, and stock prices of companies in these industries may not decline as much as securities in general. The key for the analyst is that overall economic activity manifests itself in the behavior of stocks in general—or the stock market, if you will. This linkage between economic activity and the stock market is critical.

Before an investor commits funds in the market, he must decide if the time is right to invest in securities at all; and if so, he must then decide which type of security to purchase under the circumstances.[2] Thus, he must decide whether to purchase common stocks, options, preferred stocks, bonds, or some combination thereof. We will explore the relevance of broad economic variables such as national income and defense expenditures to the investor or analyst considering the purchase of common stocks. In the process, we will place major emphasis on the techniques most frequently employed by business economists as they go about their business of short-term economic forecasting. These are important for the security analyst or investor to know because he will be utilizing much of the output of the economists' efforts as a basis for his own opinion about the impending economic environment. In this respect, the analyst can better evaluate economic forecasts if he has at least some knowledge of alternative economic forecasting tools—not only the techniques but also their advantages and shortcomings. The

---

[2]Obviously, timing (which we consider to include both the *what* and *when* issues) is of critical importance not only in a purchase decision but also in the sell decision; however, in order to ease the explanation of the relevant factors, we will restrict our discussion to the purchase question and leave it to the reader to adapt the methodology discussed in the text to the sell decision.

Furthermore, as an adjunct to the timing issue, the economic forecast of the analyst can be compared with the overall market's behavior as reflected in stock prices. If the analyst's expectations are markedly different from the apparent consensus market forecast, an investment action may be warranted. The reader should recall that if one accepts the efficient-market hypothesis, this will occur only in rare instances—and then for the good only if the investor analyst is particularly astute and skillful.

techniques we will examine and evaluate include the use of surveys, key economic indicators, diffusion indexes, econometric model building, and the opportunistic model building. First, let us discuss the relationship of economic forecasting to the stock-investment decision more fully.[3]

ECONOMIC FORECASTING AND THE STOCK-INVESTMENT DECISION

If an investor purchases the stock of an automobile manufacturer that is selling near an all-time high, and shortly thereafter the automobile workers go on strike for a long period of time, the investor will surely suffer a large paper loss on his investment. Certainly, if the investor had waited until the strike was close to being settled, other things being equal, his purchase price would have been considerably lower and his potential capital gains greatly enhanced. In analyzing the economy, a careful analyst would have considered the potential impact of an impending automobile workers' strike.

However, there is yet another important reason for considering the economic environment before taking an investment action. As we have seen, research has discovered that approximately half the variability in stock prices is explained by the movement of the overall market. In investment jargon, this common or market effect is known as *systematic risk*. Furthermore, it is intuitively appealing to reason that the total market or some index of market performance is related to overall economic performance. That is, the success of the economy will ultimately include the success of the overall market.[4] For without a positive and healthy economic environment, corporations in general will find it difficult to flourish over time, and investors' holding-period returns will suffer. This in turn will adversely affect an index of overall stock-market performance.

Above and beyond these broad, general relationships, we should observe that future prospects of specific economic industries and firms will be tied to future developments in specific economic series, because profits are based on key economic factors. For example, labor-intensive industries will be tied to labor costs and conditions, most firms involved with transforming material and producing a final product will be tied to the costs of raw materials, savings and loan associations will be affected by the course of interest rates and the demand for mortgages, and leisure-

---

[3]Throughout this chapter we should keep in mind that the exact cause-and-effect relationships between macroeconomic variables and the stock market are not known. However, we know that they are related, and thus the economic environment must be considered.

[4]Notwithstanding this, we will observe shortly that an index of 500 common-stock prices is classified as a leading indicator, with a median lead time of four months. However, it is still possible for individual economic components, such as disposable income, population, expenditures on defense, and income distribution by age group, to lead corporate sales, earnings, and the stock prices of certain industries and companies. Furthermore, if business conditions can be forecast far enough ahead, even in a general fashion, they will lead stock prices, thus *leading a leading indicator.*

products firms will be affected by the availability of leisure time and consumer disposable income.

Thus, we see the importance of relating economic phenomena to security price movements. To equip the security analyst and investor better for this undertaking, we will, in the next few sections, discuss several commonly used forecasting techniques, with major emphasis on the sources of this information, their potential usefulness to the analyst, and their limitations. (See the accompanying box for six trends the editors of *Business Week* see as important for the 1990s.)

FORECASTING TECHNIQUES

Short-Term versus Long-Term Economic Forecasts

First, let us define some terms in the manner in which a business forecaster uses them. When he speaks of a *short-term forecast,* he is generally referring to one covering a period of up to three years, although frequently he means a much shorter period, such as a quarter or several quarters. An *intermediate forecast* refers to a three- to five-year period ahead. And finally, a *long-term forecast* refers to a period more than five years, and frequently ten or more years, in advance.

We noted in an earlier chapter that one of the differences between investment and speculation is the time horizon of the individual in question. That is, the speculator is interested in very short-term holds of securities in order to realize quick capital gains. On the other hand, the investor is interested in situations that will yield adequate returns in both dividends and capital gains for their risk class over a period of several years. However, we also observed earlier that even in the true investment situation, the investor or analyst must constantly review each security's performance both in an absolute sense and in a relative sense—relative to the market. Furthermore, he must regularly observe the state of the stock market, the money and capital markets, and the economy in general in order to ascertain if basic economic conditions have changed sufficiently to warrant his changing his investment strategy. This is another reason for viewing the macroeconomic picture—namely, to de-

---

INVESTING FOR THE 1990S: SIX TRENDS THAT POINT TO A TREASURE TROVE OF STOCK OPPORTUNITIES

JEFFREY M. LADERMAN

Forget about what the stock market is going to do today, tomorrow, or even next year. Instead, think about investing for the longer term. Where do you start? First, identify the economic, social, and technological forces that will dominate the next decade. Then, figure out what kinds of companies could profit from those trends. That's how you'll find the stars of the 1990s.

In this Special Report, we focus on six crucial trends that will play out in coming years and pinpoint companies that are poised to benefit from them. [See the following list.] Of course, there's always danger in forecasting—especially when trying to envision the sweep of a new decade. In late 1979, most investment strategists thought OPEC had the West over an oil barrel. The seers said the 1980s would see $100-a-barrel oil and energy stocks were a sure bet. As it turned out, oil prices peaked around $40 early in the decade, and a barrel now goes for about $20. Everyone overestimated the cartel's power and underestimated consumers' ability to conserve.

The forces that BUSINESS WEEK's editors have identified will not evaporate so swiftly. Nothing is more certain than aging, so we explore the investment ramifications of the age wave that will hit the 1990s—the maturing of the baby-boom generation and the growth of "senior-seniors"—the 75-plus generation.

Two themes concern the reshaping of America's physical landscape—improving the environment and rebuilding the nation's decaying infrastructure. True, these needs were emerging years ago. But not enough was done. Today, the needs have escalated, and so has the political will to tackle the problems.

In a not-so-different vein, new legislation and deregulation are finally allowing a major overhaul of the U.S. banking system. Besides the problems of Third World loans and failing thrifts, there are just too many banks for the system to operate efficiently. That's beginning to change rapidly.

Powerful economic and political forces are ushering in a new era in world trade. Yes, trade pacts can be undone. But the benefits of trade are evident around the world. And governments, be they capitalist or socialist, have little choice but to speed up the process.

We also look at the changing face of the computer industry, for which investors once held high hopes. Today, the stock market treats it like a wasteland. But computers may be one of the most unusual contrarian plays for the 1990s, and consequently, one of the most alluring.

So, welcome to the 1990s—and happy investing.

- REBUILDING There's money to be made in repairing the infrastructure—if you're patient.
- TRADE As trade barriers melt and new pacts are formed, the race will go to those who think global.
- ENVIRONMENT The great cleanup is about to begin, and companies that do the dirty work will sparkle financially.
- BANKING Fewer restrictions and more buyouts make superregionals the ones to watch.
- COMPUTERS Desktops are becoming the rage, but minicomputers and mainframes are far from relics.
- THE AGE WAVE The fortysomething set will spend more, and senior-seniors' health care needs will soar.

tect the relatively most attractive industries at a given moment. Thus, even for the pure investor with a long time horizon, we see that this long period is broken into several short-term periods. In other words, his initial long-term forecast can be broken down into a series of short-term forecasts that are constantly reviewed and revised. Therefore we will focus on a one-year horizon throughout our analysis.

In this chapter we will discuss only short-term forecasting techniques, realizing that when these various short-term forecasts are put side by side, they constitute a check for consistency with an independently arrived-at long-term forecast.

Alternative Techniques of Short-Term Business Forecasting

Central to all forecasting techniques is an understanding of the national income and product accounts, which summarize both the receipts and the expenditures of all segments of the economy, whether government, business, or personal. These macroeconomic accounts taken together measure the total of economic activity in the United States over some specified period of time. By definition, the total of the final expenditures must equal the total of the receipts in the economy. This total quantity is known as the *gross national product,* or GNP for short. Thus, to give it a formal definition, GNP is the *total value of the final output of goods and services produced in the economy.* The various approaches we are about to discuss are used in conjunction with forecasting GNP for short periods in advance, as well as for forecasting various components of GNP over similar periods of time.

It would be of no small interest to an analyst to have knowledge in advance of impending moves, particularly in those components of GNP that are most closely related to the industry or firm he is investigating. For example, if the analyst were considering a defense-oriented company or the defense industry, he would be very interested in a forecast of federal expenditures for defense. If he were examining a consumer-oriented firm, he would undoubtedly be interested in a forecast of disposable personal income and per capita real GNP. (Real GNP is GNP adjusted for price-level changes.) Certainly, forecasts of the rate of population growth, the rate of GNP growth, and thus the rate of growth in per capita GNP would also be important to a consumer-oriented firm's future prospects.

The matter of business forecasting is rather complex and quite specialized. As a result, it is not likely that the security analyst or investor will be called upon to make his own complete forecast of the entire economy, or for that matter a complete forecast of any individual sector in the economy. Nonetheless, it will undoubtedly be necessary for him to use, in his decision-making process concerning securities, economic forecasts or information that a business forecaster uses as a starting point; and thus, it is a prerequisite to knowledgeable and successful investing that he be able to understand and evaluate economic inputs and forecasts that are furnished to him.

To this end, we will next turn our attention to a brief review of major reputable approaches to short-term business forecasting. Our purpose will not be to turn the reader into a professional forecaster, but rather to equip him with the knowledge of the sources of this type of information and to help him understand the value, advantages, and limitations of these approaches.

ANTICIPATORY SURVEYS

Perhaps the most logical place to start a forecast is to ask prominent people in government and industry what their plans are with respect to construction, plant and equipment expenditure, and inventory adjustments, and to ask consumers what their future spending plans are. To the extent that these people plan and budget for expenditures in advance and adhere to their intentions, surveys of intentions constitute a valuable input in the forecasting process. The President's budget, *Business Conditions Digest,* and the *Survey of Current Business,* all of which are U.S. government publications, provide valuable insights for the analyst to assist him in forecasting future economic events.

Inasmuch as we are living in a decentralized economy (that is, an economy in which economic decisions are made by individual entities rather that dictated to them by a centralized government), a survey of intentions must be based upon elaborate statistical sampling procedures. Furthermore, adequate facilities must be provided for the processing and tabulation of the results of the questionnaires. As a result, the use of surveys in forecasting is of recent vintage when compared with several of the other approaches we will discuss shortly; and because of this lack of history of performance, each forecaster must decide the relative usefulness of the various surveys for his purposes. That is, the analyst must decide which surveys overestimate and which underestimate the actual observed results, so that he can determine how the survey results need to be adjusted before inclusion in his individual forecast. This leads us to a most important point—that survey results should not be thought of as forecasts in themselves, but rather as a consensus that the forecaster can use in framing his own forecast.

Perhaps the greatest shortcoming of intention surveys is that the forecaster has no guarantee that the intentions will be carried out. For this reason, the survey approach is most reliable for short-term forecasts that are continually monitored. External shocks such as strikes, political turmoil, or government action can cause sudden changes in intentions. But to the extent that intentions do become translated into final action, this survey approach provides a most valuable insight to the business investor.

Despite the shortcomings of anticipatory surveys, a great plus is their abundance and easy availability even to a noninstitutional investor. To name only three, *Fortune, Business Week,* and the *Survey of Current Business* are key sources of survey results and are publications that many investors either subscribe to or can easily consult at a local library.

BAROMETRIC OR INDICATOR APPROACH

Another forecasting tool is the barometric or indicator approach. It has its foundations in work pioneered by Wesley C. Mitchell, Arthur F. Burns, and Geoffrey H. Moore, at the National Bureau of Economic Research (NBER). Currently, the U.S. Department of Commerce, through the Bureau of Economic Analysis (BEA), has published in its *Business Conditions Digest* data on more than 100 cyclical indicators, classified according to cyclical timing and economic process. For example,

there are ten series dealing with production and income, of which two are leading indicators of business cycle peaks and eight are coincident indicators.

The cyclical-timing classification is either leading, roughly coincident, or lagging. The leading indicators are those time series of data that historically reach their high points (peaks) or their low points (troughs) in advance of total economic activity; the roughly coincident indicators reach their peaks or troughs at approximately the same time as the economy; and finally, the lagging indicators reach their turning points after the economy has already reached its own. The BEA has painstakingly examined historical data in order to ascertain which economical variables have led, lagged after, or moved together with the economy. In order to facilitate the use of the indicator approach, the BEA has developed a "short list" of indicators, consisting of twelve leading, four roughly coincident, and six lagging indicators. In addition, as needed, the BEA revises its composite indexes of leading, coincident, and lagging indicators to reflect changes in the components, changes in methodology, updated statistical factors, and historical revisions to component data. The current composite index of leading, coincident, and lagging indicators is summarized in Table 4–1.

Table 4-1

INDEXES OF ECONOMIC INDICATORS

Composite Index of Leading Indicators
  1. Average weekly hours of production workers (manufacturing)
  2. Average weekly initial claims for unemployment insurance
  3. Manufacturers new orders (consumer goods and materials industries)
  4. Vendor performance—slower deliveries diffusion index
  5. Contracts and orders for plant and equipment
  6. New private housing units authorized by local building permits
  7. Change in manufacturers' unfilled orders (durable goods industries)
  8. Change in sensitive materials prices
  9. Stock prices, 500 common stocks
  10. Money supply (M2)
  11. Index of consumer expectations

Composite Index of Coincident Indicators
  1. Employees on nonagricultural payrolls
  2. Personal income less transfer payments
  3. Industrial production
  4. Manufacturing and trade sales

Composite Index of Lagging Indicators
  1. Average duration of unemployment
  2. Ratio of trade inventories to sales
  3. Change in index of labor cost per unit of output
  4. Average prime rate charged by banks
  5. Commercial and industrial loans outstanding
  6. Ratio of consumer installment credit outstanding to personal income
  7. Change in consumer price index for services

From *Survey of Current Business*, U.S. Department of Commerce, February 1991.

An explanation of the economic rationale behind the indicator approach is helpful. For example, the rationale for the average workweek of production workers in manufacturing being expressed in hours is that before aggregate business activity picks up, the length of the workweek of production workers will increase. That is, before a company goes out and hires new workers, it will offer overtime to current workers, thereby utilizing them more intensively. So we see that a leading indicator may be leading because it measures something that foreshadows a change in productive activity.

The indicator approach is most valuable in suggesting the *direction* of a change in aggregate economic activity; however, it tells us nothing of the magnitude or duration of the change. Unfortunately, even with all this data available, forecasting cycles and turning points is difficult. Often, what appears initially as a significant change turns out after the fact to have been an aberration. Also much time lapses while the government collects and processes the data. To compound the difficulties, outright errors frequently occur in the data. The accompanying box and sidebar from *Fortune* addresses this very issue and correctly states not only problems inherent in shaky statistics but the danger from overanalyzing data that is wrong.

MONEY AND STOCK PRICES

In recent years the monetarist notion of economics has grown increasingly more popular.[5] Although not universally accepted, this monetary theory in its simplest form states that fluctuations in the rate of growth of the money supply are of utmost importance in determining GNP, corporate profits, interest rates, and, of interest to us, stock prices. Monetarists contend that changes in the growth rate of the money supply set off a complicated series of events that ultimately affect share prices. In addition, they maintain that these monetary changes lead stock price changes: "Changes in monetary growth lead changes in stock prices by an average of about nine months prior to a bear market and about two or three months prior to bull markets."[6] These lead times are averages and are based on historical data. It cannot be said whether these average relationships can and will persist for future periods.

Research in the area of monetary theory has led many analysts, both economic and security, to consider changes in the growth rate of the money supply when preparing their forecasts. However, some contemporary thinking states that the stock market leads changes in the money supply.

Today there is strong sentiment that sound monetary policy is a necessary ingredient for steady economic growth and stable prices.

[5]This section draws from Beryl W. Sprinkel, *Money and Markets: A Monetarist View* (Homewood, Ill.: Richard D. Irwin, 1971).
[6]*Ibid.,* p. 221.

WHY THE ECONOMIC DATA MISLEAD US

LOUIS S. RICHMAN WITH JOHN LABATE

It could be the biggest infrastructure problem of all. Once the envy of the world, America's system for gathering and interpreting economic statistics has fallen into disrepair. The resulting mismeasurements make it harder than ever to understand what's happening to the economy, both in the short run and over the long haul.

Over the past decade, the statistics may have *understated* annual economic growth and productivity gains by a percentage point or more, argues Michael Darby, a former Treasury official who teaches at UCLA's graduate school of business. Annual consumer price inflation may have been *overstated* by as much as 1.8%. Unemployment? It's impossible to say what the rate really is.

Such knowledge gaps create endless opportunities for bad policy decisions. If growth is faster than generally assumed, should the Clinton Administration back away from its plans to stimulate the economy? Then again, if inflation is only 1% after all, America has probably reached Federal Reserve Chairman Alan Greenspan's goal of effective zero inflation, leaving room for fiscal and monetary stimulus that could spur small-business growth. One can only guess.

How did we reach this sorry state? Lay part of the blame on penny-pinching. Real government spending on data gathering and analysis, some $2 billion in 1992, has barely grown since the late 1970s, though the economy today is nearly 30% larger and infinitely more complex. Washington's otherwise laudable efforts to reduce the burden of paperwork on business has made it more difficult to gather data detailed enough to ensure better accuracy. And shrunken companies can't spare the people to feed data to government statisticians.

But there's a more important problem: The statisticians are analyzing yesterday's news. The loosely coordinated efforts of the half-dozen or so agencies that crank out most of the data haven't kept pace with enormous technological and structural changes that have transformed the economy.

The federal reporting system was developed and refined over decades to detect the cyclical swings of a manufacturing-based economy largely isolated from the rest of the world. Now companies routinely turn out new goods tailored to specific market niches, greatly expanding consumer choice and shortening product life cycles. Much activity has shifted to harder-to-measure small businesses. And globalization has blurred the boundaries between the American economy and the rest of the world. Says Harvard University economist Zvi Griliches: "Our data are weakest in precisely those areas where economic change has been most dynamic, such as technological innovation, the service sector, and trade."

The divergence between the two economies—the one the government measures and the rapidly evolving one economists and business people are struggling to understand—is widening. Whole industries from biotechnology to telemarketing hatched and flourished in the 1980s. But you wouldn't know it from the government's Standard Industrial Classification (SIC) system, the business categorization scheme that planners, marketers, and economists use to track their industries' performance.

Though the Office of Management and Budget (OMB) revised the 1,005 classifications in 1987 for the first time in a decade, they remain hopelessly out of date. OMB finally created a separate category for semiconductors, but it lumps advanced microprocessors together with photovoltaic cells and simple memory chips. Electronic vac-

uum tubes, meanwhile, get a category of their own. Anyone interested in following the plodding progress of the "nonrubber footwear" industry can find details on no fewer than four different varieties. But telemarketing is grouped together with 134 other business services such as wig styling and window trimming. OMB has started a project to completely overhaul the code, but results aren't likely until 1997 at the earliest. Meantime, the putative data the government collects for industry groups are almost certainly misleading.

Mismeasurement of inflation is the biggest source of economic distortion; the errors affect productivity calculations, long-term wage data, and the GDP growth rate itself. If measurements of price changes by the Department of Labor's Bureau of Labor Statistics (BLS) overstate the inflation rate, real growth of output will be understated except in the few cases, such as autos, where the agency actually analyzes in detail the units produced. Result: Productivity and incomes will seem to stagnate. This overstatement of inflation is precisely what appears to be happening, particularly in the measurement of the consumer prices that make up about two-thirds of the GDP deflator. (Government purchases and payrolls, capital equipment, and construction account for the balance.)

While few experts think the distortions are as large as UCLA's Darby estimates, he's not totally alone. A Federal Reserve Board working paper suggests that in recent years inflation may have been exaggerated by about one percentage point. And many other economists, such as Harvard's Griliches and Robert Gordon of Northwestern, have no doubt that the official data misrepresent the economy's true strength to some degree. Says Gordon: "We have been preoccupied with problems such as slow productivity growth, the competitiveness of U.S. industry, and stagnating real wages. But the trends in income and productivity are not nearly as bad as the numbers make them look."

Each month the BLS dispatches 450 inspectors, most of whom work part time, throughout the land to gather standardized price data on everything Americans buy or rent, from apples and apparel to apartments, appliances, and appendectomies. But today's consumers change their buying patterns too rapidly for the BLS shoppers to keep up. Because the bureau adjusts the products and retail outlets it surveys only gradually over a five-year period, it is slow to detect how swiftly those preferences shift.

Major case in point: BLS has largely missed the huge swing from full-price food retailers to grocery wholesalers and discount outlet clubs such as Cub Foods, Sam's Club, and Costco. Looking at food sales alone, for example, the bargain outlets increased their share of the total from 3.2% in 1980 to 16.2% in 1992, according to *Progressive Grocer,* a food trade publication. As measured by the BLS, food prices rose at an annual 4.2% during the Eighties. But the food inflation index doesn't pick up the savings consumers are enjoying. The result, says Marshall Reinsdorf, a BLS economist, is that the actual inflation rate was 1.7 percentage points lower. More recently the bureau has overlooked the trend by consumers to substitute far less costly private-label store brands for virtually identical big-name-brand products; the generics have grown from 12.5% to 14% of total supermarket dollar sales volume since 1989.

Government economists are also too slow to recognize how new technologies and better product quality pump up consumers' effective buying power. Penicillin was left out until 1951, though it had been in common use for several years, and its price had dropped by 99%. The common pocket calculator, introduced in 1970, didn't show up in BLS's market basket until eight years later, when it had become 90% cheaper than the earliest models. Says Harvard's Griliches: "Whole generations of new goods come and go before the data collectors can measure their impact on prices, productivity, and growth." Thus

(continued)

BLS misses years of price *deflation* even after fast-growing new products have become pervasive throughout the economy.

The distortions compounded manyfold in the 1980s with the information and communications technologies that revolutionized so many factories and offices. Says Henry Kelly, a senior associate at the Office of Technology Assessment in Washington: "Information technology is now 40% of all capital goods investment. But if the price deflators don't reflect its decreasing true cost as the equipment becomes more powerful, the real value of that investment is badly understated."

Economists at the Commerce Department's Bureau of Economic Analysis (BEA) are slowly beginning to adjust. In 1985 the bureau, with help from IBM, revised its methods for calculating the computer price indexes by taking into account increases in computing speed. As a result, computer prices adjusted for quality changes are plunging at a rate of 12% a year.

But in most other areas, the task of adjusting price indexes is monumentally incomplete. The producer price index, which contains thousands of values for such pedestrian products as bolts, flanges, valves, and cleats, still has no accurate measure for semiconductors or for communications equipment, a $58-billion-a-year industry and the biggest category of producer durables.

Some economists, like Martin Baily of the University of Maryland and Northwestern's Robert Gordon, finger mismeasurement as one of the main suspects in the great productivity mystery. The rapidly expanding service sector has created almost all of the economy's new jobs. Measuring productivity in services is treacherously difficult—particularly so for such large sectors as financial services, whose output is hard to define. The government's methods are painfully primitive—and in some cases useless.

Commerce Department statisticians estimate output in financial service businesses, for example, as the value of the labor employed to create it. But labor productivity is by definition total output divided by total labor inputs. So the crude official calculations make it mathematically impossible for productivity to grow at all.

When Baily and Gordon took a close look at the securities industry, they found a lot of productivity growth. In 1973 the average volume of shares traded by the industry's 209,000 employees totaled 5.7 million daily. By 1987 trading volume had grown to an average 63.8 million shares a day—a better than 11-fold increase though industry employment had only doubled. "Instead of zero productivity growth," they conclude, "growth was rapid and accelerating in the 1980s." Baily and Gordon also found serious measurement problems for the supposedly unproductive real estate and insurance industries.

Such mismeasurement helps explain the puzzle of why heavy investments in computers have not visibly lifted productivity. Over the past decade, for example, grocery wholesalers and retailers purchased more information technology—computers, scanners, and the like—than all aircraft manufacturers, with virtually no measured productivity payoff. But the official measurements don't account for the vast proliferation in services that computer power made possible. Example: Electronic tracking of inventories, which allows retailers to offer consumers a far richer choice of products while shrinking their inventory/sales ratios.

Indeed, a new study by the McKinsey Global Institute, the research unit of the McKinsey & Co. management consulting firm, found that productivity in major service industries is far higher in the U.S. than it is in Europe and Japan. In banking, for example, it's nearly 50% higher than in Europe, largely because American banks were quicker during the 1980s to apply computer technology to their back-office clearing op-

erations, install automated teller machines, and adopt new, more efficient organizational structures.

Perhaps the biggest lacuna is the poor quality of data on America's trade flows and international financial transactions. Until the early 1970s, imports and exports were so small a part of total activity that economists could almost regard the current account balance as a rounding error. No more. Over the past two decades the value of U.S. imports and exports has more than doubled as a share of GDP, to 11% last year.

The very factors that expanded trade are making the job of measuring it far harder. Falling tariffs and other barriers, cross-border industrial alliances, and cheap, fast communications foil the auditing systems that were set up in a time when trade was much more tightly controlled. Dun & Bradstreet chief economist Joseph Duncan headed the statistics branch at the Office of Management and Budget during the mid-1970s. Says he: "Our methods of gathering and reporting trade data were designed for a mercantilist economy."

Here again the result is almost certainly an understatement of America's strength. Because most imported goods arrive in U.S. ports accompanied by detailed shipping and customs documents, the Commerce Department captures their value reasonably well. But a commission of the National Academy of Sciences finds that exporters have strong incentives to lowball the value of the products they send abroad, minimizing the tax bite on reported profits or reducing insurance costs. Software makers, for example, quite logically insure for the value of the plastic in their diskettes rather than for the knowledge inscribed on them. The overworked International Trade Division at Commerce lacks the manpower to perform more than a cursory audit on exports.

The most underreported part of trade is fast-growing U.S. service exports. "Despite significant recent improvements by the Commerce Department, the data are still poor," says University of Wisconsin economist Robert Baldwin, who last year headed the National Academy of Sciences panel that examined the quality of U.S. international data. What value do American exporters place on their services? How to get service companies, most of them small, to report their foreign sales? How many globe-hopping consultants, lawyers, or architects leave their fees in overseas banks? Government statisticians have only the dimmest idea. Official estimates for 1991, the last full year available, showed the U.S. as having a $45 billion surplus in service exports, but the true number is undoubtedly larger—perhaps far larger.

So if inflation is cooler, productivity growing more briskly, and foreign trade healthier than the official measurements show, the economy must be in much better shape than we think? Not necessarily. Some mismeasurements have *overstated* growth, partly offsetting the damping effects of the errors based on inflation. While it's often noted that manufacturing continues to account for 22% of real GDP as it did in the 1950s, today's manufacturing needs a lot more service support. The Office of Technology Assessment figures that the share of activities such as advertising, legal services, insurance, security, and communications that go into final output has nearly doubled. These intermediate services—OTA calls them "transactional businesses"—are now as large a proportion of GDP as goods production. Much of them amount to input that eludes measurement.

University of Nebraska economists Scott M. Fuess Jr. and Hendrik van den Berg have calculated the economic impact of this transactional activity by subtracting the measured growth in output that can be attributed to it. The fast growth of the transactions, they say, has sapped productivity. Thus, measured economic growth is less robust

(continued)

that it appears. Their conclusion: Real per capita GDP grew a quarter percentage point a year less between 1983 and 1989 than the average 2.9% computed by the Commerce Department.

The growth figure may be further inflated because the government is measuring output from the new economy that used to go unrecorded. Fuess and van den Berg estimated that many married women who joined the labor force in the 1980s turned to the market for services such as child care and household maintenance, formerly produced as unmeasured housework (although as Zoë Baird showed us, not all of this output gets into the statistics). That added nearly another three-tenths of a percentage point to measured per capita economic growth.

Since jobs are Topic A today, the unemployment rate is among the most critical of statistics. The world's largest ongoing monthly data-gathering exercises are the BLS's surveys of businesses and households on the number of jobs and the unemployment rate. Yet the accuracy of the official numbers is problematic—and especially so during hard times.

The employment picture has been particularly murky. Last November the survey of businesses reported that total employment grew by 417,000 in the first ten months of 1992. But separate data gathered by local BLS offices from state departments of employment showed the job base shrinking by 149,000. Since then, the state offices have been registering higher growth than the national figures.

Both estimates are suspect. The nationwide figures are adjusted to include finger-in-the-wind estimates of the net number of jobs created by new business formations minus those lost to closings. The state data, meanwhile, have been compromised by budget cuts. Only the year-end reconciliation of federal tax withholding forms filed by all employers will determine which estimates were closer to the mark. They will be available this spring.

Attempts by BLS to measure unemployment by monthly surveys of some 60,000 representative households have been bedeviled by demographic and structural shifts. Among other questions the survey cannot answer: How many of the "unemployed" work in the underground economy? What proportion of the 84 million Americans putting in 35 or more hours a week and counted as full-time workers actually hold two or more part-time jobs? Might not many laid-off managers adopt the less ego-bruising label "self-employed" to mask the harsh reality of joblessness? BLS has refined its survey methods for the first time since 1967 and will begin probing these weak spots next year. Until it does, the true unemployment rate could be higher—or lower—than the official data report.

What to do about the crumbling statistical infrastructure? More money is needed, but any change has to begin with some basic reengineering—starting with the abolition of unneeded work. In 1991 the Department of Agriculture spent as much to gather numbers on farm production, which accounts for just 3% of GDP, as the BLS, the BEA, and the Treasury Department *combined* spent on data gathering.

The statistical agencies could also stretch the resources they do have by making better use of technology. Instead of sending its agents scurrying out to price oranges at fruit stands, for example, BLS could get timely readings of changes in prices and preferences by tapping into the electronic scanning data now widely used by retailers and their suppliers.

As always, change will have to come from the top. Michael Boskin, chairman of George Bush's Council of Economic Advisers, laid out a promising proposal. The principal goals: Harmonize U.S. accounts with those of other countries, introduce into the price indexes more quality adjustments for new products and technologies, improve the measurement of service sector output, and refine the Labor Department's surveys of changes in employment. The cost: a modest $200 million or so extra by 1997. Instead, Congress balked—for example, it cut the $30 million increase in outlays requested for 1992 to $18 million.

Action on the Boskin initiative would help. So would continuous research into new measurement methods and closer coordination among the agencies. The U.S. could learn much from the Canadians, whose centralized data office, Statistics Canada, is the industrial world's acknowledged champ at economic measurement. Americans need to know what's happening in their *real* economy—not in the statistical artifact that's being monitored today.

Source: *Fortune,* March 8, 1993, pp 108-114.

ECONOMETRIC MODEL BUILDING

Econometrics is the field of study that applies mathematical and statistical techniques to economic theory. As such, it is the most precise and scientific of the approaches we have discussed thus far because, in applying this technique, the user is forced to specify in a formal mathematical manner the precise relation between the independent and dependent variables. Thus, in using econometrics, the forecaster must quantify precisely the relationships and assumptions he is making. Naturally, one of the key advantages of this approach is that the forecaster must think through clearly all the interrelationships of the economic variables; and for his reward he is yielded a forecast that gives him not only direction but magnitudes. In short, his method yields him a precise figure; even so, however, his forecast is not better than his underlying understanding of economic theory, his application of it, the quality of his data input, and the validity of his assumptions.

Econometric model building involves the specification of a system of simultaneous equations containing both endogenous and exogenous variables. *Endogenous variables* are those determined by the system of equations; *exogenous variables* are those determined outside the system of equations. Therefore, at least one equation is needed to determine a forecast value of each endogenous variable. Values of the exogenous variables are predetermined.

Generally speaking, the well-known econometric models, such as the FRB/MIT (Federal Reserve Board/Massachusetts Institute of Technology), the Michigan, the Pennsylvania, and the Brookings models, are extremely complex; that is, they contain many equations. Their results, both new and revised, are reported regularly in the financial press, such as the *Wall Street Journal.*

Some of the problems with the econometric approach are these: (1) Large computer facilities and vast amounts of clerical and programming support are needed to maintain and update the system. (2) Frequently, the overall forecast is more reliable than the individual components of the forecast. (This is because errors tend to cancel themselves out in the overall forecast.) (3) Because of the vast amounts of data that must be collected, processed, and prepared for inclusion in the model, delays occur in making the results available to the public. Needless to say, this time lapse is potentially more troublesome to the security analyst than to the business forecaster. (4) Generally, these models are useful only for very short-term forecasts.

However, as stated earlier, the beauty of this approach is that it yields a blueprint of the economic system that is based on precisely stated factors that can then be used to yield a definite forecast figure.

For Economists, Life Is Getting Tougher

Encouraged by a recent string of stronger economic data, forecasters are growing more confident that 1993 will produce a solid expansion. Can we count on them to be right? Most failed to foresee either the recession that began in July 1990 or the swoon of late 1991, and they were forced to lower their initial 1992 prediction of 2.5% GNP growth to a meager 1.6%. The December announcement by the experts who date business cycles that the slump hit bottom way back in March 1991 seemed like a bad joke to the many Americans who felt as if the country was *still* in recession.

What went wrong? First, the Commerce Department's 11 leading indicators, which supposedly anticipate economic activity three to six months ahead, gave little warning that the economy was headed toward a slump before Iraq's invasion of Kuwait in August 1990. Then, contradictory 1992 employment readings from the Bureau of Labor Statistics' national surveys and local offices compounded forecasters' problems (see story). Finally, the economists had to wrestle with both the peculiarities of this recession, including historically high debt loads and corporate downsizing (i.e., gross layoffs), and the structural changes that government data don't measure adequately.

To their credit, the forecasters saw that job losses and the debt workout would sap the recovery's vitality. But their reading of the slump might have been sharper had the Bureau of Economic Analysis continued to publish some important measures of these big structural shifts. Alas, budget cuts claimed many, such as the employment layoff rate, which tracked announced corporate payroll reductions. University of Chicago economist Victor Zarnowitz, a business cycle expert, thinks the agency has been pound foolish: "The savings have been negligible, but the losses of information are huge."

Similarly, economists can no longer find how much consumer credit banks extended in the previous month and how much was repaid. In an effort to reduce paperwork burdens, the Fed now asks only for the net change in credit outstanding. Here the savings seem less than negligible: The banks generate the data anyway.

Most forecasts have tracked the economy reasonably well during expansions. From 1983 through 1989, the average of the 51 private forecasters' year-ahead predictions compiled in *Blue Chip Economic Indicators* newsletter fell within seven-tenths of a percentage point of the actual growth. But as the quality and relevance of the official data continue to deteriorate, the job will only get harder.

OPPORTUNISTIC MODEL BUILDING

Opportunistic model building (or GNP model building, sectoral analysis, or any other of the often-used titles for this approach) refers to the most eclectic and perhaps most widely used forecasting method.[7] The forecaster using this approach draws from any and all of the methods already discussed in his quest for an accurate economic forecast. Its similarity to other approaches lies in its use of the na-

---

[7]Much of the material in this section parallels the discussion contained in two classics in this area of study: William F. Butler and Robert A. Kavesh, "Judgmental Forecasting of the Gross National Product," in Butler and Kavesh eds, *How Business Economists Forecast*, Englewood Cliffs, N.J.: Prentice Hall, 1969 and Lewis and Turner, *Business Conditions Analysis*, New York: McGraw-Hill, 1967, particularly chaps. 17–24. Refer to these works for a comprehensive treatment of this fascinating subject.

tional accounting framework to achieve a short-term forecast; its difference arises from its great flexibility and reliance on informed judgments. Perhaps this method can best be appreciated by understanding how it is applied in practice.

Initially, the forecaster must hypothesize total demand, and thus total income, during the forecast period. Obviously, this will necessitate assuming certain environmental decisions, such as war or peace, political relationships among various groups in the economy, any imminent tax changes, the rate of inflation, and the level of interest rates. After this work has been done, the forecaster begins building a forecast of the GNP figure by estimating the levels of the various components of GNP. That is, he must fill in the numbers for consumption expenditures, gross private domestic investment, government purchases of goods and services, and net exports.

Generally, the forecaster will begin with the easiest figure to come by and work toward the most complex. He usually begins with an estimate for the government sector, broken down into federal expenditures and state and local expenditures, with the federal portion being further broken down into defense and nondefense expenditures. The various government publications, including the federal budget itself and the *Annual Economic Report of the President,* provide very useful sources of information for the forecaster. Further insight can be gained in conversations with key government employees. State and local expenditures can be arrived at rather simply, merely by extrapolation of past data, because they have risen by a fairly stable percentage year after year.

Gross private domestic investment is broken down into business expenditures for plant and equipment, residential construction, and changes in the levels of business inventories. The most difficult to forecast accurately is the change in business inventories; this figure changes drastically over the business cycle.

The next sector to be forecast is that of net exports. This is a particularly difficult number to come by, for the forecaster must consider not only domestic but also international, political, and foreign economic problems.

The last sector to forecast in opportunistic model building is the personal consumption factor. Traditionally, this sector is subdivided into three components: durable goods minus automobiles, automobiles, and nondurable goods and services. This sort of breakdown allows the forecaster to find any stable relationships between economic variables, such as between disposable income and expenditures on nondurables. Inasmuch as durables and automobiles tend to fluctuate vigorously over the business cycle, the forecaster should analyze these components separately.

After the forecaster has acquired totals for these four major categories, he adds them together to come up with his GNP forecast. However, his work is not yet completed, for he must then test this total for consistency with an independently arrived at a priori forecast of GNP, as well as test the overall forecast for internal consistency. The former consistency check might necessitate retracing some of the steps in order to bring the two forecasts into line with each other. Thus, he may have to approximate successively the various subcategories, as well as the final estimate of GNP. The internal consistency check arises because of the interrelatedness of the GNP accounts. For example, consumption by individuals implies a level of savings that affects business investment, which further affects productive activity

and thus incomes, which will once again affect savings. While these circular effects take place, other factors such as interest rates, unemployment, and inflation will be affected. Thus, the forecaster must ensure in the light of all these relationships that both his total forecast and his subcomponent forecast make sense and fit together in a reasonable economic fashion.[8] In short, opportunistic model building employs all these techniques, plus a vast amount of judgment and ingenuity in an attempt to build a comprehensive forecast.

This versatile approach to forecasting is at once the greatest asset to opportunistic model building and its greatest liability, for with the advantages that accrue to the economist by mobilizing a variety of forecasting tools and adding judgment come the weaknesses of these techniques. Unfortunately, although the weaknesses can be lessened though selective combination, they cannot be entirely eliminated. Notwithstanding the possible shortcomings of business forecasting, the analyst must still consider and incorporate economic data in his investment decision-making process. Several key sources that summarize forecasts of key research organizations, banks, and economists are the Federal Reserve Bank of Philadelphia's "Predictions for 19—," published in January of each year, and the Federal Reserve Bank of Richmond's "Business Forecasts," published in February of each year. In addition, the *New York Times* and the *Wall Street Journal*, among others, publish many forecasts as they are released.

Potential Usefulness of Economic Forecasts

This chapter has presented a number of interesting paradoxes. Perhaps the most interesting is that we attempted initially to get a handle on future stock price behavior by predicting economic behavior. However, we learned that stock prices are in fact one of the leading indicators for the market taken as a whole. Therefore, this poses a bit of a dilemma if we are attempting to forecast the stock market using the economy because the stock market itself is a leading indicator of the economy. There are, however, several ways out of this chicken-or-egg type of situation. First, we can attempt to forecast the economy far enough into the future so that it will be before even the stock price series is able to forecast the economy. A second possibility would be to develop an economic series that leads the economy by a period of time longer than the stock prices themselves lead the economy. In effect, the leading indicator approach as well as the use of money supply statistics have been attempts at achieving this very objective.

By now, at least two key points are apparent about economic forecasting: (1) It is an extremely arduous and difficult process, even for specialists; and (2) because of this, an analyst must critically evaluate such forecasts and not accept them blindly.

---

[8]Another method of checking for this internal consistency is to forecast what the distribution of incomes will be—between wages, interest, salaries, and so on—under his forecast level of GNP and the various subclassifications, and check to see if these relationships make economic sense.

International Economic Factors

Because the global economy is growing at a very rapid rate, it has become increasingly important for the analyst to consider the international economic environment in addition to the domestic economic environment. First, the company the analyst is working on may sell into many other countries or conversely his firms might import component parts from other areas of the world. As mentioned, the world is becoming increasingly interdependent.

A key issue the analyst will need to consider is exchange rates. The *exchange rate* is the rate at which one's domestic currency can be converted into foreign currency that is, currency of another country. The analyst forecasting a domestic corporation doing business in several different countries will have to consider the U.S. exchange rates with the currency of each country. Exchange rates affect the international competitiveness of domestically produced goods. Conversely, they also affect the competitiveness of foreign-produced goods sold in the United States. If the dollar appreciates relative to the Japanese yen, then Japanese goods become cheaper for U.S. customers to purchase because each dollar can purchase more yen. On the other hand, if the dollar appreciates, it will cost Japanese consumers more yen to purchase goods priced in terms of U.S. dollars. Thus, exchange rates can affect imports, exports, and the rate of inflation domestically.

As U.S. companies reach their limits of domestic growth, they will look to other markets in other countries for expansion and contribution of those growth rates. Mature companies will reach out so as not to stagnate. This will mean that the performance of their foreign operations will become increasingly important to their sales, earnings, P/E ratio, and share-price performance. The accompanying box discusses Southeast Asia as a potential booming emerging market for U.S. corporations.

AN ILLUSTRATION OF AN ECONOMIC ANALYSIS

In order to understand more clearly the E-I-C framework, in the next several chapters we will apply the techniques discussed in these chapters to the same business example. For analysis purposes, we will examine the restaurant industry and McDonald's Corp., because this industry and company are widely known and contain a variety of areas of analytical interest. In this section we will analyze economic data relevant to this industry in order to ascertain if the expected economic environment will be favorable for the restaurant industry in general and for the fast-food sector of the industry in particular.

The forecasts of business conditions of any given year are by themselves difficult to construct. To compound the difficulties further, we have to consider the continuing worries about the rate of inflation; uncertainty as to the future course of interest rates; the international monetary and political situations; and the reality of a large and growing federal budget deficit. In addition to these problem areas, the fast-food sector of the restaurant industry and McDonald's in particular are also

Missing Out on a Glittering Market

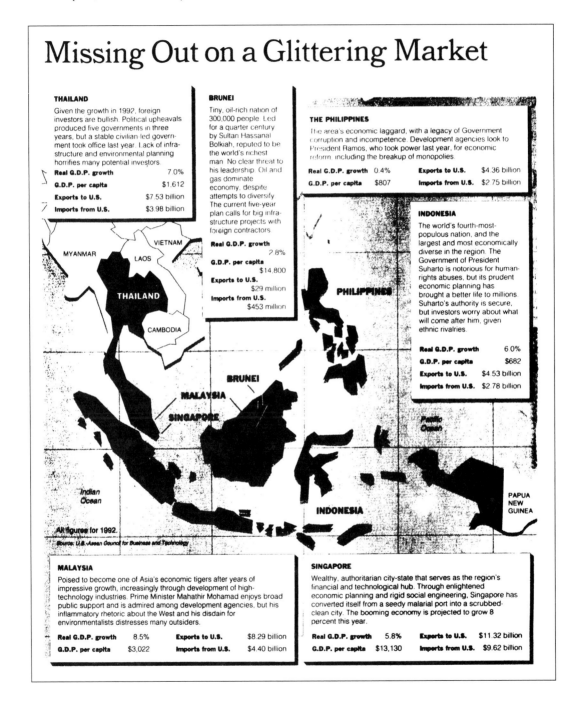

THAILAND

Given the growth in 1992, foreign investors are bullish. Political upheavals produced five governments in three years, but a stable civilian-led government took office last year. Lack of infrastructure and environmental planning horrifies many potential investors.

Real G.D.P. growth	7.0%
G.D.P. per capita	$1,612
Exports to U.S.	$7.53 billion
Imports from U.S.	$3.98 billion

BRUNEI

Tiny, oil-rich nation of 300,000 people. Led for a quarter century by Sultan Hassanal Bolkiah, reputed to be the world's richest man. No clear threat to his leadership. Oil and gas dominate economy, despite attempts to diversify. The current five-year plan calls for big infrastructure projects with foreign contractors.

Real G.D.P. growth	2.8%
G.D.P. per capita	$14,800
Exports to U.S.	$29 million
Imports from U.S.	$453 million

THE PHILIPPINES

The area's economic laggard, with a legacy of Government corruption and incompetence. Development agencies look to President Ramos, who took power last year, for economic reform, including the breakup of monopolies.

Real G.D.P. growth	0.4%	Exports to U.S.	$4.36 billion
G.D.P. per capita	$807	Imports from U.S.	$2.75 billion

INDONESIA

The world's fourth-most-populous nation, and the largest and most economically diverse in the region. The Government of President Suharto is notorious for human-rights abuses, but its prudent economic planning has brought a better life to millions. Suharto's authority is secure, but investors worry about what will come after him, given ethnic rivalries.

Real G.D.P. growth	6.0%		
G.D.P. per capita	$682		
Exports to U.S.	$4.53 billion		
Imports from U.S.	$2.78 billion		

All figures for 1992.

Source: U.S.-Asean Council for Business and Technology

MALAYSIA

Poised to become one of Asia's economic tigers after years of impressive growth, increasingly through development of high-technology industries. Prime Minister Mahathir Mohamad enjoys broad public support and is admired among development agencies, but his inflammatory rhetoric about the West and his disdain for environmentalists distresses many outsiders.

Real G.D.P. growth	8.5%	Exports to U.S.	$8.29 billion
G.D.P. per capita	$3,022	Imports from U.S.	$4.40 billion

SINGAPORE

Wealthy, authoritarian city-state that serves as the region's financial and technological hub. Through enlightened economic planning and rigid social engineering, Singapore has converted itself from a seedy malarial port into a scrubbed-clean city. The booming economy is projected to grow 8 percent this year.

Real G.D.P. growth	5.8%	Exports to U.S.	$11.32 billion
G.D.P. per capita	$13,130	Imports from U.S.	$9.62 billion

MISSING OUT ON A GLITTERING MARKET

PHILIP SHENON

Les Musial assumed that Malaysians lived in "straw huts or something" when the Chrysler Corporation dispatched him to Southeast Asia last year to help open its first manufacturing operation in the region in more than a decade.

Chrysler made him feel no more comfortable about the assignment when a company doctor presented him with 10 pounds of medicines—"for malaria, for tropical diseases"—apparently in the belief that local supplies might be lacking.

But Mr. Musial's qualms about Malaysia were upended the minute he landed at the marble-lined international airport here in the capital and began driving into one of the most modern cities in Asia, with residential neighborhoods that could be mistaken for California suburbs.

"I saw the skyscrapers, lots of skyscrapers, and the manicured lawns," he said. "There were good, new cars on the road. I thought that the technology and the industry would be in the beginning stages. But then you see the factories, and they are so advanced that you could put them anyplace on earth."

Mr. Musial was seeing for himself what many American business leaders have not yet seen, or have chosen to ignore—that Southeast Asia is in the midst of an economic revolution that in several nations is creating glittering wealth where once there had been only abject poverty, and that Americans are welcome to profit from it.

Over the last decade, Southeast Asia has been the fastest-growing economic region on earth. Collectively, the major non-Communist nations of the region—Indonesia, Malaysia, Singapore, Taiwan, Thailand and the Philippines—already have a vast manufacturing base, and they are quickly creating a market here for imported goods. Among the more than 400 million people of Southeast Asia, a large and growing middle class is clamoring for American goods—even as the market for American products has faltered in Japan and in Europe.

So why aren't more American companies here?

American businesses offer several answers to that question—from the perception of widespread corruption among government bureaucrats in the region to the frustrations of doing business halfway round the world from the home office. But the larger reason that Americans shy away may be simple ignorance about the opportunities here.

An Ambassador's Plaints

"We've really had to beat on American companies to get them out here," said John Wolf, the United States Ambassador to Malaysia, recounting his frustration in trying to persuade American companies to open marketing offices here and to bid on big government infrastructure projects, including this city's new $3 billion airport. "The place is in the chokehold of the Japanese, even though there is a fantastic potential for Americans."

To be sure, American investment in Southeast Asia has grown substantially in recent years, but the pace of Japanese investment has been much faster.

According to the Japanese Finance Ministry, that nation's cumulative investment in Asia, most of it in Southeast Asia, has tripled from $20 billion in 1985 to $60 billion at the end of last year. The latest total is almost double the $32.2 billion that the Commerce

Department shows American companies have invested in the region, although the figures are not perfectly comparable because of different statistical methods.

The companies that account for most of the new American investment in the region are the same giants—including Exxon, I.B.M., Coca-Cola—that have been operating in Southeast Asia for years. More than 40 percent of American investment in Southeast Asia is in a single industry: petroleum.

In July, Chrysler began manufacturing right-hand-drive Jeep Cherokee utility vehicles in a plant just outside Kuala Lumpur, the company's first manufacturing operation in Southeast Asia since it pulled out in the late 1970's to deal with a severe domestic slump. Kmart announced last month that it would open stores in Singapore in its first large venture in Southeast Asia.

Yet Chrysler and Kmart are the exceptions to what American diplomats and members of the American business community here say is a distressing rule.

"There is an amazing lack of understanding as to the potential of Southeast Asia," said Roger Bertelson, general manager for Malaysia for Motorola, which has four factories in Malaysia and employs 12,000 people. With high-technology investments like Motorola's, Malaysia is now the world's largest exporter of computer chips.

"There needs to be a swift kick in the rear end for American businesses," said Robert D. Orr, the former American ambassador to Singapore, the futuristic city-state that functions as the hub of Southeast Asia's economic miracle. "I just don't think they understand what has happened in Southeast Asia."

Impressive Numbers

The numbers bear out the opportunities. The economies of the six nations that make up the Association of Southeast Asian Nations—Indonesia, Malaysia, Singapore, Thailand, the Philippines and Brunei—have collectively experienced annual growth of 7 percent over the last decade. They grew 5.3 percent last year—still impressive in light of the recession among Asean's large Western trading partners.

With 328 million people and a gross domestic product of more than $350 billion, the six Asean nations are already the fifth-largest export market for the United States, after Canada, Japan, the European Community and Mexico. Adding neighboring Taiwan and Hong Kong, Southeast Asia is a $600 billion economic powerhouse.

The export markets for American goods in Japan and Europe have stagnated since 1990, but the export market to the Asean nations has grown by more than 26 percent, reaching $24 billion last year.

There is still wrenching poverty in Southeast Asia, Cambodia, Laos and Myanmar (formerly Burma) remain among the poorest nations on earth and after years of upheaval, the Philippines has fallen far behind its non-Communist neighbors. But the overall trend in Southeast Asia is one of solid growth, stable governments and open markets.

The region's largest nation, Indonesia, home to 184 million people, has seen per capita income rise from $250 in 1985 to nearly $650 today, and seems likely to see it double again within a decade.

Despite concern that Indonesia could someday fragment along ethnic lines—there are scores of major ethnic groups and hundreds of languages among Indonesia's 13,000 islands—American investors already in the country say the risk seems far off, and they speak with enthusiasm about the Government's prudent economic planning, vast natural resources and cheap labor.

Malaysia is poised to become one of Asia's next economic tigers, notably through the development of high-technology industries. Singapore, with its enlightened economic planning and rigid social engineering, has emerged as the region's financial and technological center. Thailand's economy continues to grow rapidly despite political upheavals and a succession of recent governments.

And Vietnam, with 70 million people and a well-educated, low-wage labor force, is widely thought by foreign investors to be on the verge of an economic boom that will accelerate if President Clinton follows through on hints that he will lift, at least partly, an American trade embargo that dates from the Vietnam War.

In a few stretches of Southeast Asia, incomes approach, or even surpass, those of Western European nations. In Singapore, the per capita income is more than $15,000. In tiny, oil-rich Brunei, it is more than $17,000—wealth for buying imports.

Robert E. Driscoll, president of the U.S.-Asean Council, a Washington-based trade group that represents American companies doing business in the region, said that among Southeast Asians, "There is a cachet to owning American." Still, American business has largely ceded the market to Japanese competitors.

Detroit's Regret

In Bangkok, Jakarta and Singapore, Southeast Asia's yuppies crowd expensive department stores bearing the names of Japanese retailing giants. The upper end of the small appliance market is virtually monopolized by Japanese brands, as is the auto market.

Detroit's decision in the 1970's to shut down Southeast Asian manufacturing operations just as the automobile market here was about to explode "was a shortsighted decision made on the basis of huge domestic losses and a need to restructure at home," Mr. Driscoll said. And now the price is being paid, as a generation of newly affluent Asian car-buyers buy Japanese.

The reluctance of more American businesses to establish operations here perplexes the Southeast Asians. "You have to be an absolute fool not to make money here," said Noordin Sopiee, director of Malaysia's Institute for Strategic and International Studies. "Our markets are open to you. Many people speak English. We watch your television shows."

He attributes the American absence from the market to a basic American ignorance about Asia, particularly Southeast Asia. "They don't think of us," he said of Americans.

Mr. Orr, the former ambassador to Singapore, recalled attending a March 1992 dinner in Manhattan held to drum up interest in Southeast Asian investment among prominent New York bankers and executives. "The dinner became a little testy because many of the people in the room were quite defensive," he said. "They kept saying they were wary of Southeast Asia after getting their fingers burned in South America and in other third-world countries."

No Latin America

Comparisons between the prudently planned economies of today's Southeast Asia and the disastrous, debt-laden economies of South America in the 70's and 80's are distressing to those who know this region. The dinner was evidence to Mr. Orr that "people just don't understand the indigenous wealth of Southeast Asia and what is happening there."

(continued)

The reasons for the absence of new American investors go beyond simple ignorance. Widespread government corruption in the region has frightened away many potential American investors who are justifiably wary of violating American laws that forbid the payment of kickbacks and bribes abroad. Few large government projects in Indonesia, the Philippines or Thailand are won by foreign contractors without at least the whiff of corruption or insider connections.

Still, American executives operating here say that the corruption is no more prevalent in Southeast Asia—and may actually be less so—than in other parts of the developing world.

"An awful lot of American companies refuse to engage in corrupt practices and succeed in Southeast Asia," said Mr. Driscoll of the U.S.-Asean Council. "It may take a little bit longer to get business done. You may lose a couple of contracts. But once you've learned the business system, it's a problem that can be overcome."

Other potential investors shy away because of the inconvenience of doing business halfway around the world from most of the United States. It is easier for a New York investor to search out business opportunities in Brussels, seven hours flying time, than in Bangkok, 19 hours, and most Americans have ancestral ties with Europe, not Asia.

"It is not as difficult to do business in Asia as some potential investors seem to think it is," said Mr. Bertelson of Motorola. "But in Asia it does take patience. Relationships are very important here. And the relationships take time. Unfortunately, Americans are not the most patient people."

As a result of their impatience, many American businesses are missing out on what is in general a liberal, welcoming climate for foreign investors and exporters. In the larger nations of Southeast Asia, foreign investors can own 100 percent of a business in most industries; there are government guarantees that foreign-owned businesses will not be nationalized; the governments are flexible about allowing foreign companies to send their profits home.

When they do consider Asia, many potential American investors think not about Southeast Asia but about China or Japan.

But investment in China carries risk. While the Chinese economy's annual growth rate is now approaching 13 percent, many economists warn that it may be on the verge of overheating. Corruption is a growing problem. And the protectionist barriers are far higher in Japan than in the large nations of Southeast Asia.

"Japan is a huge market, but there are many more obstacles to getting into it," said Phil Curran, managing director for the Thailand division of Digital Equipment, the computer maker. "The argument you can make for Thailand, Malaysia, Indonesia and Singapore is that you can hit the ground running, you can get productive quicker, and you can start taking your money out quicker."

In contrast to Digital's upheavals at home in the United States, its operation in Thailand has grown phenomenally since it began in 1988. Business in Thailand grew 46 percent last year, reaching $70 million. A recent survey of 3,000 Asian business people, most of them in Southeast Asia, found that more than 50 percent had invested in desktop computers in the last year.

Why Eastern Europe?

The commercial counselor in the American Embassy in Kuala Lumpur, Paul Walters, said that among many Americans, "there is almost a fear of the unknown about Asia."

> In the United States, he said, he encountered companies that were moving quickly in Eastern Europe, where there is only a small fraction of the industrial capacity and affluence of Southeast Asia.
>
> "I see these companies spending all of their time in Eastern Europe, even though there's no money in Eastern Europe to speak of," he said. "And in the end, nothing comes of it. If these same companies came to Southeast Asia, they'd find the people here are ready to deal with them—and have the money to spend."
>
> *Source: New York Times,* September 12, 1993. Reprinted with permission.

affected by beef prices. This in turn is affected by grain and weather conditions for grain and their impact on the growing of herds of cattle. This particular dependence on beef prices is caused by the fact that beef products such as hamburgers are the mainstay of McDonald's limited menu. We anticipate that beef prices will be fairly stable through 1994.

Disposable Income Demographic Factors and Demand

Although some uncertainty exists regarding the economic outlook for 1994, the general expectation is for real GDP growth in the 2 to 4 percent range. Furthermore, despite some concerns about excessive levels of inflation, the overall feeling is that 1994 will be in the 3 percent range. Such an economic scenario of real growth and modest inflation, coupled with the new tax legislation of 1993, should result in increases in disposable income and, in turn, discretionary income. Also we see consumer confidence improving slightly in 1994. This type of economic environment bodes fairly well for the food-away-from-home industry.

Since World War II, the demand for food consumed away from home has escalated significantly more than the demand for food consumed at home for the same period. This trend, when combined with other demand factors and steady price increases, has provided an excellent environment for large increases of sales for fast-food restaurants. Furthermore, we expected that disposable income and consumer discretionary spending would continue to increase in the 1990s; however, we felt that the rate of increase would be slower than it was in the early 1980s. The reason, of course, is slower economic growth in the late 1980s.

There has been a long-term, virtually constant relationship between disposable income and consumer spending on food eaten away from home. Inasmuch as such basic economic relationships are very slow to change because of our forecast of an increase in disposable income, an increase in sales for the restaurant industry is forthcoming for at least 1994 and probably for the next few subsequent years.

Another relevant factor relating to demographics is the rapid rate of increase in the proportion of women in the labor force. We expect that the number of female employees will continue to increase in the near future. This phenomenon should lead to increased dining out by families. On the other hand, although the number of younger people in the population has been increasing in recent years, this teen market, so to speak, will grow at a slower rate in the period ahead and

therefore will be a negative influence on demand for fast food. Furthermore, as teens become the twenty- to thirty-year-olds of the population, they will require a greater diversity in eating experiences when they dine out. This will lead to some decrease in the rate of increase of meal sales of the fast-food sector of the market. These trends will be apparent abroad as well. McDonald's should continue to benefit from its foreign operations.

Other Economic Factors

Two somewhat related factors that must be considered, particularly regarding industries that are building new physical facilities, such as restaurants, are construction costs and interest rates. These can be significant influences in expanding industries because they cut into profits and therefore affect earnings per share, dividends, and share prices. Inflationary pressures will continue to increase construction costs in terms of materials used in construction and in terms of the wages of workers in the construction trades, which are for the most part unionized. Should construction costs continue to rise, and if firms in the industry still want to expand their physical plants, these additional costs could affect future profits. However, firms such as McDonald's could use substitute building materials and construction designs, which probably lower construction costs. Furthermore, interest costs will cut into profits of firms that need to borrow money to finance the new construction although interest rates are currently near record lows in the United States.

Another potential negative influence on the fast-food industry is the existence of price competition and couponing. Consumers are very value oriented, while at the same time demanding better service. This could be a negative influence for the industry as a whole. Because of McDonald's size, however, it could benefit at the expense of weaker competitors.

The energy crisis experienced several years ago should not affect this industry for the next few years because gasoline prices are not expected to increase significantly. Furthermore, the bulk of McDonald's sales are in restaurants located near large population centers. One does not have to drive very far to eat at McDonald's and, therefore, if gasoline does increase in price, the influence on McDonald's should be minor and perhaps even slightly positive.

One final consideration relates to the value of the U.S. dollar relative to foreign currencies. Most economic observers believed that the dollar will be stronger in 1994 and continue to strengthen against most major foreign currencies. Factors contributing to these expectations included the low rate of inflation and the expectation of relatively slow economic growth in 1994. Such ongoing relative strength of the U.S. dollar would be unfavorable to a company such as McDonald's, which has a significant and growing international aspect to its business. However, McDonald's growth abroad is at a high rate so the unfavorable currency exchange will serve as a drag on a very positive affect.

On balance, 1994 looked like a fairly positive year for the economy and the restaurant industry, particularly the fast-food sector. In the next chapter we will ex-

amine this industry in some detail, as we continue toward our goal of price, dividend, and earnings estimates of McDonald's Corp.

SUMMARY

In this chapter we assessed the importance of short-term economic forecasting in the decision-making process surrounding the purchase of common stocks. In order to understand and appreciate the forecasting task, we discussed and critically evaluated several major economic forecasting techniques—anticipatory surveys, indicators, econometric models, and opportunistic model building. All these techniques had distinct advantages as well as disadvantages, but on balance they have been successful for forecasts up to a few quarters in advance. For the security analyst or investor, the anticipated economic environment, and therefore the economic forecast, is important for making decisions concerning both the timing of an investment and the relative investment desirability among the various industries in the economy. Internation economic factors were also discussed.

In the next chapter we will continue our efforts to forecast price and dividend information for our holding-period-return calculations by discussing and applying useful techniques of industry analysis.

QUESTIONS AND PROBLEMS

1. Compare and contrast the survey, indicator, and econometric approaches to forecasting.

2. What fiscal and monetary policies would you suggest for an economy in a deep recession? Why?

3. What is *opportunistic model building?*

4. Would you suppose that GNP forecasts for next year prepared by major universities, banks, and research organizations would be quite similar? Why or why not? Get three major GNP forecasts for next year and see.

5. What economic factors do you think must directly affect defense-oriented industries and thus would be most important to forecast properly?

6. What economic factors would you be most interested in forecasting if you were an analyst investigating major consumer durable-goods sales for next year?

7. If you were told that more families than ever before would have second cars next year and that the expected lives of cars had increased, which industries do you suppose would benefit most?

8. It has often been said that common stocks are a good "hedge against inflation." Why do you suppose people think this way? Are you inclined to agree or disagree with this sentiment?

9. If you were designing an equation to forecast corporate capital spending for an econometric model, what variables do you suppose would be useful in explaining the level of corporate capital spending?

10. How might one classify industries within a business cycle framework?

11. a. What are three examples of key leading economic indicators (excluding stock prices)?
    b. What is the rationale for the use of diffusion indexes to accompany forecasts using leading indicators?

12. What is the significance of a diffusion index with a large, positive reading?

13. The "cumulative" nature of business cycles suggests that various sectors of the economy react to changes in economic conditions to produce revivals and recessions in aggregate economic activity. Suppose that Congress passed a public works program totaling $4 billion. This program would create a net addition to government spending with no offsetting increase in taxes or decrease in other previously scheduled government spending. Assuming that the economy is in the *initial* stages of recovery, indicate the sectors of the economy and the components of GNP that would be most immediately affected and describe their reaction.

14. If the dollar was appreciating worldwide, what do you think the affect would be on U.S. auto producers? Why?

15. A government budget deficit that is *least* likely to be inflationary is one that:
    a. occurs even though the resources of the economy are fully employed.
    b. is caused by tax revenues falling as the result of a business recession.
    c. is financed by borrowing, perhaps indirectly, from the central bank.
    d. is caused by a sharp increase in governmental transfer payments while the economy is operating at its full-employment output level.

16. If increased borrowing by the government drives up the real interest rate in the United States, then:
    a. U.S. investors will increase their investments abroad.
    b. U.S. exports will expand relative to imports.
    c. an inflow of loanable funds from abroad will occur.
    d. the U.S. dollar will depreciate in the foreign exchange market.

17. According to the supply-side view of fiscal policy, if the impact of tax revenues is the same, does it make any difference whether the government cuts taxes by either reducing marginal tax rates or increasing the personal exemption allowance?
    a. No, both of the methods of cutting taxes will exert the same impact on aggregate supply.
    b. No, people in both cases will increase their saving expecting higher future taxes thereby offsetting the stimulus effect of lower current taxes.
    c. Yes, the lower tax rates alone will increase the incentive to earn marginal income and thereby stimulate aggregate supply.
    d. Yes, interest rates will increase if marginal tax rates are lowered, whereas they will tend to decrease if the personal exemption allowance is raised.

18. If the Federal Reserve wanted to reduce the supply of money as part of an anti-inflation policy, it might:
   a. increase the reserve requirements.
   b. buy U.S. securities on the open market.
   c. lower the discount rate.
   d. buy U.S. securities directly from the Treasury.

19. If both monetary and fiscal policy became much more expansionary, Keynesians and monetarists would agree that:
   a. the change in fiscal policy would primarily affect the rate of unemployment, whereas the change in monetary policy would primarily affect the price level.
   b. the natural rate of unemployment would increase.
   c. output and employment would be temporarily stimulated if the policy were not anticipated.
   d. the natural rate of unemployment would decline.

20. "Import quotas will create jobs, increasing the employment level of a nation." Economic analysis indicates that this statement is in the:

	Short Run	*Long Run*
a.	true	false
b.	false	true
c.	false	false
d.	true	true

REFERENCES

BLACK, F. "The ABCs of Business Cycles." *Financial Analysts Journal* (November–December 1981).

BOOTH, J., and D. OFFICER. "Expectations, Interest Rates, and Commercial Bank Stocks." *Journal of Financial Research* (Spring 1985), pp. 51–58.

KRUTZMER, P. "Monetary vs. Fiscal Policy: New Evidence on an Old Debate." *Economic Review,* Federal Reserve Bank of Kansas City (Second Quarter 1992), pp. 21–30.

NYEMIRA, M. P. and G. FREDMAN. "An Evaluation of the Composite Index of Leading Indicators for Signaling Turning Points in Business and Growth Cycles." *Business Economics* (October 1991), pp. 49–55.

SPRINKEL, B. *Money and Markets: A Monetarist's View,* Homewood, Ill.: Richard D. Irwin, 1971.

CHAPTER 5

INDUSTRY ANALYSIS

Investing is a business of relative changes. When the economic outlook is assessed, along with the direction of changes in the overall market for stocks, the analyst must realize that even though industry groups and/or individual companies may find it difficult to "buck the trend," they do not necessarily respond to the same degree. For example, it is widely assumed that heavy-goods industries fare worse in economic recessions than do consumer-goods industries. Heavy-goods industries include automobiles (and related industries such as rubber, steel, and glass) and machinery. Consumer-goods and service industries include utilities (telephone, power), food, and banks. Recessions or expansions in economic activity may translate into falling or rising stock markets with different *relative* price changes among industry groups.

For the analyst, industry analysis demands insight into (1) the key sectors or subdivisions of overall economic activity that influence particular industries, and (2) the relative strength or weakness of particular industry or other groupings under specific sets of assumptions about economic activity. The analyst with an economic forecast that he has developed from scratch, or a set of figures that he has developed from forecasts prepared by others, is now ready to apply this information to an appropriate industry. Before demonstrating this, however, let us look at some definitions of an industry.

ALTERNATIVE INDUSTRY CLASSIFICATION SCHEMES

Webster's Dictionary defines an *industry* as "a department or branch of a craft, art, business, or manufacture." And more specifically:

> [a] group of productive or profit-making enterprises or organizations that have a similar technological structure of production and that produce or supply technically substitutable goods, services, or sources of income.[1]

[1]*Webster's Third New International Dictionary* (Springfield, Mass.: Merriam, 1966), pp. 1155–56.

Although at first glance these definitions seem neat and clear-cut, they are not. First, it may seem desirable to break industries down by their products; however, defining a product is no easy chore.

Industry Classification by Product

Are glass containers in the same industry as metal containers? Is steel in the same industry as aluminum? Is a fast-food chain in the same industry as a chain of restaurants?

In one sense, a container is a container, and the substance from which it is constructed should not cause the product to appear in a separate industry for an industry analysis; however, the firms producing these different products might be very dissimilar in the other products that they produce.[2] Between the steel and aluminum industries, the economics, technology, and refinements are so substantially different that analyzing them as separate industries is advisable. Substantial differences also exist between the mode of operation in a limited-menu, fast-food, take-out type of restaurant and that of a limited-menu, sit-down type or a legitimate full-menu restaurant.

By now it should be clear that pinpointing an industry is not easy, and the investigator needs to have a clear goal in mind so that he can properly classify firms into industries for his specific purpose. For example, if the goal were to reach an estimate of sales for the industry, the analyst might want to consider similar products and products that could be substituted for the item in question (glass containers for metal, or aluminum containers for steel). But if he were calculating comparative costs of the industry, he might consider only those firms with similar manufacturing processes, for only such a comparison would be meaningful. For instance, the analyst might compare the costs of one candy producer with those of another candy producer but not with those of a toy manufacturer.

Industry classification by product does not present a terribly acute problem for the astute analyst when he is classifying firms with basically one product or a homogeneous group of products. The problem worsens considerably, however, when he deals with a firm that has a diversified product line. Unfortunately, today the latter case is the rule rather than the exception. Our illustration later in this chapter will serve to highlight this problem.

SIC Classification

In order to provide an organized reporting framework for the vast amount of data collected by the federal government, the Standard Industrial Classification (SIC) was developed. The following passage from the *SIC Manual* describes the system.

---

[2]In an antitrust case, the Supreme Court prevented the merger of Continental Can (metal containers) with Hazel-Atlas Glass (glass containers), on the grounds of a possible lessening of competition. Thus, a key issue in this case was the delineation of the container industry.

The SIC is the statistical classification standard underlying all establishment-based federal economic statistics classified by industry. The SIC is used to promote the comparability of establishment data describing various facets of the U.S. economy. The classification covers the entire field of economic activities and defines industries in accordance with the composition and structure of the economy. It is revised periodically to reflect the economy's changing industrial organization.[3]

The SIC is subdivided as follows:[4]

INDUSTRIAL DIVISION		MAJOR GROUPS
A	Agriculture, forestry, and fishing	01–09
B	Mining	10–14
C	Construction	15–17
D	Manufacturing	20–39
E	Transportation, communications, electric, gas, and sanitary services	40–49
F	Wholesale trade—durable goods	50–51
G	Retail trade	52–59
H	Finance, insurance, and real estate	60–67
I	Services	70–89
J	Public administration	91–97
K	Nonclassifiable establishments	99

The major groups detailed in the table and identified by two-digit codes are further subdivided into three-digit industry groups and, finally, into four-digit industries. For example, under industrial division G, retail trade, major group 57 is home furniture, furnishings, and equipment stores, industry group 571 is home furniture and furnishings stores; this consists of industry numbers 5712, furniture stores; 5713, floor covering stores; 5714, drapery, curtain, and upholstery stores; and 5719, miscellaneous home furnishings stores.

Using SIC codes, industry information, such as the number of firms classified in the industry, number of employees, value of shipments, and capital expenditures, can be found and analyzed. This information is useful in detecting changing industrial patterns and developments over time, such as expansion or contraction of the industry.

Although the census provides valuable information to the industry analyst, it is not without its drawbacks. For example, the methodology employed in classifying firms into the various categories is not consistent over the entire spectrum of the U.S. economy.

---

[3]*Standard Industrial Classification Manual* (Washington, D.C.: U.S. Government Printing Office, 1987).
[4]*Ibid.*

Industry Classification According to Business Cycle

Another way of classifying industries is in a cyclical framework, that is, by how they react to upswings and downswings in the economy. The general classifications in this framework are growth, cyclical, defensive, and cyclical-growth.

Growth industries are generally characterized by expectations of abnormally high rates of expansion in earnings, often independent of the business cycle. Frequently this type of situation is associated with a major change in the state of technology or an innovative way of doing or selling something. In the early part of the twentieth century, industries such as automobiles and airplane manufacturing were considered the growth groups. In the 1940s, 1950s, and 1960s, the growth industries were associated with photography, color television, computers, pharmaceuticals, office equipment, and sophisticated communications equipment. In recent years the growth industries have dealt with such items as cellular phones, genetic engineering, and environmental/waste management.

Cyclical industries are considered to be those most likely to benefit from a period of economic prosperity and most likely to suffer from a period of economic recession. We shall see later in this chapter that consumer and manufacturer durables, such as refrigerators and drill presses, are these types of products. This is because their purchase can be postponed until personal financial or general business conditions improve. These industries, then, are considered cyclical.

Defensive industries are those, such as the food-processing industry, hurt least in periods of economic downswing. We will see later that consumer nondurables and services, which in large part are those items necessary for existence—such as food and shelter—are products in defensive industries. Defensive industries often contain firms whose securities an investor might hold for income. Defensive stocks might even be considered countercyclical, because their earnings might very well expand while the earnings of cyclical stocks are declining.

The investment press and brokerage firms have coined yet another classification, that of *cyclical-growth industries*. Obviously, these possess characteristics of both a cyclical industry and a growth industry. An example in this classification would be the airline industry. Airlines, according to some, grow tremendously, then go through periods of stagnation and perhaps even decline, and then resume their growth—often because of changes in technology, such as the introduction of a new type of aircraft.

THE ECONOMY AND THE INDUSTRY ANALYSIS

In the preceding chapter we saw how various techniques of economic forecasting could be brought to bear upon the investment decision. Specifically, we observed how various approaches could be used to forecast components of gross national product (GNP), and we noted that for the investment decision it was often as significant to predict the direction of any change in these sectors as it was to predict their actual level. An example or two will highlight this concept.

When the GNP is growing, unemployment is relatively low (4 to 5 percent), and the general economic climate is optimistic; an economic forecast based upon any of the approaches already discussed would probably show high and increasing levels of expenditures on consumer durables, inventory, and plant and equipment. Because business is buoyant and it is generally expected that this will continue, businessmen accumulate inventory in anticipation of still higher sales levels, and they also increase their capacity through plant and equipment expenditures. At the same time, on the consumer's side of the market, individual households are experiencing high levels of personal discretionary income (income available for luxuries), and they are free to spend some of this money on such things as residential housing, automobiles, and other consumer durables. Indeed, if prior economic periods had been far less booming than those just described, expenditures on various durables, having been postponed, could now become exaggerated.

It would be desirable at such a time to buy securities of firms in industries most likely to benefit from these purchasing patterns. As you will recall in the opportunistic-model-building approach, the forecaster would arrive at specific estimates of the broad categories we have just mentioned. It is easy to see how such an economic forecast can be helpful, not only in selecting industries that will benefit in a period of general economic prosperity but also in selecting those that will benefit in periods when only certain sectors of the economy are expanding. Much academic research has substantiated the importance of sound industry analysis to successful investment analysis. Examples of the latter type would be defense industries in a period when the federal government is boosting the economy through large national-defense expenditures, and also those industries that will be hurt least during a period of economic downswing—such as those producing food, something that is always necessary.

Another way of gauging the economy's performance with special regard to specific industry classifications is to examine regularly the statistics contained in the monthly *Federal Reserve Bulletin.* By examining the behavior of the various series over time, the analyst can gain insights into important economic developments in many industries and important industry subsectors. An increase in manufacturing could necessitate additional capital spending to add overall manufacturing capacity. If additional capacity comes on-line, price competition could become more prevalent if an occurrence, such as an economic downturn, results in decreased demand for manufactured products. These are but two of the possible implications of the noted increase in capacity utilization. Many more undoubtedly exist. Although such tentative conclusions can be derived from even such a superficial analysis, such observations should be incorporated into the analyst's overall data base of information.[5]

---

[5]Meaningful analysis of much of the information contained in the *Federal Reserve Bulletin* requires comparison with earlier time series and great familiarity with the behavior of these series.

KEY CHARACTERISTICS IN AN
INDUSTRY ANALYSIS

In an industry analysis, any number of key characteristics should be considered at some point by the analyst. In this section we will enumerate and discuss several of these: past sales and earnings performance, the permanence of the industry, the attitude of government toward the industry, labor conditions within the industry, the competitive conditions as reflected in any barriers to entry that might exist, and stock prices of firms in the industry relative to their earnings.

Past Sales and Earnings Performance

One of the most effective steps in forecasting is assessing the historical performance of the industry in question. Certainly, two factors with a central role in the ultimate success of any security investment are sales and earnings; therefore, in order to gain a perspective from which to forecast, looking at the historical performance of sales and earnings is helpful.

One important factor the analyst might uncover is that the history of the industry is very brief. This finding alone might make him more cautious about a commitment in this industry, because if the industry has not proved its ability to weather a variety of economic growth prospects, the opportunity of getting in on the ground floor might be a paramount consideration.

The historical record of the industry is crucial for yet another reason—namely, the calculation of both average levels and stability of performance in both sales and earnings, including growth-rate calculations. Even though past average levels or past variability may not be repeated in the future, the analyst needs to know how this industry has reacted in the past. With knowledge and understanding of the reasons behind past behavior, he is better able to assess the relative magnitudes of performance in the future.[6]

A related factor that the analyst must also consider is the cost structure of the industry—that is, the relation of fixed to variable costs. The higher the fixed-cost component, the higher the sales volume necessary to achieve the firm's break-even point. Conversely, the lower the relative fixed costs, the easier it is for a firm to achieve and surpass its breakeven point.

The attached box illustrates how a new "niche" can develop in an industry that has quite a track record and still have the potential for investment profits.

---

[6]We saw in Chapter 3 how the mean and variance forecasts are important outputs of security analysis and inputs to portfolio analysis. Briefly, the analyst forecasts the future level and stability of the firm's earnings, prices, and return. We will use the mean and standard deviation of return to reflect the anticipated level and stability of the security's performance.

Permanence

Another important factor in an industry analysis is the relative permanence of the industry. Permanence is a phenomenon related to the products and technology of the industry, whereas the historical record just discussed deals with the behavior of the numbers without regard to the factors that underlie them. If the analyst feels that the need for this particular industry will vanish in an extremely short period of time, it would seem foolish to invest funds in the industry. Sometimes an industry fades from the scene because of a replacement industry that eliminates or dimin-

---

BETWEEN THE TOES OF GIANTS

ERIC HARDY AND ROBERT ROSENSTEIN

Software companies couldn't be happier about the collapse in computer hardware prices, since cheap hardware expands the population of software buyers. Sales of U.S.-based software and service vendors have climbed at an 18% compound annual rate over the past three years, to an estimated $25 billion last year.

Five giants—Microsoft, Lotus, Borland, WordPerfect and Novell—own 71% of the PC software market. These companies have their strength in operating system, spreadsheet, database, word processing and networking software. Since everybody knows this, their stocks are, to put it mildly, fully priced. But those basic programs aren't the whole software story. Dean Witter analyst Timothy McCollum points out that the average user of a Windows operating system will also buy two to four Windows-specific programs, programs that don't have to come from Microsoft.

Home education is one of the fastest-growing software segments, but Microsoft, Lotus and Borland aren't big in it. It is little outfits like Software Toolworks that are selling programs to help you learn how to forecast the weather, touch-type, or play the piano or chess.

Smaller software companies are an excellent way to participate in the computer sector, says Daniel Leonard, whose Financial Strategic Technology Fund rose 11% over the last 12 months. His $256 million portfolio includes not a single hardware maker but does have Oracle Systems, which sells database management software, and Banyan Systems, which sells computer networking software.

Don't go into these stocks looking for any Ben Graham-style values; price/earnings ratios as high as Microsoft's (which is 29) are not uncommon. Realizing this, Leonard looks especially for high growth rates in sales and earnings to select potential winners.

The table lists 15 small software companies—those with sales under $200 million and market capitalizations under $500 million. Each firm is expected to increase profits this year and has a price/sales ratio no greater than 6.4. In this ratio, price means the sum of debt outstanding and market value of common stock.

Software Publishing has sales of $156 million and a price/sales ratio of 0.9 (to Microsoft's 8.1). Its Harvard Graphics is a leader in PC graphing and charting. Aldus Corp., a vendor of desktop publishing products for business applications, is a little more expensive at 1.5 times sales but enjoys a better profit margin.

SECOND-STAGE SOFTWARE

COMPANY/ SOFTWARE PRODUCTS	RECENT PRICE	EARNINGS PER SHARE		P/E 1993 (EST.)	SALES ($MIL)*	SALES GROWTH[†]	PRICE/ SALES[‡]
		LATEST 12 MOS	1993 (EST.)				
Systems Center/ networking	8	$–1.15	$0.64	12.5	$126	35%	0.9
Phoenix Technologies Ltd./compatibility tools	5⅛	0.20	0.45	11.4	71	10	0.9
Software Publishing/ graphics, word processing	11⅞	0.02	1.10	10.8	156	15	0.9
Ross Systems/business services	10½	0.21	0.42	25.0	76	NA	1.3
Aldus/desktop publishing	17	0.62	0.84	20.2	168	28	1.5
Continuum/insurance	19⅜	0.85	0.89	21.8	126	24	1.7
Marcam/production aids	18¾	0.93	1.14	16.4	80	NA	1.9
Frame Technology/ desktop publishing	13	0.19	0.73	17.8	42	NA	2.0
Easel/graphics	10	–0.52	0.29	34.5	28	NA	2.0
Software Toolworks/ education, entertainment	7½	–0.61	0.23	32.6	103	106	2.0
Intersolv/programming aids	8¾	0.56	0.72	12.2	79	55	2.1
Electronics for Imaging/ desktop publishing	16¼	0.74	0.83	19.6	16	NA	3.5
Cerner/health care	42¾	1.29	1.64	26.1	75	22	4.3
Sulcus Computer/ information retrieval	16¼ 8	0.74 0.36	0.83 0.60	19.6 13.3	16 18	NA 104	3.5 4.7
Caere/optical character recognition	20	0.68	0.83	24.1	32	NA	6.4

*Latest fiscal year.
[†]Compound annual rate, past three years.
[‡]Debt plus market value of common equity, divided by sales.
Sources: Institutional Brokers Estimate System; Value Line Database Service via Lotus One Source.
Products of these 15 fledgling software firms complement Lotus or Microsoft packages without necessarily competing with them.

Source: Reprinted with permission from *Forbes* magazine, March 15, 1993. %c Forbes Inc., 1993.

ishes the need for the original industry. Certainly the rise of the automobile caused a decline in the importance of the carriage and the buggy whip, the growth of popularity of margarine hurt the demand for butter, and so on. In this age of rapid technological advance, the degree of permanence of an industry has become an ever more important consideration in industry analysis.

The Attitude of Government toward the Industry

It is important for the analyst or prospective investor to consider the probable role government will play in the industry. Will it provide support—financial or otherwise? Or will it restrain the industry's development through restrictive legislation and legal enforcement? For example, if the government feels that foreign competition is too severe for a particular domestic industry, it can impose restrictive import quotas and/or tariffs that would tend to assist the domestic industry. Conversely, if the government feels the domestic industry is becoming too independent, it can remove any existing barriers and thus aid foreign competition. Furthermore, government can assist selected industries through favorable tax legislation.

As government becomes more influential in attempting to regulate business and to advocate consumer protection, the permanence of the industry might well be affected—not in that government interference will necessarily drive it out of business, but in that profits of the industry can be substantially lessened. Sometimes an industry declines in importance because of legal restrictions that are placed upon it.

Labor Conditions

As unions grow in power in our economy, the state of labor conditions in the industry under analysis becomes ever more important. That is, if we are dealing with a very labor-intensive production process or a very mechanized capital-intensive process where labor performs crucial operations, the possibility of a strike looms as an important factor to be reckoned with. This is particularly true in industries with large fixed costs, for fixed costs such as rent and insurance continue even when production is curtailed. If a strike occurs in such an industry, for example, steel manufacturing, the large fixed costs would cut deeply into profits earned before and after the strike.

In a labor-intensive industry, the variable costs would undoubtedly dominate the fixed costs; however, even here, the loss of customer goodwill during a long strike would probably more than offset the possible advantages of low fixed costs. That is, customers would find other suppliers, and even the low fixed costs might be difficult for the firm to cover.

Competitive Conditions

Another significant factor in industry analysis is the competitive conditions in the industry under study. One way to determine the competitive conditions is to observe whether any barriers to entry exist. Three general types of barriers are: (1) a product-differentiation edge that forestalls the entry of competition, (2) absolute-cost advantages, and (3) advantages arising from economies of scale.

Product-differentiation advantages generally arise when buyers have a preference for the products of established firms or industries, such as in patent medicines

and breakfast cereals. Because existing firms or industries have such an advantage, a new entrant is not likely to be able to charge as high a price as they do. Furthermore, a new entrant would probably have to expend large sums of money on sales and promotion expenses in order to procure an acceptable sales level.

By *absolute-cost advantages,* we refer to the fact that established firms or industries are able to produce and distribute their products at any level of production or distribution at a lower cost than any new entrant can. These advantages arise from such things as patents, ownership of resources or other key raw materials, and easier access to necessary equipment, funds, or management skills. With this combination of circumstances, the established firms clearly are more likely to have considerably wider profit margins than their newer competition.

Economies of scale are found in industries in which it is necessary to attain a fairly high level of production in order to obtain economically feasible levels of cost—such as in producing automobiles. A firm attempting to break into such an industry would, under normal circumstances, have to obtain a significant share of the market if it expects to have a competitive cost structure relative to existing firms.

The investment implication when examining an industry that has significant barriers to entry should be clear. An analyst or prospective investor would like to see that the industry in which he is considering investment seems to be well protected from the inroads of new firms; if the industry were protected by product differentiation, not only would it be difficult for new firms to enter it but it would also be exceedingly difficult for new industries to develop in competition with the market currently owned by the existing industry.

More Illustrations of Competitive Conditions Creating Investment Opportunities

Industries can often provide investment profits in unexpected ways. We have talked about earnings, P/E, and dividends leading to holding-period profits. However, some industries can lead to profits because of undervalued assets for example. Department stores might be losing money from continuing operations but might be of value to a purchaser because of the vast amount of real estate they own in prime locations across the United States. The same is true of railroads, which often own vast amounts of land under and around their tracks.

Some industries are exceedingly competitive and successful firms within such industries need superior management for the firms to stay competitive. On the other hand, a firm in an industry that is less competitive might continue to be successful with an average management group. An investor must be keenly aware of the industry environment the firm is operating in—computers versus cement, for example.

If an industry has an opportunity for developing a niche, exciting opportunities might be found. The preceding box illustrated the potential of small software developers possibly being such a niche. The publishing industry, particularly newspapers, is such an example. A newspaper in a large market can be an exclusive franchise. Often, a metropolitan area might have one dominant newspaper. Such a

paper can receive virtually all dollars spent on print advertising in the area. Papers such as the *Washington Post, Los Angeles Times,* and the *Boston Globe* represent examples of papers that dominate local markets. Investors who recognize the potential profits inherent in such a situation have the opportunity to earn large profits on their share purchases of media stocks in the 1970s. The cable television industry is another example for possible niche plays within the communications industry.

Marketing trends can be helpful in finding industries and companies for stock investment ideas. In the 1980s dress became more casual and comfortable. Industries such as apparel and sneakers would be interesting to explore. Companies such as Gap, The Limited, and Nike might be explored. Consumers collected comic books. This could prompt exploration of firms that could benefit in this industry—Marvel, for example. In other words, the investor must be alert to the trends and other nuances that affect buying habits to help discover industries with large upside potential.

INDUSTRY SHARE PRICES RELATIVE TO INDUSTRY EARNINGS

Having evaluated the various characteristics of past sales and earnings, industry permanence, government attitude, labor conditions, and industry competitive conditions, the analyst must ultimately reach a considered investment decision. However, even if all indications are that the industry has very favorable future prospects, this does not necessarily imply that funds should be committed to it immediately. A decision to purchase is not made based only on the current status and future prospects, but also on the current prices of securities in the industry, their risk, and the returns they promise.

At this point we will refer to only the price consideration. If the price is very high relative to future earnings growth, these securities might not be a wise investment. Conversely, if future prospects are dim but prices are low relative to a fairly level future pattern of earnings, the stocks in this industry might well be an attractive investment. Frequently, when an industry develops because of technology or some other such reason, investors become overzealous in their desire to purchase securities of firms in this new industry. Thus, these share prices are bid to very high levels, with the consequence that the P/E ratio soars. So it can be seen that the "market psychology" can be a crucial factor in both raising prices to exorbitant levels and depressing prices to unreasonable levels, depending on how the market evaluates the industry's future prospects.

RESTAURANT INDUSTRY EXAMPLE

Following the order of presentation, let us determine the key characteristics of the restaurant industry.

1. ***Past sales and earnings performance.*** Table 5–1 contains selected past sales and earnings performance data as compiled by Standard & Poor's in its industry survey of the restaurant industry. Note that in the table only selected companies are included in this series of data. However, S&P believes that these companies are representative of the industry as a whole.

   Sales of the industry as defined by S&P have grown dramatically since 1979, more than a twofold increase. A similar trend trend is evident in operating income. This trend would be even more dramatic had the series been extended back into the 1950s and 1960s. However, even with this selected period from 1979 to 1987 has obviously been a growth industry.

2. ***Permanence of the industry.*** Eating away from home has been popular for many years. The restaurant industry and in particular the fast-food industry, however, is relatively new, having experienced its greatest growth in the post-World War II period. As long as people continue to be sociable creatures and desire a change of pace, eating away from home will be a habit that persists. Furthermore, as both husband and wife continue to work, the need to dine out occasionally will remain. Those who travel for pleasure and business also must have meals away from home. The eating-away-from-home habit has spread to foreign countries as well. As the restaurant industry (particularly fast-food restaurants) expand into foreign markets, the permanence and growth of the industry will be further advanced.

3. ***The attitude of government.*** Compared with most other industries government intervention in the restaurant industry is minimal. This in part is because this industry is relatively free from issues that cause political controversy. The fast-food sector of the industry in particular is staffed primarily by young, minimum-wage workers and is therefore not generally encumbered by unions, union restrictions, and potential labor law problems.

Table 5–1

PAST SALES AND EARNINGS PERFORMANCE,
FAST-FOOD RESTAURANTS

RESTAURANTS

The companies used for this series of per-share data are: Church's Fried Chicken; Jerrico Inc. (5-6-87); Luby's Cafeterias (added 5-15-85); McDonald's Corp.; Shoney's Inc. (added 1-30-85); Wendy's Int'l. (added 3-3-82). Denny's Inc. (deleted 1-30-85); Gino's Inc. (deleted 3-3-82); Howard Johnson (deleted 6-25-80); Marriott Corp. (deleted 5-25-83).

	1979	1980	1981	1982	1983	1984	1985	1986	1987
Book value	14.94	17.07	20.52	24.00	29.85	33.98	36.30	39.44	46.23
Return on book value %	18.88	20.80	20.32	19.88	19.53	20.01	19.37	16.99	16.79
Working capital	0.28	d1.02	d1.16	d1.51	d1.69	d3.15	d4.27	d4.06	d4.61
Capital expenditures	6.57	8.00	8.52	13.34	9.32	12.42	14.67	14.63	15.45

Source: Standard & Poor's *Industry Surveys* (New York: Standard & Poor's Corp., March 16, 1989).

The industry to date has been relatively free of antitrust vulnerability. There has been little involvement of federal authorities in the area of pricing policies, and to date there has been no significant involvement regarding pollution. The only potential governmental interference that might be foreseen would be in the form of local zoning restrictions on the construction of more buildings and the form that these buildings and related signs may take. Also the issue of environmentally friendly packaging could become an issue.

4. *Labor conditions.* While labor costs in the fast-food sector of the industry are high as a percentage, the level of wage rates is notoriously low. As stated, the vast majority of the workers at fast-food restaurants are paid at minimum-wage rates. Recent increases in the minimum wage as well as the relative shortage of qualified employees should continue to impact profit margins for this sector of the restaurant industry.

5. *Competitive conditions.* Because of the high returns on investment, as evidenced in Table 5–1, and because of the abundant opportunities for rapid physical expansion, the fast-food sector of the restaurant industry has experienced rapidly escalating, intensified domestic competition. Thus, one could characterize this industry as increasingly competitive. This has caused the key chains to launch massive advertising and marketing campaigns to maintain and perhaps increase their market share. In addition, promotional gifts, contests, and prizes have been initiated to lure customers. Couponing has become an important means of competing.

In addition to the large advertising and promotional expenditures, the companies have been forced to upgrade continually the decor of the facilities, maintain extremely fast service, and provide good value for the customer's money. Also, because of the availability of the facilities, member firms have attempted to expand their menus to attract customers throughout the day and into the evening. Traditionally, these establishments have catered to a lunch business; however, several key member firms have now introduced a breakfast menu and are attempting to increase dinner business by introducing new varieties of beef dishes such as steak sandwiches, and chicken dishes such as chicken "nuggets." In addition, salads are now being offered for the weight- and health-conscious customer. Obviously, in expanding menus while attempting to maintain profit margins, the various chains will need to intensify their advertising and marketing campaigns and causing an already competitive industry to become even more so.

The large chains that dominate the industry benefit from a perceived product differentiated from individual industry units that are not affiliated with a national chain. They attempt to guarantee uniform quality and uniform service throughout all members of the chain in both company-owned and franchised restaurants. Furthermore, the large chains have an additional advantage through their highly trained management teams that help achieve operating economies and effectuate efficient food delivery systems.

6. *Industry share prices relative to industry earnings.* The restaurant industry has enjoyed rapid growth in earnings, as can be seen from examining Table

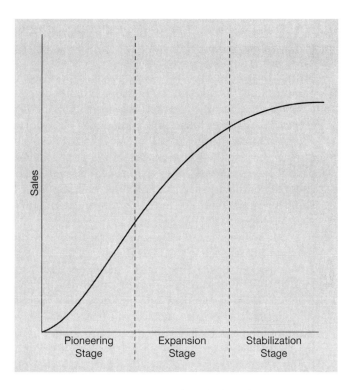

FIGURE 5–1   Industrial Life Cycle

5–1. As a result of this and the bull market that existed through much of the mid and late 1980s, the P/E multiples have increased fairly steadily. See the price-earnings ratios line of Table 5–1. Interestingly, despite the October 1987 market crash, the 1987 industry low P/E still exceeded the high P/E for the years 1979–84.

Overall, based upon our review of the key characteristics of the fast-food sector of the restaurant industry, the outlook for industry into the 1990s is mildly optimistic.

INDUSTRY LIFE CYCLE

Thus far in this chapter, we have discussed several pertinent factors that should be considered in an industry analysis. A framework within which we can place many of these considerations is known as the *industry life-cycle theory.* The life of an industry can be separated into the pioneering stage, the expansion stage, the stagnation stage, and the decay stage.[7] These stages are illustrated in Figure 5–1.

[7]For convenience, we will combine the stagnation and decay stages and refer to them as the *stabilization stage.*

Pioneering Stage

The pioneering stage is typified by rapid growth in demand for the output of the industry. In fact, in this earliest stage, demand not only grows but grows at an increasing rate. As a result, a great opportunity exists for profits, and thus venture capital comes into the industry. As large numbers of firms attempt to capture their share of the market, there arises a high business mortality rate; many of the weaker firms attempting to survive in this new industry are eliminated, and a lesser number of firms survive the initial phases of the pioneering stage. Firms are eliminated in part because of price competition, heavy losses resulting from startup costs, and generally hard nonprice competition stemming from such things as attempts to develop a brand name, a differentiated product, or a market edge as a result of product image that has been created.

Many firms are lured into the industry as a result of profit opportunities, and they compete vigorously with each other. The result is a constant shifting of the relative positions of the firms in the industry. Thus, the analyst will have a difficult task at this stage selecting those firms that will remain on top for some time to come. Even if the analyst can recognize an emerging industry in the pioneering stage, he will probably not invest at this point in the industry's development because of the great risks involved and because of the tremendous difficulty in selecting the survivors. However, the astute analyst will not even consider investment in the industry in the pioneering stage but will rather observe the industry's maturity and will wait for the expansion stage before he commits funds.

Expansion Stage

The expansion stage is characterized by the appearance of the firms surviving from the pioneering stage. These few companies continue to get stronger, both in share of the market and financially. Their competition in the expansion stage usually brings about improved products at a lower price. These firms continue to expand, but at a more moderate rate of growth than that experienced in the pioneering stage. As a result, these now stronger, steadier, more efficient firms become more attractive for investment purposes. While they are still growing, they have the aura of stability about them. They invest on themselves to sustain growth. In fact, in the expansion stage, many companies establish the precedent of paying dividends (although they may be small), making them an even more desirable investment.

Stabilization Stage

The growth of the industry, which had moderated in the expansion stage, begins at some point to moderate even further and perhaps even begins to stagnate. In other words, the ability of the industry to grow appears to have been lost. Sales may be increasing at a slower rate than that experienced by competitive industries or by the overall economy. The investment opportunities within the industry may

diminish, and member firms may pay larger dividends and may be deemed "cash cows."

Symptoms of this stage include changing social habits, high labor costs, changes in technology, and stationary demand.

The investment implication as these events take place is to dispose of one's holdings as soon as the industry begins to pass from the expansion stage to the stabilization stage, for after knowledge of the transition becomes widespread, the stock's price may be depressed. However, an industry may only stagnate intermittently before resuming a period of growth (e.g., airlines, in the view of some analysts), thereby starting a new cycle by, say, the introduction of a technological innovation or a new product. Thus, the investor or analyst must monitor industry developments constantly.

Although our exposition of the industry life-cycle theory seems to imply that it is easy to detect which stage of development an industry is in at any point in time, this is not necessarily so, for often the transition from one stage to the next is slow and unclear, making it detectable only by careful analysis. Nonetheless, this approach is useful in a somewhat crude way, and at the same time it gives the analyst insight into the apparent merits of investments in a given industry at a given time. In fact, one investment advisory service states, "In judging the probable future trend of an individual stock it is therefore more important to project the trend of its industry group than to project the trend of the general market. . . ."[8]

Despite the intuitive attractiveness of the industry life-cycle framework, it should be noted that it is only a *general* framework, and therefore, one will meet exceptions to the stereotype presented here. The analyst must be careful not to attempt to force all situations encountered in practice into the pioneering, expansion, and stabilization molds. Furthermore, the investment-policy implications mentioned in conjunction with the foregoing analysis serve as only a general guideline. Due heed must be paid to the current price of the security relative to its future earnings prospects.

International Investing as an "Industry" Choice

Many students of the U.S. stock market see it as a mature "industry." Certainly relative to securities available in other countries with newly emerging capital markets and vast populations, U.S. companies may not seem as exciting to an investor. Notwithstanding the above, investing abroad has substantial risks—such as currency fluctuation risks, potential governmental and social instability or uncertainty, and different accounting reporting standards. Many mutual funds have appeared that allow individual investors to invest globally while passing the handling of the above risk to professional managers. See the attached box for discussion of some of these issues and a statistical listing of some of the funds available. We will explore this topic in more depth later in Chapter 20.

[8]George A. Chestnutt, Jr., *Stock Market Analysis: Facts and Principles* (Greenwich, Conn.: Chestnutt Corp., 1971), p. 12.

BEARISH ON AMERICA

ROBERT LENZNER

Except for that nasty jolt in October 1987, most investors under 40 have never experienced anything but bull markets. They think stocks return 9% or better as a matter of course. They are in for a big shock, says Barton Biggs, Morgan Stanley's chief investment officer. Says Biggs: "We have all been spoiled by the 12 fat years we have just lived through."

Convinced that the U.S. stock market has gotten way ahead of itself, Biggs is telling his clients to move their money overseas. He recommends investors cut U.S. equities to 18% of their investment assets. Since common stocks constitute 62% of Morgan Stanley's recommended asset allocation model *(see chart),* this means Morgan Stanley recommends investors keep less than one-third of their equity money in U.S. equities.

This is pretty strong stuff coming from a man who has been remarkably perceptive in calling major turns in recent years. In summer of 1980, with the Dow in the 800s, he recommended Morgan Stanley clients load up on U.S. stocks. In April 1987 Biggs got bearish. By December 1987 he again recommended U.S. stocks.

In neither case did Biggs call the precise turn. The great Reagan bull market didn't really get under way until 1982, and Biggs was six months early on the October 1987 massacre. Those who took his advice, however, have no reason to complain, especially since so many of his clients are huge pension funds, which need months to accumulate or liquidate their positions. In any case, better too soon than even a week too late. "We got cautious too early in '87," Biggs says. "When you're running big money you have to be early. Sometimes it takes a month to get out."

Why does Biggs want to move money out of the U.S.? Three reasons. One is that he thinks the U.S. stock market has gotten way ahead of itself after quadrupling in a dozen years. And he sees much greater opportunity for investment abroad. The third reason is that he is appalled by what he sees going on in Washington.

"We want to get our clients' money as far away from Bill and Hillary as we can," Biggs tells FORBES. "The President is a negative for the U.S. market. I'm embarrassed that I voted for him and contributed money to his campaign."

Biggs, who is registered as a Republican, doesn't take seriously the Administration's assertion that its tax increases and so-called spending cuts will shrink the federal budget deficit by anything like the half-trillion dollars Clinton claims. Once the markets understand that the deficit is going to stay staggeringly high, interest rates will go up again, which can only be bad for the U.S. stock market. Biggs: "The first sign of trouble will be when the yield on 30-year Treasurys rises by 50 to 100 basis points. Stocks will begin falling when the market comes to grips with the chaos in Washington and the chances that the deficit is not going to be reduced substantially."

Clintonomics aside, Biggs argues that the U.S. stock market is near the top of its composite valuations since World War II, and due for a fall that could range from 20% up to 50% of the main stock market averages. The market has returned on average about 15% a year over the past dozen years, way above the 9% that stocks have traditionally returned. To get back to the long-term trend line, stocks will inevitably show below-average or even negative returns for a while.

"We're telling our clients: You've had an incredible run. Returns on financial assets have been way above average." If the market decides to get back quickly to its long-term trend line, it could have a precipitous drop. Says Biggs: "If there is a regression to the mean in the stock averages, it practically amounts to a cosmic event."

How cosmic? Hold on to your hat! "If the S&P 500 stock index registers one of its average cyclical declines experienced since World War II, it could fall 20% to 35%," says Biggs. This would mean a drop in the Dow Jones industrial average to somewhere between 2800 and 2275. That's with a run-of-the-mill cyclical bear market, but Biggs reminds us that there are also secular bear markets, declines that go much further and last longer. "We're due for a secular bear market. It's been 20 years since the last one. Then, the decline could be 50%, as it was in the 1970s."

Pushed, Biggs says he leans toward the belief that the decline will be of the lesser, cyclical variety. "A secular bear market will happen when sentiment turns from caution to optimism," he says. He's encouraged that the rising market of 1992 and 1993 hasn't been accompanied by euphoria. Equity mutual funds have over 10%, or $55.5 billion, of their assets in cash, and the advisory services are mixed in their bullishness.

But even if the drop is at the lower end of his band, at, say, 20%, it means that you can't expect much from U.S. stocks for a good while. Why stick with them, then, when markets abroad look so much more promising? "I'm not predicting the timing," he says, but adds that people who follow his advice are already selling U.S. stocks. "It will take months to reallocate the portfolio holdings of the $40 billion in assets under management handled by Morgan Stanley. We have already sold the brand-name consumer stocks."

While the U.S. has had a tremendous bull market, the European markets have been sluggish or worse, and the markets in emerging industrial countries are still small. Biggs says: "I believe the S&P 500 index, which has been returning a 14% annual rate of return the past five years, and the Morgan Stanley Capital International EAFE [Europe, Australia and the Far East] index, which grew by a measly 1% a year over the last five years, will reverse their performance over the next five years. It doesn't take a genius to see that this relationship is due for a change. You'll probably make 10% in Europe and 17% to 18% in Asian and other emerging nation stocks over the next half-dozen years."

Biggs especially likes the emerging markets, even though many of them have already performed spectacularly well the past few years. "According to the latest World Bank and International Monetary Fund figures, emerging nations are 41% of the world economy but only 7% of the world stock market capitalization, and amount to less than 1% of U.S. institutional equity holdings," says Biggs.

Biggs points out that these industrializing countries represent a bigger proportion of the world economy than their GDP figures indicate. "I believe the World Bank and IMF figures, which use purchasing power parities to compute countries' economic output, are the most accurate barometer of these nations' ranking. On this scorecard, China ranks as the world's third-biggest economy, India the sixth, Brazil the ninth and Mexico the tenth in the world." But you would never realize these countries were so important just from looking at the current capitalization of their stock markets.

Morgan Stanley likes the markets in Thailand, Singapore, the Philippines, Hong Kong, Taiwan, China, Indonesia and India. "I believe that Southeast Asian markets

(continued)

selling from 12 to 18 times earnings today will be selling at 20 to 30 times earnings in three years," says Biggs. The largest Thai position of Morgan clients is in Bangkok Bank Ltd.

Biggs' two favorite emerging markets? China and India—with a combined population of roughly 2 billion people—account for 20% of the Morgan Stanley emerging markets portfolio. Biggs sees pluses and minuses in both nations. "In the short run the potential is greater in China because it is a dictatorship, while India is a coalition democracy. I believe China should grow 8% to 10% a year, while India will grow by 6%. Nevertheless, India has a developed stock market ruled by British law and accounting, while, by comparison, China has a minuscule stock market with very primitive trading facilities."

But the negatives don't scare him. "I am especially bullish on China because it recently devalued its currency by 20%, getting rid of an artificial official exchange rate and going to a market exchange rate. Their economy is going to be open and deregulated. A country famous for mandarin bureaucracy suddenly went to a free open currency. Our Chinese positions are in the Hong Kong stock market, which is a call on China." Some of Morgan Stanley's largest Hong Kong holdings are China Light & Power, Citic Pacific Ltd., Hutchison Whampoa and HSBC Holdings Plc.

And India? "What I like about India is that industry is growing much faster than the economy as a whole, which is held back by agriculture and subsidized industry. Speculative excesses have been wrung out of the stock market because of scandal and the recent Bombay bombings. I think the average price/earnings multiples on Indian stocks will go from 13 times earnings to 20 times earnings because the long-term sustainable earnings growth in the country is 18% to 20%."

Biggs also sees high potential in three other emerging markets—Indonesia, Brazil and Turkey. "Not only are the Brazil and Turkey markets cheap. We believe their politicians understand the values of free markets. Above all else, emerging markets are where the real growth is in the world." The largest Indonesian holding is Indocement Tunggal.

What markets should investors be cautious about? "Pakistan and the Philippines may not make it or do as well, because they really haven't emerged yet. The governments there need to make progress on privatization, deregulation, opening the economy to competition and reducing tax rates to get people into the markets. With these developing economies you see trickle-down economics working, prosperity at the top working its way down through the entire population. But if governments are populist or corrupt, trickle-down economics doesn't work."

Latin America? "We like Mexico, but the trouble is we're not early. I'd rather buy Telebrás, the Brazilian telephone company, than Telmex," the Mexican telephone stock Morgan Stanley has held for three years. "Telebrás is selling at $32, with a book value of $42 a share. Of course, seven months ago it was selling at $11, and it could go back to $11. But I think it's a superb play on the Brazilian economy."

If he's so bullish on Asia, why does Biggs recommend putting more money into Europe?

"Europe is growing slowly, but equities are cheap and fairly valued there. The U.S. market is selling at 10.1 times cash earnings while Germany is selling at 4.2 times, Italy, 3.8 times, Austria, 4 times and France, 6.5 times. I particularly like Italian stocks because they are selling at a third the multiple on cash earnings as in the U.S. Also, I think we've seen the worst of the scandal and demoralization of the political system. I think we're at the start of the mending process in Italy.

"Germany is very cheap because there are going to be institutional changes related to taxes and market structure that will be more friendly to equity holders. Eventually Germany will significantly reduce its capital gains tax of over 50%. It will encourage companies to report their true asset values, as Deutsche Bank did when it came over here to spell out some of its specific hidden reserves. In time, also, Germany will change its corporate law to make it difficult for Deutsche Bank to own 15% to 20% of many large companies. This will force them to sell, unlocking long-term holdings and freeing up capital for new investments."

Shifting money abroad from the U.S. is well and good for pension funds, which don't pay capital gains taxes. But what is the individual investor to do if he or she is sitting on big capital gains? Selling U.S. stocks to buy foreign stocks would involve paying a third or more of the paper profits to federal and state governments in capital gains taxes.

"Don't worry about paying the 28% capital gains tax," advises Biggs, "because you're better off making the right strategic decision and paying the taxes than staying because of the tax implications."

Investing abroad, of course, involves currency risks. Morgan Stanley hedges half of its currency exposure in its European market holdings and half of its yen position. But it doesn't hedge the other Asian markets because those currencies are informally pegged to the dollar. The Indian rupee depreciates about 5% a year, so the firm doesn't bother hedging currency risk on its Indian shares.

If Biggs' advice makes sense to you but you're not a big institutional investor with access to research on foreign markets, what should you do? That's no longer much of a problem because there are so many mutual funds, both open-end and closed-end, that specialize in foreign stocks. As Biggs points out, portfolio allocation strategy accounts for over 90% of the variable returns of private pension funds, so making the decision to invest abroad is more important for an investor than the ability to pick the hottest stocks in Bangkok or Buenos Aires. Funds are a handy and relatively economical way to make that decision. And you can be darned sure that as investing abroad becomes more popular, there will be plenty more such funds; Morgan Stanley has just launched several new funds. For a listing of such funds that invest overseas, see the table below.

Source: Reprinted with permission of *Forbes* magazine, July 19, 1993. © Forbes Inc., 1993.

(continued)

AROUND THE WORLD

PERFORMANCE UP MARKET	DOWN MARKET	FUND	(800) NUMBER	TOTAL RETURN ANNUAL AVERAGE 5/88-5/93	LAST 12 MOS	YIELD (%)	ASSETS 3/31/93 ($MIL)	WEIGHTED AVERAGE P/E	MEDIAN MARKET CAP ($BIL)	ANNUAL EXPENSES PER $100	MANAGER
GLOBAL											
		Dreyfus Global Investing—A	242-8671	—*	8.6%	0.6%	$49	20.5	$2.2	NA	Fiona Biggs
		Janus Worldwide	525-8993	—*	9.7	1.0	327	19.8	6.1	$1.73	Helen Hayes
		Kidder Global Equity	238-7753	—*	7.5	none	130	20.7	12.8	1.62	Ralph R Layman
B	C	Lexington Global	526-0056	7.7%	13.3	0.5	64	21.4	3.7	1.52	Caesar Bryan
A	C	Scudder Global	225-2470	13.3	12.6	0.7	478	18.3	3.2	1.59	Multiple managers
		Scudder Global Small Cos	225-2470	—*	14.9	0.5	74	23.1	0.4	1.50	Multiple managers
		Smith Barney World—Intl Eq	544-7835	13.6	4.3	0.1	161	30.2	2.6	1.56	Maurits Edersheim
B	B	USAA Invest—Cornerstone	382-8722	9.5	18.2	2.8	621	23.4	4.6	1.18	Harry W Miller
C	C	Vanguard Intl Growth	662-7447	5.7	6.1	1.9	963	29.4	15.5	0.58	Richard R Foulkes
A	B	Vanguard US Growth	662-7447	16.6	1.1	1.2	1,907	17.7	18.0	0.48	Multiple managers
FOREIGN											
		Financial Series—Intl Growth	525-8085	4.5	5.0	0.8	46	23.4	15.5	1.36	Multiple managers
		Financial Strategic—Europe	525-8085	6.9	-10.6	1.8	136	14.3	12.5	1.29	Multiple managers
	D	Financial Strategic—Pacific	525-8085	3.3	15.6	0.4	43	17.0	7.9	1.78	Multiple managers
A		Harbor International	422-1050	15.6	4.1	1.1	1,015	23.8	11.8	1.28	Hakan Castegren
		IAI International	945-3863	7.0	6.0	0.3	59	26.9	15.7	1.98	Roy Gillson
B		Japan Fund	535-2726	2.4	27.4	0.1	462	32.2	19.7	1.45	Elizabeth Allan
C		Kleinwort Benson Intl Eq	233-9164	6.6	-1.4	0.2	59	18.8	7.9	1.88	Multiple managers
C	A	Lexington World Emerging	526-0056	9.6	5.9	1.2	33	18.5	3.2	1.89	Multiple managers
		Nomura Pacific Basic	833-0018	6.0	24.0	0.1	46	38.3	15.9	1.46	Takeo Nakamura
		T Rowe Price European Stock	638-5660	—*	-5.1	1.7	188	15.7	12.5	1.48	Martin G Wade
		T Rowe Price Intl Discovery	638-5660	—*	3.0	0.9	187	19.3	0.2	1.50	Martin G Wade
B	B	T Rowe Price Intl Stock	638-5660	9.6	5.4	1.6	2,184	20.6	12.5	1.05	Martin G Wade
		T Rowe Price New Asia	638-5660	—*	15.7	1.3	442	22.7	8.7	1.51	Martin G Wade
C	B	Scudder International	225-2470	9.3	10.3	2.2	1,179	21.0	10.3	1.26	Multiple managers
		20th Century Intl Equity	345-2021	—*	5.8	2.9	292	26.1	9.7	1.91	Multiple managers
		USAA Investment—Intl	382-8722	—*	10.7	0.9	48	17.2	15.5	1.69	David G Peebles
B		Vanguard/Trustees' Eq—Intl	662-7447	7.4	9.9	2.1	728	21.7	4.6	0.43	Jarrod Wilcox
B		Warburg, Pincus Intl Eq	888-6878	—*	10.3	0.4	131	29.5	11.8	1.50	Richard King

*Fund not in operation for full period. NA: Not available.

Sources: CDA/Wiesenberger; Morningstar; Forbes

For those who want to put some money abroad, these open-end mutual funds invest in non-U.S. stocks. They all charge no sales loads and have annual expenses of less than $2 per $100 of assets. Performance ratings include three up-and-down cycles since 1982.

EXTERNAL SOURCES OF INFORMATION
FOR INDUSTRY ANALYSIS

Federal Government

The federal government publishes a wide variety of data that can be useful during the industry phase of the analysis. It is well worth the time to thumb through the *Census of Manufacturers, Federal Reserve Bulletins,* and *Survey of Current Business* in order to appreciate more fully the wealth of information, helpful in the economic as well as industry analysis, available in these government sources. Many private services use these government-furnished data in their own security-analysis efforts.

Investment Services

Many investment services are available to furnish the investor or analyst with valuable industry and corporate information. The ones we highlight in this section are perhaps the best known.[9]

STANDARD & POOR'S

Standard & Poor's regularly covers a number of different industries in two ways: a basic analysis and a current update of the basic analysis. The basic analysis provides an in-depth report on all facets of the industry and the firms comprising the industry. A revised basic analysis is published approximately every year. The current update, entitled *Current Analysis and Outlook,* is published roughly every quarter.

Standard & Poor's also publishes the *Security Price Index Record,* containing indexes of the S&P's groupings, which are helpful when performing an industry analysis.

THE VALUE LINE

The *Value Line* also publishes industry data but in a considerably more condensed form than does Standard & Poor's. Figures 5–2 shows a basic analysis for the restaurant industry and shows a typical *Value Line* industry report. Such a report is followed by separate pages of data for each major firm in the industry. Note that along with descriptive material, the report contains composite statistics of the industry and a graph of the relative strength of the industry's share prices compared to the *Value Line* index of 1,500 stocks. This type of analysis coupled with the discussion like on pages 140–143 form an industry analysis.

---

[9]The *Wall Street Journal, Barron's,* the *Commercial and Financial Chronicle,* and *Predicasts* are among other key sources of investment information.

Stocks in the Restaurant Industry have performed about in line with the Value Line arithmetic index over the past three months. With this issue we are bringing in *Cracker Barrel Old Country Store* and dropping coverage of *Frisch's Restaurants*. Industry dynamics appear to be unchanged with value remaining the primary selling point.

Not A Bad Quarter

The restaurant industry has advanced more quickly than the Value Line composite over the past three months. This is a significantly better performance than the March-to-June stretch, when the restaurant composite slid 6%, versus a flat performance for the broader averages.

Overall, the business dynamics within the industry remain the same. Consumers are keeping an eye on their wallets and purses, and the stronger players in the segment are growing by taking market share away from the weaker ones. Food prices, especially beef, rose in the second quarter, but we think that commodity costs will be stable through the rest of the year. Meanwhile, the recent one-percentage point increase in the corporate tax rate (from 34% to 35%) will likely be offset largely by the targeted jobs tax credit and the elimination of FICA charges on tips.

In this issue we are initiating coverage of *Cracker Barrel Old Country Store*. Based in the Southeast, this chain operates a restaurant/gift shop combination that uses a country store motif. Overall, family restaurant chains are facing increased competition from both fast feeders that are pushing prices lower to capture more cost-conscious consumers, and casual theme chains that are increasingly becoming family friendly. But *Cracker Barrel* has been a successful combatant by focusing on high traffic areas (where fewer chains compete) and by maintaining high service standards.

Value Is King

Value remains the primary tool for gaining market share, in our opinion. While pricing is a major factor in measuring value, many chains are putting more emphasis on improving service. At the fast-food level, for instance, *McDonald's* is installing equipment to accommodate special orders more easily and to serve hotter food. It is also giving crew members more autonomy to respond to customer needs. Addressing the problems of a dissatisfied customer is especially

important in full service restaurants. And many chains are training their servers to detect potential problems and head them off. For instance, a free dessert may well keep a customer coming back even if he waited too long for his entree. Until fairly recently, such a gesture may have been discouraged by a management concerned with cost controls. But increasingly, operators are recognizing the long-term benefits of the small expense.

Measuring Sales

A closely followed measure of restaurant performance is same-store sales. Indeed, this is often a more accurate indicator of performance than total sales. That's because revenues from new restaurants may lift the top line, but business at the established restaurants has more of an effect on the bottom line. A case in point is the June-quarter results of *Ryan's*. This chain of steak houses reported a 12% gain in revenues, but a decline in profits. A 2.8% drop in same-store sales during the quarter meant that fixed costs were taking up a greater portion of the top line. The resulting pressure on margins (along with cost pressures from higher beef prices) more than offset earnings contributions from new units, which accounted for the sales gains.

Often in our comments, we look at components of same-store sales, especially traffic counts and menu prices. For instance, *Luby's* recently inaugurated television advertising in a few key markets, which helped lift same-store sales by 3% in August. Customer counts rose 4.2%, but the average guest check was down by 1.2%. The decline was likely the result of more patrons ordering the Lu Ann platter (a combination entree, two vegetables, and a bread at a special low price), which was being featured in the advertising. But the higher customer traffic more than offset the average guest check reduction.

Investment Advice

In general, restaurant companies reinvest their retained earnings in new units. Therefore, most operators in this segment pay either a low or no dividend. Our restaurant composite is dominated by *McDonald's*, which represents about 70% of the group's market capitalization. But because that company is in the fast-feed segment, its influence is felt less by chains in the full service area.

William G. Barr, CFA

Composite Statistics: Restaurant Industry

1989	1990	1991	1992	1993	1994		96-98
12504	13560	14122	15222	16600	17720	Sales ($mill)	26270
21.4%	22.4%	22.7%	22.6%	22.8%	23.0%	Operating Margin	24.5%
629.2	788.5	838.5	905.8	935	990	Depreciation ($mill)	1250
1035.3	1155.2	1245.0	1386.4	1565	1755	Net Profit ($mill)	2800
36.5%	35.4%	34.0%	34.3%	34.5%	34.5%	Income Tax Rate	34.5%
8.3%	8.5%	8.8%	9.1%	9.4%	9.9%	Net Profit Margin	10.7%
d592.7	d759.0	d606.3	d732.8	d795	d730	Working Cap'l ($mill)	d590
5185.9	5663.0	5543.4	4293.7	4330	4375	Long-Term Debt ($mill)	5965
5124.9	6038.3	7076.4	8479.6	9200	10660	Net Worth ($mill)	16605
12.3%	12.1%	11.9%	12.6%	11.5%	11.0%	% Earned Total Cap'l	11.5%
20.2%	19.1%	17.6%	16.3%	17.0%	16.5%	% Earned Net Worth	17.0%
17.2%	16.1%	14.9%	14.7%	14.5%	14.5%	% Retained to Comm Eq	15.5%
18%	18%	19%	17%	19%	18%	% All Div'ds to Net Prof	15%
15.0	14.7	15.2	17.8	*Bold figures are*		Avg Ann'l P/E Ratio	14.0
1.14	1.09	.97	1.08	*Value Line*		Relative P/E Ratio	1.08
1.2%	1.2%	1.1%	.9%	*estimates*		Avg Ann'l Div'd Yield	1.2%

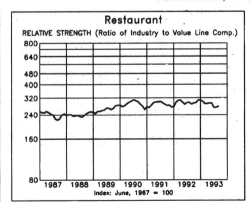

Restaurant

RELATIVE STRENGTH (Ratio of Industry to Value Line Comp.)

Index: June, 1967 = 100

FIGURE 5–2   Sample Value Line Industrial Analysis (*Source:* Value Line Investment Survey (New York: Value Line Publishing, March 31, 1989).)

On a weekly basis, the *Value Line* ranks the probable market performance of industries over the next twelve months, and in the case of individual stocks, their probable performance over the next twelve months and the next three to five years. See Figure 5–3 for *Value Line's* industry rankings in November 1993.

FORBES

The early-January issue of *Forbes* contains its "Annual Report on American Industry." This report includes a number of rankings of profitability, growth, and stock-market performance of more than 700 U.S. corporations. Of interest here are its rankings of major industry groupings, from which the analyst can see which groups appear to be on the move.

TRADE PUBLICATIONS

Virtually every major U.S. industry has at least one trade association, which in its publications reports much data pertaining to the industry it represents. The analyst can locate these sources, as well as references to various industries in other publications, by checking the *Business Periodicals Index* and the *Science and Technology Index,* as well as secondary sources already mentioned in this chapter.

FUNK AND SCOTT INDEX

The Funk and Scott Index of Corporations and Industries provides a valuable indexing service for the investor or analyst seeking published industry and company information. This service, published monthly, lists articles appearing in more than 700 trade and business publications. Funk and Scott index this information by SIC and by company name. The researcher can then consult the various cited articles and obtain information on the industry, company, or competition of the firm under investigation.

OTHER OBSERVATIONS ON INDUSTRY ANALYSIS

Throughout this chapter we have enumerated a number of relevant quantifiable and nonquantifiable factors, and have alluded to others, that should be considered when performing an industry analysis. Now let us point out several additional considerations: the composition of the industry's population, the distribution of income and wealth among the population, any evolving buying habits of consumers, and foreign and domestic production competition. These pieces of information are not always easy to come by, but the analyst who takes the trouble to develop *all* necessary information will find it worth the effort.

We observed earlier that the market psychology is an important, if at times seemingly irrational, factor that must be dealt with in an industry analysis. That is to say, within a short period of time, an industry's relative attraction as an investment opportunity can change from an extremely desirable, conservative, undervalued situation to a highly risky, potentially overpriced situation.

THE VALUE LINE
Investment Survey

Part 1
Summary & Index

File at the front of the *Ratings & Reports* binder. Last week's *Summary & Index* should be removed.

November 26, 1993

TABLE OF SUMMARY-INDEX CONTENTS

The Median of Estimated **PRICE-EARNINGS RATIOS** of all stocks with earnings	The Median of **ESTIMATED YIELDS** (next 12 months) of all dividend paying stocks under review	The Estimated Median **APPRECIATION POTENTIAL** of all 1700 stocks in the hypothesized economic environment 3 to 5 years hence
16.6	**2.5%**	**55%**

	Price-Earnings Ratios			Estimated Yields			Appreciation Potential	
26 Weeks Ago*	Market Low 12-23-74*	Market High 9-4-87*	26 Weeks Ago*	Market Low 12-23-74*	Market High 9-4-87*	26 Weeks Ago*	Market Low 12-23-74*	Market High 9-4-87*
16.3	4.8	16.9	2.5%	7.8%	2.3%	65%	234%	40%

*Estimated medians as published in *The Value Line Investment Survey* on the dates shown.

ANALYSES OF INDUSTRIES IN ALPHABETICAL ORDER WITH PAGE NUMBER

Numeral in parenthesis after the industry is rank for probable performance (next 12 months).

*Reviewed in this week's edition.

In three parts: This is Part 1, the Summary & Index. Part 2 is Selection & Opinion. Part 3 is Ratings & Reports. Volume XLIX, No. 11.
Published weekly by VALUE LINE PUBLISHING, INC. 711 3rd Avenue, New York, N.Y. 10017-4064

FIGURE 5–3 Value Line Investment Survey

During 1988 several industry groups became popular candidates for takeover by other companies. For example, food companies and pharmaceutical companies became "rumor candidates" and thus very active issues as speculators attempted to predict which industry member would be taken over next. When this occurred, the affected company's common stock price fluctuated dramatically. When this kind of fervor hits the market, it takes a cool analyst to discern whether the potential growth prospects of the industry have been fully discounted or whether the growth warrants purchase in the midst of such an uproar. In other words, even the best of growth situations can be bought at too high a price and thus bring a low or negative return to the investor. And even low- or no-growth industries, when bought at a very low price, can bring respectable returns. This situation arises because the market seems to value highly industries on the verge of tremendous growth in earnings, and to value low those industries that have already achieved their growth and have stabilized. That is, stocks on the verge of growth generally sell at high P/E ratios, and stocks that have come to the end of their growth pattern generally sell at low P/E ratios.

Before we continue our illustration of the application of industry-analysis techniques, it is necessary to place the importance of an industry analysis in the proper perspective. Its benefits can be fully realized only if it occurs along with a properly conceived economic analysis and company analysis.

A good economic analysis informs the investor about the propriety of a current stock purchase, regardless of the industry in which he might invest. If the economic outlook suggests purchase at this time, the economic analysis along with the industry analysis will aid the investor in selecting the proper industry in which to invest. Nonetheless, knowing when to invest and in which industry to invest is not enough. It is also necessary to know which companies in which industries should be selected. We turn our attention to this topic in the ensuing three chapters.

SUMMARY

In this chapter we first discussed alternative industry-classification schemes, observing that different schemes are appropriate for different purposes. Next, we observed how the economic analysis could best be meshed with the industry analysis. Key characteristics of the industry that the analyst needs to consider include the past sales and earnings performance of the industry, its permanence, the attitude of government toward the industry, labor conditions prevalent in the industry, industry competitive conditions, and the industry P/E levels. We illustrated this part of the analysis with an extended example using the fast-food industry. The concepts of an industry life cycle, end-use analysis, regression analysis, and input-output analysis were explained. Finally, we noted some sources of industry information.

QUESTIONS AND PROBLEMS

1. If you were attempting to forecast the sales of the candy industry, what classification scheme would you use?

2. What is a cyclical industry?

3. Of what value is the past sales and earnings performance of an industry in forecasting the future prospects of the industry?

4. What domestic industries do you suppose will decline in importance in the next decade? Why?

5. Why do you suppose only three automobile manufacturers in the United States almost completely dominate the auto industry?

6. How high would industry share prices have to go relative to industry earnings before you would decide that the shares were overpriced for investment purposes? Explain.

7. Of what use is the industry-life-cycle approach to an industry analyst?

8. How would you go about forecasting the sales of domestically produced beer next year? What variables are most important in determining the demand for beer?

9. Based on the latest Standard & Poor's *Basic Analysis* of the aerospace industry, would you recommend stock purchases in the group? Why?

10. The analysis of sales growth is generally the starting point in estimating earning power potential for an industry (and firms therein). Further, on a perspective basis, it is common to look at an industry from an industrial-life-cycle point of view.

    a. Assume that two companies in an industry have identical rates of sales growth. Why might an analyst nevertheless consider the sales record of one superior to that of the other?

    b. Which stage of the industrial life cycle is the most attractive from an investment point of view?

11. What are the three most critical variables one might "track" in forecasting the outlook for the fast-food industry?

12. Why should an investor consider investing in industries outside of the United States?

13. Give an example of an industry you feel has positive competitive conditions for your selection as an industry to invest in. Why have you selected this industry?

14. Select an industry that may be ripe for investment because it has significant undervalued assets on its books.

15. Select an industry or industry sector that has a niche to exploit for profits. Explain your choice.

16. Identify a significant marketing-driven development during the current year that may lead or has led to an investment opportunity. Explain your selection.

17. Name three sources of industry data available in many libraries. Obtain an example from each of the three sources for an industry of your choice. Based

on information in those sources *above,* would you recommend it for investment potential for someone with a three-year investment time horizon?

18. If you were told that the housing industry was going to have a good year, what other industries do you think would be positively affected either concurrent with this event or shortly thereafter? Explain your answer.

19. If you were considering for investment an industry with high fixed costs and high profit margins, what other factors would you want to explore before deciding to invest in this industry? Why?

20. If you were considering for investment an industry with low fixed costs and low profit margins, what other factors would you want to explore before deciding to invest in this industry? Why?

21. What geographic region outside the United States would you consider the most advantageous for investment consideration if you had a three-year time horizon? Why?

DISCLOSURE PROBLEM

We have said that generally mature industries will tend to have higher dividend payout ratios than rapidly growing industries. The newer, rapidly growing industries will tend to invest funds in themselves rather than pay them out to shareholders. Select an example of each type of industry and using *disclosure,* test this contention by calculating relevant ratios for three companies in each industry you selected.

COMPANY ANALYSIS: MEASURING EARNINGS

The most immediately recognizable effect of economic and industry influences on a specific company is probably the impact on revenues. The sales of some industries (steel, autos) tend to move in tandem with the business cycle; others (food, telephone, utilities) are relatively immune from the cycle; still others (such as housing) move countercyclically. From the viewpoint of the individual company, adjustments to changes in the general business cycle can be different from those of the industry in general. Product mix and pricing peculiar to specific firms can cause total revenues to respond more or less to broad economic and industry impact. Diversified product lines, for example, allow a company to spread cyclical effects.

Revenue changes in firms in the same industry with identical product mix and pricing policies may lead to different relative changes in costs. As we saw in Chapter 3, a company in which fixed costs absorb a large percentage of total costs may have difficulty curtailing expenses during economic declines and responding as demand increases. A firm with a large proportion of its total costs variable may respond better, both up and down. In the end, the latter firm may show better earnings (revenue minus costs). The relationship of revenues and expenses to economic and industry changes, and the resulting earnings, is the focal point of the company analysis.

The next three chapters will demonstrate how an analyst estimates return and risk for specific stocks. This chapter examines the nature and sources of relevant information about companies that is required to make judgments about return and risk. Chapters 7 and 8 demonstrate how to translate that information into expectations about holding-period yields.

INTRODUCTION

Many pieces of information influence investment decisions. Investors need to know the characteristics of various investment alternatives and must keep in-

formed on the institutions and markets where they are available. Up-to-date information is required on the status of and trends in the economy, particular industries, and firms.

The United States is a nation known for an abundance of widely available and rapidly disseminated information of almost every sort imaginable. This flood of information creates problems for the investor; he must continuously sample, sift, and sort messages and events for "good" information. Success in investing will be largely dependent on (1) discovering new and credible information rapidly and in more detail than others do, and (2) applying superior judgment to ascertain the relevance of the information to the decision at hand. *The true test of an analyst's worth lies in his ability to develop a system of security analysis that couples original insight and unique ways of forming expectations about the prospects for individual companies.* Varied public and private sources of information must be analyzed.

Superior judgment comes from the capacity to take information and (1) see given relationships more clearly, or (2) perceive more interrelationships. Judgment depends pretty much upon one's store of knowledge and experiences. The task of security analysis is largely a matter of sifting, sorting, and rearranging data on markets, the economy, industries, and firms. By applying various tools of analysis to the data, the investor formulates expectations and judgments about the alternatives open to him.

This chapter is concerned with two broad categories of information: internal and external. Internal information consists of data and events made public by firms concerning their operations. It mainly takes the form of interim and annual reports to shareholders, and public and private statements of the officers and managers of the firm. The principal information sources generated internally by a firm are its financial statements. The analyst does not, of course, limit inquiry to information provided by accountants; ingenious and competent analysts sample widely from many kinds of information.

External sources of information are those generated independently outside the company. They provide a supplement to internal sources by (1) overcoming some of the bias inherent in company-generated information, and (2) providing information simply not found in the materials made available by companies themselves.

INTERNAL INFORMATION

The Key Role of Financial Statements

An overwhelming weight is placed by analysts and investors on the information contained in the financial statements of firms. One critical reason for this reliance lies in the vouchsafed nature of the statements because their form and content is controlled under a variety of rules, regulations, and statutes. The vast majority of these statements are attested to by independent auditors. In sum, investors tend to accept financial statements as the closest thing to complete credibility in infor-

mation available to them. In the private and public statements of company officers, there is little chance of corroborating what is said. Very often the true significance of such pronouncements is clouded by some degree of enthusiasm and loyalty.

Financial Statements as Proxies of Real Processes

Accounting is a proxy that has been developed for representing *real* processes and *real* goods. Accounts and statements are devices created to summarize certain types of information about real corporate goods and processes.

As such, these statements, to a large extent, form the basis for action by investors, potential investors, creditors, and potential creditors of the corporation. Because of this, analysts must understand in a general way how these statements are prepared so that they can better interpret their true meaning. A good beginning point for investment analysis and ultimately investment decision making is to be aware of the historical record of the firm in a financial sense. This historical record of the firm's earnings and financial position can often give the analyst insight into the inner workings of the firm and thus assist him in projecting the future. This investigation of the past is a vital step taken by the investment analyst.

Someone once said, however, that accounting statements are like the tips of icebergs: What you see is interesting, but what you do not see is significant! A good investment analyst must judge financial statements as they meet the tests of (1) correctness, (2) completeness, (3) consistency, and (4) comparability.

Correctness, or accuracy, is normally established through the presence or absence of an "unqualified" auditor's certification. Nearly all public corporations retain public accounting firms to audit and certify the fairness of financial statements. Unaudited statements are not necessarily inaccurate or fraudulently prepared; they simply lack the intrinsic credibility of audited statements accompanied by the signed opinion of a certified public accountant (CPA).

Completeness is a matter of disclosure. Inasmuch as accounting is only a proxy of real goods and processes, it cannot and does not pretend to tell everything. Many, many bits of information about a business were never intended to be incorporated into established financial reports and statements. The Securities and Exchange Commission (SEC), the American Institute of Certified Public Accountants (AICPA), and the Financial Accounting Standards Board (FASB) have worked together, and at times at odds, in dealing with the matter of full disclosure. The vital emphasis placed upon financial statements by analysts and investors, always hungry for more and better information, is creating increasing pressure for making more and more information available in different forms.[1]

---

[1]Many have suggested that the form of the income statement should be changed to assist analysis. Traditional expense breakdowns do not explain dynamic changes in costs as volume changes. Fixed and variable cost division would be more informative for marginal analysis. Other cost segregations used by managements could also help investors.

Auditors are charged with the primary responsibility of ensuring that changes in reporting over time are justified and brought to the attention of the public. *Consistency* is vital in making comparisons of the performance of a firm over time. Data constructed differently at various points in time lack meaningful continuity unless reconciled prior to analysis.[2]

No area of accounting information has created more debate and difficulties for the analyst than *comparability.* Using audited financial statements for a firm, most of the time an analyst can work toward more complete and consistent information on his own. However, investment decision making involves comparing alternatives—or, as it were, *comparing the data derived from the financial statements of different firms.* The problem: Are the financial statements of different firms prepared under the same ground rules? Is it valid to make choices between two companies on the basis of financial information if the information is not generated on a uniform basis?

Accounting for revenue, costs, and profits is not done under a set of rigid rules whereby each event and transaction, regardless of the firm, is handled in one way only. To the extent that accounting provides options in handling certain transactions, comparability diminishes.

One set of accounting rules in the name of uniformity is perhaps an unrealistic ideal. Highly flexible accounting practices have grown up over the years to recognize the wide diversity of circumstances within American business. However, from an analyst/investor point of view, the need for uniformity is obvious because investment decisions are the product of comparative analysis of data for the determination of relative values.

In the following pages we will examine the principal financial statements made public by corporations. Our goal is neither to teach accounting nor to cover every one of the many areas of interest in financial reporting. We do want to focus on critical problem areas—the sources of an analyst's difficulties in interpreting financial statements. A good analyst must train himself to understand the kinds of flexibility permitted in accounting and the effects of this flexibility on his interpretation of what he sees. Further, an analyst must learn to rely upon the *total* impact of all financial statements taken as a unit over time. The auditor's opinion is a critical part of the financial statements, as are the notes to the statements. In short, the prudent analyst will look at the statements "taken as a whole" and will understand how the major statements are interrelated. There is danger in looking at single figures on individual statements in an isolated year. Finally, and perhaps most important, reported financial data (especially reported earnings) need to be examined carefully and interpreted in the light of other generally available information.

The results of our exploration into financial statements should enable the analyst to work with the interrelationships contained in the various statements in forming expectations about earnings, dividends, and stock prices.

---

[2]See pronouncements of the FASB for a detailed treatment of this complex subject.

Operating Results: The Income Statement

Three major financial statements comprise the backbone of internal information available to the analyst: the statement of income and retained earnings, the balance sheet, and the statement of cash flows. Accompanying notes to these statements are also crucial and are less important than the statements themselves.

In the early 1900s, security analysts placed primary emphasis on the evaluation of the corporation's balance sheet. In fact, it would not be unfair to say that emphasis was almost exclusively placed on the financial strength or weakness of the company. As the years went by, this emphasis on the evaluation of the balance sheet began to shift toward an emphasis on the income statement. This shift continued until the early 1970s. Again, it would not be unfair to say that in these years major emphasis was placed on earnings and earnings per share as reflected in the income statement. The growth rate of these earnings was also of vital importance to the analyst. However, in the mid-1970s it became apparent that looking at the income statement and the earnings figures to the detriment of the balance sheet was no longer a prudent thing to do. And so, today analysts look very closely at both the balance sheet and the income statement as well as the statement of cash flows. In fact, in today's merger and leveraged buyout-filled environment, this last statement—and derivatives thereof—have become an increasingly popular analytical tool.

In the sections that follow we will discuss each of these statements—namely, the statement of income and retained earnings, the balance sheet, and the statement of cash flows. Our discussion will point out certain trouble spots that the security analyst should be aware of when examining these various statements. Because these trouble spots are often very complex to analyze—even for a trained accountant—we strongly feel that an analyst should realize that these problem areas exist so that he will at least proceed with caution and will be aware of potential pitfalls in any analysis. With this general warning, let us proceed with our analysis of these statements.

INCOME-STATEMENT FORMAT

The Accounting Principles Board (APB) has suggested the format shown in Table 6–1 for a statement of income and a statement of retained earnings. The income statement provides an analysis of significant factors that have contributed to and affected the earnings for the period. The statement of retained earnings bridges the gap between the income statement and the position statement (balance sheet), in the sense that the net income on the income statement is reflected in the retained-earnings part of the stockholders' equity on the balance sheet. The usual changes in retained earnings are the net income or loss for the period, dividends declared, and corrections of net income for prior periods.

The income statement is a key financial statement by which analysts judge management's performance. It is used perhaps more than any other statement in

Table 6-1

COMPARATIVE STATEMENT OF INCOME AND
STATEMENT OF RETAINED EARNINGS

STATEMENT OF INCOME
YEARS ENDED DECEMBER 31, 19X0, AND DECEMBER 31, 19X1

	19X0	19X1
Net sales (net of trade discounts, returns, and allowances)		
Other income (e.g., rents, interest, dividends, royalties)		
Costs and expenses:		
Costs of goods sold (cost of merchandise sold during period)		
Selling expenses (creating sales, storing goods and delivery, including depreciation)		
Administration and general expenses (administering overall activities, including depreciation)		
Financial management expenses (interest on borrowed money)		
Other deductions (items extraneous to primary operations)		
Income tax (federal, state, and local)		
Income before extraordinary items (per share: (19X0: 19X1:)		
Extraordinary items, less applicable income tax (per share: 19X0: ; 19X1:) (usually, nonrecurring and not related to primary operating activity of the business)		
Net income (per share: 19X0: ; 19X1:)		

STATEMENT OF RETAINED EARNINGS
YEARS ENDED DECEMBER 31, 19X0, AND DECEMBER 31, 19X1

	19X0	19X1
Retained earnings at beginning of year:		
As previously reported (on prior-period balance sheet)		
Adjustments (corrections of income reported in prior periods; e.g., settlements of law and tax suits, and for carelessness or imprudence in valuing assets at end of earlier periods)		
As restated		
Net income (last line of statement of income)		
Cash dividends on common and preferred stock (shown separately)		
Retained earnings at end of year		

attempting to assess the future. Past earnings reported on the income statement are very often used as a base for predicting future performance. Thus a major job for the analyst is to probe principal areas of the income statement to assess their impact on earnings.

The nature of a company is a principal determinant of the extent to which a particular item is likely to have significance with respect to earnings. For example, the choice of depreciation method has considerable impact upon the earnings of an airline, which has almost all its assets in equipment. The choice of deprecia-

tion method is less significant, although not unimportant, for a bank because most bank assets are in securities and loans. The analyst is forced to examine almost every item of revenue, expense, and resulting earnings on the income statement. Elements of the statement of retained earnings, particularly charges for prior periods, should be investigated. Let us address ourselves to some major problem areas on the income statement and statement of retained earnings.

EARNINGS FROM REGULAR OPERATIONS

The analyst must recognize that earnings from regular, normal operations reflect the major thrust of a business, and so these earnings should be segregated from earnings (or losses) resulting from infrequent, unusual, or nonrecurring events. Because earnings from these regular, normal operations are more apt to be continuing for some reasonable period, their separate disclosure is important to the analyst in judging and forecasting the future. Obviously, the assumption is made that these recurring types of transactions are a better base on which to build or forecast than nonrecurring or infrequent types of transactions. However, as can be seen in Table 6–1, so-called extraordinary gains or losses do sometimes occur in the operations of a business. Fortunately, however, the accounting profession has specifically defined how these items are to be treated in the financial statements.

Extraordinary items need to arise from material transactions that are both unusual in nature and occur infrequently in the operating environment of the business. The *environment* of the business would include such things as the characteristics of the industry in which the firm operates, the geographic location of the facilities of the corporation, and the role of governmental regulations in the corporation's affairs. As can be seen, this definition very narrowly describes what can properly be called an extraordinary item. For example, a loss resulting from an earthquake in certain sections of California might not be considered an extraordinary item; however, damage caused by an earthquake in Connecticut would be considered an extraordinary item. As shown in Table 6–1, the extraordinary item would be listed separately and would be listed net of any income tax effects.

APB *Opinion No. 30* also deals with the problem of properly disclosing information related to disposals of certain major segments of the business. Any income or loss from such discontinued operations must also be separately disclosed in the financial statements. If a corporation in the same year had normal operations, had extraordinary items, and disposed of a segment of its business, three different income figures would be disclosed in the income statement. The first would probably be labeled "income from continuing operations." Then a separate section for the discontinued operations would probably be included, which would lead to another income figure labeled "income before extraordinary items." Finally, a section for disclosing the extraordinary items would be included, which would lead to a final figure labeled "net income." Therefore, the analyst must be careful to select the proper income figure to use as a basis for any forecast.

THE MATCHING PRINCIPLE

Accounting is based upon many "rules of the road" called *generally accepted accounting principles.* An important rule applied to income statements that concerns the analyst is what accountants call the *matching principle.* In simple terms, the matching principle requires that expenses be reflected in the same period as the revenues to which they are related. Various accounting methods have been devised, some rather scientific and others somewhat arbitrary, for matching costs and revenues. The utility of accounting information on the investment analyst is impaired if (1) expenses and revenues are improperly matched, or (2) methods employed are switched over time.

The process of matching costs and revenues is only approximate and often yields to expediency. Do we really know the rate at which a machine depreciates? In what order did inventory really flow out of the plant? Will a particular expenditure benefit this period alone, or several future periods? If several periods, how many? Judgment in prorating expenses and recognizing revenues is needed within clearly drawn guidelines. Let us examine some key statement areas in which the matching problem creates difficulties in analysis.

INTANGIBLES.   Many assets are developed or purchased that lack a physical or tangible character. Some, such as patents, copyrights, and franchises, have limited life by law. Others, such as goodwill, trademarks, and secret processes or formulas, have an indeterminate life. In the past, some companies have written off intangibles immediately; others have set them up with no amortization; still others have written them off over lives determined by expediency.

APB *Opinion No. 17* has helped to clarify the ground rules for recording and amortizing intangibles. In essence, it says that purchased intangibles are to be set up at cost and amortized on a straight-line basis over *estimated* useful lives not to exceed forty years. And the *Opinion* specifies certain factors to consider in estimating useful life.

The accompanying two boxes illustrate some practical issues and problems in accounting for goodwill.

PENSION COSTS.   Every company pension plan requires accounting for past, present, and future costs. Under APB *Opinion No. 8,* companies were effectively able to control the amount of pension costs to be recognized in their financial statements through a variety of means. The FASB recently issued new standards for pension accounting that have served to remove much of the discretion previously granted to pension-plan sponsors, thereby reducing the amount of management control over pension cost.[3]

However, pension accounting is a very complex area and is still in an evolving transitional mode. Analysts are well advised to gain a thorough understanding of the area and of the specific pension accounting policies utilized by the company

---

[3]Financial Accounting Standards Board, *Statement of Financial Accounting Standards No. 87, Employers' Accounting for Pensions* (Stamford, Conn.: FASB, 1985).

GOODWILL IS MAKING A LOT OF PEOPLE ANGRY: WRITE-OFFS OF INTANGIBLE ASSETS ARE GIVING SERVICE COMPANIES A BIG PAIN IN THE EARNINGS

JEFFREY M. LADERMAN, WITH LEAH J. NATHANS IN NEW YORK, MARK MAREMONT IN LONDON, AND TED HOLDEN IN TOKYO

When Philip Morris Cos. gobbled up Kraft Inc. for $12.9 billion last year, it acquired a passel of prizes that are household names to nearly every shopper in America: Velveeta cheese and Chiffon margarine, to mention just a few. Wall Street has applauded vigorously, sending Philip Morris stock up more than 50%. But according to accountants, Philip Morris was taken to the cleaners. The fair value of the Kraft assets, say the bean counters, was only $1.3 billion. The difference, a staggering $11.6 billion, or 90% of the purchase price, is a wispy, intangible asset known as goodwill.

There are scores of issues on which investors and accountants part company, but few are as contentious—or important—as the treatment of goodwill. And in an era of megadeals, the balance sheets of U.S. companies are piling it up at a torrid pace. Because of the Kraft deal, Philip Morris' goodwill climbed to $15 billion from $4 billion. That's nearly triple its net worth (table). And for many other companies, especially those in consumer products and media, goodwill is becoming an ever larger piece of the balance sheet. At Gannett, Dow Jones, and PepsiCo, goodwill and other intangibles make up more than 80% of net worth.

"Slippery Concept."

All that goodwill is bad news for reported earnings. U.S. corporations must "amortize" or write it off—without the benefit of a tax deduction. That puts American companies at a disadvantage when bidding against foreign buyers for acquisitions. In Britain, companies don't amortize goodwill at the expense of earnings. In Japan, West Germany, and Canada, they do, but the write-off is cushioned by tax breaks. "If there's a more slippery concept [in accounting,] I don't know of it," says Robert Willens, an accounting analyst at Shearson Lehman Hutton Inc.

No one's advocating doing away with goodwill entirely. Indeed, it's a "plug" number that makes a balance sheet balance. When one company buys another, the fair value of the physical assets go into the inventory or plant, property, and equipment accounts. The remainder is called goodwill, also known as "going concern value," and is classified as an intangible asset. In that light, it makes sense. Kraft spent decades building up its food products, and consumer loyalty to the Kraft label is a valuable asset.

But will the value of the Kraft name decline to zero in 40 years? That's how Philip Morris has to treat it, deducting $290 million a year from earnings—about $1.25 a share. While assets such as machines deteriorate visibly, it's not so easy to pinpoint when an intangible is losing value. The write-off is "ludicrous," says Hans G. Storr, Philip Morris' chief financial officer. "It's camouflaging real income."

The goodwill rules also have a vastly different impact on different industries. In capital-intensive businesses, the bulk of the purchase price can be attributed to physical assets. Goodwill is not a major factor, and the write-off does not chew up earnings.

But in consumer products and media, the bulk of the purchase price is goodwill. If Time Inc. succeeds in buying Warner Communications Inc., nearly $11 billion of its $14

billion bid will result in goodwill. The write-off—and it could be more than $300 million annually—will throw Time's reported earnings into the red for several years, even though it takes no cash out of the till. "We have an accounting system that works fine for bricks and mortar," says Lee Seidler, senior managing director at Bear, Stearns & Co. "But it penalizes service companies."

Companies didn't always have to write down their goodwill. Prior to 1970, goodwill was carried at cost and cut only when there was evidence that the asset's value was diminishing. That's essentially what some would like to see today. "If you take care of it, the asset lasts indefinitely," says Roman L. Weil, professor of accounting at the University of Chicago Graduate School of Business. "But bad management can destroy it quickly, too."

Accountants made the write-off of goodwill mandatory because some managers were loath to recognize that the value of intangibles, such as brand names, had eroded. "The goodwill writeoff is only a compromise," says Arthur R. Wyatt, a partner at Arthur Andersen & Co. "But no one's yet come up with a better solution."

Unfair Advantage.

U.S. companies can also be hurt by the goodwill write-off in international deals. Seidler, among others, thinks that goodwill helped two British advertising giants, Saatchi & Saatchi PLC and WPP Group PLC, swallow up U.S. advertising agencies. As service businesses, nearly all the purchase price of the companies wound up as goodwill. The British don't have to charge it off before reporting earnings on their profit-and-loss statement. Instead, they turn directly to the balance sheet and deduct the goodwill from retained earnings. That can make a company look precariously leveraged. To remedy that problem, a few aggressive British companies have begun to shore up their balance sheets by creating an entry called intangible assets, just as it's called in the U.S. But they don't have to amortize it. The bottom line: Since the accounting for acquisitions doesn't penalize earnings, the British can outbid the U.S.

That advantage is under fire in Britain. The British Accounting Standards Committee is weighing a proposed move to a U.S.-style treatment of goodwill. That would coincide with a proposal from the International Accounting Standards Committee, which has proposed a goodwill rule that would write off the asset over five years, though the period could be extended to as much as 20 years if the company could justify it. If adopted in the U.S., that standard would be even more punishing on reported profits.

Of course, some dealmakers say that goodwill's distortion of profits doesn't matter much, because the smart money knows what's going on anyway. "We've never backed off an acquisition because of the goodwill," says Douglas H. McCorkindale, chief financial officer of Gannett Co., the media giant.

Still, McCorkindale says it has taken a long time for Wall Street to realize that goodwill "is an accounting charge without any substance." That could be true for Gannett, Philip Morris, and a few others. But if scores of companies started reporting big losses just because of goodwill, shareholders would surely start screaming.

How Goodwill Weighs on the Balance Sheets

When one company buys another, the difference between the purchase price and the fair value of the physical assets is goodwill. Most companies put it under the heading of intangible assets

(continued)

COMPANY	INTANGIBLE ASSETS	
	MILLIONS OF DOLLARS	PERCENTAGE OF NET WORTH
Viacom	$2,468	721%
Fruit of the Loom	908	352
Tele-Communications	3,143	261
Philip Morris	15,071	196
Coca-Cola Enterprises	2,935	188
Baxter International	2,705	87
Gannett	1,526	85
Dow Jones	964	83
Pepsico	2,582	82
Shearson Lehman Hutton	1,758	76
Capital Cities/ABC	2,217	73
Eastman Kodak	4,610	68
McGraw-Hill	507	55
General Electric	8,552	46
Waste Management	838	38
Chrysler	2,688	35
American Home Products	643	22
Xerox	1,089	20
General Motors	5,392	15
IBM	717	2

Data: Standard & Poor's Compustat Services Inc.

Source: Reprinted from July 31, 1989, issue of *Business Week* by special permission, copyright © 1989 by McGraw-Hill, Inc.

GOODWILL GAMES

AMY FELDMAN

Many a company would like to do what Supermarkets General Holdings Corp. just did. In one swoop the parent of Pathmark supermarkets and Rickel home-improvement stores wrote off $600 million in goodwill.

The company, which had 1992 revenues of $4.3 billion, made its move just before filing for a public offering in March. Supermarkets General probably figured that the writeoff, by boosting reported earnings, would make the issue easier to sell.

Goodwill, of course, comes with an acquisition. It is the difference between what you pay and the current value of the net assets you acquire. Thus what you pay for a brand name or reputation counts as goodwill—a so-called intangible. Under current accounting rules, U.S. companies must amortize goodwill for reporting purposes over as many as 40 years. It's a drag on earnings year after year, and until this year there was no tax benefit, since the amortization of goodwill has not been tax-deductible, as depreciation of other assets is.

Companies have argued again and again that this accounting treatment puts them at a disadvantage: Their British and German counterparts, for example, can write off goodwill against equity immediately and thus not crimp their future earnings.

How did Supermarkets General get away with its writeoff? By finding a loophole. Seems the language governing all this is murky. The accounting rule actually says that goodwill should be reevaluated more or less continually and reduced if need be. Certainly, a company that decided to sell or wind down a business it had previously acquired could get rid of the associated goodwill. The rule also gives a break to companies that suffer losses over several years and expect only lackluster results in the future. They, too, can write off part or all of the goodwill on their books.

Supermarkets General, formed in a 1987 leveraged buyout by Merrill Lynch Capital Partners, has been losing money for six years. Supermarkets General told the Securities & Exchange Commission and the company's accountants at Deloitte & Touche that its total operating income for the next 35 years, the duration of the remaining goodwill, would not reach $600 million, the amount of goodwill remaining.

A dire forecast, you might say, for a company about to tap the public markets. But you can be sure Supermarkets General peddled a different story to investors. The dismal performance was based on results at the end of 1992. But in March Supermakets General announced a restructuring that would slash debt, spin off the Rickel stores and offer to the public about one-third of the new company.

The restructuring gave a whole new look to the company's past and future. The company told investors to look at income after the effects of the restructuring. Instead of the flat sales and net losses it reported last year, Supermarkets General said that now Pathmark's net income was $42 million.

"Supermarkets General essentially told the SEC to ignore the restructuring in calculating the goodwill impairment, but told investors to feel good about it," says Lehman Brothers accounting expert Robert Willens. The accountants and SEC went along.

Before the writeoff, the goodwill amortization costs were $17 million per year. The writeoff eliminated the charge, enhancing aftertax income by that amount. Figure at 11 times earnings the change adds about $200 million to Pathmark's valuation. Pretty neat. Take a $600 million bookkeeping hit and increase the company's market value by $200 million.

Any company that posted losses in recent years but is now restructuring may be able to follow in Supermarkets General's lead. The recession and disappointing results from many LBOs give managements a plausible argument for writing down goodwill.

Now, if only the SEC and the Financial Accounting Standards Board would get the message and eliminate this accounting monstrosity once and for all for everybody.

Source: Reprinted with permission of *Forbes* magazine, September 13, 1993.

under analysis through a review of appropriate literature as well as a detailed review of the notes to the financial statements.

IMPLICATIONS OF INVENTORY COSTING METHODS

Two areas that deserve special attention are accounting for inventories and fixed assets. For the majority of businesses, these items amount to a major slice of total expenses during an accounting period.

Goods available for sale during the year either are sold or remain in inventory. Accountants generally subtract a value for ending inventory from goods available for sale in order to arrive, indirectly, at the cost of what was sold.

Accounting convention permits placing a value upon inventory in any of a number of ways. The most widely known methods are LIFO (last-in, first-out) and FIFO (first-in, first-out). LIFO assumes that the last units produced are the first sold; FIFO assumes that older units are sold first. There are no problems created by either method when prices remain the same, period to period. The difficulty arises when prices change.

LIFO assesses recent costs against sales and includes earlier costs in inventory. During periods of rising prices, the effect is to diminish profits and create a low carrying value for inventory. The result is deferral of income taxes. FIFO assesses sales with costs in the order of their origin. The cost of earlier units is charged against sales, and inventory includes recent purchases. Inventory is valued near current market value. When prices rise, profits are higher than with LIFO. The result is that taxes are paid as profits are reported, unlike LIFO, where taxes are deferred until inventory is liquidated.

Consider the following example: Allen Co. buys a product at the prevailing market price and sells it at a price 10 cents higher. The purchase price remains constant during the year. Assume that no expenses other than the cost of goods sold are incurred during the year. Let us see the effects of LIFO and FIFO inventory valuation upon (1) reported earnings, and (2) the position statement:

Units of beginning inventory (cost = $.50)			1,000
Units purchased during year (cost = $.75)			1,000
Units sold (at $.85)			1,000

	LIFO		FIFO
Sales		$850	$850
Cost of sales:			
Beginning inventory	$ 500		$ 500
Purchases	750		750
Goods available for sales	$1,250		$1,250
Less: Ending inventory:			
LIFO: (1,000 at $.50)	$ 500		
FIFO: (1,000 at $.75)			$ 750
Total cost of sales		$750	$500
Pretax profits		$100	$350
Taxes (50%)		$ 50	$175
Ending inventory		$500	$750

Rising purchase prices caused profits to be three and one-half times larger than under FIFO, and on the position statement FIFO inventory is 50 percent larger. The resulting numbers would be altered if prices and/or total sales were changed.

Most analysts would agree that during periods of advancing prices, LIFO provides a more conservative statement of income, with earnings less distorted and

patterns more easily identified, whereas FIFO tends to overstate earnings. Conversely, during periods of falling prices, the effects on the position and income statements would be the opposite.

So choice of inventory valuation method is important to the analyst, depending as it does upon the movement of prices and the nature of the industry. Firms that have large proportions of total assets devoted to inventories can affect reported earnings through the inventory method chosen. Other things being equal, firms prefer smoothed profits rather than fluctuating profits. Smoothed profits tend to produce level share prices. LIFO permits smoothing of income, while FIFO accentuates ups and downs. The analyst should be aware of the quite different effects of LIFO and FIFO on earnings, taxes, and the carrying value of inventory as price levels change.

If the results for Allen Co. under FIFO and LIFO depicted results for two different firms with equal operating results and dissimilar inventory valuation methods, it is easy to see that the company using FIFO enjoys three and one-half times the pretax profits of its counterpart. However, the LIFO company pays less than one-third the taxes of the FIFO company. Which company is economically better off?

DEPRECIATION ACCOUNTING

Net income reported on the financial statements can be affected by depreciation accounting. Depreciation recognizes that an asset will be exhausted at some point. In general, fixed assets are charged off against revenues they help create. From an analytical point of view, a problem arises in the rate at which a fixed asset is written off. Moreover, in the same firm, not all assets are depreciated on the same basis, and shifts in rate of charge-off take place over time.

The amount of annual charge for depreciation depends primarily upon the original cost of the asset, its estimated useful life, and its estimated salvage value at the end of its useful life. Fixed assets are depreciated under accounting convention on the basis of use or the basis of time. When depreciation is based upon the passage of time, so-called straight-line and/or accelerated bases of depreciation can be employed.

The straight-line method writes off depreciation uniformly over the useful life. The accelerated method recognizes that assets do not depreciate equally year by year. More likely the value of services from a fixed asset declines at an irregular rate. In other words, accelerated depreciation would permit the charge-off to be larger in the beginning and become progressively smaller.

Among the more significant benefits of this kind of charge-off is the delay in tax payments. For example, larger write-offs in the beginning reduce taxable income and, correspondingly, taxes. In later years the smaller depreciation charges result in higher taxable income, and therefore higher taxes, than with the straight-line method. Unless tax rates change appreciably over time, the *total* tax bill is the same under both methods of depreciation. However, considering the "time value" of money, accelerated depreciation affords a relative advantage over straight-line because tax payments are postponed.

In the straight-line method, the annual charge for depreciation would be calculated as

$$\text{Straight-line depreciation} = \frac{\text{Original cost} - \text{Estimated salvage}}{\text{Estimated useful life}}$$

Accelerated methods do not permit the firm to write off any more depreciation in the aggregate than does the straight-line; the rate of write-off is simply accelerated. A popular method is the declining-balance method.[4] Double-declining balance allows a charge-off of twice the straight-line rate the first year. In the second year, this doubled rate is repeated, not on original cost but on the "declining balance" (original cost less first year's depreciation), and so on. By this method, the asset is never completely written off, but the tax laws permit switching to straight-line whenever the company wishes. The only limitation is that total depreciation may not exceed the original cost of the asset.

Let us see the impact of using normal and accelerated depreciation in a common example. A company acquires $300,000 in new equipment with an estimated life of five years and no salvage value. Annual depreciation under straight-line would be $\frac{1}{5}$, or 20 percent. Declining-balance would permit $\frac{2}{5}$, or 40 percent, of undepreciated original cost each year:

YEAR	STRAIGHT-LINE DEPRECIATION	DOUBLE-DECLINING-BALANCE DEPRECIATION
1	$60,000	$120,000
2	60,000	72,000*
3	60,000	43,200
4	60,000	32,400[†]
5	60,000	32,400
Total	$300,000	$300,000

*40% ($300,000 − $120,000) = $72,000.

[†]The company reverts to straight-line depreciation here. During the fourth year, accelerated depreciation would be $25,920. Reversion to straight-line provides larger depreciation.

The different effects upon pretax profits should be obvious. If tax rates remain unchanged, taxes will be the same in the aggregate; however, they are postponed under accelerated depreciation (declining-balance).

Not all companies use the same method of computing depreciation, nor are estimates of useful life and salvage value uniform. All this is further complicated by frequent changes in depreciation guidelines by Congress and the tax authorities.

[4]Sum-of-the-years'-digits is another popular accelerated method. The digits in the estimated useful life are added together to get a denominator (e.g., 5 years is 1 + 2 + 3 + 4 + 5 = 15). First year's charges are $\frac{5}{15}$, second year's are $\frac{4}{15}$, and so on.
Under the current Internal Revenue Code a special form of accelerated depreciation, ACRS (accelerated cost recovery system) depreciation, is allowed. The code contains tables that specify the percentage depreciation allowed each year for tax purposes.

The result is great difficulty for the analyst in comparing data for a single company over time, as well as in comparing companies.

PROVISION FOR INCOME TAXES

The matching principle requires that income taxes be offset against related income, or that tax savings be offset against a related loss. Thus, in Table 6–1, income taxes related to operating income are shown separate from taxes related to extraordinary items. Just as ordinary and extraordinary income are offset by appropriate taxes, ordinary and extraordinary losses would be offset by taxes that are refundable.

During years when a loss is shown and no prior-year income is available, the tax savings could be utilized in offsetting possible income in future years. Such tax savings are, however, contingent upon future earnings and are noted in footnotes to the financial statements rather than being carried as contingent assets. If future periods produce net income, this income is reduced by appropriate taxes, and the carryover savings from prior years is shown in the income statement as extraordinary income. This procedure avoids clouding the true picture of earnings.

Certain items are treated differently on the financial statements and in the tax returns of companies. The tax expense shown on the income statement conforms to the income reported on the statements, rather than to the income reported to the tax authorities. For example, it is both legal and quite common to use accelerated depreciation on tax returns and straight-line on the financial statements. The result is that tax savings now from accelerated depreciation will be offset by higher taxes in later years. It is customary to set up a long-term or deferred tax liability for the savings, which is converted into a current liability in the future period in which the later tax is due.

Referring to our earlier example involving depreciation, recall that we contrasted depreciation under straight-line and declining-balance for new equipment costing $300,000 with a useful life of five years and no salvage value. Let us see what the tax effects would be:

YEAR	(A) STRAIGHT-LINE DEPRECIATION ON STATEMENTS	(B) DECLINING-BALANCE DEPRECIATION ON TAX RETURN	(C) ADDED TAXES OR (SAVINGS) AT 50% RATE USING (B)
1	$ 60,000	$120,000	($30,000)
2	60,000	72,000	(6,000)
3	60,000	43,200	8,400
4	60,000	32,400	13,800
5	60,000	32,400	
Total	$300,000	$300,000	

Assume that net income before depreciation and taxes in year 1 was $500,000. The tax rate is 50 percent. Using accelerated depreciation on the tax return results in a tax bill of $190,000 [½($500,000 − $120,000)]. Straight-line depreciation on the income statement for stockholders reporting would result in taxable income of $220,000 [½($500,000 − $60,000)]. To "normalize" the effect of the dif-

ference between the tax expense shown ($220,000) and taxes actually owed ($190,000), a $30,000 deferred liability would be shown on the balance sheet. In year 2, the difference between tax expense and taxes owed would be $6,000. The deferred tax liability account at the end of year 2 would be $36,000 ($30,000 + $6,000). Between year 3 and the end of year 5, the deferred tax liability would reduce to zero.

Earnings per Share

In order to determine earnings per share, the analyst must first calculate the number of common shares outstanding, as follows. First, the number of shares issued is reduced by the number of treasury shares; these are common stock sold at one time but subsequently repurchased by the company, often with the intention of reissue. Second, a weighted average is used when stock transactions involving asset accounts have taken place during the period. For example, if 1 million shares are outstanding at the beginning of the period, and 200,000 shares are sold July 1 (midyear) for cash (an asset), the weighted-average number of shares would be 1.1 million [1,000,000 + ½(200,000)].[5]

Third, when stock transactions take place that do *not* involve assets, such as stock dividends or splits, the new number of shares is treated as being effective from the beginning of the year. For example, 1 million shares are outstanding. In November a 20 percent stock dividend is declared. The weighted-average number of shares at year-end would still be 1.2 million.

Once we have determined the number of common shares outstanding, the net income after taxes is customarily translated into a per-share-of-ownership equivalent, in order to compare firms on a common-size basis. Firms A and B may each have earnings of $1 million. However, if A has 1 million shares outstanding and B has only 500,000, firm A would have earnings per share of $1, and B of $2.

The increasing use of securities that are convertible into common shares and of stock options through warrants creates the overhang, or contingent creation of new common shares, as conversion privileges, warrants, or other options are exercised. The existence of such contingent shares is now being recognized in financial reporting by the calculation of two supplementary earnings-per-share figures. One is called *primary earnings* per share, the other *secondary* or *fully diluted earnings* per share. Primary earnings per share reflects the assumption that all options and warrants are exercised, but reflects convertible securities *only* if at the time of issuance their value by the market was mostly due to conversion privilege. For example, if a convertible bond issue is sold at a price that yields investors 6 percent to maturity while similar bonds without conversion rights are selling to yield 10 percent, it might be said that the convertible bonds were purchased more for their option feature than as straight bonds. The other earnings per share (EPS) figure, fully

---

[5] 200,000 shares sold April 15 would be outstanding for 8½ months, or about 7/10 of a year. Weighted-average total shares would be 1 million plus 140,000, or 1,140,000.

diluted or secondary earnings per share, assumes that *all* options, warrants, and convertibles were turned into stock. In effect, secondary earnings would represent the most conservative statement of EPS and would be less than or equal to primary earnings per share.

For the analyst, it is important to recognize (1) that there are multiple earnings-per-share figures, and (2) that secondary earnings per share represent the most reasonable statement of earnings, taking into account all contingent shares. Below are shown abbreviated statements for 19X8 for a company with convertible bonds and preferred stock outstanding. Regular earnings per share are shown.

INCOME STATEMENT		BALANCE SHEET	
Operating income	$4,200,000	4% convertible bonds (convertible	
Interest expense	400,000	into 500,000 shares of common)	$10 million
Earnings before taxes	$3,800,000		
Taxes (50%)	1,900,000	5% preferred (convertible into	
Net income	$1,900,000	500,000 shares of common)	$5 million
Preferred dividends	250,000		
Earnings to common	$1,650,000	Common (1,600,000 shares)	$8 million
Earnings per share	$1.03		

If we assume that the preferred at the time of issue was *not* sold mainly because of the conversion option but the bonds were, then primary earnings per share would be:

Operating earnings		$4,200,000
Taxes (50%)		2,100,000
Net income		2,100,000
Preferred dividends		250,000
Earnings to common		1,850,000
Shares:		
Bonds	500,000	
Common	1,600,000	2,100,000 shares
Earnings per share		$.88

Fully diluted or secondary earnings per share (all convertibles assumed converted) would be:

Operating earnings		$4,200,000
Taxes (50%)		2,100,000
Earnings to common		2,100,000
Shares:		
Bonds	500,000	
Preferred	500,000	
Common	1,600,000	2,600,000 shares
Earnings per share		$.81

INTERIM EARNINGS REPORTS

Quarterly reports to stockholders are an effort to provide disclosure of the continuous nature of corporate developments. The Financial Analysts Federation surveys reveal that the majority of investment analysts regard interim data of equal or greater importance than annual data. In the main, quarterly reports are used by analysts to update and adjust projections of future performance. However, problems arise when using these reports.

Quarterly reports are generally not audited. This creates problems with respect to outside, independent control over proper matching of revenues and expenses. Income can be "managed" by not segregating nonrecurring income, or by cutting off sales and related costs at different times. The brief time period involved in quarterly reports creates problems of proper estimation and proration of many items that are difficult enough to assess on an annual basis. Shortened time periods lead to more arbitrary period allocations. Further, interim reports do not contain information on changes in accounting methods and retroactive adjustments.

The usual interim or quarterly financial report is a very abbreviated earnings statement and balance sheet. The analyst would no doubt have more confidence in interim data if full and complete statements (including a funds statement) were provided, with an auditor's certification. Although the SEC has discussed requiring quarterly financial statements to at least be reviewed by outside auditors, no definitive requirement has yet been issued.

OTHER TOPICS

The analyst should be familiar with several other key areas in income statement analysis. However, these topics also have a profound influence on the balance sheet, and we will therefore defer the discussion of these recent developments in financial statement analysis and deal with them in a separate section later in this chapter. The topics that will be discussed include accounting for foreign currency transactions, reporting the financial results of various segments of a business enterprise, and deferred income taxes. Let us now turn our attention to the balance sheet.

NASTY SURPRISES

PENELOPE WANG

Manufactured Homes, Inc., looked like a steady winner for most of 1987. In the first nine months the North Carolina prefab house manufacturer reported pretax earnings of $10.6 million on sales of $148.2 million. But in its fourth quarter the company abruptly booked an enormous $8.5 million loss reserve for credit sales, wip-

ing out those earlier quarterly earnings and ending the year with an anemic pretax $1.6 million.

Was management as surprised as investors? No. Manufactured Homes had been understating its potential credit losses. The outside auditing firm of Peat Marwick Main & Co. believed that to be the case months earlier, and had urged an increase in loss reserves. Management resisted—and management got its way, since corporate quarterly, or 10–Q, reports, unlike annual reports, do not require auditor approval. Come the fourth quarter, the company at last had to bite the bullet. Says Glenn Perry, partner at Peat Marwick, "If we had a requirement to formally review quarterly data, we wouldn't have had a surprise fourth-quarter adjustment."

The situation at Manufactured Homes is not unique. "Misleading quarterly statements have been a persistent problem, particularly among smaller companies," says Glen Davison, deputy chief accountant at the Securities & Exchange Commission. Indeed, last year the SEC took enforcement actions against several companies, including Stereo Village and Cali Computer Systems, largely because of false or misleading quarterly reports.

But these actions were taken after the horse was gone; now the SEC is preparing to close the barn door. In the next month or so the commission is expected to release a proposal requiring that all quarterly reports be "reviewed" on a timely basis by outside auditors. The rule could go into effect as soon as early 1990.

What does the SEC have in mind when it says "review"? As commission officials explain it, outside auditors would check the numbers in quarterly statements and, based on prior auditing experience with the firm, would then question senior management about items that seem out of line. Such problem areas might include unusually large inventories compared with year-ago figures, or steadily increasing accounts receivable. The SEC proposal, in addition, would require the auditors to submit a letter saying that the numbers were reviewed, which would be included on the 10–Q report.

Unlike a full-scale audit, a quarterly review would not require accountants to examine documentation or seek third-party corroboration about management's numbers. Nonetheless, the SEC proposal is an important step in the right direction to tighten lax reporting rules. Currently, only large, actively traded public companies must publish audited quarterly data, and at that, only once a year in their annual 10–K financial reports to shareholders. Gaylen N. Larson, group vice president of Household International, comments: "The key is simply to encourage outside accountants to discuss judgmental issues with senior management."

Will this prevent future unpleasant surprises? Not all of them. "Even audits can fail to turn up fraud or mismanagement, so how can a review make a difference?" asks Thornton O'glove, publisher of *The Quality of Earnings Report,* an institutional research newsletter. "Too often auditors are ready to sign off on anything that seems halfway reasonable." Moreover, many smaller companies complain that the increased costs of the review effort would outweigh any benefits.

There is some slight merit in these complaints, but not much. In these days of jumpy markets, unpleasant surprises can cost investors dearly, souring them permanently on the stock market. "The value of the quarterly is becoming just as important to the public as the annual report," comments Household's Larson. "So why not spread out the auditing effort through the year rather than just at the year-end?"

Source: Reprinted by permission of *Forbes* magazine, January 23, 1989. © Forbes Inc., 1989.

Financial Position: The Balance Sheet

The level, trend, and stability of earnings are powerful forces in the determination of security prices. This *flow* of earnings is depicted on the income statement. The *stock* of assets and the claims to those assets that provide the fuel for those earnings are revealed on the balance sheet. The balance sheet shows, at a given point in time, the assets, liabilities, and owners' equity in a company. It is the analyst's primary source of information on the financial strength of a company.

Assets include properties and rights to properties, both tangible (such as buildings) and intangible (such as patents and goodwill). Liabilities are debts that are payable on demand or over specified future periods. They are evidenced by simple invoices or rather lengthy legal documents, such as mortgages. The equity of stockholders represents the excess of assets over liabilities at the balance-sheet date.

Modern accounting principles dictate the basis for assigning values to assets. Liability values are set by contracts. When assets are reduced by liabilities, the "book value" of stockholders' equity can be determined. This book value invariably differs from current value in the marketplace because market value is dependent upon the earning power of assets and not their cost or value in the accounts.

THE COST PRINCIPLE

For the most part, the accounting concept of conservatism requires that assets be carried at original or historical cost when they are first acquired. During subsequent time periods, they may be valued at cost or market, whichever is lower.

Income-statement and reported-earnings problems can stem from the rate at which assets are written off against related revenues, a matter we discussed under inventory and depreciation accounting. In addition, the framework of historical cost does not make reference to the changing purchasing power of the dollar. When inflation occurs, historical-dollar accounting can be unrealistic and deficient.

First, the income statement fails to express all items in dollars of the same purchasing power. For example, revenues closely represent current dollars, whereas FIFO inventory costing would represent "old" dollars. Needless to say, over time interperiod comparability is destroyed.

Second, assets and stockholders' equity reflect an admixture of items shown in dollars of different purchasing power. For example, FIFO inventory procedures might tend to show inventories in near-current dollars, but fixed assets may be worth many times their carrying value. These distortions in asset groups are similarly reflected in the stockholders'-equity section of the balance sheet. The erosion of the purchasing power of the dollar affects measurements using the balance sheet and influences "real" earning power.

BALANCE-SHEET FORMAT

See Table 6-2 for a balance-sheet format. It is in *account form,* with assets on the left side of the page and liabilities and stockholders' equity on the right side. Total assets equals total liabilities plus stockholders' equity.

Table 6–2

BALANCE SHEET

DECEMBER 31, 19X0, AND DECEMBER 31, 19X1

ASSETS	LIABILITIES AND EQUITY
Current assets:	Current liabilities:
Cash and securities	Accounts payable
Receivables	Accrued wages
Inventories	Taxes payable
Prepaid expenses	Long-term liabilities:
Permanent investments:	Long-term notes
Investments in other companies	Bonds payable
Realty held for investment	Stockholders' equity:
Fixed tangible assets:	Capital stock
Buildings	Additional paid-in capital
Land	Retained earnings
Machinery and equipment	
Furniture and fixtures	
Fixed intangible assets:	
Goodwill	
Patents	
Deferred charges to expense:	
Organization costs	
Total Assets	Total Liabilities and Stockholders' Equity

Discussion of other problems the analyst faces in using the balance sheet will be explored in the analysis of fixed-income securities in Chapter 10.

Notes to Financial Statements

Most accounting statements deal with rather arbitrary cutoff points in time.[6] Thus, *accounting statements cannot be considered complete* without parenthetical references and notes that not only clarify the data in the body of the statements but also introduce new information not conveniently admissible within the statements proper.

Quite often, valuation bases for assets are shown next to the item caption or in footnotes. Parenthetical references should be examined to note where assets have been pledged and the related liability secured.

Footnotes to the balance sheet often show many of the following items of importance to the analyst.[7]

1. Contingent liabilities for taxes, dividends, and pending lawsuits.

---

[6]Calendar and fiscal years are based upon custom and operating convenience.

[7]J.A. Mauriello, *Accounting for the Financial Analyst,* rev. ed., C.F.A. Monograph Series (Homewood, Ill.: Richard D. Irwin, 1971), p. 35.

2. Particulars on options outstanding, leases, loans, and other financing arrangements.

3. Changes in accounting principles and techniques, including bases of valuation, and the dollar effect on income.

4. Facts of importance occurring between the balance-sheet data and date of submission of statements that might have a material effect on the statements. Examples include refinancing, proposed mergers, and changes in capitalization.

The analyst will find a wealth of information in these parenthetical references and footnotes that can shed light on the company under analysis.

Statement of Cash Flows

In November 1987 the FASB issued new standards requiring a company to provide, as part of a complete set of financial statements, a statement of cash flows in place of the statement of changes in financial position.[8] A variety of factors led to the issuance of the new standards. First, information about a company's cash flows has become increasingly recognized as a very useful analytical tool in all types of investment and credit decisions. In addition, the statement of changes in financial position suffered from a variety of flaws, including ambiguity of terms and lack of consistency and comparability, which limited its analytical usefulness.

According to the FASB, the purpose of the statement of cash flows is

. . . to provide relevant information about the cash receipts and cash payments of an enterprise during a period.

The information provided in the statement of cash flows, if used with related disclosures and information in the other financial statements, should help investors, creditors and others to (a) assess the enterprise's ability to generate positive future net cash flows; (b) assess the enterprise's ability to meet its obligations, its ability to pay dividends, and its need for external financing; (c) assess the reasons for differences between net income and associated cash receipts and payments; and (d) assess the effects on an enterprise's financial position of both its cash and noncash investing and financing transactions during the period.[9]

The basic ingredients for the statement of cash flows come from the balance sheet, income statement, statement of retained earnings, and certain other supplementary data. Table 6–3 shows very simple income and position statements, and Table 6–4 is a statement of cash flows prepared from Table 6–3 for the Douglas

---

[8]Financial Accounting Standards Board, *Statement of Financial Accounting Standards No. 95, Statement of Cash Flows* (Stamford, Conn.: FASB, 1987).
[9]*Ibid.*, p. 2.

Table 6–3

SIMPLIFIED INCOME AND COMPARATIVE BALANCE SHEETS
($ IN THOUSANDS)

DOUGLAS CORP.
INCOME STATEMENT
YEAR ENDED DECEMBER 31, 19X1

Net Sales	$1,000
Expenses (including taxes)	775
Net income	$ 25
Dividends paid	100
Transferred to retained earnings	$ 125

DOUGLAS CORP.
COMPARATIVE BALANCE SHEETS
DECEMBER 31, 19X0, AND DECEMBER 31, 19X1

	19X1	19X0	CHANGE
Assets:			
Current assets:			
Cash	$ 150	$ 120	+30
Receivables	150	200	−50
Inventories	200	180	+20
Total current assets	$ 500	$ 500	
Tangible fixed assets:			
Plant and equipment	$1,935	$1,700	+235
Less: Accumulated depreciation	(500)	(350)	+150
Net tangible fixed assets	$1,435	$1,350	+85
Total Assets	$1,935	$1,850	
Liabilities and stockholders' equity:			
Current liabilities:			
Accounts payable	$ 150	$ 125	+25
Accrued taxes and wages	35	105	−70
Total current liabilities	$ 185	$ 230	
Long-term liabilities:			
Nonconvertible bonds	$ 300	$ 295	+5
Convertible bonds	150	200	−50
Total long-term liabilities	$ 450	$ 495	
Stockholders' equity:			
Capital stock	$ 170	$ 150	+20
Additional paid-in capital	580	550	+30
Retained earnings	550	425	+125
Total stockholders' equity	$1,300	$1,125	
Total Liabilities and Stockholders' Equity	$1,935	$1,850	

Table 6–4

DOUGLAS CORPORATION: STATEMENT OF CASH FLOWS, YEAR ENDED DECEMBER 31, 19X1 ($ IN THOUSANDS)

Cash flows from operating activities:		
Net income		$225
Adjustments to reconcile net income to net cash provided by operating activities:		
Depreciation	150	
Changes in assets and liabilities:		
Decrease in accounts receivable	50	
Increase in inventories	<20>	
Increase in accounts payable	25	
Decrease in accrued wages	<70>	
Total adjustment		135
Net cash provided by operating activities:		360
Cash flows from investing activities:		
Purchase of fixed assets	<335>	
Proceeds from sale of fixed assets	100	
Net cash used in investing activities:		<235>
Cash flows from financing activities:		
Payment of dividends	<100>	
Proceeds from issuance of bonds	5	
Net cash used in financing activities:		<95>
Net increase in cash:		30
Cash at beginning of year		120
Cash at end of year		$150

Supplemental disclosure of cash-flow information
Cash paid during the year for:

Interest	$ 50
Income taxes	$150

Supplemental schedule of noncash investing and financing activities
Additional common stock was issued upon the conversion of $50 of convertible bonds.

Note: The statement of cash flows is prepared using the indirect method of FASB No. 95. For information on the direct method, which provides more specific information on cash receipts and cash expenditures, the reader should consult FASB No. 95 or any recent basic accounting text.

Corp. Certain detail on transactions not found directly in the income statement or balance sheet is required to prepare the statement of cash flows. This information appears in Table 6–4 but cannot be traced directly to Table 6–3.

The statement of cash flows displays changes in working capital, as well as changes traced to noncurrent assets, long-term liabilities, and stockholders' equity. Let us examine Table 6–4. There are three main subdivisions in the statement: cash flow from operating activities, financing activities, and investing activities.

The primary cash flow from operating activities will generally consist of income for the period. Other operating activities providing or using cash have been defined by the FASB to consist of all transactions not specifically defined to be an investing or financing activity. The more common of these items would include the add-back of noncash depreciation expense and changes in working capital accounts. Cash flows from investing activities include, among others, the proceeds or disbursements relating to the sale or purchase of equity investments in other companies and the proceeds or disbursements for the sale or purchase of property, plant, and equipment by the enterprise. Cash flows from financing activities include the proceeds from the sale of equity securities or the issuance of debt, and the disbursement of cash for dividends, stock repurchases, or repayment of debt.

USE OF STATEMENT BY ANALYST

The statement of cash flows discloses clearly and individually the significant operating, financing, and investing activities of the company during an accounting period, giving the analyst an overall view of the financial management of a company and its policies. The statement may help to answer some of the following questions.

1. How much cash was generated from operations?
2. How were dividends possible despite a loss for the period?
3. How can the company be experiencing cash-flow problems while reporting such large profits?
4. Why are dividends not larger (or smaller)?
5. How were fixed-asset additions financed?
6. Why was additional debt financing necessary?
7. What was the change in working capital and how was it financed?

Comparing statements over the past provides insight into patterns that may or may not be followed in the years ahead. The statement of cash flows is a valuable supplement to the balance sheet and income statement. The analyst should probe it thoroughly.

Consolidated Financial Statements

Very often, certain operating units of a parent company are not owned 100 percent. That is, the voting common stock is shared with third parties, often other companies. Where 50 percent or more of the voting common stock is held by the parent company, the company held is referred to as a *subsidiary*. Less than 50 percent control results in an *affiliated* company. An *associated* company is a company owned jointly by two other companies.

A holding company may own anywhere from a small fraction up to 100 percent of another company. Where the percentage of ownership exceeds 50 percent, accountants strongly recommend that company statements be consolidated. Al-

though there are certain refinements in the process, consolidation means adding the statements of the companies together. The portion of the equity that is not owned by the consolidator, or holding company, is shown as a "minority-interest" liability on the balance sheet. Net income on the statement of income is reduced by the portion accruing to minority interests.

Where ownership of voting common stock is between 20 and 50 percent, the accounting profession adopts the view that the holding company has effective control of dividend policy of the subsidiary. Thus the initial cost of the investment in the subsidiary stock is shown separately as a long-term investment under *Assets* on the holding company's balance sheet. As time passes, the investment account is adjusted upward for the holding company's share of subsidiary profits, and downward for its share in subsidiary losses and for dividends received. This is referred to as the *equity method* of accounting for subsidiaries. For ownership of less than 20 percent, if it can be shown that the holding company and the affiliate are two separate units and that effective control is not exercised by the holding company, then the *cost method* of accounting for subsidiaries is permitted. The investment in affiliate shares is shown at cost on the balance sheet. Dividends received are treated as income.

The essential difference between the cost and equity methods is that the former does not generally adjust the investment up and down for profits and losses, less dividends. More significantly, on the income statement only dividends received are shown, and not the parent's portion of total income. This latter provision can lead to abuses, by which dividend declarations by subsidiaries or affiliates can be regulated to affect the parent's earnings. The following example illustrates the use of the *equity method* of accounting for subsidiaries.

EXAMPLE.   The Melicher Corp. purchased 40 percent of the voting common stock of the Rush Co. one year ago, at a cost of $5 million. At that time, Melicher's balance sheet showed "Investments in affiliates, $5,000,000." During the past year, Rush had after-tax earnings of $250,000. It declared dividends on common shares of $100,000. The holding company's share of profits and dividends is $100,000 and $40,000 respectively. Melicher would show the net difference between its share of profits and dividends received, $60,000, as an addition to its investment account. The account would now show a total of $5,060,000. The reason for netting profits and dividends received can be seen in another way. Rush Co. will show an increase in its assets and retained earnings of $150,000, or after-tax earnings of $250,000 less dividends of $100,000 paid. Melicher's share of these assets and retained earnings is 40 percent, or $60,000.

The Auditor's Opinion

Investors and investment analysts look to an independent certified public accounting firm to attest to the financial statements we have been discussing. The certified public accountant (CPA), after conducting his examination, renders an opinion on the financial statements. An example of the general wording of an auditor's typical "unqualified" opinion follows:

We have audited the balance sheet of MLK Corp. as of December 31, 19X8, and the related statement of earnings, stockholders' equity, and cash flows for the year then ended. These financial statements are the responsibility of the company's management. Our responsibility is to express an opinion on these financial statements based on our audits.

We conducted our audits in accordance with generally accepted auditing standards. Those standards require that we plan and perform the audit to obtain reasonable assurance about whether the financial statements are free of material misstatement. An audit includes examining, on a test basis, evidence supporting the amounts and disclosures in the financial statements. An audit also includes assessing the accounting principles used and significant estimates made by management, as well as evaluating the overall financial statement presentation. We believe that our audits provide a reasonable basis for our opinion.

In our opinion, the financial statements referred to above present fairly, in all material respects, the financial position of MLK Corp. as of December 31, 19X8, and the results of its operations and its cash flows for the year then ended in conformity with generally accepted accounting principles.

This unqualified opinion, which would generally be addressed to the board of directors of the corporation, often is mistakenly taken as a *guaranty* from the CPA that the statements are 100 percent accurate. This is *not* true. You will note that the opinion explicitly states that the financial statements are the responsibility of management. The auditor has reviewed the content of the statements and has not prepared or guaranteed these statements. Furthermore, the opinion goes on to say that the examination was conducted in accordance with certain prescribed auditing standards and that the auditor performed those tests he considered necessary. Thus the reader is made aware of the existence of specific rules that auditors must follow, and the fact that the auditor *does* exercise subjective opinion in judgment. Nonetheless, the fact that the auditor does issue this type of opinion should give some consolation to the reader that these statements and notes have been subjected to stringent external review.

When circumstances do not permit the issuance of such an unqualified opinion, the auditor has a number of other types of opinions that he can issue. The board of directors of the corporation or its auditing committee, however, would usually prefer that the auditor issue an unqualified opinion, and they therefore tend to cooperate with the auditor in every way possible so that he can do so.[10]

We have already discussed many key accounting conventions or *generally accepted accounting principles*. These rules become "generally accepted" in two main ways: (1) by authoritative pronouncements from such bodies as the FASB and the SEC, and (2) by widespread usage and custom among respected CPAs.

---

[10]The reader who is interested in learning more about the other types of possible opinions should consult the AICPA's *Statements on Auditing Standards* (New York: AICPA, 1977), or any basic auditing textbook.

STILL PUSSYFOOTING

SUBRATA N. CHAKRAVARTY

It used to be that when auditors caught their corporate clients lying, the Form 8–K protected both parties from an embarrassing public row. Form 8–K? That's the document that management must file with the Securities & Exchange Commission explaining why it has changed auditors. Generally the departing auditor must also comment on management's explanation.

These filings used to be as dull and unrevealing as minutes from a Rumanian agricultural committee meeting. But they're getting a lot less so. A rule implemented by the SEC last year, but only now showing up in filings, requires outside auditors to be much more specific on why they resign an account. And if you miss the 8–K, don't worry: The substance of the auditor/client disagreements must now also be reported in a company's annual proxy statement.

This makes for some spicy reading. Consider this passage from the 8–K filed in May 1988 by New York's Bombay Palace Restaurants, Inc. (FORBES, *Aug. 22, 1988)*:

"On Apr. 18, 1988, Peat Marwick advised the company that it could no longer rely on the representations of management and thus resigned as the company's auditors." And in an extraordinarily blunt follow-up letter to the SEC, the auditors said they had discovered "invoice documentation prepared by the company to be false and inaccurate."

In sum, Peat Marwick Main & Co. was saying, they dropped Bombay Palace because management lied. The SEC's enforcement division began an investigation of Bombay Palace in January.

"We're not making a legal judgment," says Peat Marwick's Associate General Counsel John Shutkin. "We came to a conclusion about the integrity of management." In other words, we don't trust the rascals.

Are the accountants finally becoming what many people have long thought them to be: corporate policemen, responsible for digging out managerial wrongdoing? The answer here is definitely no. Independent auditors don't—can't—check every transaction and every invoice. The cost of doing so would be prohibitive.

What that means, of course, is that the auditor's letter certifying a company's books merely signifies that the auditors came across no specific instances of wrongdoings and found no reasons for distrusting management's words. It doesn't guarantee that everything is kosher; only that the auditor found nothing that wasn't kosher. "What the reader [of financial statements] infers is that the opinion letter is a Good Housekeeping Seal of Approval [of the accuracy of the financial statements]," says John Shank, Noble Professor of management accounting at the Tuck School of Business at Dartmouth. "But what the opinion really says is vacuous and innocuous: "We did what auditors do, and nothing came to our attention that would suggest that things are not okay."

For an example of how pussyfooting the auditor's opinion can sometimes be, look at Convenient Food Mart, Inc., a Rosemont, Ill.-based chain of retail convenience stores. In an 8–K filed in February, management reported that the company's auditors, Laventhol & Horwath, had conducted a study of the company's internal controls back in the spring of 1988. That study concluded that Convenient Food Mart's internal accounting system was such a mess that Laventhol couldn't be sure of the accuracy of the company's financial statements. Nevertheless, Laventhol issued an unqualified opinion on the company's 1987 results. Then, three months later, after management began an investigation

of its books, Laventhol withdrew that opinion. The company later restated its results to reflect numerous accounting errors. In January 1989 Laventhol quit the account altogether. In other words, Laventhol's certification was meaningless. Both Laventhol and the company are being sued.

Should the accountants take responsibility for rooting out managerial messes and evildoings? Peat Marwick's Shutkin says this is not practical, given current auditing standards. "You can perform an audit entirely consistent with Generally Accepted Auditing Standards and not detect a fraud that exists," says Shutkin. "That's simply the way life is."

Source: Reprinted with permission of *Forbes* magazine, August 21, 1989. © Forbes Inc., 1989.

We will now discuss some new reporting requirements which the accounting profession feels are necessary in order to better inform the investment community.

Key Changes in Generally Accepted Accounting Principles Affecting Investment Analysis

In the sections that follow we will briefly describe several major recent developments and changes in generally accepted accounting principles. The reader should understand that these are merely some of the changes that have occurred that affect the financial statements. However, we believe we have selected those specific changes whose effect will be most widely felt in the investment community.

ACCOUNTING FOR FOREIGN CURRENCY

In 1981 the FASB restated standards of financial accounting and reporting for the translation of foreign currency transactions and foreign currency financial statements.[11] The FASB felt that because of the U.S. dollar devaluations and the institution of "floating" exchange rates, standards reflecting these financial dealings needed to be developed.

FINANCIAL REPORTING FOR SEGMENTS OF THE BUSINESS ENTERPRISE

In December 1976 the FASB issued its *Statement No. 14, Financial Reporting for Segments of a Business Enterprise.*[12] The FASB recognized that businesses have continually broadened their base of operations into various industries, foreign countries, and various markets within countries. The FASB felt that it was necessary for financial statements to include information about the corporation's busi-

---

[11]Financial Accounting Standards Board, *Statement of Financial Accounting Standards No. 52, Foreign Currency Translation* (Stamford, Conn.: FASB, 1981).

[12]Financial Accounting Standards Board, *Statement of Financial Accounting Standards No. 14, Financial Reporting for Segments of a Business Enterprise* (Stamford, Conn.: FASB, 1976).

ness as it occurred in different industries, in different countries, and to various major customers when the firm issues a *complete* set of statements that present financial position, and so forth. *Statement No. 14,* perhaps more than any other statement that the FASB has issued to date, reflects the accounting profession's growing awareness of the need for various types of information for various reasons—particularly among the investment community. It is of considerable interest to students of the securities markets to note the wording the FASB used in explaining why it had issued *No. 14:*

> Financial statement users point out that the evaluation of risk and return is the central element of investment and lending decisions—the greater the perceived degree of risk associated with an investment or lending alternative, the greater is the required rate of return to the investor or lender. If return is defined as expected cash flows to the investor or creditor, the evaluation of risk involves assessment of the uncertainty surrounding both the timing and the amount of the expected cash flows to the enterprise, which in turn are indicative of potential cash flows to the investor or creditor. Users of financial statements indicate that uncertainty results, in part, from factors unique to the particular enterprise in which an investment may be made or to which credit may be extended. Uncertainty also results, in part, from factors related to the industries and geographic areas in which the enterprise operates and, in part, from national and international economic and political factors. Investors and lenders analyze factors at all of those levels to evaluate the risk and return associated with an investment or lending alternative.
>
> Information contained in an enterprise's financial statements constitutes an important input to that analysis. Financial statements provide information about conditions, trends, and ratios that assist in predicting cash flows. In analyzing an enterprise, a financial statement user often compares information about the enterprise with information about other enterprises, with industry-wide information, and with national or international economic information in general. Those comparisons are helpful in determining whether a given enterprise's operations may be expected to move with, against, or independently of developments in its industry and in the economy within which it operates.
>
> The broadening of an enterprise's activities into different industries or geographic areas complicates the analysis of conditions, trends, and ratios and, therefore, the ability to predict. The various industry segments or geographic areas of operations of an enterprise may have different rates of profitability, degrees and types of risk, and opportunities for growth. There may be differences in the rates of return on the investment commitment in the various industry segments or geographic areas and in their future capital demands.[13]

The principal disclosure requirements of *Statement No. 14* are sales and revenue, operating profit or loss, and identifiable assets. Information relating to these

---

[13]*Ibid.,* pp. 27–28.

Exhibit A

X COMPANY—CONSOLIDATED INCOME STATEMENT, YEAR ENDED DECEMBER 31, 19X7

Sales		$4,700
Cost of sales	$3,000	
Selling, general, and administrative expense	700	
Interest expense	200	3,900
		800
Equity in net income of Z Co. (25% owned)		100
Income from continuing operations before income taxes		900
Income taxes		400
Income from continuing operations		500
Discontinued operations:		
Loss from operations of discontinued West Coast division (net of income tax effect of $50)	70	
Loss on disposal of West Coast division (net of income tax effect of $100)	130	200
Income before extraordinary gain and before cumulative effect of change in accounting principle		300
Extraordinary gain (net of income tax effect of $80)		90
Cumulative effect on prior years of change from straightline to accelerated depreciation (net of income tax effect of $60)		(60)
Net income		$ 330

Source: Copyright © by Financial Accounting Standards Board, High Ridge Park, Stamford, CT 06905, U.S.A. Reprinted with permission. Copies of the document are available from the FASB.

specific items must be identified with specific industry segments. This required information must be presented in the body of the financial statement, or in its footnotes, or in a separate schedule that is clearly an integral part of the financial statements. The example in Exhibits A and B are taken from FASB *No. 14* and indicate what this new information and notes for this new information should look like.[14]

To be identified as a recordable segment, an industry segment must be significant to the business as a whole. An industry segment must be recorded separately if it satisfies one or more of the following tests:

1. Its revenue (including both sales to unaffiliated customers and intersegment sales or transfers) is 10 percent or more of the combined revenue (sales to unaffiliated customers and intersegment sales or transfers) of all of the enterprise's industry segments.

2. The absolute amount of its operating profit or operating loss is 10 percent or more of the greater, in absolute amount, of:

   a. the combined operating profit of all industry segments that did not incur an operating loss, or

[14]*Ibid.*, pp. 53–56.

Exhibit B

X COMPANY—INFORMATION ABOUT THE COMPANY'S
OPERATIONS IN DIFFERENT INDUSTRIES,
YEAR ENDED DECEMBER 31, 19X7

	INDUS-TRY A	INDUS-TRY B	INDUS-TRY C	OTHER INDUS-TRIES	ADJUST-MENTS AND ELIMI-NATIONS	CONSOLI-DATED
Sales to unaffiliated customers	$1,000	$2,000	$1,500	$ 200		$ 4,700
Intersegment sales	200		500		$(700)	
Total revenue	$1,200	$2,000	$2,000	$ 200	$(700)	$ 4,700
Operating profit	$ 200	$ 290	$ 600	$ 50	$ (40)	$ 1,100
Equity in net income of Z Co.						100
General corporate expenses						(100)
Interest expense						(200)
Income from continuing opera-tions before income taxes						$ 900
Identifiable assets at December 31, 1977	$2,000	$4,050	$6,000	$1,000	$ (50)	$13,000
Investment in net assets of Z Co.						400
Corporate assets						1,600
Total assets at December 31, 1977						$15,000

See accompanying note.

Note: The company operates principally in three industries, A, B, and C. Operations in Industry A involve production and sale of (describe types of products and services). Operations in Industry B involve production and sale of (describe types of products and services). Operations in Industry C involve production and sale of (describe types of products and services). Total revenue by industry includes both sales to unaffiliated customers, as reported in the company's consolidated income statement, and intersegment sales, which are accounted for by unaffiliated customers, as reported in the company's consolidated income statement, and intersegment sales, which are accounted for by (describe the basis of accounting for intersegment sales).

Operating profit is total revenue less operating expenses. In computing operating profit, none of the following items has been added or deducted: general corporate expenses, interest expense, income taxes, equity in income from unconsolidated investee, loss from discontinued operations of the West Coast division (which was a part of the company's operations in Industry B), extraordinary gain (which relates to the company's operations in Industry A), and the cumulative effect of the change from straight-line to accelerated depreciation (of which $30 relates to the company's operations in Industry A, $10 to Industry B, and $20 to Industry C). Depreciation for Industries A, B, and C, respectively, was $80, $100, and $150. Capital expenditures for the three industries were $100, $200, and $400, respectively.

The effect of the change from straight-line to accelerated depreciation was to reduce the 1977 operating profit of Industries A, B, and C, respectively, by $40, $30, and $20.

Identifiable assets by industry are those assets that are used in the company's operations in each industry. Corporate assets are principally cash and marketable securities.

The company has a 25 percent interest in Z Co., whose operations are in the United States and are vertically integrated with the company's operations in Industry A. Equity in net income of Z Co. was $100; investment in net assets of Z Co. was $400.

To reconcile industry information with consolidated amounts, the following eliminations have been made: $700 of intersegment sales; $40 relating to the net change in intersegment operating profit in beginning and ending inventories; and $50 intersegment operating profit in inventory at December 31, 1977.

Contracts with a U.S. government agency account for $1,100 of the sales to unaffiliated customers of Industry B.

Source: Copyright © by Financial Accounting Standards Board, High Ridge Park, Stamford, CT 06905, U.S.A. Reprinted with permission. Copies of the complete document are available from the FASB.

b. the combined operating loss of all industry segments that did incur an operating loss.

3. Its identifiable assets are 10 percent or more of the combined identifiable assets of all industry segments.[15]

Clearly, the impact of FASB *Statement No. 14* on financial statement users has been monumental. This new information greatly assists analysts not only in examining and understanding the past performance of the business as a whole but also in forecasting the future. While consolidated information is important, understanding the makeup of this consolidated information as defined in FASB *Statement No. 14* greatly benefits the investment community.

DEFERRED INCOME TAXES

Deferred income taxes generally arise whenever a revenue or expense item is recognized for financial accounting purposes in a different period than when it is recognized for tax accounting purposes. Some of the more common causes of deferred income taxes include using accelerated depreciation for tax purposes and straight-line depreciation for financial accounting purposes, and recognizing revenue under the accrual method for financial accounting purposes while using the installment method for tax purposes.

Recent years have seen growing concern regarding the nature of the deferred-tax-liability account. Will the liability shown on the balance sheet ever require an outflow of funds? The general answer to this question is no. As long as companies continue expanding their fixed assets, the new, higher tax depreciation related to these new assets will offset the lower tax depreciation on the older assets. As a result, while a review of the specific circumstances is needed, analysts generally treat the deferred tax liability as a type of quasi-equity rather than a true liability of the company.

While the FASB has not yet addressed the issue of the nature of the deferred-tax-liability account, in 1987 it issued new standards regarding deferred tax accounting.[16] These new standards require the use of the liability method to calculate deferred taxes. This method is balance-sheet oriented, as opposed to the old deferral method, which was highly income-statement oriented. Readers of financial statements are urged to review current accounting texts to obtain a more detailed understanding of the differences and the implications for financial statement analysis.

Published Financial Forecasts

In recent years, analysts and regulatory agencies have been pressing to have accounting statements and annual reports provide greater utility to investors. It has been suggested, for instance, that companies provide forecasts of future operations

---

[15]*Ibid.,* p. 10.

[16]Financial Accounting Standards Board, *Statement of Financial Accounting Standards No. 96, Accounting for Income Taxes* (Stamford, Conn.: FASB, 1987).

in annual reports, alongside traditional historical information. The primary item, of course, that investors would like projected or forecast is earnings for the year ahead. The merits, legalities, and ethics of such a move will no doubt take some time to resolve.

In October 1985 the AICPA published "Financial Forecasts and Projections." This statement provides standards the accountant must apply when issuing reports containing either forecasts or projections of financial data.

Officially Filed Information

Public companies are required to file certain information with the SEC. In the main, public companies are those listed on the organized securities exchange and traded over-the-counter that meet certain size tests (assets and number of shareholders). These filings take the form of periodic reports, proxies, financial statements, and other information.

Three periodic reports must be filed with the SEC: Form 8–K reports various events as they occur—acquisition and disposition of assets, changes in securities (amounts), defaults on senior securities, issuance of options, revaluation of assets, and other material events. Form 10–Q is a quarterly report containing financial information in summary form. Form 10–K is an annual report containing certified financial statements and certain detailed supporting schedules not normally seen in annual reports provided to the public. These financial statements include notes on the basis for computing depreciation and certain details on leases, funded debt, management stock options, and inventory classification, among other items.

These periodic reports provide expanded information for analysts and investors. They are available from private firms that have reproduced the reports on microfilm or microfiche, from the SEC, and, often, from the company itself. Reproduction, handling, and postage costs must be considered.[17]

INTERNATIONAL ACCOUNTING ISSUES

International investing has its own unique set of potential problems. Investors often cite a lack of information, disparate accounting standards, illiquidity, and what might be called "sovereign risks" as disincentives to internationalization.

LIMITED AVAILABILITY OF INFORMATION

In many instances, the quality and quantity of information on foreign companies available from either corporate financial reports or in-depth research coverage by the financial community fall short of that in the United States. Although a cost is clearly associated with the collection and analysis of information on foreign stocks, as noted earlier, those with the patience and ability to understand the value of un-

---

[17]For example, a complete 10–K report may be fifty pages long.

deranalyzed securities and thus exploit market inefficiencies also have correspondingly greater opportunities to achieve higher returns.

DISPARATE ACCOUNTING STANDARDS

A company's financial reports may be clear and complete, and there may be adequate research coverage of its situation. But how can you value its stock against that of a competitor in a different country if company A in Germany sets aside earnings in special reserves or reports on a full-replacement-cost accounting basis, whereas company B in the United States or Japan does not? Clearly, disparate accounting principles can severely distort the picture.

Generally speaking, accounting principles in Canada and the United Kingdom are close to those in the United States. Additionally, some overseas firms report also on U.S. or U.K. standards, particularly those whose shares are traded in the United States or London. Currency and interest-rate differentials, as well as the growing internationalization of many companies' businesses, have often behooved managements to seek financing in markets outside their own. If companies wish foreigners (particularly Americans) to invest in them, they clearly have to provide their accounts in a manner to which those foreigners can relate.

The number of practices that differ country to country is quite large; fortunately, most of them are nonmaterial. Several, however, can have considerable impact in determining a company's income or its balance sheet valuations. These typically relate to accounting for goodwill, depreciation, discretionary reserves, inflation, currency translations, consolidated subsidiaries, and taxes. Also, in Japan and Europe, companies report on a "parent-company" basis, not consolidated, and also can make large allocations to reserves to shelter income. Swedish companies, for example, are not allowed to use accelerated depreciation for income-tax purposes—clearly increasing their income-tax liability. However, they can allocate portions of revenues into certain "untaxed" reserves; that is, these allocations are deductible for income-tax purposes, thereby diminishing income-tax liability. Are these reserves to be considered a future liability akin to deferred taxes? (They become taxable only when reduced from one accounting period to another.) Or are they a "somewhat restricted" portion of stockholders' equity? Are earnings to be considered after these reserve allocations are deducted or before?

Although a detailed discussion of all differences is not within the scope of this chapter, Table 6–5 provides a sketch of some of the differences alluded to herein.

LIQUIDITY CONSTRAINTS

One common complaint among investors is the difficulty in accumulating substantial positions in foreign equities because of smaller market capitalizations and less well-developed trading strategies abroad. U.S. brokerage firms are increasing their participation in the international arena, and their trading expertise and willingness to commit capital should do much to lessen such problems for their customers. Many foreign markets are regarded as small and less liquid than those of the United States. The United States alone accounts for nearly 45 percent of

Table 6–5

SYNTHESIS OF ACCOUNTING DIFFERENCES

ACCOUNTING PRINCIPLES	U.S.	AUSTRALIA	CANADA	FRANCE	GERMANY	JAPAN	NETH.	SWEDEN	SWITZ.	U.K.
1. Marketable securities recorded at the lower of cost or market?	Yes	Yes	Yes	Yes	Yes	Yes	Yes	Yes	Yes	Yes
2. Provision for uncollectible accounts made?	Yes	Yes	Yes	No	Yes	Yes	Yes	Yes	Yes	Yes
3. Inventory costed using FIFO?	Mixed	Yes	Mixed	Mixed	Yes	Mixed	Mixed	Yes	Yes	Yes
4. Manufacturing overhead allocated to year-end inventory?	Yes	Yes	Yes	Yes	Yes	Yes	Yes	Yes	No	Yes
5. Inventory valued at the lower of cost or market?	Yes	Yes	Yes	Yes	Yes	Yes	Yes	Yes	Yes	Yes
6. Accounting for long-term investments: less than 20 percent ownership: cost method.	Yes	Yes	Yes	Yes*	Yes	Yes	No	Yes	Yes	Yes
7. Accounting for long-term investments: 21–50 percent ownership: equity method.	Yes	No (G)	Yes	Yes*	No (B)	No (B)	Yes	No (B)	No (B)	Yes
8. Accounting for long-term investments: more than 50 percent ownership: full consolidation.	Yes	Yes	Yes	Yes*	Yes	Yes	Yes	Yes	Yes	Yes
9. Both domestic and foreign subsidiaries consolidated?	Yes	Yes	Yes	Yes	No**	Yes	Yes	Yes	Yes	Yes

KEY: Yes—Predominant practice.
Yes*—Minor modifications, but still predominant practice.
No**—Minority practice.
No—Accounting principle in question not adhered to.
Mixed—Alternative practices followed with no majority.
B—Cost method is used.
G—Cost or equity.

Source: Used by permission from Frederick D.S. Chois and Vinod B. Bavishi, "Diversity in Multinational Accounting," *Financial Executive* (August 1982). © 1982 by Financial Executive Institute.

world capitalizations. Nine countries account for about 90 percent of total world stock capitalizations outside the United States (Japan, Switzerland, West Germany, Italy, United Kingdom, Canada, France, Netherlands, Australia). Some large investors are concerned about being able to accumulate meaningful holdings in foreign markets. For example, in the Netherlands and Switzerland, it is estimated that the top ten companies account for 65 to 75 percent of total market capitalization. This means there are fewer medium and smaller listed companies available. On the other hand, the turnover of shares in foreign markets has been increasing substantially over time. This speaks to the issue of liquidity and depth. By contrast, notice the breadth of the U.S. and Japanese markets. The growth of share turnover in foreign markets has increased. These size and liquidity problems suggest, at the very least, a certain amount of patience when buying and selling in foreign markets.

SOVEREIGN RISKS

Sovereign risks are related to events specific to a national marketplace—disruptive political, sociological, or psychological developments that do not have direct parallels in this country. In the political area, for example, the possibilities of nationalization of local companies, expropriation of the interests of foreign investors, restrictions on withdrawal of capital, or punitive taxation may have a dramatic impact on the valuation of the securities in that market. This poses a special challenge for international investors who must monitor not only local economies but also the general climate in evaluating foreign markets, stocks, and prospects of risk or reward. Also, as we will detail in the following section, currency can have a negative as well as a positive impact on the performance of foreign stockholdings.

Currency Relationships and Returns on Foreign Stocks

U.S. investors choose not to own foreign equities in local currencies and prefer to settle their international trade in U.S. dollars. This introduces what can be either another element of risk or a positive foreign-exchange "kicker" into the performance equation, depending on changes in exchange rates after the time of purchase. Foreign-exchange rates fluctuate for a number of reasons:

- the relative strengths of the respective economies—growth in gross domestic product, balance of payments position, the rate of inflation, etc.;
- real interest rate differentials;
- technical (supply and demand) and seasonal factors (e.g., year-end corporate foreign exchange needs); and
- political and regulatory developments.

Exchange-rate volatility has captured the headlines with increasing frequency in recent years—first with the strong upward surge of the U.S. dollar vis-à-vis the major foreign currencies and lately with its trending in the opposite direction.

CURRENCY RISK-REWARD EFFECTS

When the dollar strengthens, investing overseas becomes cheaper. However, a dollar investor's return on capital is diminished if the dollar appreciates further. The reverse is true when the dollar weakens: Investing abroad becomes more expensive, yet a decline in the U.S. dollar relative to the home currency of the foreign holding will enhance returns.

Thus, exchange rates figure importantly in international performance, as illustrated in the following example. A U.S. investor buys 1,000 shares of a Japanese company in Tokyo at Y830 (Y = yen) per share when the dollar is equivalent to Y253 and pays $3,280 (Y830 times 1,000 divided by Y253). A month later, seeing that the stock has gone up to Y850, he decides to sell the shares and take a profit. However, in the meantime, the exchange rate has moved against him to Y260 per $1.00. Consequently, he receives only $3,270 on the sale. Because of the change in the exchange rate, the 2.4 percent rise in the Japanese stock in yen terms translates into a 0.3 percent decline on a dollar basis. What the investor thought would be a profit turned into a loss.

However, if over the same time frame the yen had strengthened from Y253 to Y245 per $1.00, the proceeds from the sale would have been $3,470. The 2.4 percent rise in the yen price of the 1,000 shares of the Japanese stock would then result in a 5.8 percent appreciation in dollar terms. This points out the reason for any heightened interest in foreign equities as a play on an anticipated weakening of the dollar.

JAPANESE STOCK

THE EFFECT OF CURRENCY FLUCTUATIONS ON CAPITAL GAINS			
	DECEMBER 19X1	DECEMBER 19X2	CAPITAL GAIN
Japan			
Japanese ordinary share price	Y727	Y904	24.3%
United States			
Exchange rate yen/$U.S.	Y232	Y252	
Price Japanese stock in $U.S.	$3.13	$3.59	14.7
Germany			
Exchange rate yen/deutsche mark	Y85	Y80	
Japanese stock in deutsche marks	DM8.55	DM11.30	32.2

EXTERNAL INFORMATION

External sources that the analyst can turn to for basic company information are prepared by investment services and brokerage firms. Three of the major services, to which even the novice investor will often turn for valuable information, are Standard & Poor's, Moody's, and *Value Line.*

Figure 6–1 is a report taken from the Standard & Poor's *Stock Reports*. This report concerns a firm on the New York Stock Exchange, but S&P also publishes similar reports on all American Stock Exchange firms and selected over-the-counter securities. These reports contain a report on the firm's operation and recent developments, information on the firm's financing, and pertinent share-price data, as well as other financial data. New reports are issued for this loose-leaf service at frequent intervals.

Moody's *Handbook of Common Stocks,* published quarterly, contains approximately the same type of information as the *S&P Stock Reports*. A reproduction from Moody's is shown in Figure 6–2.

The *Value Line Investment Survey,* in conjunction with the *Industry Reports,* lists excellent one-page summary sheets of member firms. As can be seen in Figure 6–3, these reports are abundant in extremely valuable information. Along with information similar to that contained in Moody's and Standard & Poor's (although contained in a different format), the *Value Line* projects key income-statement data several years in advance, computes betas (the measure of relative responsiveness of the stock's price to the market, to be examined in Chapter 16), and provides an insider index (which measures insiders' decisions to buy the stock relative to their decisions to sell), historical growth rates, and *Value Line* ratings on performance, income, and safety. The use and significance of these ratings are explained by *Value Line* in Figure 6–4.

In addition to these easily accessible services (most libraries subscribe to them), there is another source that all interested investors can obtain in some form from a stockbroker: Standard & Poor's *Stock Guide* and *Bond Guide.* Both these guides are published monthly and contain key skeletal information on all listed stocks and bonds and many unlisted securities. The *Stock Guide* provides a brief statement of the nature of the firm's business, selected accounting information, and selected price data on the stock. The *Bond Guide* contains many other items of interest and information on the firm's business, key bond provisions, investment-times-interest-earned ratios, the amount of debt outstanding, the S&P bond rating, and price data on the various bond issues of the firm.

Certainly an investment decision should not be based on such sketchy data. Their use is primarily to act as a screening device for the investor. He may decide that the firm is so unappealing to him that it's not even worth a trip to the library for more research information. On the other hand, the security may look interesting and worthy of some research. At the library, after consulting the sources already mentioned, the investor may decide to probe still further. To aid him, we recommend the use of the *Wall Street Journal Index,* the *Business Periodicals Index,* and the *Funk and Scott Index of Corporations and Industries.*[18]

The annual *WSJ Index* contains an alphabetical listing of firms mentioned in the *Wall Street Journal* during the year. Under the firm's name are listed key words from the title of the story, plus documentation concerning the issue, page, and col-

---

[18]All three indexing services publish monthly supplements to their annual volumes.

1447K McDonald's Corporation

Income Data (Million $)

Year Ended Dec. 31	Revs.	Oper. Inc.	% Oper. Inc. of Revs.	Cap. Exp.	Depr.	Int. Exp.	Net Bef. Taxes	Eff. Tax Rate	[3]Net Inc.	% Net Inc. of Revs.	Cash Flow
1992	7,133	2,290	32.1	1,171	493	393	[2]1,448	33.8%	959	13.4	1,437
[1]1991	6,695	2,022	30.2	1,129	457	418	[2]1,299	33.8%	860	12.8	1,297
1990	6,640	1,944	29.3	1,613	444	417	[2]1,246	35.6%	802	12.1	1,232
1989	6,065	1,772	29.2	1,556	390	332	[2]1,157	37.2%	727	12.0	1,113
1988	5,521	1,573	28.5	1,489	335	267	[2]1,046	38.3%	646	11.7	981
1987	4,853	1,413	29.1	1,059	292	225	959	42.7%	549	11.3	839
1986	4,144	1,173	28.3	965	248	189	848	43.4%	480	11.6	725
1985	3,695	1,065	28.8	830	208	157	782	44.6%	433	11.7	636
1984	3,366	966	28.7	672	185	135	707	45.0%	389	11.6	571
[1]1983	3,001	840	28.0	682	165	123	628	45.4%	343	11.4	508

Balance Sheet Data (Million $)

Dec. 31	Cash	Assets	Curr. Liab.	Ratio	Total Assets	% Ret. on Assets	Long Term Debt	Common Equity	Total Cap.	% LT Debt of Cap.	% Ret. on Equity
1992	437	865	1,545	0.6	11,681	8.3	3,176	5,984	9,911	32.0	17.4
1991	220	646	1,288	0.5	11,349	7.8	4,267	4,537	9,837	43.4	19.7
1990	143	549	1,199	0.5	10,668	8.1	4,429	3,984	9,306	47.6	21.6
1989	137	495	1,017	0.5	9,175	8.5	3,901	3,349	8,064	48.4	21.8
1988	184	516	1,004	0.5	8,159	8.6	3,111	3,413	7,067	44.0	20.5
1987	183	484	856	0.6	6,982	8.5	2,685	2,917	6,042	44.4	20.5
1986	205	473	799	0.6	5,968	8.8	2,131	2,448	5,089	41.9	20.7
1985	155	369	663	0.6	5,043	9.4	1,638	2,187	4,297	38.1	21.0
1984	75	255	514	0.5	4,230	9.9	1,268	1,943	3,638	34.9	21.1
1983	66	231	430	0.5	3,727	9.8	1,171	1,755	3,225	36.3	21.0

Data as orig. reptd. 1. Refl. acctg. change. 2. Incl. equity in earns. of nonconsol. subs. 3. Bef. spec. item(s).

Business Summary

McDonald's operates, licenses and services the world's largest chain of fast-food restaurants. At December 31, 1993, there were 9,283 units in the U.S. and 4,710 in more than 60 other countries or overseas territories. Of the international units, 72% were in Japan, Canada, Germany, England, Australia or France. Contributions by geographic area in 1992 (latest available) were:

	Revs.	Profits
United States	53%	56%
Europe/Africa	31%	26%
Canada	8%	6%
Pacific	6%	9%
Latin America	2%	3%

Units in operation at year-end were:

	1993	1992	1991	1990
Company	2,699	2,551	2,547	2,643
Franchisees	9,832	9,237	8,735	8,131
Affiliates	1,462	1,305	1,136	1,029
Total	13,993	13,093	12,418	11,803

The restaurants offer a substantially uniform menu, including hamburgers, fries, chicken, fish, specialty sandwiches, beverages and desserts. Most units also serve breakfast.

MCD owns or leases a substantial amount of the real estate used by franchisees in their operations. Fees from franchisees to MCD typically include rents and service fees, often totaling at least 11.5% of sales. Licensees make sizable investments in startup costs.

Dividend Data

Dividends were initiated in 1976. A dividend reinvestment plan is available. A new "poison pill" preferred stock purchase right was adopted in 1988.

Amt. of Divd. $	Date Decl.	Ex–divd. Date	Stock of Record	Payment Date
0.10¾	May 28	Jun. 1	Jun. 7	Jun. 18'93
0.10¾	Aug. 17	Aug. 25	Aug. 31	Sep. 17'93
0.10¾	Oct. 19	Nov. 23	Nov. 30	Dec. 17'93
0.10¾	Jan. 18	Feb. 22	Feb. 28	Mar. 18'94

Capitalization

Long Term Debt: $3,563,400,000 (9/93).

7% Conv. Preferred Stock: $678,000,000 principal amount, incl. about $179 million owned by ESOP.

Common Stock: About 353,012,412 shs. (6/93; no par).
Institutions hold some 65%.
Shareholders: 378,000.

FIGURE 6–1 McDonald's Corp. (*Source:* Standard & Poor's Corp., December 10, 1992)

McDonald's Corp. 1447K

NYSE Symbol MCD Options on CBOE In S&P 500

Price	Range	P–E Ratio	Dividend	Yield	S&P Ranking	Beta
Feb. 23'94	1994					
60⅜	62⅜–55⅛	21	0.43	0.7%	A+	1.08

Summary

Aggressive expansion and creative merchandising over the years have enabled McDonald's to maintain its position as the dominant force in the fast-food industry. International operations are expected to fuel much of MCD's sales and operating profit growth. However, a "value" strategy appears to be helping sales in the U.S., where about 66% of MCD's systemwide units are located.

Current Outlook

Earnings for 1994 are estimated at $3.35 a share, up from 1993's $2.91.

A near-term increase in the $0.10¾ quarterly dividend is likely.

In 1994, double-digit profit growth is expected from international operations. Further benefits from economies of scale are likely as MCD's presence in various foreign markets continues to grow. In 1993, MCD's international growth was partly masked by adverse effects from currency fluctuation. From the U.S., a moderate profit increase is expected in 1994.

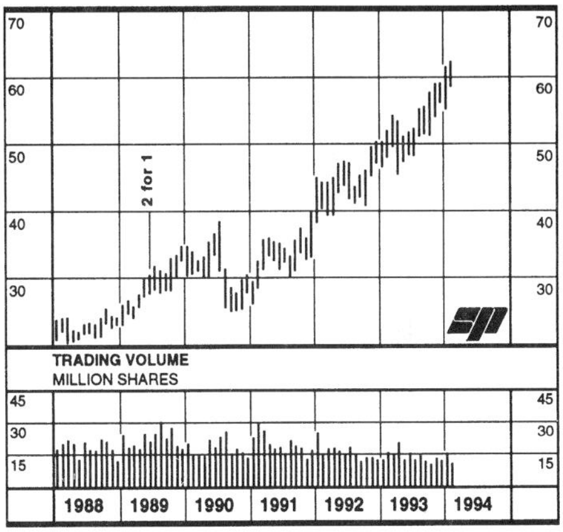

Revenues (Million $)

Quarter:	1993	1992	1991	1990
Mar.	1,654	1,618	1,558	1,509
Jun.	1,878	1,774	1,671	1,659
Sep.	1,944	1,913	1,737	1,769
Dec.	193	1,828	1,730	1,703
	7,408	7,133	6,695	6,640

Revenues for 1993 (preliminary) increased 3.9% from thos eof the prior year. Operating profit rose 6.6%, and interest expense declined 15%. With a higher tax rate, net income was up 13%. After preferred dividends, which increased due to a stock issuance in late 1992, common share earnings (2.0% fewer shares) increased 12%, to $2.91, from $2.60.

Common Share Earnings ($)

Quarter:	1993	1992	1991	1990
Mar.	0.57	0.51	0.46	0.43
Jun.	0.78	0.69	0.63	0.59
Sep.	0.85	0.79	0.71	0.67
Dec.	0.72	0.61	0.54	0.51
	2.91	2.60	2.35	2.20

Important Developments

Jan. '94— MCD said that it planned to spend up to $1 billion on common stock repurchase within the next three years. Also, MCD plans to open between 900 and 1,200 new restaurants in each of the next several years. Of these, about two-thirds would be in locations outside the U.S. Meanwhile, in 1993, MCD's worldwide systemwide sales (including franchises and affiliates) increased 7.8%, year to year, including a 7.1% rise from the U.S. From international markets, such sales were up 8.8%, but would have risen 13% if currency exchange rates had remained stable. MCD said that in 1993, currency fluctuation lowered per share earnings by $0.09. Also, MCD's tax rate was increased by federal legislation. In October 1993, MCD completed a U.S. rollout of a McGrilled Chicken sandwich.

Next earnings report expected in late April.

Per Share Data ($)

Yr. End Dec. 31	**1993**	1992	[1]1991	1990	1989	1988	1987	1986	1985	1984
Tangible Bk. Val.	**NA**	15.38	11.62	10.02	8.35	8.25	7.03	5.84	5.25	4.60
Cash Flow	**NA**	3.96	3.62	3.43	3.00	2.60	2.21	1.89	1.64	1.44
Earnings[2]	**2.91**	2.60	2.35	2.20	1.95	1.72	1.45	1.24	1.11	0.98
Dividends	**0.423**	0.393	0.363	0.333	0.303	0.273	0.243	0.215	0.196	0.169
Payout Ratio	**15%**	15%	15%	15%	15%	16%	17%	17%	18%	17%
Prices—High	**59⅛**	50⅜	39⅞	38½	34⅞	25½	30⅝	25⅝	18¼	12½
Low	**45½**	38¼	26⅛	25	23	20⅜	15¾	16¼	11⅜	9⅛
P/E Ratio—	**20–16**	19–15	17–11	18–11	18–12	15–12	21–11	21–13	16–10	13–9

FIGURE 6–1 (continued)

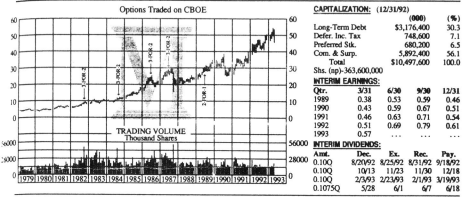

MC DONALD'S CORPORATION

LISTED	SYM.	LTPS♦	STPS♦	IND. DIV.	REC. PRICE	RANGE (52-WKS.)	YLD.	'92 YR.-END PR.	DIV. ACH.
NYSE	MCD	118.3	103.6	$0.43*	48	54 - 41	0.9%	48¾	16 yrs.

INVESTMENT GRADE. CONSISTENT EARNINGS GROWTH WILL NOT BE INTERRUPTED AS WORLDWIDE EXPANSION CONTINUES.

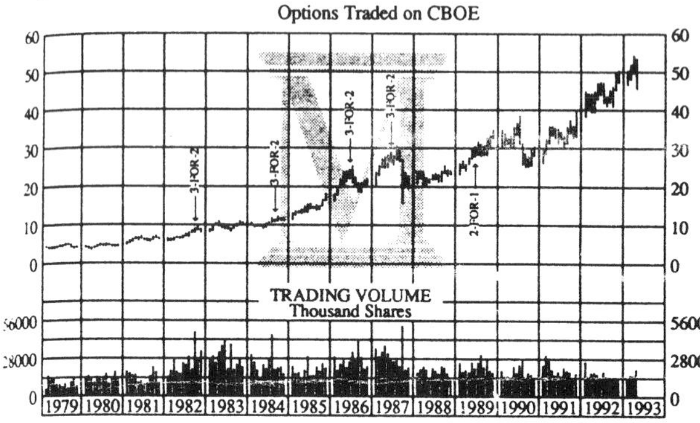

CAPITALIZATION: (12/31/92)

	(000)	(%)
Long-Term Debt	$3,176,400	30.3
Defer. Inc. Tax	748,600	7.1
Preferred Stk.	680,200	6.5
Com. & Surp.	5,892,400	56.1
Total	$10,497,600	100.0

Shs. (np)-363,600,000

INTERIM EARNINGS:

Qtr.	3/31	6/30	9/30	12/31
1989	0.38	0.53	0.59	0.46
1990	0.43	0.59	0.67	0.51
1991	0.46	0.63	0.71	0.54
1992	0.51	0.69	0.79	0.61
1993	0.57	...	...	...

INTERIM DIVIDENDS:

Amt.	Dec.	Ex.	Rec.	Pay.
0.10Q	8/20/92	8/25/92	8/31/92	9/18/92
0.10Q	10/13	11/23	11/30	12/18
0.10Q	2/3/93	2/23/93	2/1/93	3/19/93
0.1075Q	5/28	6/1	6/7	6/18

BACKGROUND:

McDonald's develops, licenses, leases and services a worldwide system of restaurants. Units serve a standardized menu of moderately priced food consisting of hamburgers, cheeseburgers, chicken sandwiches, salads, desserts and beverages. As of 12/31/92, there were 9,001 units operated by franchisees, 2,510 units operated by the Company, and 1,209 units operated by affiliates. There are 12,752 MCD restaurants in 59 countries. Revenues in 1992 were derived from: Company owned units sales, 44%; and franchised restaurants, 56%. Independent operators normally lease on a 20-year basis with rental derived as a percentage of sales, with a minimum fixed rent.

RECENT DEVELOPMENTS:

For the quarter ended 3/31/93, net income jumped 16% to $218.3 million compared with $187.4 million for the comparable period in 1992. Total revenues rose 2% to $1.65 billion, while systemwide sales grew 6% to $5.24 billion due to the addition of 91 new restaurants as well as to higher sales at existing restaurants. The rate of increase for revenues continued to lag that of systemwide sales due to weaknesses in foreign currencies and the franchising of certain Company-operated restaurant businesses in the U.S. Operating income increased as a result of higher sales, but was diluted by higher selling and administrative expenses.

PROSPECTS:

The Company's operations in the U.S. should benefit from ongoing efforts to reduce operating costs. MCD's domestic business will gain from continuing evaluation of its value program which permit MCD to introduce several new menu strategies and increase customer traffic. International business remains a key contributor to growth due to expansion. MCD plans to accelerate new restaurant openings over the next several years, ranging from 700-900 units yearly. The planned repurchase of up to $700 million in shares will directly boost earnings per share.

STATISTICS:

YEAR	GROSS REVS. ($mill.)	OPER. PROFIT MARGIN %	RET. ON EQUITY %	NET INCOME ($mill.)	WORK CAP. ($mill.)	SENIOR CAPITAL ($mill.)	SHARES (000)	EARN. PER SH.$	DIV. PER SH.$	DIV. PAY. %	PRICE RANGE	P/E RATIO	AVG. YIELD %
83	3,062.9	24.1	19.6	342.6	d198.5	1,171.3	400,486	0.85	0.15	17	11 - 8⅛	11.3	1.5
84	3,414.8	24.3	19.4	389.1	d259.7	1,268.2	393,130	0.97	0.17	17	12⅜ - 10¾	11.8	1.6
85	3,760.9	24.5	19.3	433.0	d294.0	1,696.3	385,335	1.11	0.20	18	18¼ - 11¼	13.3	1.3
86	4,240.1	24.1	19.1	479.7	d326.7	2,189.7	379,658	1.24	0.22	18	25½ - 16⅛	16.7	1.0
b87	4,893.5	23.7	18.8	a549.1	d372.6	2,685.8	377,712	a1.44	0.243	17	30½ - 15⅝	18.5	1.1
88	5,566.3	21.0	18.9	645.9	d487.2	3,176.7	375,476	1.71	0.273	16	25½ - 20⅜	13.3	1.1
89	6,142.4	26.4	20.5	726.7	d522.0	3,901.0	362,000	1.95	0.314	16	34⅞ - 23	14.8	1.1
90	6,776.0	24.0	19.2	802.3	d649.7	4,428.7	359,100	2.20	0.333	15	38½ - 25	14.4	1.0
91	6,695.0	23.4	17.8	859.6	d641.9	4,565.5	358,600	2.35	0.363	15	39⅞ - 26⅛	14.0	1.1
92	7,133.3	26.1	16.3	958.6	d679.9	3,856.6	363,600	2.60	0.393	15	50⅜ - 38¼	17.0	0.9

♦Long-Term Price Score — Short-Term Price Score; see page 4a. STATISTICS ARE AS ORIGINALLY REPORTED. Adjusted for 3-for-2 stock splits, 9/84, 6/86 and 6/87; and 2-for-1, 6/89. a-Before accounting credit of $47.4 million ($0.13 a share) to reflect cumulative effect on prior periods of an accounting change. b-Reflects change in method of accounting for certain income taxes.

FIGURE 6-2 Sample Page of *Moody's Handbook of Common Stocks*. (*Source:* Moody's Investor Service, Inc., 1992)

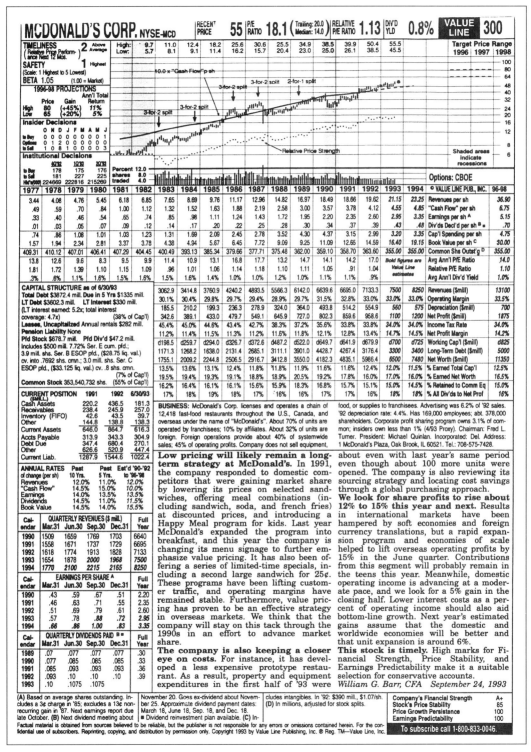

FIGURE 6–3 Sample Page of *Value Line Investment Survey*. (*Source*: Value Line Publishing, September 24, 1993).)

201

TO SELECT A SUITABLE COMMON STOCK BY THE
VALUE LINE METHOD, PROCEED AS FOLLOWS:

FIRST: Decide on the degree of risk you are willing to assume All stocks involve risk But some are safer, that is to say, less risky, than others.

Risk is measured by the characteristic volatility of the stock's price around its own long term trend. The narrower the band of fluctuation around trend, the safer the stock, the wider the band, the less safe, or the riskier.

Stocks ranked 1 (highest) for Safety are relatively the least volatile.

Stocks ranked 2 (above average) are less safe than the 1's but safer than stocks ranked 3 (average), 4 (below average) or 5 (lowest).

Stocks ranked 5 (lowest) are the riskiest, or least safe.

Stocks ranked 4 are riskier than average but not so risky as those ranked 5 (lowest).

Those ranked 3 are of average safety (i.e., risk).

SECOND: Pick out from among the stocks with acceptable Safety Ranks those whose current dividend yields appear attractive to you. You can select by referring to the weekly Summary Index of this Service where all 1550 stocks monitored by Value Line are listed in alphabetical order together with their recent prices, dividend yields, Safety Ranks and Performance Ranks. On the first page of the Summary Index you will find the average yield of all dividend-paying stocks. It will serve as a reference point.

Dividend yield may be desirable for some persons, not for others. Where there is a division of interest, as in a trust which may distribute only the dividend income to beneficiaries, reserving capital growth for the remaindermen, dividends obviously are important. Furthermore, many conservative investors shrink as a matter of habit from "invading principal", including appreciation of principal. For them, dividend income is the only true income. On the other hand, to the investor in a high tax bracket, as well as the investor who looks to "total return" (which is the sum of dividend payments and capital appreciation) dividend yield may appear to be the less important portion of return. High dividend yields generally signal low appreciation potential because they indicate that the market foresees relatively little further dividend growth in the future. For the vast majority of stocks over a long period of years, capital appreciation has far outweighed the dividend as a factor in total return.

THIRD: Having picked a list acceptable in terms of safety and current yield, cull out from that list the stocks ranked 1 (highest) and 2 (above average) for Performance in the next 12 months. Select one of these and hold it until its rank falls to 3 (average) or lower (4 or 5). Then sell and replace it with another stock ranked 1 or 2 culled from a list that then also offers an acceptable Safety Rank and yield. The policy of selling as soon as a stock falls to a Performance rank of 3 or lower may be too rigidly aggressive for all accounts. Capital gains tax liability and brokerage expense should be taken into account; and where stocks sell extremely low in relation to their 3 to 5 year appreciation potentiality, performance within the next 12 months might reasonably be assigned a lesser weight in the judgment of some investors. Still the general rule is worth observing when buying, concentrate on stocks ranked 1 or 2 for Performance in the next 12 months; when selling take aim at stocks ranked 4 or 5 for Performance. When a stock falls to a rank 3 (average) for Performance in the next 12 months, bear in mind that in the coming year it will probably perform no better, but no worse either, than the average of all 1550 stocks.

FIGURE 6–4   How to Select Stocks for Your Portfolio (*Source:* "How to Select Stocks for Your Portfolio," *Value Line Investment Survey* 29, no. 19 (New York: Value Line, February 15, 1974)

umn in which the story appeared. The interested investor can then go to the sources and read up on the company.

The *Business Periodicals Index* provides an alphabetical listing by key word, industry, and company of all stories carried by major business publications that are covered by the index. From it, researchers can readily locate much information on the industry, firm, and firm's products in which they are interested, for they can track down the stories and read up on almost all published data they need to know.

The *Funk and Scott Index* provides a similar but more specific kind of service. It indexes data on companies, products, and industries from more than 750 publications—many of them specialized trade journals. Furthermore, this information is accessible numerically from Standard Industrial Classification (SIC) as well as alphabetically by company name. The SIC is useful because researchers will find references to all firms in that particular classification in one place. Using the alphabetical listing, they can zero in on firms of particular interest to them regardless of the SIC.

SUMMARY

Armed with economic and industry forecasts, the analyst is ready to look at the shares of specific companies.

Company information is generated internally and externally. The principal source of internal information about a company is its financial statements. The analyst must screen quarterly and annual reports of income, financial position, and cash flows in order to assure himself that such statements are correct, complete, consistent, and comparable. The use of accounting reports can be influenced by options to treat certain transactions in different ways. Further, accounting statements taken as a whole over time can reveal critical information to the trained eye that is not seen by casual analysis of specific statements in isolation, or for only a single year.

Our examination of financial statements highlighted the income statement, statement of retained earnings, balance sheet, and statement of cash flows. We saw the continuing importance attached to the income statement as a prominent source of evidence regarding management performance, particularly in reference to earnings. We also noted the increased emphasis being placed on analysis of cash flows.

Many popular and widely circulated sources of information about companies emanate from outside, or external, sources. These sources provide supplements to company-generated information by overcoming some of its bias, such as public pronouncements by its officers. External information sources also provide certain kinds of information not found in the materials made available by companies themselves.

QUESTIONS AND PROBLEMS

1. What four major tests must financial statements meet to have utility for investment analysis?

2. What advantages and disadvantages would probably accompany a move toward complete uniformity in accounting, where every transaction, regardless of the firm, is handled in one way only?

3. In what ways will a company behave differently with respect to its accounting if it chooses to concentrate on (a) maximizing earnings, or (b) minimizing taxes?

4. Prepare a table similar to the one shown on page 201, using sum-of-the-years'-digits depreciation. How do you account for any differences in the pattern of added taxes or savings? Which method would you advocate, declining-balance or SYD?

5. Distinguish between primary and secondary earnings per share. Why is such a distinction important to a common-stock investor?

6. With all the concern shown for the income statement, of what significance to an investor is the book value of assets and the amount of debt on the balance sheet?

7. Refer to the financial statements of McDonald's Corp. in the Appendix to this chapter. What specific insights into company operations are offered by examining the consolidated statement of cash flows for the year ended December 31, 1992, that are not readily seen on the balance sheet and income statement for the same period?

8. The Rush Co. example in the text highlighted accounting for a subsidiary in which Melicher Corp. held only 40 percent of the voting stock. What changes would occur on the balance sheet of Melicher if it owned 70 percent of the Rush stock?

9. What are some significant bits of investment information about a company that are not normally found in standard financial statements?

10. What does an auditor's "unqualified" opinion really mean?

11. In what ways, if any, does FASB *Statement No. 14* prove useful to investors or security analysts?

12. Which *one* of the following would best explain a situation where the ratio of "net income to total equity" for a firm is higher than the industry average, while the ratio of "net income to total assets" is lower than the industry average?
   a. Net profit margin is higher than the industry average.
   b. Debt ratio is higher than the industry average.
   c. Asset turnover is higher than the industry average.
   d. Equity multiplier must be lower than the industry average.

13. Which *one* of the following best explains why a firm's ratio of "long-term debt to total capital" is lower than the industry average, and its ratio of "income before interest and taxes to debt interest charges" is lower than the industry average? The firm:
   a. pays lower interest on its long-term debt than average.
   b. has a high ratio of total cash flow to long-term debt.

c. has more short-term debt than average.

d. has a high ratio of current assets to current liabilities.

14. Which *one* of the following combinations of accounting practices will lead to the highest reported earnings in an inflationary environment?

Depreciation Method	*Inventory Method*
a. straight-line	FIFO
b. double-declining-balance	LIFO
c. double-declining-balance	FIFO
d. straight-line	LIFO

15. Straight-line depreciation:

a. results in higher total tax payments over the life of an asset than acceler-ated depreciation.

b. results in a decreasing return on equity over the asset's life.

c. introduces a built-in increase in return on investment over the asset's life.

d. recognizes the increasing rate of obsolescence of an asset with the passage of time.

16. The cash flow data of Palomba Pizza Stores for the year ended December 31, 19X1, is as follows:

Cash payment of dividends	$35,000
Purchase of land	14,000
Cash payments for interest	10,000
Cash payments for salaries	45,000
Sale of equipment	38,000
Retirement of common stock	25,000
Purchase of equipment	30,000
Cash payments to suppliers	85,000
Cash collections from customers	250,000
Cash at beginning of year	50,000

a. Prepare a statement of cash flows for Palomba in accordance with SFAS 95 showing:

- net cash provided by operating activities,
- net cash provided by or used in investing activities, and
- net cash provided by or used in financing activities.

b. Discuss, from an analyst's viewpoint, the purpose of classifying cash flows into the three categories listed above.

DISCLOSURE PROBLEM

Consult *Disclosure* and obtain the McDonald's Corp. annual report for 1993 and report significant insights into the company's operations for 1993 as reflected in its statement of cash flow.

APPENDIX
■
Financial Review

On the following pages (Figure 6–5) are presented financial highlights, statements, and historical statistics for McDonald's Corp. and its consolidated subsidiaries taken from its 1992 annual report. This information is provided so that the reader may note key items on the statements that were mentioned in this chapter and observe how accounting reporting standards are implemented in an audited financial statement of a major publicly held U.S. corporation. Further, these statements and statistics will serve as part of the basic data for use in subsequent chapters.

McDonald's Corporation
CONSOLIDATED STATEMENT OF INCOME

(In millions of dollars, except per common share data)	Years ended December 31, 1992	1991	1990
Revenues			
Sales by Company-operated restaurants	**$5,102.5**	$4,908.5	$5,018.9
Revenues from franchised restaurants	**2,030.8**	1,786.5	1,620.7
Total revenues	**7,133.3**	6,695.0	6,639.6
Operating costs and expenses			
Company-operated restaurants			
Food and packaging	**1,688.8**	1,627.5	1,683.4
Payroll and other employee benefits	**1,281.4**	1,259.2	1,291.0
Occupancy and other operating expenses	**1,156.3**	1,142.4	1,161.2
	4,126.5	4,029.1	4,135.6
Franchised restaurants—occupancy expenses	**348.6**	306.5	279.2
General, administrative and selling expenses	**860.6**	794.7	724.2
Other operating (income) expense—net	**(64.0)**	(113.8)	(95.3)
Total operating costs and expenses	**5,271.7**	5,016.5	5,043.7
Operating income	**1,861.6**	1,678.5	1,595.9
Interest expense—net of capitalized interest of $19.5, $26.2, and $36.0	**373.6**	391.4	381.2
Nonoperating income (expense)—net	**(39.9)**	12.3	31.6
Income before provision for income taxes	**1,448.1**	1,299.4	1,246.3
Provision for income taxes	**489.5**	439.8	444.0
Net income	**$ 958.6**	$ 859.6	$ 802.3
Net income per common share	**$ 2.60**	$ 2.35	$ 2.20
Dividends per common share	**$ .39**	$ .36	$ .33

The accompanying Financial Comments are an integral part of the consolidated financial statements.

FIGURE 6–5   McDonald's Corp. Annual Report for 1993 (*Source:* McDonald's Corp., *1992 Annual Report to Stockholders* ([place]: , 1994). Reprinted with permission.

McDonald's Corporation
CONSOLIDATED BALANCE SHEET

(In millions of dollars)	December 31, **1992**	1991
Assets		
Current assets		
Cash and equivalents	$ **436.5**	$ 220.2
Accounts receivable	**245.9**	238.4
Notes receivable	**33.7**	36.0
Inventories, at cost, not in excess of market	**43.5**	42.6
Prepaid expenses and other current assets	**105.1**	108.8
Total current assets	**864.7**	646.0
Other assets and deferred charges		
Notes receivable due after one year	**99.0**	123.1
Investments in and advances to affiliates	**399.7**	374.2
Miscellaneous	**330.7**	278.2
Total other assets and deferred charges	**829.4**	775.5
Property and equipment		
Property and equipment, at cost	**12,658.0**	12,368.0
Accumulated depreciation and amortization	**(3,060.6)**	(2,809.5)
Net property and equipment	**9,597.4**	9,558.5
Intangible assets—net	**389.7**	369.1
Total assets	**$11,681.2**	$11,349.1
Liabilities and shareholders' equity		
Current liabilities		
Notes payable	$ **411.0**	$ 278.3
Accounts payable	**343.3**	313.9
Income taxes	**109.7**	157.2
Other taxes	**74.8**	82.3
Accrued interest	**133.3**	185.7
Other accrued liabilities	**203.1**	201.4
Current maturities of long-term debt	**269.4**	69.1
Total current liabilities	**1,544.6**	1,287.9
Long-term debt	**3,176.4**	4,267.4
Security deposits by franchisees and other long-term liabilities	**225.2**	224.5
Deferred income taxes	**748.6**	734.2
Common equity put options	**94.0**	
Shareholders' equity		
Preferred stock, no par value; authorized—165.0 million shares; issued—5.8 and 9.9 million	**680.2**	298.2
Common stock, no par value; authorized—1.25 billion shares; issued—415.2 million	**46.2**	46.2
Additional paid-in capital	**260.2**	201.9
Guarantee of ESOP Notes	**(271.3)**	(286.7)
Retained earnings	**6,727.3**	5,925.2
Foreign currency translation adjustment	**(127.4)**	32.3
	7,315.2	6,217.1
Common stock in treasury, at cost; 51.6 and 56.5 million shares	**(1,422.8)**	(1,382.0)
Total shareholders' equity	**5,892.4**	4,835.1
Total liabilities and shareholders' equity	**$11,681.2**	$11,349.1

The accompanying Financial Comments are an integral part of the consolidated financial statements.

FIGURE 6–5   (continued)

McDonald's Corporation
CONSOLIDATED STATEMENT OF CASH FLOWS

(In millions of dollars)	Years ended December 31, 1992	1991	1990
Operating activities			
Net income	$ 958.6	$ 859.6	$ 802.3
Adjustments to reconcile to cash provided by operations			
Depreciation and amortization	554.9	514.2	493.3
Deferred income taxes	22.4	64.7	70.8
Changes in operating working capital items			
Accounts receivable increase	(29.1)	(40.9)	(26.6)
Inventories, prepaid expenses and other current assets (increase) decrease	2.2	.4	(32.1)
Accounts payable increase (decrease)	.8	(22.7)	(14.5)
Accrued interest increase (decrease)	(27.4)	27.5	(1.7)
Taxes and other liabilities increase (decrease)	(68.2)	85.2	80.5
Other—net	11.7	(64.8)	(71.0)
Cash provided by operations	1,425.9	1,423.2	1,301.0
Investing activities			
Property and equipment expenditures	(1,086.9)	(1,128.8)	(1,570.7)
Sales of restaurant businesses	124.5	159.8	130.8
Purchases of restaurant businesses	(64.1)	(30.1)	(81.9)
Notes receivable additions	(31.8)	(38.8)	(46.2)
Property sales	52.2	58.6	39.5
Notes receivable reductions	78.5	53.1	61.2
Other	(71.1)	(13.5)	(55.2)
Cash used for investing activities	(998.7)	(939.7)	(1,522.5)
Financing activities			
Notes payable and commercial paper net borrowings supported by line of credit agreements	17.0	(676.7)	987.9
Other long-term debt borrowings	509.5	1,004.1	1,070.7
Other long-term debt repayments	(1,041.5)	(606.9)	(1,561.0)
Treasury stock purchases	(79.7)	(109.2)	(160.3)
Preferred stock issuances	484.9	100.0	
Common and preferred stock dividends	(160.5)	(148.3)	(133.3)
Other	59.4	30.9	23.4
Cash provided by (used for) financing activities	(210.9)	(406.1)	227.4
Cash and equivalents increase	216.3	77.4	5.9
Cash and equivalents at beginning of year	220.2	142.8	136.9
Cash and equivalents at end of year	$ 436.5	$ 220.2	$ 142.8
Supplemental cash flow disclosures			
Interest paid	$ 395.7	$ 368.1	$ 370.5
Income taxes paid	$ 531.6	$ 313.5	$ 326.5

The accompanying Financial Comments are an integral part of the consolidated financial statements.

FIGURE 6–5   (continued)

McDonald's Corporation
CONSOLIDATED STATEMENT OF SHAREHOLDERS' EQUITY

(Dollars and shares in millions, except per share data)	Preferred stock issued Shares	Amount	Common stock issued Shares	Amount	Additional paid-in capital	Guarantee of ESOP Notes	Retained earnings	Foreign currency translation adjustment	Common stock in treasury Shares	Amount
Balance at December 31, 1989	7.0	$200.0	415.2	$46.2	$158.9	$(199.2)	$4,545.5	$ (29.0)	(53.3)	$(1,172.0)
Net income							802.3			
Common stock cash dividends ($.33 per share)							(119.3)			
Preferred stock cash dividends ($2.01 per share)							(14.0)			
ESOP Notes payment						2.7				
Treasury stock acquisitions									(4.9)	(156.5)
Translation adjustments (including tax benefits of $27.4)								75.7		
Stock option exercises and other (including tax benefits of $13.7)	(.1)	(.3)			14.8				2.1	26.5
Balance at December 31, 1990	6.9	199.7	415.2	46.2	173.7	(196.5)	5,214.5	46.7	(56.1)	(1,302.0)
Net income							859.6			
Common stock cash dividends ($.36 per share)							(129.7)			
Preferred stock cash dividends ($2.01 for Series B and $1.74 for Series C)							(19.2)			
Preferred stock issuance	3.0	100.0			(.2)	(100.0)				
ESOP Notes payment						8.1				
Treasury stock acquisitions									(3.4)	(116.7)
Translation adjustments (including taxes of $1.0)								(14.4)		
Stock option exercises and other (including tax benefits of $15.9)		(1.5)			28.4	1.7			3.0	36.7
Balance at December 31, 1991	9.9	298.2	415.2	46.2	201.9	(286.7)	5,925.2	32.3	(56.5)	(1,382.0)
Net income							**958.6**			
Common stock cash dividends ($.39 per share)							**(141.8)**			
Preferred stock cash dividends ($2.01 for Series B, $2.32 for Series C and $.16 for Series E depositary share), (net of tax benefits of $6.4)							**(14.7)**			
Preferred stock issuance		**500.0**			**(15.1)**					
Preferred stock conversion	**(4.1)**	**(118.0)**			**22.9**				**3.2**	**95.1**
ESOP Notes payment						**12.6**				
Treasury stock acquisitions									**(1.9)**	**(92.3)**
Translation adjustments (including taxes of $21.2)								**(159.7)**		
Common equity put options issuance										**(91.5)**
Stock option exercises and other (including tax benefits of $29.7)					**50.5**	**2.8**			**3.6**	**47.9**
Balance at December 31, 1992	**5.8**	**$680.2**	**415.2**	**$46.2**	**$260.2**	**$(271.3)**	**$6,727.3**	**$(127.4)**	**(51.6)**	**$(1,422.8)**

The accompanying Financial Comments are an integral part of the consolidated financial statements.

FIGURE 6–5   (continued)

McDonald's Corporation
FINANCIAL COMMENTS

Summary of significant accounting policies

Consolidation
The consolidated financial statements include the accounts of the Company and its subsidiaries. Investments in 50% or less owned affiliates are carried at equity in the companies' net assets.

Foreign currency translation
The functional currency of each operation outside of the U.S., except for those located in hyperinflationary countries, is the respective local currency.

Income taxes
In 1992, the Company adopted Financial Accounting Standards Board Statement No. 109, Accounting for Income Taxes. The effects were not material, as the Company had previously adopted Statement No. 96. Accordingly, prior year amounts have not been reclassified to conform to Statement No. 109.

Property and equipment
Property and equipment are stated at cost with depreciation and amortization provided on the straight-line method over the following estimated useful lives: buildings—up to 40 years; leasehold improvements—lesser of useful lives of assets or lease terms including option periods; and equipment—3 to 12 years.

Intangible assets
Intangible assets consist primarily of franchise rights reacquired from franchisees and affiliates, and are amortized on the straight-line method over an average life of 29 years.

Financial instruments
Non-U.S. Dollar financing transactions generally are effective as hedges of long-term investments in the corresponding currency. Interest-rate exchange agreements are designated and generally are effective as hedges of the Company's interest-rate exposures. The carrying amounts for Cash and equivalents and Notes receivable approximated fair value. For noninterest-bearing security deposits by franchisees, no fair value is provided as these deposits are an integral part of the overall franchise arrangements.

Statement of cash flows
The Company considers all highly liquid investments with short-term maturity dates to be cash equivalents. The impact of changing foreign currencies on Cash and equivalents was not material. Certain prior year amounts have been reclassified to conform to the current year's presentation.

Number of restaurants in operation

	1992	1991	1990	1989
Operated by franchisees	8,654	8,151	7,578	7,135
Operated under business facilities lease arrangements	583	584	553	438
Operated by the Company	2,551	2,547	2,643	2,691
Operated by 50% or less owned affiliates	1,305	1,136	1,029	898
Systemwide restaurants	13,093	12,418	11,803	11,162

Franchisees operating under business facilities lease arrangements have options to purchase the businesses. The results of operations of restaurant businesses purchased and sold in transactions with franchisees and affiliates were not material to the consolidated financial statements for periods prior to purchase and sale.

Due to an increase in the Company's ownership, the Company consolidated affiliates in South Korea, Hungary and Chile in 1992, which increased Total assets and liabilities by $22.5 million. The consolidation of the Hawaii and Venezuela affiliates increased Total assets and liabilities by $51.4 million in 1991. In addition to other consideration, in 1991 the Company issued 160,000 shares of 5% Series D Preferred Stock at $100.00 per share as part of the Hawaii acquisition. Each share is entitled to one vote and is redeemable by the Company under certain circumstances at the redemption price of $100.00 per share. The redemption value of these shares, along with future consideration, was included in Security deposits by franchisees and other long-term liabilities.

Other operating (income) expense—net

(In millions of dollars)	1992	1991	1990
Gains on sales of restaurant businesses	$(43.1)	$ (64.0)	$(60.6)
Equity in earnings of unconsolidated affiliates	(29.5)	(57.5)	(32.0)
Net losses from property dispositions	18.1	9.9	6.2
Other—net	(9.5)	(2.2)	(8.9)
Other operating (income) expense—net	$(64.0)	$(113.8)	$(95.3)

Gains on sales of restaurant businesses are recognized as income when the sales are consummated and other stipulated conditions are met. Proceeds from certain sales of restaurant businesses and property include notes receivable.

FIGURE 6–5   (continued)

Property and equipment		
(In millions of dollars)	December 31, **1992**	1991
Land	**$ 2,440.0**	$ 2,375.8
Buildings and improvements on owned land	**4,906.0**	4,774.3
Buildings and improvements on leased land	**3,423.7**	3,293.2
Equipment, signs and seating	**1,467.2**	1,516.4
Other	**421.1**	408.3
	12,658.0	12,368.0
Accumulated depreciation and amortization	**(3,060.6)**	(2,809.5)
Net property and equipment	**$ 9,597.4**	$ 9,558.5

Depreciation and amortization were: 1992—$492.9 million; 1991—$456.9 million; 1990—$443.9 million. Contractual obligations for the acquisition and construction of property at December 31, 1992, amounted to $180.8 million.

Debt financing

Line of credit agreements

The Company has a long-term line of credit agreement for $700.0 million, which remained unborrowed at December 31, 1992, and which continues indefinitely unless terminated by the participating banks upon advance notice of at least 18 months. The Company decreased this line by $300.0 million from December 31, 1991. Each borrowing under the agreement bears interest at one of several specified floating rates, to be selected by the Company at the time of borrowing. The agreement provides for fees of .15 of 1% per annum on the unused portion of the commitment. At December 31, 1992, certain subsidiaries outside of the U.S. had unused lines of credit totaling $846.9 million; these were principally short-term and denominated in various currencies at local market rates of interest.

Exchange agreements

The Company has entered into agreements for the exchange of various currencies. Certain of these agreements also provide for the periodic exchange of interest payments. These agreements, as well as additional interest-rate exchange agreements, expire through 2002 and provide for an effective right of offset; therefore, the related receivable and liability are offset in the financial statements. The counterparties to these exchange agreements consist of a diverse group of financial institutions. The Company continually monitors its positions and the credit ratings of its counterparties, and adjusts positions as appropriate.

At December 31, 1992, the Company also had short-term forward foreign exchange contracts outstanding with a U.S. Dollar equivalent of $133.1 million in various currencies, primarily the French Franc.

Aggregate maturities

Included in the 1994 maturities are $700.0 million of notes maturing within one year, as 1994 is the earliest time at which the banks can terminate the line of credit agreement, which supports the classification in Long-term debt. Under certain agreements, the Company has the option to retire debt prior to maturity, either at par or at a premium over par. During 1992, $191.0 million was retired prior to maturity.

Guarantees

Included in Long-term debt at December 31, 1992, was $181.9 million of 7.67% ESOP Notes, Series A (Notes), and $93.9 million of 7.30% ESOP Notes, Series B (Notes), issued by the Leveraged Employee Stock Ownership Plan (LESOP), with payments through 2004 and 2006, respectively, which are guaranteed by the Company. The Company has agreed to repurchase the Notes upon the occurrence of certain events.

The Company also has guaranteed certain foreign affiliate loans of $164.2 million at December 31, 1992. The Company also was a general partner in 42 domestic partnerships with total assets of $155.0 million and total liabilities of $87.7 million at December 31, 1992.

Fair values

The carrying amounts for Notes payable and short-term forward foreign exchange contracts approximated fair value at December 31, 1992. The fair value of the remaining debt obligations (excluding capital leases), including the net effects of currency and interest-rate exchange agreements, was estimated using quoted market prices, various pricing models or discounted cash flow analyses. At December 31, 1992, the fair value of these obligations, which were primarily used to finance property and equipment, was $3.5 billion compared to a carrying value of $3.3 billion. The Company currently has no plans to retire any of these obligations prior to maturity, with the exception of $200.0 million of 8⅞% Debentures which were redeemed on January 21, 1993; a related loss of $16.0 million was recorded in 1992 when the redemption notice was given.

The Company believes that the fair value of Total assets is higher than their carrying value.

FIGURE 6–5   (continued)

Debt obligations

The Company has incurred debt obligations principally through various public and private offerings and bank loans. The terms of most debt obligations contain restrictions on Company and subsidiary mortgages and long-term debt of certain subsidiaries. The following table summarizes these debt obligations:

(In millions of U.S. Dollars)	Maturity dates	Interest rates (1) December 31		Amounts outstanding December 31		Aggregate maturities by currency for 1992 balances					
		1992	1991	1992	1991	1993	1994	1995	1996	1997	Thereafter
Fixed—original issue		8.9	9.0	$2,002.8	$2,054.3						
Fixed—converted via exchange agreements (2)		6.9	7.9	(1,174.7)	(677.3)						
Floating		4.0	5.5	214.6	381.4						
Total U.S. Dollars	1993-2014			1,042.7	1,758.4	$272.4	$ 583.2	$ 52.2	$(35.6)	$(16.1)	$186.6
Fixed		10.8	10.8	489.6	687.0						
Floating		7.8	10.9	275.3	177.2						
Total Pounds Sterling	1993-2002			764.9	864.2	165.7	83.5	30.3	145.2	15.1	325.1
Fixed		7.4	7.5	366.9	389.4						
Floating		11.5	9.6	19.3	20.6						
Total Deutsche Marks	1993-1998			386.2	410.0	20.0	205.8	91.5	18.9	49.8	.2
Fixed		9.9	9.6	293.2	323.4						
Floating		10.1	9.6	165.6	122.5						
Total French Francs	1993-2002			458.8	445.9	27.5	136.0	53.7	54.4	55.7	131.5
Fixed		12.9	12.4	155.7	200.3						
Floating		6.2	8.5	64.3	52.3						
Total Australian Dollars	1993-2000			220.0	252.6	27.6	70.5	1.3	58.2	1.1	61.3
Fixed		11.4	11.0	175.7	205.1						
Floating		7.4	8.5	56.7	50.7						
Total Canadian Dollars	1993-2021			232.4	255.8	4.4	79.2	68.3	78.8	.3	1.4
Fixed		5.8	6.1	120.2	100.2						
Total Japanese Yen	1997-2002			120.2	100.2					80.1	40.1
Fixed		8.6	9.3	361.5	264.9						
Floating		12.3	10.4	154.3	172.8						
Total other currencies	1993-2001			515.8	437.7	162.8	130.6	62.4	22.2	9.3	128.5
Debt obligations including the net effects of currency and interest-rate exchange agreements				3,741.0	4,524.8	680.4	1,288.8	359.7	342.1	195.3	874.7
Net asset positions of currency exchange agreements (included in Miscellaneous other assets)				115.8	90.0		38.3	6.1	12.8	1.1	57.5
Total debt obligations				$3,856.8	$4,614.8	$680.4	$1,327.1	$365.8	$354.9	$196.4	$932.2

(1) *Weighted average effective rate, computed on a semi-annual basis.*

(2) *A portion of U.S. Dollar fixed-rate debt has been converted into other currencies and/or into floating-rate debt through the use of exchange agreements as described on the previous page. The rates shown reflected the fixed rate on the receivable portion of the exchange agreements. All other obligations in this table reflected the gross effects of these and other exchange agreements.*

FIGURE 6–5　(continued)

Leasing arrangements

At December 31, 1992, the Company was lessee at 2,105 restaurant locations under ground leases (the Company leases land and constructs and owns buildings) and at 2,151 locations under improved leases (lessor owns land and buildings). Land and building lease terms are generally for 20 to 25 years and, in many cases, provide for rent escalations and one or more five-year renewal options with certain leases providing purchase options. The Company is generally obligated for the related occupancy costs which include property taxes, insurance and maintenance. In addition, the Company is lessee under noncancelable leases covering offices and vehicles.

Future minimum payments required under operating leases with initial terms of one year or more after December 31, 1992, are:

(In millions of dollars)	Restaurant	Other	Total
1993	$ 246.5	$ 35.0	$ 281.5
1994	241.7	33.4	275.1
1995	229.1	29.6	258.7
1996	218.7	26.1	244.8
1997	216.8	24.2	241.0
Thereafter	2,073.6	166.6	2,240.2
Total minimum payments	$3,226.4	$314.9	$3,541.3

Rent expense was: 1992—$320.2 million; 1991—$283.6 million; 1990—$256.8 million. Included in these amounts were percentage rents based on sales by the related restaurants in excess of minimum rents stipulated in certain lease agreements: 1992—$26.1 million; 1991—$26.3 million; 1990—$27.3 million.

Franchise arrangements

Franchise arrangements, with franchisees who operate in various geographic locations, generally provide for initial fees and continuing payments to the Company based upon a percent of sales, with minimum rent payments. Among other things, franchisees are provided the use of restaurant facilities, generally for a period of 20 years. They are required to pay related occupancy costs which include property taxes, insurance, maintenance and a refundable, noninterest-bearing security deposit. On a limited basis, the Company receives notes from franchisees. Generally the notes are secured by interests in restaurant equipment and franchises.

(In millions of dollars)	1992	1991	1990
Minimum rents			
Owned sites	$ 538.7	$ 494.5	$ 439.8
Leased sites	353.3	303.7	250.9
	892.0	798.2	690.7
Percentage fees	1,120.6	970.4	914.0
Initial fees	18.2	17.9	16.0
Revenues from franchised restaurants	$2,030.8	$1,786.5	$1,620.7

Future minimum payments based on minimum rents specified under franchise arrangements after December 31, 1992, are:

(In millions of dollars)	Owned sites	Leased sites	Total
1993	$ 584.4	$ 383.5	$ 967.9
1994	574.8	377.6	952.4
1995	564.4	361.0	925.4
1996	553.3	347.4	900.7
1997	541.8	335.7	877.5
Thereafter	5,155.5	3,095.7	8,251.2
Total minimum payments	$7,974.2	$4,900.9	$12,875.1

At December 31, 1992, Net property and equipment under franchise arrangements was $5.5 billion (including land of $1.7 billion), after deducting accumulated depreciation and amortization of $1.6 billion.

Profit sharing program

The Company has a program for U.S. employees which includes profit sharing, 401(k) (McDESOP), and leveraged employee stock ownership features. McDESOP allows employees to invest in McDonald's common stock by making contributions which are partially matched by the Company. Assets of the profit sharing plan can be invested in McDonald's common stock, or among several other alternatives. Certain subsidiaries outside of the U.S. also offer profit sharing, stock purchase or other similar benefit plans. Total U.S. program costs were: 1992—$38.8 million; 1991—$46.4 million; 1990—$50.4 million. Total plan costs outside of the U.S. were: 1992—$14.0 million; 1991—$9.8 million; 1990—$10.9 million. The Company does not provide any other postretirement benefits.

Stock options

In 1992, shareholders approved the McDonald's 1992 Stock Ownership Incentive Plan, under which 18.0 million shares of common stock are reserved for issuance. At December 31, 1992, no shares were issued under the plan. Under the 1975 Stock Ownership Option Plan, options to purchase common stock are granted at prices

FIGURE 6–5   (continued)

not less than fair market value of the stock on date of grant. Substantially all of these options become exercisable in four equal biennial installments, commencing one year from date of grant, and expire ten years from date of grant. At December 31, 1992, 26.2 million shares of common stock were reserved for issuance under this plan.

(In millions, except per common share data)	1992	1991	1990
Options outstanding at January 1	23.7	21.6	19.7
Options granted	5.8	5.5	4.9
Options exercised	(3.8)	(2.6)	(1.9)
Options forfeited	(.6)	(.8)	(1.1)
Options outstanding at December 31	25.1	23.7	21.6
Options exercisable at December 31	7.7	7.8	7.0
Common shares reserved for future grants at December 31	19.1	6.3	10.9
Option prices per common share			
Exercised during the year	$9 to $45	$6 to $34	$5 to $29
Outstanding at year-end	$9 to $48	$9 to $34	$6 to $34

Capital stock

Per common share information
Income used in the computation of per common share information was reduced by preferred stock cash dividends (net of tax benefits in 1992) and divided by the weighted average shares of common stock outstanding during each year: 1992—363.2 million; 1991—358.1 million; 1990—359.0 million. The effect of potentially dilutive securities was not material.

Preferred stock
In December 1992, the Company issued $500.0 million of Series E 7.72% Cumulative Preferred Stock; 10,000 preferred shares are equivalent to 20.0 million depositary shares having a liquidation preference of $25.00 per depositary share. Each preferred share is entitled to one vote under certain circumstances, and is redeemable at the option of the Company beginning on December 3, 1997, at its liquidation preference plus accrued and unpaid dividends.

In September 1989 and April 1991, the Company sold $200.0 million of Series B and $100.0 million of Series C ESOP Convertible Preferred Stock, respectively, to the LESOP. The LESOP financed the purchase by issuing Notes which are guaranteed by the Company and are included in Long-term debt, with an offsetting reduction in Shareholders' equity. Each preferred share has a liquidation preference of $28.75 and $33.125, respectively, and is convertible into a minimum of .7692 and .8 common

share (conversion rate), respectively. Upon termination, employees are guaranteed a minimum value payable in common shares, equal to the greater of the conversion rate; the fair market value of their preferred shares; or the liquidation preference plus accrued dividends, not to exceed one common share. Each preferred share is entitled to one vote and is redeemable at the option of the Company three years after issuance and, under certain circumstances, is redeemable prior to that date. In 1992, 4.1 million shares of Series B stock were converted into 3.2 million common shares.

Common equity put options
In December 1992, the Company sold 2.0 million Common equity put options which are exercisable in April 1993 at an average price of $46.98 per share. The exercise price of $94.0 million was classified in Common equity put options and the related offset was recorded in Common stock in treasury, net of premiums received, at December 31, 1992.

Shareholder rights plan
In December 1988, the Company declared a dividend of one Preferred Share Purchase Right (Right) on each outstanding share of common stock. Under certain conditions, each Right may be exercised to purchase one two-hundredths of a share of Series A Junior Participating Preferred Stock (the economic equivalent of one common share) at an exercise price of $125.00 (which may be adjusted under certain circumstances), and is transferable apart from the common stock ten days following a public announcement that a person or group has acquired beneficial ownership of 20% or more of the outstanding common shares, or ten business days following the commencement or announcement of an intention to make a tender or exchange offer, resulting in beneficial ownership by a person or group of 20% or more of the outstanding common shares.

If a person or group acquires 20% or more of the outstanding common shares, or if the Company is acquired in a merger or other business combination transaction, each Right will entitle the holder, other than such person or group, to purchase at the then current exercise price, stock of the Company or the acquiring company having a market value of twice the exercise price.

Each Right is nonvoting and expires on December 28, 1998, unless redeemed by the Company, at a price of $.005, at any time prior to the public announcement that a person or group has acquired beneficial ownership of 20% or more of the outstanding common shares. At December 31, 1992, 2.1 million shares of the Series A Junior Participating Preferred Stock were reserved for issuance under this Plan.

FIGURE 6–5 (continued)

11-YEAR SUMMARY

(Dollars rounded to millions, except per common share data and average restaurant sales)	1992	1991	1990	1989	1988	1987	1986	1985	1984	1983	1982
Systemwide sales	$21,885	19,928	18,759	17,333	16,064	14,330	12,432	11,001	10,007	8,687	7,809
U.S.	$13,243	12,519	12,252	12,012	11,380	10,576	9,534	8,843	8,071	7,069	6,362
Outside of the U.S.	$ 8,642	7,409	6,507	5,321	4,684	3,754	2,898	2,158	1,936	1,618	1,447
Systemwide sales by type											
Operated by franchisees	$14,474	12,959	12,017	11,219	10,424	9,452	8,422	7,612	6,914	5,929	5,239
Operated by the Company	$ 5,103	4,908	5,019	4,601	4,196	3,667	3,106	2,770	2,538	2,297	2,095
Operated by affiliates	$ 2,308	2,061	1,723	1,513	1,444	1,211	904	619	555	461	475
Average sales by restaurants open at least one year, in thousands	$ 1,733	1,658	1,649	1,621	1,596	1,502	1,369	1,296	1,264	1,169	1,132
Revenues from franchised restaurants	$ 2,031	1,787	1,621	1,465	1,325	1,186	1,037	924	828	704	620
Total revenues	$ 7,133	6,695	6,640	6,066	5,521	4,853	4,143	3,694	3,366	3,001	2,715
Operating income	$ 1,862	1,679	1,596	1,438	1,288	1,160	983	905	812	713	613
Income before provision for income taxes	$ 1,448	1,299	1,246	1,157	1,046	959	848	782	707	628	546
Net income	$ 959	860	802	727	646	549*	480	433	389	343	301
Cash provided by operations	$ 1,426	1,423	1,301	1,246	1,177	1,051	852	813	701	618	505
Financial position at year-end											
Net property and equipment	$ 9,597	9,559	9,047	7,758	6,800	5,820	4,878	4,164	3,521	3,183	2,765
Total assets	$11,681	11,349	10,668	9,175	8,159	6,982	5,969	5,043	4,230	3,727	3,263
Long-term debt	$ 3,176	4,267	4,429	3,902	3,111	2,685	2,131	1,638	1,268	1,171	1,056
Total shareholders' equity	$ 5,892	4,835	4,182	3,550	3,413	2,917	2,506	2,245	2,009	1,755	1,529
Per common share											
Net income	$ 2.60	2.35	2.20	1.95	1.71	1.45*	1.24	1.11	.97	.85	.74
Dividends declared	$ .39	.36	.33	.30	.27	.24	.21	.20	.17	.14	.12
Total shareholders' equity at year-end	$ 14.77	13.48	11.65	9.81	9.09	7.72	6.45	5.67	4.94	4.38	3.78
Market price at year-end	$ 48¾	38	29⅛	34½	24⅛	22	20¼	18	11½	10½	9
Systemwide restaurants at year-end	13,093	12,418	11,803	11,162	10,513	9,911	9,410	8,901	8,304	7,778	7,259
Operated by franchisees	9,237	8,735	8,131	7,573	7,110	6,760	6,406	6,150	5,724	5,371	4,911
Operated by the Company	2,551	2,547	2,643	2,691	2,600	2,399	2,301	2,165	2,053	1,949	1,846
Operated by affiliates	1,305	1,136	1,029	898	803	752	703	586	527	458	502
U.S.	8,959	8,764	8,576	8,270	7,907	7,567	7,272	6,972	6,595	6,251	5,918
Outside of the U.S.	4,134	3,654	3,227	2,892	2,606	2,344	2,138	1,929	1,709	1,527	1,341
Number of countries at year-end	65	59	53	51	50	47	46	42	36	32	31

*Before the cumulative prior years' benefit from the change in accounting for income taxes.

FIGURE 6–5 (continued)

REFERENCES

CHOIS, F., and R. LEVICH. "International Accounting Diversity: Does It Affect Market Participants?" *Financial Analysts Journal,* July/August 1991, pp. 73–82.

FLEMING, P. "The Growing Importance of International Accounting Standards." *Journal of Accountancy,* September 1991, pp. 100–106.

COMPANY ANALYSIS: FORECASTING EARNINGS

INTRODUCTION

In Chapter 6 we reviewed the primary sources of information, internal and external, about firms. We discovered that the principal sources of internal information about a firm were its financial statements. However, the analyst must be aware that there is more to financial statements than meets the eye. More than anything else, a good analyst must understand the impact of different acceptable methods of accounting for items on the position statement and the statement of income.

The income statement is perhaps used more than any other to assess the future of the firm, and earnings per share has become a key figure on this statement. Strong evidence indicates that earnings have a direct and powerful effect upon dividends and share prices, so the importance of forecasting earnings cannot be overstated. A Niederhoffer and Regan study suggests that stock prices are strongly dependent upon earnings changes, both absolute and relative to analysts' estimates. They discovered that the common characteristics of the companies registering the best price changes included a forecast of moderately increased earnings and a realized profit gain far in excess of analysts' expectations. The worst-performing stocks were those characterized by severe earnings declines, combined with unusually optimistic forecasts.[1] The accuracy of earnings forecasts is of enormous value in stock selection.

This chapter has two aims: First, using financial statements, we will examine the "chemistry" of earnings. The various ingredients in the financial statements can be related in such a way that the analyst is able to visualize the critical aspects of a firm's operations that dictate the level, trend, and stability of earnings. Second, we will look at traditional methods employed by analysts in assessing the outlook for revenues, expenses, and earnings in the firm over a forward holding period, given the economic and industry outlook. The methods that will be explained are (1) the return-on-investment (ROI) approach, (2) the market-share/profit-margin

---

[1]Victor Niederhoffer and Patrick J. Regan, "Earnings Changes, Analysts' Forecasts, and Stock Prices," *Financial Analysts Journal* 28, no. 3 (May–June 1972), pp. 65–71.

approach, and (3) an independent, subjective approach to the forecast of revenues and expenses.

In Chapter 8 we will examine some newer techniques used in forecasting revenues, expenses, and ultimately earnings; and we will take up the forecasting of dividends and the market price of a share of stock at the end of the holding period.

Let us begin this journey through the next two chapters by taking a look at the ingredients that produce earnings in the firm.

THE CHEMISTRY OF EARNINGS

One of the most effective ways of getting "inside" earnings is to explore the financial statements for all possible explanations of a change, or lack of change, in earnings. Changes in reported earnings can result from changes in methods of accounting, as we saw in Chapter 6. Beyond this, they result from changes (1) in the operations of the business, and/or (2) in the financing of the business—that is, changes in productivity or in the resource (asset) base.

The efficiency or profitability with which a firm uses its assets is a key influence on earnings levels and growth. Better-managed companies typically have higher profits (net income) per dollar of assets than do poorly managed firms. The other key to earnings levels and growth lies in how fast a firm increases its asset base and the sources it uses for financing expansion. Debt and equity sources each have a unique effect upon earnings growth.

Our task of earnings analysis will be greatly facilitated by using a simple accounting model to focus on (1) what effect a change in a specific variable will have on earnings, and (2) whether each variable can be expected to cause a sustainable influence on earnings over long periods.

Asset Productivity and Earnings

Every firm has an aggregate of invested capital in the form of assets. These assets are used by management to generate revenues and net income. The funds necessary to acquire assets come from debt and equity sources of financing. Firms strive to operate in such a way as to provide shareholders the best possible return per dollar invested.

In balance-sheet terms, firms seek to maximize the return on total funds provided (assets). Should all financing be provided from equity money (no debt financing), the return on assets and equity are the same. To the extent that borrowed money is used to provide assets, return on equity will depend upon the relationship between return on total capital and the cost of borrowed funds.

Separation of the investment and financing activities of the firm makes the problem a bit clearer. Shown below are an income statement and a balance sheet in abbreviated form:

INCOME STATEMENT ($ IN MILLIONS)		BALANCE SHEET ($ IN MILLIONS)			
Sales	$100	Assets	$50	Liabilities	$25
− Operating Costs	88			Equity	25
= EBIT	12				
− Interest Expense	2				
= EBT	10				
− Taxes	4				
= EAT	6				
÷ No. of shares	5				
= EPS	$1.20				
DPS	.84				

We have used some shorthand to distinguish earnings at various stages:

EBIT = earnings before interest and taxes

EBT = earnings before taxes

EAT = earnings after taxes

EPS = earnings per share

DPS = dividend per share

Let us set aside the effects of taxes and financing for the moment. The productivity of total assets can be seen as:

$$\text{Return on assets} = \frac{\text{EBIT}}{\text{Assets}} = \frac{12}{50} = 24\%$$

The $50 million provided the firm (without reference to source of funds—debt or equity) generated a 24 percent return before considering distribution of these earnings to the tax collector, creditors, and shareholders. In general, the greater the return on assets, the higher the market value of the firm, other things being equal.

The return on assets, however, is only the end product of a mixture of events within the firm. If we think of the normal operating cycle of a company as analogous to the functioning of a wheel, we are better able to dissect the forces that contribute to the return on assets. See Figure 7–1 for the ordinary operating cycle

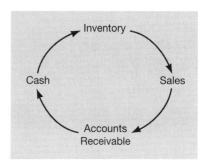

FIGURE 7–1   Operating Cycle for a Firm

for a firm, starting with placing cash into inventories. These inventories are then sold to create revenues. Deducting operating costs from revenues (sales) provides a profit. Thus, each time the operating cycle or wheel goes around, a profit (or loss) results. The key to overall return on funds committed to the enterprise is (1) the number of times per year the wheel spins around, and (2) the profits that emerge with each spin. Thus, a refinement of the return-on-assets concept is to say that it is the product of the turnover of assets into sales (number of spins of the operating wheel), or intensity of utilization of assets in creating sales, and the margin of profit from each spin, or the profit productivity of sales. In the lexicon of finance, we say that the return on assets is the product of the *turnover* of assets and the *margin* of profit:

$$\text{Return on assets} = \underset{\text{(Turnover)}}{\frac{\text{Sales}}{\text{Assets}}} \times \underset{\text{(Margin)}}{\frac{\text{EBIT}}{\text{Sales}}}$$

or, as before:

$$\text{Return on assets} = \frac{\text{EBIT}}{\text{Assets}}$$

Two firms in the same or even different industries can quite possibly earn comparable returns on assets. However, they may have totally different (1) turnover of assets, and/or (2) profit margins on sales. For example, consider the basic character of a jewelry store and a supermarket. They may enjoy similar returns on assets, but jewelry stores turn over their goods very slowly, while supermarkets enjoy an operating cycle that is quite rapid. Yet supermarkets enjoy only modest profit margins, and jewelry-store margins are much higher. So it is conceivable that the following relationship might apply:

	RETURN ON ASSETS	=	TURNOVER	×	MARGIN
Jeweler	.15	=	.5	×	.30
Supermarket	.15	=	15.0	×	.01

Within the same industry, firms with slightly different product mixes and/or operating characteristics might earn competitive returns on assets through skillful compensations for deficiencies in margin or turnover. For example, take two jewelers who differ in the type of merchandise they offer for sale. Jeweler A deals in expensive jewelry, watches, and precious stones; jeweler B specializes in costume jewelry. Jeweler A might have a higher margin but lower turnover than B, but both may enjoy equal returns on assets. Thus:

	RETURN ON ASSETS	=	TURNOVER	×	MARGIN
Jeweler A	.15	=	.5	×	.30
Jeweler B	.15	=	1.0	×	.15

In sum, the productivity of total funds provided the firm is the product of the management's ability to (1) generate sales and revenues in relation to this package of funds or its intensity of utilization of assets, and (2) increase the profitability that results from each dollar of sales created.

In our hypothetical company, the return on assets is broken down as follows:

$$\text{Return on assets } (R) = \text{Turnover } (T) \times \text{Margin } (M)$$

R	$=$	T	$\times$	M
.24	$=$	$\dfrac{100}{50}$	$\times$	$\dfrac{12}{100}$
.24	$=$	2	$\times$	.12

So far, so good. But we have sidestepped taxes and distinctions in the sources of financing.

Earnings and the Role of Financing

The sources of funds available to firms are numerous. In the main, they are either borrowed money or equity funds. Some borrowed money is essentially cost-free—for instance, tax and wage accruals, and trade credit paid on time. Other borrowed money, such as bank loans and bond issues, has a readily identifiable dollar interest cost. Equity funds have explicit and implicit costs. The most readily identifiable explicit cost of equity money is the dividend paid. Of course, we know by now that shareholders expect capital gains in addition to dividends when they purchase common shares. However, capital gains must be thought of more as an implicit cost of equity money. For the time being at least, it may help to think of the requirements of those who provide equity money as stated in the form of an earnings return per dollar of equity capital employed by the firm.

DEBT FINANCING AND EARNINGS

Among the many reasons for debt financing, the most important is the leverage provided to common-stock holders. In Chapter 3 the notion of financial risk or financial leverage taught us a simple axiom: If you can earn more on borrowed money than you have to pay for it, you come out ahead—provided that you borrow within prudent limits. If you borrow money from your banker at 10 percent and place the funds in another bank to earn 5 percent interest on a savings account, your road to ruin is assured. It would be far better if you had the same deal at a 4 percent cost of borrowing.

The *productivity* of funds was called *return on assets*. The *cost* of borrowed funds is called the *effective interest rate:*

$$\text{Effective interest rate } (I) = \frac{\text{Interest expense}}{\text{Total liabilities}}$$

$$= \frac{2}{25} = 8\%$$

The firm in our example has total liabilities of $25 million. The company may have $5 million in debts with no explicit interest cost and a $20 million bond issue outstanding that bears a rate of interest of 10 percent. The weighted-average, or "effective," cost of borrowed money is thus 8 percent because some debt bears no direct cost and the remainder costs 10 percent ($0\% \times \$5$ million $+ 10\% \times \$20$ million $= \$2/\$25$ million $= 8\%$).

Relating the return on assets to the effective cost of funds indicates whether the firm is able to earn more than its direct cost of borrowing funds. Now, let us relate the productivity of borrowed funds to their effective cost:

Benefits of borrowed money = Return on assets − Effective interest rate

or

Benefits of borrowed money = $R - I$

In our example:

$$R - I = .24 - .08 = .16, \text{ or } 16\%$$

The borrowing of money at a fixed cost and the use of these funds to earn a return on assets is known as employing *leverage*. Leverage can also be used with preferred stock or any form of fixed-cost financing. As long as $R - I$ is a positive difference, leverage is being used to the firm's advantage. The importance of maximizing the difference between R and I is obvious. The necessity to avoid $R < I$ is equally apparent. Less obvious, however, is a reasonable answer to a simple question: If a firm enjoys a positive difference of $R - I$, why not push the mix of total funds acquired to the maximum limit of debt funds and minimize the financing that is done through equity sources? More simply, if you can borrow funds at an effective cost of 8 percent and earn 24 percent on money, why not borrow as much as you possibly can in order to enhance the return on your own funds (equity)?

First, as borrowed funds increase relative to equity funds in the total financing mix, borrowing costs (I) increase, and increase more rapidly than the amounts borrowed. For example, increasing debt funds from $25 million to $30 million ($+20$ percent) could result in an increase in interest on the additional $5 million to 15 percent from the prior rate of 10 percent ($+50$ percent). Thus, while $R = 24\%$, the difference ($R - I$) will shrink. The reason the rate of interest would rise is that creditors are now providing relatively more funds than are owners (equity), and therefore, proportionately more of the risks of the business are being shouldered by the creditors. Creditors will require greater compensation in the form of higher interest rates (and perhaps controls over the business—an indirect cost).

Table 7–1

PERCENTAGE RETURNS FOR SHAREHOLDERS UNDER
ALTERNATIVE CAPITAL STRUCTURES*

PERCENT RATE OF RETURN ON ASSETS (R)	LIABILITY/EQUITY RATIO (L/E)			
	0	½	1	2
− 4	− 4	− 8	− 13	−22
0	0	− 2	− 5	−10
4	4	3	3	2
5	5	5	5	5
7	7	8	9	11
9	9	11	13	17
10	10	12	15	20

*Assumes 5 percent interest rate (i) on debt.

Second, when the cost of debt financing rises—directly and indirectly—so will the cost of equity funds. The employment of leverage causes the *quantity* of earnings available to the owners to increase whenever leverage is employed successfully ($R > I$). However, as more debt is employed relative to equity funds, the *quality* of earnings can deteriorate.

We see in Table 7–1 the return on shareholders' equity at book value as the result of differing rates of return on assets and capital structures (L/E). The assumption in the table is that debt costs 5 percent (I), and taxes on income are ignored.

Example: Assume $L/E = 2$.

$$\text{Rate of return on equity} = R + (R - I)L/E$$
$$= -4 + [(-4) - (+5)]2$$
$$= 4 + (-9)2$$
$$= -4 + (-18)$$
$$= -22$$

Note that when the return on assets equals the interest rate on borrowed funds (5 percent), the return to shareholders is independent of the degree of financial leverage; that is, L/E. On the other hand, if the rate of return on assets is greater than (less than) the interest rate, the stockholders' percentage return is increased (decreased) by leverage. Furthermore, the increased volatility of shareholder returns increases with the expansion of L/E, or the degree of financial leverage. Note that over the range of return on assets shown, the range of shareholder returns expands from the range (−4% to +10%) to (−22% to +20%) as we move from no leverage to a 2:1 ratio. This increase in variation or range can affect the P/E on the stock

downward or increase the cost of equity capital. In addition, equity costs might increase because the risk of bankruptcy is greater. With no leverage, a series of years of −4 percent returns on assets can injure a firm; however, with L/E of 2, a series of −4 percent returns on assets leads to −22 percent on equity and accelerates the risk of ruin to stockholders markedly.

The greater volatility of earnings (up *and* down) owing to increased leverage can, at certain levels of debt financing, cause the market to pay less per dollar of earnings. Suppose the quantity of earnings is increased 10 percent owing to expanded leverage, but the market pays 15 percent less for the earnings because of their lower presumed quality or stability. In effect, the result is that a lower price per share is experienced. Thus, we might say that the cost of equity capital has increased along with the higher interest cost of debt. In other words, earnings before and after taxes might increase through the expansion of borrowed capital, but the market might pay less for these increased earnings owing to a perceived (real or imagined) deterioration in the stability (quality) of these earnings. Lower stock prices suggest that shareholders are really *worse* off because of additional borrowings!

Finally, while the difference between R and I is decreasing as more debt is raised and the improved earnings are worth less to stockholders, the likelihood that R will remain constant or increase as funds employed expand is questionable. R itself may become progressively more difficult to maintain (or improve) as a firm gets larger.

If it were not for the relationships noted—(1) higher I, (2) higher cost of equity (lower share prices), and (3) strain on R—we would observe many more firms than we do with debt pushed as close as possible to 100 percent of total funds.

The proportions of debt and equity financing in the total mix of funds can be measured in a variety of ways.[2] We shall simply relate debt to equity as:

$$\text{Debt/Equity} = \frac{\text{Total liabilities}}{\text{Equity}}$$

In our example, total company funds come to $50 million. Debt represents $25 million and equity $25 million. Thus the debt-equity ratio is 25/25, or 1. Translated into words, this means that the firm has $1 of debt for each $1 of equity capital. Suppose the $50 million had been split between $32 million in debt and $18 million in equity. The debt-equity ratio would be 32/18, or 1.77:1—in words, $1.77 in debt for each $1 in equity. The higher the debt-to-equity ratio, the greater the leverage being employed, and conversely, the lower the equity funds in a relative sense. Thus, larger amounts of debt relative to equity funds leads to increased leverage, or "trading on the equity."

The difference between the return on assets and the effective interest rate on borrowed capital yielded a percentage amount. We were originally concerned with an ultimate explanation of earnings in dollar form. To convert back:

[2]Some authors use Debt/Total assets. This measure relates debt to total funds employed.

$$\text{EBT} = (R)(A) - (I)(L)$$

$$= (\text{EBIT/Assets}) \, (\text{Assets}) - (\text{Interest/Liabilities}) \, (\text{Liabilities})$$

$$= \text{EBIT} - \text{Interest}$$

where:

A = assets
L = total liabilities

$$\text{EBT} = (.24) \, (\$50) - (.08) \, (\$25)$$
$$= \$12 - 2$$
$$= \$10$$

Equation 7.1 can be recast to enable us to isolate and relate R, I, and L/E in the following manner: Because $A = L + E$, where E = equity, then:

$$\text{EBT} = (R) \, (L + E) - (I) \, (L)$$

and simplifying yields

$$\text{EBT} = (RL) + (RE) - (IL)$$

To isolate $(R - I)$ and L/E, further simplification yields

$$\text{EBT} = (RE) + (RL) - (IL)$$
$$= (RE) + L(R - I)$$

Dividing each element on the right side of the equation by E while multiplying the entire right side by E maintains the integrity of the equation, so[3]

$$\text{EBT} = \left[\frac{RE}{E} + \frac{L(R - I)}{E} \right] E$$

$$= [R + (R - I)L/E]E$$

$$= [.24 + (.24 - .08)25/25]\$25$$

$$= (.24 + 16)\$25$$

$$= (.40)\$25$$

$$= \$10$$

We can now appreciate not only the importance of $R - I$ but the magnification of the difference depending upon L/E. In our example, if total assets (\$50) had been

---

[3]Consider the following: $1 + 2 = 3$. If we divide and multiply by, say, 2, we get $(\frac{1}{2} + 1) \times 2$, or $1\frac{1}{2} \times 2 = 3$.

divided into debt = $40 and equity = $10 and $(R - I)$ remained unchanged (a questionable assumption), then:

$$EBT = [.24 + (.24 - .08) \, 40/10]\$10$$

$$= [.24 + (.16) \, 4]\$10$$

$$= (.88)\$10$$

$$= \$8.8$$

With debt $40 and equity $10, EBT is only $8.8. With debt and equity each at $25, EBT was $10. However, if we relate EBT to equity (EBT/Equity), the answers are 8.8/10, or 88 percent, versus 10/25, or 40 percent. Stated in the latter form, we can visualize the point that when the difference $R - I$ is positive, larger values of L/E magnify the difference.

In sum, at this juncture we have been able to define earnings before taxes as follows:

$$EBT = [R + (R - I)L/E]E$$

Equity Financing and Earnings

Most firms obtain equity financing from (1) the issuance of new shares, and/or (2) retention of earnings.

The issuance of stock occurs through a cash sale or through an exchange for shares in another firm. The effect of issuing new shares depends primarily upon the relationship of the sale price to the asset value of outstanding shares. Asset value is determined in the following manner:

$$\text{Asset value per share} = \frac{\text{Assets}}{\text{Number of common shares}}$$

In our example, 5 million shares are assumed to be outstanding. The value of assets is $50 million. The asset value per share of stock is $10($50/5).

To see the earnings effect of new shares, let us assume we sell 1 million new shares at either $15, or $10, or $5 per share:

	NEW SHARE PRICE		
	$15	$10	$5
(1) Old asset base	$50.00	$50.00	$50.00
(2) Proceeds from sale of new shares	$15.00	$10.00	$5.00
(3) New asset base	$65.00	$60.00	$55.00
(4) Rate of return on assets	.24	.24	.24
(5) New EBIT (3 × 4)	$15.60	$14.40	$13.20
(6) EBIT/New shares (new total shares = 6 million)	$2.60	$2.40	$2.20

This exercise suggests that whenever new shares can be sold at a price in excess of asset value per share, earnings can be improved on a per-share basis. Earnings fall only if new shares are sold below asset value and/or if profitability declines. The level of EBIT before the assumed common-stock financing was $12 million, and the EBIT per share was $2.40. Notice that EBIT per share remains at $2.40 if new shares are sold at $10, but sales below $10 result in lower earnings per share than before the new financing and new shares sold at prices above $10 bolster earnings per share.

Even though we have been discussing the sale of new shares for cash, the same type of analysis is applicable to a merger in which the book value of assets per share received by the acquiring company exceeds the book value of the assets per share given to the stockholders of the acquired company. Furthermore, asset value per share can also be increased by retiring shares at a discount from existing book value. For example, assume that our hypothetical firm with an asset value per share of $10 is able to repurchase some of its shares in the open market at a price of $8 per share. Suppose sufficient cash is available to repurchase 1 million shares ($8 million). The new asset value per share will be $50 million less $8 million in cash, divided by 4 million remaining shares, or $10.50. This is an increase of 5 percent ($.50/$10). The ability to sustain a rate of return on assets (R) of 24 percent would cause earnings to be $42 million times .24, or $10,080,000. On a per-share basis this is $2.52 ($10,080,000/4 million), or a rise of 5 percent from the previous level of $2.40, corresponding to the percentage increase in asset value per share.

It is vital to remember that these examples of selling or exchanging stock above asset values or redeeming shares below asset values will influence earnings as a function of the ability of the company to maintain the level of the rate of return on assets ($R = 24\%$).

The ability of the firm to maintain $R = 24\%$ is a prerequisite to improved earnings. This can occur under astute management, up to a point. If the ability to sustain (or improve) the return on assets (R) were possible regardless of the size of the firm (total assets), companies whose share prices exceeded asset values would find they could improve earnings per share almost without limit simply by selling more and more and more stock.

Earnings retention provides a basic source of earnings growth. Corporations in general tend to pay out about one-half their earnings. The amounts retained increase the asset base. Our example company had earnings per share of $1.20 and paid a dividend of $0.84 per share. We can say:

$$\text{Dividend payout rate} = \frac{\text{DPS}}{\text{EPS}} = \frac{\$0.84}{\$1.20} = 70\%$$

or, alternatively,

$$\text{Retention rate} = 1.00 - \text{Dividend payout (\%)}$$

$$= 1.00 - .70$$

$$= .30, \text{ or } 30\%$$

The company's total earnings after taxes of $6 million was split into $4.2 million paid out and $1.8 million retained. The $1.8 million retained adds to the equity base and the total asset base. The maintenance of a return on assets of 24 percent, other things being equal, would add $.432 million to EBIT in the following year:

$$\text{Growth in EBIT} = \text{Retention rate} \times \text{Return on assets}$$

$$= .30 \times .24 = .072 = 7.2\%$$

or

$$g = B \times R$$

where:

B = retention rate (%)
g = growth rate of EBIT
R = return on assets

Retention and earnings growth are, once again, dependent upon maintaining the rate of return on assets.

Effects of Taxes

Our discussion so far has been in terms of earnings before taxes. The effects of taxes on income can be accommodated in our model by making the following transformation:

$$\text{EAT} = (1 - T)\,[R + (R - I)L/E]E$$

where:

T = Effective tax rate = Tax expense/EBT

The notion $(1 - T)$ is really indicating what percentage of each $1 of income is available after satisfying Uncle Sam and other taxing authorities. If $T = 60$ percent, we would say that 40 cents of every $1 of income is available after taxes ($1.00 − $.60). The lower the tax rate, the higher the percentage of income left over, and vice versa. The difference between a tax rate and an "effective" tax rate lies in the fact that not all income to the firm is taxed at the same rate. Hence, the effective tax rate is apt to be different from what the rate schedule shows for the level of EBT.

Moreover, as we learned in Chapter 6, the income reported for tax returns may be different from the income shown on the reports to shareholders. For example, a firm may have ordinary operating income of $7 million, subject to a tax rate of 50 percent. Additional income of $3 million may be subject to lower capital gains rates of, say, 25 percent. The effective tax *rate* is the total tax relative to the total income to be taxed, or $4.25/$10, or 42.5 percent. Our example firm has an effective tax rate of

$$T = \text{Tax expense/EBT} = 4/10 = 40\%$$

EAT in the example becomes:

$$\text{EAT} = (1 - T)\,[R + (R - I)L/E]E$$
$$= (1 - .4)(\$10)$$
$$= \$6$$

Earnings and Dividends Per Share

To convert EAT to a per-share basis, we need only divide it by the number of common shares outstanding:

$$\text{EPS} = \frac{\text{EAT}}{\text{Number of shares outstanding}}$$

In general, then, in terms of our total model,[4]

$$\text{EPS} = \frac{(1 - T)\,[R + (R - I)L/E]E}{\text{Number of common shares outstanding}}$$

where:

> EPS = earnings per share
> T = effective tax rate (Tax expense/EBT)
> B = retention rate [or $1 - (\text{DPS/EPS})$]
> R = before tax return on assets (EBIT/A)
> I = effective interest rate (Interest expense/Liabilities)
> L = total liabilities
> E = equity

Dividends per share can be calculated as:

$$\text{DPS} = (1 - B)(\text{EPS})$$

The value of the model can now be appreciated fully. We can see that earnings per share and changes in earnings are a function of:

1. utilization of asset base (turnover of assets);
2. profit productivity of sales (margin on sales);
3. effective cost of borrowed funds (effective interest rate);

---

[4]This model and its enrichment are the result primarily of the work of Lerner and Carleton. See E. Lerner and W. T. Carleton, *A Theory of Financial Analysis* (New York: Harcourt Brace Jovanovich, 1966).

Table 7–2

THE GROWTH CO.: INCOME STATEMENTS FOR THE YEARS
ENDED DECEMBER 31, 19X1–X3 ($ IN MILLIONS)

	19X1	19X2	19X3
Net sales	$117.0	$117.0	$116.0
Other income	1.0		3.2
Cost of sales	105.0	103.0	105.0
Earnings before interest and taxes	13.0	14.0	14.2
Interest expense	.5	.4	1.1
Earnings before taxes	12.5	13.6	13.1
Taxes	6.0	6.0	5.0
Earnings after taxes	6.5	7.6	8.1
Average shares outstanding (millions)	5.6	5.5	5.0
Earnings per share	$1.16	$1.38	$1.63
Dividends per share	.58	.65	.75

4. debt-to-equity ratio;

5. equity base; and

6. effective tax rate.

We have deliberately isolated the critical variables that determine earnings and in turn dividends. The final task we face is to (1) isolate how changes in specific variables affect earnings, and (2) examine the sustainability of each variable as a long-run influence upon earnings.

An Example: The Growth Co.

See Tables 7–2 and 7–3 for abbreviated financial statements for a company we have chosen to call the Growth Co. In Table 7–4 is a summary of values for the key variables in our model for three years of data.[5]

Table 7–3

THE GROWTH CO.: POSITION STATEMENT (ABBREVIATED),
DECEMBER 31, 19X1–X3 ($ IN MILLIONS)

	19X1	19X2	19X3
Total assets	$103	$105	$103
Current debt	21	21	21
Long-term debt	9	8	17
Common-stock equity	73	76	65
Total debt and equity	103	105	103

[5]The reader is invited to calculate several of the values in Table 7–4 to ensure understanding of earlier materials.

Table 7–4

THE GROWTH CO.: SUMMARY DATA ON KEY FINANCIAL VARIABLES, 19X1–X3

VARIABLE	19X1	19X2	19X3
Dividends per share	$.580	$.650	$.750
Earnings per share	$1.160	$1.380	$1.630
Return on assets:	.126	.133	.138
Margin	.111	.120	.122
Turnover	1.136	1.114	1.126
Effective interest rate	.017	.014	0.29
Total liabilities/equity	.410	.380	.580
Equity ($ in millions)	73.000	76.000	65.000
Number of shares (millions)	5.600	5.500	5.000
Effective tax rate	.480	.440	.380
Retention rate	.500	.530	.540

The pattern of earnings over the three-year period indicates that earnings per share have grown 18 percent per year between 19X1 and 19X3. An impressive rate of growth indeed! The big question is: Is the growth rate transitory or is it sustainable? For example, has the growth been achieved through profitability rather than shifts in funds sources? The latter is not sustainable, while the former usually is. Let us take a closer look.

The return on assets has steadily improved, year to year. The primary source is improved profit margins in the face of slower asset turnover and almost stagnant sales. Such a profit-margin improvement is a healthy sign.

Increasing use has been made of debt financing relative to equity (although the retention rate on earnings has moved upward to increase the equity base). The upward movement of the effective rate of interest on borrowed funds shows the following changes in the spread between the return on assets and the effective interest rate $(R - I)$: 19X1, .109; 19X2, .119; 19X3, .109. In effect, increased return on assets between 19X1 and 19X3 (.126 to .138) has been negated by rising debt financing and the associated interest cost. The leverage provided (L/E) has increased. This makes the product $[(R - I)L/E]$ greater in 19X3 than in 19X1. The significance, however, is that earnings are more vulnerable to decline. The relatively fixed nature of I and the possible erosion of R is the key here!

Pretax earnings have been taxed at lower effective rates over time. What are the reasons? Is some revenue taxed at capital gains rates? Have differences occurred between reporting to shareholders and to the tax authorities? In general, lower effective rates of taxation, whatever the source, are not sustainable.

Increases in after-tax earnings per share are, in large measure, the result of a dwindling number of outstanding shares. The company could be buying back its own shares. Is it possible that reduced equity is being achieved by increasing debt to take its place?

The possibilities with respect to detailed analysis can be extended. We do not suggest that this company deliberately manipulated earnings. The point is that not

all sources of improvement in earnings per share are desirable and/or sustainable. Mere earnings growth should not impress an analyst. The anatomy of earnings growth is more important.

FORECASTING VIA THE EARNINGS MODEL

Our emphasis thus far in the presentation of the ROI method has been to view it as a device for analyzing the effects of and interaction between the return a firm earns on its assets and the manner in which it is financed. However, this analytical device can be used as a forecasting tool. Once the analyst understands the inner workings of the firm's earnings-formation process, he can forecast the key variables, substitute the values into the model, and forecast EAT for the next period.

For example, assume that a firm's tax bracket is forecast to be 50 percent in 19X4, that 15 percent will be earned on its assets, and that it will pay an effective interest rate of 6 percent. Further assume that the firm will have $100 million of equity and $100 million of debt in its capital structure in 19X4. Then, if we substitute these values into the model, EAT = $(1 - T) [R + (R - I)L/E]E$, its forecast EAT will be as follows:

$$EAT = (1 - .5) [.15 + (.15 - .06)100/100]\$100$$

$$= .5[.15 + (.09)1]100$$

$$= .5[.24]100$$

$$= \$12$$

We can then subtract any forecast preferred dividends that will be paid, and divide the remainder by the projected number of outstanding common shares to arrive at EPS. This can be multiplied by the projected P/E ratio to get the projected price. To continue our example, if our firm is expected to have 3 million shares outstanding and a P/E of 15 in 19X4, then EPS will be forecast at $4($12 million/3 million) and the price per common share at $60(15 \times $4). This can be translated to HPY by subtracting the beginning per-share price, adding dividends paid in 19X4, and dividing by the beginning price. If the price at the end of 19X3 is $50 and no dividends are expected during 19X4, then the projected HPY for 19X4 is 20 percent [(60 - 50)/50].

MARKET-SHARE/PROFIT-MARGIN APPROACH

The market-share/profit-margin approach emanates directly from the industry analysis. Once the industry forecast of market shares is completed, the analyst must next decide which firms are likely to be dominant factors, pacesetters, in the industry. If an investor has his choice, he will undoubtedly select a leader rather than a follower. Thus the next logical step for the analyst is to determine what

share of the industry's total market the firm under analysis can reasonably be expected to achieve.

If the industry is established and has a track record of performance and stability, the analyst can probably make good use of the historical shares of the market attained by the competing firms. Industries such as autos, steel, oil, and copper have well-entrenched member firms. In a slightly more dynamic industry, such as household appliances, the analyst must translate the ability and aggressiveness of management relative to the competition into a forecast of market share. However, in an evolving and somewhat unstable industry, with new firms entering and leaving the market—such as the fast-food industry—the analyst's job is considerably more difficult, perhaps even impossible, using this approach. He must attempt to start with those firms that have begun to establish their permanence in the industry; then he has at least a point of reference from which to depart. He can then subjectively determine the relative strengths and weaknesses of the firm's most pressing competition. These subjective options can be translated into estimates of the probable share of the market to be attained by both the firm under analysis and the competition.

Assume that the analyst is studying an industry that produces auxiliary swimming-pool equipment—items such as lounge chairs, pads, and beach umbrellas. Industry sales for 19X2 are $10 million, and Danes Co. captured 10 percent of this market in 19X2, or $1 million in sales. The analyst forecasts a 20 percent increase in 19X3 sales for the industry because of a more favorable economic climate for leisure-time products. If he expects Danes Co. to increase its market share to 12 percent because of an aggressive campaign, what would its projected sales be? Industry sales will be $10 million plus the 19X3 increase of 20 percent ($2 million), for a total of $12 million. Danes Co. share is 12 percent; therefore, its sales will be 12 percent of $12 million, or $1.44 million.

With an estimate of sales for the company for the ensuing year, the analyst must next determine the most likely profit margin this firm can earn, given its manufacturing capacity, its total resources, and its projected level of sales. We define net-income profit margin as net income after taxes, divided by sales.[6]

The analyst must calculate the most likely net-income margin the firm is likely to achieve on each category of sales revenue. In the case of a predominantly one-product firm, the analyst multiplies the sales figures by the net-income margin to get the firm's profit from the predominating product.[7] For a multiproduct firm, the analyst multiplies the sales of each division by the appropriate profit margin to obtain the various divisions' earnings, totals these, and arrives at the firm's total earnings. These earnings are then divided by the number

---

[6]Throughout the ensuing discussion and text, we use the terms *net-income margin, net-income profit margin,* and *profit margin* interchangeably.

[7]The portion of sales arising from the other products of the firm, which are relatively unimportant compared to the predominant product, is often calculated merely by assuming a growth rate in the level of sales arising from these other products. This sales figure is multiplied by the appropriate profit margin, and this profit is added to the profit calculated above to arrive at the firm's total profit.

of common shares outstanding (after deducting any preferred dividends), to get earnings per share.

EXAMPLE 1.   Danes's sales forecast for 19X3 is $1,440,000. If its net-income margin is forecast to be 5 percent and there are 100,000 shares of common outstanding, what would projected EPS be?[8]

1. Multiply projected sales by the projected margin to get total earnings. $1,440,000 × 5% = $72,000

2. Divide earnings by common shares outstanding (Danes has no preferred stocks). $72,000 ÷ 100,000 = $.72/share

Then the EPS is multiplied by the forecast P/E ratio to get the forecast price. The price at the beginning of the period is subtracted from the ending price to calculate the price change for the period. Then the annual dividend is added to the price change, and the sum is divided by the beginning price to calculate the holding-period yield.

EXAMPLE 2.   If the P/E for the end of 19X3 is projected to be 20 and the price at the end of 19X2 was $10, what is the HPY for Danes Co.? Assume that a $.10 annual dividend is paid.

1. Multiply EPS by P/E. $.72 × 20 = $14.40.

2. Subtract the beginning price from the ending price. $14.40 − $10.00 = $4.40 price change.

3. Add dividend to price change and divide by beginning price.

$$\frac{\$4.40 + \$.10}{\$10} = \frac{\$4.50}{\$10} = 45\% \text{ HPY}$$

This approach involves forecasting only a few key variables, which are easier to get a handle on than the inputs required by the other traditional approaches, and thus it represents a realistic and practical method of forecasting. One last point is perhaps in order before proceeding.

Profit margins are apt to vary little over a very limited range of sales and operating capacity; however, they can vary drastically once the range of possible sales and capacity outcomes is broadened. In order to calculate a useful profit margin (for the relevant range), the analyst must understand the makeup and behavior of prices and costs of the firm in question. We refer, of course, to the relative importance to the firm of *fixed and variable cost*. In other words, we need first to appreciate the degree of operating leverage (the size of the fixed costs) the firm is employing before we can properly relate this information to sales and capacity fig-

---

[8]Usually, estimates of net-income margins are based upon historical performance. If any changes in the mode of operation or market conditions have occurred, the analyst modifies the historical margins to incorporate these changes. The 5 percent figure for Danes reflects this procedure.

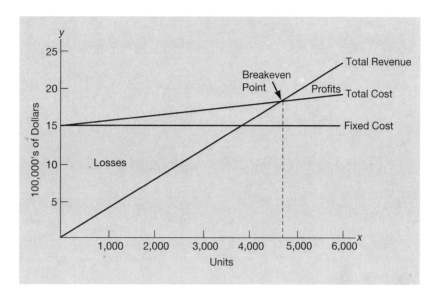

FIGURE 7–2   Break-Even Point of a High-Fixed-Cost Company

ures. To facilitate this understanding, analysts frequently employ break-even analysis and the adjunct break-even chart.

Break-Even Analysis

A central concept in the break-even analysis is the break-even point. The break-even point is a sales level at which total revenues equal total costs. To state the matter in its simplest form, a firm's total costs are made up of fixed costs plus linear variable costs. Fixed costs—for example, rent—are constant over large ranges of output over a finite time period.[9] Note in Figure 7–2, for example, that when total costs hit the y-axis, variable costs—for example, materials—vary directly in proportion to output. The more items produced, the more variable costs increase. The aspect of break-even analysis with which we are concerned here is the effect of high fixed costs versus low fixed costs on a company's profit margin, and how the profit margin changes about the break-even point (level of sales).

Figure 7–2 depicts the break-even point of a high-fixed-cost company; Figure 7–3, of a low-fixed-cost company. Observe that the break-even point (in units) is higher for the high-fixed-cost company than for the low-fixed-cost company. This is the general case. The high-fixed-cost company might be characterized as more capital-intensive (using larger amounts of equipment and machinery) than the low-fixed-cost company.

[9]All costs, given some wide dimensions, will be variable. Costs are fixed only over some "relevant" range.

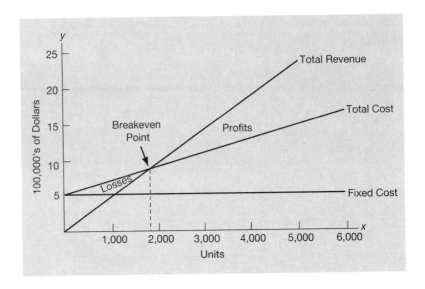

FIGURE 7–3 Break-Even Point of a Low-Fixed-Cost Company

Generally, when a firm has high fixed costs, it also has lower variable costs. The significance of this fact can be seen by examining Figure 7–2. Below the break-even point, large losses are sustained, and above the break-even point, large profits are achieved. The losses get larger as the sales volume falls significantly below the break-even point. Conversely, the profits get larger as sales move further and further above the break-even point. Graphically, this is depicted by the vertical distance between the total-revenue line and the total-cost line. This situation differs in degree rather than kind when one views the low-fixed-cost company illustrated in Figure 7–3.

Generally, when a firm has lower fixed costs, it has higher variable costs. Thus, although profits increase as sales move above the break-even point and losses increase as sales fall below the break-even point, the rate of increased profits and losses is substantially less than the rate for the high-fixed-cost company. In other words, profits and losses "explode" more rapidly in the case of the high-fixed-cost company than in the case of the low-fixed-cost company.

So we can see how important it is that an analyst properly perceive (1) the type of firm (high or low fixed costs) he is analyzing, and (2) the level of sales volume the firm is likely to achieve during the forecast period; for these factors will greatly influence the net-income profit margin the firm will achieve. This problem becomes particularly acute as the projected sales volume of the firm approaches its break-even point. A slight error in estimation in this region can have radical consequences for the success of investing in the firm's shares. This kind of analysis is helpful in determining the return on assets, *R,* if the analyst is using the earnings model discussed earlier in this chapter.

INDEPENDENT FORECASTS OF REVENUE AND EXPENSES

The ROI method skirts the issue of specifically forecasting various categories of income and expenses. The independent forecasting of revenues and expenses, sometimes called the *scientific method*,[10] directly confronts this problem. The technique generally follows one of two main routes. The first and more specific approach is to forecast each and every revenue and expense item separately. For example, the analyst would separately forecast the sales of each division and each product line of the company, as well as each of the major expense items appearing on the firm's income statement. The advantage of this approach is that it forces the analyst to become intimately familiar with the inner workings of the business—both manufacturing operations and sales and administrative operations. The main disadvantage of this method is that for a company of any size, it is an extremely time-consuming and often tedious procedure; furthermore, the danger always exists that the analyst may become so involved with the detail that he misses some broader, but very fundamental, points of interest.

The second route is to take a broader-brush approach to the forecasting problem. Here the analyst hopes to overcome the pitfalls of the "scientific" method by analyzing the forecasting category totals rather than all the individual components. For example, he would look at the sales of the various divisions as totals, rather than attempting to forecast the sales of all the individual product lines of each division. He would forecast broad categories of expenses, such as administrative and sales expenses, rather than attempting to break these down finely into categories such as salaries, rent, and insurance. The advantage of this approach is that it avoids most of the problems of the scientific approach and is more efficient. Also, it is perhaps more accurate per unit of time spent on the forecast because generally there are over- and underestimates of individual components that may be misleading when looked at separately, but that cancel out when they are combined.

When the analyst has completed his forecast of revenues and expenses by using either the specific or the broad approach just outlined, he merely subtracts expenses from the revenues, and he has his forecast of earnings. Then he determines the number of common shares that will be outstanding in the forecast period, and divides it into the forecast earnings (after deducting any preferred dividends) to get earnings per share. Next, the analyst would multiply this earnings-per-share figure by the estimated P/E ratio in order to arrive at his best estimate of price. Then he would subtract the price at the beginning of the period, add dividends, and divide by the beginning price to calculate the HPY.

EXAMPLE.   Kniffen Co. sales consist of two main divisions, one producing lounge chairs and pads, the other beach umbrellas and other miscellaneous items. Our esti-

---

[10]This term is attributed to Benjamin Graham, David L. Dodd, and Sidney Cottle in *Security Analysis* (New York: McGraw-Hill, 1962), p. 463.

mates call for $1.2 million in revenue from the lounge chair division and $240,000 from the umbrella division. These figures are based on advance orders and projected sales to new resort hotels and motels, as well as anticipated replacement orders. Manufacturing expenses are about 70 percent of total revenues; sales and administrative expenses and taxes are 25 percent of sales revenue. The other pertinent information about Kniffen is as previously noted. What is the projected HPY?

Revenues:	Lounge chair division	$1,200,000	
	Umbrella division	240,000	
	Total revenue		$1,440,000
Expenses:	Manufacturing	1,008,000	
	S&A	360,000	
	Total expenses		$1,368,000
	Net earnings		$72,000

As before, EPS = $.72, and HPY = 45 percent.

The three approaches we have discussed represent the main lines and methodology traditionally employed by security analysts when performing a company analysis. These main approaches are not mutually exclusive; they are often combined and used to complement each other. Despite the fact that they have been used with much success by many analysts for some time now, it should be pointed out that they all possess some shortcomings. To a large extent they are based on subjective evaluations made at various stages of the analysis by the analyst or investor, and quite frequently involve his estimate of the most likely figure.

In statistics, this type of estimate, which attempts to zero in on *one* number, is called a *point estimate*. For example, a weatherman might estimate that the temperature will reach a high of 72°F tomorrow; in this case, 72°F is a point estimate. When these point estimates are made in security analysis, no formal statement is generally made about their reliability. That is, the reader of such a report does not know how accurate the analyst himself thinks the forecast may be, or, for that matter, how accurate the analyst thinks will be any of a range of point estimates he may have forecast. In addition, the output generated from such traditional analysis is usually not directly usable in modern portfolio analysis. The approaches to be presented in the next chapter represent newer techniques that have been applied in the field of security analysis in an attempt to overcome these shortcomings.

EARNINGS-MODEL PROJECTION FOR McDONALD'S CORP.

The starting point for the application of the earnings model to any company is to understand the relationships among the key variables for the particular firm. As an example we will look in-depth at McDonald's Corp. McDonald's is the largest food service organization in the world. The company was founded in 1955 by Ray A.

Kroc, who bought the rights to franchise the name and operating practices of a lim-ited-menu, quick-service restaurant in San Bernardino, California, owned by two brothers, Richard and Maurice McDonald.

Of the nation's retailing organizations, McDonald's ranks among the top in profit margins and return on stockholder's equity. The name *McDonald's* is among the most widely advertised brand names in the world. In a typical day, more than 22 million customers worldwide visit a McDonald's restaurant, and it has added a new restaurant every fifteen hours for the past ten years.

McDonald's Corp. usually participates in the operation of the chain's restau-rants by operating the units itself or by franchising them to independent operators. About two-thirds of the system's 13,000 restaurants are operated by franchisees. In both cases, McDonald's usually controls the land and building in which the store operates, either by leasing the facility from a third party or by owning the property and building outright. For the most part, the company buys the land on which the stores are to be located, except in the case of shopping center locations or those in urban areas where land is not for sale.

In addition to selecting the site, McDonald's has responsibility for training the franchisee and members of his management staff and conducts periodic inspec-tions to ensure that the franchisee is fulfilling the operating requirements of the li-cense. Franchising agreements call for the prospective franchisee to pay the company an initial fee for the right to conduct business for twenty years at a site se-lected and specified by the company, and in a building the company has had built. The franchisee pays McDonald's a royalty fee of 3.5 percent of sales for the life of the franchising agreement, plus a rental to McDonald's of at least 13 percent of sales. In addition, he is required to spend a minimum of 4 percent of sales for ad-vertising and promotion of the business.

McDonald's does not sell either supplies or equipment to franchisees. It does, however, exercise the right to approve suppliers to franchisees. In practice, virtu-ally all franchisees and company-operated stores buy supplies and equipment from a very limited number of suppliers. Keystone Foods is the main supplier of ham-burger meat to domestic McDonald's. In addition, the Coca-Cola Co. or its bottlers are major suppliers of soft-drink syrup to McDonald's.

A good starting point for this analysis is to examine historical data. Table 7–5 contains this key financial data for McDonald's (MCD) for 1987–92. Table 7–6 contains the key variables for the earnings analysis for 1987–92. In the extreme right-hand column of Table 7–6 is the average value for the variables for 1987–92. Because these basic economic relationships are slow to change unless management by specific design takes steps to bring about a change, we will assume, for purposes of illustration, that those average values for 1987–92 will persist in 1993. However, we will use 34 percent as the tax rate on the basis of recent corporate tax rates.[11]

---

[11]For the time being, we ask the reader to accept our assumption of a P/E of 18 and a divi-dend of $.42 for 1993, so that we can illustrate the HPY calculation for a one-year holding period, which is calculated one year forward from the time McDonald's is selling at $48.75. In Chapter 8 we will discuss procedures for arriving at an estimate of P/E and dividends per share.

Table 7–5

MCDONALD'S CORP. FINANCIAL DATA
FOR YEARS ENDED 1987–92

($ IN MILLIONS)	1992	1991	1990	1989	1988	1987
Sales	7133	6695	6640	6066	5521	4853
Earnings before interest and taxes	1848	1717	1663	1489	1313	1184
Interest Expense	400	418	417	332	267	225
Earnings before taxes	1448	1299	1246	1157	1046	959
Income tax expense	489	439	444	430	401	410
Earnings after taxes	959	860	802	727	645	549*
Earnings available to common stock	959	860	802	727	645	549*
Common stock dividends	141.7	128.9	118.5	111.9	101.4	90.6
No. shares common stock (millions)	363.2	358.1	359.0	373.0	375.4	377.6
Assets	11681	11349	10668	9175	8159	6982
Liabilities	5789	6514	6486	5625	4746	4065
Equity	5892	4835	4182	3550	3413	2917

*Before the cumulative prior years' benefit from the change in accounting for income taxes.

Thus, an estimate for 1993 is:

$$EAT = (1 - .34)[.160 + (.160 - .06)1.37]\$5,892$$

$$= (.66)(.297)\$5,892$$

$$= (.66)(\$1,749.92)$$

$$= \$1,154.95$$

Using a forecast of 363 million common shares outstanding in 1993 yields a forecast EPS of \$3.18. Assuming a P/E of 18, a beginning share price of \$48.75, and a forecast dividend of \$0.42 yields a return of 16.6 percent, which is calculated as follows:

$$HPY = \frac{18(\$3.18) - \$48.75 + \$0.42}{\$48.75} = 16.6\%$$

This represents a point estimate of HPY, and based on this the analyst or investor would determine whether an investment in MCD is warranted.

The fact that the ROI approach forces the analyst to become very close to the inner workings of the company is a decided disadvantage as well as an advantage because it involves forecasting a number of key ratios and variables, which is very difficult to do. Thus, although in theory ROI is a nice, neat approach, in practice it is a difficult one to implement with high degree of accuracy.

Table 7–6

MCDONALD'S CORP. EARNINGS ANALYSIS (1987–92)

	1992	1991	1990	1989	1988	1987*	AVER-AGE
Dividend per share	.39	.36	.33	.30	.27	.24	
Payout rate (DPS/EPS)	15.0%	15.3%	15.0%	15.4%	15.8%	16.6%*	15.52%
Earnings per share	2.60	2.35	2.20	1.95	1.71	1.45*	
Tax rate(taxes/EBT)	33.8%	33.8%	35.6%	37.2%	38.3%	42.8%	36.92%
Rate of return on assets (EBIT/assets)	15.8%	15.1%	15.6%	16.2%	16.1%	17.0%	16.00%
Profit margin (EBIT/sales)	25.9%	25.6%	25.0%	24.6%	23.8%	24.4%	24.90%
Asset turnover (sales/assets)	.61	.59	.62	.66	.68	.70	.64
Total debt/equity	.98	1.35	1.55	1.58	1.39	1.39	1.37
Interest rate (interest/ total debt)	6.9%	6.4%	6.4%	5.9%	5.6%	5.5%	6.10%

*Before the cumulative prior years' benefit from the change in accounting for income taxes.

INDEPENDENT FORECAST OF REVENUE AND EXPENSES FOR MCDONALD'S CORP.

Four major factors should allow McDonald's to post 15 percent per-share earnings growth over the 1993–95 period: increasing same-store sales (4 to 6 percent), additional unit expansion (7 to 8 percent), additional profits from the international market (2 to 3 percent), and continued cost-control efforts.

Same-Store Sales

Sales in existing restaurants should continue to increase at a 4 to 6 percent compound annual growth rate, fueled by new product introductions, extended hours, new promotions, continued expansion of drive-throughs, and price increases. In 1992, average sales for all restaurants open were $1.672 million. This represents a 4.2 percent increase over 1991 levels.

McDonald's continues to add both drive-throughs and playgrounds to existing units in order to improve sales and also includes them in new restaurants. The incremental sales gains from drive-throughs (in restaurants that have them, drive-throughs account for half of total sales) have motivated McDonald's to expand the concept to include extended drive-throughs and tandem menu boards, which serve additional customers during high-volume periods. Due to favorable returns on investment, the company has also aggressively added playgrounds.

Sales increases are also expected to result from further menu expansion. The company's recently introduced McGrilled chicken sandwich, which has been well

EMPTY TABLES

MARCIA BERSS

It's 6 p.m. in Northbrook, a Chicago suburb, and the local McDonald's is mostly empty. It's a different scene nearby at Chili's, a casual dining chain owned by Brinker International. The place is teeming with families with kids, McDonald's core market, busily chowing down things like hamburgers and chicken. Dinner here costs a few bucks more than at McDonald's, but there's a wider food selection, better ambiance, and table service.

The contrast is giving McDonald's management fits. In tests in Dayton, Ohio, Rochester, N.Y. and other towns, McDonald's tried tempting families with pizza, pasta offerings and a skinless roast chicken entrée.

The dinner bell never rang. This spring the world's largest food server (1992 systemwide sales, $21.9 billion) admitted defeat and canned the dinner test.

Without dinner, McDonald's looks close to topped out in the U.S. For the last five years McDonald's Corp.'s U.S. revenues have stagnated at about $3.8 billion. Domestic operating earnings are up 4%, to $1.04 billion, but that's mostly because McDonald's has been cutting costs aggressively through such tactics as opening smaller outlets that cost about 20% less to build.

Cost-cutting can't go on indefinitely, and McDonald's is getting close to the bone. It must continue to boost domestic earnings to keep funding its major growth engine, foreign expansion.

The problem is obvious, even if the solution isn't. McDonald's gets 55% of its revenues at lunch, 25% during breakfast and only 20% at dinner. Which means all that expensive space is vastly underutilized during what should be a strong part of the day.

For a while McDonald's hoped pizza would do the trick. Three-quarters of the restaurant pizza eaten in the U.S. gets scarfed down in the evening. Pizza is much cheaper to make than hamburgers. But McDonald's threw in the mozzarella. Says McDonald's spokesman Chuck Ebeling: "Pizza has proved to be elusive. We haven't figured that one out."

McPizza tasted pretty good, and unlike most McDonald's fare was custom-made to order. The company put everything it had into making it go, even cutting production time from five minutes to three minutes. It applied to pizza lessons learned at breakfast two decades ago, when it surrounded the disappointing Egg McMuffin with supporting offerings like Big Breakfast and hotcakes. The breakfast business boomed. McDonald's tried the same technique with dinner, adding pasta meals and roast chicken, both with good nutritional images, to round out its menu.

Why didn't the new offerings fill those empty dinner tables? Irrational as it seems, image is more important than nutrition, price or convenience. McDonald's has a lunch and breakfast image. People see it as a purveyor of fast finger food that can be eaten on the run. They seem to regard dinner as a relaxed family event, not a quick refueling squeezed between soccer practice and homework.

Then, too, half of McDonald's sales are made at the drive-through window, and while it's easy to munch a Big Mac behind the wheel, try slurping spaghetti marinara on the freeway ramp. "People came for hamburgers," says Ebeling.

Not that McDonald's didn't try to modify the image. Television commercials pushed McDonald's as a dinner solution for people with busy schedules. One spot

showed a mother chauffeuring her kids from school to soccer and dance lessons, and stopping off at McDonald's for dinner on the way home, spending time talking to her kids instead of cooking. Still, the tables remained empty at night.

McDonald's is not alone among the fast food companies in suffering from deserted evening restaurants. Concedes Dave Thomas, the founder and senior chairman of the number three chain, Wendy's: "Our business is sandwiches. It's a lunch item."

McDonald's isn't giving up on dinner. The stakes are too high. But while some 500 of McDonald's 9,000 U.S. outlets continue to sell McPizza—after all, these franchisees spent up to $50,000 each on pizza ovens—the grand dinner rollout awaits further tinkering. For example, McDonald's couldn't come up with a tomato sauce recipe appealing to all regional tastes; some like their spaghetti sauce sweet, others spicy.

Says McDonald's Ebeling: "It's back in the test kitchen for now."

Source: Reprinted with permission from *Forbes* magazine, December 6, 1993.

received, represents another demonstration of the company's ability to introduce successfully new and varied products. A new product called McStuffins, a hollowed-center French bread stuffed with various fillings, is being tested. Promotional activities should continue at their current expanded level, serving to both increase sales and squeeze the competition. McDonald's is also testing the use of credit cards at certain locations. Tests have indicated that the average bill increases when a credit card is used.

Unit Expansion

Unit expansion is expected to contribute 7 to 8 percent to McDonald's earnings growth, with the rate of international unit growth continuing to exceed the rate of domestic unit growth. We expect 300 new store openings in 1993 in the United States and at least 600 new store openings internationally. There are currently 4,500 international units open. McDonald's sees the potential for 17,000 units outside the United States.

The company continued its expansion efforts in 1992 opening 675 new restaurants. The company planned to accelerate growth with the addition of between 700 and 900 restaurants through 1992. We expect the company to open between 900 and 1,200 new stores over the next several years; the bulk of these stores will be outside the United States. There should be an increased reliance on specialty locations such as hospitals, schools, military bases, malls, turnpikes, and other nontraditional locations for the company's domestic unit expansion.

Although the domestic market continues to hold promise, the international market seems to contain most of the long-term unit growth prospects for McDonald's. New unit openings in the international markets should more than continue at a rapid pace, with new restaurant openings continuing to increase to over 500 in 1993. New international restaurant openings should account for two-thirds of new

systemwide openings by 1993. Operating income growth from international operations should grow in the 20+ percent range.

International Profits

Profits from international operations are expected to generate gains of 2 to 3 percent in per-share earnings over the next five years. Continued revenue increases with franchised operations and anticipated increases in affiliated profitability should also add to the company's per-share earnings. Lower average cost structures, improved existing-unit sales, and a larger number of units in a given market are expected to result in additional profits in the international market.

The initial costs associated with new international ventures can be substantial. Adequate suppliers must be located; qualified personnel must be trained; semivariable and fixed costs (associated with supervisory personnel, advertising costs, and other general and administrative costs) must initially be allocated over a smaller base of operations; and economies of size in relation to bulk purchasing abilities must be delayed. McDonald's has patiently endured the initial losses that arise from these forces in order to establish an international presence. However, as a market becomes profitable, McDonald's has accelerated unit expansion in that market, resulting in overhead and system costs being spread over more units and profit margins expanding rapidly. This strategy has paid off, and the company's international profit margins have expanded and will continue to do so. The only possible negative impact we see is from unfavorable currency fluctuations, which could affect our 20+ percent growth in operating income from international operations.

Cost Control

Finally, modest per-share earnings growth is expected to result from cost-control efforts at the store and corporate levels. At the store level, food costs and labor costs as a percentage of sales should stabilize over the next several years. McDonald's has significantly covered the development costs of new domestic stores by lowering building costs through a new building design. In addition, the company has developed an even less costly prototype building for smaller sites or smaller population markets. In addition, McDonald's has a unique advantage over its competitors on an investment basis because it has already established global economics of scale.

One additional comment on the McDonald's data presented in this chapter should be made. The company has apparently adopted a policy of splitting the stock periodically to keep the stock affordable for individual investors. The reader is cautioned to adjust the McDonald's financial data appropriately if splits occur. Considering the growth and the discussion above, we forecast $2.95 EPS for McDonald's for 1993 using the independent forecast of revenue and expenses method. This compares with our forecast of $3.18 EPS using the earnings-model approach and historical financial data.

SUMMARY

In this chapter we have shown how company information can be used to calculate holding-period yields. Three traditional techniques for the forecasting of revenues and expenses were examined—the ROI approach, the marketshare/net-income-margin approach, and the so-called scientific approach. It was noted that all three yield point estimates, with no statement of their likelihood of occurrence. In the next chapter, newer, more sophisticated techniques will be analyzed.

QUESTIONS AND PROBLEMS

1. What is the relationship between industry analysis and company analysis?

2. Assume that the return on assets of J. G. Co. is forecast to be 20 percent. The effective interest rate is forecast at 9 percent, the tax rate at 50 percent, and the capital structure is expected to be $10 million. If J. G. Co. is financed with 70 percent equity and 30 percent debt, what will be your forecast of EAT?

3. What are the advantages and disadvantages of the ROI technique as a forecasting device?

4. What potential uses do you see for the ROI approach other than as a forecasting device?

5. Discuss the market-share/net-income-margin approach to company earnings analysis.

6. Allgent Corp. has two divisions. Division A captures 10 percent of industry sales, forecast to be $50 million. Division B will capture 30 percent of its industry's sales, which are expected to be $20 million. Allgent's division A has traditionally had a 5 percent net-income margin, and division B has had an 8 percent net-income margin. Allgent has 300,000 shares of common stock outstanding, which sell at $30. If you require at least a 20 percent, one-year return, and you expect the P/E to be 10 next year, would you purchase Allgent common at this time based on your one-year forecast?

7. How would you go about forecasting a firm's market share and net-income margin a year in advance?

8. How would you go about forecasting the earnings of the local pizza shop via an independent forecast of revenues and expenses?

9. In analyzing any company using each of the three traditional approaches to company analysis, would you expect your forecasts of return to be the same under all the methods? Why or why not?

10. Determine the sales composition of Minnesota Mining and Manufacturing (3M) Co. for 1992 from sources such as Standard & Poor's, Moody's, *Value Line,* or the firm's annual report. How would you expect the revenues for the various sectors to change in 1993, based on 1992 figures and your prediction of economic and industry conditions during 1992?

11. Following are data for Johnson Products:

($ IN MILLIONS)	19X1		EST. 19X2
Assets	$600	Revenues	$660
Liabilities:		Operating exps.	594
Short-term (1989)	25	EBIT	66
8% Debentures	125	Interest	16
10% Bonds (1999)	50	EBT	50
Common stock ($5 par)	100	Taxes	20
Surplus	300	Dividends	5

    a. Provide the following information for an analysis of earnings:
       i. Asset turnover
      ii. Effective interest rate
     iii. Effective tax rate
     iv. Financial leverage (debt/equity)
      v. Dividend payout rate
    b. What growth rate of EBIT can be expected?

12. The following data pertain to the Northwoods Corp.:

Shares outstanding (millions)	5.0
Effective tax rate	50%
Annual depreciation ($ in millions)	$2.0
Total debt ($ millions)*	$60
Total stockholders' equity ($ in millions)	$60
Last dividend (per share)	$.72
Rate of return on equity	15%
EBIT/assets	20%
Market price of stock ($)	$20
EAT/sales	12.5%

*Current liabilities	$6.0
10%, first-mortgage bonds (1995)	24.0
12%, subordinated debenture bonds (2010)	30.0

    a. What is the firm's implied growth rate of EBIT? Earnings per share?
    b. Suppose that the data above persist into the near future and investors require a rate of return (discount rate) on this stock of 13 percent. Is the stock a "bargain" in theory? Explain.
    c. Suppose that $20 million in additional capital is to be raised and is evenly divided between 10 percent bonds and new shares sold at $20 per share. EBIT/assets continues at its present rate. What is the new earnings per share?

13. If a firm enjoys a positive difference between the rate of return on assets and the effective interest rate paid on borrowed funds, why shouldn't it push the

mix of total funds acquired to the maximum limit of debt funds and minimize the financing that is done through equity sources?

14. In 1992 Scoville Inc. had assets of $600 million and EBIT of $90 million on sales of $750 million. In 1989 the company earned $3 per share and paid a dividend of $1.50. What rate of growth in EBIT is implied in these relationships?

15. Selected financial information for Figgie International, Inc., is shown. Trace the sources of the change in earnings between 1991 and 1992.

YEARS ENDED DECEMBER 31	1992	1991
($ IN MILLIONS)		
Net Sales	$1,200.2	$1,053.1
Operating expenses	1,087.3	961.4
Operating profit	112.9	91.7
Other income, net	3.8	6.3
Interest expense, net	(18.5)	(9.7)
Income before provision for income taxes	98.1	88.3
Provision for income taxes	36.3	38.9
Net income	61.9	49.3
Earnings per common share	$9.03	$7.02
Common shares outstanding (weighted average) (in thousands)	6,850	7,025
Working capital	$272.7	$227.6
Property, plant and equipment, net	246.3	216.9
Total assets	1022.0	868.0
Long-term debt	200.0	106.8
Stockholders' equity	365.8	321.5

16. The following data were reported by Ridge Corp. for fiscal 1988 and 1992.

($ IN MILLIONS)	FISCAL 1988	FISCAL 1992
Total assets	$415.3	$953.8
Net sales	455.0	1,061.8
Net income after taxes	44.0	80.2
Income taxes	31.8	52.2
Interest charges	4.1	25.3
Dividend payments	4.0	16.6
Equity capital	274.1	557.5
Common shares	17.7	18.6

From the data provided, what are the sources of sustainable growth in earnings per share? Why are these sources of sustainable growth?

17. What specific information included in the data below might explain the tendency for the stock price of Bottle Co. to "stagnate" between 1986 and 1988.

	1988	1987	1986	1985	1984
Dividend per share	$1.62	$1.58	$1.42	$1.26	$1.11
Payout rate (DPS/EPS)	53.8%	65.8%	39.3%	39.4%	38.9%
Earnings per Share (EAT/no. of shares)	$3.01	$2.40	$3.61	$3.20	$2.85
Book value per share (Equity/no. of shares)	$19.18	$17.68	$17.91	$15.65	$13.89
Rate of return on equity	15.9%	13.6%	20.3%	20.4%	21.0%
1 – effective tax rate	67%	50%	61%	59%	61%
Rate of return on assets	13.2%	14.9%	17.2%	18.1%	17.6%
Profit Margin (EBIT/sales)	7.7%	8.3%	9.9%	10.3%	10.0%
Gross profit margin	57.5%	56.1%	53.9%	52.6%	52.0%
Total asset turnover	1.70	1.79	1.73	1.75	1.76
Financial leverage (total debt/equity)	1.59	1.54	1.47	1.39	1.28
Effective interest rate	6.5%	6.8%	6.3%	6.3%	4.5%
Stock price (at year-end)	$38	$36	$36	$27	$25

18. The value of the components affecting the ROE of Merck & Co. for 1985 are indicated in Exhibit 1 below. Selected 1990 income statement and balance sheet information for Merck can be found in Exhibit 2 below.

    a. Calculate *each* of the *five* ROE components for Merck in 1990. Using the *five* components, calculate ROE for Merck in 1990. Show all calculations.

    b. Based on your calculations, describe how *each* ROE component contributed to the change in Merck's ROE between 1985 and 1990. Identify the major underlying reasons for the change in Merck's ROE.

Exhibit 1

MERCK & CO.
1985 ROE COMPONENTS

Tax burden (net income/pretax income)	.628
Interest burden (pretax income/EBIT)	.989
Operating (or profit) margin	.245
Asset turnover	.724
Financial leverage	1.877

Exhibit 2

MERCK & CO.
1990 SELECTED FINANCIAL DATA

($ IN MILLIONS)

<u>Income Statement Data</u>

Sales revenue	$7,120
Depreciation	230
Interest expense	10
Pretax income	2,550
Income taxes	900
Net income	1,650

<u>Balance Sheet Data</u>

Current assets	$4,850
Net fixed assets	2,400
Total assets	7,250
Current liabilities	3,290
Long-term debt	100
Shareholders' equity	3,860
Total liabilities and shareholders' equity	7,250

COMPANY ANALYSIS:
APPLIED VALUATION

This chapter has three major parts. The first concludes our discussion of earnings forecasting begun in Chapter 6 and considers methods of forecasting dividends and determining price-earnings (P/E) ratios. The second part of the chapter briefly examines a number of alternative stock selection techniques. The third part of the chapter combines all our efforts at forecasting earnings, dividends, and P/E ratios to show applied valuation in practice.

In the preceding chapter we analyzed three traditional approaches to the forecasting of company earnings and holding-period yield. We observed that each of these techniques yielded a single estimate of earnings and HPY. In effect, a probability of 100 percent is attached to the outcome.

However, analysts are seldom so certain of the infallibility of their forecasts. Furthermore, modern portfolio analysis requires that we forecast not only the *expected return* but also the *expected risk* of an investment. In this chapter we will present three modern techniques of analysis: regression analysis, trend analysis, and decision-tree analysis, collectively, they attempt to overcome the weakness of, while building their conceptual foundations on, the more traditional tools. These techniques are appealing for yet another reason—they are inherently useful, for they can be applied on a limited scale even by the investor who does not have a computer.

The final part of this chapter will be devoted to applying several approaches to stock valuation to determine the value of McDonald's Corp. common stock. These approaches will parallel our earlier discussion of valuation in Chapter 3. The approaches are: (1) P/E ratio models, and (2) the dividend discount model.

REGRESSION AND CORRELATION ANALYSIS
IN FORECASTING REVENUES AND EXPENSES

As explained in Chapter 5, *regression analysis* allows the user to examine the relationship between two variables in the case of simple linear regression, and the rela-

tionship of several variables in the case of multiple linear regression. Correlation analysis permits the user to test for the "goodness of fit" between these variables.[1] Many of the usages of regression analysis discussed earlier in conjunction with industry analysis can be translated to the company level. For example, many of the applications of regression analysis for end-use analysis and the regression on industry sales of economic variables such as gross national product (GNP), disposable income, and indexes of industrial production can be adapted to company analysis by regressing the same variable against items such as company or division sales. Furthermore, experience may have taught the analyst certain relationships not only between external economic variables and company sales but also between internal company variables and external industry variables. Also, relationships may exist among industry, economic, and firm variables and company expenses. These relationships can then be used to build rather sophisticated systems of regression equations.

One advantage of using regression analysis in this way over the methods discussed in the preceding chapter is that the point estimates that are derived by this method are based on a somewhat rigorous statistical and economic foundation. Furthermore, the analyst is forced to think through the various problems of the company and the various complex interrelationships between internal and external variables and company revenues and expenses.[2] Another advantage over more traditional approaches is that correlation analysis permits the analyst to have a very specific measure of the explanatory power of the regression equation; and thus he has a means for assessing the reliability of his point estimates. Correlation analysis tells the analyst how well the independent variable "explains" the dependent variable in the regression equation.

TREND ANALYSIS

In conjunction with regression analysis, the technique of *trend analysis* can also be very useful. Frequently, trend analysis of time series utilizes regression analysis. For the sake of simplicity, we differentiate the two by referring to regression analysis when we are studying the degree of correspondence between two "real" variables, and we speak of trend analysis when we examine the behavior of an economic series over time (times series). Thus, in the case of trend analysis, we are looking at only one "real" variable (such as earnings), which is being regressed over time—that is, over a period of years. This is how the name *trend analysis* evolved.

See Figure 8–1 for trend analysis applied to a series of earnings per share of a company. The equation of the "fitted" straight line might then be used to forecast the next year's earnings. For example:

---

[1]The reader is urged to review the portions of Chapter 5 in which these techniques were introduced.

[2]In addition, it is possible that more stable, systematic relationships will be found between the company and some macroeconomic variable than will be found between the industry and the same macroeconomic variable.

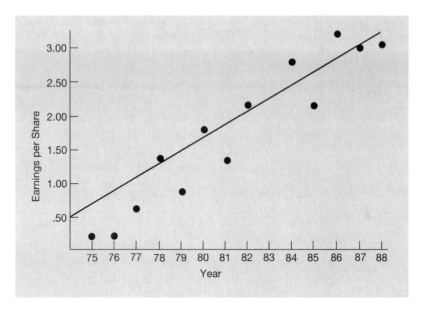

FIGURE 8–1   Trend Line Fitted to Earnings per Share

$$\text{Year } x \text{ EPS} = a + bx$$

where a and b have been calculated from the regression analysis and the underlying conditions will remain stable for the forecast period. Therefore, if 1975 = 1, 1976 = 2, 1977 = 3, and so on, the EPS for 1989 would be calculated as:

$$\text{Year } 15 = a + b(15)$$

Frequently analysts employ trend analysis by plotting the data on a special kind of graph paper, semilogarithmic or semilog paper, in order to reveal starkly different growth rates. The advantage of plotting the information on semilog paper as opposed to plotting on arithmetic graph paper can be seen by examining Figures 8–2 and 8–3.

In an arithmetic graph, such as Figure 8–2, equal distances on an axis represent equal absolute quantities. In this example, each demarcation on the y-axis represents $.10 of earnings per share. Because of this construction, companies A, B, C, and D seem to have achieved identical patterns of growth in earnings per share between 1985 and 1988 because the trend lines are parallel. However, if we examine the data carefully, we see that this is an illusion. Company A's earnings per share have increased from $.10 to $.20, or 100 percent during the period, company B's earnings have increased from $.30 to $.40, or 33% 13 percent, company C's earnings have increased from $.50 to $.60, or 20 percent, and company D's earnings have increased from $.80 to $.90, or 12% 12 percent. Thus, even though their trend rates are parallel, their performances during 1985–88 have in fact been drastically different.

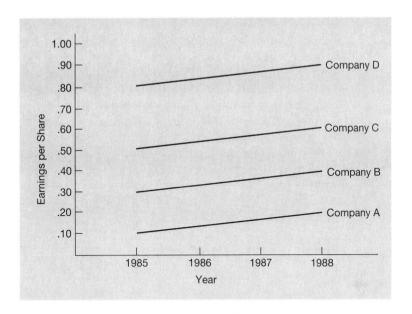

FIGURE 8–2 Arithmetic Graph for Depicting Trends in Growth Rates

Semilogarithmic graphs attempt to overcome this optical illusion. In a semilogarithmic chart, one axis, usually the *x*-axis, is drawn as in the arithmetic graph. The difference lies in how the other axis, usually the *y*-axis, is constructed. Here, equal distance between demarcations represents equal percentage changes rather

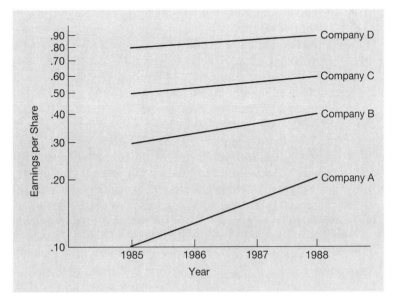

FIGURE 8–3 Semilogarithmic Graph for Depicting Trends in Growth Rates

than equal quantities. Figure 8–3 contains the same information as that in Figure 8–2, but this time on semilog paper. The reader can observe that when this is done, the four companies' trend lines are no longer parallel. In fact, the slopes of the four trend lines are radically different—as they should be. Thus the semilogarithmic graph clearly demonstrates the different growth patterns in companies A, B, C, and D and does so accurately. Here the different slopes clearly point out the difference in growth patterns of 100, 33%13, 20, and 12%12 percent. Generally, semilogarithmic graphs are very useful in comparing and visually demonstrating different growth rates among different companies. As a forecasting device, these trend lines can be used by merely extending them for the next period and then reading off the forecast on the *y*-axis. Clearly, this is a crude method that should be used only as an approximation, and only then when the underlying conditions are expected to remain stable during the forecast period.

DECISION TREES

The traditional approaches to company analysis were criticized because they lacked an objective measurement of quality. That is, they were based to a large extent on subjective analysis and resulted in a point estimate, which did not carry along with it a formal measure of probability. Even though subjectivity has not been and cannot be removed entirely from the investment process, and the investor's or analyst's judgment will always be required, the newer techniques that have been presented thus far overcome the problem to some extent because they are based upon formal statistical tools and often economic rationale as well.

Nonetheless, an important disadvantage still remains with these newer techniques: The output of the various regression models still yields a point estimate. Furthermore, this estimate of earnings, dividends, or price still does not carry a statement of the probability of actual occurrence.[3] Techniques are available that attempt to overcome this shortcoming.

Whenever alternative actions or probabilities exist in an investment environment, there should be some way of assessing the probabilities that the various outcomes will occur. When a sequence of these decisions must be made, and the probability of a particular sequence's occurring is desired, the probabilities of occurrence of the various independent outcomes must be multiplied together. An example of two independent outcomes might be the temperature in Hawaii and the size of trout in a Rocky Mountain stream. Needless to say, the more alternatives that exist, and the more intermediate steps between the original decision and the final solution of a complex problem, the more complex these calculations become. Obviously, the expected value of each of the outcomes will be different, depending on the sequence of events that actually occurs. *Decision-tree analysis* is a technique aimed at formalizing and simplifying the procedure involved in the solution of such problems.

---

[3]However, the analyst can calculate—or have the program calculate—a standard error of the estimate, which can be used to determine the likelihood that a value within a range of values about the estimate will occur. See a basic statistics text.

PROBLEM AREAS IN IMPLEMENTATION OF NEWER TECHNIQUES

Thus far in this chapter, we have examined the newer analytical techniques of company analysis. However, we have not addressed some of the problems that face the security analyst or investor when he attempts to make use of these tools. In this section we must face up to these difficult issues.

Regression Analysis to Forecast Revenues and Expenses

In order to implement regression analysis for the forecasting of revenues and expenses, it is necessary to develop plausible economic relationships between revenues and expenses of the firm and other economic variables, such as GNP, national income, some index of industrial production, per capita consumption of the firm's output, and so on. Generally, these relationships will be developed after examination of past data, the application of economic rationale to explain logical relationship, and the application and testing of these two items. After the initial testing has been completed, the analyst will undoubtedly find some relation between independent (influencing change) and dependent (affected by the influencing factors) variables that he feels will yield sufficiently good results correlatively. He may be willing to base his stock recommendation upon these relationships. When these relationships have been selected, monitored, and put in final form, the user will apply these various systems of equations to the analysis in order to generate forecasts of revenues and expenses.

Unfortunately for the investor or analyst, isolating key explanatory variables is a time-consuming process, and one requiring a thorough understanding of the firm's mode of operation as well as the structure and performance of its industry. But for those able to isolate these key relationships, the payoffs can be great—both in dollars and in personal satisfaction.

Decision Trees

Decision-tree analysis, as presented earlier, attempts to enumerate the various possible combinations of events that culminate in the formation of share price and the probabilities of the various events occurring. Specifically, this can involve the forecasting of such things as revenues, expenses, shares outstanding, and P/E ratio, together with their probabilities of occurrence. This process necessitates that the analyst seek out all information he can get concerning these variables, and any others he wishes to add to the analysis, so that a more realistic set of outcomes and associated probabilities can be obtained. In addition to the price outputs that are generated in the specific decision-tree model we have discussed, it is possible with the proper statement of the end points of the branches of a decision tree to construct a cumulative probability distribution. That is, a distribution could take the

following form (the values are hypothetical): There is a 30 percent probability that the share price of the firm in question will be at least $60, there is a 45 percent probability that the share price will be at least $50, and there is a 90 percent probability that the share price will be at least $25. In other words, as the combination of events becomes ever more pessimistic, the probability of accuracy of the final outcome increases. This is a very useful output of the technique, for it gives the analyst a "feel" for the underlying price-formation process.

GENERATING THE NECESSARY INPUTS

Up to this point we have said very little about the problems of generating the necessary inputs to decision-tree analysis—or for that matter, simulation. Without going into great detail, let us introduce this required step in the implementation of decision-tree analysis.

First, one must know enough about the firm to establish the possible outcomes that may occur. This information undoubtedly stems from insight into the workings of the firm in question and, perhaps more likely, insight into the workings of the industry or industries in which the firm is involved. With this understanding of the firm and its industry and a knowledge of historical sales volume, prices, revenues, and costs, the analyst is in an excellent position to estimate the likelihood of the various alternative outcomes. It is not at all unrealistic to expect this knowledge of the analyst. The research organizations of large brokerage firms and large financial institutions have been traditionally organized along industry lines, with a research analyst or group of analysts assigned to a specific industry—such as construction, shoes, and lodgings. This practice, in effect, creates industry experts whose sole job is to become intimately familiar with the inner workings of the industry and the firms comprising it. These industry experts keep abreast of all the latest developments within the industry. In addition, they visit the various companies they follow and interview senior management. The results of their activities, coupled with addresses by company officials at analysts' meetings, round out the analyst's main sources of information.

For those investors who are attempting to reach their own considered judgment, there is opportunity to receive this knowledge in the form of reports from the industry experts at a number of institutions, such as Standard & Poor's, Moody's, *Value Line,* and a variety of brokerage firms. In addition, the *Wall Street Transcript* regularly publishes these addresses of speakers at the analysts' luncheons, as well as brokerage reports on key corporations. With this variety of expertise assembled, by surveying a number of sources investors can reach a consensus opinion without doing all the legwork themselves. Furthermore, by knowing what constitutes good research, investors will be in a position to assess its quality before they evaluate a recommendation.

Ultimately, then, analysts or investors using decision-tree analysis arrive at a forecast of a number of possible prices of the shares one period in advance, together with the probabilities of each outcome's occurring. In addition, these ana-

lysts or investors can construct a cumulative frequency distribution of price and holding-price yield that gives them an even firmer grasp on the range of the most likely outcomes one period in advance.

Several key issues, however, still need to be confronted. How does the quality of a firm's management enter the analysis? Where does the all-important P/E ratio come from? And how about the dividend payout ratio? These are the topics of the next several sections.

MANAGEMENT IN COMPANY ANALYSIS

Before we can complete our company analysis and make a final decision or an investment action, we need to determine whether management is capable of carrying out its policies so that our expectations are fulfilled.

The future developments that will affect the variables we have discussed in the past several chapters will be in the hands of company management, so the analyst must have faith in the ability of the management of a company he favors. Management should have clear-cut goals in mind and strategies for achieving them. Obviously, among the key end points that will measure management's success will be the earnings per share, dividends, and share price. In order to assess the likelihood that management will achieve the desired end point of the analysis, the analyst can take a number of steps.

First, the analyst can look at past performance of management to see if his past expectations and management's past hopes have been fulfilled. Second, through interviews with management, he can learn something about their backgrounds, experience, motivations, and outlook on such things as the firm's future research and development expenditures, plans for product improvement, marketing strategy, future competition, sales, and profits. In the course of these interviews and his firsthand observations of the firm in operation, he must take note of management's ability to plan, to organize, and to select, motivate, and control personnel.

In the realm of planning, the analyst should ascertain whether clear-cut corporate objectives have been specified. Organization comprises a well-outlined arrangement of duties, including who has what authority and what responsibility. Good personnel selection is management's knowledge of how to recruit, develop, and keep the right people for the right jobs—including the ability to motivate them to do their best in these jobs. Control involves a series of communication devices, such as budgets and reports, that permit management up and down the organization chart to keep tabs on corporate activities.

When this research is coupled with discussion with others who are familiar with the management of the company under analysis, the analyst can get an idea of how much faith he can place in management, and thus how likely it is that his forecast will be fulfilled. He will manifest his conclusion about management abilities in the P/E ratio he assigns to the firm's stock.

Alternative Stock-Selection Techniques

Generally speaking, equity investment strategy has two major categories: active and passive. Active strategies involve attempts at picking undervalued stocks and, by implication, placing bets against the market consensus. Passive strategy is basically a buy-and-hold approach to stocks.

ACTIVE EQUITY MANAGEMENT

In this section of the chapter we review briefly a number of currently used active equity-selection techniques. The specific approach used by the analyst will vary depending upon the methodology he favors. However, in this section and in the sections to follow, all the techniques involve active involvement in the selection of the individual stocks for his portfolio. After this brief review of a number of approaches we will, for the balance of the chapter, devote more time to two very widely used active equity selection techniques.

GROWTH-STOCK APPROACH.   The basic premise of the growth-stock approach is that those companies who have above-average earnings growth over a period of time will tend to produce stock values that will lead to above-average returns for the investor. Therefore, the analyst must select those stocks that have historically had the highest above-average earnings growth and that he feels will also continue to have above-average earnings growth. He must also be careful to avoid selecting those stocks whose price already adequately reflects the high historic or projected growth rates in the earnings of the firm. Because we are talking about growth rates in this approach, the stocks selected can be either small, medium, or large companies. The size of the company alone is not indicative of the historic or projected growth rates in earnings of the company. Stocks selected on the basis of high growth rates or high anticipated growth rates in earnings tend to have high amounts of both systematic and unsystematic risk.

UNDERVALUED STOCK APPROACH.   Practitioners of this approach are sometimes called managers seeking high yield. They tend to look for companies that have either high dividend yields, low market-to-book-value ratios, or low price-earnings ratios. In times of economic uncertainty there tends to be an increasing emphasis on seeking such high-yield investments. This stems from the desire to achieve high current income. This can be accomplished through the holding of stocks that pay high current dividends. A variation of this approach is often used by some analysts. This alternative approach is called purchasing out-of-favor stocks.

Out-of-favor stocks tend to be stocks that have low P/E ratios. At various times in the economic cycle certain stock groups—that is, stocks whose basic businesses are in certain sectors of the economy—tend to be out of favor. For example, at a given point in the cycle, maybe automobile stocks or steel industry stocks are not popular. This means investors shy away from owning these stocks because they feel the economic environment is not conducive to solid business in these industries. When this occurs and there are very few buyers around and maybe lots of

sellers, the prices of these securities tend to drop; sometimes they drop way out of line with the earnings of these companies. This then causes a deterioration in their P/E ratios, and when their P/E ratios become very low, these analysts jump in to buy the out-of-favor stocks.

SMALL CAPITALIZATION APPROACH.   In recent years, because of some statistical studies that we will discuss in the chapter on efficient markets and also because of changes in regulations concerning the management of pension funds, there has been a growing attraction of securities in smaller companies. Traditionally, institutional investors have primarily sought the largest companies in the S&P 500 Index and have shied away from the smaller companies in the S&P 500 Stock Index, on the American Stock Exchange, and in the over-the-counter market. However, in the 1970s and 1980s, many of these smaller-capitalization companies have performed extremely well; thus a "new" approach is to seek investment in smaller companies that have potential to grow rapidly.

MARKET-TIMER APPROACH.   The portfolio manager who is a market-timer varies the proportion of certain types of stocks in his portfolio depending on where he views the stock market to be at a particular time. He may vary the proportion of his portfolio in stocks versus bonds versus cash or he may vary the proportion of stocks he holds in specific industries—for example, durable goods sector stocks or consumer goods stocks. At certain times in the market he will favor one of these sectors versus the other. Such a market-timer approach can then either rotate the number of stocks in a portfolio or specific groups of stocks in a portfolio.

All the approaches discussed thus far can be called active equity-management strategies because in each case the analyst or portfolio manager is making affirmative decisions regarding the securities selected based on his philosophy of investment. In the next section we will look at a passive equity-management approach. Under this approach the analyst merely attempts to mirror the performance of the market. This approach will be discussed at more length in Chapter 20 when we discuss index funds.

PASSIVE EQUITY MANAGEMENT

A passive approach to investing in stocks normally manifests itself in an attempt to buy the "market"—that is, acquire a representative cross section of the market for stocks. The most popular way to achieve this has been by owning a representative sample of the S&P 500 Stock Index stocks. It is not necessary to own all 500 stocks in the S&P Stock Index. A number of mutual fund groups offer *index funds,* which mechanically invest in a representative cross-section of stocks underlying an index. The most widely known among these are the Vanguard Index–500 Portfolio and the Colonial U.S. Equity Index Trust. Both funds mirror the S&P 500 Stock Index. The S&P 500 stocks are not the only ones known. Funds indexed to smaller stocks, international securities, and bonds are available.

Index funds have two main advantages. First, they provide investors with a broadly diversified way to participate in the stock market. Second, investment can

be done at less cost—lower brokerage and management costs—because stocks in index funds are not actively traded (Vanguards management expenses are a mere .26 percent of assets). Computers do most of the work.

Index funds have their limitations. Because passive implies that they are virtually unmanaged, their performance will mirror the moods and swings of the stock market. They look good in strong bull markets, but investors must be prepared for a scary—and expensive—downhill slalom when the overall market slumps.

Index funds will tend to underperform the index they seek to emulate for two reasons. First, because they do not tend to own all the stocks in the index they mirror, there is a tracking error. The size of this error depends upon how well statistical sampling in the purchase of stocks works out.[4] Second, the existence of brokerage fees (to invest new money or redeem fund shares) and management fees will reduce returns.

DETERMINING A PRICE-EARNINGS RATIO

Thus far, our analysis has focused on determining a forecast of earnings per share. This was translated into price by applying the "appropriate" P/E ratio as multiplier. The forecast price was then a central figure in the HPY calculation. We now need to zero in on the critical questions, "What is an appropriate P/E ratio?" and "Where does it come from?"

The most commonly used P/E multiplier is defined as the closing price of the stock, divided by the reported earnings of the most recent twelve months. Thus, if the closing price of the stock was $50 and earnings for the last four quarters totaled $2, the P/E multiplier would be 25. Generally, the P/E is based upon the current price—that is, the closing price of the stock on the day the analysis is being conducted. Thus, the P/E can change daily.

The multiplier, or P/E, is primarily determined by the riskiness of the firm and the rate of growth in its earnings. Low P/E ratios are typically associated with low earnings growth and cyclical businesses, and high P/E ratios are typically associated with high earnings growth and noncyclical businesses. The S&P 500 Stock Index, which represents a cross section of stocks with average risk and growth prospects, might sell in the range of twelve to fifteen times earnings. A high-growth company may sell at a P/E of 30. On the other hand, a slower-growing company in a cyclical business, may sell at a P/E of 7.

The analyst seeks various rules of thumb for selecting an appropriate P/E ratio that can be applied to a company's earnings to determine his valuation for its shares. The resulting price is compared with current market prices to assess bargains or overpriced stocks—at least, superficially. For example, if XYZ is expected to earn $10 per share and normally sells at a P/E ratio of 12, the analyst might conclude that a fair price is currently $120. If the stock is currently selling for $110,

[4]The top 150 companies in the S&P 500 Stock Index with the largest market value account for about 75 percent of the total value of the Index.

some analysts might consider it undervalued. Should the stock sell for $130, it might be judged overpriced (overvalued).

Actual and "Normal" Price-Earnings Ratios

The determination of the current P/E on a stock must be followed by a standard of comparison, invariably taken from the historical record of the stock. The analyst may ascertain the median or *mean* P/E for a stock, its *range* over time, and the P/E relative to the "market" P/E (e.g., Dow Jones Industrial Average [DJIA] or S&P 500 Stock Index). More weight can be given to the recent past. This provides boundaries within which the P/E should fall (assuming nothing has changed drastically) and indicates whether the stock is tending to sell at the upper limits of expectation (high end of P/E range) or lower limits (low end of range). Industry P/E ratios provide some guidelines; however, different companies in the same industry frequently carry quite different P/E ratios.

Bing found that several techniques are favored by analysts in determining proper multiples. In the majority of cases, he found that analysts (1) used time horizons from one to three years, and (2) preferred to use several techniques in combination rather than sticking rigidly to one. Seventy-five percent of the analysts surveyed used "normal" multiplier rules of thumb under the following techniques:

1. They compared current actual P/E with what they considered normal for the stock in question.

2. They compared price times estimated future earnings (one to three years out) with what they considered a normal multiplier for the stock in question.

3. They compared the multiplier and the growth of earnings of individual stocks with industry group multiple and earnings growth.[5]

The lingering question is, of course: What is a "proper" or "normal" P/E? Historical data on the S&P 400 Industrial Price Index sheds some light on the subject. Over the thirty-one-year period from 1957 to 1987, the S&P 400 P/E ranged from a high of 23 in 1961 to a low of 7 in 1979. The mean P/E for this period was 14. Given that this long period covers several economic and stock market cycles, it is reasonable to suggest that a market P/E in the 12–15 range would appear "normal."[6]

The principal determinants of a standard P/E for a stock would be determined by the extent to which the following variables exceed or fall below S&P averages:

[5]R. A. Bing, "Survey of Practitioners' Stock Evaluation Methods," *Financial Analysts Journal* (May–June 1971), p. 56.

[6]Data on the index are published by Standard & Poor's, *The Analysts Handbook*.

1. expected five-year growth of earnings;
2. dividend payout ratio;
3. sales stability;
4. institutional ownership of stock (e.g., mutual funds, etc.); or
5. financial leverage (use of debt financing).

In practice, analysts frequently attempt to view the P/E ratio on a given stock in relation to the P/E ratio prevailing on some broad market index. The most common market gauge is S&P 400 Stock Index. Once a sense of the relationship is attained, the analyst will attempt to estimate the P/E that will be applicable to the "market" over a forward period and derive a P/E for the stock based thereupon. In other words, how does the multiple (P/E) on the stock behave in relationship to the market?

The annual earnings per share for the stock is related to the high, low, and closing price of the stock for the year. Thus we get a P/E ratio based on the high, low, and closing price for the year. The resulting P/E in each case is divided by the S&P 400 price-earnings ratio to determine a *price-earnings relative* (i.e., stock P/E relative to the S&P P/E ratio). Suppose that the S&P P/E ratio were 10 and the calculated P/E for a stock were 15. The P/E relative would be:

$$\frac{\text{Stock P/E}}{\text{S\&P Index P/E}} = \frac{15}{10} = 1.5$$

This in effect says that for the measurement period involved, the stock sold at a P/E that was one and one-half times the "market" P/E.

Statistical Analysis of Price-Earnings Ratios

Analysts equate normality with experience conditioned by recent history and intuition. The analyst's job remains essentially unstructured, and analytical approaches are highly individualist and eclectic, and therefore somewhat unstable. In an attempt to bring some scientific evidence to the problem of "normality" in P/E's, several studies have been conducted, using statistical techniques to achieve solutions. Correlation analysis has been prominent among these techniques. When using correlation analysis, the analyst selects factors or variables that he believes are the main influences on the price of stock. The aim of correlation analysis is to determine the nature and extent to which the variables chosen explain stock price.

Whitbeck and Kisor studied a number of stocks over the same time span. They speculated that differences in P/E ratios between stocks could be explained by (1) projected earnings growth, (2) expected dividend payout, and (3) the variation in the rate of earnings growth, or growth risk.[7] Bower and Bower used a similar approach for a different time period with another sample of firms. They used earnings growth and payout as variables but divided risk into subcomponents, in-

[7]V. S. Whitbeck and M. Kisor, Jr., "A New Tool in Investment Decision-Making," *Financial Analysts Journal* (May–June 1963), pp. 52–62.

cluding marketability of the stock, its price variability, and its conformity with the market (how it moved with the market).[8]

Whitbeck and Kisor applied their statistical technique to a cross section of 135 stocks to explain differences in individual P/E ratios. They concluded that P/E is an increasing function of growth and payout and inversely related to the variation in the growth rate. In other words, higher P/E ratios were associated with higher growth and payout and less variation in the growth rate. Bower and Bower showed results similar to Whitbeck and Kisor's for a cross section of stocks. They saw the same positive effects of earnings growth and payout. However, their examination of risk was more detailed. They discovered that higher P/E ratios were associated with more rapid earnings growth and higher dividend payout; lower P/E ratios with less marketability, greater conformity to market price movements, and higher price variability.

Malkiel and Cragg studied the effects of historical growth of earnings, dividend payout ratio, and the stock's rate of return relative to the market in determining P/E. Earnings growth was found to have a positive effect on the P/E. The closer a stock's return followed that of the market, the more negative the P/E effect. The dividend payout effect was not clear; in some years, the higher the payout the higher the P/E, but this was not true for all years.[9]

PROJECTING DIVIDENDS

At this juncture we have gathered all the numbers we need to compute the projected HPY, except for the dividend. We already have the projected price, beginning price, and necessary tax and commission information. The starting point for the dividend calculation is the earnings projection because dividends ultimately stem from earnings. The projected figure for earnings per share available to common is multiplied by the *payout ratio* (the percentage of EPS that is paid out as a dividend) to arrive at projected dividends.

This seems relatively simple; all we need is the payout ratio. Empirical studies have produced several interesting findings: (1) companies appear to have a predetermined payout ratio that they attempt to adhere to over the long run; (2) dividends are raised only if corporate management feels that a new, higher level of earnings can be supported in the future; and (3) managements are extremely reluctant to cut the absolute dollar amount of cash dividends.[10] We might apply these findings to the problem at hand—namely, projecting dividends.

---

[8]R. S. Bower and D. H. Bower, "Risk and the Valuation of Common Stock," *Journal of Political Economy* (May–June 1969), pp. 349–62.

[9]B. G. Malkiel and J. G. Cragg, "Expectations and the Structure of Share Prices," *American Economic Review* 60, no. 4 (September 1970), pp. 601–17.

[10]See John Lintner, "Distribution of Income of Corporations," *American Economic Review* (May 1956), pp. 97–113; John A. Brittain, *Corporate Dividend Policy* (Washington, D.C.: Brookings Institution, 1966); and Eugene F. Fama and Harvey Babiak, "Dividend Policy: An Empirical Analysis," *Journal of the American Statistical Association* (December 1968), pp. 1132–61.

First, we must keep in mind the evidence that firms have a long-run payout ratio. This means, for example, that on balance over time, a firm with a target payout of 50 percent is likely to pay out $1 in dividends if the EPS is $2; however, the *long-run average* need not be the figure decided upon in any one year.[11] The analyst must look at any trend in earnings, as well as at the absolute level of recent cash dividends. For example, suppose that our firm with the 50 percent target payout had earnings of $.90 in 1984, $1.00 in 1985, $1.10 in 1986, $1.20 in 1987, and $1.40 in 1988, and had paid $.45, $.45, $.50, and $.50 in cash dividends during the first four of these years, respectively. We must decide if management feels strongly enough about the growth rate in earnings [note that it rose between 1987 and 1988, from 9 percent ($.10/$1.10) to 17 percent ($.20/$1.20)] to raise the absolute dollar dividend from $.50 to, say, $.65 or $.70. It appears that management will at least raise the dividend; the question is, By how much? Will the payout again approach the 50 percent long-run target? (It has not been at that level since 1984.) If management is optimistic about future prospects, the $.70 dividend may well come about. Projecting dividends, much like projecting a P/E ratio, requires experience, insight, and sound judgment.

Present-Value Approach

ONE-YEAR HOLDING PERIOD

The value of a common stock at any moment can be thought of as the discounted value of a series of uncertain future dividends that may grow or decline at varying rates over time. It is easiest to start with common-stock valuation where the expected holding period is one year. The benefits any investor receives from holding a common stock consists of dividends plus any change in price during the holding period. Suppose that we buy one share of the Olsen Co. at the beginning of the year for $25. We hold the stock for one year. One dollar in dividends is collected at year-end, and the share is sold for $26.50. The rate of return achieved is the composite of dividend yield and change in price (capital gains yield). Thus, we get:

$$\text{Dividend yield} = \frac{D}{P} = \frac{\$1}{\$25} = .04$$

$$\text{Capital gains yield} = \frac{\$26.50 - \$25.00}{\$25} = .06$$

The total rate of return achieved is .04 + .06 = .10, or 10 percent. How might we express this same notion in terms of present values? Thus:

$$P_0 = \frac{D_1}{1 + r} + \frac{P_1}{1 + r}$$

[11]The analyst can zero in on a target-payout ratio by computing the average payout over a number of recent fiscal years.

where:

D_1 = dividend to be received at the end of year 1
  r = investor's required rate of return or discount rate
P_1 = selling price at the end of year 1
P_0 = selling price today

Therefore,

$$\$25 = \frac{\$1.00}{1 + r} + \frac{\$26.50}{1 + r}$$

Will r = .10 balance the equation? At a required rate of return of 10 percent, the dividend is worth $.909 today,[12] and the selling price has a present value of $24.091 ($26.50 × .909). The combined present value is $.909 + $24.091 = $25.00.

Should a rate of return of 15 percent have been required, the purchase price would have been too high at $25. (The $1 dividend is assumed fixed, and the selling price of $26.50 remains constant.) To achieve a 15 percent return, the value of the stock at the *beginning* of the year would have had to be:

$$P_0 = \frac{\$1.00}{1 + .15} + \frac{\$26.50}{1 + .15}$$

$$= \$.87 + \$23.04$$

$$= \$23.91$$

An alternative approach would be to ask the question: At what price must we be able to sell the stock at the *end* of one year (if the purchase price is $25 and the dividend is $1) in order to attain a rate of return of 15 percent?

$$\$25 = \frac{\$1.00}{(1 + .15)} + \frac{P_1}{(1 + .15)}$$

$$\$25 = \$0.87 + .87P_1$$

$$\$24.13 = .87P_1$$

$$\$27.74 = P_1 \text{ (selling price)}$$

MULTIPLE-YEAR HOLDING PERIOD

Consider holding a share of the Olsen Co. for five years. In most cases the dividend will grow from year to year. To look at some results, let us stipulate the following:

---

[12]Dividends are generally received quarterly. Our example assumes receipt once each year, at year-end.

g = annual expected growth in earnings, dividends and price = 6%
e_0 = most recent earnings per share = $1.89
d/e = dividend payout (%) = 50%
r = required rate of return = 10%
P_0 = price per share
P/E = price-earnings ratio = 12.5
N = holding period in years = 5

Given these stipulations, the present value of a share of stock can be determined by solving the following equation:

$$P_0 = \left(\sum_{n=1}^{n} \frac{[(e_0)(d/e)](1 + g)^n}{(1 + r)^n} \right) + \left(\frac{(P/E)[(e_0)(1 + g)^{N + 1}]}{} \right)$$

This imposing formula says, sum the present value of all dividends to be received over the holding period, and add this to the present value of the selling price of the stock at the end of the holding period to arrive at the present value of the stock.

Let us write out the string of appropriate numbers. Because the current earnings per share (e_0) are $1.89 and the dividend payout (d/e) is 50 percent, the most recent dividend per share is e_0 times d/e, or $1.89 times 50 percent, or $.945. This was stipulated in the beginning of the problem. After one year, the dividend is expected to be $.943 times $(1 + g)^1$, where g = .06. So the first year's dividend will be $1. The process is repeated for years 1 through 5 as follows:

DIVIDEND YEAR 1	DIVIDEND YEAR 2	DIVIDEND YEAR 3	DIVIDEND YEAR 4	DIVIDEND YEAR 5
$ .943$(1.06)^1$	$ .943$(1.06)^2$	9.43(1.06)^3$	$ .943$(1.06)^4$	$ .943$(1.06)^5$
$1.00	$1.06	$1.12	$1.19	$1.26

The values of $(1.06)^t$ can be found in a compound sum of $1 table. The next step is to discount each dividend at the required rate of return of 10 percent. Thus:

$$\frac{\$1.00}{(1.10)^1} + \frac{\$1.06}{(1.10)^2} + \frac{\$1.12}{(1.10)^3} + \frac{\$1.19}{(1.10)^4} + \frac{\$1.26}{(1.10)^5}$$

The values for the string $(1.10)^t$ can also be found in the appropriate factor table. The string of fractions reduces to:

$$\frac{\$1.00}{1.10} + \frac{\$1.06}{1.21} + \frac{\$1.12}{1.333} + \frac{\$1.19}{1.464} + \frac{\$1.26}{1.611}$$

The sum of these numbers is:

$$\$.909 + \$.876 + \$.844 + \$.813 + \$.783 = \$4.225$$

Thus, the present value of the stream of dividends is equal to $4.225 over the five-year period if the required rate of return is 10 percent and the dividends grow at a rate of 6 percent per year. Although the number of dollars of dividends is $5.63, their present value is only $4.225 as indicated because the dividends grow at only 6 percent and the investor requires a 10 percent rate of return.

The price of the stock at the end of the holding period (year 5) is the last part of our equation. Let us assume that the current price of the stock is $25, forecasted earnings per share (e_1) are $2.00 [$1.89(1.06)], and the P/E ratio is 12.5. Holding P/E at 12.5, the earnings, expected to grow at 6 percent per year, should amount to $2.68 [$1.89(1.06)^6] for year 6. Thus:

$$\text{Selling price at the end of year 5} = (12.5)[(\$1.89)(1.06)^6]$$

$$= \$33.45$$

The present value of the selling price is $33.45/(1.10)^5, or $20.78. Adding the present value of the stream of dividends to the present value of the expected selling price of the stock yields $4.22 + $20.78, or $25.00.

Notice that throughout this explanation, the variables g, d/e, and P/E are estimated by the analyst or investor. The current price of the stock (P) and current earnings (e_0) are observed. Equation 8.1 is solved for the rate of return (r). Let us illustrate our efforts up to now with a real-world example.

EXAMPLE: MCDONALD'S CORP. STOCK.   Let us estimate the return on McDonald's stock as an investment to be held for five years. McDonald's operates the largest fast-food restaurant system in the country. Assume that its common stock could have been purchased at the beginning of 1990 for $30. A thoroughgoing analysis of expected future earnings, dividends, and P/E ratio has provided the following predictions:

YEAR	EARNINGS PER SHARE	DIVIDENDS PER SHARE
1990	$2.27	$.36
1991	2.61	.41
1992	3.00	.48
1993	3.45	.55
1994	3.97	.63

At the end of 1994 the stock will sell for an estimated $60.

What rate of return would equate the flow of dividends and the terminal price shown above back to the current price of $30? Alternatively stated, what yield or return is required on an investment of $30 in order that an investor may withdraw dividends each year as indicated above and be able to remove a final balance of $60 at the end of five years?

In effect, we want the rate of return that will solve the following:

$$\$30 = \frac{\$.36}{1 + r} + \frac{\$.41}{(1 + r)^2} + \frac{\$.48}{(1 + r)^3} + \frac{\$.55}{(1 + r)^4} + \frac{\$.63}{(1 + r)^5} + \frac{\$60}{(1 + r)^5}$$

where r is the rate of return. Calculating the rate that will solve the equation is a somewhat tedious task, requiring trial-and-error computation. Let us turn the equation into columnar form and try a discount rate:

YEAR	RECEIPT	16% PRESENT VALUE FACTOR	PRESENT VALUE
1	$ .36	.862	$ .31
2	.41	.743	.30
3	.48	.641	.31
4	.55	.552	.30
5	.63	.476	.30
5	60.00	.476	28.57
			$30.09

At 16 percent, this stream of receipts has a present value of $30.09, which is close to the market price of $30. The investor must decide if 16 percent is a satisfactory return, given the alternative investment opportunities and the investor's attitude toward risk in holding McDonald's stock.

What happened to earnings? We instinctively feel that earnings should be worth something, whether they are paid out as dividends or not, and wonder why they do not appear in the valuation equation. In fact, they do appear in the equation but in the correct form. Earnings can be used for one of two purposes: They can be paid out to stockholders in the form of dividends or they can be reinvested in the firm. If they are reinvested in the firm they should result in increased future earnings and increased future dividends. To the extent earnings at any time, say time t, are paid out to stockholders, they are measured by the term D_t and to the extent they are retained in the firm and used productively they are reflected in future dividends and should result in future dividends being larger than D_t. To discount the future earnings stream of a share of stock would be double counting because we would count retained earnings both when they were earned and when they, or the earnings from their reinvestment, were later paid to stockholders.[13]

CONSTANT GROWTH

The simplest extension of what we have been doing assumes that dividends will grow at the same rate (g) into the indefinite future. Under this assumption the value of a share of stock is:

[13]Also see T. Estep, "A New Method for Valuing Common Stocks," *Financial Analysts Journal* (November–December 1985).

$$P = \frac{D(1+g)}{1+r} + \frac{D(1+g)^2}{(1+r)^2} + \frac{D(1+g)^3}{(1+r)^3} + \ldots + \frac{D(1+g)^N}{(1+r)^N} + \ldots$$

where N approaches infinity, this equation collapses simply to:

$$P = \frac{D_1}{r-g}$$

This model states that the price of a share of stock should be equal to next year's expected dividend divided by the difference between the appropriate discount rate for the stock and its expected long-term growth rate. Alternatively, this model can be stated in terms of the rate of return on a stock as:

$$r = \frac{D_1}{P} + g$$

The constant-growth model is often defended as the model that arises from the assumption that the firm will maintain a stable dividend policy (keep its retention rate constant) and earn a stable return on new equity investment over time.

How might the single-period model be used to select stocks? One way is to predict next year's dividends, the firm's long-term growth rate, and the rate of return stockholders require for holding the stock. The equation could then be solved for the theoretical price of the stock that could be compared with its current price. Stocks that have theoretical prices above their actual price are candidates for purchase; those with theoretical prices below their actual price are candidates for sale.

Another way to use the approach is to find the rate of return implicit in the price at which the stock is now selling. This can be done by substituting the current price, estimated dividend, and estimated growth rate into Equation 8.1 and solving for the discount rate that equates the present price with the expected flow of future dividends. If this rate is higher than the rate of return considered appropriate for the stock, given its risk, it is a candidate for purchase.

Let us illustrate the use of a single-period model with McDonald's stock. At the end of 1990 the stock sold for $30 a share. Earnings of $2.61 per share with $.41 dividend are projected for 1991. Analysts are estimating McDonald's long-term growth rate at 15 percent and its dividend payout rate at 15 percent. If we assume that 16 percent is an appropriate discount rate for McDonald's, we would compute a theoretical price of:

$$P = \$.41/(.16 - .15) = \$41$$

While McDonald's stock would seem to be undervalued selling at $30 a share, notice the sensitivity of this valuation to both the estimate of the appropriate discount rate and the estimate of the long-term growth rate. For example, if the growth rate were 14 percent rather than 15 percent, the theoretical value would be only $20.

It seems logical to assume that firms that have grown at a very high rate will not continue to do so infinitely. Similarly, firms with very poor growth might im-

prove in the future. While a single growth rate can be found that will produce the same value as a more complex pattern, it is so hard to estimate this single number, and the resultant valuation is so sensitive to this number that many analysts have been reluctant to use the constant growth model without modification.

TWO-STAGE GROWTH

The most logical further extension of the constant-growth model is to assume that a period of extraordinary growth (good or bad) will continue for a certain number of years, after which growth will change to a level at which it is expected to continue indefinitely. Firms typically go through life cycles; during part of these cycles their growth is much faster than that of the economy as a whole. Automobile manufacturers in the 1920s, manufacturers of hand calculators in the 1970s, and computer manufacturers in the 1980s are examples.

A hypothetical firm is expected to grow at a 20 percent rate for ten years, then to have its growth rate fall to 4 percent, the norm for the economy. The value of the firm with this growth pattern is determined by the following equation:

Present price = PV of dividends during above-normal growth period

+ value of stock price at end of above-normal growth period discounted back to present

$$P_0 = \sum_{t=1}^{N} \frac{D_0(1 + g_s)^t}{(1 + r_s)^t} + \frac{D_{N+1}}{r_s - g_n} \frac{1}{(1 + r_s)^N}$$

where:

g_s = above-normal growth rate
g_n = normal growth rate
N = period of above-normal growth

Consider a company whose previous dividend was \$.71 (D_0 = \$.71), with the dividend expected to increase by 15 percent a year for ten years and thereafter at 10 percent a year indefinitely. If a stockholder's required rate of return is 16 percent, what is the value of the stock? On the basis of the calculations in Table 8–1 the value is \$18.75, the present value of the dividends during the first ten years plus the present value of the stock at the end of the tenth year.

The Capitalization or Multiplier Approach

Judging from current practice, the capitalization or multiplier approach to valuation still holds the preeminent position. The multiplier is a shortcut computation to find the present value. The analyst estimates earnings per share for the year ahead. He divides this figure into the current market price of the stock, and the result is an

Table 8-1

CALCULATING THE VALUE OF A TWO-STAGE GROWTH STOCK

Assumptions:

a. Required rate of return = 16%

b. Growth rate is 15% for ten years and 10% thereafter ($g_s = 15\%$, $g_n = 10\%$, and $N = 10$).

c. Last year's dividend was $.71 ($D_o = \$.71$).

Step 1. Find the present value of dividends during the rapid-growth period.

END OF YEAR	DIVIDEND $.71 (1.15)^t$	PVIF = $1/(1.16)^t$	PV
1	$ .82	.862	$.71
2	.95	.743	.71
3	1.10	.640	.70
4	1.25	.552	.69
5	1.45	.476	.69
6	1.66	.410	.68
7	1.90	.354	.67
8	2.18	.305	.66
9	2.51	.263	.66
10	2.88	.226	.65

$$\text{PV of first ten years' dividends} = \sum_{t=1}^{10} \frac{d_0 (1 + g_s)^t}{(1 + r_s)^t} = \underline{\$6.82}$$

Step 2. Find the present value of the year 10 stock price.

a. Find the value of the stock at the end of year 10:

$$P_{10} = \frac{d_{11}}{r_s - g_n} = \frac{\$2.88 (1.10)}{.06} = \$52.80$$

b. Discount P_{10} back to the present:

$$PV = P_{10} \left[\frac{1}{1 + r_s} \right]^{10} = \$52.80 \,(.226) = \$11.93$$

Step 3. Sum to find the total value of the stock today:

$$P_0 = \$6.82 + \$11.93 = \$18.75$$

earnings multiplier. The terms *multiplier* and *price-earnings ratio* are used interchangeably. Thus:

$$\text{Earnings multiplier} = \text{P/E ratio} = \frac{\text{Current market price}}{\text{Estimated earnings per share}}$$

The multiplier, or P/E ratio, is primarily determined by the riskiness of the firm and the rate of growth in its earnings. High multipliers are associated with

high earnings growth. The DJIA might sell in the range 9 to 11 P/E. It represents a cross section of stocks with average risk and growth prospects. McDonald's may sell at a P/E of 15, because of its high rate of earnings growth. AT&T may sell at a P/E of 11, because of average growth.

The analyst seeks various rules of thumb for selecting an appropriate P/E ratio that can be applied to a company's earnings to determine value for its shares. The resulting price is compared with current market prices to assess bargains or overpriced stocks. For example, if Standard Oil of California is expected to earn $6 per share next year and normally sells at a P/E of 8, the analyst might conclude that a fair price is currently $48. If the stock is currently selling for $40, it is undervalued; if it is selling for $55, it is overpriced (overvalued).

The determination of the current P/E on a stock must be followed by a standard of comparison, taken from the historical record of the stock in question. The analyst may ascertain the median or mean P/E for a stock, as well as its range over time. More weight can be given to the recent past. This provides boundaries within which the P/E should fall (range) and indicates whether the stock is tending to sell at the upper limits of expectation (high end of P/E range) or lower limits. Industry P/E's provide some guidelines; however, different companies in the same industry frequently carry quite different P/E's.

Applied Stock Valuation

Let us now apply several approaches to stock valuation to determine the fundamental value of McDonald's Corp.'s common stock at year-end 1992. The actual closing market price at that time was $48.75.

The approaches we will use parallel our discussion of valuation above the P/E model and the dividend discount model. The P/E model will be applied in two ways, both of which will utilize an earnings forecast. They will differ in the manner in which the P/E ratio is derived. The dividend discount model will estimate dividends for a significant time into the future using multiple growth rates for those dividends. The resulting dividend stream will be discounted back to the current (year-end 1992) market price of the stock.

Basic P/E Approach to Valuation

Now we have the necessary ingredients to formulate an appropriate P/E ratio and dividends for McDonald's to combine with our earlier earnings estimates. These ingredients will allow us to determine the value of McDonald's shares.

Prior to 1976 McDonald's had not paid a cash dividend because vigorous expansion had caused the company to rely heavily on internal financing to support the addition of new units. Since 1976 the annual dividend paid has increased gradually. In recent years, the dividend payout rate has settled in around 15 percent. See Table 8–2 for dividend information for McDonald's for 1988–92.

Table 8–2

MCDONALD'S CORP.: HISTORICAL DIVIDEND INFORMATION

YEAR	DIVIDEND PER SHARE	DIVIDEND PAYOUT RATE
1992	.39	15%
1991	.36	15.3%
1990	.33	15.0%
1989	.30	15.4%
1988	.27	15.8%

Based on recent trends of quarterly dividends it is reasonable to assume that the annual dividend will be \$.42 for 1993 and \$.45 for 1994. These amounts are in line with what we perceive to be a continuation in dividend payout of 15 to 16 percent of earnings. In Figure 8–4 we see the P/E range for McDonald's during 1983–92 and the P/E ratio of the Standard & Poor's 500; note that it has fluctuated with the market over the five-year period. McDonald's P/E increased steadily during the bull market until the stock market crash in October 1987, when its P/E

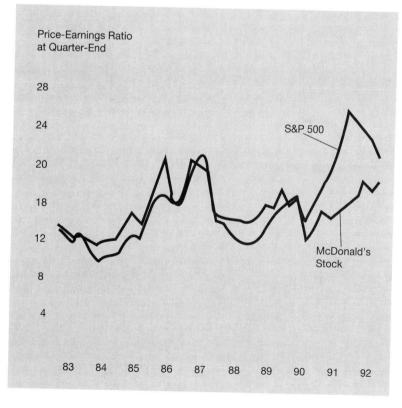

FIGURE 8–4   McDonald's Corp. Price-Earnings Ratio vs. Standard & Poor's 500 Price-Earnings Ratio, 1983–92 (*Source:* McDonald's Corporation.)

plunged along with most other stocks. Since that time, its P/E has once again risen steadily. It would appear that, using average prices, over the entire period the P/E for McDonald's will be roughly 110 to 115 percent of the S&P 500 P/E ratio. Based upon our earlier examination of the economic outlook for 1993, we predict that the S&P 500 P/E ratio will be about 16 to 17. Thus, a reasonable estimate for the P/E to use with our earnings forecast for McDonald's is one ranging from 17 to 19.

Our earlier estimate (in Chapter 7) of earnings per share for McDonald's suggested an EPS of approximately $3.06 for 1993, the average of the two methods used. Our expected dividend for 1993 is $.42, and the closing price of the stock at year-end 1992 is $48.75. Our price estimate for the stock at the end of 1993 uses a P/E of 18 and estimated earnings of $3.06, or a price of $55.00. These numbers lead to an estimated return for a one-year holding period as follows:

$$\text{Expected return} = [D_1 + (P_1 - P_0)]/P_0$$
$$= [\$0.42 + (\$55.00 - \$48.75)]/\$48.75$$
$$= 13.7\%$$

The reasonableness of the expected return of about 14 percent must be gauged in light of the risk associated with holding McDonald's shares, as well as a consideration of other alternative investment opportunities.

DOLLAR-COST AVERAGING AS A WAY TO TIME PURCHASES

Assuming that a decision to buy McDonald's has been made, the question becomes when and how the purchase should be made. Timing has long been a problem that has challenged investors. Buying at prices that are too high limits the return that can be obtained. Likewise, selling out at low prices will often result in losses. But stock prices do fluctuate, and the natural tendencies of investors often cause them to react in a way opposite to one that would enable them to benefit from these fluctuations. Ideally, investors should buy when prices are low, and then sell these securities when their prices rise to higher limits of their fluctuations. But investors are hesitant to buy when prices are low for fear that prices will fall lower, or for fear that prices won't move upward again. When prices are high, investors are hesitant to sell because they want to maximize their profits, and feel that the price may rise further. It requires discipline to buy when stock prices are low and pessimism abounds, and to sell when stock prices are high and optimism prevails!

Most investors have the discipline to carry out such a course of action *if* they know the course of the future fluctuations. But these fluctuations have proved very difficult, if not impossible, for most investors to forecast. Mechanical portfolio-management techniques have been developed to ease the problem of timing and minimize the emotions involved in investing. These techniques are referred to as *formula plans.*

Formula plans assume that stock prices fluctuate up and down in over time. Empirical evidence does seem to show that cycles exist and that cycles are closely related to movements in economic activity. Formula plans represent an attempt to

exploit these price fluctuations and make them a source of profit to the investor. Formula plans are efforts to make the decisions on timing automatic. They consist of predetermined rules for *when* purchases will be made and *how large* the purchases will be. Formula plans eliminate the emotions that surround timing decisions, such as pessimism and optimism, because the rules and plan of action are predetermined. The rules will often call for specified action that is contrary to what the investor would otherwise do and contrary to what the majority of the investors in the market are doing. The *selection* of a formula plan and the determination of the appropriate ground rules cause the investor to consider and outline his investment objectives and policies. The *implementation* of a formula plan relieves the pressures on the investor to forecast fluctuations in stock prices.

Dollar averaging requires that investors invest a constant-dollar sum in a specified stock or portfolio of stocks at periodic dates, regardless of the price of the stocks. This technique is especially appropriate for investors who have periodic sums to invest or who are otherwise in the process of *building a fund.*

Dollar averaging helps the investor avoid buying securities at high levels. If dollar averaging is executed over a complete cycle of stock prices, the investor will obtain his shares at a lower average cost per share than the average price per share of the stock over that same period. This phenomenon results from the fact that the constant-dollar sum purchases more shares at lower prices than at higher prices.

Dollar-averaging plans can vary according to the length of intervals between investments. The size of the dollar sum invested must be large enough to keep the percentage of commission costs relatively low if possible, and this may require the intervals between investments to be fairly long. For best results from the plan, however, the shorter the interval the better. The shorter interval makes it less likely that the investor will miss the opportunity to purchase stocks at low prices resulting from downward fluctuations.

The capacity of the dollar-averaging plan to achieve a lower average cost per share works most dramatically shortly after the program is started, when the fund is still small. As the program continues for long periods of time and the total fund becomes very large, the incremental addition of each new investment at various prices is averaged over many shares, and the effect on the average cost per share is greatly diluted. This is the reason that it is sometimes better for an investor to switch to one of the other formula plans when his fund becomes large.

In Table 8–3 we show purchases of shares in the lower range of a fluctuation of the same size (50 to 40). However, as the total size of the fund grows, the new shares purchased lowers the average cost per share by a smaller amount (from 50 to 48.2, versus from 50 to 44.4). As the total size of the fund becomes even larger, this effect will become even smaller.

The fact that dollar averaging enables investors to acquire the shares below their average price is not as important as the growth of the value of the shares over the long term (see Table 8–4). Dollar-averaging programs are generally considered most useful over long terms, such as five to fifteen years, periods enabling stock prices to complete numerous cycles and to achieve the long-term growth that is anticipated. Higher volatility leads to higher profits in a dollar-averaging plan over entire cycles, but advocating high volatility seems questionable, particu-

Table 8–3

EXAMPLE OF CHANGING EFFECTS OF DOLLAR
AVERAGING AS FUND SIZE INCREASES

DATE	DOLLAR VALUE OF INVESTMENT	TOTAL VALUE OF INVESTMENT	PRICE OF STOCK	NUMBER OF SHARES PURCHASED	TOTAL SHARES	AVERAGE COST PER SHARE
1/x4	$1,000	$1.000	$50	20	20	$50
1/x5	1,000	2.000	40	25	45	44.4
.	.	.	.	.	.	.
.	.	.	.	.	.	.
.	.	.	.	.	.	.
1/y4	1,000	11.000	50	20	220	50
1/y5	1,000	12.000	40	25	245	48.2

larly concerning the application of dollar averaging for savings plans, in which investors would seek low levels of risk. Dollar averaging is not advocated for use by anyone who might need to withdraw funds from the investment program on short notice. Such a situation can lead to losses if the investor has to liquidate the holdings at low prices. If an investor can meet these requirements, dollar averaging can obtain favorable results if the proper stocks are chosen and timing of liquidation is successful.

Example of a Dollar-Cost-Averaging Plan

In Table 8–5 we display the results of a hypothetical dollar-cost-averaging program using McDonald's. The example assumes monthly investments of $200 from January 1988 through July 1989. For the period considered, the average cost per share is lower than the average market value of a share in July 1989. As indicated in our earlier explanation of dollar-cost averaging, these favorable results are a function of the cycle in the shares over the period under consideration and the somewhat modest total investment of only $3,546. A graphical representation of dollar cost averaging is shown in Figure 8–5.

SUMMARY

In this chapter we have discussed several newer techniques of company analysis—regression analysis and the related tools of trend and correlation analysis, and decision-tree analysis. We have noted the strengths of these approaches as well as potential troublespots; however, on balance, we have concluded that they are superior to the more traditional techniques. In short, the newer methods have the strengths of the traditional methods while attempting to overcome their shortcomings.

Table 8-4

EXAMPLE OF DOLLAR-COST AVERAGING

INSTALL-MENT (1)	REGULAR INVEST-MENT (2)	STOCK PRICE (3)	SHARES PURCHASED (2) ÷ (3) = (4)	TOTAL SHARES OWNED Σ(4) = (5)	TOTAL AMOUNT INVESTED Σ(2) = (6)	TOTAL VALUE OF INVESTMENT (3)(5) = (7)	AVERAGE PRICE PER SHARES [Σ(3)] ÷ (1) = (8)	AVERAGE COST PER SHARE (6) ÷ (5) = (9)
1	$1,000	$25	40	40	$1,000	$1,000	$25	$25.0
2	1,000	20	50	90	2,000	1,800	22½	22.2
3	1,000	20	50	140	3,000	2,800	21⅔	21.4
4	1,000	30	33⅓	173⅓	4,000	5,200	21¾	23.0
5	1,000	25	40	213⅓	5,000	5,320	24	23.5
6	1,000	30	33⅓	246⅔	6,000	7,400	25	24.3
7	1,000	30	33⅓	280	7,000	8,400	25⁴⁄₇	25.0

Table 8–5

DOLLAR-COST AVERAGING ILLUSTRATED WITH MCDONALD'S CORP. COMMON STOCK

PAYMENT NUMBER	MONTH ENDING	REGULAR INVESTMENT	STOCK PRICE	SHARES PURCHASED*	TOTAL SHARES OWNED	TOTAL AMOUNT INVESTED	TOTAL VALUE OF INVESTMENT	AVERAGE PRICE PER SHARE	AVERAGE COST PER SHARE
1	Jan. 1988	$200	$22.63	8.0	8.0	$181	$181	$22.63	$22.63
2	Feb.	$200	$23.13	9.0	17.0	$389	$393	$22.88	$22.89
3	Mar.	$200	$21.75	9.0	26.0	$585	$566	$22.50	$22.50
4	Apr.	$200	$21.63	9.0	35.0	$780	$757	$22.28	$22.27
5	May	$200	$22.63	8.0	43.0	$961	$973	$22.35	$22.34
6	June	$200	$22.88	8.0	51.0	$1,144	$1,167	$22.44	$22.42
7	July	$200	$22.50	8.0	59.0	$1,324	$1,328	$22.45	$22.43
8	Aug.	$200	$21.88	9.0	68.0	$1,520	$1,488	$22.38	$22.36
9	Sept.	$200	$23.75	8.0	76.0	$1,710	$1,805	$22.53	$22.50
10	Oct.	$200	$23.50	8.0	84.0	$1,898	$1,974	$22.63	$22.60
11	Nov.	$200	$23.25	8.0	92.0	$2,084	$2,139	$22.68	$22.66
12	Dec.	$200	$24.13	8.0	100.0	$2,277	$2,413	$22.80	$22.77
13	Jan. 1989	$200	$26.25	7.0	107.0	$2,461	$2,809	$23.07	$23.00
14	Feb.	$200	$25.38	7.0	114.0	$2,639	$2,893	$23.23	$23.15
15	Mar.	$200	$25.75	7.0	121.0	$2,819	$3,116	$23.40	$23.30
16	Apr.	$200	$27.50	7.0	128.0	$3,012	$3,520	$23.66	$23.53
17	May	$200	$29.88	6.0	134.0	$3,191	$4,003	$24.02	$23.81
18	June	$200	$29.25	6.0	140.0	$3,366	$4,095	$24.31	$24.04
19	July	$200	$30.00	6.0	146.0	$3,546	$4,380	$24.61	$24.29

*Rounded to nearest whole share.

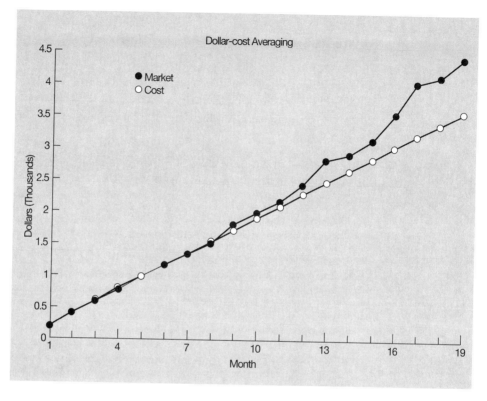

FIGURE 8–5   Graphical Representation of Dollar-Cost Averaging

Traditional valuation techniques using "normal" P/E ratios along with fore-casts of expected dividends and earnings allow us to determine whether a stock is "fairly" valued at a point in time. Such approaches allow us to evaluate a stock for a short-term horizon. Moreover, an approach combining the dividend discount model (with or without variable growth rates) can also be helpful in evaluating a stock for a longer-term holding period.

QUESTIONS AND PROBLEMS

1. What is the primary shortcoming of the traditional approaches to company analysis?

2. How should an analyst go about selecting variables to use in a regression dur-ing the company-analysis phase of his security evaluation procedures?

3. What variables do you think might "explain" the sales of a steel manufac-turer? Why?

4. Differentiate between trend analysis and regression analysis.

5. Why are semilog graphs useful in plotting growth rates?

6. What are the pros and cons of using decision trees?

7. If you were a junior security analyst in a conservative research department, how might you try to convince management to experiment with more modern techniques of company analysis?

8. What determines an appropriate P/E for the analyst to use? Why is this important?

9. What variables have been found to be useful in "explaining" P/E ratios?

10. Would you expect firms in the same industry to have approximately the same P/E ratios? Explain.

11. How might you forecast a firm's dividend for the next year? Forecast U.S. X's dividend for next year using this approach.

12. Based on your analysis of U.S. X performed above, what is your forecast of a one-year holding-period yield for U.S. X, beginning with yesterday's price?

13. Tijuana Tom is a rapidly growing entrant in the fast-food industry. The company operates a chain of Mexican-food restaurants in the southwestern United States. The company expects to sustain an earnings growth rate of 30 percent per year while retaining all earnings to finance growth. To date, earnings volatility has been about 20 percent around the trend. The stock sells at $50 today on earnings estimated at $2.00 per share for the year ahead. Use the comparative P/E model in the text to determine the "fair" value of Tijuana Tom's stock.

14. Why is it believed that the average cost per share of shares purchased under a dollar-cost-averaging plan will be lower than the average price per share of the same stock during the period of the plan's usage? Is this always true?

15. At what point in the building of a portfolio is the impact of dollar-cost averaging greatest? Why? Prove this by making up an example of your own.

C A S E

■

Philip Morris Companies

The director of research asks O'Hara to make a valuation recommendation to guide Green Securities in the possible addition of the Philip Morris stock to its portfolios. In response to current trends in valuation techniques, Green has established a strict, dual-approach valuation format. All analysts' recommendations must be structured around both approaches.

QUESTIONS

1. As a first approach, the director of research consistently reminds his analysts that excellent companies often do not make excellent investments, and that, regardless of numerical valuation analysis, individual stock prices usually reflect consensus-forming forecasts, that in turn determine stock prices. He requires anticipatory, nonconsensus valuation analysis as the first segment of any analyst's recommendation.

Using *only* the data shown in Exhibit 4, analyze the attractiveness of Philip Morris common stock on the basis of an anticipatory, nonconsensus valuation approach.

Exhibit 1

PHILIP MORRIS COMPANIES
BALANCE SHEETS
AS OF DECEMBER 31, 1988
($ IN MILLIONS)

	1988	1987
ASSETS		
Cash and cash equivalents	$ 68	$ 90
Accounts receivable	2,222	2,065
Inventories	5,384	4,154
Current assets	$ 7,774	$ 6,309
Property, plant & equipment (net)	8,648	6,582
Goodwill (net)	15,071	4,052
Investments	3,260	3,665
Total assets	$34,753	$20,608
LIABILITIES & STOCKHOLDERS' EQUITY		
Short-term debt	$ 1,259	$ 1,440
Accounts payable	1,777	791
Accrued liabilities	3,848	2,277
Income taxes payable	1,089	727
Dividends payable	260	213
Current liabilities	$ 8,233	$ 5,448
Long-term debt	17,122	6,293
Deferred income taxes	1,719	2,044
Stockholders' equity	7,679	6,823
Total liabilities & stockholders' equity	$34,753	$20,608

2. As the second approach of the required recommendation format, analysts must (1) closely relate forecasted, long-term earnings per share growth to stock price, and (2) incorporate the 20 percent required return used by the firm to compare common stocks with alternative investments.

Using *only* the information provided in Exhibit 4, and the constant growth dividend discount model, analyze the Philip Morris stock and determine its attractiveness on this basis.

Exhibit 2

PHILIP MORRIS COMPANIES
INCOME STATEMENT
FOR THE YEAR ENDED DECEMBER 31, 1988
($ IN MILLIONS)

Sales	$31,742
Cost of goods sold	(12,156)
Selling and administrative expenses	(14,410)
Depreciation expense	(654)
Goodwill amortization	(125)
Interest expense	(670)
Pretax income	$ 3,727
Income tax expense	(1,390)
Net income	$ 2,337
Dividends declared $941 million	

Exhibit 3

PHILIP MORRIS PURCHASE OF KRAFT
ALLOCATION OF PURCHASE PRICE
($ IN MILLIONS)

Accounts receivable	$758
Inventories	1,232
Property, plant & equipment	1,740
Goodwill	10,361
Short-term debt	(700)
Accounts payable	(578)
Accrued liabilities	(530)
Long-term debt	(900)
Purchase price (net of cash acquired)	$11,383

Exhibit 4

PHILIP MORRIS COMPANIES
VALUATION DATA

	AMOUNT	PERCENTAGE CHANGE FROM PRIOR YEAR
Current stock price	$115.00	–
1988 Earnings per share	10.03	29%
1988 Dividends per share	4.05	29
Current annual dividends per share	4.50	11

COMPARATIVE WALL STREET DATA	ESTIMATED EARNINGS PER SHARE (EPS)				PROJECTED LONG-TERM GROWTH RATE		CURRENT RECOMMENDATION
	1989	% INCREASE	1990	% INCREASE	EPS	DIVIDENDS	
Firm A	$11.70	17%	$14.00	20%	20%	20%	Buy
Firm B	11.85	18	13.80	16	20	18	Buy/Hold
Firm C	11.80	18	14.25	21	18	16	Attractive
Firm D	12.00	20	14.20	18	15	15	Long-Term Buy
Firm E	11.60	16	13.90	20	15	15	Current Buy
Green Securities	$11.40	14%	$12.75	12%	14%	15%	

REFERENCES

BARRY, C. and R. JENNINGS. "Information and Diversity of Analyst Opinion." *Journal of Financial and Quantitative Analysis* (June 1992) pp. 169–83.

BEAVER, W., and D. MORSE. "What Determines Price-Earnings Ratios?" *Financial Analysts Journal* (July–August 1978).

BENEISH, M. "Stock Prices and the Dissemination of Analysts' Recommendations" *Journal of Business* (October 1991) pp. 393–416.

BING, R. "Survey of Practitioners' Stock Evaluation Methods." *Financial Analysts Journal* (May–June 1971).

CHUGH LAL C., and JOSEPH W. MEADER. "The Stock Valuation Process: The Analysts' View." *Financial Analysts Journal* (November–December, 1984), pp. 41–48.

ELLIS, CHARLES D. "Ben Graham: Ideas as Mementos." *Financial Analysts Journal* (July–August 1982), p. 41.

FARRELL, JAMES L., JR. "The Dividend Discount Model: A Primer." *Financial Analysts Journal* (November–December 1985), pp. 16–25.

MURRAY, ROGER F. "Graham and Dodd: A Durable Discipline." *Financial Analysts Journal* (September–October 1984), p. 18.

PHILBROCK, D. and W. RICKS. "Using Value Line and IBES Analyst Forecasts in *Accounting Research*" (Autumn 1991) pp 397–417.

OPPENHEIMER, HENRY R. "A Test of Ben Graham's Stock Selection Criteria." *Financial Analysts Journal* (September–October 1984), p. 68.

SORENSEN, ERIC, and DAVID A. WILLIAMSON. "Some Evidence on the Value of Dividend Discount Models." *Financial Analysts Journal* (November–December 1985), p. 60.

STATMAN, MEIR. "Growth Opportunities vs. Growth Stocks." *Journal of Portfolio Management* (Spring 1984), p. 70.

STREBEL, PAUL J., and AVNER ARBEL. "Pay Attention to Neglected Firms!" *Journal of Portfolio Management* (Winter 1983), p. 37.

CHAPTER 9

BOND ANALYSIS: RETURNS AND SYSTEMATIC RISK

Because of their fascination with the potential rewards normally associated with investing in stocks, investors often lack an interest in or an understanding of fixed-income securities as an investment vehicle. After all, bonds pay a fixed-interest income, and one expects that their price will not be subject to wide fluctuations. The rather straightforward type of analysis required in bond investing centers on quality and safety and certainly lacks the appeal of discovering the wonder stock of the future.

THE STRATEGIC ROLE OF BONDS

Portfolio management can be viewed as a two-level process. It includes the macro decision regarding the proportion of the portfolio to hold in the available asset classes (e.g., stocks and bonds) and the micro decision of which individual securities to hold that will comprise the respective components. Our initial interest in this chapter will be in the role that bonds can play in the macro analysis. For most of recent history, investors looked to bonds for certainty of income. Bonds served as a kind of anchor to the winds of adversity. For those who find less volatility more emotionally acceptable or for those who realize their investment needs are more modest than those promised by an all-equity portfolio (over the long term), bonds tend to represent an important investment alternative in the portfolio asset allocation decision. If minimizing risk is the only objective, then investment in Treasury instruments will achieve a return which is accepted as being "risk-free." If maximizing return is the only objective, then investment in the higher expected return asset is the answer. Given the usual range of alternatives, this choice is common stock. The real problem arises when a trade-off is desired between return and risk.

For the long sweep of time, bond returns are less than stock returns; however, bond investment involves less risk. The implication is that, although stocks might be expected to outperform bonds over sufficiently long periods of time, the associ-

ated risk may also be greater. Whether the risk preference of the investor can tolerate the associated intraperiod risk is a significant issue.

The total risk of a portfolio may be thought of as the individual risk of each investment and its correlation or tendency to move relative to each other. For example, if one had two assets of the same return and individual risk, there would be benefits to holding both assets if there were a tendency for one asset to counteract the volatility of the other.

There has been a historical positive, albeit low, correlation between stocks and corporate bonds. The implication of this relationship is that combining stocks and bonds in a portfolio can help reduce the portfolio's risk, perhaps more than proportionate to the reduction in overall return. Thus, bonds not only possess lower risk than stocks, they also can be useful when combined with stocks in a portfolio.

Finally, bonds have a place for an ever-increasing number of investors who do not wish to buy-and-hold. For those investors interested in capitalizing on bond price movements, bond trading can offer every bit of the excitement normally associated with trading in stocks.

THE MARKETS FOR DEBT SECURITIES

The bond market is chiefly over-the-counter in nature, and today's bond market offers issues to suit any investor. The bond market is normally separated into two issuer segments: domestic (government and corporate) and international.

GOVERNMENT BONDS

Federal Government Bonds

The U.S. Treasury issues bonds, notes, and bills. All Treasury obligations are of the highest quality because they are backed by the full faith and credit of the U.S. government. This feature, along with their liquidity, makes them very attractive. Treasury notes carry maturities of two to ten years, whereas Treasury bonds have maturities of ten to thirty years. Treasury notes and bonds are sold in $1,000 denominations (two- to three-year notes are sold in $5,000 minimums). Interest income is subject to normal federal income tax, but is exempt from state and local taxes. All government notes and bonds today are issued as noncallable securities.

Agency bonds are debt securities issued by various agencies and organizations of the U.S. government, such as the Tennessee Valley Authority, Federal Farm Credit Banks, and the Government National Mortgage Association (GNMA). They are not obligations of the U.S. Treasury so they customarily provide yields that are above the rates for Treasury instruments.

Two types of agency issues are available: government-sponsored and federal agencies. Although only six government-sponsored organizations exist, the number of federal agencies exceeds two dozen.

Most of the government agencies in existence today were created to support either agriculture or housing. Although these issues are not direct liabilities of the U.S. government, they are all viewed as moral obligations of the U.S. government (indeed, would Congress ever allow one to default?). Also, as with Treasury securities, agency issues are normally noncallable or carry long-call deferment.

Municipal Bonds

Municipal bonds are the issues of states, counties, cities, and other political subdivisions (e.g., school, water, and sewer districts). These bonds carry $5,000 denominations and are often issued serial in form. The issue is broken into a series of smaller bonds, each with its own maturity date and interest rate. Municipal bonds are brought to the market as either general obligation or revenue bonds. General obligation bonds are backed by the full faith, credit, and taxing power of the issuer (e.g., the state of Texas or the city of New Orleans). Revenue bonds, in contrast, are serviced by the income generated from specific income-producing projects (e.g., airports, college dormitories, toll roads). The vast majority of municipals out today are revenue bonds (about two-thirds of the new-issue volume).

The distinction between a general obligation and a revenue bond is an important one because the issuer of a revenue bond is obligated to pay principal and interest only if a sufficient level of revenue is generated (no cars on the toll road, no interest payments). General obligations must be serviced regardless of the level of tax income generated by the municipality. Thus, while revenue bonds involve a lot more risk than general obligations, they provide higher yields.

CORPORATE BOND MARKET

Utilities dominate the U.S. corporate market. The other important segments include industrials (second to utilities), transportation, and financial issues. Almost every bond has a single maturity date. Maturities range from twenty-five to forty years, with public utilities generally near the longer end and industrials in the twenty-five- to thirty-year range. Shorter term notes are popular during periods of higher interest rates when issuing firms want to avoid long-term obligations.

Generally, the average yields for industrial bonds will be the lowest of the three corporate sectors, followed by utilities, with yields on transportation bonds generally being the highest. Yields differ between utilities and industrials because the large supply of utility bonds means that their yields must rise to attract the necessary demand.

Some corporate bonds have unique features or security arrangements. The issuer of a mortgage bond grants to the bondholder a mortgage lien on some piece of property, or possibly all of the firm's property. Such a lien provides greater security to the bondholder and a lower interest rate for the issuing firm. Additional mortgage bonds can be issued, assuming certain restrictions related to earnings or assets are met by the issuer.

As an alternative to pledging fixed assets, a borrower can pledge stocks, bonds, or notes as collateral. The bonds secured by these financial assets are termed collateral trust bonds.

Equipment trust certificates are issued by railroads, airlines, and other transportation firms; the proceeds are used to purchase equipment (e.g., freight cars, locomotives, and aircraft), which serve as collateral for the debts. Serial maturities range from one to about fifteen years. The use of serial maturities reflect the nature of the collateral, which is subject to substantial wear and tear and tends to deteriorate rapidly.

High-Yield Corporate Bond Sector

Bonds are normally graded from A (highest quality) to C (in default). High-yield bonds, commonly called junk bonds, are issues with quality ratings below triple B (BBB). Bond issues in this sector of the market either were rated investment-grade (BBB and higher) at the time of issuance but have been downgraded subsequently (fallen angels) to noninvestment grade, or at the time of issuance were rated as noninvestment grade (born bad). One of the best-known examples of the latter is RJR Nabisco. The downgrading of RJR came about because of a leveraged buyout (LBO) that took the company private and substantially increased its debt-to-equity ratio.

LBO financing and recapitalizations often result in highly complex debt structures. In these situations, the heavy interest payment burden the corporation must make places severe cash-flow drain on the firm. To reduce this burden, firms involved have debt structures that permit the avoidance of cash interest payments for a period of time. Three types of deferred-interest payment structures exist: deferred-interest, step-up, and payment-in-kind.

Deferred-interest bonds are the most common type of deferred coupon structure. These bonds sell at a deep discount from par value and do not pay interest for a period of three to seven years. Step-up bonds pay interest, but the interest rate is low for the initial period before it increases to a higher coupon rate. Finally, payment-in-kind (PIK) bonds give the issuer an option to pay cash at an interest payment date or to give the bondholder a similar bond. By similar, we mean a bond with an identical coupon rate and a par value equal to the amount of the coupon payment that would have been paid. The period during which the issuer can make this choice varies from five to ten years.

INTERNATIONAL FIXED-INCOME INVESTING

The term *international bonds* is often used to describe several types of bonds with a variety of characteristics relating to issuer or buyer domicile, the location of the primary trading market, and/or currency denomination. Insofar as price movements are concerned, the most important characteristic is currency denomination. Regardless of the domicile of the issuer, the buyer, or the trading market, prices of

issues denominated in U.S. dollars (*U.S. pay*) are affected principally by the direction of U.S. interest rates, whereas prices of issues denominated in other currencies (*foreign pay*) are determined primarily by movements of interest rates in the country of the currency denomination. Thus analysis of international bond investing must be separated into two parts—U.S. pay and foreign pay.

The U.S.-pay international bond market can in turn be divided into issues for which the primary trading market is in the United States (*Yankees*) and issues for which the primary trading market is abroad (*Eurodollars*). The other portion of the U.S.-pay international bond market encompasses those foreign-domiciled issuers who register with the Securities and Exchange Commission (SEC) and borrow U.S. dollars via issues underwritten by a U.S. syndicate for delivery in the United States. The principal trading market is in the United States, although foreign buyers can and do participate. From the standpoint of the U.S. investor, foreign-pay international bonds encompass all issues denominated in currencies other than the dollar. A variety of types of issues are available to the U.S. investor, but in all cases the primary trading market is outside the United States. Securities sold by a particular issuer within the country of issue and in that country's currency are typically termed *domestic issues*. These may include direct government issues or corporate bonds. Corporate bonds clearly carry an additional risk beyond currency, interest-rate, and sovereign risks—that of company credit risk and marketability. In addition, in some countries, all securities in their domestic bond market are subject to withholding tax on interest when sold to nonresidents, unless the rate is reduced or eliminated by a tax treaty with the country of the buyer.

Another market is termed the *foreign bond market,* which indicates issues sold primarily in one country and its currency by a borrower of a different nationality. The *Yankee market* is the U.S.-dollar version of this market. Other examples are the *Samurai market* (yen-denominated bonds issued in Japan by non-Japanese issuers), and the *Bulldog market* (U.K. sterling-denominated bonds issued in the United Kingdom by non-British entities). Compared with the size of the domestic bond markets, these foreign bond markets are quite small, and liquidity can be limited.

Rationale for International Bond Investing

The rationale for foreign-pay international bond investing is threefold. First, more than one-half of the total global bond market is represented by bond markets outside the United States. This is far too large an asset class to be ignored. Second, the credit-quality profile of many borrowers in the international market is generally higher than that in the United States. This derives from several factors, such as the preponderance of sovereign (e.g., Kingdom of Sweden), government supported (e.g., Gas de France), and supranational organizations (e.g., World Bank) that finance in these markets. Furthermore, many countries have a greater willingness to support and aid companies that encounter difficulties because of smaller size and greater industrial concentration.

Third, international bonds can enhance an investor's total rate of return compared with what is available from alternative U.S. domestic bond investments. The

composition of return will, however, be variable between income, domestic price change, and foreign currency change. A fourth rationale for international bond investing is diversification. The inclusion of foreign bonds in a portfolio should reduce the risk or volatility of returns of a portfolio otherwise invested solely in U.S. fixed-income securities. The fundamental reason for this is that foreign bond markets are not perfectly correlated with the U.S. bond market. This should be obvious, for the dynamics of the business cycle differ by country, as does the role of monetary policy in the arsenal of a government's economic weapons. Institutional or structural forces, government financing practices, and tradition mean that the role of buyers and sellers differs among fixed-income markets.

SPECIALIZED BONDS

High and volatile interest rates have driven some borrowers to become increasingly innovative in structuring the terms of their debt issues. The principal objective of issuers is to lower the interest rates they must pay. Some want to borrow long term when the threat of inflation makes lenders prefer shorter maturities. To achieve these objectives, issuers have had to add inducements ("sweeteners" or "kickers") to bonds. In other cases certain lending segments that have been outside the normal channels of the bond market have altered their practices in order to enter into this market.

A number of specialized types of bonds have appeared in recent years. Among the more interesting are : mortgage-backed securities, puttable bonds, floating-rate instruments, and zero coupon bonds.

Mortgage-Backed Securities

Mortgage-backed securities allow investors to invest in residential mortgage assets without having to become involved in the administratively burdensome processes of mortgage origination and/or servicing. In general, a mortgage-backed security represents a pro rata and undivided claim, generally evidenced by a certificate. Investors receive periodic payments consisting of interest and principal amortization from a pool of mortgages with very similar characteristics. The mortgages in the pool stand as collateral for this claim.

Two broad categories of mortgage-backed securities exist: mortgage-backed bonds and pass-through securities. Pass-through securities, as the name implies, pass through to the ultimate investor a fractional share of monthly payments received on the underlying mortgages in the pool, consisting of principal amortization and interest as these are received or scheduled to be received (including prepayments on those mortgages).

A unique feature of pass-through securities is that the cash flow received each month by investors is uncertain due to the unpredictable nature of prepayments by the mortgagor. This cash flow uncertainty has been unattractive to some investors

(although the monthly flow-through feature itself has been attractive to others). Mortgage-backed bonds have payments that are structured so as to be similar to conventional bonds, such as semiannual interest payments and known maturities. Some pass-throughs are backed by Veterans Administration (VA) and Federal Housing Administration (FHA) mortgages and others by conventional mortgages.

The prototype and most common pass-through security is issued by the GNMA, or "Ginnie Maes" for short. Ginnie Maes are backed by VA and FHA mortgages, which are in turn guaranteed by the U.S. government. Federal Home Loan Mortgage Corp. (FHLMC) participation certificates are backed by conventional mortgages. Private pass-through securities are issued by savings and loan associations, commercial banks, mortgage bankers and other mortgage companies, and private mortgage insurance companies on first mortgages that they either have originated or have purchased from the originator or a mortgage lender. Although private pass-throughs provide no government guarantee, most private issues utilize mortgage-pool insurance purchased from a private mortgage insurance company to insure against losses due to default by mortgagors.

Collateralized mortgage obligations (CMOs) were developed to offset some of the problems with mortgage pass-throughs. The main innovation of the CMO instrument is the segmentation of the irregular mortgage cash flows into securities that are short-, medium-, and long-term mortgage collateralized bonds. The bonds are serviced with the cash flows from these mortgages. Rather than the straight pass-through arrangement, however, the CMO creates a series of bonds with varying maturities to appeal to a wider range of investors. A standard CMO has four classes, or tranches. The first three classes receive interest as it is accrued. Principal payments are different. The first class receives all principal payments on the underlying mortgages until such securities are entirely paid. At that time, the second class begins to receive principal payments and is entitled to all of them until that class is paid. At this point, the third class receives all principal payments until it is completely repaid.

The last class is an accrual security, known as a *Z bond*. Its holders receive no interim interest payments. Rather, interest accrues at a stated coupon rate. Cash payments on a Z bond begin only after the earlier classes have been retired. At that point its holders receive payments from whatever collateral remains in the pool. Due to mortgage prepayments, the timing and magnitude of payments to the Z-bond holders are highly uncertain.

Another security that can be created in a CMO is a residual class. As the name implies, this class comes after the Z class. The residual security has no stated interest rate or face value. Rather, it receives any cash flows that remain after interest and principal payments have been paid on prior classes and all administrative expenses have been paid. Any excess paid at the end is due to (1) overcollateralization of the mortgage pool; (2) interest payments by mortgagees exceeding the coupon payments on the CMO bonds; and (3) reinvestment income arising from mortgage payments being monthly whereas coupon payments on the bonds are quarterly or semiannual. Obviously, the residual class bears greater risk than any other class in a CMO. It is like equity.

Put Privileges

Option tender bonds—for convenience, referred to as issues with put options—give holders the right to sell back their bonds to the issuers, normally at par. Issues with puts are aimed both at investors who are pessimistic about the ability of interest rates to decline over the long term and at those who simply prefer to take a cautious approach to their bond buying.

In addition to being able to get out of their positions, investors derive a collateral benefit from owning bonds with puts. In the period before the put becomes effective, these issues should tend to hold their value to a greater degree than straight bonds of comparable maturity if interest rates rise. The reason, of course, is that the put privilege acts as a floor under the market price of the bonds.

The Brevard County Housing Finance Authority of Florida sold almost $150 million of 9 percent tax-exempt bonds due February 1, 2013, that give holders the right to sell the bonds back to the Authority on February 1, 1986, and each succeeding February 1. The bonds were sold at par and would be bought back at par if tendered.

Investors purchasing the Brevard bonds relinquish a substantial amount of interest in return for the put feature. The issue's 9 percent coupon interest is low compared to coupons of more than 11 percent available on straight municipal bonds with a three-year maturity at the time of issuance.

But the put privilege means that, after February 1, 1986, the issue will trade as though it were a one-year note paying 9 percent interest.

Floating Rates

Whether they are named floating-, adjustable-, or variable-rate, these issues have the same underlying concept. The interest rate paid to holders changes periodically, sometimes as often as once a week, but usually once or twice a year. In most instances, the rate has been based on formulas that involve the discount rate on three- or six-month U.S. Treasury bills.

But when the interest rate of an intermediate- or long-term issue is based on the yield of a three- or six-month money-market instrument, many institutional bond buyers shun the issue. The reason is that short-term rates fluctuate to a far greater degree than long-term, and these investors do not want to gamble that today's high short-term yields will remain a part of the economic scene for the next five or ten years.

One solution devised by issuers has been to tie the interest on floating-rate bonds to a combination of short- and long-term yields on stipulated securities. General Motors Acceptance Corp. (GMAC) offered investors a ten-year $250 million adjustable-rate issue whose interest is tied to the yield of U.S. Treasury notes maturing in ten years.

Until mid-November 1982, the GMAC notes paid 13.45 percent interest, but on each November 15 starting in 1982, the annual rate was established at 107.2 percent of the two most recent weekly average yields on ten-year Treasury notes. If,

for example, on November 15, 1996, that average was 10 percent, the GMAC notes would pay 10.72 percent for the following twelve months. The rate is adjusted again on November 15, 1997, and so on.

The advantage of owning these GMACs is that in periods when intermediate-term rates rise, the annual refixing of the interest will act as a floor under the market price, especially because GMAC has put no ceiling on the rate it will pay.

But if intermediate-term rates experience a lengthy decline, the notes have several disadvantages: (1) just as the interest rate has no ceiling, it has no floor, so your yield could fall to a low single-digit number; (2) the annual rate adjustment will act as a lid on the market price of the notes; (3) GMAC might redeem the issue prior to maturity and sell a new issue at the then-prevailing lower rates.

Extendible Notes

The extendible note is in some respects like floating-rate issues. It also permits the issuer to borrow money at a lower rate than would be required by a bond with a conventional long maturity.

IBM has extendible notes. The company has the right to redeem (call) all or part of the issue during a one-year period starting December 15, 1986. If the notes are not called, holders have the right to cash them in on December 15, 1987, and on every December 15 thereafter.

The interest rate is set each mid-December in line with then-current interest rates. Each succeeding December 15, adjustments will be made to a rate established by the company in its discretion without limitation. If holders are not satisfied with the rate, they can cash in their notes and get a price of par (100).

Notes that both are extendible and have floating rates are also on the market.

Original-Issue Discount Bonds

One of the new debt species—the long-term, original-issue deep-discount bond—is designed to appeal more to tax-exempt institutional investors such as pension funds than to the average individual.[1] That is so because the difference between the discounted price at which the bonds are sold and the $1,000 paid at maturity is not viewed as a capital gain by the Internal Revenue Service. Instead, the tax rules require that the discount be taxed as ordinary income spread over the life of the bond. Individual investors can only realize capital gains at maturity if the discount is not an original-issue discount.

The advantage to institutions is that the deep-discount price virtually guarantees that they have locked in a high yield for the life of the bond—usually 30 years—because it is most unlikely that any issuer would retire an original-issue deep-discount bond prior to maturity. Issuers of such bonds benefit by succeeding

---

[1] Certain zero coupon bonds have successfully found their way into individual retirement accounts.

in borrowing for the long term when they might otherwise have difficulty in doing so and by paying substantially less coupon interest than they would otherwise have to pay.

Martin-Marietta Corp. sold a deep-discount issue maturing in 2011 at a price of 53.835 percent of par and paying coupon interest of 7 percent. Original purchasers of the bonds obtained a respectable 13 percent current yield and a yield-to-maturity of 13.25 percent.

The $175 million of Martin-Marietta bonds were so well received that the sale was quickly followed by other issues. Northwest Industries offered $125 million of thirty-year 7 percent bonds at a price of 52.75 and Trans-America Financial sold a $200 million 6.5 percent thirty-issue whose price was only about 48 percent of par. In addition, GMAC offered $400 million of 6 percent thirty-year bonds at a price of 44.51 percent of par.

BOND MARKET PERFORMANCE RESULTS

Figure 9–1 shows the track of interest rates on U.S. Treasury bonds from 1973 through 1992. It is easy to see that the rising trend in rates from 1973 until 1981 represented painful capital losses for bondholders. However, the period from 1981 through 1992 represented a reversal of fortune for bondholders. Interest rates declined dramatically during the period and bond prices rose.

Table 9–1 shows the results of investing in stocks and bonds between 1981 and the end of 1992. These results assume an investor purchases a package of bonds on January 1 each year and sells these bonds on December 31 each year. Salomon Brothers is a large investment firm that tracks indexes of bond returns. It

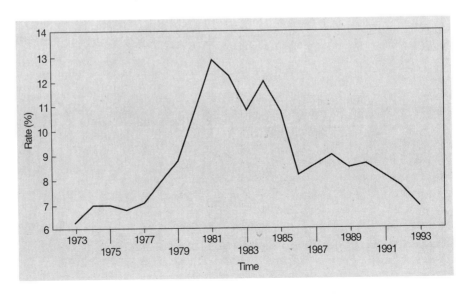

FIGURE 9–1   Rates on U.S. Treasury Bonds, 1973–93

TABLE 9–1

Annual Rates of Return on Bond and Stock Indexes, 1981–92

INDEX	RATE OF RETURN	STANDARD DEVIATION OF RETURNS	CORRELATION WITH S&P 500 INDEX
Broad Bonds	13.68%	6.85%	0.46
Treasuries	14.28%	11.40%	0.49
Corporates	15.48%	10.34%	0.52
SP 500 Stocks	15.88%	14.22%	1.00

tracks a broad bond index (Treasury instruments, agencies, corporate and mortgage bonds), and treasuries and corporate bonds with maturities greater than ten years.

Note that the rates of return on the various bond indexes are below those on stocks, but not by a lot, and the standard deviation of returns is also less, especially when one combines categories of bonds into the broad index. Also, the low correlation between bonds and stocks highlights the diversification potential of adding bonds to a stock portfolio.

Table 9–2 extends this performance analysis to cover international bond markets for 1977–91. Data is included for the larger bond markets in the world. The return information in Table 9–2 would be that achieved by a U.S. investor. These returns include annual results from interest income and capital gains (losses) plus any impact related to currency changes. For example, the return on Japanese bonds in a given year might be 9 percent from interest income and capital gains to Japanese investors. However, if the relationship between the yen and the dollar changed throughout the year, a U.S. investor could find the net return raised or lowered significantly. Over the fifteen years shown, the British bond market afforded a U.S. investor with the best return, while the French market had the best ten-year performance.

TABLE 9–2

Selected World Bond Markets Average
Annual Returns,* 1977–91

	UNITED STATES	CANADA	UNITED KINGDOM	JAPAN	FRANCE	GERMANY
5 Years						
1977–81	–1.2%	–10.0%	16.0%	15.2%	9.0%	5.3%
1982–86	22.4	16.5	13.2	18.2	19.5	16.8
1987–91	10.3	14.6	17.5	8.8	14.2	8.6
10 Years						
1982–91	16.2	15.5	15.3	13.4	16.8	12.6
15 Years						
1977–91	10.1	11.3	15.6	14.0	11.2	10.1

*Coupon income plus capital and currency gains (losses).

Listed Bond Tables

CORPORATE BONDS

Basic information on bond trading appears regularly in the newspaper (see Figure 9–2). A key difference from the stock tables is that bond prices are shown as a percentage figure of $1,000, par value, whereas stock prices are listed in actual dollars and fractions thereof. For example, a bond price shown as 106 means 106 percent of $1,000 per bond or $1,060. A stock listed at 106 means $106 per share.

To examine the reading of these tables, look at the McDonald's Corp. bond listed in the following table.

BONDS	1	2 CUR YLD	3 VOL	4 CLOSE	5 NET CHG
McDnl	9¾99	8.9	2	109⅜	−¼

1. The *bond description* sets forth the abbreviated name of the issuer, the interest rate, and the year of maturity. In this illustration the issuer of the bond is the McDonald's Corp., the interest rate is 9¾ percent of the bond's $1,000 face value, and the bond must be redeemed in the year 1999. The specific month and day of maturation cannot be determined from these tables. Interested investors must refer to a research service that provides such information.

2. The *current yield* is a function of the investor's annual interest dollars and the latest value of the bond. The analytical formula is the annual interest divided by the current market value shown in column 4. Therefore, the current yield for this debenture is

$$\frac{\$97.50 \ (9.75\% \text{ of } \$1,000)}{\$1,093.75 \ (109.375\% \text{ of } \$1,000)} = 8.9\%$$

The current yield of a convertible bond is not calculated in this bond table. It is identified by the letters "cv" appearing in this column. Investors do not normally buy convertible bonds just for their yield. They also look for a movement in the underlying stock to provide them with capital gains. Interest income is of secondary importance.

3. *Volume figures* are expressed in the number of $1,000 face-value bonds traded today. Simply add three zeros to the number in this column to find that $2,000 worth of face-value McDonald's bonds changed hands on the New York Stock Exchange (NYSE).

4. The *close* is the last price at which a transaction took place on October 7, 1993, in the McDonald's 9¾ percent bonds on the NYSE.

5. The net change, the change in value between day-to-day closing prices, is expressed as a percentage of a bond's $1,000 typical face value. Thus, a change

NEW YORK EXCHANGE BONDS

Bonds	Cur Yld	Vol	Close	Net Chg
Ens 8¾01	8.4	30	104	...
F&M 11½03	11.6	13	99	+ ¼
FairCp 12s01	13.3	75	90	+ 4
FairCp 13⅛06	14.6	35	90	+ 2
Fldcst 6s12	cv	111	80	...
FUnRE 10¼09	cv	1	101¼	− ¼
FrpMCG zr11	...	100	29½	+ 1¼
Frpt dc6.55s01	cv	12	91	+ ¼
FreptM zr06	...	55	32½	− ⅛
FremntGn zr13	...	110	37½	...
GMA 8¼06	8.0	5	102⅞	+ ¼
GMA dc6s11	6.9	108	86½	+ ¼
GMA zr12	...	12	228	− 2
GMA zr15	...	102	189⅜	− 1½
GMA 8¼16	7.8	121	106¼	...
GMA 8s94	7.7	79	104	+ ¼
GMA 7⅞97	7.8	85	101½	...
GPA Del 8¾98	11.4	190	77	...
GHost 11½02	11.1	75	104	− 1¼
GHost 8s02	cv	58	98½	− 1
Gene 10⅜03	9.9	42	104⅞	− ⅛
Genrad 7¼11	cv	37	72	+ ½
GaPw 10s16J	9.7	71	103⅛	+ ¼
GrnTrFn 10¼02	8.8	60	117	− 1¼
GreyF zr94	...	4	96 13/16	+ 1/16
Gulfrd 6s12	cv	15	95½	− 2
Hallwd 7s00	9.1	115	77	+ ½
Hlttrst 8¾05	8.7	2	100⅜	− 1½
Hertz 7s03	6.9	37	100¾	...
HmGrp 14⅞99	14.5	18	102⅝	− ⅛
HomeDp 4½97	cv	7	122	...
HudFd 8s06	cv	20	102	+ 1
Huffy 7¼cld	cv	6	123	− 1⅛
ICN 12⅞98	12.4	145	104	+ ⅞
IMC Fer 6¼01	cv	3	92¾	+ ¼
IRT Pr 7.3s03	cv	10	112	...
IllBel 7⅝06	7.4	5	102¾	+ ⅛
InldStl 9½00	9.4	3	101½	+ ⅜
IBM 8⅜19	7.4	20	112½	...
IBM 6⅜97	6.1	158	104⅛	+ ⅛
IBM 7¼02	6.8	15	107	− ¼
IBM 6⅜00	6.2	80	103⅛	...
IBM 7½13	7.2	441	103¾	+ ⅛
IPap dc5⅛12	6.0	30	86	+ 1
IntTch 9⅜96	9.4	40	99⅜	+ ⅜
Jamswy 8s05	cv	10	24½	− 1
K mart 12⅛95	...	15	109¾	− 1
K mart 8⅜17	7.9	3	106	− ⅛
KerrGp 13s96	12.8	20	101¼	+ ¼
KerrMc 7¼12	cv	1	112	− 1
Kolmrg 8¾09	cv	5	99½	+ ½
Kroger 9s99	8.6	15	105	+ ¼
Kroger 6⅜99	cv	2	128½	+ 1½
LaFrg 7s13	cv	15	109	+ ½
Leucadia 10⅜02	9.3	20	112	− 1
LglsLt 8.9s19	7.9	17	112½	+ ½
Lowes 3s03	cv	1	103½	− 1
MGM Grd 11¾99	10.5	48	112	...
MGMUA 13cldf	...	280	110 5/32	− 3/32
Manvl zr03	...	50	98	− ⅛
MarO 8.5s06	8.4	11	100⅝	− ⅝
MarO 9½94	9.3	170	101⅝	...
MarO 9¾/7s02	9.3	65	104½	+ 1⅜
Marriott zr06	...	183	43½	+ 1¼
Masco 5¼12	cv	24	103	...
vjMcCro 6½92f	cv	3	42¼	...
McDnl zr94	...	5	99 5/32	...
McDnl 9¾99	8.9	2	109⅜	− ¼

Quotations as of 4 p.m. Eastern Time
Thursday, October 7, 1993

Volume $29,010,000

SALES SINCE JANUARY 1
(000 omitted)

1993	1992	1991
$7,815,183	$9,324,436	$9,967,844

	Domestic Thu.	Domestic Wed.	All Issues Thu.	All Issues Wed.
Issues traded	364	375	366	375
Advances	135	148	135	148
Declines	133	132	134	132
Unchanged	96	95	97	95
New highs	27	22	27	22
New lows	6	5	7	5

Dow Jones Bond Averages

−1992− High	−1992− Low	−1993− High	−1993− Low		−1993− Close	−1993− Chg.	−1993− %Yld	−1992− Close	−1992− Chg.
103.89	98.41	109.69	103.49	20 Bonds	109.25	−0.18	6.21	102.54	+0.07
103.31	98.45	105.59	102.30	10 Utilities	105.26	−0.27	6.78	102.78	....
105.14	97.26	113.88	104.58	10 Industrials	113.25	−0.08	5.64	102.29	+0.13

Bonds	Cur Yld	Vol	Close	Net Chg
PacBell 6⅞23	7.0	166	98⅞	− ⅛
PGE 7½s04	7.2	30	103½	...
PacSci 7¾03	cv	20	101	− ½
ParCm 7s03A	7.0	109	100	+ ½
PennTr 9⅝05	9.4	105	102½	...
Pepsic 7⅝98	6.9	10	110	− 1⅞
PeryDr 8½10	cv	7	95⅝	− ⅞
Petrie 8s10	cv	42	120¼	− ¼
PhilEl 8¾94	8.5	10	103½	− ½
PhilEl 7¾23	7.4	47	104½	...
PhilEl 7⅛23	7.2	284	99¼	+ ¼
Pier1 6⅞02	cv	1	113½	+ 1
PionFn 8s00	...	330	109½	+ ¾
Pittstn 9.2s04	cv	10	105	+ 1
PogoP 8s05	cv	37	102½	...
PopeTl 6s12	cv	5	100½	− ½
PotEl 7s18	cv	1	105½	− ¾
PotEl 5s02	...	1	94¾	− ⅛
PSCol 8¾00	8.5	57	103¼	...
PSEG 7⅝00	6.9	10	111⅛	+ ½
PSEG 8½22	7.8	5	108½	...
PSEG 6⅞03	6.4	45	107	+ ¾
RJR 7⅜01	7.6	8	97⅛	− ⅜
RJRNb 10½98	9.5	70	111	+ ½
RJR Nb 8.3s99	8.4	154	99	− ⅜
RJR Nb 13½01	12.3	45	110	...
RJR Nb zr01	...	432	103¼	...
RJR Nb 8¾04	9.0	157	97⅝	...
RJR Nb 8⅝02	8.9	269	97	− ⅛
RJR Nb 7⅝03	8.4	814	90½	− ⅜
RJR Nb 8s00	8.3	1755	96½	...
RJR Nb 8¾05	9.0	657	96⅞	+ ¼
RJR Nb 9¼13	9.4	1461	98⅜	− ⅛
RLI 6s03	cv	10	102½	+ ½
Rallys 9⅞00	10.3	158	95¾	− ⅛
RalsP 9½16	9.0	5	105⅝	+ ⅛
vjRapA 12s99f	...	10	⅜	...

Bonds	Cur Yld	Vol	Close	Net Chg
Tidwtr 7s10	cv	15	107¼	− ½
TmeWar 8¾17	8.4	158	104⅛	+ ⅛
TmeWar zr02	...	38	89½	+ ⅛
TmeWar 7.45s98	7.1	44	104½	− ¼
TmeWar 9⅛13	8.4	47	109¼	− ¼
TmeWar 7.95s00	7.4	260	107½	...
TmeWar 9.15s23	8.4	141	109⅜	+ ⅜
TmeWar 8¾15	...	137	106¼	...
TmeWar zr13	...	60	39¾	− ⅛
Trnstex 10½00	10.0	5	105½	+ ¾
Trvlr 8.32s15	cv	71	102½	− ¼
Trimas 5s03	cv	7	106¾	...
TucEP 7.55s02	7.6	5	100	− ¼
TucEP 7.65s03	7.7	34	99⅞	+ ⅞
Tyco 10⅛02	9.9	270	102⅜	...
UNC 7½06	cv	10	92½	+ 1⅛
UNC 9⅛03	9.0	45	102	...
URS 8⅝04	10.1	46	85¾	− 1⅛
USAir 12⅞00	12.2	176	105⅞	− ⅛
USLICO 8½14	cv	15	106	...
USBO 7¾02	7.7	18	101	+ 1
USX 4⅝96	4.7	57	99⅜	...
USX 5¾01	cv	2	88⅝	+ ⅜
USX 7s17	cv	122	97	...
Unisys 8.2s96	8.1	209	101	− ⅞
Unisy na15s97	...	70	117¼	+ 1¼
Unisys 8¼00	cv	44	135¼	− 2¾
Vencor 6s02	...	12	94	− ½
WMS 5¾02	cv	16	114½	− ½
WasteM zr12	...	57	33½	− ⅛
Waban 6½02	cv	10	95	− ½
Wendys 7¼10	cv	17	111	...
Wendys 7s06	cv	30	145	+ 6
WstCNA 7¼15	cv	10	113¼	− 4½
WstDig 9s14	cv	49	88	+ ½
WstgE 9s09	cv	28	115	...
WilcxGb 7s14	cv	15	93½	+ 1

Explanatory Notes

(For New York and American bonds)

Yield is current yield.

cv-Convertible bond. cf-Certificates. dc-Deep discount. f-Dealt in flat. m-Matured bonds, negotiability impaired by maturity. na-No accrual. r-Registered. st-Stamped. t-Floating rate. wd-When distributed. ww-With warrants. x-Ex interest. xw-Without warrants. zr-Zero coupon.

vi-In bankruptcy or receivership or being reorganized under the Bankruptcy Act, or securities assumed by such companies.

Source: The Wall Street Journal, October 7, 1993. Reprinted by permission of *The Wall Street Journal,* © Dow Jones & Company, Inc., 1993. All rights reserved.

FIGURE 9–2 Corporate Bond Quotations

of −¼ means a decrease in value of .25 percent of $1,000 ($2.50 per bond) over the previous closing price of that issue. The McDonald's debentures due 1999 obviously closed yesterday at 109⅝ (109⅜ + ¼).

GOVERNMENT BONDS

A portion of the business section in the daily newspaper is often used to present price information for most U.S. government, government agency, and quasi-government debt securities (see Figure 9–3). Some local papers may publish such information weekly only, although the major ones print daily quotations solicited from market-makers in those issues. The listings are categorized by issuer. In the case of U.S. government securities, they are categorized by type (such as bills, notes, bonds) and arranged in order of maturity. The earliest maturation dates are first, without regard to interest rate or yield. As with securities traded over the counter, only bid and asked prices are shown, defined in increments as small as ½₂ percent of the issue's par value (½₂ amounts to $.3125 per $1,000). The figure in the column labeled *Yld.* is a yield-to-maturity, not a current yield. Yield-to-maturity will be examined shortly.

In analyzing Figure 9–3, let us focus upon the *8s* of August 1996–2001 outlined in the section headed *Treasury Bonds and Notes*.

1 RATE	2 MAT. DATE	3 BID	4 ASKED	5 CHG.	6 ASK YLD.
8s	1996-01 Aug	110:02	110:06	−2	4.16

1. These bonds pay 8 percent interest. The small letter *s* following the interest rate is the traditional way these securities are identified; that is, in the plural form. It means that there is more than one debt instrument outstanding in this series to represent the obligation characterized by this issue. The absence of an *n* after the maturation month informs us that this is a bond and not a government note.

2. What appears to be a double maturation date (1996–2001) is, in reality, advice that this issue is a *term bond*. The earlier year signifies that anytime after August 1996 until the time the bond must be redeemed in August 2001 the government can retire it at par by exercising its option to call this issue pursuant to such privilege stated in the indenture.

3. A holder anxious to sell this bond must accept the bid price of 110:02, which is 110²⁄₃₂ percent of $1,000, or 1100.63 per bond.

4. An investor interested in buying the bond must pay the offering price of 110.06, which is 110⁶⁄₃₂ percent of $1,000, or 1101.88 per bond.

5. This issue was down 2 from yesterday's bid. Net changes are always measured from day to day based upon the bid price.

TREASURY BONDS, NOTES & BILLS

Thursday, October 7, 1993

Representative Over-the-Counter quotations based on transactions of $1 million or more.

Treasury bond, note and bill quotes are as of mid-afternoon. Colons in bid-and-asked quotes represent 32nds; 101:01 means 101 1/32. Net changes in 32nds. n-Treasury note. Treasury bill quotes in hundredths, quoted on terms of a rate of discount. Days to maturity calculated from settlement date. All yields are to maturity and based on the asked quote. Latest 13-week and 26-week bills are boldfaced. For bonds callable prior to maturity, yields are computed to the earliest call date for issues quoted above par and to the maturity date for issues below par. *-When issued.

Source: Federal Reserve Bank of New York.

U.S. Treasury strips as of 3 p.m. Eastern time, also based on transactions of $1 million or more. Colons in bid-and-asked quotes represent 32nds; 101:01 means 101 1/32. Net changes in 32nds. Yields calculated on the asked quotation. ci-stripped coupon interest. bp-Treasury bond, stripped principal. np-Treasury note, stripped principal. For bonds callable prior to maturity, yields are computed to the earliest call date for issues quoted above par and to the maturity date for issues below par.

Source: Bear, Stearns & Co. via Street Software Technology Inc.

GOVT. BONDS & NOTES

Rate	Maturity Mo/Yr	Bid	Asked	Chg.	Ask Yld.
$7\frac{1}{8}$	Oct 93n	100:02	100:04	....	0.00
6	Oct 93n	100:06	100:08	....	1.12
$7\frac{3}{4}$	Nov 93n	100:15	100:17	....	1.93
$8\frac{5}{8}$	Nov 93	100:18	100:20	− 1	1.79
9	Nov 93n	100:18	100:20	− 1	2.14
$11\frac{3}{4}$	Nov 93n	100:28	100:30	....	1.52
$5\frac{1}{2}$	Nov 93n	100:11	100:13	....	2.41
5	Dec 93n	100:13	100:15	....	2.79
$7\frac{5}{8}$	Dec 93n	101:00	101:02	− 1	2.65
7	Jan 94n	101:00	101:02	....	2.81
$4\frac{7}{8}$	Jan 94n	100:17	100:19	....	2.86
$6\frac{7}{8}$	Feb 94n	101:09	101:11	....	2.88
$8\frac{7}{8}$	Feb 94n	101:31	102:01	....	2.84
9	Feb 94	102:01	102:03	....	2.79
$5\frac{3}{8}$	Feb 94n	100:28	100:30	....	2.89
$5\frac{3}{4}$	Mar 94n	101:07	101:09	....	2.96
$8\frac{1}{2}$	Mar 94n	102:16	102:18	....	2.93
7	Apr 94n	101:29	101:31	− 1	3.07
$5\frac{3}{8}$	Apr 94n	101:05	101:07	....	3.13
7	May 94n	102:06	102:08	....	3.14
$9\frac{1}{2}$	May 94n	103:22	103:24	....	3.07
$13\frac{1}{8}$	May 94n	105:26	105:28	− 1	3.05
$5\frac{1}{8}$	May 94n	101:06	101:08	+ 1	3.12
5	Jun 94n	101:07	101:09	+ 1	3.18
$8\frac{1}{2}$	Jun 94n	103:22	103:24	− 1	3.18
8	Jul 94n	103:16	103:18	....	3.21
$4\frac{1}{4}$	Jul 94n	100:23	100:25	....	3.26
$6\frac{7}{8}$	Aug 94n	102:29	102:31	....	3.28
$8\frac{5}{8}$	Aug 94n	104:12	104:14	....	3.25
$8\frac{3}{4}$	Aug 94	104:15	104:19	....	3.19
$12\frac{5}{8}$	Aug 94n	107:24	107:26	....	3.16
$4\frac{1}{4}$	Aug 94n	100:25	100:27	....	3.27
4	Sep 94n	100:19	100:21	....	3.31
$8\frac{1}{2}$	Sep 94n	104:28	104:30	....	3.27
$9\frac{1}{2}$	Oct 94n	106:00	106:02	....	3.34
$4\frac{1}{4}$	Oct 94n	100:27	100:29	....	3.37
6	Nov 94n	102:23	102:25	+ 1	3.39
$8\frac{1}{4}$	Nov 94n	105:04	105:06	....	3.38
$10\frac{1}{8}$	Nov 94	107:04	107:06	....	3.37
$11\frac{5}{8}$	Nov 94n	108:24	108:26	....	3.35
$4\frac{5}{8}$	Nov 94n	101:09	101:11	....	3.41
$4\frac{5}{8}$	Dec 94n	101:11	101:13	+ 1	3.44
$7\frac{5}{8}$	Dec 94n	104:30	105:00	+ 1	3.40
$8\frac{5}{8}$	Jan 95n	106:07	106:09	....	3.48
$4\frac{1}{4}$	Jan 95n	100:28	100:30	....	3.51
3	Feb 95	100:00	101:00	....	2.24
$5\frac{1}{2}$	Feb 95n	102:16	102:18	+ 1	3.53
$7\frac{3}{4}$	Feb 95n	105:15	105:17	+ 1	3.50
$10\frac{1}{2}$	Feb 95	109:01	109:03	....	3.51
$11\frac{1}{4}$	Feb 95n	110:01	110:03	....	3.49
$3\frac{7}{8}$	Feb 95n	100:12	100:14	....	3.55
$3\frac{7}{8}$	Mar 95n	100:12	100:14	+ 1	3.57
$8\frac{3}{8}$	Apr 95n	106:28	106:30	....	3.61
$3\frac{7}{8}$	Apr 95n	100:09	100:11	....	3.65
$5\frac{7}{8}$	May 95n	103:11	103:13	....	3.65
$8\frac{1}{2}$	May 95n	107:12	107:14	....	3.65
$10\frac{3}{8}$	May 95	110:09	110:11	....	3.63
$11\frac{1}{4}$	May 95n	111:21	111:23	....	3.61
$12\frac{5}{8}$	May 95	113:26	113:30	....	3.55
$4\frac{1}{8}$	May 95n	100:22	100:24	+ 1	3.65
$4\frac{1}{8}$	Jun 95n	100:21	100:23	....	3.69
$8\frac{7}{8}$	Jul 95n	108:23	108:25	....	3.67
$4\frac{1}{4}$	Jul 95n	100:27	100:29	....	3.73
$4\frac{5}{8}$	Aug 95n	101:17	101:19	....	3.72
$8\frac{1}{2}$	Aug 95n	108:13	108:15	+ 1	3.70
$10\frac{1}{2}$	Aug 95n	111:31	112:01	....	3.69

Rate	Maturity Mo/Yr	Bid	Asked	Chg.	Ask Yld.
$6\frac{3}{8}$	Jul 99n	107:17	107:19	+ 1	4.85
8	Aug 99n	115:26	115:28	+ 1	4.85
6	Oct 99n	105:20	105:22	+ 1	4.90
$7\frac{7}{8}$	Nov 99n	115:16	115:18	+ 2	4.89
$6\frac{3}{8}$	Jan 00n	107:21	107:23	....	4.93
$7\frac{7}{8}$	Feb 95-00	105:18	105:22	+ 3	3.50
$8\frac{1}{2}$	Feb 00n	119:07	119:09	+ 1	4.92
$5\frac{1}{2}$	Apr 00n	103:11	103:13	+ 1	4.88
$8\frac{7}{8}$	May 00n	121:25	121:27	+ 1	4.95
$8\frac{3}{8}$	Aug 95-00	108:04	108:08	− 1	3.70
$8\frac{3}{4}$	Aug 00n	121:15	121:17	+ 1	5.00
$8\frac{1}{2}$	Nov 00n	120:10	120:12	+ 1	5.05
$7\frac{3}{4}$	Feb 01n	116:04	116:06	....	5.08
$11\frac{3}{4}$	Feb 01	140:22	140:26	− 1	5.03
8	May 01n	117:29	117:31	+ 1	5.11
$13\frac{1}{8}$	May 01	150:05	150:09	− 1	5.07
$7\frac{7}{8}$	Aug 01n	117:11	117:13	+ 2	5.15
8	Aug 96-01	110:02	110:06	− 2	4.16
$13\frac{3}{8}$	Aug 01	152:27	152:31	+ 2	5.10
$7\frac{1}{2}$	Nov 01n	115:02	115:04	+ 1	5.19
$15\frac{3}{4}$	Nov 01	169:20	169:24	+ 2	5.12
$14\frac{1}{4}$	Feb 02	161:03	161:07	+ 2	5.14
$7\frac{1}{2}$	May 02n	115:12	115:14	+ 2	5.25
$6\frac{3}{8}$	Aug 02n	107:14	107:16	+13	5.30
$11\frac{5}{8}$	Nov 02	145:03	145:07	+ 1	5.30
$6\frac{1}{4}$	Feb 03n	106:11	106:13	+ 1	5.37
$10\frac{3}{4}$	Feb 03	139:09	139:13	+ 1	5.34
$10\frac{3}{4}$	May 03	139:30	140:02	+ 2	5.36
$5\frac{3}{4}$	Aug 03n	103:08	103:10	+ 3	5.31
$11\frac{1}{8}$	Aug 03	143:16	143:20	+ 1	5.36
$11\frac{7}{8}$	Nov 03	149:27	149:31	+ 1	5.39
$12\frac{3}{8}$	May 04	155:21	155:25	+ 3	5.39
$13\frac{3}{4}$	Aug 04	167:22	167:26	+ 5	5.40
$11\frac{5}{8}$	Nov 04	150:18	150:22	+ 2	5.47
$8\frac{1}{4}$	May 00-05	116:28	117:00	− 1	5.17
12	May 05	155:00	155:04	+ 3	5.50
$10\frac{3}{4}$	Aug 05	144:25	144:29	+ 3	5.53
$9\frac{3}{8}$	Feb 06	133:21	133:25	+ 4	5.56
$7\frac{5}{8}$	Feb 02-07	113:18	113:22	+ 2	5.55
$7\frac{7}{8}$	Nov 02-07	116:07	116:11	+ 3	5.56
$8\frac{3}{8}$	Aug 03-08	120:24	120:28	+ 3	5.59
$8\frac{3}{4}$	Nov 03-08	123:30	124:02	+ 3	5.60
$9\frac{1}{8}$	May 04-09	127:21	127:25	+ 3	5.61
$10\frac{3}{8}$	Nov 04-09	138:25	138:29	+ 3	5.62
$11\frac{3}{4}$	Feb 05-10	150:24	150:28	+ 4	5.62
10	May 05-10	136:23	136:27	+ 3	5.63
$12\frac{3}{4}$	Nov 05-10	161:23	161:27	+ 4	5.63
$13\frac{7}{8}$	May 06-11	173:09	173:13	+ 3	5.65
14	Nov 06-11	176:09	176:13	+ 3	5.66
$10\frac{3}{8}$	Nov 07-12	143:11	143:15	+ 1	5.81
12	Aug 08-13	160:20	160:24	+ 2	5.83
$13\frac{1}{4}$	May 09-14	175:29	176:01	....	5.78
$12\frac{1}{2}$	Aug 09-14	168:11	168:15	+ 1	5.82
$11\frac{3}{4}$	Nov 09-14	160:22	160:26	− 1	5.86
$11\frac{1}{4}$	Feb 15	160:07	160:09	+ 2	6.14
$10\frac{5}{8}$	Aug 15	153:03	153:05	+ 2	6.16
$9\frac{7}{8}$	Nov 15	144:06	144:08	+ 1	6.18
$9\frac{1}{4}$	Feb 16	136:20	136:22	+ 1	6.20
$7\frac{1}{4}$	May 16	112:12	112:14	+ 2	6.22
$7\frac{1}{2}$	Nov 16	115:12	115:14	+ 1	6.23
$8\frac{3}{4}$	May 17	131:02	131:04	+ 1	6.22
$8\frac{7}{8}$	Aug 17	132:22	132:24	+ 2	6.22
$9\frac{1}{8}$	May 18	136:10	136:12	+ 1	6.22
9	Nov 18	134:30	135:00	+ 2	6.23
$8\frac{7}{8}$	Feb 19	133:15	133:17	+ 1	6.23
$8\frac{1}{8}$	Aug 19	123:30	124:00	+ 1	6.24
$8\frac{1}{2}$	Feb 20	129:01	129:03	+ 2	6.24

Mat.	Type	Bid	Asked	Chg.	Ask Yld.
May 01	ci	67:16	67:21	+ 2	5.22
May 01	np	67:14	67:19	+ 2	5.22
Aug 01	ci	66:12	66:17	+ 2	5.26
Aug 01	np	66:10	66:15	+ 2	5.28
Nov 01	ci	65:05	65:10	+ 1	5.34
Nov 01	np	65:02	65:07	+ 1	5.36
Feb 02	ci	63:31	64:04	+ 2	5.39
May 02	ci	63:03	63:08	+ 2	5.41
May 02	np	63:03	63:08	+ 2	5.41
Aug 02	ci	62:01	62:06	+ 2	5.45
Aug 02	np	62:03	62:08	+ 2	5.43
Nov 02	ci	60:30	61:03	+ 2	5.49
Feb 03	ci	59:25	59:30	+ 2	5.55
Feb 03	np	59:28	60:01	+ 2	5.53
May 03	ci	58:24	58:29	....	5.59
Aug 03	ci	57:24	57:30	− 1	5.63
Nov 03	ci	56:25	56:31	....	5.66
Feb 04	ci	55:21	55:27	+ 2	5.72
May 04	ci	54:17	54:23	....	5.78
Aug 04	ci	53:19	53:25	....	5.80
Nov 04	ci	52:23	52:29	....	5.82
Nov 04	bp	53:04	53:09	....	5.76
Feb 05	ci	51:22	51:27	....	5.88
May 05	ci	50:30	51:03	+ 4	5.88
May 05	bp	51:16	51:22	+ 4	5.78
Aug 05	ci	49:31	50:05	+ 2	5.91
Aug 05	bp	50:18	50:23	+ 2	5.82
Nov 05	ci	48:29	49:02	− 2	5.97
Feb 06	ci	48:01	48:06	+ 2	6.00
Feb 06	bp	49:09	49:15	+ 2	5.78
May 06	ci	47:07	47:12	+ 2	6.02
Aug 06	ci	46:13	46:18	+ 2	6.04
Nov 06	ci	45:17	45:22	+ 2	6.07
Feb 07	ci	44:20	44:25	+ 4	6.11
May 07	ci	43:27	44:00	+ 4	6.13
Aug 07	ci	43:00	43:06	+ 2	6.16
Nov 07	ci	42:06	42:11	+ 2	6.19
Feb 08	ci	41:12	41:17	+ 4	6.22
May 08	ci	40:18	40:23	+ 6	6.25
Aug 08	ci	29:24	39:30	+ 6	6.28
Nov 08	ci	38:31	39:05	+ 4	6.31
Feb 09	ci	38:05	38:10	+ 4	6.35
May 09	ci	37:12	37:18	+ 6	6.38
Aug 09	ci	36:22	36:27	+ 9	6.40
Nov 09	ci	36:02	36:07	+ 8	6.41
Nov 09	bp	36:27	37:01	....	6.27
Feb 10	ci	35:07	35:12	....	6.46
May 10	ci	34:19	34:24	+ 2	6.47
Aug 10	ci	33:30	34:03	+ 2	6.49
Nov 10	ci	33:11	33:16	+ 2	6.50
Feb 11	ci	32:24	32:29	+ 6	6.51
May 11	ci	32:00	32:06	+ 2	6.55
Aug 11	ci	31:14	31:19	+ 4	6.56
Nov 11	ci	30:26	31:00	+ 4	6.58
Feb 12	ci	30:07	30:12	....	6.60
May 12	ci	29:20	29:25	....	6.62
Aug 12	ci	29:06	29:12	+ 2	6.61
Nov 12	ci	28:23	28:28	+ 4	6.61
Feb 13	ci	28:05	28:10	+ 4	6.63
May 13	ci	27:21	27:26	+ 4	6.64
Aug 13	ci	27:06	27:11	+ 4	6.64
Nov 13	ci	26:24	26:29	+ 4	6.64
Feb 14	ci	26:05	26:10	....	6.67
May 14	ci	25:24	25:28	....	6.67
Aug 14	ci	25:08	25:13	....	6.68
Nov 14	ci	24:27	25:00	+ 2	6.68
Feb 15	ci	24:13	24:17	+ 2	6.69
Feb 15	bp	24:17	24:22	....	6.66
May 15	ci	24:01	24:06	+ 2	6.68
Aug 15	ci	23:21	23:26	+ 2	6.68
Aug 15	bp	23:26	23:30	+ 2	6.65
Nov 15	ci	23:10	23:15	+ 2	6.67
Nov 15	bp	23:13	23:18	....	6.65
Feb 16	ci	22:28	23:01	....	6.68
Feb 16	bp	22:31	23:04	....	6.66
May 16	ci	22:16	22:21	....	6.68
May 16	bp	22:19	22:24	....	6.66
Aug 16	ci	22:04	22:09	....	6.68
Nov 16	ci	21:25	21:30	....	6.68
Nov 16	bp	22:04	22:09	....	6.61
Feb 17	ci	21:12	21:17	....	6.69
May 17	ci	21:01	21:05	....	6.69
May 17	bp	21:05	21:10	− 1	6.66
Aug 17	ci	20:22	20:26	....	6.69
Aug 17	bp	20:29	21:02	....	6.64
Nov 17	ci	20:11	20:15	....	6.69
Feb 18	ci	20:02	20:06	....	6.68
May 18	ci	19:23	19:28	....	6.68
May 18	bp	19:26	19:31	....	6.66

FIGURE 9–3 Treasury Bonds, Notes, and Bills Quotations (*Source: The Wall Street Journal*, October 7, 1993. Reprinted by permission of *The Wall Street Journal*, © Dow Jones & Company, Inc., 1993. All rights reserved.)

6. The $1101.88 offering price per bond is equivalent to a yield-to-maturity of 4.16 percent when one takes into account the depreciation if held until 2001, plus the interest coupon of $80 ($1,000 × 8 percent) per year.

BOND RETURNS AND PRICES

Bond returns can be calculated in a number of ways. We will examine these methods of calculating bond returns in the sections below.

Current Yield

The current yield relates the annual dollar coupon interest to the market price. It can be expressed as follows:

$$\text{Current yield} = I_n/P_o$$

where:

I_n = annual interest
P_o = current market price

For example, a bond paying $100 per year in interest that is currently selling for $800 would have a current yield of 12.5 percent:

$$\text{Current yield} = \$100/\$800 = .125, \text{ or } 12.5\%$$

The current yield exceeds the coupon when the bond is selling at a discount. The opposite is true when the bond is selling at a premium. Notice in our example that the coupon is 10 percent and the bond, selling at a discount, has a current yield above the coupon.

The drawback to the current yield is that it does not take into account the two other sources of income—reinvestment of income and capital gain (or loss). To illustrate the latter source, suppose the bond is held to maturity. At that time the issuer is obligated to redeem it for $1,000. The investor who paid $800 for the bond will realize a capital gain of $200 ($1,000 minus $800).

Look again at Figure 9–2. If the price of McDonald's 9.75 percent bonds due in 1999 closed at 109⅜ on October 7, 1993, the current yield at that time would be:

$$\frac{9.75}{109.375} = 8.9\%$$

Time-Adjusted Yield on Bonds[2]

As long as a bond is not expected to go into default, the expected return comprises of annual interest payments plus the price to be recovered at maturity or sooner. Take an example of a three-year bond with a principal value of $1,000, bearing a nominal rate of interest (coupon) of 6 percent. Assume that an investor wishes to purchase this bond for a rate of 6 percent. Because bond interest is normally paid twice a year, $60 of interest per annum would be paid in two semiannual install-ments of $30 each ($60/2). The 6 percent annual rate is thus 3 percent per six-month period (6/2). What should he be willing to pay for a series of six $30 interest payments and a lump sum of $1,000 at the end of the third year?

In general, what a bond is worth can be determined thus:

$$V = \sum_{n=1}^{2N} \frac{I_n/2}{(1 + i/2)^n} + \frac{P_N}{(1 + i/2)^{2N}} \tag{9.1}$$

where:

V = value of bond
I = annual interest (dollars)
i = required rate of interest (percent)
P = principal value of maturity
N = life of bond

It is easy to see that although bonds carry a promise to maintain a constant-dollar interest payment to maturity, I, and pay a fixed principal at maturity, P, the num-ber of years to maturity, N, and the required rate of interest, i, can vary.

The present value of the interest-payment stream of $60 per year for three years is as follows:

$$V = \frac{\$30}{1 + .03} + \frac{\$30}{(1 + .03)^2} + \frac{\$30}{(1 + .03)^3}$$

$$+ \frac{\$30}{(1 + .03)^4} + \frac{\$30}{(1 + .03)^5} + \frac{\$30}{(1 + .03)^6} = \$163$$

The present value of the principal at maturity (end of year 3) is $1,000/(1 + .03)^6 = $837. The total value of the bond is thus $163 + $837, or $1,000. In other words, a $1,000 bond is worth $1,000 today if the nominal rate and the required rate of in-terest are equal. The $1,000 value is a composite of $163 of interest payments and $837 of principal. Note that the principal is compounded twice a year, as are inter-est payments.

Suppose new three-year bonds are offered at 8 percent. Outstanding 6 per-cent bonds will continue to pay $60 per $1,000 by contract. The advance in interest rates will cause the price of the outstanding bond to fall:

[2]For a look at the many nuances of yield the reader should refer to S. Homer and M. Liebowitz, *Inside the Yield Book* (Englewood Cliffs, N.J.: Prentice Hall, 1972).

$$V = \frac{\$30}{1 + .04} + \frac{\$30}{(1 + .04)^2} + \frac{\$30}{(1 + .04)^3}$$

$$+ \frac{\$30}{(1 + .04)^4} + \frac{\$30}{(1 + .04)^5} + \frac{\$30}{(1 + .04)^6} + \frac{\$1,000}{(1 + .04)^6}$$

$$= \$948$$

Had new three-year bonds been offered at 4 percent, or less than the outstanding 6 percent bonds, the price of the 6 percent bonds would have risen to $1,056. A basic principle concerning bonds is that *prices move inversely to interest rates.*

Most people now use calculators or computers to get bond prices and yields. Pocket calculators can perform necessary price and/or yield calculations very quickly.

The McDonald's 9¾ percent bond due in 1999 was highlighted in Figure 9–2. A feel for the approximate yield-to-maturity using an 8 percent annual rate and annual compounding is as follows:

$$\text{Present value of coupons} = \$97.50 \times 4.623 = \$\ 450.74$$

$$\text{Present value of principal} = \$1,000 \times .63 \quad = \underline{\quad 630.00}$$

$$\text{Present value of bond} \qquad\qquad\qquad = \$1080.74$$

Because the bond was selling for $1,093.75, it is easy to see that the time-adjusted yield (yield-to-maturity) is slightly lower than 8 percent. It is actually 7.76 percent.

Yield-to-Call

When a bond is subject to redemption prior to maturity, the cash flow implicit in the yield-to-maturity figure is subject to possible early alteration. Most corporate bonds sold today are callable by the issuer, but with a certain period of protection before the call option can be exercised. At the expiration of this period the bond may be called in at a specified call price, which usually involves some premium over par.

To provide some measure of the return in the event that the issuer were to exercise his call option at some future point, the yield-to-call is often computed and compared with the yield-to-maturity. This computation is based on the assumption that the bond's cash flow is terminated at the *first call date* with redemption of principal at the specified call price. For a given rate, the present value of this assumed "cash flow to call" can be determined and the yield-to-call is then defined as that discount rate, which makes this present-value figure equal to the bond's market value.

For example, suppose one has a thirty-year 8¾ percent bond priced at 107¾, which is callable at 107 starting in five years. The cash-flow-to-maturity consists of sixty semiannual coupon payments of $43.75 each followed by a redemption payment of $1,000. The yield-to-maturity turns out to be 8.15 percent. The cash flow to

an assumed call in five years consists of ten coupon payments followed by a redemption payment of $1,070. Using a discount rate of 8 percent, the present value of the cash flow to call is $1,077.70, that is, close to the bond's market price:

Coupon payment (semiannual)	$43.75 × 8.1109 = $ 354.85
Redemption payment	$1,070.00 × .6756 = <u> 722.89</u>
	$1,077.74

The investor would have to choose between the higher yield-to-maturity (8.15 percent) and the lower yield-to-call (8 percent) for investment purposes. With the bond selling above par, if interest rates were expected to fall below 8 percent over the next five years, using the lower yield is both prudent and conservative.

Yield-to-call can be calculated by the following general formula:

$$P_M = \sum_{n=1}^{2NC} \frac{I_n/2}{(1 + i/2)^n} + \frac{P_C}{(1 + i/2)^{2NC}} \qquad (9.2)$$

where:

NC = number of years to first call date
P_C = call price
P_M = market price

To calculate the yield-to-call on our McDonald's 9¾ percent bonds due in 1999, we require some additional information. These bonds are not callable prior to 1996, at which time the call price is $100. Let's go forward in time to 1994. The appropriate yield-to-call calculations would be as follows, using Equation 9.2:

$$1093.75 = \sum_{n=1}^{6} \frac{48.75}{(1 + i/2)^n} + \frac{1000}{(1 + i/2)^6}$$

$$i = \text{Yield-to-call} = 6.27\%$$

For an investor who assumes that rates will fall, basing expected yield on the yield-to-call rather than the higher yield-to-maturity might be appropriate. In general, it is always wise to pay some attention to the yield-to-call calculation when the bond: (a) sells at or above par, and (b) you expect interest rates to trend lower over time.

PREFERRED-STOCK VALUATION[3]

When the term to maturity approaches infinity, as it would in the case of a perpetuity (a security that never matures), interest is paid indefinitely. Equation 9.1 becomes

[3]David Emanuel, "A Theoretical Model for Valuing Preferred Stock," *Journal of Finance* 38, no. 4 (September 1983).

$$V = \frac{I}{i} \qquad\qquad\qquad (9.3)$$

Because most preferred stocks entitle their owners to regular fixed dividends similar to interest payments, they are in fact like perpetuities. Although preferreds are often retired, this is not the usual case. The value of a preferred stock can thus be thought of in terms of Equation 9.3, where $I = D$, D signifying annual dividend payments rather than interest payments. Suppose a preferred stock paying annual dividends of $6 were sold in 1985. This preferred today, given market conditions, should be yielding 10 percent. What is it worth today?

$$V = \frac{D}{i}$$

$$= \frac{\$6}{.10} = \$60$$

The absence of a maturity in preferred stock lends perpetuity aspects to this security form. The result is greater value or price fluctuation in preferreds vis-à-vis bonds as a class.

   The yield or return can be determined by substituting price in the market for value. Assume that a $6 preferred stock is selling in the market for $75. The yield or return is:

$$\$75 = \frac{\$6}{i}$$

$$.080 = i$$

Thus, given the annual income flow, we can determine the value given the required yield or return, we can determine the yield or return given the market price.

SYSTEMATIC RISK IN HOLDING
FIXED-INCOME SECURITIES[4]

The same general categories of risk that influence common stocks also influence fixed-income securities, but the degree of their impact differs. The primary sources of *systematic* risk in holding fixed-income securities are purchasing-power and interest-rate risk.

[4]The many facets of systematic and unsystematic risk in bonds are discussed in detail in J. C. Van Horne, *Financial Market Rates and Flows*, 2d ed. (Englewood Cliffs, N.J.: Prentice Hall, 1984).

Purchasing-Power Risk

Over very broad lapses of time no single economic or financial variable appears to be more strongly positively correlated with the level of interest rates than does the commodity price trend. Either historically, in periods as long as 1900 to the present, or in less encompassing periods, such as the post-World War II era, the positive relationship seems unambiguous. The problem with this relationship lies in predicting interest rates over much shorter intervals using inflation forecasts as the major explanatory variable.

Theoretically, when commodity prices are perceived to rise, lenders require higher rates of interest to protect depreciating purchasing power of the debt payments, while borrowers are willing to repay in cheaper dollars at higher nominal rates. Some also theorize that rising commodity prices raise the level of interest rates because rising commodity prices increase nominal credit demands, thereby boosting interest rates.

To a great extent, the return expected on U.S. government securities (USGs) at any point in time will reflect the rate of inflation in the economy because the rate on USGs embodies a riskless rate plus some compensation for purchasing-power risk. Governments are devoid of business and financial risk, owing to a monopoly status and taxing powers available to ensure that debt-servicing obligations are met.

Extensive studies of interest rates by the Federal Reserve Bank of St. Louis tend to indicate that the riskless rate of interest fluctuates around 3 percent. If this is true, adding to this an allowance for the rate of price change (purchasing-power risk) might produce a fair approximation of the rate of interest on long-term government bonds.

The rate of price change is the annual percentage change in prices; we often refer to it as the change in the cost of living. If a price index begins the year at 100 and ends at 103, we say the rate of increase (inflation) is 3 percent [(103 − 100)/100]. If, from the second to third year, the index changes from 103 to 109, the rate of price change is said to be about 5.8 percent [(109 − 103)/103]. The rate of change in prices can also be downward (deflation).

The necessity to adjust the rate of interest for price changes can be seen in a simple example. Suppose you lend $100 today for a promise to be repaid $105 at the end of a year. The rate of interest is 5 percent. However, assume that prices over the next year are expected to advance 6 percent. Because of inflation, the $105 received at the end of the year has a purchasing power of only 94 percent of $105, or $98.70. You must charge 6 percent interest to allow for inflation.

The rate of inflation experienced in the United States over long time periods prior to 1992 was on the order of 2 to 3 percent. The rate was 8.5 percent compounded per annum between 1973 and 1979. Between 1982 and 1992 the rate retreated to about 3.8 percent, compounded.

The tricky part of the whole process is that long-term interest rates reflect both *expected* inflation and *uncertainty* about inflation. Rates of expected future in-

flation will not necessarily be the same as those experienced in the past, even the most recent past.

Interest-Rate Risk

Interest-rate risk can be identified as the truly overwhelming systematic risk associated with holding fixed-income securities. Interest-rate risk refers to the possibility that income and/or capital loss will result because of an increase in the level of interest rates; this is the major risk element for most high-quality, investment-grade debt securities. This risk can be illustrated by observing the impact of a change in interest rates on bonds with different coupon rates and maturities.

PRICE RISK

High-grade bond prices react to a given change in yield as a function of maturity, the coupon rate, and the general level of yields from which the change occurs. All other things being equal, with the same percentage change in yield, the *volatility* of the price of a bond *increases*

1. as the maturity lengthens (the longer the maturity, the greater the bond price volatility), but at a diminishing rate as maturity is lengthened;
2. as the coupon rate declines (the lower the coupon, the greater the price volatility); or
3. as the yields rise (the higher the yield level from which a yield fluctuation starts, the greater the price volatility).

Before exploring the structural forces that create these three determinants of volatility, let us look at Table 9–3 for the volatility effect of these three variables: maturity, coupon, and the starting level of yields.

Note in the first section of Table 9–3 the relationship between price changes and maturity. The example being used assumes a 6 percent coupon bond with a face value of $100. Notice that when the required yield is 6 percent, the bond price is 100 regardless of the number of years to maturity. As the required yield moves away from the coupon rate, notice that prices move in an inverse direction. For example, for a bond with a one-year maturity and a 6 percent coupon, if the required yield is 4 percent, the suggested bond price is 102. Similarly, if the required yield is 8 percent, the suggested bond price is 98. Note, however, that the volatility of a bond's price will increase, but at a diminishing rate, as the maturity is lengthened. Table 9–4 utilizes the data appearing in part 1 of Table 9–3.

Two coupon rates were selected and the percentage change in the price of a bond was calculated as maturity was lengthened. From Table 9–3 we saw that a 6 percent bond with a ten-year maturity would sell for 116 if the investor's required yield were 4 percent. Using the same required yield, the price at twenty years would be 127 and for thirty years, 135. In Table 9–4 the price change moving from ten to twenty years' maturity is +9.5 percent [(127 − 116)/116]; moving from

TABLE 9–3

Volatility of Bond Prices

1 Price Changes and Maturity

Face = $100   Coupon = 6%

REQUIRED YIELD (%)	YEARS TO MATURITY			
	1	10	20	30
4	102*	116	127	135
5	101	108	112	115
6	100	100	100	100
7	99	93	89	88
8	98	86	80	77

2 Price Changes and Coupon (20-year maturity)

COUPON VALUE (%)	INTEREST RATES RISE			INTEREST RATES FALL		
	7%	8%	% CHANGE	7%	5%	% CHANGE
4	68*	60	−11.3	68	87	+28.7
5	78	70	−10.5	78	100	+27.1
6	89	80	−10.0	89	112	+25.8
7	100	90	−9.8	100	125	+25.1
8	110	100	−9.5	110	137	+24.4

3 Price Changes and Level of Rates

6%, 20-year bond. Basis point change of 10% from original yield in each case.

ORIGINAL YIELD (%)	INTEREST RATES RISE				INTEREST RATES FALL			
	PRICE	NEW YIELD	NEW PRICE	% CHANGE	PRICE	NEW YIELD	NEW PRICE	% CHANGE
4	127*	4.4	121	−4.9	127	3.6	134	+5.3
5	112	5.5	106	−5.8	113	4.5	120	+6.3
6	100	6.6	93	−7.0	100	5.4	107	+7.3
7	89	7.7	83	−7.3	89	6.3	96	+8.1
8	80	8.8	74	+8.0	80	7.2	87	+9.0

*All prices are rounded for simplification. Thus, percentages will not correspond exactly.

twenty to thirty years, the percentage price change is only +6.3 percent [(135 − 127)/127]. Note that volatility changes are not linear relative to maturity.

For a given difference between the coupon rate and required yield, the longer the term-to-maturity, the greater the accompanying price change. For example, if rates move from 6 to 7 percent, the price of the bond will move to 99 if the maturity is one year; at the forty-year maturity, the price would fall to 87. Note that the *percentage* decline in price is 1 percent at one year [(99 − 100)/100] and 13 percent at forty years [(87 − 100)/100].

TABLE 9–4

Bond Price Volatility Relative to Maturity
(Percentage Change in Bond Price as Maturity Changes from):

REQUIRED YIELD	1–10	10–20	20–30
4%	+13.7	+9.5	+6.3
8%	−13.2	−7.0	−3.7

The relationship between price changes and the coupon rate is illustrated in the second section of Table 9–3. All the examples in this table assume a constant twenty-year maturity bond. A twenty-year bond with a 4 percent coupon will sell at 68 if the required yield is 7 percent. If interest rates rise to 8 percent, the bond will fall to 60. The same 4 percent coupon bond would rise to 87 if interest rates fell to 5 percent. Looking at the entire second section of Table 9–3, it is obvious that the greatest price volatility occurs in the lowest coupon bonds.

The relationship between price changes and the level of rates is illustrated in the third section of Table 9–3. Using a 6 percent, twenty-year bond throughout this table illustrates the price effects of a 10 percent change from the original yield level in each case. If the original yield is 7 percent, the suggested price for a 6 percent, twenty-year bond is 89. If interest rates rise 10 percent to 7.7 percent, the new bond price is 83. This represents a 7.3 percent decline in the bond price. Looking at the entire third section of Table 9–3, it becomes apparent that price volatility is greatest when interest rates change from a high level of yields to a lower level of yields.

REINVESTMENT RISK

Interest-rate risk has a second dimension, which is referred to as *reinvestment risk*. If, after you purchase a bond, interest rates decline (rise), it will not be possible to reinvest interest payments at the proposed yield to maturity, but they will be reinvested at lower (higher) rates and the ending sum would be below (above) what you expected. For example, suppose you purchase a one-year, 8 percent bond at $1,000 today in order to pay a $1,081.60 debt one year from now. Because coupon payments are semiannual, your plan is sound enough if you can reinvest the semiannual $40 coupon at 8 percent.

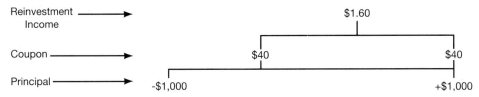

However, if interest rates drop by the semiannual payment time to, say, 6 percent, your reinvestment income will not be $1.60 ($40 × .04) but rather $1.20 ($40 × .03). Thus, a drop in interest rates causes a decline in the expected income from investing interim coupon payments. See in Table 9–5 the total realized compound

TABLE 9–5

Realized Compound Yield (8 Percent Bond Due
in Twenty Years, Purchased at Par)

REINVESTMENT RATE (%)	TOTAL REALIZED COMPOUND YIELD (%)
0	4.84
6	6.64
8	8.00
10	9.01

yield over the life of an 8 percent bond due in twenty years and purchased for $1,000 under varying assumptions relative to coupon reinvestment rates. Note that the yield to maturity of 8 percent (bond purchased at par with an 8 percent coupon) is a valid measure of the return on the bond *only* if coupons are reinvested at the calculated yield-to-maturity. For example, reinvesting coupons at 10 percent provides a lifetime yield of 9.01 percent.

Note that the price risk and the reinvestment risk resulting from a change in interest rates have opposite effects on an investor's ending wealth position. Specifically, an increase in the level of interest rates will cause an ending price that is below expectations, but the reinvestment of interim cash flow (coupons) will be at a rate above expectations. The reverse is true for declining interest rates. In Chapter 11 we will look more closely at aggressive and defensive tactics designed to capitalize on or immunize against these effects.

The following data represent realized yields based on different reinvestment rates for our McDonald's 9¾ percent bonds of 1999. Notice that if the interest payments collected are reinvested at a zero rate (put under a mattress) the realized yield would only be 6.28 percent, far less than the promised yield-to-maturity (7.76 percent). However, if interest payments are reinvested at, say, 10 percent, the realized yield would be 8.24 percent. This exceeds the promised yield-to-maturity of 7.76 percent. The realized yield will be somewhere between the reinvestment rate and the yield-to-maturity.

REINVESTMENT RATE (%)	REALIZED YIELD (%)
10	8.24
9	8.03
8	7.81
7	7.61
6	7.40
5	7.21
4	7.01
3	6.82
2	6.64
1	6.46
0	6.28

Determinants of the Interest Rate Level

Two theories attempt to explain the level and changes in the level of the market rate of interest: the loanable-funds theory and the liquidity-preference theory.

LOANABLE FUNDS

The loanable-funds theory focuses on the demand for and supply of loanable funds for a given period of time, generally one quarter or one year. The supply of loanable funds originates from household, business, and government surplus spending units (SSUs) who prefer to spend less than current income and to save. The higher the interest rate, the more SSUs are willing to loan and the more units are induced to be SSUs. The positive relationship between the supply of loanable funds and interest rates is shown in Figure 9–4 as schedule SL. When SSUs lend, they receive primary or secondary securities as evidence of their claims on deficit spending units (DSUs). Thus, the supply of loanable funds is the other side of, and equivalent to, the demand for securities.

The demand for loanable funds originates from household, business, and government DSUs, which prefer to spend more than their current income. To do so, they must borrow and, in the process, issue primary securities. The lower the rate of interest is, the more these units are willing to borrow and the more units are induced to be deficit spending units. The demand for loanable funds is thus inversely related to interest rates. This is drawn in Figure 9–4 as schedule DL. The demand for loanable funds is equivalent to the supply of securities. The equilibrium interest rate occurs where $SL = DL$. This is shown as rate i_0. The corresponding equilib-

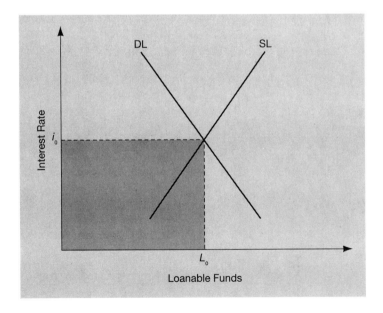

FIGURE 9–4   Interest-Rate Determination by Loanable-Funds Theory

rium amount of loanable funds (or securities) is L_0. Other things equal, increases in the demand for loanable funds increase interest rates, and increases in the supply decrease interest rates. Expectations of an acceleration in the rate of inflation will raise interest rates by increasing the demand for loanable funds at every interest rate and decreasing the supply.

The loanable-funds theory is frequently used to predict interest rates in various financial sectors as well as the basic interest rate. DSUs come in a large variety of types, requiring loanable funds for a large variety of purposes and time periods in a large variety of amounts. Hence, at any one time, large number of financial instruments that differ in maturity, default risk, and other features are outstanding. Likewise, SSUs are an equally diverse group. Some prefer to make more risky loans rather than less risky loans or longer-term rather than shorter-term loans, and others prefer the opposite. By deriving the demand for and supply of loanable funds for each type of security or financial sector, the equilibrium interest rate in each sector can be determined.

The ability to predict interest rates by sector makes the loanable-funds theory particularly important to many practitioners in the financial markets who limit their activities to only a few sectors, such as short-term money-market instruments, mortgages, or municipal securities. Tables projecting the supply and demand in important sectors by quarter or year are prepared regularly by a number of major financial institutions to assist analysts in predicting interest rates.

These tables, referred to as sources and uses of funds or flow-of-funds tables, divide the supply of loanable funds between those made available by financial intermediaries and those made available by SSUs directly. All loanable funds are ultimately derived from SSUs. Some are lent to DSUs directly in the private financial market and others indirectly in the intermediation market through commercial banks, savings and loan associations, insurance companies, and other intermediaries. It is useful for analysts to know how the funds are channeled. Using such a table, they can identify "pressure points," where the supply of funds appears inadequate (overabundant) relative to the demand, causing interest rates in this sector to increase (decrease) relative to rates in other sectors.

LIQUIDITY PREFERENCE

The liquidity-preference theory derives the equilibrium basic interest rate from the demand for and supply of money at any given time. Spending units are postulated to demand money balances to be held for liquidity to spend later. The demand for money balances is directly related to the income or wealth of the holder; the greater the income, the greater the demand for money. However, to the extent that money promises no or little return, holding money balances incurs an opportunity cost. The higher the interest rate, the higher the opportunity cost and the smaller the demand for money balances. Thus, the quantity of money demanded is related inversely to the interest rate.

The supply of money in the United States is effectively determined by the Federal Reserve System (the Fed), which does so by changing either the dollar amount of cash reserves financial institutions have available or the minimum re-

quired ratio of cash reserves to deposits that they have to hold. Thus, at first approximation, the quantity of money at any moment may be assumed to be determined by the Fed. The equations for the demand for and the supply of money may be specified in functional form as follows:

$$\overset{+\ -}{DM = f(Y,\ i)} \tag{9.4}$$

$$SM = M$$

where:

$$
\begin{aligned}
DM &= \text{demand for money balances}\\
SM &= \text{supply of money balances}\\
Y &= \text{gross national product}\\
M &= \text{money supply}\\
i &= \text{market rate of interest}
\end{aligned}
$$

The sign above a variable indicates the direction of its relation with the dependent variable on the left side of the equation. A plus sign indicates that the relation is direct; a minus that it is inverse. In equilibrium, the demand for money is equal to the supply of money:

$$DM = SM$$

Substituting,

$$\overset{+\ -}{f(Y,\ i) = M}$$

and solving for i,

$$\overset{-\ +}{i = f(M,\ Y).}$$

But, as discussed earlier, the nominal interest rate is also affected by people's expectations of the rate of price change. Thus, the complete liquidity-preference theory may be written as:

$$\overset{-\ +\ +}{i = f(M,\ Y,\ P_E)} \tag{9.5}$$

where P_E is the rate of change in the price level expected at the beginning of the loan period for the same period as the term to maturity of the loan. The equation indicates that the level of nominal market interest rates varies directly with income and price expectations and inversely with money supply. That is, increases in income and/or expectations about the future rate of inflation exert up-

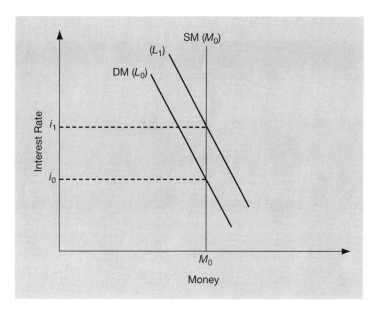

FIGURE 9–5   Interest-Rate Determination by Liquidity-Preference Theory

ward pressure on interest rates, while increases in money supply exert downward pressure.

Also as discussed earlier in this chapter, if prices are not expected to change, the nominal interest rate is equal to the real interest. Thus, Equation 9.5 explains real, not nominal, interest rates and underlies the assumption in the Fisher effect that the real rate remains constant when expectations of inflation do not change. The real rate is assumed to be affected only by changes in aggregate income and in aggregate money supply by the Fed, not by changes in the rate of inflation.

The determination of the equilibrium interest rate under the liquidity-preference theory is shown graphically in Figure 9–5. The demand for money balances for given levels of income and price expectations is shown as schedule L_0. As shown in Equation 9.4, the demand varies inversely with market interest rates, so the schedule slopes downward to the right because at first approximation, the supply of money may be assumed to be determined completely by the Fed without regard to the level of interest rates. The supply schedule is shown as completely vertical at M_0. The equilibrium interest rate is given by the intersection of the L_0 and M_0 schedules at i_0. If income and/or price expectations increase, the demand for money increases and the L schedule shifts out the right, say to L_1. Interest rates rise to i_1. If the Fed increases the money stock, the M schedule shifts to the right, and interest rates decline. The initial change in interest rates brought about by a change in the money supply is likely to be only temporary.

The Term Structure of Interest Rates

Interest-rate levels, direction, and patterns can be analyzed in three categories: short term, medium term, and long term. Short-term fluctuations often last from a few weeks to a few months.[5] Long-term movements or secular trends can last from several business cycles to several decades. Medium-term or cyclical trends roughly coincide with trends of the business cycle. Our discussion has concerned itself mainly with the last.

For a given bond issuer, such as the U.S. government (USG), the structure of yields that is observed for bonds with different terms to maturity (but no other differences) is called the *term structure of interest rates*. In more everyday financial parlance, a diagram of the rates prevailing on a class of securities that are alike in every respect except term to maturity provides us with a *yield curve*. The most common portrait of yields plotted against time, or yield curve, is for marketable USGs.

The record of interest rates, when viewed according to term to maturity, suggests that at times short rates are above long rates, and vice versa. We want to explain the possible determinants of such changes in the term structure of interest rates. In Figure 9–6 we show interest rates on governments by term to maturity at two different points in time. Why do these disparate configurations exist?[6]

One of the most frequently noted behavior patterns concerning the term structure is the observation that, over the business cycle, short-term rates have a greater magnitude of variation than long-term rates have. Over the course of a complete cycle from recession to peak and back to recession, the level of rates will move upward and downward; however, the shorts will move more frequently and to a greater extent than the longs.

The lower curve (at March 15, 1988) is a classic upward-sloping configuration reflecting a time when interest-rate levels were relatively low. In one year, rates had tightened up considerably, as evidenced by the yield curve on March 15, 1989. The *level* of rates rose sharply and the *shape* of the yield curve turned flat. Notice the relative movements in short and long rates between the two dates. For example, very short-term rates (one year or less) moved up from around 6 to 9 percent. Very long rates (thirty years) rose from about 8.5 percent to around 9.1 percent.

From an operational point of view, an investor must recognize that (1) short-term *rates* do fluctuate more violently than long-term rates over a business cycle, (2) long-term *prices* are apt to fluctuate more than short-term prices, (3) the shape of the curve at recession, recovery, and boom phases moves from upward to horizontal to downward sloping; the short end becomes progressively more shallow (differences between very short and three years' rates become narrow); and the long end tends to remain level as it rises or falls.

---

[5]Studies of seasonal factors suggest that they have a strong influence on short-term rates and negligible effects on long-term rates. Between 1951 and 1960, Conrad found tendencies for highs in December and lows in June or July. See J. W. Conrad, *The Behavior of Interest Rates* (New York: National Bureau of Economic Research, 1966), pp. 53–54.

[6]E. A. Dyl and M. D. Joehnk, "Riding the Yield Curve: Does it Work?" *Journal of Portfolio Management* (Spring 1981).

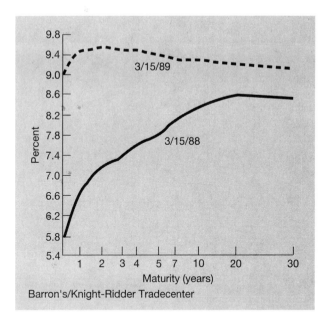

FIGURE 9–6   U.S. Treasury Yield Curve (*Source: Barrons*, March 20, 1989.)

The Shape of the Yield Curve

Financial theory states that any long-term interest rate is the expected value of future short-term interest rates. An investor makes a choice between buying a long-term instrument or buying a short-term instrument and rolling it over based on what he thinks rates will be at the time of reinvestment. The yield on the 30-year bond should thus be the expected average yield of the next 120 three-month Treasury bills.

In the real world, another complication arises. Because three-month Treasury bills can be cashed in at any time with no risk, they provide more liquidity than thirty-year bonds. In a risk-free world, this would make no difference because the risk of interest rates falling would balance the risk of interest rates rising. If investors are risk-averse, however, the long-term bond yield would average somewhat higher than the yield on short-term instruments. This has certainly been true during the postwar era: Since 1953, the thirty-year bond has yielded 52 basis points more on average than the bond-equivalent yield on one-year Treasury bills. In other words, the yield curve has a positive bias.

If the yield on long-term instruments is lower than that on short-term instruments, it implies that individuals expect that, on average, interest rates will be falling over the period of the bond. Investors might expect interest rates to fall over the near term for three reasons: (1) they think inflation will drop substantially, reducing the inflation premium; (2) they expect the federal deficit to be reduced, thus lowering real interest rates; or (3) they expect the economy to slow down or move

into recession, cutting the private demand for capital and thus lowering real interest rates.

In general, the yield curve inverts not because long-term bond yields fall, but because short-term interest rates rise. It should be noted, though, that the thirty-year bond is a somewhat misleading indicator of the yield curve inversion. The popularity of bond issues for stripping, along with the termination of the twenty-year issue and the Treasury's need to skip the August auction, has created a shortage of long-term bonds. This shortage has artifically depressed the thirty-year bond yield relative to other long-term interest rates; the thirty-year Treasury is now yielding 20 basis points less than the ten-year note. This part of the inversion is thus due to technical supply factors, not to any underlying expectation that the outlook beyond ten years is different than that for the first ten.

It is also true that an inversion of the yield curve does not mark the peak of the interest rate cycle. On average, interest rates continue to rise for another seven months after the yield curve inverts. Only when the economy turns down do interest rates normally slide.

CAUSES OF TERM STRUCTURE

The term structure of interest rates, sometimes referred to as the *yield curve,* isolates the differences in interest rates that correspond solely to differences in term-to-maturity. As a first approximation, we can measure the term structure by measuring the relationship between the yields-to-maturity on government debt instruments and their terms-to-maturity. By focusing on government debt instruments, we control for differences in yield that might arise from credit risk.

Three hypotheses commonly cited to explain the term structure of interest rates are (1) the expectations hypothesis; (2) the liquidity-premium hypothesis; and (3) the segmented-market hypothesis, also known as the preferred-habitat hypothesis. The *expectations hypothesis* holds that the current term structure of interest rates is determined by the consensus forecast of future interest rates. Suppose that the interest rate for a one-year instrument is 6 percent and that the rate of interest for a two-year instrument is 7 percent. According to the expectations hypothesis, this term structure arises from the fact that investors believe that a one-year instrument one year in the future will yield 8 percent, because an investor could achieve the same return by investing in a one-year instrument today and a one-year instrument one year from now as he could achieve by investing in a two-year instrument today. If the investor believes that the one-year rate one year in the future will exceed 8 percent, he will prefer to roll over consecutive one-year instruments as opposed to investing in a two-year instrument today. But if he anticipates that the one-year rate one year ahead will be less than 8 percent, he will opt for the two-year instrument today.

According to the expectations hypothesis, an upward sloping yield curve indicates that investors expect interest rates to rise. A flat yield curve implies that investors expect rates to remain the same. A downward sloping yield curve indicates that investors expect rates to fall.

YIELD CURVE AS A RECESSION INDICATOR

The yield curve inverts when investors expect interest rates to decline. Historically, interest rates have fallen either because the economy has moved into recession or because inflation rates have dropped (which usually occurs because the economy has first gone into recession). The yield curve thus indicates recession because it inverts only when traders expect a recession or major economic slowdown.

Given that an inversion primarily reflects expectations of a downturn, it is no surprise that one has preceded each of the last six recessions. Expectations do not, however, always translate into realities. The clearest exception was in the late 1960s: the yield curve first inverted in December 1965, but the recession did not occur until four years later.

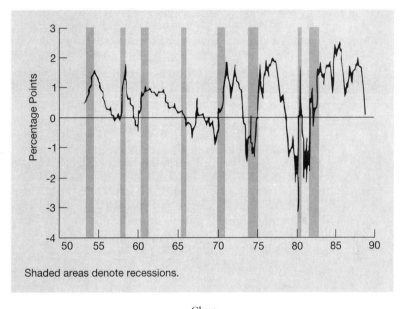

Shaded areas denote recessions.

Chart
The Spread Between the Ten-Year Treasury Bond Yield and the One-Year Treasury Bill Yield
(Percentage Points) (*Source:* DRI/McGraw-Hill, *U.S. Review*, March 1989.)

It is implausible that the expectations hypothesis fully accounts for the term structure of interest rates. When the term structure of interest rates slopes upward, according to the expectations hypothesis, investors expect interest rates to rise. Historically, the term structure has had an upward slope about 80 percent of the time. It seems unlikely that investors have expected interest rates to rise with that degree of frequency.

The higher historical returns of long-term bonds relative to shorter-term instruments lend credence to an alternative explanation of the term structure—the *liquidity-premium hypothesis*. This hypothesis holds that investors are not indiffer-

ent to risk. They recognize that a bond's price is more sensitive to changes in interest rates, the longer its maturity, and they demand compensation for bearing this interest-rate risk. Thus, bonds with longer maturities typically offer a premium in their yields relative to shorter-term instruments in order to induce investors to take on additional risk. The extent of the premium increases with term-to-maturity but at a decreasing rate.

The notion that yields on longer-term instruments reflect a liquidity premium is consistent with the observations that the yield curve usually has an upward slope. Even when investors anticipate that interest rates will remain the same or decline slightly, a liquidity premium could still cause long-term rates to exceed short-term rates.

A third explanation of the term structure of interest rates is the *segmented-market hypothesis,* which holds that groups of investors regularly prefer bonds within particular maturity ranges in order to hedge their liabilities or to comply with regulatory requirements. Life insurance companies, for example, have historically preferred to purchase long-term bonds, whereas commercial banks have favored shorter-term instruments. To the extent the demand of one group of investors increases relative to the demand of one groups of investors increases relative to the demand of the other group, yields within the maturity range where relative demand has risen will fall relative to the yields within the maturity range where there is slack in demand.

SUMMARY

The contractually fixed nature of interest on bonds and dividends on preferred stocks is such that any changes in required holding-period yields occur through market-price changes, which result from changes in systematic and unsystematic risk factors. Perceived increases (decreases) in risk lead to lower (higher) market prices.

Changes in interest rates are the most powerful forces affecting prices of fixed-income securities. This systematic risk factor is really two-dimensional: First, the level of interest rates may move up or down. Second, as the level of rates changes, securities that differ in maturity dates may not move up or down to the same extent; short-term rates may move above long-term rates, or vice versa.

Forecasting the level of interest rates requires insight into business activity, prices, and employment for the period ahead. Along with predicting the economic outlook and price and employment prospects, the analyst needs to gauge the natural forces of supply and demand in financing this outlook. Monetary and fiscal policy must be predicted as a force that will augment or upset projections of business activity, prices, and employment.

As the level of interest rates is forecast to move up or down (or remain relatively stable), the shape of the yield curve may change. The underlying cause of differing shapes in the yield curve seems to be investor expectations of the future course of interest rates. Even though other factors are involved, it appears that if

expected future short-term rates are above current short-term rates, then the yield curve will slope upward. Similarly, if expected short rates are below current short rates, the yield curve will slope downward. Alternative explanations serve to modify somewhat this rather simple explanation.

QUESTIONS

1. When we speak of the "moral" obligation of the federal government to back agency bonds, what do we mean?

2. How are federal and state government (muni) bonds treated for income tax purposes?

3. Do revenue bonds have a higher or lower promised return than general obligation bonds? Why is this so?

4. Examine the bond quotation in Figure 9–2 for PepsiCo 7 5/8, 98. Indicate the following for the day of the quotation:

   a. coupon interest rate,

   b. year of maturity,

   c. current yield,

   d. volume of trading,

   e. price on Wednesday, October 6.

5. What is a Eurobond? How does it differ from a Yankee bond?

6. Why would a U.S. investor wish to consider investing in international bonds?

7. What are "junk" bonds? What is a PIK feature often found in junk bonds?

8. Would a put privilege be superior to a floating interest rate in a bond? Explain.

9. What are the relative advantages and disadvantages to a U.S. investor of buying U.S.-pay versus foreign-pay bonds?

10. Between 1960 and 1980 the average annual returns (income plus price change) for international bonds in Germany and Japan were relatively average. How was it that U.S. investors in these markets were able to capture handsome returns?

11. What are the differences between mortgage-backed securities and U.S. Treasury bonds? Between mortgage-backed securities and corporate bonds?

12. Suppose that Treasury securities due in two years are quoted to yield 8 percent and one-year Treasury instruments are quoted to yield 6 percent. According to the expectations theory of the term structure of interest rates, what rate is the market expecting on one-year Treasury instruments one year from today?

13. Why is the current yield not a true measure of a bond's return?

14. Assume that interest rates are expected to fall substantially. Under the circumstances, which is a better measure of return, the yield-to-call or the yield-to-maturity on a fixed-income security? Explain.

15. Contrast the current yield calculation and the calculation of yield-to-maturity in terms of their usefulness to investors in decision making.

16. Under what specific circumstances would continuous reinvestment in one-year bonds provide superior total income relative to a onetime purchase of a twenty-five-year bond?

17. **a.** What is meant by the term *reinvestment risk*.

    b. Is reinvestment risk greater when the current market rate is 5 percent or 12 percent? Why?

    c. What are the differences in the reinvestment risk between a 5 percent coupon bond selling at 78 to yield 8.5 percent and a 9 percent coupon bond selling at 103 to yield 8.5 percent.

    d. Is the reinvestment risk different between two 9 percent bonds, one due in 2000 and the other due in 2016? Why?

18. What is the significance to an investor of a flat yield curve (long rates are the same as short rates)?

19. Would expectations hypothesis support a negative sloping yield curve? Why?

20. Is the existence of downward-sloping yield curves proof that the liquidity-preference idea is invalid? Why?

21. Assume the following average yields on U.S. Treasury bonds:

TERM-TO-MATURITY	YIELD
1 year	10%
5 years	9%
10 years	8%
15 years	7%
25 years	6%

Given the yield curve implied by the above data, discuss how each of the three major hypotheses of the term structure of interest rates would explain the shape of the curve.

PROBLEMS

1. Assume that you lend a friend $200 at 4 percent interest. The loan plus interest is to be repaid at the end of one year. The level of consumer prices is expected to advance 8 percent during the year.

    a. How much money will you receive at the end of one year?

    b. What is the true purchasing power of the money you receive?

2. The current interest rate on quality corporate bonds is 8 percent on a $1,000 instrument due in one year. Suppose that one-year rates drop to 7 percent because of shifts in supply and demand. What should the price of the 8 percent bond be to adjust to an 7 percent market?

3. Using the present value method, what is the yield-to-maturity on a 12 percent, fifteen-year bond, selling for 120?

4. Using present-value tables and Equation 9.1 determine:

   a. The present worth of a bond where $P_n = \$1,000$, $I = \$100$, $N = 15$, and $i = 12$.

   b. Assume the same data as above, except that $N = 2$. Determine the present worth of the bond.

   c. Compare your answers in parts (a) and (b). How do you account for the effect of merely reducing the life of the bond in part (b)?

5. Set up the equation for determining the rate of interest (i) implied by a 6 percent, twenty-two-year bond selling at $895 (principal at maturity is $1,000).

6. Prove the entry in Table 9–3, which states that the return on a 6 percent bond due in ten years and selling at 86 is about 8 percent.

7. Calculate the realized compound yield for a 10 percent bond with twenty years-to-maturity and an expected reinvestment rate of 8 percent, purchased for $1,000.

8. Odom Corp. has a 16 percent debenture bond outstanding that matures in twenty years. The bond is callable in ten years at 116. It currently sells for 125. Calculate each of the following for this bond:

   a. current yield

   b. yield-to-call

   c. yield-to-maturity

9. A bond is available at a price of 102. The bond has a coupon of 15 percent and matures in twenty years. The bond is callable in five years at 111. Interest rates are expected to trend downward over the foreseeable future.

   a. What is the yield-to-maturity on this bond?

   b. What is the yield-to-call on the bond?

   c. Which yield calculation should an investor regard as the most important for decision-making purposes? Why?

10. Conaway Corp. has a 10 percent bond outstanding that will mature in ten years. Jay Byrd has purchased several of these bonds at par. He expects to place the interest payments he receives in a desk drawer at home because he does not trust financial institutions. Calculate the yield-to-maturity and the realized compound yield for Mr. Byrd. Why do these two yields differ?

11. Calculate the yield-to-call for a 10 percent, ten-year bond that is callable for $1,050 five years from now. The current market price of the bond is $970.

12. Calculate the information requested for each of the following $1,000 par value zero coupon bonds, assuming semiannual compounding.

BOND	MATURITY (YEARS)	YIELD TO MATURITY	PRICE
1	20	12%	?
2	?	8%	$601
3	9	?	350

13. Boudreaux Inc. has issued a $1,000 par value zero coupon bond with an 8 percent yield to maturity that is due in fifteen years. Assuming semiannual compounding:
   a. What is the price of the bond today?
   b. What will the price of the bond be in three years if interest rates remain constant at 8 percent?
   c. What will the price of the bond be in three years if interest rates rise to 10 percent?

14. The yield to maturity on a 10 percent, fifteen-year bond is 12%. Calculate the price of this bond.

15. Today you are offered two Treasury bonds. Both bonds have ten years to maturity, pay coupons semiannually, and have a $1,000 face value. Bond A pays a 12 percent coupon while bond B pays a 10 percent coupon. Market interest rates for these types of bonds are 11 percent today. You forecast market interest rates for these types of bonds will decrease to 10.5 percent soon. If your forecast is correct, then you plan to buy bonds today and sell them when rates drop. Limited resources only allow you to purchase one bond. If your forecast is correct, which bond should you purchase today and sell later? (Justify your answer by determining the percentage changes of each bond.)

16. Calculate the yield-to-call for a 10 percent, ten-year bond that is callable for $1,050 five years from now. The current market price of the bond is $970.

17. The yield to maturity on a 10 percent, fifteen-year bond is 12 percent. Calculate the price of this bond.

REFERENCES

BEIDLEMAN, C., ed. *The Handbook of International Investing.* Chicago: Probus Publishing, 1987.

BIERMAN, H. "Investing in Junk Bonds." *Journal of Portfolio Management* (Winter 1990).

BRICK, J. R., H. K. BAKER, and J. A. HASLEM, eds *Financial Mcrkets Instruments and Concepts.* 2d ed. Reston, Va.: Reston Publishing, 1986.

COX, J., J. INGERSOLL, and S. ROSS. "A Re-examination of Traditional Hypotheses about the Term Structure of Interest Rates." *Journal of Finance* (September 1981).

FABOZZI, F. J. *Bond Markets, Analysis and Strategies.* Englewood Cliffs, N.J.: Prentice Hall, 1993.

The Handbook of Fixed-Income Securities, 3d ed. Homewood, Il.: Business One Irwin, 1991.

Federal Reserve Bank of Richmond, *Instruments of the Money Market.* 8th ed. Richmond: Federal Reserve Bank of Richmond, 1990.

First Boston Corp. *Handbook of Securities of the United States Government and Federal Agencies.* 35th ed. New York: First Boston Corp., 1990.

IBBOTSON, R. G., and L. B. SIEGEL. "The World Bond Market: Market Values, Yields, and Returns." *Journal of Fixed-Income,* June 1991.

VAN HORNE, J. C. *Financial Market Rates and Flows.* 4th ed. Englewood Cliffs, N.J.: Prentice Hall, 1993.

WILSON, R. S., and F. J. FABOZZI. *The New Corporate Bond Market.* Chicago: Probus Publishing, 1990.

YAGO, GLENN. *Junk Bonds.* New York: Oxford University Press, 1991.

BOND ANALYSIS: UNSYSTEMATIC RISK

I n forecasting purchasing-power and interest-rate risk, what we are really talking about are expectations concerning the outlook for the price of commodities and of money. These major sources of risk in fixed-income securities explain why it is that the level and time shape of interest rates shift.

There are also influences that create risk and explain why certain classes of fixed-income securities, such as governments and corporates, or different subgroups of corporates, may move in general harmony with interest rates, but not in a parallel or synchronous fashion.

Investors must learn to react not to a single yield curve but to a whole family of them. The yield curve for corporates might have the same shape as that for governments on any given day, but it could be at a different level and less stable. Each type of bond has a different yield curve, and they change every day.

The analytical thrust of high-grade bond selection differs markedly from common-stock selection, although earning power is the fundamental basis of value for both. High-grade bond selection emphasizes continuity of income and protection against loss of principal, whereas common-stock selection emphasizes earnings and dividend growth and capital appreciation potential.

Losses in high-grade bonds arise from either of two factors: changes in the level of interest rates or impairment in quality. Market fluctuations due to interest-rate changes may be short run or long run, but in any event the original principal is recovered at maturity and the only loss is an opportunity cost in maximizing income.

An impairment in quality causes a greater loss in market value, which may become permanent in case of default. Quality impairment arises principally from a decline in earning power relative to the level of debt and fixed charges (or an increase in debt and fixed charges relative to earning power), which may portend future financial difficulties. Normally, a decline increases sensitivity to interest-rate changes, so that market price fluctuation is typically greater for lesser-quality bonds than for the highest-quality issues.

Secondary-quality bonds may improve in quality over time due to increased earnings and asset protection, or they may be paid at maturity despite underlying

uncertainties. Such bonds will provide an extra return in capital appreciation in addition to interest. The task of analysis is to weigh the risk of uncertainty of payment relative to the potential return, just as for common stocks.

BUSINESS AND FINANCIAL RISK

Corporate bonds sell at higher yields than governments, mainly because of business and financial risk. Within the generic group called *corporate bonds,* yield differentials, or "spreads," exist. Business and financial risk are absent from government bonds because of the monopoly status of the government and its ability to meet debt-servicing requirements through taxation. For corporates, the concepts of business and financial risk are generally combined in a single term, *default risk.*

Default in a legal sense is the failure of the issuer to meet the terms of the debt contract. In investment terms, default refers to the probability that the return realized will be less than promised, rather than to total loss. For example, if you buy an 8 percent bond for $1,000 to hold ten years to maturity, you expect $80 in interest each year and the return of principal at the end of ten years. Assume—an unlikely event—that interest payments are delayed ten years, at which time accumulated interest and principal are paid in full. You *realize* less than 8 percent because of the time value of money. The $1,800 ($800 interest plus $1,000 principal) you receive at the end of the tenth year provides a realized return of only about 6 percent.[1]

Default is a matter of degree, from the simple *extension* of time to make an interest payment, to legal *liquidation* of the debtor to settle accumulated interest and principal. An extension occurs when creditors voluntarily allow extension of maturity and/or postponement of interest payments. Liquidation may occur when a number of successive interest payments are missed owing to underlying problems of management. When it appears that the borrower has no hope of turning the situation around, liquidation proceedings are instituted. Creditors hope to recover some portion of the original principal advanced, plus back interest.

Between extension and liquidation, we have the practice called *reorganization.* A financial reorganization involves the issuance of new securities of the reorganized company for defaulted bonds. In such a case, the nature of interest and/or sinking-fund payments is such that the company cannot generate sufficient cash from operations to meet these requirements. So new securities with revised payment schedules, in amount and/or timing, replace the defaulted securities in the hope that the cash strain is relieved.

These varied degrees of default stem largely from inadequate liquidity and/or earnings. The former case is a manifestation of weak cash-flow management. The earnings problem results from some combination of (1) an inadequate revenue-operating cost relationship (business risk), and/or (2) too much borrowed capital (financial risk).

[1]$1,000 \times (1 + r)^{10} = $1,800$
$$r = 6\%$$

TABLE 10-1

Ratings by Investment Agencies

MOODY'S INVESTOR'S SERVICE

Aaa	Best quality
Aa	High grade
A	Higher medium grade
Baa	Lower medium grade
Ba	Possess speculative elements
B	Generally lack characteristics of desirable investment
Caa	Poor standing; may be in default
Ca	Speculative to a high degree; often in default
C	Lowest grade

STANDARD & POOR'S CORP.

AAA	Highest grade
AA	High grade
A	Upper medium grade
BBB	Medium grade
BB	Lower medium grade
B	Speculative
CCC–CC	Outright speculation
C	Reserved for income bonds
DDD–D	In default, with rating indicating relative salvage value

Default Ratings by Independent Agencies

Bond-investment agencies evaluate the quality of bonds and rank them in categories according to relative probability of default. For the typical investor, this evaluation somewhat simplifies the task of assessing default risk. The principal rating agencies are Moody's Investors Service and Standard & Poor's Corp.[2]

The bond categories are assigned letter grades. The highest-grade bonds, whose risk of default is felt to be negligible, are rated triple A (Aaa or AAA). The rating agencies assign pluses or minuses (e.g., Aa+, A−) when appropriate to show the relative standing within the major rating categories. In Table 10–1 are the ratings used by the two leading rating agencies, with brief descriptions of each. See Table 10-2 for more detailed descriptions of the ratings of Standard & Poor's Corp.

Not all bonds are rated by the agencies. Small issues and those placed privately are generally not rated. For those bonds that are rated, the competing ser-

---

[2]Preferred stocks are also rated by the agencies, but not on a basis consistent with bond ratings. For example, Standard & Poor's preferred-stock ratings are not necessarily graduated downward according to the issuer's debt. Preferred ratings refer to relative security of dividends and prospective stability of yield.

TABLE 10–2

Standard & Poor's Corporate Bond Ratings

AAA   Debt rated AAA has the highest rating assigned by S&P. Capacity to pay interest and repay principal is extremely strong.

AA   Debt rated AA has a very strong capacity to pay interest and repay principal and differs from the higher rated issues only in small degree.

A   Debt rated A has a strong capacity to pay interest and repay principal although it is somewhat more susceptible to the adverse effects of changes in circumstances and economic conditions than debt in higher rated categories.

BBB   Debt rated BBB is regarded as having an adequate capacity to pay interest and repay principal. Whereas it normally exhibits adequate protection parameters, adverse economic conditions or changing circumstances are more likely to lead to a weakened capacity to pay interest and repay principal for debt in this category than in higher rated categories.

BB, B, CCC, CC   Debt rated BB, B, CCC, or CC is regarded, on balance, as predominantly speculative with respect to capacity to pay interest and repay principal in accordance with the terms of the obligation. BB indicates the lowest degree of speculation and CC the highest degree of speculation. While such debt will likely have some quality and protective characteristics, these are outweighed by large uncertainties or major risk exposures to adverse conditions.

C   The rating C is reserved for income bonds on which no interest is being paid.

D   Debt rated D is in default, and payment of interest and/or repayment of principal is in arrears.

PLUS (+) OR MINUS (−)   The ratings from "AA" to "B" may be modified by the addition of a plus or minus sign to show relative standing within the major rating categories.

Source: Standard & Poor's *Bond Guide* (New York: Standard & Poor's Corp., June 1977), p. 6.

vices generally rank the same bond in the same rating category; seldom do they disagree by more than one grade.[3] Overall, the evidence indicates a close correspondence between rating category and subsequent default experience.

Ratings, however, do not totally solve the investor's problem of default-risk discrimination between bonds. First, fully 90 percent of all rated bonds fall into the top four rating categories—not a very detailed distinction for making choices. Second, although the agencies seldom differ widely in their evaluation and classification, they do occasionally differ. Third, and of considerable importance, ratings are changed (up or down) slowly. Under constant review, they are altered only when the agencies deem that sufficient changes have occurred. Thus, letter grades assigned by rating agencies serve only as a general, somewhat coarse form of discrimination.[4]

[3]Louis Brand, former head of Standard & Poor's bond department, estimated that S&P and Moody's disagreed on ratings of about one in twenty utility bonds and one in ten industrial bonds. See H. C. Sherwood, "How They'll Rate Your Company's Bonds," *Business Management* 29 (March 1966), pp. 38–42 ff.

[4]The classic article describing how one rating service evaluates debt can be seen in H. Sherwood, *How Corporate and Municipal Debt is Rated* (New York: John Wiley and Sons, 1976).

In the sections that follow, we will consider key factors in the bond-rating process that analysts examine to verify and refine default ratings. The major factors include earnings power and financial leverage.[5]

Major Factors in the Bond-Rating Process[6]

Depending on the nature of the issuer, the factors that go into a long-term debt rating may vary tremendously. However, four basic areas of investigation are common to most issuers:

1. indenture provisions;
2. earnings power and leverage;
3. liquidity; and
4. management.

Indenture Provisions

The *indenture* spells out in rather lengthy detail the rights and obligations between the lender and borrower and does, in many instances, require the borrower to maintain certain levels of retained earnings, working capital, debt in relation to assets, etc.

An important indenture provision would be a limitation on the creation of additional debt. This so-called debt test is usually found in indentures of companies at the lower end of the investment-grade scale.

Another important indenture provision is the restriction on sale and lease-back of assets. This should be fairly tight for obvious reasons.

But the indenture is only a part of the legal framework surrounding a financing. For example, inquiries also cover such areas as the following:

- Are any assets subject to, or may they be subjected to, a prior claim of creditors?
- What is the nature of off-balance-sheet guarantees and commitments, both current and future?
- What is the impact of external regulation on creditor rights?

[5]Fisher found that risk premiums on bonds were related to (1) earnings variability of the firm, (2) the length of time it was solvent, (3) the debt-to-equity ratio, and (4) the market value or marketability of its debt issue. In effect, companies of long standing, with relatively stable earnings, whose bonds are highly marketable and covered by a large equity cushion, sell at lower default-risk premiums than their counterparts with opposite traits. See L. Fisher, "Determinants of Risk Premiums on Corporate Bonds," *Journal of Political Economy* 67 (June 1959), pp. 217–37.

[6]Continuous information on the rating of new debt and the rerating of old debt can be found weekly in Standard & Poor's Corp., *Credit Overview: Corporate and International Ratings.*

Earnings Power and Leverage

The assessment of corporate *earnings power* is vital for three reasons: (1) it is the best indication of the financial health of the organization, (2) it is the springboard for future growth because the retention of earnings is the basis for future capital investment, and (3) it is the best tangible measurement for determining the success of management's efforts. But an important secondary aspect to earnings power is that it may dictate the amount of leverage an issuer may employ in its business. An example may illustrate this point:

> A company has financed its assets with 60 percent debt and 40 percent equity and earns a return of 18 percent pretax, preinterest on its assets. Assuming imbedded interest costs of 10 percent, it will cover its interest charges 3.00 times. On the other hand, if it earns only 9 percent return on assets, still enough to cover its interest charges 3.00 times and provide equal protection for creditors, its capitalization could only contain 30 percent debt.

But the foregoing illustration is an oversimplification because it does not take into account critical analytical judgments, many of which are subjective in nature:

- Are the return levels indicated sustainable? What has been the track record? Are there cyclical trends impacting on these results?
- What is management's plan for the future? Are there new business entries or acquisitions planned that could impact profit return levels?
- What is the regulatory and political environment? Will additional capital have to be provided for nonproductive assets?
- What is the quality of earnings? What has been the return on sales? Are profit margins increasing or decreasing? What is the trend in competition? What is the nature of the company's accounting?

Those are some of the areas of in-depth analysis, but they, too, do not address the following important questions concerning the quality of assets:

- Does the company maintain amounts of cash and marketable securities in excess of its operating requirements? Under "normal" conditions, this would tend to lower the company's return on assets, but it obviously enhances its liquidity.
- Are inventory and receivables levels realistic in view of the economic outlook?
- Are assets undervalued on the books as they are for many natural resource concerns?
- Are fixed assets overvalued in terms of traditional earnings power? What are the replacement values?
- Are accounting policies in line with industry norms?

Finally, the analyst must look behind the traditional leverage measurements to determine off-balance-sheet liabilities, such as unfunded pension obligations and lease rental liabilities not capitalized.

Liquidity

Liquidity is broadly defined to include not only balance sheet measurements of current or "quick" assets in relation to liabilities but also to include the concept of access to cash. Corporations have three sources of cash other than the turnover of current assets:

- internal cash generation—i.e., net income plus depreciation and amortization plus deferred taxes;
- the sale of equity or the incurrence of debt; and
- the sale of fixed assets.

The existence of "excess" liquidity is directly related to the company's ability to generate sufficient funds internally to meet requirements for expansion, dividends, and debt repayments. Where anticipated cash disbursements exceed this ability to generate cash, then we consider the existence of excess cash to be only a temporary phenomenon. For example, a major corporation recently sold a subsidiary for cash. At the same time, this company anticipated temporary reinvestment of these funds in higher-yielding but less-liquid assets and also announced its intention to diversify from its traditional business. Because ratings are long-term assessments, not much weight in the rating process is given to the temporary existence of high liquidity.

The three aforementioned ongoing sources of cash generation deserve further comment as to how they relate to the rating process.

- *Internal cash flow:* When internal cash generation of funds is considered as a source of debt repayment, we must consider other demands on such funds as well. These include dividends and "mandatory" reinvestments, such as working capital, equipment, and "brick and mortar," all of which are necessary to keep the enterprise competitive.
- *External financing:* The ability of U.S. corporations to raise equity capital from time to time has been highly tenuous. It is considered prudent financial management for companies to maintain adequate short-term financing capability to avoid the necessity of a permanent financing at an inopportune time. The least desirable time for companies to sell debt or equity is when they must.
- *Sale of fixed assets:* The actual sale of long-term assets is obviously a highly unusual method to raise cash. It may be considered somewhat of an admis-

sion that such assets are not capable of generating sufficient near-term cash in relation to the seller's needs.

Management

The final broad area of analytical endeavor involves an assessment of *management*. As critical as this might be, the task is somewhat alleviated by the nature of many companies that are rated. Most are large, well-established, efficiently run organizations with a track record of developing capable senior and middle management talent. Their substantial financial resources enable them to attract younger talent with excellent academic or work credentials.

On the other hand, situations do occur where the quality, strength, and depth of management may not be presumed, such as the following:

- where the company is in a state of flux reflecting increasing competitive pressures. In short, the profit pattern is erratic;
- where the company is involved in an actual acquisition program involving a large number of unrelated enterprises;
- where the company is quite small, closely held, or has a relatively short track record;
- where management talent is constantly being acquitted from outside, as opposed to being developed internally;
- where there is an obvious concentration of policy formation and operations decision making; or
- where the company has failed to perform as well as its major competitors over an extended period of time.[7]

EARNINGS POWER

Heavy burdens of fixed-interest and preferred-dividend payments have led many companies into default and eventual bankruptcy. The degree of default risk is measured in two ways by analysts: (1) earnings-coverage ratios, and (2) capitalization ratios. Each of these will be explored in turn.

Earnings coverage rests on income relative to charges on debt and preferred stock. The higher the income relative to charges, the lower the risk of default, other things being equal. This income-charges relationship is normally cast in ratio terms, income/charges.

---

[7]It is not unusual for bonds to be rated differently by competing bond-rating services. A look at the impact of this phenomenon is in P. Liu, and W. T. Moore, "The Impact of Split Bond Ratings on Risk Premia," *Financial Review* (February 1987).

EARNINGS AND CHARGES—BONDS

The income referred to is generally EBIT (earnings before interest and taxes). Because interest is a tax-deductible expense, it is logical to compare it with earnings before taxes.[8]

The *level of income* used in the computation of earnings-coverage ratios deserves serious consideration. The most important consideration here is: What level of income will be most representative of the amount that will actually be available in the *future* for the payment of debt-related fixed charges? An average earnings figure encompassing the entire range of the business cycle, and adjusted for any known factors that may change it in the future, is most likely to be the best approximation of the average source of funds from future operations that can be expected to become available for the payment of fixed charges. Moreover, if the objective of the earnings-coverage ratio is to measure the creditor's maximum exposure to risk, then the proper earnings figure to use is that achieved at the low point of the enterprise's business cycle.[9]

The *total charges* on bonds usually amount to the sum of the annual interest charges on all debts. Although a company may have several bonds outstanding with different priorities to income (and assets), such as mortgage bonds and debentures, we generally do not calculate a separate mortgage-bond coverage and debenture-bond coverage. Ability to meet interest payments on mortgage bonds but not debentures can put the company into bankruptcy. Then the mortgage bondholders are in jeopardy as well. The chain of bond priorities is only as strong as the weakest link.

Let us illustrate our earnings-*coverage-ratio* idea. The income statement of ABC, Inc., shows its EBIT to be $25 million. The company has outstanding a 6 percent, first-mortgage bond issue in the amount of $50 million. In addition, an 8 percent debenture-bond issue is outstanding in the amount of $25 million. Total interest payments would be $5 million (6 percent of $50 million, plus 8 percent of $25 million). Earnings coverage would be calculated as follows:

$$\text{Interest coverage on all bonds} = \frac{\text{EBIT}}{\text{Interest charges on all bonds}}$$
$$= \frac{\$25 \text{ million}}{\$5 \text{ million}} = 5$$

The earnings coverage is said to be five times. The larger this ratio, the better. We must recognize, however, that the significance of this coverage is enhanced by gauging it (1) over a period of years, future as well as past, and (2) against some standard to ascertain whether it is high or low, good or bad.

The adequacy of the ratio must be related to the volatility and other characteristics of earning power. Coverage ratios in cyclically sensitive businesses such as

[8]It is customary to exclude extraordinary and/or nonrecurring income from earnings. Such extraordinary items cannot be assumed to occur regularly or predictably.

[9]Various methods used in rating bonds are examined in J. Ang and K. Patel, "Bond Rating Methods: Comparison and Validation," *Journal of Finance* (May 1975).

autos, machinery, or chemicals should average higher than for more stable businesses such as food or drugs. If a company is to enjoy a high credit rating, it should show sufficient coverage so that even under the worst of foreseeable conditions, there is a cushion against unexpected adversity. Companies in this position will continue to enjoy adequate credit standing and have access to financial markets under even the most adverse conditions.

DEBT-SERVICE ANALYSIS.   The use of borrowed capital also typically requires cash outlays to discharge part or all of the principal of the debt in future years. Serial maturities or sinking funds are the typical contractual covenants that indicate cash requirements for this purpose. Although payments on debt principal may represent a regular flow of cash out of the company, they are not reflected on the income statement. Investor protection can be impaired by the inability of the issuer to meet sinking-fund or amortization requirements because these are also legal obligations, just like regular interest. Therefore, the analyst should make some determination of the issuer's capacity to cover total requirements, including both interest payments and annual debt reduction. Coverage of both is essential.

In this light, it is customary to determine *debt-service coverage* by the following:

$$\frac{\text{EBIT}}{\text{Interest charges on bonds} + [\text{Sinking-fund payments}/(1 - \text{Tax rate})]}$$

Because sinking-fund payments are not expenses but return of principal, they are not reported on the income statement. Hence, they must be paid out of after-tax dollars. This is the reason for the mathematical setup in the denominator of the fraction. Thus, for a company in the 40 percent tax bracket to cover $300,000 for sinking-fund payments, $500,000 must be earned before taxes ($500,000 less $200,000 in taxes is $300,000). Hence, for ABC, Inc., let us assume that a 40 percent tax rate applies, and that the $25 million in 8 percent debentures calls for an annual sinking-fund payment of $300,000. Debt-service coverage could be calculated as

$$\frac{\$25}{\$5 + [\$0.3/(1 - .4)]} = \frac{\$25}{\$5 + \$.5} = \frac{\$25}{\$5.5} = 4.5$$

EARNINGS AND CHARGES—PREFERRED STOCK

Preferred-stock dividends are paid after interest. Recognition of this fact means that preferred dividend coverage must include in the total charges all prior interest. Preferred dividend requirements could be added to interest charges, if any, and this sum could be divided into earnings. However, complications arise.

Preferred dividends are paid after taxes, whereas bond interest is paid before taxes. Adding both together is like mixing apples and oranges. Either preferred dividends must be adjusted to a pretax basis or interest payments must be adjusted to an after-tax basis. The former is preferable. At a tax rate of 50 percent, a corporation needs $2 in EBIT to pay $1 in preferred dividends; only $1 of EBIT is needed to pay $1 in interest because interest is a pretax expense. In general, to adjust preferred dividends to a pretax basis:

$$\text{Pretax preferred dividend requirement} = \frac{\text{Preferred dividends}}{1 - \text{Tax rate}}$$

In other words, at a 40 percent tax rate, a company has to earn $5 million before taxes to pay $3 million in preferred dividends [$3 million/(1 − .4) = $5 million].

After adjustment for the tax factor, earnings coverage on preferred dividends becomes:

$$\text{Preferred dividend coverage} = \frac{\text{EBIT}}{\text{Interest} + [\text{Preferred dividend}/(1 - \text{Tax rate})]}$$

Assume that ABC, Inc., has EBIT of $25 million and the balance sheet shows (dollars in millions):

Current assets	$90	Current liabilities	$30
		6% first-mortgage bonds	$50
		8% debentures	25
Fixed assets	$140	8% preferred stock	25
		Common equity	100

Total interest was determined earlier to be $5 million. Preferred dividends are determined in dollars as 8 percent of $25 million, or $2 million. Assuming a tax rate of 40 percent, total charges are covered:

$$\text{Preferred dividend coverage} = \frac{\text{EBIT}}{\text{Interest} + [\text{Preferred dividends}/(1 - \text{Tax rate})]}$$

$$= \frac{\$25}{\$5 + (\$2/.6)} = \frac{\$25}{\$5 + \$3.33} = \frac{\$25}{\$8.33} = 3 \text{ times}$$

Note that where a company has both bond and preferred-stock financing, the coverage of the preferred is always lower than the coverage on the bonds.[10]

Capitalization

Financial leverage or risk can also be measured on the balance sheet. Capital from each of varied sources—debt, preferred stock, and common stock—can be related in percentage form to total funds. To the bondholder or preferred stockholder, the greater the percentage of total funds that common stockholders provide, the better. Extending our ABC, Inc., example (reported in millions of dollars):

---

[10]Note the fallacy in subtracting interest from EBIT and dividing the result by adjusted preferred dividends. The result is $20/$3.33 = 6 times. Recall that bond interest coverage was 5 times. Preferred dividends cannot be better protected than bond interest.

6% first-mortgage bonds	$ 50
8% debentures	25
8% preferred stock	25
Common equity	100
Total long-term capital	$200

Capitalization ratios, at book value, can be stated as:

Long-term bonds	37.5%	(75/200)
Preferred stock	12.5	(25/200)
Common equity	50.0	(100/200)
Total	100.0%	

If the ABC bonds were being analyzed, the relevant capitalization ratio would consider preferred and common stock as junior in standing to bonds. In this case, a bondholder would note that his equity "cushion" is 62.5 percent (125/200) of total long-term funds. For preferred stockholders, the cushion is 50 percent (common equity). Bondholders and preferred stockholders desire a strong common-equity base to cushion their position.[11]

The rating services and analysts look at capitalization in alternative ways to the percentage breakdown of long-term capital shown above. Financial risk can be measured on the balance sheet by total debt/equity (20/80 = .25). This is interpreted as $.25 of debt for every $1 of equity. The ratio long-term debt/total capital would merely relate long-term debt to the total of long-term debt plus preferred stock and common equity. Obviously, the lower this ratio or any capitalization ratio such as debt/equity, the better protected the bondholders, since the equity cushion would be larger in the event of adversity.

Total assets	$100	Liabilities (debt)	$20
		Equity	80
		Total debt and equity	$100

The ratio net tangible assets/long-term debt is used as an indication of the asset protection afforded to the debt of a company. Net tangible assets are total assets less intangibles, current liabilities, investment tax credits, and deferred taxes. A ratio of 400 percent means that every dollar of long-term debt has $4 of tangible assets (at book value) in support. By the time a corporation declares bankruptcy, the assets have often been dissipated. On the other hand, book values can be understated.

---

[11]At times, preferred stock has no par value or has a nominal value, such as $1 per share. Preferred stockholders would be entitled to more on liquidation of the company—say $50 maximum per share. To compute capitalization ratios, it is appropriate to show preferred stock at liquidation value. Any difference between nominal value and liquidating value would come from a reduction of surplus accounts. The result is to lower the common-equity percentage of total funds.

Leases

An analytical complication arises when a company leases some or all of its fixed assets. Instead of borrowing long-term funds to buy buildings and equipment, many companies lease them.[12] Financial analysts call this "off-balance-sheet" financing, referring to the fact that because leased facilities are not owned, their cost is typically not carried as an asset. More important, at most only current lease installments appear as a liability. In effect, two companies may be utilizing the same amount of fixed assets, one leasing and the other owning. They may generate identical profits, but they will show different debt outstanding and interest charges, as well as different earnings coverage and capitalization ratios.

Payments under a lease are designed to cover three basic ingredients required by the lessor or the landlord: (1) depreciation on the property, (2) interest expense on the borrowing, and (3) a profit margin. Only interest expense plus profit margin is analogous to bond interest.

Analysts attempt to make financial statements of companies comparable. When companies lease property, fixed charges and long-term debt must be adjusted upward. How? A rule of thumb is to assume that about one-third of a lease payment represents interest payments.[13] Dividing this amount by prevailing rates available to the company on long-term debt at the time the lease was arranged in effect "capitalizes" the lease. This capitalization provides us a debt-value equivalent represented by the lease.[14]

Suppose ABC, Inc., makes lease payments of $4.5 million on a building. At the time of the lease arrangement, the company could have borrowed at 6 percent (the rate on its mortgage bonds). With the suggested rule of thumb:

$$\frac{\frac{1}{3} \times \$4.5 \text{ million}}{.06} = \frac{\$1.5 \text{ million}}{.06} = \$25 \text{ million}$$

The $25 million is the equivalent amount of debt represented by the lease. When the building was built, if ABC had borrowed money at 6 percent rather than

[12]For analytical purposes, use of the alternative of borrowing rather than selling stock stems from the debtlike nature of most lease contracts.

[13]The inclusion of a portion of lease (rental) expense (deemed to be an interest factor representative of leases) is typically performed only for "financing leases." These are defined by the Securities and Exchange Commission (SEC) as noncancelable leases that (1) cover 75 percent or more of the economic life of the property, or (2) assure the lessor a full recovery of his initial investment plus a reasonable return. For years prior to 1973 it was necessary to rely on conventions such as capitalizing total lease rentals. Since 1973 the SEC has required that notes to the financial statements of annual reports show how these leases are capitalized. Generally, these leases are capitalized at the present value of gross minimum rentals based on the interest rate implicit in the terms of the lease. The use of the one-third total net rental payments is an inexact method.

Refer to the footnotes to the financial statements of McDonald's Corp. (Chapter 6) to see how lease commitments are reported.

[14]It would be best to use present-value calculations using the term-to-maturity of the lease. However, most financial data available to the investor do not include all the terms of lease contracts to make this refined calculation possible.

signing a lease agreement, annual interest expense would be $1.5 million higher than shown in the income statement, and long-term debt on the balance sheet would be greater by $25 million.

Revised coverage and capitalization ratios for ABC would be determined by adding back one-third of the lease payments to EBIT on the income statement. This has the effect of raising EBIT. Interest expense is then raised by $1.5 million. Thus:

$$\text{Interest + lease expense coverage} = \frac{\text{EBIT} + \frac{1}{3}\text{ lease payment}}{\text{Interest} + \frac{1}{3}\text{ lease payment}}$$

$$\frac{\text{EBIT (revised)}}{\text{Interest on bonds (revised)}} = \frac{\$25 + \$1.5}{\$5 + \$1.5} = \frac{\$26.5}{\$6.5} = 4.1$$

Our earlier bond coverage of five times has been reduced. Because defaults on lease payments have legal consequences, the revised coverage of 4.1 times adds meaning to our default-risk measurement using earnings coverage. Preferred-dividend coverage would have to be adjusted accordingly.

Lease (rental) payments would have to be reflected in a revised debt-service coverage ratio. The interest coverage computation included only that portion of leases (rentals) that is attributable to the interest factor. As a long-term obligation, from a contractual point of view, the interest portion is indistinguishable from the principal portion (the remaining two-thirds, as it were). Consequently, debt-service coverage should account for the entire amount of leases (rentals), rather than only the interest portion. Thus:

$$\frac{\text{EBIT + Lease payments}}{\text{Interest + Lease payments} + [\text{Sinking-fund payments}/(1 - \text{Tax rate})]}$$

$$= \frac{\$25.0 + \$4.5}{\$5 + \$4.5 + \$.5} = \frac{\$29.5}{10.0} = 2.95$$

Similarly, revised capitalization ratios would recognize the added $25 million debt equivalent:

Long-term debt	$75.0	33.3%	(75/225)
Debt equivalent	25.0	11.1	(25/225)
Preferred stock	25.0	11.1	(25/225)
Common equity	100.0	44.5	(100/225)
	$225.0	100%	

The common-equity cushion was calculated earlier to be 50 percent.

The methods employed to adjust for leases are admittedly somewhat crude. Security analysts and accountants have grappled with the problem of widespread, adequate lease-disclosure standards for many years. More and more companies are providing some information on leases in footnotes to financial statements. We are still some way from having the kind of detail necessary to sound analysis, but at

least the methods presented here are significantly better than making no adjust-ment for leases at all.

Liquidity

Adequate earnings coverage does not mean that adequate cash will be on hand to make actual payments required on bonds and preferred stock. Companies rich with earnings can be cash-poor.

The amount of cash and working capital (current assets minus current liabili-ties) a company has will provide a good indication of its ability to ride out a general recession or a temporary decline in its particular industry and still make interest, dividend, and sinking-fund payments. The size of its cash and working capital will also indicate its ability to finance improvements or expand sales volume without resorting to further borrowing.

The analyst is interested in (1) the size and (2) the character of the company's liquid position. Levels of cash and sources of cash should be examined. Stable or increasing cash positions are desired, generated mainly internally, rather than from outside sources such as bank borrowing. Analysts want to be certain that the com-pany's dividend policy is in line with the industry. Over-liberal dividends weaken defenses against business downturns and benefit only common-stockholders.

Liquidity connotes the ability to meet obligations as they mature and to sus-tain current operations. The liquidity position of a company may be thought of as a reservoir into which cash is deposited from revenues and cash flows out to pay obli-gations incurred for expenses and expansion. When the reservoir gets too low, it may be replenished in the first instance from liquidation of short-term financial as-sets or by borrowing in the capital market or from banks or by sales of equity. If these avenues are not available, a financial crisis develops. Often a weakness in one type of cash resource is quickly followed by weakness in the others. The bond-holder's interest in the company's liquidity is directed toward the overall financial position and ability to meet debt maturities without recourse to a refunding opera-tion in the capital market, which might happen to be congested at the time.

Several key funds items interest the analyst as measures of basic cash flow in the business on a long-run basis. *Internal funds* are defined as retained earnings plus depreciation, the change in deferred taxes, and, where material, minority in-terest. Also where material, we remove undistributed earnings of unconsolidated subsidiaries accounted for by the equity method. In an extreme situation, dividends could be stopped to increase cash flow as defined, but usually the capacity to pay dividends is one evidence of financial strength and hence we use retained earnings. This is a conservative measure because it excludes other sources of funds; impor-tantly, any increase in payables and accruals. *Funds used* are capital expenditures plus the change in receivables and inventories. There are other uses of funds, of course, but these are the principal expenditures necessary for the operation and growth of the business.

Companies that keep these two totals in balance seldom need to raise new capital. An occasional imbalance may be financed by temporary bank credit. Often

the excess of funds used over internal cash flow may be funded steadily into debt while holding the debt ratio constant. However, sustained excesses of funds used over internal cash flow and a rising debt ratio can be a danger signal.

The bondholder is interested in appraising the company's ability to repay debt out of internal cash flow, in comparison with other uses of funds. This has been shown to be an important measure of credit quality and liquidity.

A key ratio is cash flow/long-term debt. Cash flow is synonymous with total funds from operations, or net income plus extraordinary items, deferred taxes, and depreciation. Generally, the higher the ratio the better for the debtholder. The ratio is an indication of the cash available from operations that could be used to service debt. For example, if the ratio were 200 percent, cash flow for the year was two times the outstanding long-term debt at year-end. The reciprocal is often used to indicate the number of years it would take, theoretically, to repay long-term debt. The 200 percent figure indicates a reciprocal of 50 percent—suggesting it would take six months to repay long-term debt from cash flow. Obviously, the timing of the cash flow is not the same for each month of the year.

Among the conventional tests of the adequacy of liquid resources are the current ratio (current assets/current liabilities) and working-capital adequacy (current assets minus current liabilities/long-term debt).

Expanding our data on ABC, Inc., will illustrate these tests of liquidity (reported in millions of dollars):

Cash	$ 6.0	Current liabilities	$ 30.0
Total current assets	90.0	Long-term debt	75.0
Fixed assets	140.0	Preferred stock	25.0
		Common equity	100.0

Current ratio $= 90/30 = 3.0$

Working capital/long-term debt $= 60/75 = .8$

Working capital/long-term debt (including lease equivalent) $= 60/100 = .6$

Generalizing about what constitutes high or low cash and working-capital ratios is difficult. A standard of 2-to-1 is often set for the current ratio. However, liquidity requirements are largely dependent upon the industry in question.

Net income is generally not a reliable measure of funds provided by operations that are available to meet fixed charges. The reason is, of course, that fixed charges are paid with cash or, from the longer-term point of view, with funds (working capital), while net income includes items of revenue that do not generate funds as well as expense items that do not require the current use of funds. Thus a better measure of fixed-charges coverage may be obtained by using as numerator funds obtained by operations rather than net income. This figure can be obtained from the statement of changes in financial position, which is now a required financial statement and should, consequently, be generally available.

Under this concept the coverage ratio could be computed by dividing funds provided by operations by fixed charges (i.e., interest, sinking-fund, and lease payments).

A TALE OF TWO CREDITS

News that Caterpillar Tractor Co. (Grant's, July 2, 1984), one of the Street's premier inflation plays, lost 31% more in the third quarter than it had in the year-ago period and that, as the Journal reported, further massive cuts are likely to be necessary if (the company) is to post a profit next year, raises some interesting questions about the nature of risk and the efficiency of markets. As the table shows, the rise of the dollar and the slump of the earth-moving business have taken their toll on Cat's balance sheet. As recently as 1981 (the year of its last profit), the company was covering its interest charges four times over; in the 12 months ended in June, it failed to cover them once.

Not every major American industrial corporation has suffered the Caterpillar (Cat) disease, as the table shows. Goodyear Tire & Rubber Co., for one, is making money and enhancing its balance sheet, the strength of the dollar notwithstanding. In 1981, it covered its interest expense by less than three times; at midyear 1984, it covered it by more than six times.

Caterpillar is troubled, whereas Goodyear is profitable. One might expect that the rating agencies and the bond market would have drawn some hard distinctions between the two credits. The distinctions are these. In July, Moody's downgraded the senior debt of Cat from A1 to A2, while reaffirming its confidence in Cat's ability to remain "a major competitor in world markets." In September, Moody's upgraded the senior debt of Goodyear from A3 to A1. Thus, the net difference between the companies amounts to one-third of one grade.

In early July 1984, a yield quote for Caterpillar Tractor 8.60s of 1999 was 12.45%, and Goodyear Tire 8.60s of 1995 were at 12.40%. Net difference: five basis points.

Is everybody awake out there?

Caterpillar Tractor Co.

	1984*	1983	1982	1981	1980	1979
Cash flow/total debt (%)	18.6	8.8	13.9	60.4	69.9	51.5
Total debt/capital (%)	41.2	40.2	42.8	31.9	28.6	31.6
Pretax interest coverage (×)	0.44	(0.62)	(0.45)	4.57	5.60	6.22

Goodyear Tire & Rubber Co.

	1984*	1983	1982	1981	1980	1979
Cash flow/total debt (%)	86.8	73.1	46.3	30.5	26.1	21.7
Total debt/capital (%)	20.8	21.9	30.9	37.9	40.6	44.9
Pretax interest coverage (×)	6.2	4.8	3.0	2.8	2.4	2.1

*12 months ended June 30.

Source: Grant's Interest Rate Observer (October 22, 1984).

The Security Contract: Indenture Provisions[15]

Bond indentures and preferred-stock contracts spell out the legal rights of holders and the restrictions under which a company must operate once it has issued bonds and/or preferred stocks.[16] The many covenants of these lengthy and complex legal documents are designed to insure against the kind of bad housekeeping that may lead to default. These various "thou-shalts" and "thou-shalt-nots" specify what a company may do while it is among the living as well as what happens if it dies. *Analysts and investors should look to see that contracts contain certain protective covenants.*

Security contracts do not ensure rising sales and profit margins. However, they can attempt to (1) control the total amount of debt and preferred-stock financing relative to common equity—a prime source of default—and (2) protect priorities to interest or dividends and principal payments in the event of default.

Controls that attempt to minimize default risk and maximize recovery in bond issues are generally stated in the areas of sinking funds, collateral, additional funded debt, and dividend restrictions. Comfort seems to lie in knowing that principal will be recaptured on a regular payments schedule (sinking fund) and/or that certain assets are pledged to support principal (collateral). Further, current bondholders want to exercise a degree of control over the amount of debt permitted over future time periods (additional funded debt). Dissipation results when too many creditors vie for limited earnings and/or assets. Dividend restrictions protect future ability to generate interest payments.

Periodic repayment of principal between date of issuance and the final due date has several advantages to investors. First, it provides greater assurance that the company will not default than does the promise of payment of the total issue in one lump sum at a distant due date. Second, with preferreds, this buy-back method lends price support to a security that, unlike bonds, has no nominal maturity. Third, if earnings are steady, piecemeal retirement enhances earnings and asset coverage on the remaining principal. On the other hand, however, as interest rates fall, a sinking-fund buy-back can take from an investor a security with an attractive yield.

An annual sinking-fund payment is usually made on corporate bonds to provide funds to buy them back through the marketplace or random call. Less frequently, the funds are placed in an escrow account (at interest) to retire the entire issue at once. Municipal bonds are normally divided into parts, each part having a different maturity date. This is a serial-maturity arrangement. The holder knows exactly when his bond is due (avoiding the chance aspects of sinking funds). Sinking-fund arrangements are designed to cope with investor fears of default risk. Serial bond issues are designed to match the repayment ability of the issuer.

---

[15]The importance of bond indenture provisions is examined in T. S. Y. Ho and R. F. Singer, "Bond Indenture Provisions and the Risk of Corporate Debt," *Journal of Financial Economics* (December 1982).

[16]For other details on features found in bond indentures and preferred-stock contracts, review Chapter 1.

Indentures normally provide for additional debt financing if certain tests are met. Added debt is given no more than an equal, and often junior, security position to debt previously issued. A common test to be met before new debt financing can occur is to relate net tangible assets to total old and new debt.[17] A rule might be that new debt can be issued only if, after the issue, net tangible assets amount to at least two and one-half times as much as current and proposed debt. Suppose a company has $100 million in net tangible assets and $25 million in long-term debt. Its ratio of net tangible assets to debt is 4:1. A proposed new long-term debt issue of $25 million would bring the ratio to 2½:1 (125/50).[18]

If additional debt is to be backed by collateral, it is common to provide equal or lesser standing to other lienholders. This feature is important when debentures (unsecured bonds) are used. If mortgage bonds are sold subsequent to a debenture issue, debentures are commonly given equal and proportionate secured standing.

Dividend restrictions attempt to avoid excessive payout, which weakens the equity base and liquidity. In some instances, dividends may be limited to retained earnings subsequent to the issuance of a particular bond issue, or subsequent earnings plus some stipulated amount of accumulated earnings.

Owners of preferred stocks normally enjoy equal claim to assets and dividends behind bondholders. Rarely, a "prior" preferred receives first claim to income and assets; this might be called a "first" preferred. Preferred issues protect against issuance of subsequent debt and preferred stock of equal or greater rank by veto rights. In such a case, the votes of, say, two-thirds of the preferred holders are required to approve prior or parity securities *unless* total debt and preferred-stock charges are covered to a specified extent (maybe two and one-half times fixed charges), and/or common-stock equity is not less than preferred-stock equity after new preferred is sold (that is, common equity ≥ preferred equity).

It is standard for preferred-stock contracts to provide for cumulation of dividends. In other words, if dividends are missed, they must be made up before any dividends can be paid on common shares. Moreover, when a certain number of dividends are missed, preferred-stockholders can elect a number of directors to prevent further difficulties. This voting right is contingent upon missing dividends and is relinquished when arrears are cleared up.

Tests of Corporate-Bond Risk: A Review Example

In Table 10–3 we see single-year data for Patriot Industries. Table 10–4 is a summary of key tests of default risk bearing on the bonds and preferred stock of the company if they were being analyzed on the statement dates. This example is included to assist the reader in pulling together the many strands of analysis introduced so far.[19]

[17]Net tangible assets are net assets less intangibles, such as patents, copyrights, and goodwill.
[18]Note that an asset-to-debt ratio is a sort of asset-coverage counterpart to the earnings-coverage ratio.
[19]To illustrate certain points, some statement items have been placed and/or combined in a manner contrary to good accounting practices.

TABLE 10–3

Patriot Industries, Financial Statements for the Year 199X

INCOME FOR THE YEAR ENDED DECEMBER 31, 199X
($ IN MILLIONS)

Revenue*	$101.2
Cost of sales	78.0
Depreciation	10.0
Lease payments[†]	1.0
EBIT	12.2
Interest expense	2.2
EBT	10.0
Income taxes[‡]	4.7
EAT	5.3
Preferred dividends	1.2
Earnings available to common	4.1
Common dividend	2.1

POSITION STATEMENT
DECEMBER 31, 199X ($ IN MILLIONS)

Cash	$ 2.0	Current debt	$ 10.0
Other current assets (net)	60.0	4% first-mortgage bonds	10.0
Fixed assets	88.6	4½% debenture bonds[§]	40.0
		6% cumulative preferred	20.0
		Common stock ($1 par)	.6
		Surplus accounts	70.0
Total assets	$150.6	Total debt and equity	150.6

*Includes pretax long-term capital gains on sale of land, $1.2 million.
[†]Financial lease. Borrowing equivalent cost = 8%.
[‡]Tax rates on income: ordinary income = 50%; capital gains = 25%.
[§]Annual sinking fund of $2.4 million.

Key items to note include the following:

1. Extraordinary income (land sale) is included in revenues. Exclude $1.2 from EBIT as nonrecurring, leaving EBIT = $11. (Note: Income taxes of $4.7 include $.3 from 25 percent tax on land sale of $1.2.)

2. Regarding lease payments, a net lease might assume that one-third the payment is equivalent to interest. Capitalized at a borrowing cost of 8 percent (.33/.08), this gives a long-term debt equivalent of $4.17. Add one-third of the lease payment to previously adjusted EBIT, and the interest portion to interest expense. EBIT = $11.33; Long-term debt = $54.17; Interest and lease payment = $2.53.

3. Pretax preferred dividend adjustments should use a tax rate of 50 percent, not the effective rate on the income statement (Income tax/EBT = 4.7/10.0 = 47%). (See item 1.) Pretax preferred dividend is $1.2/.5, or $2.4.

TABLE 10–4

Key Measures of Risk on Fixed-Income Securities

RATIO	CALCULATION	RESULT
Coverage ratios:		
Interest coverage	$[(11)+(.33)]/[(2.2)+(.33)]$	4.60
Preferred dividend coverage	$[(11)+(.33)]/[(2.53)+(2.4)]$	2.30
Debt-service coverage	$[(11)+(1)]/[(2.2)+(1)+(4.8)]$	1.50
Capitalization ratios:		
Long-term debt/total capital	54.17/144.77	.37
Net tangible assets/long-term debt	140.6/54.17	2.60
Liquidity ratios:		
Current ratio	62/10	6.20
Working capital/long-term debt	52/54.17	.96
Cash flow/long-term debt	$(4.1+10.0)/54.17$	.26

Municipal-Bond Analysis

Two principal types of municipal securities are general-credit obligations and revenue bonds. *General-obligation bonds* are backed by the full taxing power of the municipality. *Revenue bonds,* however, are backed only by the revenue of the specific project for which they were issued. A toll-road bond issue is an example of a revenue bond. Because of the greater risk of revenue bonds, they must provide higher yields-to-maturity.

Municipal securities, like corporates, are subject to default risk and are rated by Moody's and S&P as to their probability of default.

GENERAL-OBLIGATION BONDS

The general factors that must be considered in assessing default risk on municipals are the taxing base, existing debt in relation to this base, and the variability of tax revenues. Several common ratios can be used to judge the relative risk of default.

First, what is the amount of tax-dependent debt relative to the assessed valuation of taxable real estate? The wealth and income of a community can be measured roughly in terms of property values. The resulting ratio is a debt-to-property-value measure. Care must be taken in making comparisons to ensure that assessment methods are standardized. Communities normally take market values of property and reduce them to assessed value by some percentage multiplier. One may assess property at 60 percent of market value and another at 80 percent. High-quality bonds would normally fall in a range of 8 to 10 percent for debt-to-assessed-value. In a sense, this measure is a rough equivalent of a debt-to-asset ratio for corporates. The reciprocal is an asset-coverage ratio.

Second, debt per capita is also measured. The number of residents of a community does not necessarily represent the number of taxpayers, so care must be taken not to use this ratio in isolation.

Third, debt service as a percentage of the community's budgeted operating expenses can be measured. Debt service refers to the sum of annual interest plus debt retirement. This ratio is a roundabout equivalent of interest-coverage ratios on corporates. Instead of using earnings or revenues as with corporates, however, it measures the community's burden in paying for debt service relative to other operating costs out of tax receipts.

Revenue Bonds

Revenue bonds bear risks similar to those of corporate bonds. Interest and principal must be paid from earnings, so earnings-coverage ratios become vitally important. The investor must assess the future revenue-generating ability of the project (e.g., toll road or sports stadium).

To illustrate some elements of municipal bond analysis let us look at Massachusetts's general obligation bonds and those of Florida. Massachusetts bonds were downgraded from Aa/AA+ (Moody's/S&P) in early 1989 to Baa/BBB while Florida maintained its Aa/A rating. The data below provides some data on both states to provide a sense of why Massachusetts's bonds are downgraded in bond rating to a lower level than Florida's.

YEAR	DEBT PER CAPITA		DEBT AS % REAL ESTATE VALUATION		DEBT AS % PERSONAL INCOME	
	MASS.	FLA.	MASS.	FLA.	MASS.	FLA.
1991	$1,111	$385	1.55%	1.08%	4.55%	2.06%
1990	935	387	1.30%	1.16%	4.00%	2.17%
1989	874	391	1.38%	1.24%	3.94%	2.30%
1988	700	412	1.10%	1.36%	3.36%	2.50%
1987	653	398	1.73%	1.37%	3.42%	2.58%
1986	625	304	1.64%	1.10%	3.55%	2.07%
1985	588	279	2.00%	1.06%	3.61%	1.99%

Note the rising debt load per capita and as a percentage of real estate valuation (since 1988) and personal income in Massachusetts and the opposite trend in Florida. In 1989 the average spread of Baa/BBB over Aa/AA municipal bonds was 50 basis points. You can see how Massachusetts was hurt in that its borrowing costs in effect went up 1/2 percent (50 basis points) due to a lowered bond rating.

Default Risk and Market Yields[20]

We present in Figures 10–1 and 10–2 the pattern of the structure of yields on governments, municipals, and corporates over time. The general correspondence of governments and various grades of corporates is in line with basic differences in underlying default risk and premiums.

[20]The relationship between ratings and return experience is seen in J. S. Fons, "The Default Premium and Corporate Bond Experience," *Journal of Finance* (March 1987).

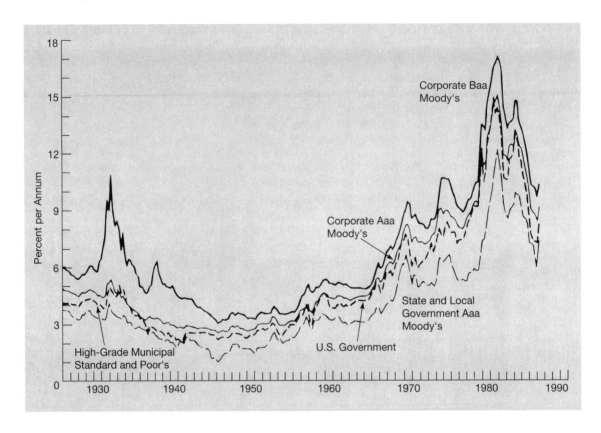

FIGURE 10–1   Long-Term Bond Yields (Quarterly Averages) (*Source:* Board of Governors of the Federal Reserve System, *Historical Chart Book,* 1988.)

The reader should be warned that default risk alone does not explain the differentials or spreads in yields. Identical agency ratings of quality can disguise differentials among industrial, finance, and electric and gas utility bonds, and even among issues within these categories.

Differences in taxation can be seen in the low levels of yields on municipals. Certain situations that exist with corporates provide different tax situations in the same rating category. Call features and differences in degree of marketability are other factors that are hidden in Figure 10–1.

NONRISK FACTORS INFLUENCING YIELDS

Certain qualities inherent in bonds, common stocks, and preferred stocks have nothing in particular to do with risk in its traditional definition. Some of these factors result from *laws,* some from *terms in security contracts,* and others from the way *securities markets* function.

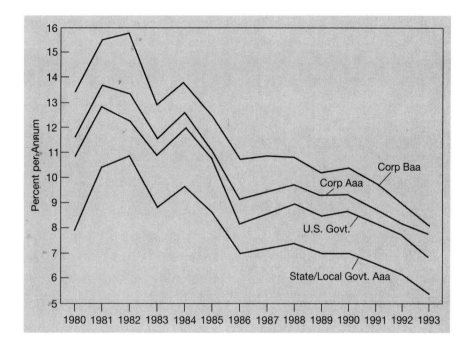

FIGURE 10–2   Long-Term Bond Yields (Annual Averages), 1980–93

Each of these factors might make a security desirable to some investors and not to others. The more desirable a particular factor or factors might be to an investor, the more he will pay for a security that bears it, other things being equal. Conversely, if an investor is neutral or can get along without a particular feature, he will not pay more to obtain it. Investors who are averse to a given quality in a security will be willing to buy it only at a lower price. In all cases, the change that results from a willingness or unwillingness to pay for a particular quality has an effect on a security's yield or return.

Three principal ownership qualities are of interest to us: marketability, call features, and taxation of returns.

Marketability

Differences in yield for various securities may result from differences in marketability. *Marketability* refers to the ability of the owner to convert to cash. This conversion process relies upon price realized and time required to sell the security. Price and time are interrelated because selling a security quickly if enough price concession is given is often possible. For securities, marketability is the ability of the seller to sell a significant volume of the securities in a short period of time without significant price concessions (which include the matter of transaction costs).

The more marketable a security, the greater the investor's ability to execute a large transaction near the quoted price.

Usually, marketability of a security is judged by the difference between the quoted bid and asked prices in relation to the level of prices because the percentage difference depends upon the price level. For example, if we express bid-asked differentials as a percentage of the bid price, a $1 spread on a bid of $10 is 10 percent. The same $1 spread on a bid of $100 is only 1 percent. The bid price is the price the dealer stands ready to buy a security for; the asked price is the price he is willing to sell the security for. The smaller the spread, expressed as a percentage of the bid price, the more marketable the security.

Dealer spreads are similar to a retailer's markup: They must cover expenses, risk of loss, and a profit. In general, as with any fast-moving merchandise, securities with a large volume of transactions carry narrower markups or spreads. Competition keeps dealers from taking larger markups than required by expense, risk, and a reasonable profit.

Investors find advantages in more marketable securities because the cost of buying and selling them is less. A highly marketable preferred stock might be quoted as 50 bid, 50½ asked. The ½-point spread is the markup. If you bought 100 shares for $5,050 and sold them again for $5,000, the service charge would be $50. (Of course, the quotes would probably not stay constant.) The cost of buying and selling the security is 1 percent of the bid price ($50/$5,000). Consider another case where a preferred is quoted as 100 bid, 102 asked. If you purchased 50 shares at $5,100 and resold at the bid price for $5,000, you would pay a service fee of $100. This is double the dollar and percentage cost in the first example.

It is quite common for investors to refer to a stock or a bond as having a "thin" market. The connotation is that there is not much of the security for sale at the asked price, and not much sought at the bid price. If you place an order to buy or sell a relatively large block, it may be executed at a price materially different from the price of the last transaction. The converse is thought of as a "broad" market, in which one can sell large amounts at once with little or no effect upon the quoted price. Poorly marketable securities have thin markets. Buying or selling small blocks in a market dominated by large trades can lead to similar marketability problems.

The marketability of a security can be judged by observing the bid-asked spread over several different time periods. Securities of small, unseasoned companies listed on the over-the-counter market are commonly thought to have less marketability than those of large, seasoned companies listed on the New York Stock Exchange. This is only a generalization. Each case must be considered individually. Frequently, "thin" markets are referred to in regard to stocks that have small numbers of shares in active supply. Large percentages of shares might be held by family trusts, or the companies may be small and have few shares issued and outstanding.

Small investors who purchase bonds must assess marketability very closely. The bond markets are dominated by large institutional holders who tend to buy and sell in blocks in the millions of dollars. The bid-asked prices appearing in the financial press will most probably be for transaction sizes (in dollars) that reflect institutional supply and demand. For example, the latest quote on a corporate bond

is 100 bid and 100¼ asked. If you wish to buy or sell $2,000 worth, the dealer might quote you 99½ bid and 101 asked because the published quotes reflect a market of transactions many times greater than yours. Yours is, in a sense, an odd-lot order.

One final comment is in order relative to the marketability of an issue. Certain liquidity problems or trading difficulties can be encountered as the bond gets older, that is, as it approaches maturity. These bonds typically begin to move into the portfolios of permanent investor types who tend to hold them to maturity.

Thus, differences in return (yield) between different securities are caused not only by differences in default risk but also by differences in marketability. The lower the marketability, the greater the yield an investor would demand and vice versa.

Seasoned Versus New Issues

Bonds that have been outstanding for some time are generally referred to in the bond trade as *seasoned*. The yields on older, seasoned issues will typically be below those on *new* issues, with the difference depending upon the level of interest rates. The yields on new issues frequently exceed those on seasoned issues of the same quality and maturity when interest rates are high. The reason for these higher yields is that underwriters do not want to hold the new issues in inventory because of the associated carrying costs and the danger of a further rise in the level of interest rates. Their behavior is such that they mark down the prices on new issues (higher yields) vis-à-vis seasoned issues. In addition, older, lower-coupon bonds tend to sell at a discount. Their inherent tax advantages and call protection cause their prices to be bid up (lowering yields). These tax and call advantages will be discussed shortly.

Overall, the spread between seasoned and new issues is a function of the level of interest rates and can vary anywhere from 0 to 50 basis points (seasoned issues are below new issues by this amount). The higher the level of interest rates, the larger will be the spread.

A study by Martin and Richards suggests that the yield differential between new and seasoned corporate bond issues exists but does not decline with the passage of time.[21] They suggest that coupon and call differences explain virtually all the observed differences in yields. The implication of this research is that there is no seasoning process and, more important, buying new rather than seasoned bonds is unlikely to result in above-average returns.

The Call Feature

Many issuers put terms in the contract giving them the right to redeem or *call* the entire outstanding amount before maturity, subject to certain conditions. Most Treasury securities, including all debt sold since 1985, are not callable, which makes Treasury issues very attractive, even though their yields are lower than

[21]J. D. Martin and R. M. Richards, "The Seasoning Process for Corporate Bonds," *Financial Management* (Summer 1981), pp. 41–48.

those on corporate bonds and mortgage-backed securities. Some long-term Treasury issues sold before 1985 are callable five years before their maturity date. Most long-term municipal issues are callable in ten years, but issues with original maturities less than ten years generally are not callable.

Corporate bonds have no set call rules. Among bonds due in ten years, some are callable and some are not. Long-term issues from utilities or telephone companies typically cannot be paid off with lower-cost debt for five years, but that has not prevented calls by other means, financed from maintenance funds, property funds, or special sinking funds.

In the case of corporate bonds and preferred stocks, the call price is usually above the face or par value of the security and decreases over time. For example, an 8 percent, twenty-five-year bond issue may be callable initially at 108 (108 percent of par). The call price might decline by $\frac{1}{4}$ percent per year (108, 107.75, 107.50, and so on). The initial call price is commonly the equivalent of one year's interest plus the par value of the bond.

The call feature modifies maturity and thereby affects a security's relative yield. The call feature is exercisable immediately or it is deferred for some time. The most widely used deferred-call periods are five years for public utility bonds and ten years for industrial bonds. During the deferment period, the investor is protected from a call by the issuer.

The issuer pays a premium for the option of calling the bonds before their nominal maturity. The option to call provides the issuer with flexibility. If interest rates decline significantly, the issuer does not have to wait until maturity to refinance but can call the bonds and reissue others at a lower interest cost. The call may also be exercised to eliminate any protective covenants in the bond contract that have become unduly restrictive.

The call feature does not come free. When interest rates are high and expected to fall, the call feature is likely to have significant value. Investors will be unwilling to invest in callable bonds unless yields are more than those of bonds that are noncallable or unless call is deferred, other things being equal. Borrowers are willing to pay a premium in yield for some sort of call privilege. When rates are expected to rise, the call feature has negligible value to the issuer. The spread between immediately callable and deferred call bonds may narrow close to zero.

Thus, the threat of a call feature to an investor is dependent upon his expectations that interest rates will fall significantly during the life of the bond or preferred-stock issue. Accepting securities with immediate call privileges will tend to provide more return (yield) than accepting some deferral period. In periods of high interest rates, this can mean a difference of $\frac{1}{4}$ percent in yield. Whether the risk of call is worth the extra $\frac{1}{4}$ percent is principally a function of the outlook for interest rates and whether the issuer feels he will be able to refund the bonds at a profit (savings).

Another strategy for approaching the call-risk problem is to buy deep-discount bonds—bonds that sell well below par or face value.[22] The principal reason for this condition is that they bear coupon rates far below prevailing rates required

---

[22]It is important to recognize the fact that a bond selling far below its face value is not necessarily in trouble.

in the market. Using bond-yield tables, we can show that in a market where the returns on ten-year AAA bonds are 8 percent, a newly issued ten-year AAA bond with an 8 percent coupon would sell for 100, whereas an older bond with a 4 percent coupon, due in ten years, would sell at 73. The 4 percent bond provides most of its required return of 8 percent through appreciation in price at maturity.

If market rates fall to 6 percent, the 8 percent bond will move to 115, and the 4 percent bond to 85. But the 8 percent bonds are in danger of call, whereas the 4 percent bonds are still far below their probable call price. The investor must realize, however, that the deep-discount aspects of bonds are really attractive on two counts: call protection and tax advantages. Because ordinary interest income is taxed at regular tax rates and long-term capital gains (increases in principal values) are taxed at lower capital gains rates, deep-discount bonds possess tax-savings appeal.

SINKING FUNDS

Sinking funds have been designed to provide for the retirement of a certain portion of a bond issue through purchases by the issuing corporation at predetermined regular intervals. Nearly all industrial bonds have sinking funds. Although less frequently used by electric utilities in the past (less than 50 percent), investor pressure has built recently to force the increasing inclusion of a sinking fund in new utility issues.

The sinking fund provides two broadly defined benefits to an investor. The orderly retirement of debt by the corporation should provide the bond investor increasing credit safety because the amount of debt outstanding is reduced and the pressure on the company to refinance a large amount of debt at maturity is moderated. A second important benefit is that the sinking fund provides an additional element of liquidity to the issue through regular purchase activity to meet sinking-fund requirements.

As a result, investors have traditionally held the notion that the existence of a sinking fund provided some extra value over and above what would be the bond's market value at any given point in time. Within the context of rising interest rates over the last twenty-five years, the sinking fund has indeed provided extra value to the bondholder. The mere fact that a sinking fund shortens the average life of the bond, thereby providing the investor an opportunity to reinvest at a higher yield earlier has provided substantial incremental value.

However, when interest rates reach high levels, the existence of the sinking fund may actually reduce the relative value of the bonds because the potential exists for bonds to be retired at par if rates subsequently fall and prices rise.

Because the sinking fund is placed in a bond issue largely for the benefit of the investor, the typical sinking-fund price is a *maximum* of par value plus any accumulated interest. Thus, if interest rates rise subsequent to the issuance of a bond, the bond will tend to fall below par. Because issuers are obliged to pay no more than the par value of the bond for sinking-fund purposes, they will generally satisfy the sinking-fund requirement by purchasing bonds in the open market. This injects demand into the market for the bonds and, depending upon the size of the sinking

fund, provides support for the bond price. If interest rates fall subsequent to the is-suance of a bond, the bond will rise in price above par value. Again, because the maximum price to be paid for the bond for sinking-fund purposes is the par value, the question remains: What is the most equitable way to repurchase bonds if the required sinking-fund price is below the market price? Typically, bonds will be re-deemed by random lot. That is, bonds are selected randomly by bond number, and a sufficient number are repurchased to satisfy the sinking-fund requirement. Thus, in a period of declining interest rates, the operation of a sinking fund injects a lot-tery risk into the holding of such bonds. You may have purchased a bond at, say, 102 only to see it called at 100.

Therefore, the presence of a sinking fund in a bond issue is a mixed blessing. It may provide the bondholder with some peace of mind that a regular redemption schedule is in place and provide some price support for the bond in a period of ris-ing interest rates. However, if interest rates decline subsequent to the issuance of a bond, an investor may have his bond called away for sinking-fund purposes and be faced with a knotty problem of reinvestment at lower rates.

An examination of public-utility bond offerings between 1977 and 1982 showed that the value of a sinking fund varied with the default risk of the issuer as well as with market expectations of future interest-rate movements. Evidence also supported the notion that sinking funds improve the liquidity of a bond issue. For example, if interest rates are low, sinking-fund bonds sell for a lower reoffering yield than similar nonsinking-fund debt, and the value of the sinking fund increases as credit quality declines. High interest rates bring about penalty yields on sinking-fund bonds compared to nonsinking-fund issues. The lower the quality of the issue, the *less* costly the sinking-fund provision.[23]

Tax Factors

Chapter 2 dealt with the broad question of taxes. Here we will discuss the tax ef-fects primarily related to bonds and preferred stocks. In particular, we will explore the tax impact of (1) discount bonds, (2) municipal and government bonds, and (3) preferred stocks.

DISCOUNT BONDS

As noted, discount bonds are bonds selling below their par, or face, value. These bonds provide not only a large measure of call protection but also certain tax advantages.

Interest, dividends, and capital gains are currently taxed at the same rate. However, interest and dividends are taxed on an ongoing basis, whereas the tax on capital gains can be postponed. The greater the discount on a bond, the greater its

---

[23]See David S. Kidwell, M. W. Marr, and J. P. Ogden, "The Effect of a Sinking Fund on the Reoffering Yields of New Public Utility Bonds," *Journal of Financial Research* (Spring 1989).

tax deferral attraction and the lower its yield relative to what it would be if the coupon were such that the bond sold at par. A simple example will illustrate the tax implications.

Consider two bonds of identical maturity and quality. The first can be bought with an 8 percent coupon to yield 9 percent to a twenty-year maturity. The second twenty-year bond has a 3 percent coupon and sells at a sufficient discount to provide an added 6 percent in capital gains, so the total yield to maturity is also 9 percent. An investor in the 33 percent tax bracket would realize 6 percent after taxes on both bonds; however, the tax on the appreciation of the 3 percent bond is postponed. The 3 percent bond should be priced to yield less than 9 percent to maturity because of the tax-deferral advantage (and, of course, the potential call protection).

U.S. government securities afford an excellent illustration of this tax issue. They are all of equal (and highest) quality, and most are not callable. Bonds with similar maturities should sell at differing yields to maturity based upon coupon differences. The following prices and yields on U.S. Treasury securities in late September 1993 illustrate the point:

MATURITY	COUPON	PRICE*	YIELD TO MATURITY
May 1996	4.25	100.26	3.93
May 1996	7.63	109.12	3.97

*For example, 109.12 is $109\frac{12}{32}$ percent of par ($1093.75 per $1,000 par).

The lowest coupon yields 16 basis points less than the highest coupon bond due to the tax-deferral advantage.

GOVERNMENTS AND MUNICIPALS

Unlike the case with all other categories of securities, interest income (but *not* capital gains) from state and local government securities is exempt from federal income taxes. This unique tax status accounts for the fact that municipal-bond yields are lower than those of other securities. Most states do not tax income from their own bonds, or income from bonds of their political subdivisions. Thus, from an overall tax standpoint, there are advantages to buying municipals issued in the state of residence of an investor.

Typically, municipal bonds will yield less than taxable bonds, depending on the level of interest rates. Because the tax exemption on municipal bonds applies only to the interest, discount and premium municipal bonds are less attractive than municipal bonds selling at par. Therefore, discount and premium municipal bonds will not sell at the same yield-to-maturity as municipal bonds selling at par.

Commercial banks are large holders of municipal bonds, particularly at times when the demand for loans is soft. Investment in municipal bonds serves as a substitute when the demand for consumer and business loans is weak. When the level of interest rates is high, banks generally sell municipal bonds to meet loan demand. This has a tendency to force down the prices on municipal bonds and therefore raises the level of rates. Thus, yields on municipal bonds during such periods will

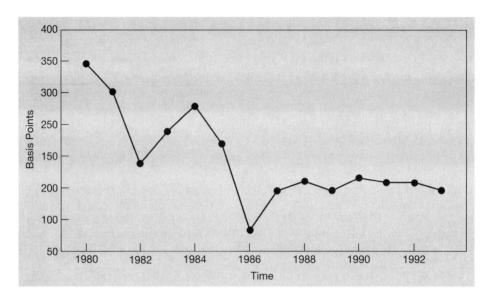

FIGURE 10–3   Yield Spread between Treasuries and Munis, 1980–93 (*Source:* Moody's Bond Record, Moody's Investors Service (June 1989).

tend to rise faster than yields on taxables; that is, the spread between municipals and taxable bonds narrows. Conversely, when the demand for consumer and business loans falls, the reverse occurs; that is, banks tend to purchase municipal bonds, and this demand raises the price of municipal bonds and lowers their yields. The spread between municipal yields and taxable bonds widens.

In addition to the federal income tax, the federal tax on estates has an impact upon Treasury securities. The estate tax is levied on assets upon the death of the owner. Certain Treasury bonds, if owned by the deceased, are redeemable at par if the proceeds are used to pay federal estate taxes. These are referred to as *flower bonds*. A $1,000-par government bond purchased at $800 would be worth $1,000 in settlement of estate taxes. For this reason, qualifying government bonds selling at discounts have a special attraction above and beyond the capital gains implications.

Note in Figure 10–3 the yield distinction between high-grade governments and high-grade municipals over time. The spread in yields, or differential, has ranged from 75 to 350 basis points (¾ to 3½ percent), owing almost entirely to the difference in taxation of these two categories of bonds under the ever changing federal income tax law.

PREFERRED STOCKS[24]

Federal tax laws provide that intercorporate dividends shall not be excessively taxed. One corporation receiving dividends from another and, in turn, paying div-

---

[24]For a detailed historical perspective on the use of preferred stock, see Donald E. Fischer and Glenn A. Wilt, Jr., "Non-Convertible Preferred Stock as a Financing Instrument, 1950–1965," *Journal of Finance* 33 (September 1968), pp. 611–24.

TABLE 10–5

			Examples: 9 Percent Dividend (or Yield)					
EFFECTIVE TAX RATE		PERCENT DIVIDEND SUBJECT	PERCENT OF DIVIDEND (OR YIELD) PAID IN TAX		PERCENT REMAINING AFTER TAX		DIVIDEND RATE (OR YIELD) (%)	AFTER-TAX DIVIDEND (OR YIELD) (%)
35%	×	30	=	10.5	thus	89.5	× 9.00	8.06
25%	×	30	=	7.5	thus	92.5	× 9.00	8.32

idends to its own shareholders could be faced with double taxation. Taxing the dividend to the ultimate shareholder would amount to triple taxation. To alleviate this chain of taxation, intercorporate dividends are taxed at very low rates.

A substantial portion of dividends received on preferred or common stocks held by corporations may be deducted when they compute their taxable income. Under existing federal income tax law, such investors (including, in certain cases, life insurance companies and mutual savings banks) are entitled to a deduction equivalent to 70 percent of dividends received on certain preferred-stock holdings. New-money issues are those sold to raise funds for the first time, rather than to redeem existing financing. For corporations in the 35 percent tax bracket, with only 30 percent of such dividend income taxable, 10.5 percent of the dividends on such issues will be paid in taxes (.35 × .30), thus providing an after-tax return equal to 89.5 percent of the dividend.

For financial institutions that have an effective tax rate of 25 percent, slightly more than 92 percent of the dividend on industrial or new-money utility preferred stocks is retained after tax (see Table 10–5).

These calculations are made in Table 10–5. To make similar calculations for effective tax rates other than 35 percent or 25 percent, substitute the appropriate effective tax rate in the first column and compute as shown.

In Table 10–6 we display pretax yields that enable corporations to determine yield needed on interest-bearing obligations to equal the after-tax yield on 70 percent tax-exempt preferreds. For example, using the 35 percent tax-rate section, if a taxpaying institution were to purchase a preferred stock yielding 9 percent (see left-hand column), it would have to receive a 12.39 percent yield on a government or corporate bond or on a mortgage, or an 8.06 percent yield on a tax-exempt issue, in order to obtain the same after-tax yield as is received on the preferred issue on a 9 percent basis.

INVESTING IN PREFERRED STOCKS.   The small investor has been effectively priced out of the market for preferred stocks, because of the advantage taxable institutions have of excluding 70 percent of dividends received from income. Bond interest, other than that on municipals, is fully taxed. For institutional investors, the relative after-tax yields on high-quality corporate bonds and high-grade preferred stocks is obvious. A tax rate of 50 percent applied to an 8 percent bond and an 8 percent preferred stock gives an after-tax yield of 4 percent on the bond and 7.4 percent on the preferred stock. This is more than enough difference to overcome any perceived differences in risk.

TABLE 10–6

Preferred Stock Equivalent Yield Table (35 Percent Tax Rate)

YIELD ON PREFERRED ENTITLED TO 70% EXEMPTION	YIELD NEEDED TO EQUAL AFTER-TAX RETURN ON 70% EXEMPT PREFERRED ON:	
	BONDS, MORTGAGES* (100% TAXABLE)	TAX-EXEMPT OBLIGATIONS†
6.00	8.26	5.37
6.50	8.95	5.82
7.00	9.64	6.27
7.50	10.33	6.71
8.00	11.02	7.16
8.50	11.70	7.61
9.00	12.39	8.06
9.50	13.08	8.50
10.00	13.77	8.95
10.50	14.46	9.40
11.00	15.15	9.85
11.50	15.83	10.29

*(Yield $\times$ .895)/.65
†Yield $\times$ .895

See Table 10–7 and Figure 10–4 for the yields on high-quality corporate bonds and preferred stocks over time. Preferreds generally yield *less* than bonds, with the average differential being about 87 basis points. The underlying causes are

TABLE 10–7

Yields on High-Grade Bonds and Preferred Stocks

YEAR	(1) Aaa CORPORATE BONDS	(2) PREFERRED STOCKS	(3) SPREAD (2) – (1)
1980	11.94	10.60	134
1981	14.17	12.36	181
1982	13.79	12.53	126
1983	12.04	11.02	102
1984	12.71	11.59	112
1985	11.37	10.49	88
1986	9.02	8.76	26
1987	9.38	8.37	101
1988	9.71	9.23	48
1989	9.26	9.05	21
1990	9.32	8.96	36
1991	8.77	8.17	60
1992	8.14	7.46	68
1993	7.73	6.55	118

Source: Federal Reserve Bulletin.

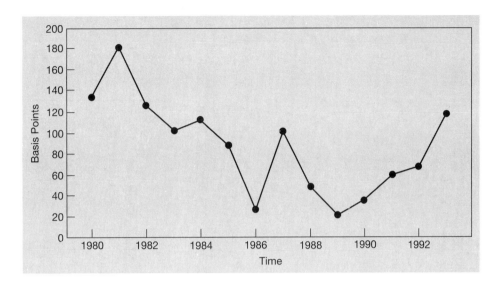

FIGURE 10–4   Yield Spread: Corporate AAA − Preferred, 1980–93

the tax anomaly and the diminishing supply of available preferred stocks. For the small investor without the income tax exclusion on preferreds, it hardly seems worth taking more risk and getting a lower return than on bonds.

DEFAULT RISK IN McDONALD'S LONG-TERM DEBT

Table 10–8 shows, in summary form, financial data and certain ratios applying to McDonald's Corp. Interest coverage fell rather consistently from 1983 until 1988 and has reversed quite impressively since 1990. This reversal is the combined result of lower interest rates in the market, expanding earnings, and a reduction of long-term borrowing by the company.

The ratio of debt to total invested capital in 1992 was the lowest in fifteen years, implying that more than two-thirds of McDonald's long-term capital now comes from equity financing. Cash flow has improved to the point where McDonald's could pay off its long-term debt in less than a half year (cash flow/long-term debt in 1992 was at about 45%). The company's ability to generate cash relative to requirements has strengthened as the corporation has matured. McDonald's policy of owning rather than leasing real estate sites stabilizes its long-term occupancy expenses and gives the corporation a pool of undervalued assets.

The negative working capital position of McDonald's (and its current ratio below 1.0) appears an area of concern at first blush. However, negative working capital is not a threat because the current assets are highly liquid (a cash business

TABLE 10-8

Financial Data and Ratios Relative to Credit Risk Bearing Upon Long-Term Debt of McDonald's Corp.
($ in millions)

	1992	1991	1990	1989	1988	1987	1986	1985	1984	1983
Earnings before interest and taxes	$2,235	$2,070	$1,977	$1,740	$1,286	$1,162	$1,021	$939	$843	$751
Interest expense	$374	$391	$381	$302	$237	$203	$173	$157	$135	$123
Cash flow (funds from operations)	$1,426	$1,423	$1,301	$1,246	$1,177	$1,051	$852	$758	$673	$580
Cash and equivalents	$436	$220	$143	$137	$184	$183	$205	$155	$75	$66
Current assets	$865	$646	$549	$495	$516	$483	$472	$370	$255	$231
Net tangible assets	$8,998	$8,958	$8,390	$7,270	$6,210	$5,341	$4,406	$3,717	$3,142	$2,782
Current liabilities	$1,545	$1,288	$1,199	$966	$1,003	$856	$799	$663	$514	$430
Long-term debt	$3,176	$4,267	$4,429	$3,902	$3,111	$2,685	$2,131	$1,638	$1,268	$1,171
Total invested capital	$10,137	$10,061	$9,469	$8,209	$7,067	$6,042	$5,088	$4,298	$3,639	$3,224
Ratios:										
Pretax interest coverage (EBIT/interest)	5.98	5.29	5.19	5.76	5.43	5.72	5.90	5.98	6.24	6.11
Debt/total invested capital	31.3%	42.4%	46.8%	47.5%	44.0%	44.4%	41.9%	38.1%	34.8%	36.3%
Cash flow/long-term debt	44.9%	33.3%	29.4%	31.9%	37.8%	39.1%	40.0%	46.3%	53.1%	49.5%
Net tangible assets/long-term debt	283.3%	209.9%	189.4%	186.3%	199.6%	198.9%	206.8%	226.9%	247.8%	237.6%
Working capital/long-term debt	-21.4%	-15.0%	-14.7%	-12.1%	-15.7%	-13.9%	-15.3%	-17.9%	-20.4%	-17.0%
Current ratio (curr. assets/curr. liabilities)	0.56	0.50	0.46	0.51	0.51	0.56	0.59	0.56	0.50	0.54
S&P bond rating	AA	AA	AA	AA	AA	AA	AA	AA	AA	AA

with high-quality franchisee receivables). Also, its current liabilities are owed to a limited group of suppliers of meat (Keystone Foods) and soft drinks (Coca-Cola), and the company can apply a lot of leverage to delay supplier payments if necessary.

SUMMARY

Yields differ on various kinds of bonds and preferred stocks. A rational way to view these differences is to isolate differences in risk associated with each. Market yields on U.S. government securities reflect compensation for the pure cost of lending or borrowing money without risk, plus compensation for purchasing-power risk. The structure of yields on corporates and municipals can be examined by differences in default risk and certain nonrisk variables influencing yield.

Investors are aided in assessing relative risks of default by established, independent rating agencies. However, the investor is well advised that these broad default ratings are only guides and provide, at best, a rough discrimination between bonds. Detailed analysis of the factors likely to contribute to default can pay handsome rewards. These factors mainly relate to asset and earnings coverage on bonds and preferreds.

Nonrisk factors influence yields as the result of tax laws, various features of security contracts, and the way in which securities markets function. Not all returns from securities are taxed in a similar manner. Municipal bonds and discount bonds possess unique tax appeal. Sinking-fund and call features represent advantages and disadvantages to investors. The cost and benefits of these contractual features must be weighed in an investment decision. Not all securities have active, broad markets. As a result, conversion back to cash may result in price concessions that detract from realized yield.

QUESTIONS

1. What are bond ratings and what are they supposed to indicate?
2. Why might one bond rating service rate a bond A which another service rates the same bond A+?
3. What letter rating would Standard & Poors generally give to speculative bonds? Bonds in default?
4. Indicate the major factors that serve as ingredients in setting a letter rating for bonds. Which factor do you think is the most important?
5. Cash flow is important to the rating process. Why is internal cash flow likely to be viewed as more important than cash flow resulting from the sale of fixed assets?

6. In the formula for calculating debt service coverage, sinking-fund payments are adjusted by dividing them by (1 – tax rate). What is the purpose of this adjustment?

7. Why might an investor purchase a BB-rated bond, which is below investment grade?

8. Of what significance to investors are bonds that sell above par value?

9. Can you think of any advantages to an issuer of bonds of periodic repayments of principal via a sinking fund? Are there disadvantages to the issuer?

10. It has been argued that the loss to the federal government in income taxes because of the tax-exempt status of municipal bonds is greater than the savings in interest realized by the issuing municipalities.
   a. How could this be so?
   b. What would be the overall effects of abolition of tax exemption on municipal-bond interest after a specified date in time?

11. Table 10–6 indicates relative yields required by corporate holders of bonds and preferreds to achieve levels of indifference between them with respect to after-tax return. Prove that an 8 percent preferred entitled to 70 percent exemption provides the same after-tax yield as a taxable bond yielding 11.02 percent and a tax-exempt obligation yielding 7.16 percent to an investor in the 35 percent tax bracket.

12. Mortgages are really bonds backed by real property that are retired monthly via sinking funds. Determine the current relationship between yields on long-term Aaa corporate bonds and long term fixed-rate conventional home mortgages. How do you explain the differences if any?

13. What kinds of protective covenants should a prospective bondholder look for in a bond contract?

14. What two strategies might bond investors utilize in attempting to guard against the threat of a call feature?

Problems

1. Refer to the ABC, Inc., example on page 334. What would interest coverage be if the first-mortgage and debenture bonds were considered separately—in other words, in order of risk priority?

2. The following data are for Tartan Products (tax rate = 40 percent):

YEAR	EBIT ($ IN THOUSANDS)
1995	$4,750
1994	4,500
1993	4,500
1992	4,250
1991	4,000

Debt and Preferred Capitalization (December 31, 1995)
($ in thousands)

Long-term debt:	
10% first-mortgage bonds (due 2010)	$25,000
6% debentures (due 2023)	10,000
Preferred stock:	
$1.60 cumulative first preferred	2,000
(par value $20/share)	
8% noncumulative preferred	14,000

Analyze the default risk bearing upon the bonds and preferred stock in the greatest detail possible.

3. Obtain a recent edition of Moody's *Industrial Manual.* Examine the major contractual features of the following bonds: Ford Motor Co., 9.15 percent (due 2004); and General Motors Corp. 8.875 percent (due 2003). How do you account for the fact that these two bonds of identical maturity sell at differing prices over time?

4. Kroll, Inc., earned $100 million after interest, taxes, and preferred dividends in 1995. The company had an effective tax rate of 40 percent. Its capital structure consists in part of $25 million in 8 percent debentures and $10 million in 9 percent cumulative preferred stock. Calculate pretax coverage of interest and preferred dividends for 1995.

5. The following information applies to Tennant Aerospace Inc.:

($ IN MILLIONS)

Revenues	$200
Operating expenses:	
Variable	40
Fixed	100*
6% first-mortgage bonds (2005)	$75**
10% subordinated debentures (2013)	50**
$8 preferred stock ($50 par)	80
Common equity	600

*Includes depreciation of $25 million; tax rate = .4
**Combined sinking-fund payments of $6 mil.

a. What is a the debt-service coverage for this firm?
b. How safe are the preferred-stock holders' dividends (ignore sinking-fund payments on the debt)? Explain.

6. Toni Ortez is in the 28 percent tax bracket. Two bonds are available for sale. One is a corporate bond that sells at par an carries an 8 percent coupon rate. The other bond is a municipal bond with a 5.5 percent coupon rate that also sells at par. Assuming these bonds are both of the highest quality and are very easily traded, which bond should Ortez purchase?

7. During 1986 the following yields existed:

20-year AAA-rated bond	10.30%
20-year Treasury bond	9.05%
20-year BBB-rated bond	11.31%

During 1995 the following yields existed:

20-year AAA-rated bond	9.32%
20-year Treasury bond	8.55%
20-year BBB-bond	9.93%

   a. Calculate the yield spread between the twenty-year AAA-rated bond and the twenty-year Treasury bond for 1986 and 1995.
   b. Calculate the yield spread between the twenty-year BBB-rated bond and the twenty-year AAA-rated bond for 1986 and 1995.
   c. During which year did investors have more confidence in the nation's economy? How does the yield spread indicate this?

DISCLOSURE

1. Examine the financial statements for PepsiCo, Coca-Cola, Wal-Mart, and Kmart. Determine why:
   a. Coca-Cola bonds are rated AA and PepsiCo bonds are rated A, or
   b. Wal-Mart bonds are rated AA and those of K Mart are rated only A.

2. Calculate, to the extent possible, the relevant ratios for that bondholders would use to evaluate the creditworthiness of the bonds of the Ford Motor Co. Use the latest year only.

REFERENCES

ANG, J., and K. PATEL. "Bond Rating Methods: Comparison and Validation." *Journal of Finance* (May 1975).

DIALYNAS, C. P. "Bond Yield Spreads Revisited." *Journal of Portfolio Management,* (Winter 1988).

EDERINGTON, L. H., J. B. YAWITZ, and B. E. ROBERTS. "The Information Content of Bond Ratings." *Journal of Financial Research* (Fall 1987).

FONS, J. S. "The Default Premium and Corporate Bond Experience." *Journal of Finance* (March 1987).

HAND, J. M., R. W. HOLTHAUSEN, and R. W. LEFTWICH. "The Effect of Bond Rating Agency Announcements on Bond and Stock Prices." *Journal of Finance* (June 1992).

HO, T. S. Y., and R. F. SINGER. "Bond Indenture Provisions and the Risk of Corporate Debt." *Journal of Financial Economics* (December 1982).

KALOTAY, A. J. "An Analysis of Original Issue Discount Bonds." *Financial Management* (Autumn 1984).

KALOTAY, A. J., and G. O. WILLIAMS. "The Valuation and Management of Bonds with Sinking Fund Provisions." *Financial Analysts Journal* (March–April 1992).

LIU, P., and W. T. MOORE. "The Impact of Split Bond Ratings on Risk Premia." *Financial Review* (February 1987).

LUCAS, D. J., and J. G. LONSKI. "Changes in Corporate Credit Quality, 1970–1990." *Journal of Fixed Income* (March 1992).

McADAMS, L. "How to Anticipate Utility Bond Rating Changes." *Journal of Portfolio Management* (Fall 1980).

PEAVY, J. W., III. "Bond Ratings as Risk Surrogates—How Good Are They?" *Best's Review* (April 1980).

PERRY, L. G., G. V. HENDERSON, and T. P. CRONAN. "Multivariate Analysis of Corporate Bond Ratings and Industry Classifications." *Journal of Financial Research* (Spring 1984).

SHERWOOD, H. *How Corporate and Municipal Debt Is Rated.* New York: John Wiley and Sons, 1976.

Standard & Poor's Corp. *Credit Overview: Corporate and International Ratings.* New York, 1992.

BOND
MANAGEMENT
STRATEGIES

Bond investors may adopt passive or active approaches to the management of their portfolios. The passive approach is usually identified with a buy-and-hold strategy. Active bond portfolio management involves switching and swapping bonds as circumstances change in the markets for fixed-income securities. This chapter is concerned primarily with the necessary ingredients in a successful approach to passive and active bond management.[1]

PASSIVE OR BUY-AND-HOLD STRATEGY

A buy-and-hold strategy essentially means purchasing and holding a security to maturity or redemption (e.g., by the issuer via a call provision) and then reinvesting cash proceeds in similar securities. Ongoing cash inflows—as well as outflows—are generally present via coupon income being received and reinvested. The emphasis is on minimizing assumptions about the future level and direction of interest rates. By holding securities to maturity, any capital change resulting from interest-rate change is neutralized or ignored (by holding to maturity, the par amount of the bond will be received). Portfolio return, therefore, is controlled by coupon payments and reinvestment proceeds. Although interest-rate forecasting is largely ignored, analysis is important to minimize the risk of default on the securities held.

 The passive, or buy-and-hold, strategy is used primarily by income-maximizing investors who are interested in the largest coupon income over a desired horizon. These types of investors include retired persons, endowment funds, bond mutual funds, insurance companies that are seeking the maximum yield over an extended period of time, or other large pools of money where the size of the fund and

---

[1]An excellent, definitive book on bond strategies is D. Tuttle, ed., *The Revolution in Techniques for Managing Bond Portfolios* (Charlottesville, Va.: Institute of Chartered Financial Analysts, 1983).

large cash inflow make portfolio turnover difficult because of possible market impact. The buy-and-hold strategy was justifiable for many investors because fixed-income securities were traditionally characterized as safe assets with predictable cash flows and low-price volatility. By assuming a long-term perspective, a return in excess of inflation with interest-rate risk minimized is the objective. This is a classic example of seeking less than maximum return to avoid the inherent risk associated with the highest-return strategy.

One technique for a passive strategy is an index fund. Index funds basically provide diversification along with minimum transaction costs. This is certainly a tractable notion for equities, as exemplified by S&P 500-type and other funds. For bonds, index funds take on new meaning.

The fixed-income market is much larger than the equity market in terms of both the dollar amount and number of issues outstanding. Because of this fragmentation, replication of a significant percentage of the total market capitalization can be considered a problem. However, indexes can be selected on the basis of maturity, coupon, issuing sector, quality, or combination thereof. More than sixty-five bond market sectors exist, each of which is a potential ingredient for indexing! From the variation in return for various market cycles, the correct selection of sector to index for a particular time period can indeed make a sizable difference. However, broad replication of the market is not difficult. Although more diverse than the stock market in types and number of issues, the dominance of the systematic risk component for institutional-grade fixed-income securities provides a fairly homogeneous universe from a return-risk standpoint.

Once the desired index is chosen, the next task is forming a representative portfolio. One of the key considerations in forming such a portfolio is how many bonds it takes to obtain adequate diversification. McEnally and Boardman have shown how diversification of bonds varies with portfolio size. The effect of portfolio size parallels closely the relationship found in common stock portfolios. This suggests that once an index is selected, it can be replicated with a manageable number of securities, probably fewer than forty.[2]

BOND LADDER STRATEGY

Building a bond ladder means buying bonds scheduled to come due at several different dates in the future, rather than all in the same year. For example, an investor might buy similar amounts of bonds due in one year, two years, three years, and so on out to ten years. This process is known as *laddering* because each group on bonds represents a rung on the investment maturity ladder.

When short-term rates are much lower than longer-term rates, a well-built bond ladder is likely to produce significantly higher returns than money-market funds or bank accounts. A ladder can be an especially effective tool for someone

[2]Richard W. McEnally and Calvin M. Boardman, "Aspects of Corporate Bond Portfolio Diversification," *Journal of Financial Research* (Spring 1979).

who needs large amounts of money available on certain future dates, for example, to pay for a child's education.

While laddering will not produce as much income currently as buying the highest-yielding, long-term bonds, the diversification makes it safer. Laddering has a lot of investment merit because the investor is not making one big, concentrated bet on a single maturity. For instance, a surge in interest rates would drive down the prices of long-term bonds, producing capital losses for investors who need to sell before the bonds come due. With a bond ladder, however, if rates surge, the investor will have new money to invest every year or so at higher rates. A bond ladder also provides some protection if rates fall because the investor has locked up some high yields for longer periods.

Bond laddering is a smart investment concept for conservative individuals who are unsure of interest-rate movement and are afraid to bet on any one forecast.

Laddering has its drawbacks, though. If interest rates plunge, investors would be better off owning only long-term bonds, enabling them to lock in today's yields for as many as thirty or forty years. But for investors who cannot afford to lose principal, long-term bonds represent a high-risk gamble.

Ladders also may not make sense for investors with small amounts of money, especially for municipal and corporate bonds, because the transaction costs of buying small blocks of numerous bonds can significantly slice into the investor's take-home yield. These investors would be better off with mutual funds.

Assembling a well-built ladder requires considerable care. Corporate and municipal-bond investors should remember that many bonds can be called prior to the scheduled final maturity date.

An easy way to build a ladder for many individual investors is to purchase new Treasury issues at regularly scheduled auctions. A portfolio for someone with $25,000 might look like the following:

FACE AMOUNT	ISSUE	YIELD (%)*
$5,000	2-year note	4.25
5,000	3-year note	4.65
5,000	5-year note	5.55
5,000	7-year note	5.89
5,000	10-year note	6.06

*The average yield of this ladder is 5.28 percent.

SEMIACTIVE MANAGEMENT STRATEGY: IMMUNIZATION

A major problem encountered in managing a bond portfolio is ensuring a given rate of return to satisfy an ending funds requirement at a future specific date. If the term structure of interest rates were flat and the level of market rates never changed between the time of purchase and the future specific date when the funds were required, an investor could acquire a bond with a maturity equal to a desired

investment horizon and the ending wealth from the bond purchase would equal the promised wealth position implied by the promised yield-to-maturity. Unfortunately, in the real world the term structure of interest rates is not typically flat, and the level of interest rates is constantly changing. Because of changes in the shape of the term structure and changes in the level of interest rates, the bond investor faces interest-rate risk between the time of investment and a future holding period. Interest-rate risk comprises two risks: price risk and coupon reinvestment risk. The price risk occurs because if interest rates change prior to the end of the holding point and the bond is sold prior to maturity, the market price for the bond will differ from the expected price assuming rates had not changed. If rates increased (decreased) since the time of purchase, the price received for the bond in the market would be below (above) expectations.

The coupon reinvestment risk arises because the yield-to-maturity computation implicitly assumes that all coupon flows will be reinvested at the promised yield-to-maturity. If, after you purchase a bond, interest rates decline (rise), it will not be possible to reinvest interest payments at the proposed yield-to-maturity, but they will be reinvested at lower (higher) rates and the ending sum would be below (above) what you expected.

Note that the price risk and the reinvestment risk derived from a change in interest rates have an opposite effect on the investor's ending wealth position. Specifically, an increase in the level of market interest rates will cause an ending price that is below expectations, but the reinvestment of interim cash flow will be at a rate above expectations, so this flow will be above expectations. In contrast, a decline in market interest rates will provide a higher than expected ending price, but lower than expected ending wealth from the reinvestment of interim cash flows. It is clearly important to a bond investor with a known holding period to attempt to eliminate these two risks derived from changing interest rates. Eliminating these risks from a bond portfolio is referred to as *immunization.* A portfolio of investments in bonds is immunized for a holding period if its value at the end of the holding period, regardless of the course of interest rates during the holding period, is as large as it would have been had the interest-rate function been constant throughout the holding period. If the realized return on an investment in bonds is sure to be at least as large as the appropriately computed yield to the horizon, then that investment is immunized.

Duration

Most bonds provide coupon (interest) payments in addition to a final (par) payment at maturity. Depending upon the relative magnitudes of these payments, a bond may be more or less like others with the same maturity date. A measure of the average time prior to receipt of payment is duration.[3]

---

[3]An excellent discussion of duration and its uses may be found in R. W. McEnally, "Duration as a Practical Tool for Bond Management," *Journal of Portfolio Management* (Summer 1977), pp. 53–56.

Duration is the weighted-average measure of a bond's life, where the various time periods in which the bond generates cash flows are weighted according to the relative sizes of the present value of those flows. Specifically, duration (D) is equal to:

$$D = \frac{\sum\limits_{n=1}^{N} \frac{(n)(C_n)}{(1+i)^n}}{\sum\limits_{n=1}^{N} \frac{C_n}{(1+i)^n}}$$

where N is the life of the bond in years, C is the cash receipt at the end of year n—equal to the annual coupon except for the last year, when it is equal to the annual coupon plus the maturity value—and i is the yield-to-maturity.[4] The numerator of the expression is the weighted present value of cash receipts; the denominator is the sum of all these present values, which is equal to the total present value or price of the bond. The n in parentheses in the numerator is simply the number of years from the present when the cash is received (1, 2, 3, and so on).

Table 11–1 contains an example that should make this measure considerably more comprehensible. It shows the computation of the duration of a 7 percent coupon bond (annual interest payments) with three years to maturity that is priced at par. Here the operation of the weighting scheme is fairly evident. For instance, at maturity after three years this bond is expected to pay off $1,070, which accounts for about 87.3 percent of its current value. Multiplying the three years by .873, we

TABLE 11–1

Duration of a 7 Percent Coupon, Three-Year Bond Priced at 100

(1) YEAR	(2) CASH FLOW	(3) PRESENT VALUE OF $1 AT 7%	(4) = (2) × (3) PRESENT VALUE FLOW	(5) = (4)/Σ(4) PRESENT VALUE PRICE	(6) = (1) × (5)
1	$70	.9346	$ 65.42	.065	.065
2	70	.8734	61.14	.061	.122
3	1,070	.8163	873.44	.873	2.619
Sum			$1,000.00	1.000	2.806
Price			$1,000.00		
Duration					2.81 years

$$D = \frac{(1)\dfrac{70}{1.07} + (2)\dfrac{70}{(1.07)^2} + (3)\dfrac{1070}{(1.07)^3}}{\dfrac{70}{1.07} + \dfrac{70}{(1.07)^2} + \dfrac{1070}{(1.07)^3}} = 2.81 \text{ years}$$

[4]A good discussion of the dimensions of duration appears in G. O. Bierwag, G. G. Kaufman, and A. Toevs, eds., *Innovations in Bond Portfolio Management: Duration Analysis and Immunization* (Greenwich, Conn.: JAI Press, 1983).

find that this receipt contributes approximately 2.62 years to the duration of this bond of 2.81 years.

In contrast, single-payment bonds, which sell at a discount and do not pay coupon interest, have durations that are exactly equal to their terms to maturity. For example, if the three-year bond in the illustration above did not carry coupons but promised to pay $1,000 three years from now and currently sold for $816, it would have a duration of three years, that is,

$$
D = \frac{(3)\ \dfrac{1000}{(1.07)^3}}{\dfrac{1000}{(1.07)^3}} = 3 \text{ years}
$$

Examine calculated duration in Table 11–2 for a McDonald's Corp. bond yielding 7.76 percent with varying coupons and years to maturity. Generally, duration is shorter than term-to-maturity and increases as time-to-maturity increases and the coupon on the bond or market yields decrease. The duration of a bond is bounded by $(r + p)/rp$, where r = yield-to-maturity (in decimal form, e.g., 7.76% = .0776) and p = the number of times per year interest is paid (usually twice). Thus, a 7.76 percent bond that pays interest twice each year has a duration boundary of 10.9 years, regardless of its maturity. This is calculated as:

$$
\frac{.0776 + 2.00}{(.0776)(2)} = \frac{2.0776}{.1552} = 13.4 \text{ years}
$$

Further, take an extreme example of a long, long bond with a low coupon (which should have a long duration). A 3½ percent bond due in 100 years priced to yield 6 percent to maturity has a duration of only seventeen years (2.06/.12).

Now that we know how to calculate a bond's duration, we know how much its price will change as its yield changes without needing to resort to trial-and-error experiments. Algebraically, an approximate direct relationship between the duration of a bond and its price volatility for a change in market interest rates is:

$$
\% \text{ change in price} = -MD\left(\frac{\Delta BP}{100}\right)
$$

TABLE 11–2

Duration (in Years) for Bond Yielding
7.76 Percent (Semiannual Coupons)

YEARS TO MATURITY	COUPON RATE			
	0%	8%	10%	12%
6	6	5	4.85	4.73
10	10	7.2	6.92	6.7
20	20	5.9	5.8	5.75
30	30	6.2	6.11	6.05

where:

MD = modified duration
ΔBP = change in basis points (plus or minus)

and:

$$MD = D \backslash 1 + \frac{r}{p}$$

where:

D = duration (years)
r = market yield (decimal)
p = interest payments per year (usually two)

Our McDonald's bond has a calculated duration of 4.87 years. The modified duration on these bonds is thus:

$$MD = (4.87)/(1 + .0776/2)$$

$$= 4.87/1.0388$$

$$= 4.69$$

So, suppose these bonds are yielding 7.76 percent to maturity, and rates fall by 50 basis points to 7.26 percent. The price of the bond should rise by 2.345 percent, as follows:

$$\text{Percent change in price} = -4.69 \left(-\frac{50}{100} \right)$$

$$= +2.345$$

Because the bond sells for 1093.75 to yield 7.76 percent, it will rise to 1,119.40 to yield 7.26 percent (a 2.345 percent price rise).

In this example, the price of the bond should decline (rise) by 2.345 percent for every 1 percent (100 basis points) increase (decrease) in market rates. The important point is: The longer the duration of a bond, the greater the price volatility of the bond for a given change in interest rates; that is, a direct relationship exists between duration and interest-rate risk.

This direct relationship between duration and interest-rate sensitivity is important in actively managing a bond portfolio because it is crucial to construct a bond portfolio with maximum interest-rate sensitivity during a period when the manager expects a decline in interest rates and vice versa during a period of rising interest rates. The point is that the portfolio should be constructed with the maximum or minimum duration rather than considering only term-to-maturity. Duration is a superior measure of the time structure of bond returns because of the direct relationship between duration and interest-rate sensitivity.

A bond portfolio can be immunized against interest-rate risk if one assumption can be made. The required assumption is that if the yield curve shifts, the shift is parallel (all rates change by the same amount) or a shape-preserving shift.[5]

Given this assumption, *a portfolio of bonds is immunized from the interest-rate risk if the duration of the portfolio is equal to the desired holding period.* As an example, if the desired holding period of a bond portfolio is eight years, in order to immunize the portfolio, the duration of the bond portfolio should be set equal to eight years. In order to have a portfolio with a given duration, the weighted-average duration (with weights equal to the proportion of value) is set at the desired length following an interest payment and then all subsequent cash flows are invested in securities with a duration equal to the remaining horizon value.

The two risks discussed (price risk and reinvestment rate risk) are affected differently by a change in market rates; that is, when the price change is positive, the reinvestment change will be negative, and vice versa. Duration is the time period at which the price risk and the coupon reinvestment risk of a bond portfolio are of equal magnitude but opposite in direction.

MATURITY MATCHING: THE REINVESTMENT PROBLEM

Suppose an investor wishes to lock in prevailing interest rates for a ten-year period. Then why not buy a ten-year bond? An investor will not be protected from changes in interest rates with the purchase of a ten-year bond. A reinvestment problem arises as the reinvestment of coupon income occurs at rates below the original target yield. Table 11–3 shows the components of return on a 9 percent, ten-year bond through various holding periods.

Note that as interest rates shift and remain at the new levels for a ten-year period, the total "holding period" return on a 9 percent par bond due in ten years will vary considerably. The initial effect will appear in the value of the asset. A capital gain (or loss) will appear immediately.

As the holding period increases after a change in rates, the interest-on-interest component of total return begins to exert a stronger influence. At ten years, we note that the interest on interest exerts a dominance over capital gain (or loss) in the determination of holding-period returns.

Intuitively we know that these relationships make sense. Capital gains appear instantly, whereas changes in reinvestment rates take time to exert their effect on the total holding-period return on a bond.

---

[5]Given a five-year horizon, the initial portfolio duration will be five years; after one year, the duration should be four years; and so on, until at the end of four years it will be one year. By ensuring that the portfolio duration is rebalanced to the appropriate remaining time to the horizon, the effects of nonparallel shifts in the yield curve can be mitigated.

TABLE 11–3

Total Return on 9 Percent, Ten-Year Bond
Held through Various Holding Periods

INCOME SOURCE	INTEREST RATE AT TIME OF REINVESTMENT	HOLDING PERIOD IN YEARS			
		1	3	6.79*	10
Coupon income	7%	90	270	611	900
Capital gain (loss)		132	109	56	0
Interest-on-interest		2	25	149	355
Total return		224	404	816	1,255
Total yield		22.0%	12.0%	9.0%	8.5%
Coupon income	9%	90	270	611	900
Capital gain (loss)		0	0	0	0
Interest-on-interest		2	32	205	495
Total return		92	302	816	1,395
Total yield		9.0%	9.0%	9.0%	9.0%
Coupon income	11%	90	270	611	900
Capital gain (loss)		–112	–95	–56	0
Interest-on-interest		2	40	261	647
Total return		–20	215	816	1,547
Total yield		–2.0%	6.7%	9.0%	9.8%

*Duration of 9 percent bond purchased at par due in ten years.

Understanding the forces operating on the total return of a bond, we may now ask at what point the forces of capital gain and reinvestment rate equally offset one another in a manner similar to a break-even. If rates jump from 9 to 11 percent and a capital loss occurs today, at what point will that capital loss be made up because we are reinvesting those coupon income payments in a higher (11 percent) rate environment? The two offsetting forces of capital value and reinvestment return equally offset at the duration of the bond—in this case at 6.79 years. In order to earn the original 9 percent target return (the original yield-to-maturity at the time of purchase) in this example, the bond must be held for the period of its duration—6.79 years. If we wanted to lock in a market rate of 9 percent for a ten-year period, we would select a bond with a duration of ten years (not a maturity of ten years). The maturity for such a par bond in this yield environment is roughly twenty-three years.

From Table 11–3 we note that regardless of the interest-rate fluctuations (in the table they fluctuate from 7 to 11 percent), we are still able to earn the 9 percent total return if our holding period is 6.79 years—the duration of the bond.

Similarly, in order to control the interest-rate risk of a portfolio of bonds, we must monitor the duration of the portfolio so that the duration of the portfolio always stays on that point of break-even. Regardless of how rates fluctuate, we are able to lock in rates and effectively eliminate the reinvestment risk that is associated with the maturity-matching strategy.

Finally, the duration of a portfolio will not move in lockstep with the passage of time. Therefore, we must monitor and adjust the "duration wandering" that takes place by rebalancing the portfolio on an annual or as-needed basis. To illustrate, suppose the remaining life in the planning period has declined by a year—from ten years to nine years. The duration of that bond may have declined by less than a year—to, say, 9.2 years.

In order to neutralize the harmful effects of this tendency, we should rebalance the portfolio in order to match the duration of the portfolio with the remaining time in the planning period. Left unchecked, duration wandering will affect the performance of a portfolio. By monitoring and adjusting the portfolio's duration, we remain immunized in the face of multiple shifts in interest rates and eliminate in the process the so-called reinvestment problem.

An example of how a bond with a duration of 6.79 years is immunized against changes in interest rate risk is presented in Table 11-3.

For example, the total return is $404 and the total yield is 12 percent if rates are 7 percent and the bond is held for only three years, calculated as follows (see box):

Coupon income plus interest-on-interest	$45 \times$ future value of annuity of $1 for 6 periods at 3.5% per period. $45 \times 6.55 = 295$
Capital gain	Price of 9% bond due in 7 years in a 7% market = 1,109 Gain = 1,109 − 1,000 = 109

The total return is $1,000 + 404$, or $1,404$. Over a three-year period this amounts to 12 percent (yield) compounded per period.

Example of Immunization

An example of the effect of attempting to immunize by matching the holding period and the duration of a bond is contained in Table 11–4. It is assumed that the holding period is eight years and the current yield-to-maturity for eight-year bonds is 8 percent. Therefore, the ending wealth ratio the investor requires should be 1.8509 $[(1.08)^8]$. For example, assume that the parents of a ten-year-old plan to enroll her in college in eight years. Given the rate of inflation in college costs, they expect they will need to accumulate $18,500 at the end of eight years. Assume that they have $10,000 to invest now. They must earn 8 percent per annum to have $10,000 grow to $18,500 in eight years $[\$10,000(1.08)^8]$. The ratio of initial to ending wealth is 1.8509. This should be the ending wealth ratio for an immunized portfolio. The example considers two portfolio strategies. The first is a maturity strategy where the term-to-maturity is set at eight years. The other is a duration strategy where the duration is set at eight years. For the maturity strategy we assume that

TABLE 11–4

Maturity Strategy vs. Duration Strategy

YEAR	MATURITY STRATEGY			DURATION STRATEGY		
	CASH FLOW	REINVEST-MENT RATE	ACCUMULATED END VALUE	CASH FLOW	REINVEST-MENT RATE	ACCUMULATED END VALUE
1	$80	.08	$80.00	$80	.08	$80.00
2	80	.08	166.40	80	.08	166.40
3	80	.08	259.71	80	.08	259.71
4	80	.08	360.49	80	.08	360.49
5	80	.06	462.12	80	.06	462.12
6	80	.06	596.85	80	.06	596.85
7	80	.06	684.04	80	.06	684.04
8	1,080	.06	1,805.08	80	.06	1,845.72
				1,040.64*		

Expected wealth ratio = 1.8509

*The bond could be sold for a market value of $1,040.64. This is the value of an 8 percent bond with two years to maturity priced to yield 6 percent.

the portfolio manager acquires an eight-year, 8 percent bond. In contrast, for the duration strategy we assume the portfolio manager acquires a ten-year, 8 percent bond that has approximately an eight-year duration (actually 8.12 years), assuming an 8 percent yield-to-maturity. For purposes of the example we assume that there is a single change in the interest-rate structure at the end of year 4 and the market yield goes from 8 percent to 6 percent and remains at 6 percent through year 8.

As shown in the example, because of the interest-rate change, the wealth ratio for the maturity strategy bond is below the desired wealth ratio because of the shortfall in the reinvestment cash flow after year 4 (i.e., the interim coupon cash flow is reinvested at 6 percent rather than 8 percent). Note that the maturity strategy eliminated the price risk because the bond matured at the end of year 8. Alternatively, the duration portfolio likewise suffered a shortfall in reinvestment cash flow because of the change in market rates. Notably, this shortfall due to the reinvestment risk is offset by an increase in ending value for the bond due to the decline in market rates (i.e., the bond is sold at 104.06 because it is an 8 percent coupon bond with two years to maturity selling to yield 6 percent).

Note that if market interest rates increased during this period, the maturity strategy portfolio would have experienced an excess of reinvestment income compared to the expected cash flow, and the wealth ratio would have been above expectations. In contrast, in the duration portfolio any reinvestment cash flow excess would have been offset by a decline in the ending price for the bond. While under the latter assumptions the maturity strategy would have provided a higher than expected ending value, the whole purpose of immunization was to eliminate uncertainty, which is what is accomplished with the duration strategy.

Duration can be used as a passive or an active strategy. That is, passively it is useful in neutralizing interest-rate risk; actively, it can be employed to capitalize on

interest-rate risk. The latter use would mean that as interest rates are expected to change, an investor would seek out bonds with long durations or short durations depending upon whether the forecast is for falling or rising interest rates.

Rebalancing an Immunized Portfolio

In our illustrations of the principles underlying immunization, we assume a one-time instantaneous change in the market yield. In practice, the market yield will fluctuate over the investment horizon. As a result, the duration of the portfolio will change as the market yield changes. In addition, the duration will change simply because of the passage of time.

Even in the face of changing market yields a portfolio can be immunized if it is rebalanced so that its duration is equal to the remaining time of the investment horizon. For example, if the investment horizon is initially 5.5 years, the initial portfolio should have a duration of 5.5 years. After six months the investment horizon will be five years, but the duration of the portfolio will probably be different from five years. Thus, the portfolio must be rebalanced so that its duration is equal to five. Six months later the portfolio must be rebalanced again so that its duration will equal 4.5 years, and so on.

How often should the portfolio be rebalanced to adjust its duration? On the one hand, more frequent rebalancing increases transaction costs, thereby reducing the likelihood of achieving the target yield. On the other hand, less frequent rebalancing will result in the duration wandering from the target duration, which will also reduce the likelihood of achieving the target yield. Thus, the investor faces a trade-off: Some transaction costs must be accepted to prevent the duration from wandering too far from its target, but some maladjustment in the duration must be endured or transaction costs will become prohibitively high.

IMMUNIZATION RISK

The sufficient condition for immunization is that the duration of the portfolio be equal to the length of the investment horizon. However, a portfolio will be immunized against interest-rate changes only if the yield curve is flat and any changes in the yield curve are parallel changes (i.e., interest rates move either up or down by the same number of basis points for all maturities). Recall that duration is a measure of price volatility for parallel shifts in the yield curve. If a change in interest rates does not correspond to this shape-preserving shift, matching the duration to the investment horizon will not ensure immunization; that is, the target yield will no longer be the minimum realized yield for the portfolio.

Empirical studies of the effectiveness of immunization strategies based on duration clearly demonstrate that immunization does not work perfectly in the real world. In the first study of immunization, Fisher and Weil found that the duration-based immunization strategy would have come closer to the target yield or exceeded it more often than a strategy based on matching the maturity of the

portfolio to the investment horizon even after considering transaction costs.[6] Studies by Bierwag, Kaufman, Schweitzer, and Toevs,[7] Hackett,[8] Lau,[9] and Leibowitz and Weinberger[10] all support the theory that a duration-matched portfolio will outperform a maturity-matched portfolio. Yet, contrary to what immunization theory would lead us to expect, a common finding was that when a duration-matched strategy was employed, the realized yield was frequently below the target yield. As for the magnitude of the divergence, Leibowitz and Weinberger found that for five-year investment horizons, the realized yield did not fall below the target yield by more than 25 basis points.

The divergence of the realized yield from the target yield is due to the assumption that the yield curve is flat and changes only in a parallel fashion. Several researchers have relaxed this assumption and developed measures of duration based on a yield curve that is not flat and does not shift in a parallel fashion.

Bierwag, Kaufman, Schweitzer, and Toevs empirically examined how duration strategies based on more complex duration measures assuming different yield curve shifts would perform compared to Macaulay duration. They concluded that duration immunized almost as well as the more complex (duration) strategies and appear to be the most cost effective.[11] Lau reached the same conclusion: duration is just about as effective as the more complex duration measures.

SEMIACTIVE MANAGEMENT STRATEGY: DEDICATION

The difference between an immunized portfolio and a dedicated portfolio is that the former is a single-period strategy, whereas the latter is a multiperiod strategy. *Dedication* is concerned with financing a stream of liabilities over time. The purpose of dedication is to fund a sequence of liability payments as they come due with no interest-rate risk. The easiest way to accomplish this is by cash-matching.

Cash-matching involves four steps. First, the liability payments stream is determined. Next, the bond universe is selected according to quality criteria. Third, investor objectives and constraints are identified. Finally, the optimal portfolio is chosen. If structured properly, the portfolio would cash itself out in the sense that between every two successive liability payments, the cash flow from principal payments and coupon receipts, plus any accrued interest from a prior balance, would

---

[6]Lawrence Fisher and Roman L. Weil, "Coping with the Risk of Interest Rate Fluctuations: Returns to Bondholders from Naive and Optimal Strategies," *Journal of Business* (October 1971), pp. 408–31.

[7]G. O. Bierwag et al., "The Art of Risk Management in Bond Portfolios," *Journal of Portfolio Management* (Spring 1981), pp. 27–36.

[8]T. Hackett, "A Simulation Analysis of Immunization Strategies Applied to Bond Portfolios," unpublished doctoral dissertation, University of Oregon, 1981.

[9]Patrick W. Lau, "An Empirical Examination of Alternative Interest Rate Immunization Strategies," unpublished doctoral dissertation, University of Wisconsin—Madison, 1983).

[10]Martin L. Leibowitz and Alfred Weinberger, "Contingent Immunization—Part II: Problem Areas," *Financial Analysts Journal* (January–February 1983), pp. 35–50.

[11]Bierwag et al., "Art of Risk Management," p. 33.

be sufficient to cover the next liability payment. Liability-payment time intervals must be clearly laid out, and the portfolio must be structured to avoid call risk. A very conservative reinvestment rate is normally assumed.

Cash-matching can be described as follows. A bond is selected with a maturity that matches the last liability. An amount of principal equal to the amount of the last liability is then invested in this bond. The remaining elements of the liability stream are then reduced by the coupon payments on this bond, and another bond is chosen for the new, reduced amount of the next-to-last liability. Going backward in time, this is continued until all liabilities have been matched by the payments on the securities in the portfolio.

Table 11–5 displays a portfolio chosen to match a sequence of liability payments shown in the second-to-last column of Table 11–6. Table 11–6 provides a cash-flow analysis of sources and applications of funds. The last column in the table shows the excess funds remaining at each time period that are reinvested at the assumed 6 percent reinvestment rate supplied by the user.

For example, assume the liability due in 2018 is at year-end. To achieve the amount of 1,356, we rely upon the maturity value of bond O (1,228), shown in Table 11–5, which comes due on May 1. In addition, this bond pays one-half of its coupon income at that point (150/2). Further, the reinvestment of the principal and coupon (1,228 + 75) for eight months or two-thirds of a year at 6 percent per annum yields an added cash flow of 53 [(1,228 + 75)(.06 × .66)].

TABLE 11–5

Bond Portfolio for Cash Matching (December 31, 1994)

BOND	COUPON	MATURITY	PAR VALUE ($000)	PRICE (% PAR)	TOTAL COUPON PAYMENTS*
A	0.000%[†]	1/01/95	$517	100.00	
B	7.850%	8/27/97	$233	86.00	18.29
C	9.620%	8/15/98	$1,199	88.13	115.34
D	8.375%	12/31/99	$1,215	75.50	101.76
E	7.600%	4/20/00	$2,353	75.63	178.83
F	15.350%	5/01/02	$2,474	94.75	379.76
G	14.700%	7/22/03	$4,080	100.00	599.76
H	10.125%	11/15/07	$1,382	77.44	139.93
I	11.500%	11/15/09	$6,021	84.94	692.42
J	8.750%	11/01/12	$1,402	61.13	122.68
K	8.875%	10/15/13	$1,357	63.75	120.43
L	13.375%	8/15/14	$1,294	95.34	173.07
M	8.375%	4/01/15	$2,649	58.50	221.85
N	9.400%	7/15/17	$1,206	59.88	113.36
O	12.250%	5/01/18	$1,228	76.00	150.43
				Total	3127.91

*(Coupon)(par value).
[†]Cash.

TABLE 11-6

Cash-Flow Analysis for Cash-Flow Matching (Reinvestment Rate = 6%)

DATE [YEAR-END]	PRIOR CASH BALANCE	PLUS: INTEREST ON BALANCE	PLUS: PRINCIPAL PAYMENTS	PLUS: COUPON PAYMENTS	PLUS: REINVESTMENT OF PAYMENTS	LESS: LIABILITY DUE	EQUALS: NEW CASH BALANCE
1995			517	3,128	125	3,770	
1996				3,128	93	3,104	117
1997	117	7	233	3,128	98	3,583	
1998			1,199	3,110	120	4,429	
1999			1,215	2,994	88	4,297	
2000			2,353	2,803	185	4,170	1171
2001	1,171	71		2,714	82	4,038	
2002			2,474	2,524	180	3,900	1278
2003	1,278	78		2,334	72	3,762	
2004			4,080	2,334	181	3,624	2971
2005	2,971	181		1,734	47	3,473	1460
2006	1,460	89		1,734	47	3,330	
2007			1,382	1,734	57	3,173	
2008			6,021	1,594	89	3,012	4692
2009	4,692	286		902	28	2,849	3059
2010	3,059	186		902	28	2,682	1493
2011	1,493	91		902	28	2,514	
2012			1,402	902	42	2,346	
2013			1,357	779	42	2,178	
2014			1,294	659	51	2,004	
2015			2,649	375	134	1,837	1321
2016	1,321	80		264	9	1,674	
2017			1,206	264	42	1,512	
2018			1,228	75	53	1,356	

To the extent such matching is possible, it would indeed produce a portfolio similar to an immunized portfolio because interest-rate changes would not affect a portfolio whose payments match exactly in timing and amount the liabilities to be paid. However, given typical liability schedules and bonds available for cash-flow matching, perfect matching is unlikely.

DEDICATION WITH ZEROS

The easiest example to illustrate dedication is the use of noncoupon-bearing bonds ("zeros" or STRIPS using Treasury instruments) Assume Dick Smith is age seventy-five. He has decided to retire having worked well beyond the normal retirement age. He and his wife (also seventy-five) want to use STRIP (noninterest bearing) Treasury bonds to fund their predicted living costs for the next ten years. Their estimated pretax living costs are shown below. The numbers reflect a 4 percent annual cost-of-living adjustment and extra outlays in year 2 for a major gift to their alma mater and in year 5 for an around-the-world cruise.

YEAR	ESTIMATED LIVING COSTS ($ IN THOUSANDS)	PRICE OF BONDS	DOLLARS REQUIRED TODAY ($ IN THOUSANDS)
1	$40.0	96-24	$38.7
2	61.6	92-16	57.0
3	45.0	87-22	39.4
4	46.8	77-26	36.4
5	68.7	73-04	50.2
6	50.7	68-16	34.7
7	52.6	64-07	33.8
8	54.8	59-23	32.7
9	57.0	55-22	31.7
10	59.3	51-19	30.6
Total	$536.5		$385.4

The prices of the bonds are in thirty-seconds (e.g., 31-2 is 31.0625 per thousand dollar par value). The dollars required today is simply the price per bond (in decimal form) multiplied by the estimated living costs (e.g., 96-24 = .9675). Hence, the Smith's need $385,400 to establish a dedicated portfolio using zero-coupon Treasury instruments.

PRESSURES FOR ACTIVE BOND MANAGEMENT

There is widespread active, or decision-oriented, management of fixed-income securities. Bond investors have made these investments a viable alternative to equities. For the passive buy-and-hold investor, the investment horizon is long and the emphasis is on ensuring a steady stream of income. In contrast, actively managed

portfolios typically have a shorter time horizon, varying from a few days to a year or so. Major emphasis is focused upon price appreciation.

The growing interest in active bond management was launched by the increased volatility of interest rates. We passed from a long period of relatively stable rates in this country to more recent experience with interest rate structures that often changed quickly and even violently. For example, between 1961 and 1966 interest rates on AA utility bonds fluctuated between 4.2 and 5.7 percent—a range of only 150 basis points. In contrast, between 1971 and 1976 this fluctuation was a range of 325 basis points. What this means, of course, is that this increased volatility brings both greater opportunities as well as risks in managing fixed-income portfolios.

INGREDIENTS IN ACTIVE BOND MANAGEMENT

Incremental returns to bond portfolio management derive essentially from correctly positioning the portfolio's maturity structure, coupon, and quality to benefit from changes in the general level of interest rates. This positioning calls for major strategy decisions or judgments regarding market rates and the shape of the yield curve.

A second source of incremental return results from weighing the bond portfolio in the more favorably situated bond sectors (Treasuries, corporates, utilities, municipals). The third source involves substitutions where similar bonds are substituted for one another when their yields get out of line. Sector and substitution switching or swapping are more tactical in nature because they may be made independent of interest-rate forecast strategies and depend upon opportunities available only briefly.

Active Strategies: Rate Anticipation

Switching bonds based upon rate forecasting can be the most productive bond portfolio action. It is also the riskiest. The types of portfolio decisions required fall roughly into four categories: maturity, quality, coupon, and sector. Of these, maturity is probably most important.

MATURITY

Interest-rate expectations are an important guideline for maturity selection. Maturities should be lengthened when interest rates are expected to fall and prices to rise, and maturities should be shortened when interest rates are expected to rise.

This general rule is, however, an oversimplification because portfolio moves must be made with a view to total return, including coupon income, reinvestment rates, and price and volatility. Assumptions about the length and amplitude of bond price cycles are important. For example, if only a modest and gradual increase in interest rates were expected, accompanied by a flattening of the yield curve, a higher total return might be derived from holding longer-term bonds. As

another example, in the higher-yield ranges, price volatility of bonds with maturities of more than one or two years is very large and relatively larger for medium-maturity bonds. Consequently, an investor sensitive to cyclical fluctuations in bond prices might be better off shifting from long bonds to cash equivalents or very short bonds rather than shifting to medium maturities if he expects interest rates to rise.

The maturity structure of a bond portfolio depends heavily upon cyclical forecasts of interest rates if an investor is going to engage in active bond portfolio management. Such forecasts should consider expected interest rates for various maturities and also the expected slope of the yield curve. Moreover, such forecasts should be reviewed frequently because expected interest rates may change significantly due to changing economic expectations, Federal Reserve Board policy, and international considerations.

SECTOR

Sector transactions attempt to increase total return by anticipating changes in yield differentials between different categories of bonds, such as governments, industrials, utilities, and the like. These relationships change because of factors such as the relative supply of new issues and the outlook for specific areas of the economy. For example, the economic effects of inflation have caused general widening of yield differentials between utility bonds and many other sectors in the past several years. However, improvement in utilities' ability to cope with inflation through a more understanding regulatory environment and reduced requirements for new construction may affect their outlook favorably and cause yield differentials to narrow.

Assume that the yield spread was 25 basis points between AAA industrials versus governments; if this spread were expected to widen, the trader would swap from the industrials to the governments now, and then back to the industrials when the wider spread had occurred. During the widening of the spread, the prices of the industrials would decline relative to the governments, thereby providing a price gain via the swapping. How does one forecast such changes in the spreads? The most common forecasting method is to observe historical yield spreads at various points in the interest-rate cycle and then to adjust for current supply-and-demand effects.

QUALITY

Quality diversification is another important consideration in constructing a bond portfolio. Ratings by Moody's and Standard & Poor's help the investor differentiate between the quality of bonds, based on the ability of the borrower to pay interest and principal promptly when due. Uncritical acceptance of bond ratings is not advisable, however; these ratings have a tendency to lag behind changes in the financial characteristics of a company. Therefore, good bond research into the economic forces affecting an industry or a company as well as its financial position often can anticipate changes in credit quality and bond ratings, thereby providing investment opportunities. Even though a rating may not be changed, identifying companies near the upper or lower limits of a particular quality range can prove rewarding.

Generally, as the quality of a bond lessens, the interest rate that the issuing company must pay to its lenders increases. Because yield spreads between different-quality bonds generally narrow during an economic recovery and widen during an economic contraction, high-quality bonds should be purchased when the economy is expected to contract and lower-quality bonds acquired when an economic expansion is expected.

However, high-grade bonds have tended to lead market turns. As prices of high-grade bonds begin to decline, investors who have an income requirement continue to purchase and thus support the prices of medium-grade issues. As a result, the peak in prices of medium-grade issues often is later in the market cycle than is the peak for high-grade issues. When investors do perceive a drop in bond prices of some duration and magnitude, prices of medium-grade bonds decline rapidly. At the trough of the bond price cycle, an upturn in prices of high-grade bonds precedes an increase in the prices of medium-grade bonds. Knowledge of these characteristics, coupled with good interest-rate forecasts, can enhance the profitability of quality diversification as a bond management technique.

COUPON

Because of the downtrend and the wide fluctuations in bond prices during the past decade or so and the heavy volume of new issues, investors now have a wide selection of bonds with varying coupons. The investor may select from high-coupon bonds, ordinarily selling at a premium above par, current-coupon issues at or about par, and low-coupon issues selling at discounts. High-coupon bonds trading at or above their redemption price are often called *cushion* bonds. Although their potential for further price appreciation is restricted regardless of further declines in long-term interest rates, in a subsequent period of rising interest rates the high coupon provides a cushion against significant price declines. Yield and price relationships between bonds of different coupons change because of factors such as the supply of new issues, sinking-fund activity, call features, dealer carrying costs, and the general level and expected trend of interest rates.

Selecting the appropriate coupon for an investor can be a somewhat complex matter, depending upon the investment objectives previously established. The tax status of the investor is important; the investment return of a discount bond is higher for a taxpayer because capital gains taxes are postponed until the bond is paid at par at maturity. For a nontaxpayer (e.g., a corporate pension fund) the total return is a more important consideration. Consequently, selection of the appropriate issue would be influenced by the need for current income, the sensitivity to interim price fluctuations, and interest-rate expectations. For example, an investor seeking maximum income who is indifferent to price fluctuations ordinarily would select the high-coupon bond. The investor seeking maximum total return would be influenced by expectations for future interest rates. If an investor expects interest rates to rise, but prefers to maintain a position in long-term bonds, high-coupon issues would be his first choice; if he expects interest rates to fall, the discount bonds would be preferable. Again the significance of interest-rate expectations in portfo-

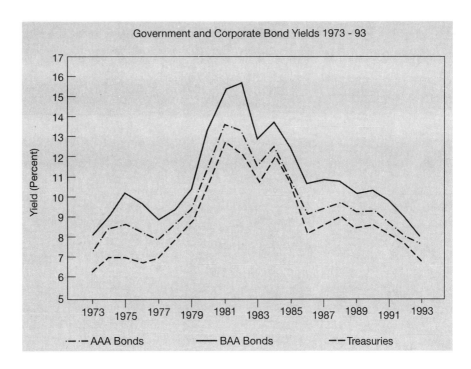

FIGURE 11-1   Government and Corporate Bond Yields 1973 - 1993

lio adjustments should be emphasized. These expectations involve not only identifying peaks and troughs but also the magnitude of the expected changes. The latter factor is important in selecting the appropriate coupon issue. For example, an interest-rate decline to a level below the trough of the previous interest-rate cycle can produce greater total returns from discount bonds than from high-coupon bonds because price appreciation of the high-coupon bond would be limited by its redemption characteristics.

QUALITY-SECTOR PREMIUMS

Figure 11–1 displays the level of interest rates on Treasury bonds and corporate Aaa and Baa bonds between 1973 and 1993. Recessions occurred between early 1980 and late 1982 and again in 1990. From late 1982 to late 1989 an unprecedented economic expansion was in progress. Note the rising level of interest rates between 1973 and 1982 and the dips in rates at the onset of each recession period.

At the same time, peaks and troughs in quality *spreads* (difference in available yield between securities with similar maturities but different quality) closely parallel related business conditions.

Troughs in quality spreads tend to occur just as a business expansion ends or a recession begins (spreads are narrowest). Spreads narrow when bankruptcies fall to a relatively low level. A period of rising prosperity tends to dull the edge of

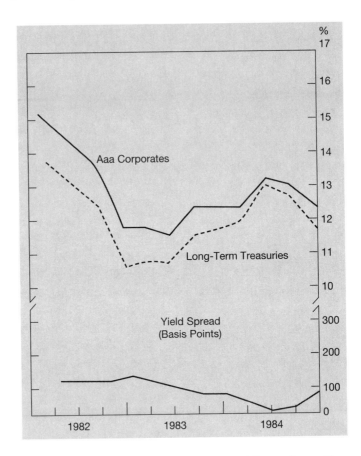

FIGURE 11–2   Yield Spreads Between Corporate and Treasury Sectors (*Source:* Moody's Investors Service, New York, N.Y. *Moody's Bond Survey* (January 21, 1985).

credit reviews as investors begin to believe they have little to fear from lending to virtually any borrower.

However, within less than a year of business recession, this sanguine view of lending abruptly reverses. Quality spreads often double within three months of a recession.

The performance of a bond portfolio can also be improved through identification of yield spreads that are out of line with historical spreads in comparable market conditions. But historical perspective indicates very strongly that yield spreads between bonds of comparable maturity are nothing more than risk premiums primarily reflecting the consensus view of future economic activity, inflation, and the general level of interest rates. Interest-rate judgments thus necessarily affect construction of the portfolio's invested position.

In Figures 11–2 and 11–3 we illustrate yield spreads between the corporate and Treasury sectors and the Aaa- and Baa-quality ratings for corporates between 1982 and late 1984. Note that from late 1983 until early 1983 the Treasury-Aaa corporate sector spread narrowed. This was caused in large part by an unusually heavy

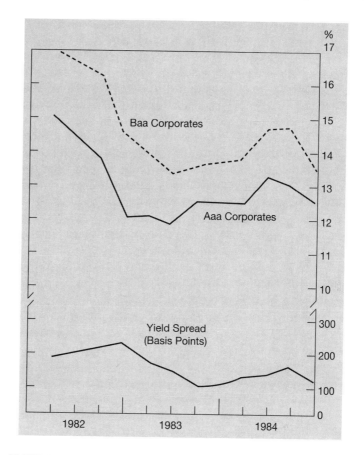

FIGURE 11–3   Yield Spreads between Aaa and Baa Corporate Ratings (*Source:* Moody's Investors Service, New York, N.Y. *Moody's Bond Survey* (January 21, 1985).

supply of Treasury securities made available to finance the burgeoning federal deficit. In fact, the spread narrowed to about 24 basis points, whereas in stable market conditions a 50-basis-point spread is usually seen.

In contrast, the gap between Baa and Aaa corporate yields continued a downtrend that started in the second half of 1982, when Aaa bonds were commanding a 250-basis-point spread over Baa corporates. This suggests that, as the economy expanded, there was a willingness by investors to seek maximum returns at some sacrifice of quality.

Sector swapping involves continually studying yield-spread relationships among different sectors in the market. When an investor detects what appears to be a transient aberration, he can dig deeper into the fundamental sources of this aberration. Market experience, widespread daily contacts, knowledge, and insights into market forces are critical. This can put one in a position to make the key judgments as to whether the existing sector relationship is, in fact, a transient aberration that will revert to more normal levels over time, or whether it is the first signal of a new trend and a new market structure.

An example of a sector-swap situation occurred when the yield on a new instrument, Government National Mortgage Association (GNMA) certificates, rose to unprecedented levels relative to both corporate and other issues. If one searches behind the statistics, the underlying cause is easily be traced to a drying up of new investable funds among thrift institutions. These had been the primary buyers of the then relatively new instrument. Because of their apparent complexity relative to straight bonds, the certificates had not yet established a wide following among pension fund managers. However, at the extraordinary attractive yields that then prevailed (and the even more attractive probable cash-flow yields), it was fairly likely that some major pension fund managers would soon overcome their initial problems with analysts and accounting for the new certificates. In fact, this is what occurred. The investor who moved quickly into GNMA certificates reaped considerable rewards as the spread relative to corporates narrowed by more than 75 basis points in the course of the next six months. The GNMA example illustrates a "new vehicle" type of sector swap. If an investor recognizes the value in a newly introduced sector, he may then reap sizable rewards as the sector becomes increasingly accepted by the market at large.

Active Strategies: Yield-Curve Anticipation

The preceding discussion placed the primary emphasis on effective rate anticipation. The Treasury yield curve on September 1, 1974, and March 1, 1975, is presented in Figure 11–4. Over this six-month period, rates not only declined, but the yield curve moved down from an inverted shape to a mildly positive shape. This effect resulted in intermediate maturities undergoing a much greater downward movement in yield than the longs. For example, the five-year maturity declined by 170 basis points, almost two and one-half times greater than the 68-basis-point improvement at thirty years. Moreover, an investment in the five-year maturity on September 1, 1974, would have moved to a 4½-year maturity over the six-month holding period, thus adding some improvement. The combination of these factors further yield improvement and shows the total return performance of the five-year investment came very close to that of the long end over this particular period.

This example indicates that the downward movement from a peaking inverted curve can lead to attractive returns from intermediate maturities. One should also note that in deteriorating markets, there can also be an upward movement effect with the result that intermediates perform worse than longs. This can hurt investors who believe that intermediates offer reduced price volatility relative to longs. On average, the intermediates, probably do have less price volatility than longs. However, strongly inverted or strongly positive yield-curve shapes are not reflective of average conditions.

A good example of the upward movement occurred in the course of 1978, when the Treasury yield curve changed significantly in both level and shape (see Figure 11–5). The change in the level of rates over 1978 ranged from approximately +100 basis points in thirty-year maturities to more than +350 basis points at the one-year point. These yield changes reshaped the yield curve.

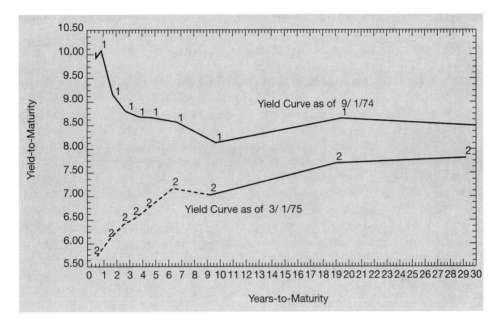

FIGURE 11–4   Historical Yield Curves

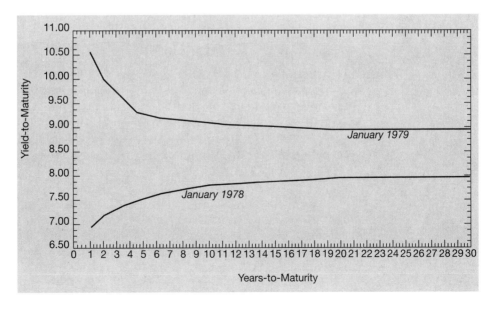

FIGURE 11–5   Yield Curves at Beginning and End of 1978

The moderately positive shape at the beginning of 1978 turned into a strongly inverted shape at year-end. One measure of this shape change is the spread of thirty-year over one-year rates. This spread began the year at about +100 basis points and ended at more than −150 basis points.

The prospects of yield-curve reshaping can add an important refinement and balance to the rate-anticipation process. For example, suppose an investor with a defensive short-term posture anticipates that the long market rates are approaching a peak. He must then determine the correct time to begin deploying at least a portion of his short-term reserves. This action may be based either on the definite belief that the peak level of rates is actually at hand or simply as a counterbalance to his uncertainty as to when and how that peak will occur. In any case once the decision has been made to commit some reserves, then the second decision must be to select the most appropriate maturity sector. If the investor believes that a good prospect exists for lower rates to be accompanied by a drop in the yield curve, then intermediate maturities should be explored as an interesting reentry vehicle on a risk-reward basis. If rates improve and the yield curve does move down to a more positive shape, then the right intermediate maturities can provide returns that are comparable to the long-term market. On the other hand, if long rates continue to rise (without a significant increase in the degree of inversion), then the shorter maturity of the intermediates will provide a certain protection against the full deterioration that would be experienced in the long market.

Finding the best distribution of maturities to take advantage of yield-curve reshaping is no simple matter. In many instances, the proper balance of return may be available only with a rather narrow range of maturities.

Active Strategies:
Mapping Expected Returns

If today's yields reflect all information about supply and demand, then an investor who buys a bond would expect his total return to reflect today's yield curve. Thus, total return would be equal to coupon income (C), amortization of premium or discount (A) and repricing because of a higher or lower yield to maturity on the yield curve as the bond ages (roll or R). Because coupon income (C) and amortization (A) are the components of yield-to-maturity (YTM), then:

$$\text{Total return} = \text{YTM} + \text{roll} = C + A + R$$

For example, from Figure 11–6(a) assume that a thirty-year bond has a yield-to-maturity of 8.5 percent at the beginning of the period with 8.4 percent expected three months later. If the bond had an 8 percent coupon, then over a horizon of one quarter:

Beginning price at 8.5% for 30 years = 94.60%

Ending price at 8.5% for 29.75 years = 94.59%

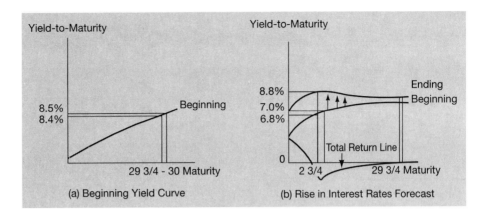

FIGURE 11–6   Yield Curve

$$\text{Ending price at 8.4\% for 29.75 years} = 95.63\%$$

$$\text{8\% coupon payment accrued} \qquad = 2.00\%$$

Thus,

$$C = \frac{\text{Coupon earned}}{\text{Beginning price}} = \frac{2.00}{94.60} = .0211$$

$$A = \frac{\text{Price change on level yield curve}}{\text{Beginning price}} = -\frac{.01}{94.60} = -.0001$$

$$R = \frac{\text{Price change due to slope}}{\text{Beginning price}} = \frac{1.03}{94.60} = .0110$$

so that the total return is

$$\text{Total return} = .0211 - .0001 + .0110 = 3.20\%$$

We know from our earlier discussions of bond price volatility that long-maturity, low-coupon bonds are the most volatile. Knowledge of these facts plus a forecast of interest rates (I) is the basis for a strategy of interest-rate anticipation. Assume that you forecast a rise in interest rates, as shown in the top two curves of Figure 11–7(b). Further, let us assume that you make a comparison between the previously considered thirty-year, 8 percent bond versus a three-year, 8 percent bond. Thus, the total return of each bond can now be viewed as:

$$\overbrace{}^{\text{Expected}} \overbrace{}^{\text{Forecast}}$$
$$\text{Total return} = C + A + R + I$$

where I for the three-year bond, for example, was calculated as $(98.06 - 102.95) \div 102.66$.

	3-YEAR	30-YEAR
Beginning yield (maturity 3, 30)	7.0	8.5
Beginning yield (maturity 2¾, 29¾)	6.8	8.4
Ending yield (maturity 2¾, 29¾)	8.8	8.7
Beginning prices	102.66	94.60
Ending prices (7.0%, 8.5%)	102.45	94.59
Ending prices (6.8%, 9.4%)	102.95	95.63
Ending prices (8.8%, 8.7%)	98.06	92.57
8% coupon payment accrued	2.00	2.00

Then,

$$C = \frac{\text{Coupon earned}}{\text{Beginning price}} = \qquad .0195 \qquad .0211$$

$$A = \frac{\text{Price change on level curve}}{\text{Beginning price}} = \qquad -.0020 \qquad -.0001$$

$$R = \frac{\text{Price change due to slope}}{\text{Beginning price}} = \qquad .0048 \qquad .0110$$

$$I = \frac{\text{Price change due to interest shift}}{\text{Beginning price}} = \qquad -.0476 \qquad -.0323$$

$$\text{Total return} = \frac{\text{Price change and coupon}}{\text{Beginning price}} = \qquad -.0253 \qquad -.0003$$

Using the previous forecast, it would be preferable to stick with the thirty-year relative to the three-year bond. This is because, although you are forecasting a rise in interest rates, the shape of the curve is forecasted to change such that intermediate maturities will be hurt more than long-term bonds. How much you shift toward the thirty-year maturity range would depend upon your confidence about your forecast, as well as the degree of risk aversion you have for incorrect forecasts.

In our discussion of rate anticipation and appropriate responses, remember that an analyst's anticipations may be already built into bond prices. For example, in large interest-rate declines, evidence shows low-coupon bonds do not experience the largest price gains. Perhaps this is accounted for by the fact that such moves are anticipated by the market generally, and that the prices of the deep-discount bonds are bid up in advance of the move. Ideally, the analyst should make forecasts of future rates and then see how the returns from specific coupon-maturity combinations behave under these anticipations given current prices.

Active Tactics: Swapping[12]

Bond substitution (swapping) is done to take advantage of temporary aberrations in the bond market due to supply and demand factors, such as long- or short-dealer positions and purchases to satisfy sinking-fund requirements. Such

[12]For a complete analysis of swaps, see M. L. Liebowitz, "How Swaps Can Pay Off," *Institutional Investor* (August 1973).

swaps may result in exchanging bonds of similar quality, sector, coupon, and maturity at relatively favorable levels. These changes are made independent of interest-rate forecasts and depend upon opportunities ordinarily available only briefly.

The expected return from any swap is usually based upon several motives, not just one; thus, swaps are really just sources of return.

YIELD PICKUP SWAP

A yield pickup swap involves the replacement of one security by another offering a higher yield but similar in all other aspects such as quality and maturity. As the name implies, the objective is to increase the total return over the life of the security.

One of the simplest and most fundamental types of swaps involves the sale of a fixed-income security and the purchase of a lower-priced security of the same or a very similar issuer that is equivalent in coupon, quality, and maturity. Often these swaps are carried out between various government agencies having similar degrees of safety. For example, the investor might execute the following transaction:

	PRICE	YIELD-TO-MATURITY
Sell: 25-year maturity, 8% bond A at	100 =	8.00
Buy: 25-year maturity, 8% bond B at	99 =	8.10
Gain in yield-to-maturity		0.10

The swap from A bonds to B bonds generates a gain of 10 points in yield-to-maturity and enables the investor to free up $10 per $1,000 bond for any desired use. An additional benefit of this type of swap comes about if the newly purchased security begins to trade on a basis similar to that of the security that was originally owned. If, after six months, interest rates have fallen to $7^3/4$ percent for securities such as the ones above, and if both the A bonds and the B bonds trade in line with these new yield levels and with each other, the original bond would have gained about three points in price (from 100 to 103), while the newly purchased bonds would have experienced a larger price gain, of four points (from 99 to 103). If the two bonds begin to trade on an equivalent basis while general yield levels remain the same or trend upward, the newly purchased bonds will still perform better.

A number of swap opportunities of this type arise when a new issue, even though it is the equivalent of seasoned issues already outstanding, declines in price after the underwriting syndicate has disbanded. In this case the investor could sell his existing holding and purchase the equivalent security at a lower price (higher yield-to-maturity). In Table 11–7 is another, somewhat more complex example of a yield pickup swap. The amount of the trade is large in order that the dollar gain offset trading costs. Moreover, because these bonds might require only 10 percent margin, the out-of-pocket cash is less than the $1 million face value.

TABLE 11–7

Example of Typical Yield Pickup Swap

Sell: $1,000,000 (par value) U.S. Treasury 5⅞ percent due August 31, 1995, at 98.375 to yield 7.70 percent

Buy: $1,060,000 (par value) Treasury bills due August 24, 1995, at 7.32 percent (discount yield) to yield 7.82 percent (coupon equivalent). Cost = 98.607

Assumption: settlement date of trade is September 16, 1994

1. If the 5⅞ percent Treasury notes are held to maturity, then the holder would receive $1,000,000 in principal plus $58,750 in interest for a total on August 31, 1995, of $1,058,750.

2. If the 5⅞ percent Treasury notes are sold and the proceeds are reinvested in $1,060,000 par value of Treasury bills due August 24, 1995, then the results would be as follows:

Sale price of 5⅞ percent notes (98⅜)	$ 983,750
Accrued interest	2,582
Total proceeds of sale	$ 986,332
Purchase price of bills	986,072
Remaining funds	$260
Maturity proceeds of bills to be received on August 24, 1995	$1,060,000

3. The two advantages of making this swap are as follows:

First advantage:	
Maturity proceeds of bills	$1,060,000
Maturity date of notes	1,058,750
Advantage of swap	$ 1,250
Second advantage:	
Maturity date of bills	8/24/95
Maturity date of notes	8/31/95
Advantage of swap	7 days*

*That is, we are able to obtain our proceeds seven days earlier and thus can reinvest these proceeds for this period of time, thereby obtaining an added advantage.

THE SUBSTITUTION SWAP

The next type of swap, the substitution swap, attempts to profit from a change in the yield spread between two nearly identical bonds. The trade is based upon a forecast change in the yield spread between the two nearly identical bonds. The bonds could be issued by the same company, but with slightly different maturities and similar coupons; or the bonds could be between two different companies in the same sector-quality-coupon category. The forecast is generally based upon the past history of the yield spread relationship between the two bonds, with the assumption that any aberration from the past relationship is temporary, thereby allowing profit by buying the bond with the lower (higher) yield if the spread is to widen (narrow); this trade is later reversed, leaving the investor in the original position, but with a trading profit from the relative changes in price.

In a substitution or replacement swap, the portfolio manager continuously analyzes the spread relationship among groups of similar types of securities. A

TABLE 11–8

Example of Typical Substitution Swap*

Sell: U.S. Treasury $6\frac{3}{4}$ percent due May 31, 1995, at 98.03125 to yield 7.97 percent.

Buy: U.S. Treasury $6\frac{7}{8}$ percent due May 15, 1995, at 98.3125 to yield 7.95 percent.

1. Above trade results in a small yield give-up.
2. However, this trade is made on the basis of past yield-spread relationships between these two issues.
3. Past records indicate that the widest spread between these two issues occurred when the $6\frac{3}{4}$s yielded 15 basis points more than the $6\frac{7}{8}$s, while the narrowest spread resulted in the $6\frac{7}{8}$s yielding 3 basis points more than the $6\frac{3}{4}$s.
4. Thus, on the basis of history, a portfolio manager should sell the $6\frac{3}{4}$s and buy the $6\frac{7}{8}$s whenever the spread relationship narrows, with the intention of reversing the swap when the hoped-for spread widening occurs at some later date.
5. In our example, this is precisely what occurs. In 30 days, the following swap was made:

Sell: U.S. Treasury $6\frac{7}{8}$ percent due May 15, 1995, at 98.28125 yield 7.97 percent.

Buy: U.S. Treasury $6\frac{3}{4}$ percent due May 31, 1995, at 97.84375 to yield 8.10 percent.

Result: Although a $\frac{1}{32}$ loss (.0315) was sustained on the $6\frac{7}{8}$s, the $6\frac{3}{4}$s were purchased at a price $\frac{6}{32}$s lower (.1875) than they were originally sold at, thereby resulting in a net profit of $\frac{5}{32}$s. (.15625) or $1,562.50 per million par value.

*This swap was based upon market prices assumed during August and September.

swap is made whenever the yield spread between two highly similar bonds reaches some extreme limit (as a result of temporary market imbalances). The portfolio manager hopes to obtain a profitable "reversal" of this swap at a later date when the spread returns to a more normal historical level. This technique usually is referred to as an arbitrage.

The major obstacle to the substitution swap is the absolute necessity to give up yield-to-maturity when required. However, this yield give-up is only temporary. A substitution swap may require giving up nominal yield for a short while with the intention of eventually being able to increase the total real return. An example is shown in Table 11–8.

SUMMARY

The management of bond portfolios historically was mostly a passive exercise. A passive strategy generally involves a buy-and-hold philosophy wherein the investor's objectives are to achieve broad diversification, predictable returns, and low management costs.

In recent years active bond management has taken center stage. Accelerating inflation, volatility in interest rates, and disappointing stock-market returns have converged as forces encouraging a search for incremental returns in the bond mar-

ket. Investors have begun to focus on correctly positioning their portfolios' maturity structure, coupons, and quality to benefit from changes in the general level of interest rates. Such strategies require decisions or judgments regarding market rates and the shape of the yield curve. Such judgments are not an integral part of a passive approach to bond management. Other active judgments are made in weighing the portfolio in the more favorably situated sectors of the bond market (e.g., Treasury instruments, utilities, and so on).

QUESTIONS

1. Describe the process of laddering a bond portfolio. What are the advantages and disadvantages of this strategy?

2. Describe three techniques that are considered semiactive or active bond management strategies.

3. What do we mean when we say that a bond portfolio is immunized?

4. Zero coupons bonds are excellent vehicles for immunizing a portfolio. Do you agree or disagree? Why?

5. Rank the following bonds in order of descending duration. Explain your reasoning. (No calculations are required.)

   a. 15 percent coupon, twenty-year, yield-to-maturity at 10 percent.

   b. 15 percent coupon, fifteen-year, yield-to-maturity at 10 percent.

   c. Zero-coupon, twenty-year, yield-to-maturity at 10 percent.

   d. 8 percent coupon, twenty-year, yield-to-maturity at 10 percent.

   e. 15 percent coupon, fifteen-year, yield-to-maturity at 15 percent.

6. How is duration on a bond related to time-to-maturity? Coupon? Do these same relationships obtain for zero-coupon bonds?

7. Refer to Table 11–3. Prove that the total return with a holding period of one year is 224 if the reinvestment rate is 7 percent.

8. What are the major issues to be considered in determining the frequency with which an immunized portfolio should be rebalanced?

9. A rate-anticipation bond strategy would emphasize which combination of coupon rate, maturity, and market sector if a bond manager expected interest rates to fall?

10. How does the difference in rates (spread) on AAA and BAA corporate bonds change over the course of a business cycle (expansion to contraction to expansion)?

11. When mapping expected returns we suggest that total expected return = yield-to-maturity plus roll. What does roll mean?

PROBLEMS

1. A bond can be acquired with a three-year maturity. The bond has a coupon rate of 8 percent and is priced in the market at 100. What is the duration of this bond?

2. A portfolio manager for an insurance company has a known liability that will occur at the end of eight years. She can either purchase an 8 percent bond due in eight years or a 4 percent bond due in ten years that would be sold at the end of eight years. Suppose interest rates make a single downward change at the end of year 6 when the market yield falls to 7 percent and remains there through year 8. Show how the purchase of the 4 percent bond is superior to the purchase of the 8 percent bond if the goal is to minimize interest-rate risk.

3. When asked what the ideal trading strategy should be when the level of interest rates is expected to decline John Towne, a retired bond investor, responds, "Buy long, low, and strong." He really means buy long maturities with low coupons of the strongest quality ratings.

    a. Why should this strategy tend to lead to superior performance?

    b. How would you advise him to amend his wisdom in light of your understanding of the concept of duration?

4. The economy has been in recession. Interest rates are beginning to move up as the Federal Reserve Board stimulates monetary growth. In each of the situations below, assuming that you had to own one of the two bonds listed, which would you prefer? Why?

    a. U.S. Treasury 11⅞ due in two years and priced at 100;

    or

    U.S. Treasury 11¾ due in twenty-nine years, priced at 96.06 to yield 12.25 percent to maturity.

    b. Texas Power and Light Co. 7½ due in twenty-one years, rated AAA, and priced at 62 to yield 12.75 percent to maturity; or

    Arizona Public Service Co. 7.45 due in twenty-one years, rated A−, and priced at 56 to yield 13.98 percent to maturity.

    c. Commonwealth Edison 2¾ due in eighteen years, rated BAA, and priced at 25 to yield 14.25 percent to maturity; or

    Commonwealth Edison 15⅜ due in nineteen years, rated BAA, and priced at 102.75 to yield 14.93 percent to maturity.

    d. Shell Oil Co. 8½ sinking-fund debentures due in nineteen years (rated AAA, sinking fund begins 9/80 at par), priced at 75 to yield 12.91 percent to maturity; or

    Warner-Lambert 8 7/8 sinking-fund debentures due in nineteen years (rated AAA, sinking fund begins ⁴/₈₆ at par), priced at 75 to yield 12.31 percent to maturity.

5. An investor has engaged in the following transactions:

   a. Sell: 8 percent, twenty-year, A-rated, gas company bond. Price = 95¼.
      Buy: 8 percent, twenty-year, AAA-rated, electric utility bond. Price = 100.
   b. Sell: 7½ percent, twenty-year, AAA-rated, food company bond. Price = 95.
      Buy: Treasury bills, ninety-day maturity. Price = 98½.
   c. Sell: 8.10 percent, ten-year, AA-rated, pharmaceutical company bond. Price = 100¼.
      Buy 8.90 percent, eight-year, AA-rated, chemical company bond. Price = 100.

   For each of these "swaps," what are the apparent underlying motivations? What are the associated risks?

6. It is August 1995. As the portfolio manager for Peoples Insurance Co. you are currently examining the fixed-income securities listed below in an environment of business contraction, declining inflation, and monetary ease. The company is in an effective tax bracket of 30 percent.

SECURITY	PRICE	YIELD-TO-MATURITY (%)
City of Sunset, 5% general obligations (2015)	57	10.00
U.S. Treasury, 8% notes (August 1997)	98½	
Durable, Inc., 10 ½% preferred stock ($25 par)*	26	
Georgia Drug Co., 0% debentures (2005)	38½	10.00
Georgia Drug Co., 11% debentures (2021)†	100	
Tasty Foods, 7% debentures (2021)‡	66	11.00

*Currently callable at par plus one year's dividend.
†Callable beginning in 1997 at 108; no sinking fund.
‡Callable beginning in 1997 at 106; sinking fund of 4 percent of issue starts 1995.

   a. Which security provides the best after-tax yield-to-maturity, Sunset or Durable? Explain.
   b. The Georgia 11 percent and the Tasty Foods bonds are both rated Aa. List reasons why these bonds are or are not properly priced relative to one another.
   c. Suppose the Peoples had a ten-year insurance policy it wished to match with an appropriate security. Does it matter whether the Georgia 0 percent or the 11 percent bonds are acquired? Explain.

7. Three bonds are being examined by an investor planning to send his daughter to college in ten years. Each bond is highest in quality.

	BOND 1	BOND 2	BOND 3
Coupon rate	0%	4%	4%
Maturity (years)	10	20	5
Yield-to-maturity	6%	6%	6%
Duration	10	13	4.5

a. Because both have the same yield, does it matter whether bond 1 or 2 is purchased? Explain.

b. Should the investor be indifferent between buying bond 2 and selling it at the end of ten years or buying bond 3 and replacing it at its maturity? Explain.

c. Assume that bond 2 is acquired at a price of 80 to yield 6 percent to maturity. Shortly thereafter, yields on similar bonds rise to 6 1/2 percent. What should the new price be on these bonds?

8. You are given the following data on U.S. Treasury securities:

	1/15/96 PRICE	YIELD-TO MATURITY (%)	TIME-TO MATURITY (YEARS)	MODIFIED DURATION
U.S. Treasury 7.875% notes 5/15/2000	95.19	9.25	4.33	2.95
U.S. Treasury 3.250% bonds 6/15/2000	81.56	8.34	4.42	3.34

a. Explain why a difference exists in the duration between the two U.S. Treasury securities.

b. Using the duration, calculate the expected total returns that will be realized on each of the two securities if held for one year under each of the following interest-rate conditions:

i. No change in interest rates.

ii. One percentage point (100 basis points) drop in interest rates.

9. Following are a number of swaps.

				MATURITY [YEARS]	CALL PRICE	MARKET PRICE	YTM*
A.	Sell	Baa	Florida Power	11.625%	18	108.2	75	15.7
	Buy	Baa	Florida Power	7.625%	19	105.2	51	15.4
B.	Sell	Aaa	AT&T Notes	13.25%	9	101.5	96	14.0
	Buy	–	U.S. Treasury	14.25%	9	None	102	13.8
C.	Sell	Aa	Bank One	0.00%	10	None	25	14.4
	Buy	Aa	Bank One	Float	27	103.9	90	–
D.	Sell	A	Texas Oil & Gas	8.25%	15	105.8	60	15.1
	Buy	–	U.S. Treasury	8.25%	22	None	66	13.0
E.	Sell	A	Exxon Convert.	6.00%	17	103.9	62	10.8
	Buy	A	Medi-Mart	11.75%	23	109.9	73	16.3

*Yield-to-maturity.

a. Identify the reason(s) investors may have made each swap.

b. Suppose an insurance company were attempting to fund a lump-sum payment to an insured client in nine years. Contrast the use of the Medi-Mart bonds or either of the U.S. Treasury securities for this purpose.

c. How do you account for the difference in the yield-to-maturity of the two Florida Power bonds?

d. Suppose the general level of interest rates were expected to drop 50 basis points (one-half of one percent) in the next ten days. Calculate the new price you expect for the Bank One bonds due in ten years.

10. The following annual coupon bonds are available:

BOND (%)	MATURITY (YEARS)	COUPON	MARKET YIELD
A	5	12%	10%
B	4	12%	10%

Compare the durations on these two bonds and discuss the implications for immunization.

11. Consider two bonds, A and B, both having face values of $10,000, yields-to-maturity of 9 percent, and four years to maturity. Bond A has a coupon rate of 10 percent and bond B has a coupon rate of 7.5 percent. Coupons are paid annually.

a. Calculate the duration of bonds A and B.

b. Explain the difference in duration between the two bonds.

12. A five-year corporate bond that pays 12 percent per year via semiannual coupons, with a 8 percent market rate and a $1,000 maturity is worth $1,162.21. The bond has a duration of four years. Based on the duration formulation:

a. Find the price of this bond if the interest rate increases 2 percent.

b. Find the price of this bond if the interest rate decreases 2 percent.

13. You receive a cash inflow of $1,500,000 and you want to invest these funds in a bond portfolio in the following manner:

BOND	% OF FUND INVESTED	DURATION (YEARS)
A	10%	10.35
B	22%	4.25
C	19%	7.50
D	7%	9.50
E	17%	12.67
F	6%	5.82
G	11%	8.50
H	8%	6.71

All of the bonds have a face value of $1,000 and a yield-to-maturity of 9 percent. What is the duration of this portfolio?

14. A bond portfolio manager is building a portfolio of bonds from three companies: Apple, General Motors, and United Airlines. These bonds wil be used to fund a pension fund outflow scheduled in six years. The current yield in the economy is 7 percent. All bonds have a $1,000 par value.

BOND	MATURITY	COUPON	DURATION
Apple	10 years	8% annual	7.35 years
General Motors	8 years	9% annual	6.15 years
United Airlines	5 years	7% semiannual	4.30 years

a. Assuming the bond portfolio manager has been instructed to keep 50 percent of the portfolio's money in Apple bonds, calculate the percentage amounts of General Motors and United Airlines bonds that need to be purchased to immunize the portfolio.

b. Now that the portfolio has been constructed, an interest-rate change occurs, increasing the current yield to 9 percent. The new durations for these bonds are:

> Apple = 7.15 years
> General Motors = 6.03 years
> United Airlines = 4.27 years

Is the bond portfolio still immunized. Why or why not?

c. Determine the new percentage amounts of General Motors and United Airlines bonds that are needed to reimmunize the portfolio (Apple remains at 50 percent of the portfolio).

C A S E

■

*Monticello Corp.**

You recently joined the investment counseling firm of Cavalier Investment Management. The Investment Committee of the firm asked you to evaluate Monticello Corp., a major holding in accounts managed by Cavalier. As part of your work on this project, you prepared a report containing the following information and data.

Monticello is a major American forest products company. Until 1990, it was entirely engaged in the manufacture and distribution of building materials, primarily wood products (e.g., lumber, plywood). During 1990, it acquired a major paper company, Great American Paper Corp., a large producer of both pulp and newsprint. The transaction was for $3.5 billion and was financed entirely with debt.

The building material distribution operations are nationwide but the manufacturing of building materials is concentrated in the southeastern United States (particularly Georgia), with 5 million acres of timberland owned to serve these facilities. The acquired paper operations are divided, with the pulp facilities in Georgia and the newsprint production in Maine.

The pulp mills (pulp is processed wood, used as the input for paper manufacturing) are low-cost producers and are near an excellent deep water port. As a result, much of the production is exported, particularly to Europe. Great American owned no nearby timberlands but the Monticello timberlands are now being utilized to supply these pulp operations.

The newsprint mills are not efficient and are in need of major capital expenditures. However, they are near 2 million acres of timberland, which were owned

*Abridged and reprinted with permission of the Association of Investment Management and Research, Charlottesville, Virginia. This case was a part of a recent CFA examination.

by Great American and now by Monticello. An additional 50,000 acres of timberland were owned by Great American (now by Monticello) that are not used in any company operations.

The paper industry is capital-intensive with large, modern mills necessary for a producer to be cost competitive. The industry's products are mostly commodities in wide use. Wood is the primary raw material, so proximity to timberlands and an ensured supply of timber through ownership or long-term contracts is important. Environmental concerns and a limitation on remaining potential sites for mills could restrict future industry expansion.

Because of the acquisition of Great American in 1990, the debt position of Monticello more than doubled as total debts increased by $5.4 billion. A result of this transaction was that both of the major rating agencies downgraded the company's debt; Moody's dropped its rating from A3 to Baa3, and S&P lowered its rating from A- to BBB-. The downgradings occurred just after the acquisition was announced and have remained unchanged since that time.

EXHIBIT 1

Monticello Corp. Years Ending December 31
($ in millions, except per share data)

	1984	1989	1991	1992	1993	1994	1995
Operational Results:							
Net sales	$4,554	$6,716	$8,603	$9,509	$10,171	$12,665	$11,000
Operating expenses	(4,242)	(6,294)	(7,747)	(8,534)	(8,824)	(11,340)	(10,290)
Interest expense	(79)	(132)	(124)	(197)	(260)	(606)	(700)
Pretax income	$ 233	$ 290	$ 732	$ 778	$ 1,087	$ 719	$ 10
Income taxes	(72)	(83)	(274)	(311)	(426)	(354)	(40)
Net income	$ 161	$ 207	$ 458	$ 467	$ 661	$ 365	$ (30)
Earnings per share	$ 1.48	$ 1.84	$ 4.23	$ 4.76	$ 7.42	$ 4.28	$ (0.35)
Dividends per share	$ 1.20	$ 0.80	$ 1.05	$ 1.25	$ 1.45	$ 1.60	$ 1.60
Average shares outstanding	108.8	112.5	108.3	98.1	89.1	85.3	86.0
Cash flow from operations	$ 350	$ 440	$ 781	$ 805	$ 1,075	$ 924	$ 630
Financial Position at Year-End:							
Current assets	$1,051	$1,291	$1,729	$1,892	$ 1,829	$ 1,766	$ 1,650
Other assets	3,266	3,575	4,141	5,223	5,227	10,294	10,465
Total assets	$4,317	$4,866	$5,870	$7,115	$ 7,056	$12,060	$12,115
Current liabilities	$710	$631	$996	$1,013	$ 924	$ 2,535	$ 2,000
Long-term debt	1,227	1,257	1,298	2,514	2,336	5,218	5,900
Other liabilities	311	675	896	953	1,079	1,332	1,400
Stockholders' equity	2,069	2,303	2,680	2,635	2,717	2,975	2,815
Total liabilities and equity	$4,317	$4,866	$5,870	$7,115	$ 7,056	$12,060	$12,115

EXHIBIT 2

Monticello Corp. Selected Financial Ratios

	1984	1989	1991	1992	1993	1994	1995
Operating income to sales	6.8%	6.3%	10.0%	10.2%	13.2%	10.5%	■
Stockholders' equity as percent of total assets	47.9%	44.1%	45.6%	37.0%	38.5%	24.7%	23.2%
Cash flow from operations to interest	5.4x	4.3x	7.3x	5.1x	5.1x	2.5x	■
Pretax interest coverage	3.9x	3.2x	6.9x	5.0x	5.2x	2.2x	■
Long-term debt to total long-term capital	34.0%	30.8%	26.6%	41.2%	38.1%	54.8%	■
Cash flow from operations to total debt	18.1%	23.3%	34.0%	22.8%	33.0%	11.9%	■
Current ratio	1.5x	2.0x	1.7x	1.9x	2.0x	0.7x	0.8x
Return on equity (based on income from continuing operations)	11.3%	13.5%	27.3%	29.5%	40.0%	24.2%	0.1%

Cavalier manages substantial bond portfolio assets, including high-yield or "junk" holdings. You have been assigned to prepare an internal analysis to evaluate the debt of Monticello, which is held widely in managed accounts. While respecting the major rating agencies and their impact on market valuation of bonds, Cavalier's investment policy requires its own independent analysis of owned securities.

1. For 1995, calculate the five missing ratios for Monticello [■] in Exhibit 2 using the data provided in Exhibit 1.

2. Justify an appropriate credit rating for Monticello's debt, using the now-completed Exhibit 2 and Exhibit 3.

3. Discuss how the use of FIFO versus LIFO in accounting for inventories might affect the rating of Monticello's debt that you determined in Question 2 above:

EXHIBIT 3

Cavalier Investment Management Credit Rating Standards

FINANCIAL RATIOS	AVERAGE RATIOS BY RATING CATEGORY			
	A	BBB	BB	B
Pretax interest coverage	5.2x	3.6x	2.4x	1.3x
Cash flow from operations to interest	7.6x	5.5x	4.1x	2.1x
Cash flow from operations to total debt	47.7%	37.1%	23.1%	9.5%
Operating income to sales	13.5%	12.1%	13.1%	9.8%
Long-term debt to total long-term capital	30.1%	37.7%	50.5%	66.1%

EXHIBIT 4

Monticello Corp. Bond Information

	BOND A (CALLABLE)	BOND B (NONCALLABLE)
Maturity	2006	2006
Coupon	11.50%	7.25%
Current price	125.75	100.00
Yield-to-maturity	7.70%	7.25%
Modified duration to maturity	6.20	6.80
Call date	2000	–
Call price	105	–
Yield-to-call	5.10%	–
Modified duration to call	3.10	–

4. As a continuation of your analysis of Monticello's debt you are asked to evaluate two specific bond issues held in Cavalier-managed accounts, shown in Exhibit 4.

5. Using the duration and yield information in Exhibit 4, compare the price and yield behavior of the two bonds under each of the following two scenarios:
   a. strong economic recovery with rising inflation expectations; and
   b. economic recession with reduced inflation expectations.

6. Using the information in Exhibit 4, calculate the projected price change for bond B if the yield-to-maturity for this bond falls by 75 basis points.

REFERENCES

AHERN, D. S. "The Strategic Role of Fixed Income Securities." *Journal of Portfolio Management* (Spring 1975).

BARNES, T., K. JOHNSON, and D. SHANNON. "A Test of Fixed Income Strategies." *Journal of Portfolio Management* (Winter 1984).

BIERWAG, G. O., G. G. KAUFMAN, and A. TOEVS, eds. *Innovations in Bond Portfolio Management: Duration Analysis and Immunization.* Greenwich, Conn.: JAI Press, 1983.

CHOIE, K. S. "A Simplified Approach to Bond Portfolio Management." *Journal of Portfolio Management* (Spring 1990).

CORNELL, BRADFORD, and KEVIN GREEN. "The Investment Performance of Low-Grade Bond Funds." *Journal of Finance,* (March 1991).

DYL, E. A. and M. D. JOEHNK. "Riding the Yield Curve: Does it Work?" *Journal of Portfolio Management* (Spring 1981).

FONG, G. and O. A. VASICEK. "Fixed-Income Volatility Management." *Journal of Portfolio Management* (Spring 1991).

FONG, G., C. PEARSON and J. VASICEK. "Bond Performance: Analyzing Sources of Return." *Financial Analysts Journal* (September–October 1983).

LIEBOWITZ, M. L. "How Swaps Can Pay Off." *Institutional Investor* (August 1973).

LIEBOWITZ, M. L. and A. WEINBERGER. "The Uses of Contingent Immunization." *Journal of Portfolio Management* (Fall 1981).

MCENALLY, R. W. "Duration as a Practical Tool in Bond Management." *Journal of Portfolio Management* (Summer 1977).

MEYER, K. R. "The Dividends from Active Bond Management" *Journal of Portfolio Management* (Spring 1975).

ROSENBERG, MICHAEL R. "A Framework for Formulating International Fixed-Income Strategy." *Journal of Portfolio Management* (Summer 1990), pp. 70–76.

TUTTLE, D., ed. *The Revolution in Techniques for Managing Bond Portfolios.* Charlottesville, Va.: Institute of Chartered Financial Analysts, 1983.

OPTIONS

The next three chapters deal with instruments that derive their value from underlying securities. These "derivatives" include options and futures. Certain options are short-term in nature (less than a year to expiration) and are issued (written) by investors. These options are the subject of this chapter. Another group of options are longer-term in nature and are issued by companies in the process of financing their activities. These options are the concern of Chapter 13. Finally, the subject of securities futures contracts is treated in Chapter 14.

An *options agreement* is a contract in which the writer of the option grants the buyer of the option the right to purchase from or sell to the writer a designated instrument at a specific price (or receive a cash settlement) within a specified period of time.

The writer grants this right to the buyer for a certain sum of money called the *option premium*. An option that grants the buyer the right to purchase a designated instrument is called a *call option*.

An option that grants the buyer the right to sell a designated instrument is called a *put option*. The price at which the buyer can exercise the option is called the *exercise price, strike price,* or *striking price*.

RATIONALE OF OPTIONS AND FUTURES DEVELOPMENT

Before describing either the fixed-income or equity offerings of futures and options, some observations regarding the history and rationale of the two markets may be useful. Both futures and options evolved quite differently, with the result that there are wide differences in the contracts that are available.

Organized exchanges began trading options on equities in 1973, whereas exchange-traded debt options did not appear until 1982. On the other hand, fixed-income futures began trading in 1975, but equity-related futures did not begin until 1982. When the nature of the markets are compared, one can immediately discern some differences that could have led to this difference in evolution. One should

also remember that the exchanges introduce contracts that they think will be successful, and thus contract design is also a function of marketing. At this point, exploring the reasons why and times when certain of the new instruments appeared on the money and capital markets scene is useful.

In the equity market, a relatively large proportion of the total risk of a security is unsystematic. At the same time, many equities exhibit a high degree of liquidity that (in the absence of epochal events such as takeovers) can be expected to be maintained for long periods of time—liquidity in the sense of being able to buy and sell relatively large amounts quickly without substantial price concessions. These two factors—large unsystematic risk and liquidity—point toward the success and viability of trading equity options on individual securities.

For the contracts to have been successful, the underlying securities had to be traded "in large size" (i.e., with large volume) and with price continuity so that option-related transactions would not cause more than minor disturbances in the market. In addition, the perpetual nature of common stock, an instrument with no maturity date, meant that successful options could remain on the exchanges for a potentially long time.

In the debt market, a much larger proportion of the total risk of securities is systematic—risk that cannot be eliminated by diversification within the debt market. Debt instruments are also finite life securities with limited marketability due to their small size relative to many common stocks. These factors favor, for the purpose of both portfolio hedging and speculation, the introduction of a derivative security that is based on some broader market rather than an individual security.

PUT AND CALL OPTIONS[1]

Options Terminology

To ensure a proper understanding of the following discussion of put and call options, certain terms must be made clear at the outset. A standard option *contract* allows the buyer to buy *100 shares* of stock at a specific price during a specific period of time, regardless of the market price of that stock. A *call* is an option contract giving the buyer the right to purchase the stock. A *put* is an option contract giving the buyer the right to sell the stock. The *expiration date* is the date on which the option contract expires—the last day on which an option can be exercised. The *exercise* (or *striking*) *price* is the price at which the buyer of a call can purchase the stock during the life of option, and the price at which the buyer of a put can sell the stock during the life of the option. Finally, the *premium* is the price the buyer pays the writer for an option contract. The term *premium* is often synonymous with the word *price.* The terms *buyer* and *holder* are synonymous, as often are *seller* and

---

[1]Two excellent options texts include J. C. Cox and M. Rubenstein, *Options Markets* (Englewood Cliffs, N.J.: Prentice Hall, 1985); and P. Ritchken, *Options* (Glenview, Ill.: Scott, Foresman, 1987).

writer. In the latter case, however, a seller of an existing option is not necessarily the writer. He might have purchased the option from a writer.

Let us review the transaction reporting techniques of the listed options market place. For simplicity of exposition, references to items shown in Figure 12–1 refer to calls exclusively. The put options that trade are identifiable in the tables by the letter *p* after the option exercise price (e.g., "McDon . . . Sep50p . . ."). The presentation is organized first by expiration month and then by exercise prices available for those issues.

To explain how to read these tables, let us analyze the activity that took place in September 50 call options of McDonald's Corp. (as highlighted in Figure 12–1).

1. McDonald's Corp. is abbreviated in the table as "McDon." Each option gives the holder a right to buy 100 shares of the underlying stock at $50 per share anytime up to the expiration date.

2. The closing price of the underlying stock on the New York Stock Exchange (NYSE) is given in the last column to allow you to compare prices of the option and the stock. On this day McDonald's closed at 54⅜ on the NYSE. The call privilege therefore has a *conversion value* of $4.38. (The conversion value is the difference between $54⅜ for the underlying stock and $50, the exercise price of the option.) The actual value of this call option is determined by the forces of supply and demand as reflected in the prices listed for the call options. If an investor exercises a September $50 call option for McDonald's, he does not automatically make a profit of $4.38 per share. His profit, if any, is the amount paid for the option privilege plus the aggregate exercise price ($54⅜ × 100 shares = $5,437.50) subtracted from the net proceeds from the sale of the stock itself. Another way to profit from this option transaction is to sell the option privilege for more money than the original cost.

3. The *expiration month* appears to the right of the company name for an option series. Although listed options have fixed expiration dates, only certain dates are made available for trading at one time.

4. The *sales figure* indicates the total number of contracts traded today in that particular series. On the Chicago Board Options Exchange (CBOE), 863 contracts for the September 50 call options were traded. Because each contract usually commands at least 100 shares of underlying stock, options on the CBOE equals 86,300 shares of stock.

5. The *open interest* is the aggregate number of exercisable contracts existing on the record from cumulative activities. Any opening writing transaction would increase the figure of 1997 contracts, whereas a closing writing transaction would reduce it.

6. The *high, low,* and *last* columns indicate that the September 50 options sold as high as 4⅝, as low as 3¾, and closed at 4½ for that week's trading. The closing (last) trade of 4½ was ½ above the prior week's last trade of 4.

Expiration dates for options in the conventional market can fall on any normal business day. In contrast, expiration dates are standardized in the listed op-

Expire date Strike price	Sales	Open Int.	Week's High	Low	Price	Net Chg.	N.Y. Close
I B M Jan 40	1172	3459	7 1/2	6	7 1/8	+ 1 3/8	45 7/8
I B M Jan 40 p	2030	6479	1 1/2	7/8	15/16	− 9/16	45 7/8
I B M Jan 45	2410	10184	4 1/8	3	3 5/8	+ 11/16	45 7/8
I B M Jan 45 p	1827	8452	3 1/2	2 3/8	2 9/16	− 1 3/16	45 7/8
I B M Jan 50	4964	11862	1 15/16	1 5/16	1 11/16	+ 7/16	45 7/8
I B M Jan 50 p	248	2838	6 5/8	5 3/8	5 5/8	− 1 3/8	45 7/8
I B M Jan 55	2860	14859	7/8	5/8	3/4	+ 1/8	45 7/8
I B M Jan 55 p	340	5531	11	9 1/4	9 3/4	− 1 3/4	45 7/8
I B M Jan 60	380	2512	3/8	1/4	1/4	...	45 7/8
I B M Jan 70	1607	13464	1/8	1/16	1/16	− 1/16	45 7/8
I B M Apr 45	238	173	5 1/8	4	4 3/4	+ 7/8	45 7/8
I B M Apr 50	755	676	2 7/8	2 1/8	2 11/16	+ 9/16	45 7/8
I B M Apr 55	745	459	1 9/16	1	1 3/8	+ 3/8	45 7/8
In Pap Sep 65	230	516	1 3/4	1/2	1/2	− 1	63 1/8
In Pap Oct 65	314	920	2 3/16	1 1/4	1 5/16	− 13/16	63 1/8
In Pap Oct 65 p	282	525	3 1/4	2	3 1/4	+ 1 1/8	63 1/8
IntRec Mar 12 1/2	440	540	1	1	1	− 1/4	10 3/4
Itel Oct 30	243	2321	3 3/8	2 1/4	2 7/16	− 15/16	32
Jackpot o Sep 18 1/8	254	285	3/8	1/4	5/16	− 5/16	17 3/8
JohnJn Sep 35	317	439	6 3/8	5 1/4	5 5/8	+ 1/4	39 7/8
JohnJn Sep 40	1146	2376	1 15/16	7/8	7/8	− 3/8	39 7/8
JohnJn Sep 40 p	1196	3242	7/8	3/8	3/4	− 1/4	39 7/8
JohnJn Sep 45	620	998	1/4	1/16	1/16	− 1/16	39 7/8
JohnJn Oct 35	409	1072	6 1/2	5 3/4	6 1/2	+ 1	39 7/8
JohnJn Oct 40	898	5502	2 5/8	1 3/4	1 3/4	...	39 7/8
JohnJn Oct 40 p	793	2230	1 5/8	1	1 5/8	+ 5/16	39 7/8
JohnJn Oct 45	919	3558	1/2	1/4	1/4	...	39 7/8
JohnJn Oct 45 p	244	634	4 5/8	3 7/8	3 7/8	− 1 1/4	39 7/8
JohnJn Jan 35 p	220	2771	13/16	9/16	13/16	− 1/16	39 7/8
JohnJn Jan 40	372	2336	3 5/8	2 3/4	2 3/4	− 3/8	39 7/8
JohnJn Jan 45	873	4794	1 3/8	7/8	7/8	− 1/4	39 7/8
JohnJn Jan 50	240	2000	7/16	1/4	3/8	+ 1/16	39 7/8
JohnJn Apr 45	737	684	2 1/4	1 5/8	2 1/8	+ 3/8	39 7/8
K mart Sep 22 1/2	378	3585	13/16	1/4	1/4	− 1/2	22
K mart Sep 22 1/2 p	371	2028	9/16	1/4	9/16	+ 1/8	22
K mart Oct 25	222	327	3/16	1/8	1/8	− 3/16	22
K mart Dec 22 1/2	205	4030	1 5/8	1	1	− 1/2	22
K mart Mar 22 1/2	587	976	1 15/16	1 5/8	1 5/8	− 3/8	22
KelyOil Sep 12 1/2	235	148	3	3/8	1/2	− 2 1/4	12 1/4
KelyOil Sep 15	585	637	1 1/4	1/8	1/8	− 7/8	12 1/4
KelyOil Sep 15 p	348	304	4 1/4	9/16	3 1/8	+ 2 1/8	12 1/4
KelyOil Nov 15	241	490	2 11/16	7/8	15/16	− 1 5/16	12 1/4
LAGear Sep 10	365	627	3/16	1/16	1/16	− 1/16	9 1/8
LAGear Oct 10	248	2193	1/2	5/16	3/8	− 1/16	9 1/8
LAC Oct 10	217	4407	1/2	1/4	5/16	+ 1/16	8 5/8
Limitd Sep 22 1/2	1235	1240	1 5/16	1/2	1/2	− 1/4	22
Limitd Sep 22 1/2 p	1472	964	1	1/4	13/16	...	22
Limitd Sep 25	234	621	5/16	1/8	1/8	...	22
Limitd Oct 22 1/2 p	383	283	1 7/16	1/2	1 1/4	+ 1/4	22
Limitd Oct 25	223	224	5/8	1/4	3/8	+ 3/16	22
Limitd Nov 22 1/2	665	3174	2 3/8	1 1/8	1 1/8	− 1/4	22
Limitd Nov 22 1/2 p	330	736	1 5/8	13/16	1 5/8	+ 1/8	22
Limitd Nov 25	566	5257	13/16	1/2	1/2	...	22
Limitd Jan 25	669	1319	1 1/2	7/8	7/8	...	22
Limitd Jan 30	247	1445	5/16	3/16	3/16	...	22
Limitd Feb 25	351	1887	1 3/8	15/16	1	− 1/4	22
Litton Sep 50	211	271	18 3/4	18 3/8	18 3/8	+ 2 1/2	64 3/4
Litton Sep 50 p	211	274	1/8	1/8	1/8	− 3/16	64 3/4
Litton Sep 70	440	402	1 1/8	1/8	1/8	− 7/16	64 3/4
Litton Dec 65	402	870	5 3/4	3	3	− 1 1/8	64 3/4
Litton Dec 70	204	1018	3 1/4	1 1/8	1 1/8	− 3/4	64 3/4
Loral Sep 55	350	...	7 7/8	7 7/8	7 7/8	+ 1/8	61 1/2
Loral Oct 55	227	273	8 3/4	7 7/8	7 7/8	+ 2 1/2	61 1/2
Loral Oct 65	270	474	1 13/16	1 3/16	1 3/8	− 7/8	61 1/2
M C I Sep 30	428	679	7/16	1/8	3/8	+ 3/16	29
M C I Oct 27 1/2	218	1635	2 1/8	1	2	+ 1	29
M C I Oct 30	664	1765	15/16	1/2	7/8	+ 7/16	29
M C I Jan 30	312	1065	1 3/4	1 1/16	1 3/4	+ 3/4	29
MTC El Sep 10	1725	2041	1 3/16	3/8	1 3/16	+ 3/4	10 5/8
MTC El Sep 10 p	205	460	15/16	1/4	5/16	− 5/8	10 5/8
MTC El Oct 10	823	340	1 9/16	11/16	1 9/16	+ 7/8	10 5/8
MTC El Nov 10	263	942	2	1	1 13/16	+ 1/2	10 5/8
McCawC Sep 40	618	2480	17	17	17	+ 2 1/4	56 7/8
McCawC Dec 40	715	99	17 3/8	17 1/4	17 1/4	+ 7/8	56 7/8
McCawC Dec 50	450	2868	8 1/8	8	8 1/8	+ 1/4	56 7/8
McCawC Dec 50 p	1930	1973	1/2	7/16	1/2	− 3/8	56 7/8
McCawC Mar 50	405	346	9	9	9	+ 2 1/2	56 7/8
McCawC Mar 50 p	1880	2867	1	7/8	1	− 3/4	56 7/8
Mc Don Sep 50	863	1997	4 5/8	3 3/4	4 1/2	+ 1/2	54 3/8
Mc Don Sep 50 p	521	1074	3/16	1/16	1/8	− 1/8	54 3/8
Mc Don Sep 55	889	3703	13/16	3/8	1/2	− 1/8	54 3/8
Mc Don Mar 55	1147	1600	3 5/8	3 1/4	3 5/8	− 1/8	54 3/8
MedCrA Sep 15	574	551	1 3/4	7/8	1 3/4	+ 1 1/16	16 3/8
Medtrn Nov 60	215	267	8 1/2	6 3/8	8	− 1	64 1/8
Merck Sep 25	2819	15	7 3/4	6 5/8	7 3/4	+ 1	33
PresRv Sep 40	564	569	2 7/16	11/16	1 3/16	− 1/16	38 3/4
Promus Sep 60	201	322	11 1/2	9 1/2	9 3/4	+ 1/4	68
Promus Sep 60 p	640	1619	9/16	1/4	3/8	− 1/4	68
Promus Sep 65	256	422	7 3/8	4 1/2	4 1/2	− 1 1/4	68
Promus Sep 65 p	744	1172	1 9/16	3/4	1 1/8	− 7/16	68
Promus Sep 70	394	897	3 7/8	1 3/8	1 1/2	− 1 3/8	68
Qualcm Sep 75	295	405	6 3/4	3 1/2	6	...	79 1/2
Qualcm Sep 80	322	304	3 3/4	2	2 1/2	− 1	79 1/2
Qualcm Sep 85	324	363	1 3/4	7/8	1	− 1 1/2	79 1/2
RdrDig Jan 35 p	250	420	1	1	1	+ 7/16	39
StJude Sep 30	220	32	2 9/16	5/8	13/16	− 2 3/16	29 1/2
StJude Sep 30 p	258	180	1 1/8	3/16	1 1/16	+ 7/8	29 1/2
StJude Oct 30 p	247	323	1 3/4	1/2	1 11/16	+ 1 1/16	29 1/2
StJude Oct 35	328	679	13/16	1/4	5/16	− 9/16	29 1/2
StJude Jan 30	243	102	4 1/4	2 1/4	2 1/4	− 2 3/8	29 1/2
StPaul Apr 95	513	507	4 1/4	3 5/8	4 1/4	...	91 1/2
SallieM Jan 45 p	390	392	3 1/8	3	3	...	45 3/4
Slumb Nov 65	359	2590	4 3/4	3 3/4	4 3/4	+ 7/8	67 1/2
Slumb Nov 70	1175	2790	1 3/4	1	1 3/4	+ 3/4	67 1/2
Slumb Feb 70	299	694	3	2 1/8	2 3/4	+ 3/8	67 1/2
Schwab Dec 30 p	829	989	2 1/2	1 7/8	1 7/8	− 1/8	33 1/4
Scimed Sep 55	311	1142	3 3/4	1 1/2	1 1/2	− 2 1/4	54 1/4
Scimed Sep 60	352	1876	1 3/16	5/16	5/16	− 3/4	54 1/4
Scimed Oct 55	202	417	5 3/8	3 1/2	4	− 1 7/8	54 1/4
Sears Sep 50	488	689	5 1/4	4 1/4	5 1/8	+ 2 1/4	54 1/2
Sears Sep 55	1235	5589	1 3/8	3/4	3/4	+ 3/16	54 1/2
Sears Sep 55 p	213	1434	1 7/8	1	1	− 2 3/8	54 1/2
Sears Oct 55	560	3210	2	1 3/8	1 3/4	+ 3/4	54 1/2
Sears Apr 50	550	545	7 1/4	6 3/4	7	...	54 1/2
SherW Sep 30 p	225	1450	1/16	1/16	1/16	− 3/4	34 1/4
SnapBv Sep 40	227	1706	18 7/8	11 7/8	15	+ 3 1/8	55 1/4
SnapBv Sep 40 p	412	3146	3/8	1/8	1/8	− 1/4	55 1/4
SnapBv Sep 45	495	2086	14 3/4	7 3/8	10 3/8	+ 3 3/8	55 1/4
SnapBv Sep 45 p	765	2181	13/16	5/16	5/16	− 5/8	55 1/4
SnapBv Sep 50	2200	3055	9 1/2	2 15/16	5 3/4	+ 2 3/4	55 1/4
SnapBv Sep 50 p	2393	3524	2	3/4	1	− 1	55 1/4
SnapBv Sep 55	3566	2329	5 7/8	1 1/8	2 5/8	+ 1 5/8	55 1/4
SnapBv Sep 55 p	2481	2302	5	2	2 3/4	− 2 3/8	55 1/4
SnapBv Sep 60	2863	2804	3	13/16	7/8	...	55 1/4
SnapBv Sep 60 p	372	339	6 5/8	1 3/16	5 3/4	...	55 1/4
SnapBv Sep 65	343	384	3/4	1/4	1/4	...	55 1/4
SnapBv Oct 40 p	282	728	15/16	1/2	15/16	...	55 1/4
SnapBv Oct 45 p	872	912	2 1/8	1	1 9/16	− 13/16	55 1/4
SnapBv Oct 50	641	759	11	4 3/4	7 1/2	+ 2 7/8	55 1/4
SnapBv Oct 50 p	784	1053	4 7/8	2 3/8	3 1/4	− 7/8	55 1/4
SnapBv Oct 55	809	1082	7 1/8	2 5/8	4 7/8	+ 2 1/4	55 1/4
SnapBv Oct 55 p	943	683	6 1/8	4	5 1/2	− 1 1/2	55 1/4
SnapBv Oct 60	1120	1067	5	2 9/16	2 13/16	...	55 1/4
SnapBv Oct 65	430	274	2 1/8	1 5/16	1 5/16	...	55 1/4
SnapBv Dec 40 p	267	2311	2 1/4	1 1/2	2	− 7/16	55 1/4
SnapBv Dec 45	303	1990	15	10 1/8	12 1/2	+ 3 1/4	55 1/4
SnapBv Dec 45 p	243	1906	3 3/4	2 5/8	3 1/2	− 1/2	55 1/4
SnapBv Dec 50	1289	2141	12 3/8	6 3/4	9 3/8	+ 2 3/4	55 1/4
SnapBv Dec 50 p	462	789	6	4 1/4	5 1/2	− 5/8	55 1/4
SnapBv Dec 55	442	569	9 1/8	4 1/2	6 5/8	+ 2 3/8	55 1/4
SnapBv Dec 60	439	628	6 3/4	1 1/8	4 1/2	...	55 1/4
SnapBv Mar 40 p	323	1463	3 3/4	2 5/8	3 3/4	...	55 1/4
SnapBv Mar 45 p	201	2299	5 3/8	4 1/2	5 3/8	− 1/2	55 1/4
SnapBv Mar 50 p	287	436	7 7/8	6 1/2	7 1/2	− 1 1/2	55 1/4
SnapBv Mar 55 p	400	368	10 1/8	8 1/4	10 1/8	− 7/8	55 1/4
Solectr Sep 40	290	1008	3 5/8	1 3/4	3 3/8	+ 1 7/16	43 1/8
Solectr Sep 45	389	292	1 1/8	3/8	1	+ 5/8	43 1/8
Solectr Oct 40	237	1516	4 5/8	2 7/8	4 5/8	+ 1 7/8	43 1/8
Solectr Oct 40 p	300	1429	2 5/16	1 1/2	1 1/2	− 1 1/2	43 1/8
Solectr Oct 45	296	1084	2 5/8	1 3/8	2 1/8	+ 15/16	43 1/8
Solectr Jan 45	430	797	3	2 7/8	3	+ 5/16	43 1/8
SwAirl Sep 35	282	485	1 7/16	5/8	5/8	− 1 1/8	34 1/2
SwAirl Sep 35 p	757	790	1 9/16	7/8	1 1/8	...	34 1/2
SwAirl Dec 40	215	340	1 7/16	1 1/16	1 1/8	− 1/4	34 1/2
Strbck Sep 50	329	519	3	1 3/16	2 9/16	+ 1 7/16	50 3/4
Strbck Sep 55	209	234	3/4	1/4	1/2	+ 1/4	50 3/4
Strbck Oct 50	556	782	4 1/4	2 3/8	4	+ 1 7/8	50 3/4
Strbck Oct 50 p	310	497	4 5/8	3	3	− 2 1/2	50 3/4
StoTch Sep 25	553	2067	7 1/4	4 7/8	5 5/8	+ 1 1/8	30 3/8
StoTch Sep 25 p	316	3610	1/2	3/16	1/4	− 3/16	30 3/8
StoTch Sep 30	4827	6829	3 3/8	1 3/8	1 7/16	+ 1/16	30 3/8
StoTch Sep 30 p	2518	2267	2	3/4	1	− 1 1/4	30 3/8
StoTch Sep 35	2479	5742	1	5/16	3/8	...	30 3/8
StoTch Sep 35 p	651	1922	5 3/4	3 3/4	5 1/4	− 1	30 3/8
StoTch Sep 40	376	3324	5/16	1/8	1/8	− 1/16	30 3/8
StoTch Oct 25 p	459	545	1	5/8	7/8	− 1/8	30 3/8
StoTch Oct 30	1105	462	4 3/8	2 3/4	3	+ 1/2	30 3/8
StoTch Oct 30 p	405	514	3 1/4	1 7/8	2 1/4	− 1 1/8	30 3/8
StoTch Oct 35	1475	1223	2 1/8	1 1/16	1 1/4	+ 1/4	30 3/8
StoTch Dec 25 p	415	1372	2 1/8	1 1/2	1 7/8	− 3/8	30 3/8

FIGURE 12–1 Options Trading, Chicago Board Options Exchange (*Source: Barron's*, September 6, 1993. Reprinted by permission of *Barron's* © Dow Jones & Company, 1993. All rights reserved.)

tions market. The exchanges initially created three expiration cycles for all listed options, and each issue was (and still is) assigned to one of these three cycles. One cycle is January, April, July, and October; another is February, May, August, and November; and the third is March, June, September, and December. This system

has been modified a bit to include both the current month and the following month, plus the next two months in the regular expiration cycle. The exchanges still use the same three expiration cycles, but they have been altered so investors are always able to trade in the two near-term months plus the next two closest months in the option's regular expiration cycle. With the January cycle, for example, the following options are available in January: January, February, April, and July; the two current months (January and February), plus the next two months in the cycle (April and July). Prices are usually reported in the financial media for only the first three maturities. In February, the available contracts would be February, March, April, and July. Finally, in March, across-the-board changes would be as follows: March, April, July, and October, and so on, as the expiration dates continue rolling over this during the course of the year. For any month of expiration, the actual day of expiration is the Saturday following the third Friday of that month.

Mechanics of Options Trading (CBOE)

Options may be purchased or sold by placing an order with a broker, as for other types of securities. Orders specify whether the order is for puts or calls, the underlying security, expiration month and exercise price, the number of contracts to be purchased or sold, and whether the purchase or sale is an *opening* or *closing* transaction (the former being intended to result in a new position as a holder and the latter to close out a preexisting writer's position). The types of orders found generally in securities markets (that is, market orders, limit orders, and so forth) are also used with puts and calls.

An innovative development in listed options is eliminating a physical instrument to prove ownership of an option. Ordinarily, no certificate is issued, transferred, or canceled in connection with a purchase or sale of any exchange-traded option. This facilitates prompt settlements of transactions and thus improves the listed option's liquidity.

Lack of a certificate means that each transaction and associated money activity must be handled as a bookkeeping entry. Additions and subtractions of option positions and related monies are inscribed on the records of participating brokers and on those of a central agency. This agency, the Options Clearing Corp. (OCC), was created to coordinate and complete operations functions for member organizations.

The success of certificateless trading results from placing the OCC between purchasing and selling brokers on each transaction. The OCC becomes holder and obligor of each option contract on behalf of the members of that transaction. It is also the only issuer of listed options, creating long and short (writing) positions in response to agreements arranged on the trading floors of the participating exchanges.

Book entry record keeping means that the OCC maintains a running total record of option positions and related monies in behalf of each clearing member's customer accounts. Options may be exercised immediately after purchase until the day before expiration. The owner of a listed option can exercise the privilege, re-

quiring performance from the contra party to the agreement. Exercise proceedings are initiated when the clearing member organization, whose ledger at the OCC shows it long on a particular option series, delivers to the OCC an exercise notice form regarding that series.

Although the OCC is the obligor for listed option contracts, it does not own the underlying stock to deliver pursuant to exercise of a call. Nor will it pay money if an investor exercises a put option. It is only an intermediary for buyers and sellers of listed option contracts. It promptly assigns any exercise notification to one of many writers of that option series whose open positions are recorded and maintained on its records. The assignment is made by computer on a random selection basis. Consequently, this procedure can result in assignment of an exercise notice to a member who initiated a writing transaction that very day.

Each member firm carrying customer accounts must also establish an equitable procedure for processing assignments made to it by the OCC. Exercise notices from the OCC must be reassigned among the firm's specific customer accounts with a writing position in that option series. Fair play dictates that an equitable internal allocation process be used that is consistent and based upon a random selection or first-in, first-out (FIFO) method.

The OCC does not automatically pair off and eliminate long positions with each sale of the same option series. Nor does it reduce or eliminate standing short positions with each purchase of the same option series. This means that in addition to basic order and execution information, each ticket must signify whether it is

1. *an opening purchase transaction:* a purchase to establish or add to a long position; the buyer is known as an option holder;
2. *an opening sale transaction:* a sale to establish or add to a short position; the seller is known as a writer;
3. *a closing purchase transaction:* a purchase to reduce or cancel a short position by the writer of that series; or
4. *a closing sale transaction:* a sale to reduce or cancel a long position by an option holder of that series.

From the foregoing list of possibilities, clearly purchasing an option does not necessarily establish a position. Nor does the sale of an option necessarily close a position. An investor may purchase an option to offset an option written. Thus, with this purchase the investor actually eliminates a short position. Similarly, an investor may write or sell an option as a way of establishing a position.

Table 12–1 lists quotations of call options for the Jinx Co. Jinx options are quoted at four different option or exercise prices ($40, $45, $50, $60) for each of three standard expiration dates (January–April–July). The exercise price of an option is set by the exchange when trading first begins in that option. For example, suppose today is February 1. All January options have just matured, and trading will start in October options. If Jinx is currently $46 per share on the NYSE, the exercise price for its October call option will probably be set at $45. This will be the only call option for Jinx for October unless Jinx stock makes a big move. If Jinx

TABLE 12–1

Hypothetical Call Option Quotations

OPTIONS AND EXERCISE PRICE	CLOSING PRICES FOR OPTIONS EXPIRING AT THE END OF:			STOCK PRICE
	JANUARY	APRIL	JULY	
Jinx/60	$\frac{1}{16}$	$\frac{1}{2}$	$\frac{3}{4}$	$46\frac{1}{2}$
Jinx/50	$\frac{1}{8}$	$1\frac{1}{2}$	$2\frac{5}{8}$	$46\frac{1}{2}$
Jinx/45	*	$3\frac{1}{4}$	$4\frac{1}{4}$	$46\frac{1}{2}$
Jinx/40	*	$6\frac{3}{4}$	$7\frac{5}{8}$	$46\frac{1}{2}$

*Unavailable.

stock dropped down to $42, for example, an additional class of Jinx October options—such as Jinx/40—could be established by the exchange. This new option would trade in addition to the Jinx/45.

Examine Table 12–1. At the time the quotations were available, the price of Jinx common stock was $46.50 per share. Those exercise prices quoted at the left that are below the prevailing price of the common stock are referred to as being "in-the-money." This means that the options have some "intrinsic" value represented by the difference between the stock price and the exercise price. Therefore, we know that the intrinsic value of Jinx/40 is $6.50, and for Jinx/45 it is $1.50 (regardless of the expiration date). Any difference between these intrinsic values and the price of the option is what is being paid for an expected rise in the price of the common that *may* lie ahead. This could be referred to as the "time' value of the option contract.

Those option contracts with an exercise price that exceeds the current market price of the stock are referred to as being "out-of-the-money." In effect, these options have no intrinsic value. The prices quoted for these options are what is being paid for any perceived time value.

DETERMINANTS OF OPTION VALUE[2]

The differences among option prices are the result of the interaction of a number of different forces. The only way we can hope to sort out their effects is to take them one at a time.

Although the same set of variables matters for both puts and calls, they do not always matter in the same way, so we will talk about calls first and then come back to puts. Here is our list of six fundamental direct determinants of option value:

1. current stock price (S),
2. striking price (K),

[2]Several option pricing models are examined in detail in R. A. Jarrow and A. Rudd, *Option Pricing* (Homewood, Ill.: Richard D. Irwin, 1983).

3. time to expiration (t),
4. stock volatility,
5. interest rates, and
6. cash dividends.

The first couple are easy to agree upon. The stock price (S) and the striking price (K) will matter before and on the expiration date. The higher (lower) the stock price, the higher (lower) the call value.

Another important determinant is the stock's volatility (dispersion of possible future stock prices). The higher the volatility, the greater the liklihood that the stock will do either very well or very poorly. These are offsetting effects for the owner of the stock, but not for the owner of a call. He will get the full dollar benefit from favorable outcomes but will avoid most of the dollar loss from the unfavorable outcomes because he will not exercise the call. Consequently, the higher the volatility over the lifetime of a call, the higher its value relative to the stock.

If time is measured in years, then time-to-expiration (t) measures the fraction of a year remaining in the life of the option. Listed options currently expire in nine months or less ($t \leq \frac{3}{4}$). One effect of a longer time-to-expiration is the same as higher volatility. Over a long period of time, a lot can happen to even a very low-volatility stock. The call premium tends to be higher the more time remaining before expiration. This premium will shrink as the expiration date nears. A call is thus a wasting asset.

The higher the interest rate (e.g., Treasury bills), the lower the value of the striking price the call buyer has contracted to pay in the event of exercise. From this effect, a higher interest rate will have the same influence as a lower striking price. Consequently, higher interest rates tend to imply higher call prices. The full impact of interest rates will also depend upon their own volatility and their correlation with stock prices.

The present value of the striking price decreases as time (t) increases, so time-to-expiration has another way of influencing the call value: First, more time is provided for changes to occur in the stock price, and second, there is an effect due to the rate of interest. For calls these two effects reinforce each other.

One other fundamental determinant of call values remains. Listed options are protected against stock splits and stock dividends but not cash dividends. This lack of cash dividend protection can be understood by looking at how dividends affect stock prices.

The average stock-price change on an ex-dividend date will be lower than the average change on other days by the amount of the dividend. For any given current stock price, higher future dividends come at the expense of lower future price appreciation. In the extreme, a final liquidating dividend would drive the stock price to zero. Ordinary dividends can be interpreted as partial liquidation of the company, with a resulting lowering of the stock price. The larger the dividend to be paid prior to expiration, the lower the call price.

These same six factors also influence put values. Other things being equal, puts should be more valuable for lower stock prices and interest rates and higher

striking prices—just the reverse of a call. However, stock volatility raises the probability of extreme outcomes and increases both put and call values.

The influence of dividends on put values is somewhat less straightforward. A purchased put (long position) is similar to a short position in a stock. Anyone short a stock does not benefit from price declines due to dividends being paid because he is required to "make good" the dividend to whomever lent the stock. However, put owners get the full benefit of price declines due to dividends. Hence, as dividends increase, a put becomes more attractive to shorting the stock. The higher the cash dividend prior to expiration, the higher the value of a put.

The only surprise is time-to-expiration. There are two contrary effects. First, greater time-to-expiration tends to increase put values by widening the dispersion of possible future stock prices. Second, greater time-to-expiration tends to decrease put values by lowering the proceeds from exercise of the put. At lower stock prices (relative to K), the second effect dominates (increased dispersion has a relatively small influence on put values). For opposite reasons, the first effect dominates. The following table summarizes our analysis of option value determinants.

| | EFFECT OF INCREASE | |
DETERMINING FACTORS	P	C
1. Current stock price (S)	↓	↑
2. Striking price (K)	↑	↓
3. Time to expiration (t)	↑	↑
4. Stock volatility	↑	↑
5. Interest rates	↓	↑
6. Cash dividends	↑	↓

Note: An arrow pointing in one direction means that the effect cannot be in the opposite direction.

Looking at the various Jinx call options in Table 12–1, notice that for any standard exercise price (e.g., Jinx/50), the market price of the option increases as the contract gets longer. For example, the Jinx/50 due in April can be purchased for $1.50. This means $1.50 per share in the standard contract of 100 shares, or a total of $150. This $1.50 plus the exercise price of $50 brings the total to $51.50, or about a $5 premium above the current market price of Jinx stock of $46.50. The premium of $5 is about 11 percent above the prevailing price of the stock ($5/$46.50). In effect, the dollar premium is calculated by adding the exercise price and the option price together and subtracting the market price of the stock. The premium for the Jinx/50 for July is about $6.125, or 13 percent ($6.125/$46.50).

The percentage premium rises as the contract grows longer and also as the amount of cash the buyer must put up gets smaller. For example, look at the July Jinx/40 and Jinx/45. The Jinx/40 sells at a 2½ percent premium and requires the buyer to put up $762.50 (7⅝ × 100 shares). The Jinx/45 sells at a premium of 6 percent but requires the buyer to put up only $425 (4¼ × 100 shares). The cash required in the latter case is about half that of the Jinx/40 option. Most option prices

are between 5 percent and 20 percent of the price of the stock, depending upon the stock's volatility as well as the particular terms of the option.

CBOE option contracts carry commissions based upon the option price, not the stock price, in accordance with regular NYSE commission schedules. A minimum commission of $25 each way (buy or sell) is charged, and option buyers are limited to owning no more than 1,000 calls (100,000 shares) on a single stock to prevent the use of call options to gain control of a firm.

Why Buy Options?

The basic reasons underlying the motivation for buying call options can be illustrated quite clearly. Following are some hypothetical quotes for listed options available for shares of the GTX Corp.:

EXPIRATION/EXERCISE PRICE	PRICE OF OPTION (PREMIUM)	STOCK PRICE
April/15	7	21½
April/20	2	21½
April/25	½	21½

The first reason may be too obvious—speculators get a hot tip on a stock but do not have the money to buy it. A call is cheaper in actual dollars. To buy an April/20 call option on GTX stock costs $200 (excluding commissions) versus $2,150 required to own 100 shares of the stock outright. The second reason is that an investor who wants to buy the stock might be afraid that it will decline in value. Buying a call rather than the stock will reduce his profit by the amount of the premium if the stock advances, but it will limit his loss to the amount of the premium if it declines sharply. In the case of GTX, if the stock were purchased outright at $21.50 and the shares declined to $18, the investor would lose $350 on the purchase of 100 shares. The maximum that could be lost on the purchase of an April/20 option is $200. While the judicious use of a stop order might reduce the loss potential through the outright purchase of common shares, one is never certain at what price a stop order will be executed.

Other investors want to take profits in a stock that they have held for a long time—either for tax purposes or simple profit-taking desires—but cannot separate themselves from their love affair with the stock that has made them so much money. A call can be bought with a percentage of the profits, although this is emotional, not intelligent, investing. A call can be bought for protection: A speculator has sold his stock short but wants to limit his loss if the stock advances. He could enter a stop order, but he then runs the risk of being whipsawed. A call would prevent that at least until expiration or the maximum loss can easily be identified. There are other more esoteric reasons for buying calls, but these are the basic ones, and the others are merely variations of these.

In summary, investors buy listed calls with the hope of selling the option at a higher price. This use is a speculation, and the buyer risks losing 100 percent of the price paid for the call. For his capital, the buyer gets an impressive array of risk opportunities. First, leverage is obtained. A small investment of hundreds of dollars in a call controls underlying stock valued in the thousands. Second, profit potential is relatively unlimited. Many times call-option prices double or triple in a week. These "quantum jump" potentials attract speculators. A third benefit is the fixed risk. The option buyer has peace of mind in knowing the limit of his loss and the knowledge that his loss can never exceed his total capital commitment. This is the speculative side of option buying.

In its simplest form, the put is used by the buyer as a safer way of betting on a decline in the stock than going short. The put increases in value as the underlying stock declines. If the buyer of the put was right about the prospects of the stock, he will get a much higher return on investment than if he had gone short. If he is wrong, he loses the entire price of the option. And if his timing was merely off, the limited loss may give him the courage to wait for the reversal to come. Of course, on the buy side, not all purchasers of puts are going to be speculating on a decline in the underlying stock. Some will be long-term investors who want to buy some insurance against a short-term or intermediate setback in appreciated stock they already hold.

Why Sell Options?

Most calls are sold by conservative investors who want additional income. An investor may own a stock for which he paid $30 and is now $40. He does not want to sell it at this level, but if he could get five points more he would be willing to part with it. He can get these five points by selling a call, but his gain is limited to those five points. On the other hand, if the stock price declines, he has the $500 premium and still owns the stock, which he would have kept anyway (although if the stock rises quickly to $45, the buyer might not exercise, waiting for higher prices, and then watch the price decline; this would prevent the seller from taking his profits). If a writer is particularly bullish on the stock, he can sell a straddle, thereby getting additional premium money for the put side, which he does not expect to be exercised. However, he is committing himself to buy stock only if that stock is declining in price, a practice that can be quite dangerous. Of course, an investor can write puts on short positions. Many writers of options write them naked (i.e., without either owning or being short the underlying stock). This is dangerous if done for one or two stocks, but if an investor utilizes substantial amounts of capital and writes puts and calls on a largely diversified group of securities, the percentage gains work out well, since, as we have already seen, most short-term options are significantly overvalued. We should point out that writing naked options well requires nerves of steel and substantial capital.

Writing puts is a sensible strategy for an individual who wants to accumulate a particular stock but believes a better buying opportunity will arise later. With XYZ selling at $50, the investor writes a put at 50 for which he receives a premium of $500, or $5 a share. If the stock drops to 40 and the put is exercised, he must buy

the stock at 50, which is offset by the premium received, so the effective purchase price is 45. This is better than 50, at which the decision was made, but worse than the 40 that could have been received if he had waited longer.

On the other hand, if the investor is wrong and the stock climbed immediately, the missed opportunity to buy at 50 is compensated by the income from the premium received.

Another investor, though, may believe the stock is going to rise. He writes the put hoping that the put will expire without being exercised and he will have made a profit from the premium without significantly encumbering any capital.

OPTION POSITIONS AND STRATEGIES[3]

Stock and Option Equivalencies

The relationship of options to stocks and to each other can be summarized as follows:

C = Call
P = Put   Long: +
S = Stock (100 shares)   Short: −

- $(+P) = (+C) + (-S)$: A long put equals a long call and short stock. If an investor is short stock, he has downside potential, but his upside risk is limited to the premium paid.
- $(+S) = (+C) + (-P)$: If an investor has a long position in a call and short position in a put, he has the economic equivalent of owning a stock because he owns the upside potential through the long call and has the risk of ownership through the short put; that is, stock will be put to him if it declines.
- $(+C) = (+S) + (+P)$: A long call equals long stock and a long put. By being long a call, an investor has the upside potential of the stock, but he has paid a premium to limit loss.
- $(-C) = (-S) + (-P)$: A short call equals short stock plus a short put. In this position, his profit is the premium on the call and his liability on the upside is unlimited.
- $(-P) = (+S) + (-C)$: A short put equals long stock and a short call. If an investor is long stock and short its call, he is in a covered writing position. This is equivalent to a short put, because he has limited his profit to the premium and have incurred the risk of ownership.
- $(-S) = (+P) + (-C)$: Short stock equals a long put and a short call. In either case, he would profit from a decline in the price of the stock and suffer from a rise in price.

[3]An excellent comparison of various option strategies appears in P. Ritchken, *Options* (Glenview, Ill.: Scott, Foresman, 1987), and R. T. Slivka, "Risk and Return for Option Investment Strategies," *Financial Analysts Journal* (September–October 1980).

Option strategies can be for speculative, hedging, or spreading purposes. *Speculation* in options involves the purchase or the sale of an option without any position in the underlying stock. Such speculation can be magnified by buying or selling options in multiples or by packaging various combinations of put and call options. *Hedging* involves attempts to manage or control risk. Such hedging frequently involves the purchase or sale of an option in conjunction with a long or short position in the stock. Hedging can be done strictly within the options market, that is, by the simultaneous purchase of one option and the sale of another. This is called *spreading*.

This section deals with the analysis of option positions using graphs, which allows us to examine the risk-reward characteristics of any holding. These graphs facilitate a profit-loss analysis of any position. A specific set of stock and option terms and prices has been selected to make the examples comparable and permit the reader to combine two or more strategies. To simplify our analysis, the following basic assumptions have been adopted.

1. A call option is available with six months remaining until expiration. It has a striking price of $100. The current price of this call is $10.

2. It is possible to buy or sell a put analogous to the call with a striking price of $100. These puts are selling at $11.

3. The common stock the investor purchases or sells short or which underlies any options he may buy or write is selling at $95 a share.

Each investment position or strategy is depicted on a standardized graph. The profit-loss line on the graph shows the dollar profit or loss the investor will experience at each possible stock price approximately six months after the position is initiated. In the case of strategies involving options, one assumes that the options will expire in six months, so the price six months out is also the price of the stock when the option expires. Any two strategies can be compared at any stock price by transferring the profit-loss line from one graph to the other or by preparing a new graph and imposing both strategies on that graph.

The discussion of various strategies and their outcomes that follows use cases that are, in effect, "pure" strategies. One can adopt intermediate strategies. For example, it is possible to purchase stock and write a lesser amount of call options. The lines in our graphs can be made to assume any slope, not merely those illustrated.

BUY SHORT-TERM DEBT SECURITIES

Figure 12–2 helps explain the use of the graphic technique. The vertical axis on the chart measures the dollar profit that the investor will realize by following this strategy. The horizontal axis lists possible prices for the hypothetical stock six months from the day the investment is initiated.

In the example illustrated here, the investor buys a short-term debt instrument paying 6 percent annually, or 3 percent over the six-month period. On a $95 investment, the interest income for six months is 3% × $95, or $2.85. As indicated

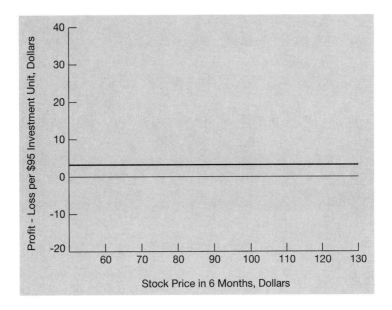

FIGURE 12–2 Purchase Short-Term Debt Securities

by the horizontal profit-loss line, income is totally independent of the price of the security.

BUY STOCK

Figure 12–3 assumes that the investor purchases 100 shares of common stock at a price of $95 per share. The profit or loss is exclusively a function of the price of the stock six months in the future. If the price of the stock falls to $75, the investor suffers a loss of $20 per share over the six-month period. If the price of the stock rises to $120, the investor receives a profit of $25. The key feature of this strategy is that the investor's profit or loss bears a direct linear relationship to the price of the stock on the date the determination of return is made. If an investor is optimistic about the probable course of stock prices in general and the price of this stock in particular, this position would be favored. If the investor is not overly optimistic, a strict long position in the stock would probably be avoided.

SELL STOCK SHORT

The graph depicting the short seller's position (Figure 12–4) is the converse of the stock buyer's graph illustrated in Figure 12–2. For every point the stock rises, the buyer gains $1 per share and the short seller loses $1 per share. If the stock declines, the short seller profits to exactly the extent that the buyer loses.

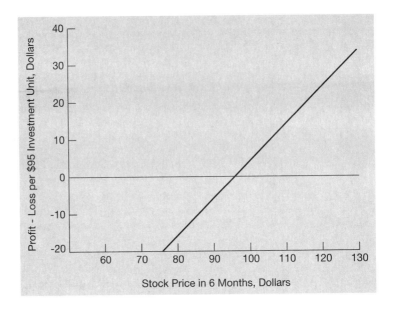

FIGURE 12–3   Purchase Stock

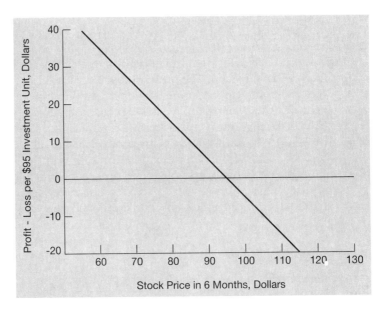

FIGURE 12–4   Sell Stock Short

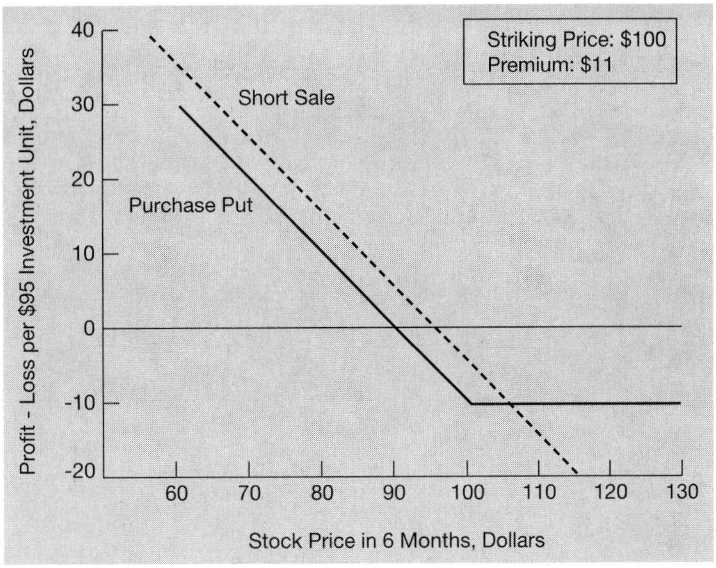

FIGURE 12–5   Purchase a Put

PURCHASE A PUT

Unless the put buyer is able to sell or exercise his put at a time when the price of the stock is below the striking price, he can lose his entire investment. To the extent that the price of the stock drops, the buyer of a put participates point for point in any decline below the striking price. In the example in Figure 12–5, the put is profitable at any price below $89 (the striking price minus the option premium, or $100 − $11), neglecting the effect of commissions.

The purchase of a put option is an alternative to short selling. A short sale of stock at $100, which subsequently falls to $89, would represent an $11 profit to the short seller (excluding commissions). For the put buyer his profit would not begin until the stock reached $89. However, the put buyer invests less cash ($1,110 versus $10,000), is not responsible for the dividend (which the short seller is), does not have to borrow stock, and pays a smaller commission. Above all, however, the most the put buyer can lose is the premium. The loss exposure for the short seller is not so finite if the stock moves up. In Table 12–2 we illustrate the relative positions of a put buyer and short seller at varying closing stock prices.

Put options can also be used for downside protection of existing stock positions. For example, an investor who bought stock at $80 that has risen to $100 may be willing to pay an option premium of several points to be assured of the right to sell the stock later for at least $100.

TABLE 12–2

Relative Positions of a Short Seller and Put
Buyer at Various Closing Stock Prices*

| | GAIN (+) OR LOSS (−) | |
STOCK AT:	SHORT SALE ($100)	PURCHASE PUT (100/11)
80	+20	+9
90	+10	−9
100	0	−11
110	−10	−11
120	−20	−11

*At $80 the investor makes $20 ($100 − $80) on the short sale. He "put" the stock to the buyer at $100, making $20, less the $11 put premium, to net $9. At $120, the short position loses $20 ($100 − 120). The put option is not exercised, and the $11 premium is lost.

BUY A CALL

With the purchase of a call (see Figure 12–6), the profit-loss line is no longer a straight line passing through the price of the stock on the day the purchase was made. The purchase of a call with a striking price of $100 at a premium of $10 would result in the loss of the entire investment if the call expired with the stock selling below the striking price of $100 per share. In addition, the investor does not even begin to make money until the price of the stock exceeds the striking price

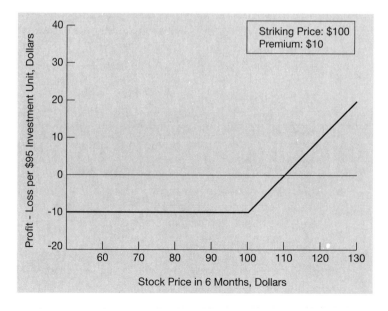

FIGURE 12–6   Purchase a Call

plus the option premium paid for the call. In this case, $100 (striking price) plus $10 (option premium) equals $110 (break-even point). However, if, for example, the price of the stock rises to $130 per share, the call buyer will have at least tripled his investment because the call option is worth at least $30 ($130 − $100).

The key advantages and disadvantages of owning a call option should be evident. Although the buyer loses his entire investment if the stock sells below the striking price when the option expires, his maximum risk exposure is limited to the amount of the option premium. This is true regardless of how low the price of the stock may fall. On the other hand, the call buyer participates in any advance in the price of the stock above the striking price. Profit increases point for point, no matter how high the price of the stock may rise over the life of the option.

SELL OR WRITE A CALL

Figure 12–7 illustrates the position of the writer of a call option who does not own the underlying stock. Such a position is referred to as uncovered, or *naked.* The uncovered writer gets to keep all of the call premium if the buyer of the option does not exercise it. The naked writing position will be profitable as long as the price of the stock does not rise above the writer's break-even point: $100 (striking price) plus $10 (call premium) equals $110 (break-even point).

The premium received by the option writer is available to him to invest in Treasury bills, reduce the debit balance in his margin account, or whatever.

The risk position of the naked call writer is such that he can never gain more than the amount of the call premium, yet his possible loss in the event of a runaway stock is substantial. The loss could easily be many times the amount of the option

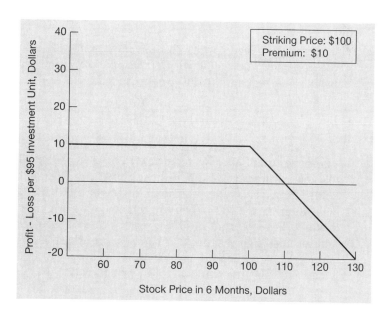

FIGURE 12–7   Sell or Write a Call

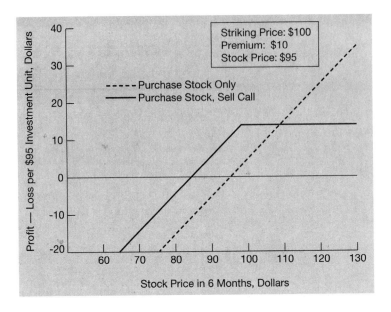

FIGURE 12–8   Purchase the Stock and Sell a Call

premium. In spite of this risk, naked writing can be an effective strategy when used intelligently.

If an investor feels strongly that a particular stock is going to decline but does not anticipate that the decline will be of such magnitude that a short sale will be highly profitable, he may elect to write naked calls. As long as his commitment in this case is not substantial relative to his resources, the profitability can be excellent, and the naked writing position can actually reduce the overall level of risk in the portfolio. The way in which this apparently high-risk strategy can reduce risk will be clear when we discuss option hedging shortly.

PURCHASE THE STOCK AND SELL A CALL[4]

This strategy is illustrated by the solid line in the graph (Figure 12–8) and is the classic posture of the covered call writer. The covered call writer buys 100 shares of the underlying stock and writes one call contract using the stock position as collateral. The call premium provides a degree of protection if the underlying stock declines during the life of the option. In return for this downside protection, the covered writer's profit is limited, in this case to $15 per share over six months, no matter how high the stock price rises. At any stock price in excess of $110 per share, the writer should have been better off not to have written the call, as indicated in owning the stock without writing a call.

[4]J. W. Yates and M. J. Alderson, "Writing Covered Call Options: Profits and Risks," *Journal of Portfolio Management* (Fall 1980).

The reasons for writing covered options are diverse. An investor may have a long-term position in the underlying stock which, for tax reasons, he is reluctant to sell even though he is not optimistic about the near-term price action of the stock. Rather than incur a large tax liability, he writes options to partially insulate himself from what he feels is a significant downside risk. If this investor's appraisal of the stock proves incorrect and it rises over the life of the option, he does not have to deliver his long-term low-cost stock. He can repurchase the option, terminating his writer's obligation and realizing an ordinary loss on the option.

Some writers write calls only on stocks they feel positive about and are willing to hold. This tactic may seem odd, for by writing the option, these investors are precluded from obtaining more than limited profit if the stock rises as they anticipate. If the stock rises above the striking price, these writers are sure to earn the option premium. When earned consistently, option premiums can provide a highly satisfactory return. The major risk in adopting this strategy is that the premium may limit the return when the stock rises by substantially more than it reduces the loss when the stock declines.

Others will write covered options only when they feel the option premium is high relative to the fair value of the option. Such persons are usually relatively neutral toward the stock but can have a strong opinion that the option is overpriced.

SELL A PUT

Just as the writer of naked calls receives 100 percent of the premium if the stock is selling below the striking price when the call expires, the seller of naked puts receives 100 percent of the put premium if the stock is selling above the striking price when the put expires. The naked put seller's reward declines as the price of the stock falls below the striking price. In the example illustrated in Figure 12–9, the seller of the naked put actually begins to lose money when the stock price falls below 89.

Writing a put can be an attractive alternative to placing a limit order to buy for an investor who basically likes a stock but expects near-term weakness. With a limit order, he may miss getting the stock by just a fraction and lose all his profit. By writing a put instead at a price below the market, he will earn the premium even if the stock goes up without first dipping down. And if his expectations turn out to be correct, he will also end up owning the stock at the lower price.

A put writer places himself in virtually the same position as a covered call writer. Assume that the covered call writer's shares are selling at a price exactly equal to the call's exercise price. Like the covered call writer, the put writer (at the same striking price) takes in a premium and loses point for point on a stock decline—although in his case the loss is not in the stock but in buying back the put. And if the stock rises, he, too, will profit by an amount limited to the option premium. The put will expire worthless, and he will not have to buy it back.

The major difference is that the covered call writer has a larger sum invested in the market, and receives dividends on his investment. The put writer, on the other hand, holds his money in cash, earning interest on it all the while—and also keeping it available to buy stock in the event it is later put to him. Another differ-

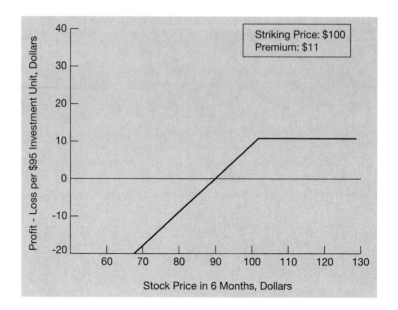

FIGURE 12–9   Sell or Write a Put

ence is that the put and call premiums may not be exactly the same. Then, too, the put writer hopes never to have to pay the commissions to buy the stock.

The essential equivalence of a naked put writer and a covered call writer can easily be seen in the example illustrated below. The example assumes the stock is at $50 and put and call options with exercise prices of 50 are available at 5. The writer of a covered call earns $500 if the stock stands still; if it falls, he will lose the amount of the decline, less $500. The naked put seller makes $500 if the stock stands still or rises. If the stock falls, he will lose the amount of the decline, less $500. Thus, the economic opportunity and risk of writing a naked put are exactly the same as writing a covered call.

WITH STOCK AT:	BUYING 100 SHARES AT 50 AND WRITING ONE $50 CALL AT 5 WILL SHOW AT EXPIRATION				WRITING ONE NAKED $50 PUT WILL SHOW AT EXPIRATION THIS CHANGE IN VALUE OF PUT:
	STOCK CHANGE	+	CALL CHANGE	= NET CHANGE	
0	−5,000		+500	−4,500	−4,500
25	−2,500		+500	−2,000	−2,000
35	−1,500		+500	−1,000	−1,000
40	−1,000		+500	−500	−500
45	−500		+500	0	0
50	0		+500	+500	+500
55	+500		0	+500	+500
100	+5,000		−4,500	+500	+500

COMBINATIONS OF PUT AND CALL OPTIONS

The simultaneous availability of puts and calls makes for some interesting combinations. Four basic kinds of options are a combination of puts and calls. A *straddle* is a put and a call on the same security at the same exercise price and for the same time period. A *strip* is two puts and one call at the same exercise price for the same period. A *spread* consists of a put and a call option on the same security for the same time period at different prices. A *strap* is two calls and one put at the same contracted exercise price and for the same period.

The buyer of a straddle is betting the premium paid that the price of the option security will deviate (either up or down) from the exercise price. The writer of a straddle accepts this bet and implicitly asserts confidence that the security's price will not vary significantly before the option expires. The buyer of a strip is betting the price of some security will change from the exercise price, but the buyer believes that the security's price is more likely to fall than it is to rise. Because a strip is two puts and a call, the buyer evidently believes a decrease in the price of the option security is more probable than an increase. A strap is like a strip that is skewed in the opposite direction. The buyer of a strap evidently foresees bullish and bearish possibilities for the optioned security with a price rise being more likely.

CALL SPREADS.   A *spread* is a trade involving the purchase of one option and the sale of another, both on the same stock. The person doing the spreading is hedging. Although spreads often become complicated, all are based on either of two patterns. If both options have the same exercise price, but one expires later than the other, we refer to this as a *time spread.* If both expire in the same month, but one exercise price is higher than the other, we have a *price spread.*[5]

To illustrate the price spread, suppose that we have three options on the same stock expiring in the same month: one at an exercise price of 50, another at 60, and a third at 70. If these options have about three months to run, and the stock is now selling at 60, we might see these prices:

Option at 70	2
Option at 60	4
Option at 50	11

Bullish spreads involve buying the more expensive option (lower exercise price) and selling the cheaper option (higher exercise price). The spread will show a profit if prices rise. For example, let us assume the 60s are selling for 4 points and the 70s for 2. If you were bullish on the stock, you might buy the 60s. Or you might prefer the bullish spread, buying the 60s and selling the 70s. You would pay out $400 and take in $200, so your net cost would be $200. If the stock is selling above 70 at the expiration date, the option at 70 that you sold will then be exercised. In

---

[5]A discussion of the techniques of option spreading is found in R. T. Slivka, "Call Option Spreading," *Journal of Portfolio Management* (Spring 1981).

turn, you may exercise the option at 60 that you bought. But your profit can never be more than $1,000, less the net cost of $200 you paid at the outset. This is an attractive ratio of risk to reward; you stand to lose $200 or make $800.

Let us examine some results of this bull spread under varying assumptions regarding the stock price:

	BULL SPREAD—GAIN (LOSS) FROM		
STOCK PRICE AT:	BUY SIDE 60 AT 4	SELL SIDE 70 AT 2	NET
55	(400)	200	(200)
60	(400)	200	(200)
62	(200)	200	0
65	100	200	300
70	600	200	800
75	1100	(300)	800

Break-even:	Stock price = Buy exercise price + difference in premiums (62).
Maximum profit:	Stock price ≥ Sell option exercise price (70). Maximum dollar profit equal to difference in exercise prices less difference in premiums: $(70 - 60) - (4 - 2) = 8 \times 100 = \$800$.
Maximum loss:	Stock price ≤ Buy option exercise price (60). Maximum dollar loss equal to difference in premiums: $4 - 2 = 2 \times 100 = \$200$.

Suppose the stock closes at 75. The option you purchased with an exercise price of 60 will be exercised. You must pay 60 per share and can sell these shares for 75, for a net of 15 less the original premium paid of 4 for a final net of 11 ($1,100). Netted together, the buy and sell sides give an $800 gain (excluding commissions). Notice that had you simply bought the 60 option at 4, the range of outcomes if the stock closed between 55 and 75 would have been between ($400) and +$1,100. Hedging your bet with the sale of a 70 at 2 (creating a spread) narrows the outcomes from ($200) to +$800. The spread is less risky than the simple purchase of a call. Beneath the table are some general rules for determining maximum profits and losses for bullish spreads as well as the break-even point.

Suppose the stock closes at 60. The person purchasing the contract with a 70 exercise price will let it expire. You gain the premium paid of 2 ($200) excluding commissions. As the buyer of a contract with an exercise price of 60, you will let it expire. Your loss of $400 is offset by the premium collected from the option you sold for $200. Net loss to you is $200. At a closing price of 75 the following occurs: The person buying the 70 from you at 2 will exercise the option, paying 70 for the stock (per share). You will have to pay 75 to buy the stock. The difference between

your cost of 75 and his payment of 70 is dampened by the original premium received of 2. The net result is a loss of 3 ($300).

If you were bearish on the stock, you might find it attractive to sell the option at 50 and buy the option at 60. You would thus take in $1,100 from your sale, and pay out $400 on your purchase. The difference would be $700, which would be credited to your account. To make the trade, you must put up margin equal to the difference in the exercise prices. In this instance, it would be 10 points, or $1,000. But you need supply only $300 of your own funds because the spread itself would give you a credit of $700. We speak of this as a *bearish spread* because it becomes profitable as the price of the stock goes down. The best outcome would be if the stock declined to 50 or lower and both options expired worthless. Then you would keep the $700 as your profit. The worst outcome would be if the stock rose to 60 and if the option at 50, which you sold, were then exercised. In turn, you could exercise the option at 60, which you bought. The purchase and sale of the stock would show a loss of $1,000 because you would buy at 60 but sell at 50. However, you would still have the $700 you took in at the outset. So your net loss would be reduced to $300.

This bearish spread, where a profit is anticipated if the stock declines, generally involves buying the lowest-priced option (highest exercise price) and selling the most expensive option (lowest exercise price). In this case we are dealing with options with the same expiration date.

Of course, it is also possible to enter into time spreads. These are trades involving the purchase of one option and the sale of another, both on the same stock at the same exercise price. The purchase and sale, however, involve different expiration dates. In using time spreads it is generally useful to sell the option with the smallest premium (closest expiration date) and to buy the option with the larger premium (later expiration date).

A bearish price spread is illustrated graphically in Figure 12–10. Specifically, this spread assumes that the investor buys the $10 option with the $100 striking price used in the previous graphs. To set up the spread, the investor writes an option having the same expiration date, but a striking price of $90, that is selling for $16, that is, $1,600 per 100-share contract. The unadjusted profit-loss line shows a fair profit if the stock declines and a loss if the stock rises.

Long-Term Options

The standard option expires in eight months or less. Long-term equity anticipation securities (LEAPS) have maturities that extend as far as two years. LEAPS are now traded on all major exchanges covering more than 100 different stocks (see Table 12–3).

LEAPS work like other option contracts, except for the extended maturity. You get this extension by paying a lot more for one of these options. Look at Table 12–3. The General Electric option due in January 1996 sells for 6.25. This option has a striking price of 110 with the stock at 95.50. This means the stock must rise to

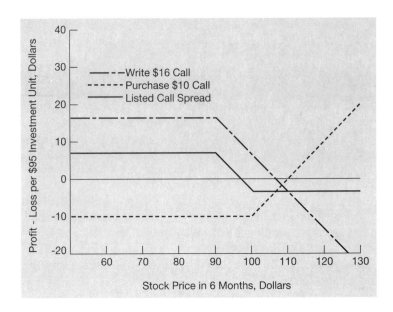

FIGURE 12–10   Call Spread

116.25 before January 1996 to make things interesting. That's a 21 percent rise! This option has a large premium.

The standard short-term option has a lot of attractions, but the biggest danger is the "time bomb" ticking away as these options move toward extinction. No fuse on LEAPS is lit until they get into the same temporal range. You on LEAPS is lit until they get into the same temporal range. You could still pick a bad stock, but at least the loss from a LEAPS would not come from a common error: choosing an option with a relatively short period until expiration. It is also worth noting that the longer time to expiration can be unattractive for a liberal dividend paying stock. A stock paying a $5 annual dividend could cost the option holder $1,000 ($5 × 100 shares × two years). As always, look before you LEAPS!

Taxes, Margin, and Commissions

Taxes

Writers (buyers) experience capital gains or losses via repurchase or expiration (selling or expiration). The short- or long-term nature of the gain or loss depends upon the holding period of the option.

Buyers of call options who exercise them have a cost basis for the purchased stock that is the striking price plus the purchase price of the call. The holding pe-

TABLE 12–3

LEAPS—Long-Term Options

LEAPS — LONG TERM OPTIONS

			–Call–		–Put–	
Option/Strike		Exp.	Vol.	Last	Vol.	Last
ABarck	20	Jan 95	94	6 7/8	...	...
23 1/2	25	Jan 95	15	4 1/4	...	...
23 1/2	30	Jan 96	1602	4 5/8	...	...
AHome	45	Jan 95	20	14 5/8	...	...
ASA	35	Jan 96	25	13 3/4	...	...
AT&T	40	Jan 95	19	18 1/2	...	...
57 3/4	50	Jan 95	19	10 1/8	32	2
57 3/4	60	Jan 95	28	4 3/4	73	6
57 3/4	60	Jan 96	43	7 1/4	...	...
AmExp	20	Jan 95	50	16	...	...
35 1/4	30	Jan 95	50	8	9	1 7/8
35 1/4	40	Jan 95	10	3	...	...
Amgen	45	Jan 95	10	5 1/4	...	...
AppleC	20	Jan 96	92	7 7/8	10	3 3/4
23	30	Jan 96	7	4 7/8	18	9 3/4
23	60	Jan 95	105	1/4	...	...
BkBost	25	Jan 95	65	4 1/2	...	...
24 7/8	30	Jan 95	359	2 5/8	...	...
Boeing	40	Jan 95	10	3 1/2	...	...
37 5/8	40	Jan 96	24	5 1/8	...	...
BrMySq	60	Jan 95	55	3 3/4	...	...
Chase	35	Jan 95	...	...	300	3 1/8
37	40	Jan 95	40	3 3/8	...	...
ChmBnk	30	Jan 95	15	16	...	...
45 1/4	40	Jan 95	24	8 3/8	...	...
45 1/4	40	Jan 96	5	10	20	3 5/8
45 1/4	50	Jan 95	50	3 3/8	...	...
Chrysl	50	Jan 95	15	7 1/4	...	...
Cisco	30	Jan 96	15	22 1/4	...	...
45	50	Jan 95	41	9 1/4	...	...
Citicp	25	Jan 95	29	15 3/8	10	5/8
38 7/8	30	Jan 95	1	11 1/8	546	1 1/2
38 7/8	35	Jan 95	40	8 1/4	14	3
38 7/8	40	Jan 95	12	5 1/2	10	5 1/8
38 7/8	45	Jan 95	23	3 1/2	...	...
CocaCl	35	Jan 95	...	...	50	1 5/8
41 1/4	40	Jan 95	10	5	4	3 1/2
Compaq	25	Jan 95	15	34 3/4	...	...
ConrPr	10	Jan 95	25	2 5/8	...	...
Digital	40	Jan 96	12	9	...	...
Disney	30	Jan 95	110	11 7/8	...	...
39 1/8	50	Jan 96	...	...	10	12
DuPont	55	Jan 95	29	1 5/8	...	...
EKodak	50	Jan 95	101	10 1/8	...	...
57 3/8	70	Jan 95	25	2 1/8	...	...
Exxon	80	Jan 95	225	13/16	...	...
FedNM	60	Jan 95	11	21 1/2	...	...
78 3/8	90	Jan 95	15	4 5/8	...	...
FordM	55	Jan 95	15	7 1/4	...	...
55 7/8	65	Jan 95	25	3 5/8	...	...
GTE	30	Jan 95	10	8 1/8	10	1/2
GaPac	45	Jan 95	10	18	25	1 1/8
GenEl	75	Jan 95	10	22 1/2	...	...
95 1/2	80	Jan 96	...	...	60	3 3/4
95 1/2	110	Jan 95	52	3 5/8	...	...
95 1/2	110	Jan 96	60	6 1/4	...	...
Glaxo	15	Jan 95	...	...	50	15/16
20	20	Jan 95	21	3 1/4	5	3
20	25	Jan 95	70	1 7/16	4	6 1/4
20	35	Jan 95	125	3/8	...	...
GnMotr	40	Jan 95	19	8 7/8	...	...
Homstk	22 1/2	Jan 96	20	4 1/4	...	...
IBM	35	Jan 95	...	...	24	1 5/8
44 1/8	40	Jan 96	205	10 1/2	100	4 1/2
44 1/8	45	Jan 95	39	5 3/4	...	...
44 1/8	50	Jan 96	19	5 5/8	...	...
44 1/8	55	Jan 95	94	2 7/16	60	12 1/2
44 1/8	60	Jan 96	104	3 1/4	100	16 3/4
44 1/8	70	Jan 95	47	3/4	...	...
Intel	32 1/2	Jan 95	...	...	40	1/2
68 3/4	40	Jan 96	15	33 1/2	...	...
68 3/4	50	Jan 95	2	23 3/4	322	15/16
68 3/4	65	Jan 95	61	14	...	...
68 3/4	65	Jan 96	12	18 1/2	...	...
68 3/4	72 1/2	Jan 95	75	10 5/8	10	11 7/8
68 3/4	80	Jan 95	32	7 5/8	1	16 1/8
JohnJn	40	Jan 96	...	...	50	5 3/4
39 5/8	45	Jan 95	26	3	...	...
39 5/8	45	Jan 96	50	4 3/4	...	...
K mart	17 1/2	Jan 95	25	7	...	...
24 3/8	25	Jan 95	12	2 1/2	...	...
Limitd	30	Jan 95	20	1 7/8	...	...
Marriot	20	Jan 96	...	...	18	7/8
33 1/4	30	Jan 95	11	6 1/8	...	...
MerLyn	80	Jan 95	...	...	53	5 1/2
97 7/8	100	Jan 95	...	...	20	13 3/4
97 7/8	100	Jan 96	50	19 1/8	50	18
Merck	30	Jan 95	133	4 3/8	1	3 3/4
30 1/4	30	Jan 96	126	5 7/8	120	4 3/4
30 1/4	40	Jan 95	288	1 9/16	...	...
30 1/4	50	Jan 96	46	1 5/16	...	...
30 1/4	60	Jan 95	70	1/4	2	30
MicrTc	60	Jan 96	17	12 7/8	...	...
Micsft	80	Jan 95	...	...	28	8 5/8
Motorla	100	Jan 95	46	14	2	13 1/4
96 3/4	120	Jan 95	95	7	...	...
96 3/4	120	Jan 96	15	12	...	...
Nike B	55	Jan 95	...	...	24	13 3/4
Oracle	50	Jan 96	...	...	18	10 1/8
58 1/2	60	Jan 96	20	19 1/8	...	...
58 1/2	75	Jan 96	...	...	18	23 1/8
PepsiC	40	Jan 95	12	4 1/4	10	4 1/8
Pfizer	70	Jan 96	17	6 1/8	...	...
PhilMr	40	Jan 95	35	9 1/4	...	...
47 1/8	50	Jan 95	61	4	...	...
47 1/8	60	Jan 95	379	1 1/2	20	14 7/8
47 1/8	80	Jan 95	25	3/8	...	...
PlacrD	15	Jan 95	15	7 7/8	...	...
21 1/4	20	Jan 95	15	5	...	...
ProctG	50	Jan 96	4	6 3/4	15	5 3/4
RJR Nb	5	Jan 96	70	1 5/16	10	1 5/16
4 1/2	5	Jan 96	...	...	210	1 5/16
4 1/2	7 1/2	Jan 95	131	1/4	...	...
StorTch	30	Jan 95	20	6 7/8	...	...
26 1/8	40	Jan 95	15	4	...	...
SunMic	25	Jan 96	20	5 3/4	...	...
Syntex	15	Jan 95	...	...	10	1 3/4
17 3/8	20	Jan 96	30	3 1/8	...	...
TelMex	35	Jan 95	10	16 5/8	...	...
50 1/8	35	Jan 95	66	16 7/8	...	...
50 1/8	40	Jan 96	...	...	80	3 1/2
50 1/8	40	Jan 96	...	...	80	3 5/8
50 1/8	45	Jan 95	35	9 7/8	...	...
Texaco	50	Jan 96	15	19	...	...
TimeW	40	Jan 95	22	6 1/2	...	...
US Surg	20	Jan 95	37	7 1/4	32	2 5/8
24 5/8	20	Jan 96	83	9 5/8	...	...
24 5/8	25	Jan 95	30	5 3/8	29	4 7/8
24 5/8	30	Jan 95	233	3 3/4	...	...
24 5/8	30	Jan 96	95	5 7/8	5	8 3/4
24 5/8	40	Jan 96	240	3 1/8	...	...
24 5/8	45	Jan 95	28	1 1/8	...	...
24 5/8	60	Jan 95	10	7/16	6	36 1/2
Unisys	10	Jan 95	10	3 1/4	...	...
Upjohn	25	Jan 95	82	5 5/8	...	...
29 1/8	30	Jan 95	15	2 7/8	32	4 1/4
29 1/8	35	Jan 95	30	1 7/16	...	...
29 1/8	35	Jan 96	40	2 3/4	...	...
WMX Tc	25	Jan 96	15	8 1/4	1	2
WalMart	22 1/2	Jan 95	140	6 1/2	20	1 1/4
26 3/4	27 1/2	Jan 95	43	3 7/8	40	3 1/2
26 3/4	32 1/2	Jan 95	748	1 7/8	...	...
26 3/4	37 1/2	Jan 95	25	7/8	9	10 5/8
WalMrt	25	Jan 96	110	6 1/2	...	...
26 3/4	30	Jan 96	100	4 3/8	5	5 1/8
Wolwth	25	Jan 95	20	3 1/2	...	...
WstgEl	10	Jan 95	5	4	20	5/8
13 1/2	10	Jan 96	...	...	20	1 1/16
13 1/2	15	Jan 96	252	11/16	...	...
13 1/2	20	Jan 96	25	1 3/16	...	...

VOLUME & OPEN INTEREST SUMMARIES
Includes all equity and index contracts.

AMERICAN			
Call Vol:	4,932	Open Int:	494,566
Put Vol:	1,252	Open Int:	308,028
CHICAGO BOARD			
Call Vol:	4,180	Open Int:	528,559
Put Vol:	2,188	Open Int:	621,710
PHILADELPHIA			
Call Vol:	623	Open Int:	209,023
Put Vol:	72	Open Int:	99,645
PACIFIC			
Call Vol:	121	Open Int:	23,141
Put Vol:	76	Open Int:	12,275
NEW YORK			
Call Vol:	16	Open Int:	32,402
Put Vol:	10	Open Int:	12,793
TOTAL			
Call Vol:	9,872	Open Int:	1,287,691
Put Vol:	3,598	Open Int:	1,054,451

Source: The Wall Street Journal, October 8, 1993.

riod of the stock starts on the day after the acquisition of the stock—it does not include the holding period of the call. Recognition of the capital gain or loss on the call is, in effect, deferred until the stock is sold—it will then be long-term or short-term, depending on the length of time the stock has been held.

Put buyers who exercise the option calculate proceeds from the sale of the stock based on the striking price minus the purchase price of the put. The resulting capital gain or loss is recognized at the time of exercise and is long-term or short-term, depending on the holding period of the stock delivered.

Exercise provides the only complication. In this case the purchased option is considered part of the resulting stock transaction, except that the holding period of the option is disregarded.

For call writers, when exercise occurs, proceeds from the sale of stock are based on the striking price plus the sale price of the call. The resulting capital gain or loss is recognized at the time of exercise and is long-term or short-term, depending on the holding period of the stock delivered.

Put writers calculate the basis for the purchased stock as the striking price minus the sale price of the put. The holding period of the stock starts on the day after acquisition of the stock—it does not include the holding period of the put. Recognition of the capital gain or loss on the put is, in effect, deferred until the stock is sold. It will then be long-term or short-term, depending on the length of time the stock is held.

For covered positions (e.g., stock plus option) or positions involving only options (e.g., spreads), the complications are many. Most arise from wash sale and short sale rules. The reader should consult suitable references on taxation to explore this complex subject.

Margin Requirements.

The minimum margin that must be maintained on a daily basis in the margin account of an uncovered (naked) writer of an option is the greater of 100 percent of the current market value of the option or $250. Margin is not required with respect to a covered writing position in an option. However, margin must be maintained with respect to the underlying stock position in the account in an amount equal to 25 percent of the current market price of the underlying stock or of the exercise price of the option, whichever is less. The NYSE's rules require an uncovered writing transaction to be margined as if the option has been exercised. This means that 30 percent of the market value of the underlying stock must be maintained in the margin account. Many brokers impose more stringent requirements upon their option-writing customers. Customer margin requirements on stock options are summarized in the following display:

Customer Margin Requirements on Stock Options
(As of July 11, 1988)

Long options:	Premium must be paid in full
Naked short options	
In-the-money:	$\pi + (.20 \times S)$
Out-of-the-money:	$\pi + MAX[(.20 \times S) - T, .10 \times S]^*$
Hedges	
Short call, long stock:	0 for call
	$.50 \times S$ for stock
Short put, short stock:	0 for put
	$1.50 \times S$ for stock

Spreads
  Long expires
    before short: Premium must be paid in full for long.
                         Short treated as naked.

  Long does not
    expire before short
      Call spreads: Premium must be paid in full for long.
                         MAX[E(long)–E(short), 0] for short.
      Put spreads: Premium must be paid in full for long.
                         MAX[E(short)–E(long), 0] for short.
  Short combinations: The greater of the naked short put or the naked short
                         call requirement plus π for the option with the lower
                         requirement.

Explanations:

π Option premium.

S   Value of underlying stock.

E   Exercise price of option.

T   Out-of-the-money amount = MAX[E–S,0] for a call.

                             = MAX[S–E,0] for a put.

*Option premium plus .20S minus T, but no less than .10S.

Source: G. Sofianos, "Margin Requirements on Equity Instruments," Federal Reserve Bank of New York, *Quarterly Review* (Summer 1988).

Option Commissions

Commissions on put and call contracts are negotiable, just as they are with stocks. To provide a sense of the order of magnitude of these commissions, we present in Table 12–4 the formula for calculating commissions used by a leading brokerage house.

TABLE 12–4

Calculation of Brokerage Commissions

TRANSACTION	COMMISSION RATE:
$ 0 – 2,500	$28.75 + 1.6% of principal
$ 2,501 – 10,000	$48.75 + .8% of principal
$10,001 +	$98.75 + 3% of principal

Minimum charge: $34.25 plus $1.75 per contract.

Maximum charge: $36 per contract for the first two contracts, plus $4 per contract thereafter, *or* one-half of principal amount (whichever is less).

All option transactions are subject to an overriding minimum of $36.

Using the schedule in Table 12–4, some sample commission calculations follow:

NUMBER OF CONTRACTS	PREMIUM	COMMISSION CALCULATION		% COST ONE WAY
1	$.9375	$28.75 + (.016 × $93.75)	= $30.25	
		Minimum:	$36.00	38.4%
20	$5.00	$48.75 + (.008 × $10,000)	= $128.75	1.29%
		Maximum: $72 + [$4 × 18]	= $144.00	
10	$20.00	$98.75 + (.003 × $20,000)	= $158.75	
		Maximum: $72 + ($4 × 8)	= $104.00	0.52%

The lesson: Purchasing low premium options and/or a small number of contracts is mighty expensive! An investor is better off purchasing more than one or two contracts on an option. In any event, option commissions are often high and can detract significantly from potential returns.

This commission schedule would be applied to the purchase, sale, or writing of an option. If you exercise an option or have an option exercised against you, the commission would be calculated by the broker using separate commission schedules for stocks. Thus, if you exercise a contract for 100 shares of stock at an exercise price of $40, the commission would be calculated based on a $4,000 transaction ($40 × 100).

McDonald's Corp. Call Options

Call options on McDonald's (MCD) stock are traded. In early September 1993, the following quotes were available:

EXERCISE PRICE	EXPIRATION MONTH		STOCK
	SEPTEMBER	MARCH	
50	4½	–	54⅜
55	½	3⅝	54⅜

The MCD/50 contract is already "in-the-money" 4⅜ points. That is, these options have an intrinsic value of $4.38. Any difference between the $4.38 value and the actual quote was what buyers were willing to pay for the time value of the option. The MCD/55 contracts were "out-of-the-money" because the striking price was above the market price of the stock. Any amount paid for the MCD/55 options was pure time value perceived by traders.

The September/55 was clearly the most speculative purchase in the set and the March/55 was the safest buy. The purchase of one March/55 contract would involve a commission of $30. For a 100-share contract this means that the round-trip cost per share is $.60[($30 × 2)/100]. The stock would have to rise to almost $59¼[55 + 3.63 + .60] for you to break even. Further, during the period between September and March, McDonald's would pay one dividend (September 30). At rates prevailing at the time this would be a total of $.10 per share ($.10 per quar-

ter). This dividend goes to the option writer (seller) under option exchange rules. If McDonald's rose above 30⅝ before late March 1994, the option buyer would begin to make money and see price leverage operating beyond that point. Would you buy or would you sell a McDonald's call option? Which striking price is best? Which expiration date is optimal? What do you think?

OPTION PRICING

Black and Scholes[6] reached the conclusion that the estimated prices of calls could be calculated with the following equation:

$$P_c = [P_s][N(d_1)] - [P_e][\text{antiln}(-R_f t)][N(d_2)]$$

where:

P_c = market value of the call option
P_s = price of the stock
P_e = striking price of the option
R_f = annualized interest rate
antiln = antilog (base e)
t = time to expiration (in years)

$N(d_1)$ and $N(d_2)$ are the values of the cumulative normal distribution, defined by the following expressions:

$$d_1 = \frac{\ln(P_s/P_e) + (R_f + .5\sigma^2)t}{\sigma \sqrt{t}} \qquad \textbf{(12.1)}$$

$$d_2 = d_1 - (\sigma \sqrt{t}) \qquad \textbf{(12.2)}$$

where:

$\ln (P_s/P_e)$ = the natural logarithm of (P_s/P_e)

and σ^2 is the variance of continuously compounded rate of return on the stock per time period.

The definitions of d_1 and d_2 are somewhat difficult to understand. They result from solving very complex mathematical equations and are admittedly not quickly grasped by the reader. Nonetheless, the basic properties of the Black-Scholes model are easy to envision. Estimated option prices vary directly with an option's term-to-maturity and with the difference between the stock's market price and the option's striking price. In addition, Equations 12.1 and 12.2 reveal that they increase with the variance of the rate of return on the stock price, reflecting the logic that greater volatility increases the chance that the option will become more valuable.[7]

[6]Fischer Black and Myron Scholes, "The Pricing of Options and Corporate Securities," *Journal of Political Economy* 81, no. 3 (May–June 1973).

[7]J. S. Butler and B. Schachter, "Unbiased Estimates of the Black-Scholes Formula," *Journal of Financial Economics* (March 1986).

The way that option premiums fluctuate as a stock price moves below or above the exercise price is important to understand. Generally, option premiums rarely move point per point with the price of the underlying stock. This happens only at parity (when the exercise price plus the premium equals the market price of the stock). Prior to reaching parity, premiums tend to increase less than point for point with stock prices. The two major reasons for this are (1) because point-for-point increase in the option premium would result in sharply reduced leverage for option buyers (reduced leverage means a reduced demand for the option), and (2) a higher option premium entails increased capital outlay and increased risk, again reducing demand.

Declining stock prices also do not normally result in a point-for-point decrease in the option premium. This is because even a steep decline in the stock price in the span of a few days has only a slight effect on one major component of an option's total value, its time value. This term-to-maturity effect exists because an option is a wasting asset. Simply, all else being equal, the more time remaining until expiration, the higher the premium will be. An out-of-the-money option will approach zero as expiration nears. An in-the-money option will be left only with its tangible value.

Volatility is the big unknown in the option formula. It is the only input that must be estimated. Part of the problem it causes is due to the fact that it changes over time. The problem may be minimized by using historical data for estimation purposes. A very rough way to get a beginning estimate is:

$$\text{Volatility} = \frac{\text{High} - \text{Low}}{1/2(\text{High} + \text{Low})}$$

where high and low reflect prices of the underlying stock over a recent period of time. The length of time used affects the volatility and may change all results and the decision made. Some people use the annual standard deviation of the rate of return for the stock as its input for volatility. The original models use the variance of the rate of return for the stock, also annualized.

Option premiums must be sufficiently high to encourage investors to write options rather than to seek alternative investments that may involve less risk. Rising interest rates therefore tend to put upward pressure on option premiums, and declining interest rates increase the present price of the exercise price; because the exercise price is a potential liability for the holder of the option, this reduces the option price. An increase in interest rate will most affect the options that have a longer time to maturity. It usually takes more than a one-percentage-point change in interest rates to cause a major change in option price. Usually, changes in other major variables such as stock price occur when interest rates change. Thus, it is many times harder to pinpoint the individual factor that caused a premium price change.

The option formula uses a low-risk security rate, such as that of certificates of deposit or prime commercial paper, of an instrument that matures at the time the option expires. This means that normally each different option maturity has a different interest rate. Note that the value of an option for a given stock does not depend on what the stock is expected to do. An option on a stock that is expected to

go up has the same value in terms of the stock as an option expected to go down. An investor who thinks the stock will go up will think that both the stock and the option are underpriced. An investor who thinks the stock will go down will not buy either the stock or the option.

COMPUTING OPTION VALUES

On September 6, 1993, a March/55 call option on McDonald's stock was quoted at $3.63, which equates to $363 per contract (100 × 3.63), excluding commissions. Let's see if the Black-Scholes model can help us determine if the March/55 call option is fairly valued.

Table 12–5 contains information useful in valuing a call option using the Black-Scholes formula. To use the formula, we need to know the stock price, time-to-expiration, striking price, volatility, and interest rate. We determine time-to-expiration by counting the number of days between today and the expiration date and dividing by 365. In this case, time-to-expiration is 195/365 = .534 years. The stock price is $54.38, and the striking price is $55. We can obtain the interest rate directly from the September 6, 1993, market price of a Treasury bill maturing at about the same time as the option. The current yield of this Treasury bill is quoted in the *The Wall Street Journal* as 3.00 percent.

The final and most difficult item to measure is the volatility or standard deviation. The information shown in Table 12–6 will allow us to estimate the volatility. The Black-Scholes formula is based on the assumption that stock prices are log normally distributed. We can apply standard statistical techniques for estimating the parameters of a normal distribution with unknown mean and variance.

From the information given in Table 12–6, we find that the estimate of annual volatility (standard deviation) is 19 percent. Now we have all the basic data for the valuation formula:

$$P_s = 54.38$$

$$P_e = 55$$

$$t = .5416$$

$$R_f = 3.00\%$$

$$\sigma = 19\%$$

$$d_1 = \frac{\ln\left(\frac{54.38}{55}\right) + (.03 + .018).534}{.19(\sqrt{.5342})}$$

$$= \frac{-.0114 + .0256}{.13888} = .1025$$

$$d_2 = .1025 - [(.19)(.7309)] = -.0363$$

TABLE 12–5

Valuing McDonald's Call Option

Valuation date: 9/6/93
Expiration date: 3/18/94
Striking price: $55
Yield on Treasury bill maturing on 3/18/94: 3.00%
Stock price: $54.375

Weekly closing prices of McDonald's stock over the period 3/3/93–8/30/93 (27 weeks)
(Data in eighths of a dollar)

March 3	50.63	July 5	49.13
8	51.38	12	48.75
15	51.50	19	49.50
22	53.50	26	48.63
29	53.25	August 2	51.50
April 5	52.38	9	51.50
12	50.50	16	53.38
19	49.00	23	54.88
26	46.13	30	53.50
May 3	48.13		
10	49.00		
17	48.63		
24	50.25		
31	49.75		
June 7	50.38		
14	50.00		
21	49.50		
28	49.38		

The values of $N(.1025)$ and $N(-.0364)$ are obtained from tables of cumulative normal distribution and are approximately .54 $(1 - .46)$ and .486 $(1 + .036)$, respectively[8] (see Table 12–7). Thus,

$$P_c = [(\$54.38)(.5408)] - [(\$55)(.9841)(.4855)] = \$3.12$$

The standard normal distribution table, Table 12–7, can be used to assess the probability that an observed value will be greater than or equal to or less than or equal to a given value. Suppose an analyst wants to know the probability of observing a value equal to or greater than −1.24. Looking in the 1.2 row/0.04 column of the table gives a value of 0.8925, which is the probability of observing a value less than or equal to −1.24. Subtract this number from 1. The answer is 0.1075; that is, a

[8]$N(d_1)$ is also called the hedge ratio. It shows the number of round lots of common stock required to balance one option contract in creating a risk-free hedge. In this example, $N(d_1) =$ 1.3617, which means that a long position in one option contract will require taking a short position of 1.3617 round lots of common stock to create a riskless hedge.

TABLE 12–6

Black-Scholes Option Valuation Model:
Determining Historical Stock Price Volatility
(Closing Prices for Twenty-Seven Weeks)

RETURN VARIANCE* = 3.61%
RETURN STANDARD DEVIATION* = 18.99%
NUMBER OF OBSERVATIONS = 26

1993 DATE	(1) CLOSING STOCK PRICE	(2) PRICE RELATIVE (PT/PT–1)	(3) LOG PRICE RELATIVE	(4) (3) LESS MEAN (3)	(5) (4) SQUARED
March 3	50.63				
8	51.38	1.015	0.0147	0.01258	0.00016
15	51.50	1.002	0.0023	0.00021	0.00000
22	53.50	1.039	0.0381	0.03598	0.00129
29	53.25	0.995	−0.0047	−0.00680	0.00005
April 5	52.38	0.984	−0.0165	−0.01859	0.00035
12	50.50	0.964	−0.0366	−0.03867	0.00150
19	49.00	0.970	−0.0302	−0.03227	0.00104
26	46.13	0.941	−0.0604	−0.06248	0.00390
May 3	48.13	1.043	0.0424	0.04032	0.00163
10	49.00	1.018	0.0179	0.01579	0.00025
17	48.63	0.992	−0.0076	−0.00970	0.00009
24	50.25	1.033	0.0328	0.03065	0.00094
31	49.75	0.990	−0.0100	−0.01212	0.00015
June 7	50.38	1.013	0.0126	0.01046	0.00011
14	50.00	0.992	−0.0076	−0.00969	0.00009
21	49.50	0.990	−0.0101	−0.01217	0.00015
28	49.38	0.998	−0.0024	−0.00455	0.00002
July 5	49.13	0.995	−0.0051	−0.00720	0.00005
12	48.75	0.992	−0.0078	−0.00989	0.00010
19	49.50	1.015	0.0153	0.01315	0.00017
26	48.63	0.982	−0.0177	−0.01985	0.00039
August 2	51.50	1.059	0.0573	0.05522	0.00305
9	51.50	1.000	0.0000	−0.00212	0.00000
16	53.38	1.037	0.0359	0.03373	0.00114
23	54.88	1.028	0.0277	0.02559	0.00065
30	53.50	0.975	−0.0255	−0.02759	0.00076

*Annualized.

10.75 percent likelihood exists that the observed value will be greater than or equal to −1.24.

Because the table is symmetric, negative values need not be shown separately. The probability of observing a value × less than or equal to −1.24 is the same as that of observing a value × greater than or equal to 1.24, Probability (x ≤ d) = Probability (x ≥ −d). The probability of observing a value × greater than or

TABLE 12–7

Values of the Cumulative Standard Normal Distribution,
N(d), for Values of d from .0 to −3.99

−d	0.00	0.01	0.02	0.03	0.04	0.05	0.06	0.07	0.08	0.09
0.0	0.5000	0.4960	0.4920	0.4880	0.4840	0.4801	0.4761	0.4721	0.4681	0.4641
0.1	0.4602	0.4562	0.4522	0.4483	0.4443	0.4404	0.4364	0.4325	0.4286	0.4246
0.2	0.4207	0.4168	0.4129	0.4090	0.4052	0.4013	0.3974	0.3936	0.3897	0.3859
0.3	0.3821	0.3783	0.3745	0.3707	0.3669	0.3632	0.3594	0.3557	0.3520	0.3483
0.4	0.3446	0.3409	0.3372	0.3336	0.3300	0.3264	0.3228	0.3192	0.3156	0.3121
0.5	0.3085	0.3050	0.3015	0.2981	0.2946	0.2912	0.2877	0.2843	0.2810	0.2776
0.6	0.2742	0.2709	0.2676	0.2644	0.2611	0.2578	0.2546	0.2514	0.2482	0.2451
0.7	0.2420	0.2388	0.2358	0.2327	0.2297	0.2266	0.2236	0.2206	0.2177	0.2148
0.8	0.2119	0.2090	0.2061	0.2033	0.2004	0.1977	0.1949	0.1922	0.1894	0.1867
0.9	0.1841	0.1814	0.1788	0.1762	0.1736	0.1711	0.1685	0.1660	0.1635	0.1611
1.0	0.1587	0.1562	0.1539	0.1515	0.1492	0.1469	0.1446	0.1423	0.1401	0.1379
1.1	0.1357	0.1335	0.1314	0.1292	0.1271	0.1251	0.1330	0.1210	0.1190	0.1170
1.2	0.1151	0.1131	0.1112	0.1094	0.1075	0.1056	0.1038	0.1020	0.1003	0.0985
1.3	0.0968	0.0951	0.0934	0.0918	0.0901	0.0885	0.0869	0.0853	0.0838	0.0823
1.4	0.0808	0.0793	0.0778	0.0764	0.0749	0.0735	0.0721	0.0708	0.0694	0.0681
1.5	0.0668	0.0655	0.0643	0.0630	0.0618	0.0606	0.0594	0.0582	0.0570	0.0559
1.6	0.0548	0.0537	0.0526	0.0516	0.0505	0.0495	0.0485	0.0475	0.0465	0.0455
1.7	0.0446	0.0436	0.0427	0.0418	0.0409	0.0401	0.0392	0.0384	0.0375	0.0367
1.8	0.0359	0.0352	0.0344	0.0336	0.0329	0.0322	0.0314	0.0307	0.0300	0.0294
1.9	0.0287	0.0281	0.0274	0.0268	0.0262	0.0256	0.0250	0.0244	0.0238	0.0233
2.0	0.0228	0.0222	0.0217	0.0212	0.0207	0.0202	0.0197	0.0192	0.0188	0.0183
2.1	0.0179	0.0174	0.0170	0.0166	0.0162	0.0158	0.0154	0.0150	0.0146	0.0143
2.2	0.0139	0.0136	0.0132	0.0129	0.0126	0.0122	0.0119	0.0116	0.0133	0.0110
2.3	0.0107	0.0104	0.0102	0.0099	0.0096	0.0094	0.0091	0.0089	0.0087	0.0084
2.4	0.0082	0.0080	0.0078	0.0076	0.0073	0.0071	0.0070	0.0068	0.0066	0.0064
2.5	0.0062	0.0060	0.0059	0.0057	0.0055	0.0054	0.0052	0.0051	0.0049	0.0048
2.6	0.0047	0.0045	0.0044	0.0043	0.0042	0.0040	0.0039	0.0038	0.0037	0.0036
2.7	0.0035	0.0034	0.0033	0.0032	0.0031	0.0030	0.0029	0.0028	0.0027	0.0026
2.8	0.0026	0.0025	0.0024	0.0023	0.0023	0.0022	0.0021	0.0020	0.0020	0.0019
2.9	0.0019	0.0018	0.0018	0.0017	0.0016	0.0016	0.0015	0.0015	0.0014	0.0014
3.0	0.0014	0.0013	0.0013	0.0012	0.0012	0.0011	0.0011	0.0011	0.0010	0.0010
3.1	0.0010	0.0009	0.0009	0.0009	0.0008	0.0008	0.0008	0.0008	0.0007	0.0007
3.2	0.0007	0.0007	0.0006	0.0006	0.0006	0.0006	0.0006	0.0005	0.0005	0.0005
3.3	0.0005	0.0005	0.0004	0.0004	0.0004	0.0004	0.0004	0.0004	0.0004	0.0004
3.4	0.0003	0.0003	0.0003	0.0003	0.0003	0.0003	0.0003	0.0003	0.0002	0.0002
3.5	0.0002	0.0002	0.0002	0.0002	0.0002	0.0002	0.0002	0.0002	0.0002	0.0002
3.6	0.0002	0.0002	0.0002	0.0001	0.0001	0.0001	0.0001	0.0001	0.0001	0.0001
3.7	0.0001	0.0001	0.0001	0.0001	0.0001	0.0001	0.0001	0.0001	0.0001	0.0001
3.8	0.0001	0.0001	0.0001	0.0001	0.0001	0.0001	0.0001	0.0000	0.0000	0.0000
3.9	0.0000	0.0000	0.0000	0.0000	0.0000	0.0000	0.0000	0.0000	0.0000	0.0000

Note: N(d) = 1.0 − N(−d).

equal to 1.24 is 1 minus the probability of observing a value $\times$ less than or equal to 1.24, $\text{Prob}(x \geq -d) = 1 - \text{Prob}(x \leq -d)$.

Because the quoted premium for the option is $3.63 and the calculated value is $3.13, this option is slightly overvalued. Of course, our estimate of volatility (standard deviation) could be wrong. In order for the option value and the market price to be equal, the volatility would have to be 22.1 percent (versus 19 percent). The former number can be derived by solving for volatility in the option valuation equation.[9]

EMPIRICAL TESTS OF THE BLACK-SCHOLES MODEL

MacBeth and Merville were able to identify common characteristics of option contracts that were overpriced.[10] They concluded that the Black-Scholes formula overvalues out-of-the-money options and undervalues in-the-money contracts. Similar studies by other investigators lead to the following general conclusions:

1. The Black-Scholes model is extremely good for pricing at-the-money options, especially when time to expiration exceeds two months and no dividends occur.

2. For deep-in-the-money and out-of-the-money contracts, significant deviations between market prices and model prices can occur.

3. Short-term (less than a month) contracts are often mispriced.

4. Options on extremely low- and extremely high-volatility stocks are often mispriced.

The biases reported in the empirical studies are not consistent over time. For example, the strike price bias from Black-Scholes values is significant and tends to be in the same direction at any point in time. However, the direction of bias may change from period to period.

Most empirical tests conducted prior to 1980 used closing prices of options. These closing prices can be very misleading and on occasion indicate that arbitrage opportunities are available. The errors in using closing prices are caused by liquidity problems, nonsimultaneity of stock and option closing prices, and the bid-ask spread.

Most option trading takes place in near-the-money short-term contracts. Low liquidity in far-from-the-money contracts increases the likelihood that the last option trade occurred some time before trading ceased in the stock. This means that the reported option price need not reflect the actual price for which an option could be bought or sold when the stock stopped trading at the end of the day.

---

[9]$4.75 = [(28.50)(.821)] - [(25)(.9731)(.7662)]$
[10]J. Macbeth and L. J. Merville, "Tests of the Black-Scholes and Cox Call Option Valuation Models," *Journal of Finance* (May 1980).

Investors who purchase (sell) options will probably get the ask (bid) price quoted in the trading pit. By looking at the closing price, the investor does not know if the trade took place at the bid, at the ask, or in between. If, for example, the spread is ½ and the closing price is 3, then if the last transaction took place at the bid (ask), the bid-ask spread is $3 - 3½(2½ - 3)$. Hence, given a closing price of 3, the bid-ask spread creates uncertainty in prices between 2½ and 3½. This spread is 33 percent of the closing price.

The overall conclusions, however, are that the Black-Scholes model provides an extremely good fit to actual data and that the pricing model does serve as a useful valuation tool.

Financial Engineering

One of the attractions of options is the ability they provide to create investment positions with payoffs that depend in a variety of ways on the values of other securities. Options also can be used to custom design new securities with desired patterns of exposure to the price of an underlying security. In this sense, options provide the ability to engage in what is referred to as *financial engineering,* the creation of investment positions with specified payoff patterns.

While the majority of financial engineering takes place for investment pools such as pension funds or mutual funds some applications have been designed for individuals. One highly successful retail product is the liquid yield option note (LYON).

A LYON is a zero-coupon, convertible, callable, and puttable bond. To illustrate how the bond works, consider the following bond. It pays no interest income and is priced at $250 with a maturity value of $1,000 in sixteen years. If it is not called, converted, or redeemed, this LYON provides a yield-to-maturity of 9 percent.

Several options may result in early retirement of the issue. First, the investor can convert each bond into four shares of underlying stock. Second, the investor can sell the bond back to the issuer at a predetermined price that rises over time. Last, the issuer can call the bond at fixed prices that also increase over time.

This combination of options results in risk-sharing that seems to be attractive to both the issuer and investors. The conversion option provides investors with the possibility of profiting from price advances in the underlying stock. At the same time, the embedded put option provides the LYON holder a protective floor. Finally, the call feature allows the issuer to call the bonds back for refinancing if interest rates drop. For other examples of ingenuity in financial engineering see the box nearby.

Even stocks have been "engineered" by dividing claims into components. This process recognizes that a stock normally pays dividends and is also expected to provide price appreciation. However, some investors prefer dividend income and others price appreciation due to risk aversion, tax bracket, and so on. This claims engineering is the financial market equivalent of market segmentation . . . or divide and prosper.

Americus Trusts allow investors to tender shares of a stock to a trust fund and receive a unit in exchange. The unit is a composite of a "prime" and a "score." These separate components need not be held together but can be separated and traded. A prime and a score can be combined back into a unit and exchange it for a share of stock.

The tendered stock is held in trust until the trust is terminated (generally five years after origination). At the termination date, the shares are divided between holders of primes and scores in accordance with specifications of the trust. This division normally depends on the stock price at the termination date.

A prime receives all dividends paid on the stock during the life of the trust as well as voting rights on the underlying shares. It also receives the market value of the stock at the termination date up to the value of the termination claim. This termination claim is set at the time the trust is established and is often 25 percent above the market price of the stock at that time. As an example, Coca-Cola primes get a maximum of $56 a share at termination. If the stock at termination is above $56, the prime holders receive sufficient shares to provide the same value as the original number of shares at $56. Thus, if the stock is at $60 at termination of the trust, 100 shares of Coca-Cola stock would be worth $6,000 ($60 × 100). The holder of the prime would get $5,600 ($56 × 100). If the shares at termination are below $56, the prime holders receive all the shares.

The score gets all the value of the stock above the termination claim as of the date of termination. If the stock is below the claim price, they receive nothing. Suppose Coca-Cola stock is at $65 and we are one year from the termination of the trust. Assume the price of the score is $11. If you buy a score, you receive a one year call on Coca Cola stock with a striking price of $56. The call is in-the-money by $9 ($65–56).

Americus Trusts were set up on over two dozen stocks in the late 1980s. They all terminated in 1992. Some other companies whose stock had an Americus Trust include American Express, Ford, IBM, and Sears.

SUMMARY

This discussion of the various options on common stocks has shown how they are similar and dissimilar. They are all dependent on the price movement, or expectations of price movement, of the associated common stock. They all vary in the length of time during which they are in effect—an important difference, because, in buying an option, the investor must predict not only a price movement but also the period within which the movement will take place.

The options discussed here give the investor varying amounts of leverage that are unobtainable by owning the common stock. They also offer somewhat more safety than the common, in that the investor need not put as much capital at risk to obtain the same reward. These features cause the options to sell at a premium, as a general rule. Thus, an investor needs to know *why* the particular option sells at a premium in order to tell if the premium is so high that it overshadows these

FINANCIAL HOCUS POCUS?

What's the latest high-yield pitch? Buy into the future payouts from winning lottery tickets. You're promised a 12% yield supposedly backed by credit-solid state lottery commissions.

A sure thing at 12%? Far from it. If nothing else scares you away, this should: Above-normal yields are always accompanied by risk of principal loss. If there were no risk, there would be no reason for the person selling the investment to raise money from the public; instead, he could borrow cheaply from a bank.

For a moment, though, let's suspend disbelief and visit Manhattan's Algonquin Hotel, where one spring morning, Dunewood Funding Corp. is pitching the high-yield virtues of buying discounted state lottery winnings.

Robert H. Shapiro, president of Dunewood, a mortgage lender, has come up with a new venture—lottery ticket brokering. "Where else can you get 12% a year and the security of an obligation backed by a state lottery commission?"

Shapiro hunts down lucky but impatient lottery ticket holders who are being paid off in installments for up to 20 years and would like to cash in some or all of their winnings for a nice, big lump sum. Outfits like Dunewood then buy out the winners' claims at a discount to future payments.

The guys in the Algonquin gallery today, for example, are told they can buy 16 annual payments of $53,000 each from a Maine lottery winner for a purchase price of $406,492. The promised yield: an annual 12% simple interest.

To the untutored eye the agreements seem bulletproof, but lottery executives are none too keen to create a free market in brokered winning tickets. Maine, Vermont, and New Hampshire, for example, adopted regulations that would limit assignments only to where they would fulfill other court-ordered "remedy" payments such as divorce settlements, bankruptcy claims or child support.

The other problem has to do with tax liabilities. Court records suggest that the lottery carveouts are structured as loans rather than outright purchases. If the IRS rules that the transaction is no loan at all, but rather an outright sale, the winner's entire lump sum could immediately become taxable to him as ordinary income. Might this expose the lottery buyer to some penalty for failing to withhold additional taxes from the lottery winner? As a buyer, you don't know. You take your chances.

****

Jersey City suffered through four mayors in two years, one of whom had to spend some time in Allenwood, a federal meditation parlor for white collar hornswogglers. The one-two punch of corruption and incompetence left the city facing a yawning deficit, a big tax hike and a 10% cutback in government employees.

Enter Bret Schundler, a former Wall Street investment banker and the first Republican mayor in this Democratic stronghold in nearly a century. Schundler teamed up with First Boston to hatch a novel way to reduce the tax bite and save jobs.

First Boston bought 2,517 property tax liens from the city which were at least six months past due. It then converted the $44 million lot into $31 million of senior notes, which it is privately placing with investors. Jersey City got a check for $25 million up front and took back a $19 million zero-coupon subordinated note. Investors get an 8¼% piece of paper which matures in less than five years. And because the portfolio of liens has an asset-to-value ratio of 25%, or more than four times the normal rate, it earned a Single-A rating from Fitch—not bad for an issue yielding about 300 basis points over Treasuries, especially with long-term junk bonds now trading in single-digit territory.

attributes of the option. This trade-off between the premium demanded and the advantages gained by the option, along with the outlook for the associated common stock, determines whether an option is an attractive buy.

QUESTIONS

1. What are the main investment attractions of put and call options? What are the key risks?

2. Define the following terms:
   a. premium;
   b. exercise price; and
   c. out-of-the-money option.

3. Is the sale of a covered call more or less risky than selling a naked call? Why?

4. Five variables are involved in estimating the value of a call option. List and discuss each of these variables. Which variable do you think is the most important?

6. A protective put is created when a long position in a stock is married to a long position in a put on that stock. What position in call options is equivalent to a protective put?

7. Carefully analyze the difference between a bull spread created from calls and a bull spread created from puts.

8. A ratio spread amounts to buying a call option and selling two call options. The exercise price of the option purchased is less than that of the two options sold. How does this strategy differ from a more regular bull or bear spread?

9. A strap is a combination of two calls and one put with the same striking price and exercise date. What does the buyer of a strap believe about the movement of the underlying stock?

10. Provide an intuitive explanation of why put premiums tend to drop when interest rates rise.

11. Explain why brokers require margins from clients when they write options but not when they buy options.

12. A company declares a 3-for-1 stock split. Explain how the terms of a call option with a strike price of $60 change.

13. If most of the call options on a stock are in-the-money, the stock price has most likely risen rapidly in the last few months. Discuss this statement.

14. Options on General Motors's stock are on a March, June, September, and December cycle. What options trade on
   a. March 1;
   b. June 30; and
   c. August 5?

PROBLEMS

1. You are interested in buying some low-priced call options. You have located an option trading at $1.50. You ask your broker to acquire fifty contracts (100 shares each). What is the commission to purchase these contracts?

2. Measuronics Corp. (MDM) is a manufacturer of computer chips. The company has call options listed on the American Stock Exchange. Recent quotes on call options are:

	JUNE	SEPT.	DEC.
MDM/260	17	24	30
MDM/280	6	13	19
MDM/300	1	6	11

The current price of the common shares is $270. No dividends are paid.

a. Assume that you engage in a bullish spread involving the Sept/280 and Sept/300 call options. What is your expected rate of return (nonannualized, excluding commissions) if Measuronics closes at $270 in late September?

b. How might one go about creating a "homemade" put if he wanted to purchase a put on Measuronics but none were quoted or available? Would such a strategy be superior to a short sale? Explain.

3. The following quotes are available on Wal-Mart (WAL) options. The stock closed on this day at 40. Wal-Mart was paying an annual dividend of $.80 per share at the time. Treasury bills were at 4 percent.

	CALLS			PUTS		
STRIKE	MAR.	JUNE	SEPT.	MAR.	JUNE	SEPT.
30	9	10	n.a.	$\frac{1}{16}$	$\frac{1}{4}$	$\frac{5}{8}$
35	4	6	7	$\frac{1}{8}$	$1\frac{1}{8}$	$1\frac{3}{4}$
40	$\frac{1}{2}$	$2\frac{1}{2}$	$3\frac{1}{2}$	$1\frac{1}{2}$	$2\frac{1}{4}$	$3\frac{1}{2}$
45	$\frac{1}{16}$	$\frac{7}{8}$	$1\frac{1}{2}$	$6\frac{1}{8}$	$6\frac{1}{4}$	$6\frac{1}{2}$

NA—Not available

a. Which call options are in-the-money?
b. Explain the rationale behind:
    i. buying a Sept/45 call rather than buying the stock; and
    ii. selling (writing) five June/40 calls when 500 shares of WAL are already held at a cost of $40 per share.
c. What factors are likely to explain the differences in the premiums quoted above for the twelve put options on WAL shares? Explain how each of these factors tends to impact the price (positive or negative).
d. Investors certainly have different expectations concerning the overall direction of the market at any given time. Match the outlook described

below in Column I with the appropriate strategy in Column II relative to the WAL options:

COLUMN I INVESTOR OUTLOOK	COLUMN II STRATEGY
1. Very optimistic	A. Buy stock and buy two June/40 puts
2. Moderately optimistic	B. Buy stock, sell Sept/40 call + Sept/45 call
3. Neutral	C. Buy Mar/35 put
4. Moderately pessimistic	D. Buy stock on margin and sell Mar/30 put
5. Very pessimistic	E. Buy stock, sell Mar/45 call

  e. Define the limits of profit and loss and an expected break-even price if you engaged in a bearish spread involving the June/30 and June/35 calls.

  f. Suppose you had $4,000 to invest. You are considering buying 100 shares of WAL or 16 calls with a strike price of 40 and a June expiration. It is now February. Compute the return on investment of both strategies if WAL stock closes in June at $0, $50, or $60.

4. Pedro Guzman is interested in Swizle Products Co. The stock is now selling at 23. Assuming no commissions or taxes, what is his dollar and annualized percentage gains from each of the following strategies if (a) the stock hits 35 in four months; (b) the stock drops to 19 in two months.

 i. buy 100 shares for cash

 ii. buy 100 shares on 60% margin

 iii. buy a six-month call at $20 for $600

5. You are generally bearish on computer stocks. You have purchsed a six-month put on Intel Corp. at 50 when the stock is at 52. The put contract costs you $200. Suppose Intel goes to 55. What is your rate of return? What is your rate of return if Intel went to 45?

6. A diagonal spread is created by buying a call with a strike price X2 and an exercise price T2, and selling a call with a strike price of X1 and an exercise price of T1 [T2 > T1]. Draw a diagram showing profit at time T1 when

 a. X2 > X1, and

 b. X2 < X1.

7. A box spread is a combination of a bull call spread with strike prices X1 and X2 and a bear put spread with the same strike prices. The expiration dates of all the options is the same. What are the characteristics of a box spread?

8. Assume that ABC stock is currently at $50. It is now July 1. Three options are quoted: Nov/55, $1; Nov/50, $5; Jan/45, $10. Ignoring commissions and dividends:

 a. List two reasons why the premium on the Jan/45 call is so much higher than the premium on the Nov/50 call.

 b. Suppose that you purchased 100 shares of ABC on June 1 at a cost of $47.50 per share. You wrote (sold) one Jan/45 on July 1. Suppose that on January 15, ABC stock was at $52.50.

i. Would the holder of the Jan/45 benefit from exercising the call? Why?

ii. If the call were exercised on January 15, what is your tax status?

c. Suppose that you do not own ABC shares. You simultaneously write one Nov/55 and buy one Nov/50. What is your annualized rate of return if ABC stock closes in November at $57.50?

9. Assume that Boeing stock is currently at $100. Two call options are quoted: Boeing/Nov/110, $1 and Jan/90, $20. Ignoring commissions:

a. Why is the premium on the January call so much higher than the premium on the November call?

b. Suppose you owned 100 shares of Boeing at a cost of $95 per share. At what price would you begin to lose money if you wrote a call on the Boeing/Jan/90?

c. If you were short Boeing, would there be any advantage in buying a call? How so?

10. You wrote an Oct/55 call option on Marriott Corp. for a premium of $1 in January. The option was written against stock held at a cost of $57 per share. Ignoring commissions and assuming the call was exercised in early October, what is your tax status on Marriott at the end of October?

11. Some of the more exotic option strategies are shown below. Draw a payoff graph similar to that shown in Figures 12–5 through 12–10 for each of the following strategies:

a. a bear put spread [buy put at strike price E2, and sell put at strike price E1 (E2 > E1)];

b. a strangle [buy put with strike price E1, and buy call with strike price E2 (E1 < E2)]; and

c. a condor [sell two different calls at strike prices E2 and E3, and buy two different call options at strike prices E1 and E4 (E1 < E2 < E3 < E4)].

12. Suppose you are using the Black-Scholes option pricing model to value a call option. The values for d1 and d2 in the model are 1.87 and 1.56, respectively. What are the appropriate values of N(1.87) and N(1.56) from Table 12–7?

13. Calculate the value of a call option with the following information: stock price = $50; exercise price = $45; interest rate = 7%; time to expiration = 90 days; standard deviation = 0.4.

14. Rollo Inc. has a call option expiring in 90 days. The risk-free rate is .10 and the variance of return on the stock is .81. The exercise price of the stock is $40 and the call option is selling at $2 out-of-the-money. What is the value of this option?

15. A straddle represents a put and call at the same striking price and exercise date on the same side of the market. Suppose a stock is at $120. You sell an April/115 call for 10 and an April/115 put for 5.

a. What is your apparent expectation about the movement of these shares?

b. At what stock price level(s) will you begin to make money on the straddle?

16. Suppose UAL stock is at 31.5. You simultaneously buy a Feb/20 call at 12 and sell a Feb/25 call at 7.5.
    a. What is your maximum profit?
    b. Your break-even price?
    c. Your maximum loss?

17. Leonardo Equipment Co. stock currently sells at $25. The company does not pay dividends. A six-month call option is available on the stock with an exercise price of $25 and a premium of $5. Treasury bills due in 182 days were just offered at auction at an annualized yield of 8 percent. The volatility of the stock (standard deviation) over the past twenty-six weeks has been about 30 percent. Evaluate the option using the Black-Scholes model.

18. Analyze carefully the difference between a bull spread created from puts and a bull spread created from calls.

19. Suppose that observations on a stock price (in dollars) at the end of consecutive weeks are as follows: 30¼, 32, 30⅛, 30¼, 30⅜, 30⅝, 33, 32⅞, 33, 33½, 33½, 33¾, 33½, 33¼. Estimate the stock price volatility.

20. What is the value of a call option on a nondividend-paying stock when the stock price is $52, the strike price is $50, the risk-free interest rate is 12 percent per annum, the volatility is 30 percent per annum, and the time to maturity is three months?

21. A call option on a nondividend-paying stock has a market price of $2½. The stock price is $15, the exercise price is $13, the time to maturity is 3 months, and the risk-free interest rate is 5 percent per annum. What is the implied volatility?

22. An investor writes 5 naked call option contracts. The option price is $3.50, the strike price is $60.00, and the stock price is $57.00. What is the initial margin requirement?

C A S E

Calipso Capital Consultants

Calipso Capital Management (CCC), an investment management firm with offices throughout Ohio, is headquartered in Cincinnati. CCC normally actively manages accounts for high-income individuals with assets of $500,000 or more. Peter Myers, managing director of CCC, thought the increased interest of clients in security options required more than routine advice because he knew that many clients did not fully appreciate the risks and hedging aspects of buying and selling puts and calls. He had personally spent many hours explaining the vocabulary and technical trading aspects of option vehicles to clients who found the area exciting but nonetheless arcane.

EXHIBIT 1

Bio-Genetics Corp. Option Quotes

STOCK PRICE : 162

STRIKE PRICE	CALLS			PUTS		
	APR	JULY	OCT	APR	JULY	OCT
140	23	—	—	—	—	—
150	16	21	25	1	4	—
160	9	14	20	3	7	—
170	3	9	13	9	10	9
180	1	5	9	—	20	11

Note: blank spaces denote option not offered or not traded.

Janet Barnes joined the firm three months ago after spending one year in Dean Witter's training program in Cleveland. She received a broad training with emphasis in options and futures instruments. Myers though Barnes would be an important member of the firm in its dealings with clients interested in securities options.

The first task that Barnes faced was preparing an analysis of various strategies in the options of Bio-Genetics Corp., a company about which a young dentist in Berea had called. The dentist owned the stock and wanted to explore various strategies to either hedge or enhance his position.

Data provided in Exhibit 1 relate to key information on Bio-Genetics puts and calls. Bio-Genetics stock is currently at 162, pays no dividends, and has a beta of 1.3. The volatility of the stock is estimated at 30 percent. The rate on two-month Treasury bills is 6 percent.

QUESTIONS

1. Which options are in-the-money? Which are out-of-the-money?

2. Compute the margin requirement for a short position in the Apr/140 call option.

3. Calculate the commission for the purchase three July/170 puts.

4. Why are investors willing to pay 1 for the Apr/180 call and also the Apr/150 put, which is closer to the current market price?

5. Assume the April options expire in one month. Are the April/160 calls fairly valued? Explain.

6. Assume the client is holding 100 shares of Bio-Genetics common long at 162. Advise the client on the relative advantages and disadvantages of selling a call against this position using:

    a. Apr/170 versus

    b. July/150 calls.

7. Would the client holding 100 shares of Bio-Genetics common be wise to simultaneously write an July/170 call while buying an July/150 put? Explain.

8. You share the client's view that the outlook for Bio-Genetics common is bullish. He has suggested that his neighbor, who does not own the common, shares his view and has just bought one July/170 call while selling one July/180 call.

    a. What is the wisdom behind this strategy?

    b. What is the maximum profit, maximum loss, and break-even price for this strategy?

9. Consider a spread that is the combination of buying one October/160 and one October/180 call while simultaneously selling two October/170 calls.

    a. What is the logic behind this strategy?

    b. Compare the profit and loss potential of this move versus the strategy in Question 8.

10. A straddle represents a put and call at the same striking price and exercise price on the same side of the market (buy or sell). Assume an April/170 straddle is purchased. Construct the payoff (profit or loss) at various stock prices for this straddle.

11. A condor represents the selling of two different calls and the purchase of two others. Suppose you use July calls. You buy a 160 and a 170 call while selling a 150 and a 180 call. What is the maximum profit and maximum loss on this strategy?

REFERENCES

BLACK, F. "Fact and Fantasy in the Use of Options." *Financial Analysts Journal* (July–August 1974).

BURGHARDT, G. and M. LANE. "How to Tell if Options Are Cheap." *Journal of Portfolio Management* (Winter 1990).

BUTLER J. S. and B. SCHACHTER. "Unbiased Estimates of the Black-Scholes Formula." *Journal of Financial Economics* (March 1986).

COX, J. C., and M. RUBENSTEIN. *Options Markets.* Englewood Cliffs, N. J.: Prentice Hall, 1985.

HANCOCK, G. D. "Futures Option Expirations and Volatility in the Stock Index Futures Market." *Journal of Futures Markets* (June 1991).

JARROW, R. A. and A. RUDD. *Option Pricing.* Homewood, Ill.: R. D. Irwin, 1983.

MACBETH, J. and L. J. MERVILLE. "Tests of the Black-Scholes and Cox Call Option Valuation Models." *Journal of Finance* (May 1980).

RITCHKEN, P. *Options.* Glenview, Ill.: Scott, Foresman, 1987.

SCARLATA, J. G. "Institutional Developments in the Globalization of Securities and Futures Markets." *Review,* Federal Reserve Bank of St. Louis (January–February 1992).

SLIVKA, R. T. "Risk and Return for Option Investment Strategies." *Financial Analysts Journal* (September–October 1980).

III."Call "Call Option Spreading." *Journal of Portfolio Management* (Spring 1981).

YATES, J. W., and M. J. ALDERSON. "Writing Covered Call Options: Profits and Risks." *Journal of Portfolio Management,* (Fall 1980).

CHAPTER 13

RIGHTS, WARRANTS, AND CONVERTIBLES

I n this chapter we consider three additional areas where options are available. The first deals with short-lived options called rights. The second group includes medium- to long-term company-issued call options known as warrants. The calls discussed in Chapter 12 were *short-term investor-issued* (written) options. The third area involves options embedded in preferred stocks and bonds enabling the owners of these securities to call away a predetermined number of shares of common stock in exchange for the underlying securities.

STOCK RIGHTS

A *right* is an option that has a very short life (a few weeks). Rights originate when corporations raise money by issuing new shares of common stock. A right enables a stockholder to buy shares of a new issue at a specified price, over a specified time period. Suppose a company has 1 million shares of common stock outstanding and has decided to issue another 100,000 shares at $80 per share. This could be done through a rights offering. Current shareholders would be given the right to maintain their proportionate share of ownership in the company, a privilege referred to as a *preemptive right* (right of first refusal). Because each stockholder receives one right for each share of stock owned, the company in our example would issue 1 million rights, and it would take ten rights plus $80 (the price of the stock) to purchase one new share of common.

Most new stock issues represent only a fraction of the existing shares. Thus, it normally takes more than one right to entitle an investor to purchase a new share. In our example, it takes ten rights. The price of the new shares is indicated in the rights and is called the exercise price. In our example, this price is $80. It is always below the prevailing market price of the stock. Assume the market price of the stock in our example is $100. The approximate value of one right can be determined as follows:

$$V_r = (P_o - P_n)/r$$

where:

V_r = value of one right
P_o = market price of existing shares
P_n = exercise price of new shares
r = number of rights to buy one new share

In our example, a right is worth: ($100–80)/10 or $2.00. Someone owning five shares of stock will be issued five rights. They are best advised to sell them or purchase enough additional rights in the open market to give them multiples of ten. Of course, the value of a right will fluctuate during the offering period as the market price of the stock moves up and down. Most important, rights not used by the expiration date become worthless.

WARRANTS

A *warrant* is a call option to buy a stated number of shares of stock at a specified price. The typical warrant has a period of a number of years during which it is exercisable. These instruments have a longer "shelf life" than the call options discussed in Chapter 12.

Warrants often originate in company reorganizations or are offered as inducements to potential investors to purchase bonds or preferred stocks offering terms less favorable than those the investors would otherwise require. But in return for accepting less favorable terms on the senior securities, such as a lower interest rate, the investor acquires an option on the possible appreciation of the common stock of the firm. He may then sell the warrants if he desires because warrants are normally detachable from the senior security and may be traded separately.

As a warrant holder, the investor has no equity rights in the firm, does not receive dividends, and does not have voting rights. The terms of the warrant are specified on the certificate. Provisions are made for the number of shares that can be purchased for each warrant, the *exercise* (purchase) price per share, and the *expiration date* of the warrant. Most warrants entitle the holder to purchase stock on a 1:1 ratio; that is, one share may be purchased per warrant. In the event of a stock split or a stock dividend, warrants are generally adjusted accordingly; investors should review these provisions carefully and should relate them to the observed behavior of the firm with respect to splits and stock dividends. The exercise price is always greater than current market price at the time the warrant is issued. This price may be fixed for the entire life of the warrant or (less commonly) it may be increased periodically. Expiration may be set for any date and, in a very few cases, warrants are perpetual; most warrants expire from five to ten years after they are issued. Warrants are usually traded as over-the-counter securities, but a number are

traded on the New York Stock Exchange (NYSE) and the American Stock Exchange (AMEX).

In some cases an investor may acquire common stock using warrants and a "usable" security rather than cash. A usable security is a bond or preferred stock acceptable at par value.

For example, Orion Pictures had a 10 percent debenture, which was usable when exercising Orion warrants (at $20 per share). Thus, each bond could be used to pay for fifty shares of Orion common ($1,000/20).

The Range of Warrant Values[1]

Prices of warrants are subject to minimum and maximum limits. The minimum value of a warrant may be identified as:

Condition	*Minimum Value*
$P_s > P_e$	$(P_s - P_e) \times N$
$P_s \leq P_e$	0

where:

P_s = current market price of the common stock
P_e = exercise price of the warrant
N = number of common shares per warrant (generally, $N = 1$)

A warrant will be worth at least the difference between the stock's market price and the warrant's exercise price; this will be the minimum value provided that the market price exceeds the exercise price. Arbitrage ensures this minimum value because at any lower warrant price an investor could purchase and immediately exercise the warrant, realizing an instantaneous risk-free profit. For market prices equal to or lower than the exercise price, the minimum warrant value is zero. Generally, the actual market value of the warrant will be greater than the minimum value.

The maximum value of a warrant is

$$P_s \times N$$

Maximum value is the value of the associated common stock; it will not be greater because the warrant offers no income potential beyond that provided by the growth of the common stock. Because warrant holders are not entitled to dividends, and because most warrants have finite lives, a warrant price at or near the maximum value is rare. In Figure 13–1 we describe these limits and trace the price

[1]An analysis of warrant pricing is found in D. Galai and M. Schneller, "Pricing Warrants and the Value of the Firm," *Journal of Finance* (December 1978).

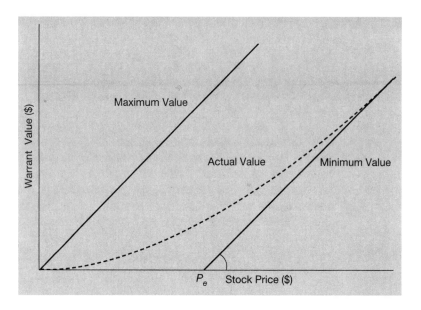

FIGURE 13–1 Relation among Maximum, Minimum, and Actual Warrant Value
(Slope depends on number of shares exchanged per warrant; if 1:1, slope = 45°)

of a typical warrant over a wide range of common stock values, with all other factors held constant. The difference between the actual price of a warrant and its minimum value is the premium over minimum value.

As the price of common stock rises above the exercise price of its associated warrant, the warrant approaches its minimum value. Thus, the premium over minimum value decreases and it ultimately vanishes as the price of the stock increases. This vanishing point tends to occur when stock price levels are about four times the exercise price of the warrant ($P_s/P_e = 4$). When the current stock price equals the exercise price, the warrant typically sells in the range 25 to 50 percent of the price of the stock. The magnitude of the premium over minimum value for any given differential between stock price and exercise price depends on a number of interrelated factors. All these factors are inputs to the valuation process that determines the investor's expected rate of return. Time remaining to expiration, stock price volatility, and leverage provided by the warrant are the factors of primary importance. Let us examine these elements more closely.

Warrant Premiums

The existence of premiums on warrants is due partly to the attractive leverage features that they offer. The lower price of warrants, which usually enjoy the same absolute change in value as the underlying common stock, enables them to return much higher profits as a percentage of investment. Suppose that warrants entitling their holder to purchase one share of PDQ at $52 are selling at $12, and that the

PDQ common is selling at $48. The warrants have a theoretical value of zero (48 − 52). As the PDQ common moves to $52, assume that the price of the warrant moves to $16. The holder of the common stock receives a holding-period yield of about 8 percent [(52 − 48)/48]. The holder of a warrant receives a 33 percent holding-period yield [(16 − 12)/12]. However, this leverage can also work against the warrant holder if the common moves downward.[2]

If a stock has any potential for rising above the option price during the life of the warrant, then the warrant will become a valuable instrument with its ability to generate high-percentage returns on investment. Thus, warrants on more volatile stocks, or stocks with higher probabilities of obtaining prices above the option price, will have higher premiums. Likewise, the longer the remaining period of the warrant, the higher the probability that the price of the common will exceed the option price, and thus the higher the premium.

The leverage effect leads one to expect a higher premium on a warrant whose associated common stock has a value that is a high multiple of the value of the warrant. Consider a warrant providing the holder the option to buy one share of stock at $10. Assume that the warrant and the stock trade on parity over time; that is, the warrant sells at its theoretical value, or a zero premium. The price relationships below reflect behavior over six years:

	PERIOD					
	1	2	3	4	5	6
Stock price	$12	$15	$30	$45	$90	$99
Warrant price	$ 2	$ 5	$20	$35	$80	$89
Stock-warrant ratio	6	3	1.5	1.29	1.13	1.11

From period 1 to 2, the stock advanced 25 percent (12 to 15) while the warrant jumped 150 percent (2 to 5); from period 2 to 3, the stock advanced 100 percent (15 to 30) and the warrant climbed 300 percent (5 to 20); and so on. Notice how leverage is operating—and how it is gradually dwindling. In the first case, the warrant moved six times as much as the stock (150/25). From period 2 to 3, the warrant moved only three times as much as the stock (300/100). The stock-warrant ratio is a kind of leverage or magnification index. As it becomes smaller, the leverage effect is diminishing.

Potential warrant holders should note that as time goes on, the remaining option period decreases (if the warrant has an expiration date), and as the price moves upward significantly, the leverage effects are lessened. These changes, as well as changing expectations for the associated stock, can result in changes in the premium a warrant commands.

---

[2]See M. K. Kim and A. Young, "Rewards and Risks from Warrant Hedging," *Journal of Portfolio Management* (Summer 1980).

TABLE 13–1

Examples of Warrants

	ATLAS CORP.	DAVSTAR INDUSTRIES	REDLAW INDUSTRIES
Expiration date	None	1997	2001
Shares per warrant	1	1	1
Exercise price (per share)	15.63	5.00	2.80
Market prices (9/6/93)			
Common	4.38	5.13	5.50
Warrant	2.00	2.50	3.50
Theoretical value of warrant*	–11.25	0.13	2.70
Stock price/Warrant price	2.19	2.05	1.57

*[(Stock price – Exercise price) × No. shares per warrant].

The existence of a positive premium on a warrant means that it will always be more beneficial for the warrant owner to sell his warrant, thus realizing its theoretical value plus its premium, than to exercise it. The reason is that in exercising it he would receive only the theoretical value. This also, however, shows that the premium associated with a warrant will shrink as its expiration date approaches, other factors remaining constant. On the expiration date, the actual value of the warrant will equal its theoretical value.

Warrant holders receive no dividends. The dividend on the common can affect the value of the warrant because this current income is forgone by the investor who chooses to hold a warrant rather than the common stock. A high dividend payout may also have an adverse effect on the price of a warrant because if the dividends were not paid out but were retained, their reinvestment could cause the market price of the stock to rise.

These are some of the factors that are thought to determine the premiums on warrants. The most important is obviously the outlook for the underlying common stock. An investor's expectations in this regard should be the prime consideration in whether he purchases a warrant. The leverage effects mentioned are a double-edged sword, with the effects on the downside being severe. After the investor determines his expectations concerning the common stock, he must then look at the warrant, determine its premium, and consider what changes in the premium, if any, might take place. The change in the value of the warrant will be made up of changes in the value of the underlying common and in the premium that the market places on the warrant.

Table 13–1 gives examples of three warrants with different life spans. The Atlas warrants afford high leverage because they have a negative theoretical value. The stock must rise to above $6.30 (almost 15 percent) before the purchaser of a warrant at $3.50 would begin to make money on the Redlaw warrants.

In Table 13–2 we display a sample of warrants in different industries with varying expiration dates.

TABLE 13–2

Samples of Warrants*

ISSUER	EXPIRATION DATE	EXERCISE PRICE	SEPTEMBER 6, 1993 STOCK PRICE	SEPTEMBER 6, 1993 WARRANT PRICE
Acceptance Insurance	January 97	11.00	14.25	4.25
Amax Gold	January 96	21.00	8.25	1.00
Atlas Corp.	None	15.63	4.38	2.00
Carter Hawley Hale	October 99	17.00	16.00	5.25
Chase Manhattan	June 96	34.61	34.38	8.13
Davstar Industries	March 97	5.00	5.13	2.50
Enquirer/Star Group	May 97	27.88	17.38	1.63
Houston Biotech	June 98	5.00	2.88	0.88
Intersystems	December 96	3.50	1.31	0.44
Laser Technology	January 98	6.00	2.63	0.44
Manville Corp.	June 98	9.40	7.38	1.38
Redlaw Industries	September 01	2.80	5.50	3.50
Sport Supply	February 97	12.50	16.75	5.00

*All warrants allow the purchase of one share of common stock.

CONVERTIBLE SECURITIES[3]

Convertible bonds and convertible preferred stocks combine the basic attributes of common stocks and corporate bonds or preferred stocks in a single security. Because they may be exchanged for common shares, convertibles participate in the growth and appreciation potential of the underlying equities. Equally significant, their status as senior securities with the obligation to pay fixed interest or dividends gives convertibles those qualities of nonconvertible senior securities that reduce risk. All convertibles possess such dual stock/bond characteristics; the extent to which one or the other attribute is more influential varies from issue to issue and even for a single issue over a period of time. Therefore, convertibles may satisfy a wide range of investment objectives.

Basic Features

The discussion that follows deals with convertible bonds. Analysis and selection of convertible preferred stock parallels the examination of convertible bonds with slightly less complication along certain lines.[4]

---

[3]Convertibles are discussed in detail in T. C. Noodings, *The Dow Jones-Irwin Guide to Convertible Securities* (Homewood, Ill.: Dow Jones-Irwin, 1973).

[4]A definitive discussion of convertible securities appears in E. F. Brigham, "An Analysis of Convertible Debentures," *Journal of Finance* (March 1966).

The number of common shares for which a bond may be exchanged (converted) is established when the bond is issued, but this number is usually subject to adjustment in the event of stock splits or stock dividends of given amounts. The number of shares of stock per bond is referred to as the *conversion rate*. The conversion price is (par/conversion rate). This price can be thought of as the strike (exercise) price. The stock value of the bond at any given point in time can be derived simply by multiplying the stock price by the conversion rate. For example, suppose a convertible bond can be exchanged for 20 shares of common stock. If the current market price of the common is $45, then the *conversion value* is $900 (20 × $45). The conversion value will change as the stock price changes.

The convertible bond will also have what is called an *investment, or straight, value.* This is its theoretical value based upon the yield-to-maturity of similar issues having no conversion feature. For example, suppose a 6 percent convertible bond due in twenty-five years is convertible into twenty shares of common stock. The common is currently at $55. Thus, the conversion value is $1,100 (55 × 20). However, suppose similar-quality bonds due in twenty-five years but without a conversion option are yielding 6 percent to maturity. This suggests an investment value for our 6 percent convertible bond of $1,000. This investment value is often regarded as a support level for the convertible bond in a declining stock market. However, the investment value also declines if interest rates rise during this period, as they usually do.

The investment value of a convertible preferred stock can be found in a similar manner. Because the preferred stock is a form of ownership, its life is assumed to be infinite and therefore the present-value factor used to find its value is not readily available. The investment value of a convertible preferred stock is assumed to equal the present value of preferred dividends over an infinite life discounted at the yield on a straight preferred stock. The present-value factor for an infinite-lived annuity is given by

$$V = \frac{D}{r}$$

where:

D = dividend on the preferred

r = appropriate discount rate or current yield on nonconvertible preferreds

An example will clarify the calculations required to find the value of preferred stock. The Strong Co. has just issued a 9 percent convertible preferred stock with a $100 par value. If the firm had issued a nonconvertible preferred stock, the annual dividend would probably have been 11 percent. Dividends are paid annually at year-end. Dividing the annual dividend of $9 (9 percent of $100) by the yields on nonconvertible preferreds, or 11 percent, yields an investment value for the preferred stock of $89 (9/.11). In other words, the straight value of the preferred stock continues.

Market Values

The *market value* of a convertible is likely to be greater than either its investment value or its conversion value. The amount by which the market price exceeds the straight or conversion value is often designated as the market *premium.* The market premium is larger the closer the straight value is to the conversion value. Even when the conversion value is below the straight value, a premium based on expected stock price movements exists. The same type of premium exists when the conversion value is above the straight value; this premium is attributed to the convertible security purchaser's expectations also. The general relationship among the straight value, the conversion value, the market value, and the market premium of a convertible bond, described in the preceding examples, is shown in Figure 13–2. The straight bond value acts as a floor for the security's value, and when the market price of the stock exceeds a certain value, the conversion value of the bond exceeds the straight bond value. Also, due to the expectations of investors about movements in the price of the firm's common stock, the market value of the convertible often exceeds both the straight and the conversion value of the security, resulting in a market premium on the security.

The notion of conversion and investment values (or the stock value of the bond and the bond value of the bond, as it were) must be compared with the actual market price of the bond to determine the extent to which the market price exceeds these levels. Consider the following for our 6 percent convertible bond that can be exchanged for 20 shares of common stock:

Market Prices:
Stock	$55
Bond	$1,200

Conversion value: $1,100 ($55 × 20 shares)
Investment value: $1,000 (to yield 6%)

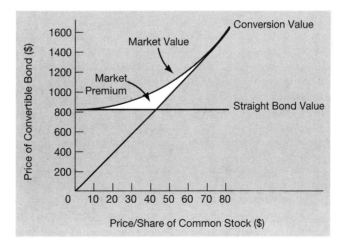

FIGURE 13–2   The Values and Market Premium for a Convertible Bond

In absolute terms the bond sells $100 above its conversion value and $200 above its investment value. In relative terms we have

$$\text{Premium over conversion value} = \frac{\text{Bond price} - \text{Conversion value}}{\text{Conversion value}}$$

$$\text{Premium over investment value} = \frac{\text{Bond price} - \text{Investment value}}{\text{Bond price}}$$

$$\text{Conversion parity price of stock} = \frac{\text{Bond price}}{\text{No. shares upon conversion}}$$

The *premium over conversion value* is 9.09 percent [($1,200 – $1,100)/$1,100], suggesting that the stock must rise about 9.09 percent for the breakeven point to be reached, or: ($55) + (.0909)($55) = $60. The *conversion parity* of the stock tells us the same thing: $1,200/20 = $60. The bond will generally sell some distance above its conversion value because investors know the leverage potential in holding the convertible bond and are looking ahead at the future price potential of the common.

The market price of a convertible bond will normally equal or exceed the conversion value of the bond; that is, negative conversion premiums are unlikely. This will be guaranteed by arbitrageurs. Let us see why. Suppose a bond is convertible into 20 shares of common stock. If the common stock were selling for $55 and the bond were selling for $1,000, the bond would be selling for $100 less than its conversion value ($55 × 20 = $1,100). Traders would see a profit opportunity in the *simultaneous* placement of orders to buy a bond and short sell 20 shares of stock (or multiples of this arrangement). They would pay $1,000 for each bond and receive $1,100 by delivering 20 shares of common stock to cover the short position—a nice $100 profit for each bond purchased. A lot of simultaneous trades of this sort will have the effect of raising the price of the bond and lowering the price of the common until an equilibrium relationship exists where the bond's conversion value is at least equal to or less than its market value.

The *premium over investment value* is 16.67 percent [($1,200 – $1,000) /$1,200], suggesting that the bond could fall 16.67 percent if the stock declined significantly before it reached a kind of price "floor."[5] Presumably, if the stock declined from $55 to, say, $40, the bond might cease falling at $1,000 even though its conversion value would be $800 ($40 $x 20 shares). However, the deterioration in the stock price very likely implies certain fundamental changes in risk surrounding the company, which will also reflect upon the quality of the bond. Increased risk in the bond might alter the required straight yield from 6 percent to a higher level, suggesting a lower investment value. Thus, the bond floor (investment value) is not necessarily a rigid value.[6]

It is also important to contrast the *current yield* on the bond and the stock to determine the relative income advantage (disadvantage) of holding one or the

---

[5]The premium over investment value is calculated using the bond price in the denominator. Some people would place the investment value in the denominator instead.

[6]An exploration of how converts have been priced over time is in R. King, "Convertible Bond Valuation: An Empirical Test," *Journal of Financial Research* (Spring 1986).

other. Suppose the underlying stock, selling currently at $55, pays an annual indicated dividend of $1.65 per share. Thus:

$$\text{Current yield on stock} = \frac{\text{Dividend}}{\text{Price}} = \frac{\$1.65}{\$55.00} = 3\%$$

$$\text{Current yield on bond} = \frac{\text{Interest}}{\text{Price}} = \frac{\$60}{\$1,200} = 5\%$$

In this instance the current yield on the stock is 3 percent and the current yield on the bond is 5 percent. In effect, the outright holding of the bond provides a higher relative income yield than the outright purchase of the common stock.

It is common to calculate a recovery or break-even period (in years) required to capture the conversion premium. This capture process is calculated as follows:

$$\text{Break-even period} = \frac{\text{Conversion premium (\$)}}{(\text{Interest income} - \text{Common dividends})}$$

Thus the break-even period determines the length of time needed to recover the conversion premium by the differential cash flow from the interest received on the convertible bond and the cash dividends available from the number of shares of common stock upon conversion. For the sample bond the conversion premium is $100. The equivalent dividend upon conversion is $33 ($1.65 × 20 shares) and the bond pays $60 in interest. Therefore, the break-even period is calculated:

$$\$100/(\$60 - \$33) = 3.7 \text{ years}$$

Convertibles Are a Compromise

Let us see where we are at this point:

Market Prices:	
Stock	$ 55
Bond	$1,200
Conversion Rate:	20 shares per $1,000 (par) bond
Values:	
Conversion	$1,100
Investment	$1,000
Parity	$ 60
Premiums:	
Conversion	9.09%
Investment	16.67%
Current Yields:	
Stock	3.00%
Bond	5.00%
Break-Even Period:	3.7 years

The central question is: Why wouldn't someone interested in capital gain (with some risk) buy the common outright at $55 and why wouldn't someone desiring current income and safety of principal buy a nonconvertible bond yielding 6 percent? Why buy this "hybrid"?

The general answer seems to be, in this case, that the buyer of the convertible would be looking for some compromise vehicle that provides a blend of current income, safety of principal, and capital gain potential. How much of each an investor wants and where he will compromise on each can only be determined by assessing (1) the bond's conversion premium, (2) the bond's investment premium, and (3) the relative current yields on the stock and the bond.

At current prices, purchase of the convertible bond provides a current yield that is higher than holding the common (5 percent versus 3 percent) but less than owning a nonconvertible issue (6 percent). Purchase of the common at $55 and a subsequent rise to, say, $66 would represent a 20 percent capital gain. Purchase of the bond at $1,200 would suggest a price of at least $1,320 (maybe slightly higher). This represents a capital gain of only 10 percent. Thus, from a capital appreciation standpoint, the bond has less potential than the common (10 percent versus 20 percent). Another compromise. With regard to the safety of principal, a 20 percent decline in the common from $55 to, say, $44 would suggest that the bond should fall to a level of only $1,000, or 16.7 percent (to its investment value). The bond has relatively more "downside" protection than the stock.

Different mixes of yield, investment, and conversion premiums will thus appeal to people with different investment objectives. The extent to which one or another of these attributes is more influential varies from issue to issue, and even for a single issue over a period of time.

As a real world example, let's look at the Boise Cascade 7.00 percent convertible debentures due in 2016. The company is in the lumber products business. Following are some relevant data on the bond and Boise Cascade stock in September 1993.

BOISE CASCADE

Bond price (Percent of bond par)	96.50
Coupon rate	7.00%
Maturity	23 years
Conversion rate (no. of shares)	22.830
Stock price	$21.75
Dividend on stock ($ annual)	$0.60
Straight bond yield	9.90%
Call price	107.00

CALCULATED VALUES:

Conversion	49.66
Investment	73.88
Premiums:	
Conversion	94.34%
Investment	23.44%

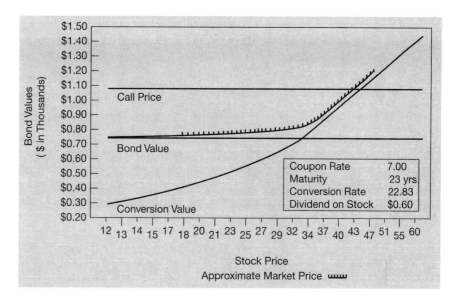

FIGURE 13–3   Convertible Bond Values (Boise Cascade due in 23 years)

Current yields:	
Stock	2.76%
Bond	7.25%
Premium recovery	8.32 years
Parity stock price	$42.27

This bond has a very "rich" conversion premium. The stock would have to advance about 94 percent (from 21.75 to 42.27) to reach parity. The premium recovery period is a very long 8.32 years. Figure 13–3 shows various values for this bond in relation to the price of Boise Cascade stock.

Risk of Call[7]

The possibility of call must be considered when investing in convertible bonds. That risk increases as the price of the common stock moves above the conversion price. A corporation that calls a convertible security expects most holders to exchange their bond for common stock instead of accepting cash (the call price). Therefore, convertible bonds are unlikely to be called until the bond is selling well above the call price and probably at little or no premium above conversion value. To continue our example, suppose the 6 percent convertible bond is callable at $1,050 and that the common sells for $60. The conversion value of $1,200 ($60 × 20 shares) is above

[7]Investor behavior in the event of a call are found in M. J. Brennan and E. S. Schwartz, "Convertible Bonds: Valuation and Optimal Strategies for Call and Conversion," *Journal of Finance* (December 1977).

TABLE 13–3

Selected Convertible Bonds

COMPANY NAME	COUPON RATE	MATURITY DATE	QUALITY RATING	SHARES PER $1,000 BOND	
Bank of New York	7.50	2001	A–	25.575	
Blockbuster Entertainment	0.00	2004	BB+	27.700	
Boise Cascade	7.00	2016	BB–	22.830	
Comptronix	6.75	2002	NR	56.340	
Cray Research	6.13	2011	BBB–	12.820	
Deere & Co.	5.50	2001	A–	30.530	
Delta Airlines	3.23	2003	B+	12.680	
Ford Motor Credit	4.88	1998	A–	71.990	
General Signal	5.75	2002	A–	25.320	
Huffy Corp.	7.25	2014	NR	65.790	
Mattel, Inc.	8.00	2001	BBB–	62.340	
Morgan, J. P.	4.75	1998	AAA	50.000	
Motorola	0.00	2009	A+	9.134	
Outboard Marine	7.00	2002	BBB–	44.940	
Pennzoil	6.50	2003	BBB	11.887	Chevron Stock
Stone Container	6.75	2007	B–	29.464	
Storage Technology	8.00	2015	B	28.369	
Sunshine Mining	9.00	2018	NR	571.428	
Time Warner	8.75	2015	BB+	20.950	
Travelers Corp.	8.32	2015	A–	19.500	
Union Pacific	4.75	1999	A	140.000	
Wendy's Int'l.	7.25	2010	BBB–	57.340	
Zenith Electronics	6.25	2011	CCC	32.000	

NR—Not rated.

the call price. What would most bondholders do if a call were made: accept $1,050 in cash or $1,200 worth of common stock? The answer is obvious.

As the price of the common passes $52.50 (conversion value = call price = $1,050), it will be difficult to justify paying any premium over conversion value for the bond. This is true since any premium paid will be lost in a call. Suppose that the common is at $60 and the bond is at $1,300. If a call is exercised at $1,050, $100 is lost because the common stock you receive is only worth $1,200.

Table 13–3 represents a broad list of convertible bonds.

Standards of Attractiveness for a Convertible

Our analysis has shown the many dimensions of convertible securities analysis. It is now useful to examine some approximate standards that should be met for a convertible to warrant serious investment consideration.

First, the convertible must meet minimum quality rating standards set by the investor. For example, many investors would consider convertible bonds rated below the "A" category unacceptable. Realistically, however, many convertible bonds carry Baa ratings and below. This may be because convertible bonds are often debentures (unsecured). Additionally, such bonds may have income and/or asset claims that are subordinated to other creditors.

Second, the purchase of convertibles is sensible only in environments in which interest rates are expected to be stable or declining. Remember, as fixed-income securities, their prices are adversely affected by rising interest rates.

Third, the premium over investment value, taking into account anticipated interest-rate changes (which will raise or lower the investment value or "floor" price), should probably not exceed 15 percent. That is, the straight value should not be more than 15 percent below the current market price. This standard helps to ensure that downside risk is not substantial.

Fourth, the conversion premium should be less than 20 percent; that is, the current price of the common stock must not be more than 20 percent below the conversion parity. This rule ensures that upside potential is meaningful and achievable. Of course, the potential price of the common stock should be well above conversion parity, probably 25 percent or more.

Fifth, the premium payback period should be reasonable. It should be possible to recover the conversion premium relatively quickly through the higher yield on the convertible security relative to the underlying common stock. A payback period of two years or less is desirable.

Convertible Strategies

Convertible-securities investment encompasses the wide variety of participants in the market. Each type of investor brings a unique perspective to the valuation process, thereby creating a wide diversity of attitudes in the marketplace. An investor in junk (low-quality) bonds may want to sell a bond equivalent when the company's prospects improve and the security begins to behave more like a hybrid. The hybrid investor who buys this security may later sell it to an equity investor when the common stock rises to the point where the security becomes an equity equivalent. Each investor is making a decision that is rational and sensible from his own perspective, yet each may feel that he has had the better side of the trade.

Convertible investors include many different types. Risk-averse types who are basically common-stock investors may wish to hold a somewhat more defensive instrument. Some income-oriented types are common-stock investors requiring more income than is provided by the common stock. Convertible specialists deal exclusively with convertible security portfolios.

Bond investors often seek equity "kickers," or low-quality bonds and other fixed-income investments where the sacrifice of a certain amount of income enables attainment of some equity exposure. Arbitragers attempt to exploit perceived disparities in the spread relationship between the common stock and the convertible security.

Each type of investor may place a different degree of emphasis on particular variables in determining which convertible securities are attractive or unattractive. The more equity-oriented investor will tend to restrict activity to the equity-equivalent end of the spectrum, whereas low-quality-bond investors will tend to be more active in the bond-equivalent range. Convertible specialists will employ the full range of securities but may have a preference for the true hybrid convertible securities, for reasons that will be discussed later. Arbitrage tends to be most easily accomplished with equity equivalent issues but can take place over a broad range of security types. In each case, the valuation tools given greatest emphasis will vary with the investor's perspective.

We have described some of the different types of investors using convertible securities. The significance of individual valuation parameters is heavily influenced by the perspective of the investor. If one is driven by a minimum-income requirement, for example, the coupon or dividend may be quite important. If one is attempting to acquire defensive characteristics in an equity portfolio, the conversion premium may be of primary importance. An investor in low-quality bonds may be concerned primarily with credit analysis and how much he is paying for the equity "kicker." Similarly, convertible specialists and arbitragers would each bring their unique perspectives to the valuation process.

What are some of the strategies these different investors might consider? One strategy is simply to view the convertible strictly as an extension of the equity selection process. In other words, first determine which common stocks are attractive and then—and only then—look at the availability of the convertibles. The convertible security's primary appeal could result from a favorable disposition to the common stock coupled with concern about the general market outlook. This strategy is essentially one of hedging against an adverse market environment. In such a case, the investor might be willing to pay slightly more than the theoretically correct value for the convertible.

In another case, the holder of a common stock may find that a convertible security is available on sufficiently attractive terms that he would prefer it to the common stock irrespective of his market view. If the analysis and valuation indicates that the convertible would share in most of the stock's appreciation while still offering significant downside protection, it might make sense to swap the common stock for the convertible. Similarly, if the income gained by using the convertible would fully absorb the premium before the bond becomes callable, a swap would make sense.

These are equity-oriented strategies. These investors will pay particular attention to valuation parameters, such as payback period, conversion premium, and call protection. They may place relatively less value on coupon and investment value.

Fixed-income-oriented investors, on the other hand, might place heavy emphasis on investment value and much less on the conversion premium. Here the strategy would be to achieve the objectives of the fixed-income portfolio (e.g., immunization) while still obtaining some exposure to the common stock, albeit distant, through the convertible. A five-year or longer payback period may be much less important than a comparison of the amount being paid in excess of investment value to the theoretical warrant value.

Convertible specialists and arbitragers will be looking for disparities in value between the convertible and the underlying common stock whenever they may occur. Although purchasing a convertible security if the common stock is expected to decline in price is generally unwise, purchasing a convertible security when the stock price outlook is indifferent might nevertheless be desirable, provided that the valuation analysis indicates that the convertible is underpriced relative to the common. One might maintain a long position in an undervalued convertible and a short position in an offsetting amount of common stock in order to exploit such undervaluations with relative indifference to the direction of stock-price changes. (Conversely, a short position can be maintained in an overvalued convertible against a long position in the common stock.)

After establishing objectives and guidelines for the use of convertible securities, perhaps the most important factor for any individual investor to bear in mind is that *other* convertible investors may have very different strategies and objectives. This may facilitate execution of his own strategies. What is perceived by one participant as an erroneous valuation may be perceived by another participant as "fair value." To a significant extent, then, a convertible security's attractiveness is in the eye of the beholder.

This is not to say that a theoretical valuation scheme aimed at estimating the "intrinsic value" of a convertible security is not worthwhile. Rather, the point is that when substantial deviations relative to such a theoretical value seem to appear, it may simply mean that another point of view is more prevalent among investors.

Practical Problems

TRADING

Most convertible bonds are traded away from the popular exchanges in what is essentially a negotiated market. Although many of the larger convertible preferred stocks and convertible bonds are listed on one of the major exchanges, the latest reported trade data will not always accurately reflect the true market conditions. This lack of visibility of the "real" market puts a premium on the ability for trades to be effectively executed.

Many of the smaller issues trade infrequently and have very few active market makers. For larger and more active issues, however, an informal network of brokers maintains a reasonable level of market efficiency. To ensure effective executions, a trader must maintain active daily surveillance of all issues in which trading activity is likely. It is only through active participation in the marketplace that actual market levels can be ascertained.

ANTICIPATING CALLS AND REDEMPTIONS

In the early 1980s, a period of high and rising long-term interest rates, very few convertible issues were called as a result of refinancing. It was generally a safe bet that a call was intended to force the holder into converting into common stock. In

more recent years, however, refinancing calls have become more common, and it is, therefore, necessary to anticipate both types of calls.

When the call is intended to "force" conversion into common stock, the issuer will normally not risk having the common stock decline sufficiently during the twenty- to thirty-day call period to make conversion unattractive. In other words, the price level of the common stock will have to be sufficiently above the conversion price of the convertible in order to provide a cushion. The size of this cushion will depend on the volatility of the stock, market conditions, the length of time that must be allowed between the announcement and the redemption, and any possible adverse reaction to the dilution that the conversion might cause. There is no simple rule of thumb for estimating the appropriate amount of cushion, but experience has shown that companies rarely force conversion unless the equity value of the convertible is at least 15 percent above the call price. In the case of more volatile issues, a 20 to 25 percent cushion may be necessary.

After a convertible security becomes callable, the most conservative assumption is that a forced conversion will take place whenever the bond price rises more than 15 percent above the call price. This enables the convertible holder to estimate the probable price action of the convertible relative to the common stock. (Because the conversion premium will normally disappear when the issue is called, the holder should assume that a convertible lacking call protection will trade at conversion parity when it is 15 to 20 percent above the call price. The corresponding stock price level is thus also determined.)

A call that is *not* intended to force conversion (i.e., a call intended to redeem the issue) will depend, in large part, on the issuer's ability to obtain capital on more favorable terms and on their internal projections of after-tax cash flows. The coupon and premium level of the existing convertible should be compared to the probable terms at which the issuer could bring a new convertible offering to market or some other measure of the issuer's marginal cost of capital. The issuer's internal cash-flow projections and probable need to obtain more capital in the future might also be important. The holder of the convertible security, to take the most conservative approach, should estimate the yield-to-call for all issues trading significantly above the call price.

DECIDING WHETHER TO REDEEM OR CONVERT

When a convertible security is called for redemption, the price of the issue will normally move very quickly to either the call price or the equity conversion value, whichever is larger. Generally speaking, the correct action will be quite obvious. Naturally, a convertible whose equity conversion value is significantly above the redemption price should not be redeemed. On the other hand, when the equity conversion value is well below the redemption price, it is clearly best to redeem. However, if the equity conversion is not too far below the redemption price, it is often wise to wait as long as possible before redeeming the security.

As an example of the value of waiting to redeem, Allied-Signal called their $6.74 convertible preferred for redemption in August 1986 at a redemption price of $57. When the call was officially announced in early July, the equity conversion

value was below the $57 redemption value. By month-end, a company announcement concerning a possible stock buy-back program briefly caused the common stock to rally above the conversion price. This gave the convertible-preferred holder an opportunity to sell shares at more than a dollar above the redemption price. The stock subsequently declined again and the preferred issue was redeemed at $57.[8]

SUMMARY

Warrants are long calls issued by companies in the process of raising capital. These instruments afford investors with longer maturities than the typical CBOE-type call and are often attached to an income-producing security.

Convertible securities represent a unique combination of equity and fixed-income attributes that offer the investor a favorable nonlinear distribution of expected returns. When equity values rise, the convertible will automatically approach the behavior of the underlying stock. During stock-price declines, the convertible will increasingly approach the behavior of a straight debt instrument.

Convertibles provide the ability to participate in the upward movement of the common stock while providing a limit to the downside as a result of the "floor" provided by the straight bond value. These instruments also provide more income than the underlying common stock.

Strategies for the use of convertible securities will tend to reflect the perspective of the investor using them. Such investors will range from risk-averse equity investors to bond investors seeking an equity "kicker." To some extent, the attraction of a convertible is in the eye of the beholder.

QUESTIONS

1. Compare the generic differences inherent in the purchase of a convertible preferred stock and the purchase of a convertible bond.

2. What are the features in a convertible bond that a fixed-income-oriented investor would be looking for? An equity-oriented investor?

3. Discuss the practical importance of a call feature in a convertible preferred stock.

4. Can you think of reasons why a convertible bond might be convertible into a security other than common stock? Convertible into the common stock of a company other than that of the issuer of the convertible bond?

5. Convertible bonds are hybrid instruments that produce a nonlinear distribution of returns. The nonlinear return distribution is essentially inherent in the security and does not depend upon the action of the investor. Explain.

[8]For a look at the relationship between risk and return on convertibles, see R. M. Soldofsky, "The Risk-Return Performance of Convertibles," *Journal of Portfolio Management* (Winter

6. Why do issuers of convertible bonds normally not automatically call these securities when they reach the call price in the market?

7. The conversion feature in a convertible bond is very similar to a long-term warrant. Could the Black-Scholes option valuation framework (see Chapter 12) be used to value this long-term warrant? Explain.

8. The Harco mutual fund buys convertible bonds while it simultaneously sells call options and buys put options on the stock of the issuing company. What is the apparent purpose of this unusual investment strategy?

9. Would a speculator want a low or high ratio of stock price/warrant price. Why?

10. Bonanza Industries has issued a convertible bond whose conversion value is substantially in excess of par value. Would a bondholder continue to hold these bonds rather than converting. Why?

11. How do we calculate the break-even or recovery period on a convertible bond. What seems to be the rationale for limiting the break-even value to two years or less when analyzing the attractiveness of a convertible bond?

12. Warrants generally originate as add-ons when a weak company is attempting to sell bonds but needs a "sweetener" to sell the bonds and/or reduce the coupon interest rate. These warrants can be made detachable or nondetachable from the host bond. *Nondetachable* means the warrant must be exercised by the bondholder. *Detachable* means that the warrant and the bond can trade separately. Which type, detachable or nondetachable, would a corporate issuer probably prefer. Why?

PROBLEMS

1. A convertible bond has the following characteristics: market price = 106, call price = 109, conversion price = 25, stock price = 28, bond investment value = 100. What is your assessment of this situation?

2. A convertible preferred stock has the following characteristics: dividend = $4.50, par value = $100, call price = $106, conversion rate = 4 shares, market price = $126. Equivalent straight preferreds are selling to yield 9 percent. The underlying common stock pays an annual dividend of $1 and sells for $28. Would you buy the convertible? Why?

3. KWIK Corp. has a 6 percent ($50 par) preferred stock outstanding that is callable at $53 and convertible into two shares of common stock. The preferred is selling for $60. The common is selling for $25 (and paying a $2 dividend). Straight preferreds are currently selling to yield 8 percent.
   a. Calculate the investment and conversion values of the 6 percent preferred stock.
   b. Assume that the preferred sold at $47. How might a speculator capitalize on this fact, other things being equal?

c. If the preferreds were called at this time, what would most holders be likely to do? Why?

4. Archway Corp. has a $10 ($100 par) convertible preferred stock selling for $108. The preferred are convertible into two shares of common stock. the common stock is currently selling for $53. Nonconvertible preferred stocks of a similar quality are currently selling to yield 10 percent. If the common stock were to fall from $53 to $45, a decline of about 15 percent, about how much would the preferred decline? Why?

5. Anthony Industries has an 11.25 percent convertible bond outstanding (2000) that is convertible into 55.5 shares of common stock. The bonds have an investment value of 670 (per 1,000 par value). The common stock currently sells for $14.50 and pays a dividend of $.44. The current price of the bonds is 965. Provide a systematic analysis of this convertible bond.

6. Consult Moody's *Manuals* or Standard & Poor's *Bond Guide* for information on Huffy 7.25 percent convertible bonds due in 2014. Perform a systematic analysis of these bonds.

7. Shale Industries is a small to medium-sized company actively engaged in the oil services industry. The company provides replacement parts for drilling rigs and has just begun to test a device that measures oil shale content in certain rock formations. The company has a $4 convertible preferred stock outstanding ($100 par). 120,000 shares are outstanding (47,500 owned by institutions). The preferred stock is callable at $102 with a conversion price of $47.17. Shale common is currently paying an indicated dividend of $1.40 on earnings per share of $2,80. Consensus opinion on Wall Street is that long-term interest rates will be flat to down over the next year. The common stock is currently selling for $14 and the preferred is at $32. Nonconvertible preferreds of companies in this industry that have similar quality ratings (Bbb) are yielding 14 percent at this time.
a. Provide a systematic analysis of the convertible preferred.
b. Assess the attractiveness of purchase of the convertible preferred at this time.

8. Hollytree Corp. has a warrant outstanding that allows the holder to acquire two shares of common stock at $20 per share for the next four years. The stock is currently selling at $17 and the warrant at $3. What is the intrinsic value of the warrant?

9. Norman Industries has a convertible bond outstanding due in ten years. This A-rated bond pays interest semiannually and its yield to maturity is 5 percent. Similar A-rated bonds that are nonconvertible are currently yielding 10 percent to maturity. Each $1,000 par value bond can be converted into twenty-one shares of common stock and is callable at 106 percent of par. The common stock is currently at $54.
a. What is the straight debt value of this bond? Conversion value?
b. Might the bond be called at this time? Why?

10. Paragram Containers has a warrant outstanding that permits the holder the right to acquire one share of stock for $30 until the year 2000. The stock is currently at $32, and the warrant is at $4. If the stock moves up to $40, what is the minimum and maximum value for this warrant?

11. Mobay Chemicals has an 8 percent convertible bond ($1,000 par) that is convertible into twenty-one shares of common any time up to the maturity date in ten years. The current yield-to-maturity on these AA-rated bonds of 5 percent compares to 10 percent on similar nonconvertible bonds. The bonds are callable at $1,060 while the common stock is selling for $54. What is the straight debt and the conversion value of these bonds?

C A S E

Brian Vandergriff

Brian Vandergriff is a portfolio manager for Southside Bank and Trust Company. He currently is considering purchasing shares of Deere (maker of farm equipment) and Zenith (a producer of electronic equipment) common stock for inclusion in several portfolios he manages. As an alternative, he also is considering purchasing Deere and Zenith convertible bonds. The portfolios under consideration are mostly equity portfolios having the objective of aggressive growth. Vandergriff expects Deere to benefit from the recent growth in demand for agricultural equipment abroad. Zenith may be on the come-back trail after its earnings growth faltered in the late 1980s. He also expects interest rates to remain stable during the next year.

CONVERTIBLE	DEERE	ZENITH
Coupon	5.50%	6.25%
Maturity [years]	8	18
Rating	A−	CCC
Conversion rate (# shares)	30.53	32
Market price (% par)	222.50	66.25
Investment value	85.43	64.95
Call price	105	106
COMMON STOCK		
Market price	72.88	6.88
Dividend	2.00	0.00
Beta	1.05	1.45

QUESTION

Analyze these two convertibles. Recommend the convertible debenture that, in your opinion, would be more desirable for purchase by an aggressive, growth-oriented investor. Justify your recommendation.

REFERENCES

ALTMAN, E. I. "The Convertible Debt Market: Are Returns Worthwhile?" *Financial Analysts Journal* (July–August 1989).

BRENNAN, M. J., and E. S. SCHWARTZ. "Convertible Bonds: Valuation and Optimal Strategies for Call and Conversion." *Journal of Finance* (December 1977).

BRIGHAM, E. F. "An Analysis of Convertible Debentures." *Journal of Finance* (March 1966).

GALAI, D., and M. SCHNELLER. "Pricing Warrants and the Value of the Firm." *Journal of Finance* (December 1978).

KEPPLER, A. MICHAEL. "The Importance of Dividend Yields in Country Selection." *Journal of Portfolio Management* (Winter 1991), pp. 24–29.

KIM, M. K., and A. YOUNG. "Rewards and Risks from Warrant Hedging." *Journal of Portfolio Management* (Summer 1980).

KING, R. "Convertible Bond Valuation: An Empirical Test." *Journal of Financial Research* (Spring 1986).

NOODINGS, T. C. *The Dow Jones-Irwin Guide to Convertible Securities.* Homewoood, Ill.: Dow Jones-Irwin, 1973.

SCHWARTZ, E. "The Valuation of Warrants: Implementing a New Approach." *Journal of Financial Economics* (January 1977).

SHELTON, J. P. "The Relation of the Price of a Warrant to the Price of Its Associated Stock." *Financial Analysts Journal* (May–June 1967).

SOLDOFSKY, R. M. "The Risk-Return Performance of Convertibles." *Journal of Portfolio Management* (Winter 1981).

FUTURES

DEFINITIONS AND COMPARISONS

An *options agreement* is a contract in which the writer of the option grants the buyer of the option the right to purchase from or sell to the writer a designated instrument at a specified price (or receive a cash settlement) within a specified period of time.

In contrast, a *futures contract* is a firm legal commitment between a buyer and seller in which they agree to exchange something at a specified price at the end of a designated period of time. The buyer agrees to take delivery of something and the seller agrees to make delivery.

The fundamental differences between futures and options are the following.

1. With futures, both parties are obligated to perform. With options only the seller (writer) is obligated to perform.

2. With options, the buyer pays the seller (writer) a premium. With futures, no premium is paid by either party.

3. With futures, the holder of the contract is exposed to the entire spectrum of downside risk and has the potential for all the upside return. With options, the buyer limits the downside risk to the option premium but retains the upside potential.

4. The parties to a futures contract must perform at the settlement date. They are not obligated to perform before that date. The buyer of an options contract can exercise any time prior to the expiration date.

STOCK INDEX FUTURES[1]

A stock index futures contract is an obligation to deliver at settlement an amount of cash equal to 500 times the difference between the stock index value at the close of the last trading day of the contract and the price at which the futures contract was originally struck. So, if the S&P 500 Stock Index is at 500 and each point in the index equals $500, a contract struck at this level could be worth $250,000 (500 × $500). If, at the expiration of the contract, the S&P 500 Stock Index is at 510, a cash settlement of $5,000 is required [(510 − 500) × 500].

No physical delivery of stocks is made. In order to ensure that sufficient funds are available for settlement, both buyer and seller are required to put up a "good faith" deposit or margin and meet variation margin calls, if any. The original margin required for an S&P 500 Stock Index futures contract depends upon whether one is a speculator (underlying stocks not owned) or a hedger (stocks owned). A speculator must put up $20,000 original margin at this time. If the S&P 500 Stock Index is at 500, the value of a contract would be $250,000 (500 × $500) so the margin requirement is about 8 percent (20,000/250,000). Recall that the original margin requirement in the stock market is 50 percent. It is easy to see that the higher leverage afforded in the stock index futures market is an essential attraction to both buyers and sellers.

The margin is not a down payment, and neither loan nor margin interest are involved. The contract is marked to the market daily, and additional cash (variation) margin may be required (or released), depending upon market movements. Thus, assume a contract is struck at 500 and the index moves up as high as 575 and down as low as 460 prior to expiration. During this time, funds are being debited and credited each day from buyer to seller. The only net exchange of cash at the expiration of the contract would be the difference between the value of the S&P 500 at the time the original contract was struck and the value at the last day of trading of the contract.

At the end of each trading session, each customer's position is marked to the new settlement prices. Each account is credited (debited) with favorable (unfavorable) price changes. Whenever the variation in settlement price brings the margin account below the maintenance level, the customer must pay in cash at least the amount needed to bring the margin account up to the original level per contract. When an account falls below the maintenance-margin level, a call is made both by phone and in writing for correction in twenty-four hours. By the same token, when the value in a margin account exceeds the original margin, any excess over the original margin may be withdrawn by the customer or used to meet variation on other positions.

For example, suppose we are dealing with one S&P 500 contract. The original margin is $20,000 and the maintenance margin is $10,000. Assume the contract is struck with the S&P 500 at 500. The next day the S&P 500 moves up to 502. The

---

[1]Detailed discussion of stock index futures can be found in F. J. Fabozzi and G. M. Kipnis, eds., *Stock Index Futures* (Homewood, Ill.: Dow Jones-Irwin, 1984).

TABLE 14–1

Contract Specifications of Stock Index Futures Contracts

INDEX (EXCHANGE)*	TRADING HOURS	CONTRACT MONTHS†	UNITS/ MINIMUM PRICE FLUCTUATION	LAST DAY OF TRADING‡
S&P 500 (CME)	8:30–3:15 (CST)	3, 6, 9, 12	500 × index/ .05 ($25)	Third Thursday
NYSE Index (NYFE)	9:30–4:15 (EST)	3, 6, 9, 12	500 × index/ .05 ($25)	Thursday preceding third Friday
Major Market Index (CBOT)	8:30–3:15 (CST)	3 current months plus 3, 6, 9, 12	250 × index/ .05 ($12.50)	First business day prior to Saturday following third Friday
Value Line Index (KCBT)	8:30–3:15 (CST)	3, 6, 9, 12	500 × index/ .05 ($25)	Third Friday
Mini Value Line Index (KCBT)	8:30–3:15 (CST)	3, 6, 9, 12	100 × index/ .05 ($5)	Third Friday

*CBOT—Chicago Board of Trade.
CME—Chicago Mercantile Exchange.
KCBT—Kansas City Board of Trade.
NYFE—New York Futures Exchange.
†The notation used in this column corresponds to the month of the calendar year (e.g., 1 is January, 2 is February, and so on).
‡All stock index futures contracts are cash settled.

buyer receives $1,000 from the seller's margin account [(502 − 500) × 500]. If during the contract life the S&P 500 moves to, say, 479, the buyer owes the seller $10,500 [(500 − 479) × 500]. A margin call is made when the amount owed exceeds $10,000 (maintenance margin falls below $10,000). Margin calls not met by the required time require selling out the customer.

The standard delivery months for index futures contracts are March, June, September, and December. Contracts are available on the Value Line Composite Average (1700 stocks) as well as the New York Stock Exchange (NYSE) Composite Index (all 1500 NYSE common stocks), and the major market index (20 Dow Jones Industrial Average [DJIA] stocks). There are contracts for the S&P 500 Stock Index and its little brother, the S&P 100 Stock Index (which uses a $200 multiple). In Table 14–1 we display specific features of major index futures contracts.

Valuation of Stock Index Futures Contracts

Unlike options, the valuation of index futures is easy to understand. No fancy valuation formulas are required. Consider an investor who wants to hold the S&P 500 stocks for the next year. He will collect dividends, and his principal value will go up

or down with the index. At some price for the futures index, this investor can get exactly the same array of outcomes by investing all his money in Treasury bills and buying a contract for future delivery of the index. It turns out that for this to be true, the futures must sell at a price equal to today's price of the index, plus a premium equal to the difference between the risk-free rate and the dividend yield on the index.

$$\text{Return to index} = \text{Index price at expiration}$$
$$- \text{ Current index price}$$
$$+ \text{ Dividends}$$
$$= I_E - I_B + D$$

$$\text{Return to futures} = \text{Futures price at expiration}$$
$$- \text{ Current futures price}$$
$$+ \text{ Interest}$$
$$= F_E - F_B + R_F$$

Because the price of the index (I_E) will equal the price of the futures (F_E) at expiration:

$$F_B = I_B + (R_F - D)$$

Today's futures price equals the price of the index, plus interest obtainable on a risk-free basis over the life of the contract, minus the dividend to be received on that index over the life of the contract.

The futures contract should be priced to reflect the "cost of carry," which is $(R_F - D)$. Thus, if the annualized risk-free rate is 13 percent and the annualized dividend yield is 6 percent, a futures contract on the index for one year should sell at an annualized 7 percent premium to the index, independent of expectations for the market.

Because the costs of purchasing an index fund are greater than the costs of buying a futures contract, the effect of transaction costs is to raise the premium at which futures should sell. Over short time intervals the cash dividends from the S&P stocks vary quite a lot, depending upon the vagaries of dividend dates and sizes. Depending on the timing of the settlement date and the initiation of a position, the relationship between dividend yield and risk-free return can vary substantially. For example, if the dividend yield exceeded the risk-free return, the future's theoretical price would be below that of the index.

In Figure 14–1 we sample the "tracking" relationship of the index and the futures contract (futures − index = spread).

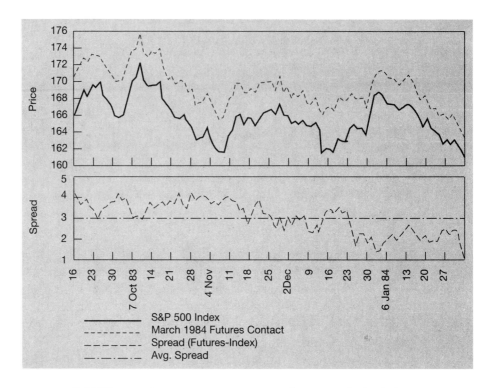

FIGURE 14–1   S&P 500 Futures Contracts, March 1984 vs. Index (Daily Data—
September 16, 1983, to February 2, 1984)

Stock Index Arbitrage

Arbitrage, or *basis trading,* is the simultaneous purchase and sale of the same commodity in two different markets in order to profit from price discrepancies between the markets. For example, we know that if the price of gold in London is $300 per ounce and the price of gold in New York is $315, an obvious opportunity exists to buy gold in London and sell in New York simultaneously to earn a profit of $15 per ounce. Economists maintain that, by eliminating intermarket differentials, arbitrage makes markets more efficient. Stock index futures arbitrage involves buying (selling) a basket of stocks and selling (buying) futures when mispricing is perceived to occur.

Stock-index arbitrage, which is not risky but requires large amounts of capital, often involves the S&P 500 futures contracts. The critical part of the arbitrage play comes in the pricing of these contracts. We saw earlier that the prime consideration in the pricing of the futures is the difference between the index dividend return and the return on alternative investments. Because the return on Treasury bills, for example, is higher than the yield of the S&P 500, the futures price should be higher than the actual S&P 500 index. The yield differential loses significance as

the futures contract approaches its expiration date, at which point the futures price and the actual index must converge. Thus, the premium gradually disappears. Market sentiment also enters into futures pricing. At times, when psychology is poor, a futures-to-index discount develops. Discounts, though, are most likely on contracts that are near expiration.

When the futures price does not accurately reflect the yield differential, the arbitrageur would buy the relatively cheap alternative and sell the relatively expensive one.

Each stock-index arbitrageur has his own entry point, which is determined by factors such as the amount of capital he has available at the time, his particular transaction costs, and the rate of return available from the arbitrage. Once the arbitrage position is established, the rate of return is guaranteed because of the merging of the futures and stock index prices at the expiration of a contract.

Let's assume the following: the time is late September, the S&P 500 index is at 505, the December 19 Treasury bill rate is 5 percent, the annual dividend yield of the S&P 500 is 3 percent, and the December S&P 500 futures contract, which expires December 19 (ninety days = .25 year), is at 507.

If the index suddenly drops to 500 but the futures contract remains at 507, a buy program would be triggered. The arbitrageur has calculated that because the premium has widened to 7 points (507–500), it has become profitable to buy stocks that replicate the index and sell (go short) the futures. This is because the value of the futures contract should be 502.5 calculated as:

$$\text{Value} = 500 + [(500)(.05)(.25)] - [(222)(.03)(.25)]$$
$$= 500 + [(500)(.05 - .03)(.25)]$$
$$= 500 + 2.50$$
$$= 502.50$$

The arbitrageur estimates that the program requires $10,234,000 for the stock purchases, which would buy him shares with a market value equivalent to roughly 39 contracts at $500 \times \$507$ per contract and $234,000 to go short an equal number of contracts (39 contracts at an assumed $6,000 down-payment price per contract).[2]

On December 19, when the contract expires, the arbitrageur must unwind his original program (sell stock, settle futures). No matter where the S&P 500 Stock Index closes on this date, his profit is the same. Let's see why.

If the S&P 500 Stock Index on December 19 closed at 490, the arbitrageur's profit is calculated as follows:

---

[2]Note that 39.45 contracts are actually required [($10 million)/(507 $\times$ 500)]. This is a slightly underhedged position.

Profit from short sale of futures $[(507 – 490) \times 500 \times 39]$	$331,500
plus	
Cash dividends received on $10 million worth of stocks $[(\$10M)(.03/4)]$	$75,000
less	
Loss on sale of stock portfolio $[(490–500)(500)(39)]$	($195,000)
Interest $[(\$10M)(.05)(.25)]$	($125,000)
Total profit (before transaction costs)	$86,500

If the S&P 500 on December 19 closed at 510, the arbitrageur's profit is calculated as follows:

Profit on sale of stock portfolio $[(510 – 500)(500)(39)]$	$195,000
plus	
Cash dividends received on $10 million worth of stocks $[(\$10M)(.03/4)]$	$75,000
less	
Loss from short sales of futures $[(507 – 510) \times 500 \times 39]$	$(58,500)
Interest $[(\$10M) (.05)(.25)]$	$(125,000)
Total profit (before transaction costs)	$86,500

The annual return (before transaction costs) in both instances is 11.86 percent, which exceeds the arbitrageur's alternative return of 5.3 percent on Treasury bills and makes the program worthwhile.

As one or more arbitrageurs buy or sell baskets of stocks comprising the S&P 500 or some cross section of the index that accurately reflects it (100 stocks often are sufficient) and concurrently sell or buy S&P 500 futures contracts, the prices of the stocks that are components of the index can swing widely. Profit-taking in arbitrage involves the reversal, or unwinding, of the positions previously taken. This *exiting*, as it is sometimes called, on occasion causes sharp movements in the stock market on days when stock-index futures and options expire.

The foregoing example is greatly simplified for purposes of illustration. In reality, stock-index arbitrage is a highly sophisticated technique requiring extensive resources, including elaborate telecommunications networks, computing facilities, and money—at least $5 million to $10 million.

Few would dispute that this so-called *program trading* has an impact, if only temporary, on the stock prices of individual companies, notably those that carry

heavy weightings in a popular arbitrage index. The reason for this is that the combined market action of a group of these companies tends to mirror that of the overall market, thus eliminating the need to replicate the basket of stocks that the index future represents. Thus, there is heavy demand for some of these major issues when arbitrageurs are selling the futures and buying the stocks.

To some extent, the reverse holds true when futures are being bought and the stocks sold as programs are initiated. The extent of impact may not be nearly so great on the downside. The reason is that a short sale of stock can occur only if the last sale was on an uptick (i.e., if the price in the last trade was higher than the trade that preceded it). In a plunging market, trades on an uptick are rare. We should note that the liquidation, or unwinding, of buy programs is not affected by the uptick rule and thus can exacerbate price movement in a declining market.

As just suggested, the impact of program trading on individual stocks can be pronounced, but indications are that the effects are short-lived.

What are the risks in arbitrage? First, there is potential tracking error; that is, your portfolio might not have a composition identical to the index underlying the futures contract you are using. Second, there are potential miscalculations regarding the stream of dividend receipts from the stocks underlying the index; for example, some stocks raise (lower) their dividends, and some pay more quickly than others from the date of dividend announcement. Third, there is market impact. The purchase or sale of large amounts of individual stocks has the potential to aggrevate the bid-asked spread on a stock (you might get in your own way!). A stock purchase of $80 million may force you to pay an eighth or quarter point in order to transact.

PORTFOLIO STRATEGIES USING INDEX FUTURES[3]

Several strategies or techniques are available where utilizing stock index futures offers implementation advantages and incremental returns to portfolios. The following suggests four such applications. Although not exhaustive, the four are representative of the types of strategic uses of stock index futures and financial futures now available to manage a portfolio.

Passive Management: Index Fund

The first application involves a common-stock index fund, a portfolio construction technique that is included in the passive-management category. A superior method of constructing an index fund (owning the "market") involves buying S&P 500 futures contracts. A numerical example will illustrate the construction mechanics.

---

[3]See S. Figlewski and S. Kon, "Portfolio Management with Stock Index Futures," *Financial Analysts Journal* (January–February 1982).

Assume we wish to structure an index fund of $10 million and that the current price of the S&P 500 future is 500. Each contract is, therefore, equivalent to a common stock exposure of 500 times $500, or $250,000. To gain exposure of $10 million in common stocks, one could easily and quickly purchase 40 ($10 million ÷ $250,000) S&P 500 futures contracts.

Such a portfolio-construction approach has many advantages. The benefits of lower transaction costs are notable. The low commission rate on futures trades and the high level of liquidity in the futures market offer the potential for significant cost savings. Second, portfolio construction via futures contracts offers the advantage of actually buying the index. When index futures are purchased, exposure to all 500 stocks is also purchased. Also, because buying a futures contract is equivalent to buying the index at all points in time, the portfolio is no longer exposed to changes in the names of the 500 stocks included in the index. The change in the composition of the S&P 500 due to the AT&T breakup illustrates that such changes may not be insignificant or trivial.

A third significant advantage of the futures approach to index-fund construction is that there are no dividends to reinvest. Periodic rebalancing of the index fund due to cash dividends is not required because the futures approach does not involve the receipt of dividends. As indicated in the section on valuation, dividends are already priced within the futures contract.

General Portfolio-Management Strategy: Deposits to a Portfolio

A second application of futures involves cash contributions (withdrawals), or a large deposit to an existing portfolio. Buying additional common stock with a sudden large cash inflow may take time—time during which one is exposed to significant market moves.

Stock index futures offer an attractive alternative. Assume on day 1 that $50 million is deposited to the portfolio. This deposit could immediately be invested in the stock market and the desired stock market exposure achieved by buying $50 million worth of futures contracts. Given the assumptions of the index-fund example, this would be accomplished by buying 200 contracts. These contracts can then be sold off as desired individual issues are purchased for the portfolio. Assume that such stock purchases occur evenly over a ten-day period from day 2 through day 11. On each of these days, a portfolio manager buys $5 million worth of attractive stocks and sells one-tenth of the futures contract position, or approximately twenty-eight contracts. The desired stock market exposure of the portfolio is maintained at all points in time.

The important point illustrated in this application is that futures offer a significant means for controlling the risk level of a portfolio and reducing exposure to unintended risks, or unintended investment judgments. For example, the investor's judgment may have been to be 95 percent invested in stocks over a certain

time period. Because of the large deposit and the time it might have taken to invest the money in attractive stocks, the portfolio may have actually been only 80 percent invested. An important penalty to incremental return would have been incurred that could have been avoided through futures contracts. Futures can be used in a similar fashion to manage portfolio withdrawals, although in the opposite way.

Beta Control

A third application, similar to the second, involves implementing an active stock market judgment. Assume that a portfolio manager has a positive outlook for the stock market and wishes to raise the exposure of the portfolio to the exposure of the market, or raise the portfolio's beta, as a consequence. An example will illustrate the alternative methods of implementing this strategic decision. Assume that the manager has a $20 million portfolio with a target beta of 1.2. Assume also that the beta of the present stock component is 1.1, with stocks currently representing 95 percent of the portfolio and with the remaining 5 percent in cash. One way to move the portfolio to the beta target of 1.2 is to sell a number of the lower beta stocks and buy an equivalent amount of higher beta stocks. This procedure maintains the stocks at 95 percent of the portfolio but raises the stock-only beta to a number such as 1.25. The result would be a portfolio with a beta of 1.2, but implementation could be a long and costly process. Not only would significant turnover be likely, but only a certain few stocks would have the required attractive characteristics.

The alternative approach is to raise the beta by buying an appropriate amount of stock index futures. Under the pricing assumptions used in the previous examples, one need purchase only eighteen S&P 500 Index futures. The appropriate number of futures to purchase (X), or 13 results from the equation:

$$(\$19 \text{ million})(1.1) + (\$250,000)(X) = (\$20 \text{ million})(1.2)$$

$$X = 13$$

The advantages of controlling beta in these circumstances by using stock index futures are the following: (1) the target beta of 1.2 can be achieved almost immediately and the portfolio can then be constructed to reflect the desired investment judgments; (2) the transaction costs are considerably lower, particularly because turnover could be very high in trading the lower beta stocks for the higher beta stocks; and (3) the optimal stock mix is maintained. This last advantage is extremely important. Presumably, the stock component with a beta of 1.1 represents the optimal mix of stocks. By selling low-beta stocks and buying high-beta stocks, the portfolio manager most likely is giving up the potential incremental return from stock-selection judgments. This loss of incremental return is avoided by achieving the portfolio target beta through buying S&P 500 futures.

TABLE 14–2

Asset-Allocation Application

| | FUND SIZE = $300 MILLION | | |
	ACTUAL MIX	TARGET MIX	NET CHANGE
Stocks	70% ($210 million)	65% ($195 million)	−$15 million
Bonds	30% ($90 million)	35% ($105 million)	+$15 million

Active Management:
Asset-Allocation Strategy[4]

A fourth futures application involves asset allocation. Assume that the manager of a large portfolio wishes to change the stock-bond mix to reflect new investment judgments. An example of this application is illustrated in Table 14–2.

Assume that the mix today of a $300 million portfolio pension fund is 70 percent in stocks ($210 million) and 30 percent in bonds ($90 million). Assume also that the manager's judgment calls for a lowering of stock exposure and a raising of bond exposure by 5 percent of total value, or $15 million in each asset category. In order to achieve the new target of 65 percent in stocks and 35 percent in bonds, the manager would have to sell $15 million of stocks and buy $15 million of bonds.

This strategy can be implemented in two ways. The traditional way would be actually selling $15 million in stocks in the market and buying $15 million in bonds. The alternative way would be to use futures, selling the equivalent of $15 million of stock exposure by selling stock index futures and buying the equivalent of $15 million of bond exposure by purchasing Treasury bond futures. If we assume that one stock index future is equivalent to $250,000 of stock exposure and one Treasury bond future is equivalent to $70,000 of bond exposure, this would involve the sale of 60 S&P stock index futures contracts and the purchase of 214 Treasury bond futures contracts.

In addition to the advantages of lower implementation costs and quicker implementation, implementing asset-allocation judgments through the use of futures has other important advantages. The first is that disruption is minimized, a particularly important consideration if fund assets are held in portfolios run by a group of external investment managers, each specializing in either stocks or bonds. By using futures to implement the stock-bond decision, the external managers are not affected; they need not even know the activity is occurring. The futures can be managed outside of the multiple manager structure.

A second advantage is that less money need be involved to alter the asset mix due to the leveraged nature of a futures contract. Assume that the manager of the

[4]See A. F. Perold and W. F. Sharpe, "Dynamic Strategies for Asset Allocation," *Financial Analysts Journal* (January–February 1988).

$300 million fund may alter the stock-bond mix within a +10 percent range around some long-term nominal mix, such as 70/30. Asset-allocation changes of this degree could be accomplished using the futures approach with margin requirements that are 10 to 15 percent of the full cost of buying and selling of stocks and bonds. More funds can therefore remain available to the specific security selection.

INDEX OPTIONS AND FUTURES

Table 14–3 contains listings of the S&P 500 Index option and index futures option contracts, respectively. The index options in Table 14–3 are all cash settlement contracts. When the option expires, usually at the close of trading on the third Friday of the contract month, the option seller pays the option buyer an amount of cash equal to the difference between the closing index price and the exercise price of the option, assuming the option is in-the-money. No delivery takes place. When the index futures options expire, the option holder receives a position in the underlying futures contract.

TABLE 14–3

Index Options
October 29, 1993 S&P 500 Index = 467.73

STRIKE PRICE	CALLS			PUTS		
	NOV.	DEC.	JAN.	NOV.	DEC.	JAN.
450	—	21.38	—	.81	—	4.13
460	9.500	12.50	14.13	2.13	4.50	6.50
465	6.125	9.00	11.63	3.50	6.00	8.50
470	3.250	6.13	9.25	5.63	8.13	—
475	1.250	3.75	—	8.25	10.00	12.25
480	.500	2.06	4.25	12.25	14.00	15.75
485	.125	—	—	17.50	—	—
490	.063	.50	1.50	—	—	—

Index Futures Options
October 29, 1993 S&P 500 Index = 467.73

STRIKE PRICE	CALLS			PUTS		
	NOV.	DEC.	JAN.	NOV.	DEC.	JAN.
460	10.05	12.45	—	2.00	4.45	6.50
465	6.30	9.00	12.10	3.25	5.95	8.10
470	3.35	6.00	9.10	5.30	7.95	10.05
475	1.50	3.70	6.55	8.45	10.60	—
480	.55	2.05	4.45	12.45	13.95	—
485	.20	1.00	2.80	—	17.85	—

PORTFOLIO INSURANCE USING FUTURES

When a stampede of institutional sell orders sent the Dow Jones Industrial Average plunging 87 points on September 11, 1987, a major part of the blame was put on something called "portfolio insurance."

To many individual investors, this investment tactic—combining powerful computer programs and mammoth transactions in the stock and futures markets—seemed like one more mystifying example of institution's strength.

Portfolio insurance is nothing more than a graduated stop-loss strategy that sells stocks as the market declines and buys as it rallies. It isn't really insurance; the idea is to limit losses while still allowing investors to participate in the market's gains. There are many forms of portfolio insurance. Certainly buying puts on individual stocks is a means of providing downside protection.

But there is a cost to portfolio insurance, and it can be substantial. Because the tactic doesn't anticipate but only reacts to market moves, investors are always in the position of buying a little high and selling a little low. In a very jumpy market, the incremental losses caused by this "whipsaw effect" could sharply depress results even if stocks ended with a gain.

To understand how the strategy works, think of a portfolio as containing a "risky" asset, such as an equity fund, and a "safe" asset, such as a money-market fund. The basic approach is to shelter the investment in the safe asset when stocks decline and expose them to more risk as stocks rise. The portfolio insurance trading plan will determine the "hedge ratio"—the portion of funds that should be in each asset at any given time to assure that the value of the total portfolio never falls below the minimum "insured" level, or floor.

The two key strategic choices for investors in designing a trading plan are the level of the floor and over what period of time they want the insurance to work. The higher the floor and the shorter the time span, the more conservative the strategy and the more it will cost.

For example, using a three-year, no-loss trading plan (no loss means that in the worst case the portfolio would be worth as much at the end of three years as it is at the beginning). Thus, even if stocks drop so that the value of the total portfolio is down 10 to 15 percent in the first year, the value would be back to its starting level at the end of the third year; this result occurs because the decline would cause a switch into money-market assets, which would earn enough in the remaining time to make up the loss.

A basic approach works something like this: Start with a 90 to 10 percent mix of stocks to cash; when stock prices rise or fall 4 percent against Treasury bills, alter the mix by 12 percent. If stocks go up 4 percent, cap out at 100 percent invested; if they fall 4 percent, lower exposure from 90 to 78 percent, and so on.

You take a starting mix and a trade barrier, such as a 4 percent move, and set an amount to be moved from one asset to the other each time that barrier is crossed.

An even simpler approach involves starting 100 percent invested, with an 80 percent floor. You set trading points to sell half your stocks when the market declines halfway to your floor; sell half of what's left in stocks when the value of the portfolio drops another quarter of the way to the floor; again, sell half of what is left when the value is one-eighth of the way from the floor, and so on. It's like a rabbit constantly jumping halfway to its hole—mathematically, it will never get there.

An investor who wants a higher floor of 90 percent, for instance, should start with 50 percent already invested in the safe asset and use the same 80 percent floor-trading plan with the 50 percent in stocks. An individual should never run a program like this with a floor higher than 80 percent; otherwise, if the market flips around, he would stand to lose a lot on volatility.

But nobody can eliminate the insidious effect of volatility. Consider what would happen under this strategy to a $100,000 portfolio if the market dropped 10 percent and then returned to its initial level.

At the low point, when the value of the portfolio fell to $90,000, the strategy would call for the investor to sell half the stocks, leaving $45,000 in money market funds and $45,000 in stocks. When stocks then rose 10 percent, the equity portion would be worth $49,500. The strategy would then call for shifting the $45,000 of money-market assets back into stocks. But the total portfolio would be worth only $94,500—a loss of 5.5 percent that would not have been incurred if the investor had simply done nothing.

If the situation kept repeating itself, the investor would give up progressively more until virtually all the portfolio was sheltered in the safe asset. The investor would then risk paying a very heavy cost in lost opportunity if the market rallied. Even under normal conditions, volatility will nibble away at an investor's return.

Stock Index Options

Most index options are European-style; that is, they may be exercised only at expiration. For the Chicago Board Options Exchange's (CBOE) S&P 100 Index options, exercise may occur at any time prior to expiration (American style). If an option buyer exercises early, he receives the difference between the closing index level on that day and the exercise price of the option. The offsetting option seller, who is obliged to make the cash payment to the buyer, is randomly chosen from all of the open short positions in that option.

The prices reported in Table 14–3 are quoted in the same units as the underlying stock index, although the value of the contract is 500 times the reported price. For example, the December 460 call option on the S&P 500 Index had a reported closing price of 12.50 on October 29, 1993, and the S&P 500 Index closed at 467.73. To buy this call, one would pay 12.50 × 500 or $6,250. The call would provide us with the right to buy 467.73 × $500 or $233,865 worth of the S&P 500 stock portfolio for an amount of cash equal to 460.00 × $500 or $230,000 on the third Friday of December 1993. Again, the contract is cash-settled, so delivery does not actually take place. If the S&P 500 Index level is, say, $480 at exercise, the call option buyer would receive in cash an amount equal to (480 – 460) × $500 or $10,000. Net profit would be $10,000 less the premium paid for the option of $6,250 (excluding commissions).

Stock Index Futures Options

Table 14–3 also contains the stock index futures quotes on the S&P 500. These options are can be exercised at any time up to the expiration date. They are denominated as 500 times the current index value and written on the index futures contract. Unlike index options, index futures options are delivery contracts in a sense. For example, ownership of the December 465 call on the S&P 500 futures would give one the right to buy the underlying December 1993 futures contract at a price of 465 at any time between October 29, 1993, and the close of trading on the third Thursday of December 1993. This option is currently in-the-money because the current price of the December S&P 500 futures is 467.73 as seen in Table 14–3. If this call were exercised on October 29, one would receive a long December S&P 500 futures position at a price of 465. A seller of the option, selected randomly, would receive the offsetting short position in the futures contract. When the futures contract is marked-to-market on that day, the long is allowed to withdraw 2.73 (467.73 − 465) × \$500 or \$1,365, and the short pays in \$1,365, but both would still have open futures positions. To withdraw fully from the market, the futures contracts established as a result of exercise would have to be sold.

An exception to the above exercise procedure occurs on the expiration date of the futures contract. Because the December futures option contract expires at the same time as the December futures contract and because the December futures contract is cash-settled to the index value at expiration, exercising the option at expiration amounts to cash settlement in that no futures position is left open.

Notice that options on futures limit losses (to the premium paid), which futures do not. Also, futures require daily settlement of margin, whereas this painful impediment does not affect options on futures.

OPTIONS VERSUS FUTURES

Do options serve portfolio management needs differently from those served by futures? The key is the risk and return potential provided by each kind of instrument. Gains and losses on open futures positions are limited only by the price of the underlying securities. Gains on an option are virtually unlimited for the purchaser (subject to the movement of the underlying stock) but limited to the option premium for the writer. Losses, on the other hand, are virtually unlimited for the writer but limited to the premium for the purchaser.

Hedging can be accomplished with either options or futures. But a single futures position can neutralize exposure in the underlying asset. Accomplishing the same hedge with options requires simultaneous put and call options in separate markets.

On the other hand, options possess characteristics that cannot be effectively simulated by positions in the futures market. In particular, the option purchaser can insure against a decline in the value of the underlying assets, while the option writer can generate income over and above the stock's dividend yield (or bond's coupon).

FUTURES ON FIXED-INCOME SECURITIES[5]

Rising interest rates are scarcely a new phenomenon, but the swings are getting wider and wilder. For example, three-month Treasury bills in 1978 traded 375 basis points higher than the level at which they sold in 1975. In the mid-1960s, 3.75 percent, or 375 basis points, represented the entire yield of a Treasury bill!

What is happening in Treasury bills, bonds, notes, and other credit instruments, in fact, bears a striking resemblance to the fluctuations that have long been part of the world of commodities, where prices traditionally gyrate in reaction to severe changes in the weather, the outbreak of war in a commodity-producing country, or the like.

The volatility of returns in the stock market during the 1930s is well known and related to the Great Depression. This volatility settled down to a much lower level after World War II. Volatility in the bond market moved along at modest levels compared to stocks through the mid-1960s, when this volatility began to move up in a pronounced fashion. The standard deviation of returns on high-grade corporate bonds has ratcheted upward to the level of common stocks. This phenomenon has been prompted in part by the rapid rise in inflation in the late 1960s and the onset of massive federal budget deficits in the 1980s, among other reasons. The increased risk (volatility) in the corporate bond market suggests increased opportunities for trading bonds as well.

In January 1976, the Chicago Mercantile Exchange (CME) began trading futures on ninety-day Treasury bills. Since that time, other successful contracts have been introduced, and volume in futures on fixed-income securities has grown sharply. Fixed-income futures have become an integral part of financing and investment and have, in a sense, transformed the whole process of interest-rate-risk management.

In the sections that follow, we will learn about actively traded futures contracts on fixed-income securities. We also provide an overview of the uses of fixed-income futures for increasing and reducing exposures to the risk of changing interest rates. First, we will cover futures on underlying instruments of less than a year in maturity when issued. Next, futures on longer-term fixed-income securities are covered. The Chicago Board of Trade (CBOT) has been most successful in the development of these long-term fixed-income futures markets.

Futures on Short-Term Fixed-Income Securities

Short-term fixed-income futures include Treasury bills, certificates of deposit, and Eurodollar futures. To facilitate matters, we will deal only with Treasury bill futures. The futures contract on Treasury bills was among the first financial instrument futures to be traded. The contract calls for delivery of bills with thirteen weeks (ninety-one days) remaining to maturity. On a typical day, volume in this

[5]A good exploration of interest rate futures in depth is in E. W. Schwarz, J. M. Hill, and T. Schneeweis, *Financial Futures* (Homewood, Ill.: Richard D. Irwin, 1986).

contract is around 10,000 to 15,000 contracts, representing $10 to $15 billion of Treasury bills—roughly four times the typical volume of $4 billion in the secondary market for Treasury bills.

The ninety-day Treasury bill is the major instrument traded in the U.S. money market. This market consists of securities maturing in under one year. A Treasury bill represents a direct obligation of the U.S. government and is the most widely used security for the financing of the federal government. Primary issues of both 91- and 182-day bills are sold in weekly auctions held on Mondays. Minimum denominations are $10,000, with multiples of $5,000 acceptable.

Treasury bills quotations generally appear in the financial press as:

MATURITY DATE	DATE: AUGUST 1		
	BID	ASKED DISCOUNT	YIELD
September 13	8.60	8.57	8.78

The maturity date of the bill is shown in the first column. Next, the annualized bid (buy from you) and asked (sell to you) discount rates appear. These are computed as follows:

$$\text{Annual discount rate} = \frac{(\text{Face value} - \text{Price})}{\text{Face value}} \bigg/ \frac{\text{Number of days to maturity}}{360} \quad \textbf{(14.1)}$$

Treasury bills are traded on a discount basis with the holder receiving the difference between the price paid and selling price, or face value, as interest. The annual discount rate of a bill maturing in forty-two days and selling for 99 percent of face value would be 8.57 percent, or

$$.0857 = \frac{100 - 99}{100} \bigg/ \frac{42}{360}$$

The discount rate does not properly represent the actual yield. Yield measures the return based on the actual price paid. Because this price is less than the face value, the yield always exceeds the quoted discount rate. The formula for the yield uses a full 365-day year:

$$\text{Yield} = \frac{(\text{Face value} - \text{Price})}{\text{Price}} \bigg/ \frac{\text{Number of days to maturity}}{365}$$

For a Treasury bill in the preceding example, the annual yield would be 8.78 percent versus a discount rate of 8.57 percent:[6]

---

[6]Notice that the asked price converts to 99. The bid price should be lower and is, in fact, 98.997

$$\left[.086 = \frac{100 - x}{100} \bigg/ \frac{42}{360} \right].$$

$$.0878 = \left. \frac{100 - 99}{100} \right/ \frac{42}{365}$$

FUTURES CONTRACT CHARACTERISTICS. Treasury bill futures call for delivery of $1 million in face value of ninety-one-day bills and are available for delivery dates in March, June, September, and December for up to two years from the current date. Open interest (contracts outstanding) in the two near-term contracts generally represents more than half of the total available. The last day of trading is the day before the first day of the delivery month when the Treasury bill issued as a one-year bill has thirteen weeks remaining to maturity.

A sample of Treasury bill futures contract price quotations is shown next.

	OPEN	HIGH	LOW	SETTLE	CHG.	DIS-COUNT SETTLE	CHG.	OPEN INTER-EST
DATE: AUGUST 1								
September	89.45	89.53	89.30	89.34	–.12	10.66	+.12	21,050
December	88.95	89.12	88.93	88.94	–.05	11.06	+.05	13,460

For each delivery date, the opening, high, low, and settle price are shown, as is the change in price from the settlement price of the previous day. The annualized discount rate and the change in this rate are also given. Open interest (number of contracts outstanding) and daily volume figures are shown.

The discount rate as defined in Equation 14.1 is subtracted from 100 to determine the futures price quotation. The actual price to be paid at delivery for a ninety-one-day bill is based on an adjustment of the trading price to reflect the ninety-one-day maturity:

$$\begin{array}{l} \text{Price paid} \\ \text{at delivery} \\ \text{(as a percent} \\ \text{of face value)} \end{array} = 100 - (\text{Discount rate} \times 90/360)$$

or

$$= 100 - [(100 - \text{Price quoted})90/360]$$

Treasury bill futures trading is done in terms of prices; yields are the basic unit of the Treasury bill cash market. The use of prices allows the future to be put on the same price basis as futures on other deliverable instruments. The minimum price index change (or discount rate change) is .01 percent of the price index, or 1 basis point. This corresponds to a $25 change in the actual value of the futures contract. If the discount rate in the near Treasury bill future changed from 10.66 to 10.67, the value of the futures contract would drop $25. The maximum price fluctuation is set at 60 basis points, or $1,500 (60 × 25). This limit can be expanded in the event of unusual circumstances by the exchange.

Uses of the Treasury Bill Futures Market. Theoretically, any individual or institution exposed to short-term interest rate risks or wishing to profit from correct forecasts of short-term rates would be motivated to participate in the Treasury bill futures market. In practice, the major users of the market have tended to be institutions that are experienced in short-term lending or borrowing, such as banks, brokerage houses, and securities dealers. Other major participants include those who have a significant stake in movements of short-term interest rates. The latter include business and governmental units who maintain large positions in cash-equivalent securities, who engage in large and frequent issues of commercial paper, and who rely on short-term lending from bankers at variable lending rates. Individuals who speculate on movements of Treasury bill rates or on the relation of Treasury bill rates to other short-term securities, foreign and domestic, are also users of this market.

Arbitrage/Speculation

One can broadly describe the different types of Treasury bill futures transactions as arbitrage, speculation, or hedging activity. One group that has been an extensive user of the Treasury bill futures market is the government securities dealers. Most large money-center and investment banks and brokerage firms have dealer operations in which traders make active markets in government bonds.

Most bond dealers describe their activity as a strategy called interest-rate arbitrage. Dealing in government securities involves constantly buying and selling large amounts of Treasury bills and engaging in repurchase agreements to finance security inventories. Dealers are in an excellent position to analyze Treasury bill futures prices by considering whether they are out of line with forward interest rates or the cost of carrying their security inventory. In circumstances where observed price discrepancies exceed transaction costs, the dealers will engage in arbitrage: buying in the cheaper market and selling in the more expensive market. They thus help perform the very important function of keeping prices in the Treasury bill futures market in their proper relationship to those in the cash market.

Individual investors and institutions with sufficient risk capital to trade in futures will often use Treasury bill futures to speculate on short-term interest-rate movements. This normally involves buying (selling) futures in anticipation of lower (higher) interest rates. Because of the great leverage associated with futures and the requirement to mark-to-market, the risks of speculation are substantial.

Hedging[7]

A large amount of hedging activity occurs in the Treasury bill futures markets. Most of this is initiated by corporations. The side of the market they are in (buy versus sell) depends on whether they are hedging an existing investment in a portfolio of money-market securities, an anticipated future investment, or a short-term security issue. Careful hedgers of Treasury bill futures monitor their net short-term

---

[7]See G. Gay, R. Kolb, and R. Chiang, "Interest Rate Hedging: An Empirical Test of Alternative Strategies," *Journal of Financial Research* (Fall 1983).

cash position at various maturities and place the hedging trades accordingly. Most large institutions have sizable amounts of both short-term liquid assets and liabilities. Their exposure to interest risk will depend on the gap between the amounts and maturities of their short-term position. Some institutions prefer to hedge only specific positions in short-term investments or borrowings because of the greater ease with which they can define their interest-rate-risk exposure thereby reducing it with specific futures contracts.

A summary of the characteristics of short-term fixed-income futures contracts is given in Table 14–4.

FUTURES ON LONG-TERM SECURITIES

This section is concerned with financial futures calling for delivery of long-term fixed-income securities. A summary of characteristics of long-term fixed-income futures is given in Table 14–4. Currently, these futures contracts all call for delivery of securities either issued or guaranteed by the U.S. government (i.e., U.S. Treasury bonds, U.S. ten-year Treasury notes, and mortgage pass-through certificates guaranteed by the U.S. government [GNMAs]. Futures contracts on other fixed-income securities and indexes are in the planning stages. We will restrict our discussion to U.S. Treasury bond futures.

The existing fixed-income futures markets developed well before cash settlement was a possibility. The most successful contract, futures on U.S. Treasury bonds, has a deliverable instrument with a very liquid market; dealer positions are easily financed by repurchase agreements and default risk is nonexistent.

Futures on four- to six-year Treasury notes were introduced in June 1979 but had little success. In May 1982, the CBOT began trading a new note contract calling for delivery of Treasury obligations maturing in 6.5 to 10 years from contract delivery. This contract has been more successful.

FUTURES CONTRACT CHARACTERISTICS.   Treasury bond futures call for delivery of Treasury bonds with $100,000 face value at any time during the delivery period. These bonds must have a maturity date or call date no sooner than fifteen years from the delivery date. There are always several bonds acceptable for delivery. For example, any bond maturing or callable after September 2010 would be acceptable for delivery into the September 1995 futures contract. Treasury note futures are also based on $100,000 face value per contract. Deliverable notes are those maturing no less than 6.5 years and no more than 10 years from the delivery date.

Price quotations in the Treasury bond futures market are based on a bond with an 8 percent coupon rate and a twenty-year maturity. The actual amount paid or received at delivery will be determined by this price, accrued interest, and a conversion factor that adjusts the futures price for the characteristics of the particular bond being delivered. These conversion factors are equal to the ratio of the price of a deliverable bond, assuming an 8 percent yield, to the delivery price of the futures contract. A detailed discussion of conversion factors is beyond the scope of this book.

TABLE 14–4

Interest Rate Futures Contracts Specifications

SECURITY (EXCHANGE)*	TRADING HOURS	CONTRACT MONTHS†	UNITS/ MINIMUM PRICE FLUCTUATION	LAST DAY OF TRADING	DELIVERABLE GRADE‡
Treasury bond (CBOT)	8:00–2:00 (CST)	3, 6, 9, 12	$100,000/ 1/32 ($31.25)	7 business days prior to last business day of month	Nominal 8% coupon with 15 years to maturity or first call date
10-year Treasury note (CBOT)	8:00–2:00 (CST)	3, 6, 9, 12	$100,000/ 1/32 ($31.25)	7 business days prior to last business day of month	Nominal 8% coupon with 6.5 to 10 years to maturity
5-year Treasury note (CBOT)	8:00–2:00 (CST)	3, 6, 9, 12	$100,000/ 1/32 ($31.25)	7 business days prior to last business day of month	Any of the four most recently auctioned 5-year Treasury notes
91-day Treasury bill (CME)	7:20–2:00 (CST)	3, 6, 9, 12	$1,000,000/ .01 ($25.00)	Business day preceding issue date of new 91-day Treasury bill	Any of the three Treasury bills 91 days from maturity
Eurodollar time deposit (CME)	7:20–2:00 (CST)	3, 6, 9, 12 plus current month	$1,000,000/ .01 ($25.00)	Second London business day before third Wednesday	Cash-settled

*CBOT—Chicago Board of Trade.

CME—Chicago Mercantile Exchange.

†The notation used in this column corresponds to the month of the calendar year (e.g., 1 is January, 2 is February, and so on).

‡All interest rate futures contracts other than the Eurodollar contract call for delivery of the underlying security.

The actual invoice price at delivery is determined as a function of the conversion factor applicable to the bonds delivered.

$$\text{Invoice amount} = \$100,000 \times \begin{array}{c}\text{Settlement price} \\ \text{of futures}\end{array} \times \begin{array}{c}\text{Conversion} \\ \text{factor for} \\ \text{bonds delivered}\end{array} + \begin{array}{c}\text{Accrued} \\ \text{interest}\end{array}$$

Bonds may sell in the cash-bond market at prices above or below the converted price of the futures contract (futures price × conversion factor). The bond that is "cheapest to deliver" (i.e., for which the difference between the invoice price and the market price is the most positive) is the bond that Treasury bond futures traders focus on in making their transaction decisions. As an example, we show invoice prices (ignoring accrual interest) for two bonds acceptable for delivery into the September 1993 future.

In Table 14–5, based on July 20, 1993, prices, the bond that is cheapest to deliver at the invoice price is the 7⅝ percent coupon. Both bonds would be delivered at a loss at this time. The loss of 1³⁄₃₂ associated with the 7⅝ percent coupon is the lowest.

The same procedure is used in invoicing Treasury note contracts. Here an 8 percent, ten-year note is used as the standard note for exchange futures price quotations. Knowing the cheapest-to-deliver Treasury bond or Treasury note at any time is critical to constructing trading strategies for Treasury bond futures. Speculators and arbitrageurs analyze the relative prices of cash futures using the cheapest-to-deliver bond as the benchmark for the cash market price.

Valuation of Fixed-Income Futures

The valuation of fixed-income futures contracts is not considered in depth here due to its very complex and arcane nature. We will restrict our discussion to the pricing of Treasury bill futures contracts because they are the easiest to understand.

TABLE 14–5

Comparison of Invoice Prices Deliverable Treasury Bonds

BOND	(1) PRICE	(2) TIME TO FIRST CALL‡	(3) CONVERSION FACTOR	(4) INVOICE PRICE*	(4) − (1)
7⅝ 2007-12 February†	71¹⁴⁄₃₂	18 years, 8 months	.9641	70¹¹⁄₃₂	−1³⁄₃₂
7⅞ 2007-12 November	73¹⁰⁄₃₂	19 years, 5 months	.9878	70³⁄₃₂	−1⁷⁄₃₂

Invoice price* = Futures settlement × Conversion factor price
As of July 20, 1993   72.969 × .9641 = 70.344
(Future = September 1993)   72.969 × .9878 = 72.079

*Ignores accrued interest differences.
†Cheapest to deliver—delivery occurs at loss of 1³⁄₃₂ versus loss of ⁷⁄₃₂ with other bond.
‡The time to first call is rounded to the nearest quarter in determining the conversion factor.

Initially, however, it is appropriate to highlight some of the underlying fundamentals that contribute to the valuation complexity associated with many fixed-income futures contracts. The valuation of fixed-income futures contracts is both easier and more complex than the simple procedures used with stock-index futures. First, the income received from the underlying securities is more certain with fixed-income securities (or not even an issue, as with Treasury bills sold on a discounted basis). In contrast, the timing and amount of the separate cash dividends in a basket of stocks is highly uncertain. Second, delivery differs between stock-index and fixed-income futures contracts. Stock-index futures contracts allow for cash settlement rather than physical delivery of securities at the expiration (settlement) date. Fixed-income futures normally involve physical delivery of underlying securities. Further, some fixed-income futures allow for alternative securities to be delivered. The seller may have the option to deliver the security with the highest invoice price as compared to its purchase cost in the cash market (called the cheapest-to-deliver contract). Moreover, futures sellers can choose to execute delivery on any day in the contract month.

The Carry-Cost Model of Futures Prices

The simplest process for valuation of futures applies to those contracts that call for delivery of a security that has a liquid cash market, has a supply that is relatively fixed in quantity (or highly predictable), and provides no intermittent cash flows such as interest or dividends. An example of a future that meets most of these criteria is the Treasury bill future.

The carrying-cost concept of futures pricing links current prices of futures to current cash prices and to the cost of "carrying" deliverable securities until the futures contract expires. This linkage is possible because purchasers and sellers of Treasury bills view the cash and futures market as a competing means of acquiring and selling these securities. When prices in either the cash or futures market are cheap relative to the other market after reflecting carrying costs, marginal purchasing will occur in the market with the lowest price and selling will occur in the market with the highest price. The trader with the cheapest access to funds will dominate the price-setting mechanism in the marketplace.

Assume that on December 20, 1995, investors A and B expect to be buying and selling Treasury bills, respectively, near the end of March 1997. Any cash available in the interim earns .8 percent interest per month or approximately 9.6 percent per annum. This is also the cost of borrowing funds. The buyer of the Treasury bills anticipates an increase in price (lower rates) prior to March and thus wishes to lock in an interest return by buying a 180-day Treasury bill today or by buying a 90-day Treasury bill on March 20 via the Treasury bill future, whichever is cheaper. Table 14–6 contains an analysis of these alternatives. If the buyer purchases a 180-day bill on December 20 instead of a 90-day March Treasury bill future, the total expenditure will be 95.20 plus 2.40 in interest expenses for financing costs the period of December 20 to March 20, for a total of 97.60

TABLE 14–6

Futures vs. Cash Market Transactions and Carrying Costs

ASSUMPTIONS: .8% MONTHLY INTEREST RATE (9.6% PER ANNUM)

DECEMBER 20	DECEMBER 20 TO MARCH 20	MARCH 20
A. 1. Buy 180-day Treasury bill: annual discount rate 9.6%, price 95.20	3 months financing cost .8 × 3 = 2.40	Total cost of Treasury bill: 95.20 + 2.40 = 97.60 Total cost of Treasury bill: 97.70
2. Buy March Treasury bill future: annual discount rate of 9.2%, price 97.70	Interest cost = 0	

Savings from buying Treasury bills in cash market =
97.70 − 97.60 = .10, or 10/$10,000 Treasury bill

B. 1. Sell 180-day Treasury bill: annual discount rate 9.6%, price 95.20	3 months interest revenue from investing cash	Total cash from Treasury bill sale:
2. Sell March Treasury bill: annual discount rate 9.6%, price 97.70	.8 × 3 = 2.40	95.20 + 2.40 = 97.60 Total cash from Treasury bill sale: 97.70

Savings from selling Treasury bill in futures market at
97.60 = .10, or $10/$10,000 Treasury bill

(prices are expressed in terms of percent of par value). The March Treasury bill future at 97.70 is thus more expensive. Investor A would attempt to buy the Treasury bill now in the cash market.

Investor B expects prices to fall (interest rates to rise) between now and the March 20 selling date for a 180-day Treasury bill he now owns. He thus would like to set a selling price based on either the cash or futures market price as of December 20. The March futures price of 97.70 is attractive to him relative to the 97.60 that he could receive if he sold the Treasury bill in the cash market today and invested the proceeds at .8 percent per month. He will therefore place an order in the futures market to sell the March contract.

Eventually, selling pressure in the futures market will force the futures price to fall to a level where no clear advantage exists to buying in the cash market and selling in the futures market. If this does not occur, 10 basis points or $10/$10,000 Treasury bills can be earned risk-free for each Treasury bill purchased in the cash market on December 20 and sold via the March 20 futures contract.

The relationship expressed in the preceding example above can be restated as (ignoring interest compounding):

$$FP_t \cong CP + (CP \times r \times t)$$

(14.2)

Futures prices = Cash price + Carrying costs

where:

FP_t = current price of a futures contract calling for delivery in t months
CP = current price of a security deliverable into the future contract
r = rate of interest per month
t = number of months until delivery

Note that we use a basic time period of a month in the formulas and examples. These could be easily restructured in terms of a daily interest rate and days until delivery.

In the example just given, the futures price should be no higher than 97.503, or

$$97.503 = 95.20(1 + .008)^3$$

The futures price (FP_t) will equal the price of the deliverable security CP plus the cost of financing the purchase of that security for t months until delivery at the monthly interest rate r. From another perspective, we can say that the futures price equals the amount that would be accumulated if one delayed purchase of the Treasury bill until the delivery of the futures and deposited the cash price (CP) in the bank to earn r interest for t months. (Both of these statements are true as long as the cost of financing equals the interest earned).

Other implications can be analyzed as well. The difference between the futures and cash prices should approximate the carrying cost as a percentage of the securities' face value. This difference between the cash and futures prices is often referred to as the *basis*. For financial futures, the basis is primarily a function of the financing costs of the cash security. Similarly, the difference between the rate implied by the futures price and the rate on a Treasury bill deliverable into the future (180-day) should equal the financing rate for the period prior to futures delivery. Finally, the sum of the rate on a 90-day bill ($r_{0.1}$) and a future calling for delivery in 90 days ($R_{1.2}$) should approximate the rate of a 180-day Treasury bill ($r_{0.2}$). This result is an approximation because it ignores the compounding of interest on a monthly basis.

Similar relationships should exist in the prices of Treasury bill futures for different delivery months. If the March Treasury bill futures are "cheap" relative to the June futures, a trader could buy Treasury bills with the March futures, sell the bills with the June futures, and pay the three months of carrying charges. This will be profitable as long as the spread between the prices of the two futures contracts is higher than these carrying charges. This is illustrated as follows:

$$FP_{t_2} = FP_{t_1} (1 + r)^{(t_2 - t_1)}$$

(14.3)

$$97.93 = 97.70 (1 + .008)^3$$

where:

t_1 = 3 on the September future
t_2 = 6 on the December future

The price spread between the two futures prices, given monthly carrying charges of $r = 0.8\%$, should be equal to .24 percent of the $1 million face value $[(.24\% = (1.008^3 - 1) \cong (97.93 - 97.70)].$

Thus, we would expect Treasury bill futures contracts of different delivery months to be priced in a pattern that reflects the market's assessment of the relevant carrying (financing) charges.

Strategies Using Fixed-Income Futures

Myriad strategies can be employed using fixed-income futures. We will consider three: changing duration, enhancing yield, and hedging.

CHANGING THE DURATION OF THE PORTFOLIO

Investors with strong expectations about the direction of the future course of interest rates will adjust the duration of their portfolio to capitalize on their expectations. Specifically, if they expect interest rates to increase, they will shorten the duration of the portfolio; if they expect interest rates to decrease, they will lengthen the duration of the portfolio. Also, anyone using a structured portfolio strategy (e.g., immunization) must periodically adjust the portfolio duration to match the duration of some benchmark.

Although investors can alter the duration of their portfolios with cash-market instruments, a quick and less expensive means for doing so is to use futures contracts. By buying futures contracts on Treasury bonds or notes, they can increase the duration of the portfolio. Conversely, they can shorten the duration of the portfolio by selling futures contracts on Treasury bonds or notes.

The formula that can be used to approximate the number of futures contracts necessary to adjust the portfolio duration to a new level is:

$$\text{Approximate number of contracts} = \frac{(D_T - D_I)\, P_I}{D_F P_F}$$

where:

D_T = target modified duration for the portfolio
D_I = initial modified duration for the portfolio
D_F = modified duration fo the futures contract[8]
P_I = initial market value of the portfolio
P_F = market value of the futures contracts

[8]The duration of a futures contract cannot be determined using standard calcuations. There are no definable cash flows—futures are pure volatility—so percentage volatility and modified duration are infinite. A long position adds volatility and a short position in futures reduces volatility in a portfolio. Some have suggested determining the volatility of a futures contract relative to yield changes in the underlying security and adding (subtracting) this volatility to (from) long (short) positions. The result will be net volatility. From this value, an implied duration may be computed. Thus, it is not necessary to have an actual duration value of a futures contract, yet the effect on portfolio duration can be determined.

Notice that if the investor wishes to increase the duration, then D_T will be greater than D_I and the above equation will have a positive sign. This means that futures contracts will be purchased. The opposite is true if the objective is to shorten the portfolio duration.

YIELD ENHANCEMENT

A cash-market security that is the deliverable for a futures contract can be synthetically created by using a position in the futures contract. The yield on the synthetic security should be the same as the yield on the cash market security. If there is a difference between the two yields, it can be exploited to enhance the yield on the portfolio.

To see how, consider an investor who owns a twenty-year Treasury bond and sells Treasury futures that call for the delivery of that particular bond three months from now. Although the maturity of the Treasury bond owned is twenty years, the investor has effectively shortened the maturity of the bond to three months because it will be delivered then. Consequently, the long position in the twenty-year bond and the short futures position are equivalent to a long position in a three-month riskless security. It is riskless because the investor is locking in the price that he will receive three months from now—the futures price. By being long the bond and short the futures, the investor has synthetically created a three-month Treasury bill. What return should the investor expect to earn from this synthetic position? It should be the yield on a three-month Treasury bill. If the yield on the synthetic three-month Treasury bill is greater than the yield on the cash-market Treasury bill, the investor will realize an enhanced yield by creating the synthetic short-term security described.

In an efficient market, opportunities for yield enhancement should not exist very long. But even in the absence of yield enhancement, synthetic securities can be used by investors to hedge a portfolio position that they find difficult to hedge in the cash market either because of lack of liquidity or other imposed constraints.

HEDGING

Hedging with futures involves employing a futures position as a temporary substitute for transactions to be made in the cash market at a later date. Hedging attempts to eliminate price risk by trying to fix the price of a transaction to be made at a later date. If cash and futures prices move together, any loss realized by the hedger from one position (whether cash or futures) will be offset by a profit on the other position. When the profit and loss from each position are equal, the hedge is referred to as a *perfect hedge.*

In practice, hedging is not that simple. The amount of the loss and profit from each position will not necessarily be identical. The outcome of a hedge will depend on the relationship between the cash price and the futures price when a hedge is placed and when it is lifted. The difference between the cash price and the futures

price is called the *basis*. The risk that the basis will change in a way that adversely impacts the hedge is called *basis risk*.

In most hedging applications, the bond to be hedged is not identical to the bond underlying the futures contract. This kind of hedging is referred to as *cross hedging*. There may be substantial basis risk in cross hedging. An unhedged position is exposed to price risk, the risk that the cash market price will move adversely. A hedged position substitutes basis risk for price risk.

A short (or sell) hedge is used to protect against a decline in the cash price of a fixed-income security resulting from an increase in interest rates. To execute a short hedge, futures contracts are sold. By establishing a short hedge, the hedger has fixed the future cash price and transferred the price risk of ownership to the buyer of the futures contract. As an example of why a short hedge would be executed, suppose that an investor knows that bonds must be liquidated in forty days to make a $5 million payment to the beneficiaries of a fund. If interest rates rise during the forty-day period, more bonds will have to be liquidated to realize $5 million. To guard against this possibility, the hedger will sell bonds in the futures market at the exercise price to lock in a selling price.

A long (or buy) hedge is undertaken to protect against an increase in the cash price of a fixed-income security resulting from a decline in interest rates. In a long hedge the hedger buys a futures contract to lock in a purchase price. An investor may use a long hedge when substantial cash contributions are expected and he is concerned that interest rates will fall. Also, an investor who knows that bonds are maturing in the near future and expects that interest rates will fall can employ a long hedge to lock in a rate. In both cases, a fall in interest rates means that when the proceeds are received, they must be invested at a lower interest rate.

Futures Contracts on Fixed-Income Indexes

At the time this chapter was written, there was only one futures contract on bond market indexes, the Muni Bond Index contract traded on the CBOT. The early popularity of this index contract probably reflected the need for greater liquidity and hedging vehicles in the municipal-bond marketplace.

There are probably several reasons for the absence of additional index contracts in the fixed-income market when the equity market has several successful ones. The first is that constructing a meaningful index that could be used as the basis for such a contract is difficult. Although such indexes do exist, such as a Salomon Brothers High-Grade Corporate Bond Index and the Lehman Government/Corporate Bond Index, they are not as straightforward as the more popular equity indexes because of the over-the-counter nature of corporate-bond trading and the relative illiquidity in the market. Prices entered into the index calculations are often traders' estimates of where such bonds would trade if there had been trades, and thus there is some subjectivity in the indexes. Second, because of the generally high correlation

in movement of securities in the fixed-income market, one can view a high-grade bond futures contract, such as the Treasury bond contract, as a sort of index contract, thus reducing the need for a specific index contract.

Fixed-Income Option Contracts

OPTIONS ON FUTURES CONTRACTS

Options on three fixed-income futures contracts are actively traded—Treasury bonds, Treasury notes, and Eurodollar deposits. However, the most popular fixed-income option contract is the option on Treasury bond futures. This option has, as its name implies, Treasury bond futures contracts as the underlying security; both puts and calls are traded. If a call holder elects to exercise, he receives a long position in the underlying futures contract at the guaranteed strike or exercise price, and the call writer becomes short at that same price. Because the option contract is likely to be in-the-money (that is, the price of the underlying futures contract is greater than the call option's strike or exercise price) if exercised, the call writer must immediately pay to the exerciser what is called the mark-to-market variation margin, or the margin required of the call writer equal to the difference in price between the strike price and the current market price of an in-the-money call option when it is exercised. A similar transaction occurs with the exercise of puts, except that the put buyer acquires a short position (by selling the futures contract to the put writer) at the strike price. In effect, at exercise, the call (put) holder buys (sells) the contract from (to) the option writer at the strike price, but, as in any futures trade, there is no "cost" except for the initial margin that must be put up on the futures contract.

Several potentially confusing elements need to be explained. First, although as many as eight different bond futures contracts can be trading at one time, options are available on only the three with the nearest delivery dates. Second, the option's stated maturity corresponds to the delivery month of the futures contract. That is, only a March option is available on the March futures contract and only a June option is available on the June futures, and so on. Finally, the options expire in the month prior to their stated maturity—that is, in the month preceding delivery of the contract underlying the option. Thus, the March bond futures option expires in February, the June option in May, and so forth. The reason for this is to prevent the expiring options from interfering with or being affected by the delivery process in the futures market. The prices of the options are quoted in points and sixty-fourths. Thus a price of 1–45 represents $1^{45}/_{64}$ points, or 1.703125.

It may appear from the sound of "options on futures" that this is the ultimate leveraged instrument, but this is not the case. The option trades very similarly to the way in which an option on an 8 percent long-maturity Treasury bond would trade if one were available. In fact, if one thinks of the Treasury bond futures contract price as simply an index of the government market, the essence of the option contract is captured. The only real difference occurs as a result of exercise, something that is not possible in index options. Exercising actually increases the leverage (and the attendant downside risk potential) by converting the option position into a futures position.

FOREIGN FUTURES MARKETS

Stock index contracts are available in the United Kingdom, Brazil, Australia, Hong Kong, and Singapore. Futures or forward markets for individual stocks also exist in some stock markets such as Rio de Janeiro and Paris. The most active contracts are described in Table 14–8. These indexes are usually broadly based to allow for broad participation in the market.

Listed options markets can found all over the world and are growing quickly. International links between options exchanges have also developed. For example, the European Options Exchange (EOE) in Amsterdam is linked to exchanges in Montreal, Vancouver, and Sydney, allowing around-the-clock trading in gold, silver, and currency options.

SUMMARY

Futures contracts on securities differ from options in some important ways. The most significant differences include the absence of premiums on futures, the duty of both parties to the contract to perform at the settlement date, and exposure of the futures holder to the full spectrum of downside risk coupled with the potential for all the upside return.

TABLE 14–8

Major Stock Index Contracts Worldwide

CONTRACT	INDEX SPECIFICATIONS	FUTURES VALUE MULTIPLIER
TFE, TSE 300	Weighted index of top 300 Canadian stocks on TSE	Canadian $10 × index
LIFFE, FTSE 100	Weighted index of top 100 British stocks on London Stock Exchange*	£25 × index
SFE, all ordinary	Weighted index of top 250 Australian stocks	Australian $100 × index
HFKE, Hang Seng	Weighted index of top 33 shares on Hong Kong Stock Exchange	Hong Kong $50 × index
Nikkei-Dow Jones Osaka and SIMEX	Unweighted index of top 225 shares on Tokyo Stock Exchange	¥1000 × index
Tokyo, TOPIX	Weighted index of Japanese Stocks on TSE	¥10,000 × index
MATIF CAC 40	Weighted index of top top 40 French stocks	FF200 × index

*The futures price quotation is the index divided by ten.

Stock index futures owe their existence to the volatility of the stock market and the lack of insurance contracts on stock portfolios. They provide a low-cost, efficient means for dealing with systematic or market risk in a portfolio—either for speculation or risk-control purposes.

Interest-rate futures provide an effective mechanism for coping with the largest source of systematic risk in holding fixed-income securities, interest-rate risk.

The close association between the price movements of futures contracts and the underlying cash instrument permit traders and investors to hedge price uncertainty, to arbitrage differentials between cash and futures, and to speculate on stock market and interest-rate changes.

QUESTIONS

1. What is meant by the term "cheapest-to-deliver" when discussing Treasury bond futures contracts. How is the cheapest-to-deliver bond normally identified?

2. Differentiate options from futures in terms of
   a. risk and return exposure;
   b. rights/obligations of the parties to the contract.

3. Which of the dollars widely available stock index futures contracts has the smallest unit and minimum price fluctuation? The largest?

4. Stock index futures contracts should be priced above the current market value of the index to reflect the cost-of-carry. What does this term *cost-of-carry* mean? How do rational investors normally behave when the cost-of-carry is less than its theoretical value?

5. What is *program trading?* What triggers it? What is the potential impact of program trading on individual stocks?

6. Assume you hold a portfolio valued at $25,000. It consists of ten stocks with roughly equal dollar commitments to each stock. It is your expectation that the market is weakening and about to fall dramatically. Discuss the wisdom of using S&P 500 Stock Index futures to hedge your portfolio against a market decline.

7. Distinguish *stock index options* from *stock index futures options.*

8. An investment banker generally purchases securities from an issuing company at a fixed price and resells them to investors at a marked-up value. This is referred to as underwriting. The inability to resell the securities above cost can result in a loss to the investment banker. Describe how an investment banker might use interest-rate futures for loss protection in underwriting a bond issue.

9. You expect interest rates to decline in the next two months. How could you use interest-rate futures to benefit from this forecast?

10. What is the idea behind the use of portfolio insurance. What are the strategic choices required for its successful its implementation?

11. Distinguish between a *perfect hedge* and a *cross hedge.*

PROBLEMS

1. The S&P 500 Stock Index was at $500 in early November. At the same time, futures contracts on the index with a settlement date of March were trading at $510.

  a. Suppose you purchased one futures contract and the index closed at $515 on the settlement date. What was your gain (loss), ignoring commissions?

  b. Why do the futures contract sell at 10 points above the cash (index) price?

2. The S&P 500 Stock Index is at $490. The underlying stocks are expected to produce a dividend yield of 5 percent over the coming year. Treasury bills due in six months were recently offered to yield 8 percent. What is the theoretical value of a futures contract with a settlement date six months from now?

3. The Reliable Insurance Co. has a portfolio that consists of $10 million in cash-equivalents yielding 8 percent and $40 million in equities with a dividend yield of 4 percent. The market had run up 20 percent in the last twelve months and the company is seeking to adjust its equity exposure to $20 million because it anticipates a moderate market decline over the next three to four months. On January 24, the chief investment officer has ordered the sale of S&P 500 April futures contracts. The value of the S&P 500 Stock Index on that date was 500. On April 15 the S&P 500 Stock Index had fallen to 450 and the April futures contract was at 454.

  a. Should the company buy or sell futures contracts to adjust its portfolio? How many contracts must be bought or sold?

  b. Was the hedge effective?

4. It is January 14, 1996. A banker is contemplating the fact that the bank expects to issue $1 million in one-year certificates of deposit three months from now. He is concerned about locking in today's rates because he feels that rates will be higher in three months. The current CD rate is 9 percent. The June 1996 Treasury bill futures contract is closest to his time horizon and the last quoted settlement price was 92.

  a. Would he establish a long or short position?

  b. How many contracts would he need to buy (sell) to hedge his certificate position?

  c. Calculate his profit (loss) on April 12, 1996, if the June Treasury bill contract is at 90 and $1 million in certificates are issued with a rate of 10 percent.

5. An arbitrageur observes that a 91-day Treasury bill yields 9.20 percent, a 182-day bill yields 9.8 percent, and a futures contract requiring delivery of a 91-

day bill 3 months hence is priced to yield 10.2 percent. What, if any, action should he take?

6. You are seeking to trade ninety-day Treasury bill futures. A bill future has been located that sells for a yield of 13 percent. A single contract is purchased. Three days after the transaction, contract yields have risen to 14 percent. The broker required an initial $4,000 in the trading account.
   a. What is the status of your trading account balance at the end of the third day?
   b. What is your dollar return if interest rates on ninety-day bills drop to 12 percent?

7. Suppose that the Federal Reserve Board has just raised the discount rate from 12 to 13 percent. You expect Treasury securities to experience rising interest rates with longer-term Treasuries rising less than shorter-term instruments. A six-month Treasury bill futures contract is quoted at 87.27 and an eighteen-month contract is at 88.25. Given your expectations, what action should you take?

8. What is the annual discount rate on a Treasury bill due in forty-five days with a face value of $100,000 that is quoted at a price of $99,500?

9. The Town of Mansfield Public Employees Pension Fund is worth $100 million. 90 percent of the fund is in common stocks and the remainder is in cash equivalents. The current beta on the fund is 1.00. Appropriate S&P Stock Index futures are quoted at 500. The manager of the fund wishes to elevate the fund's beta from 1.00 to 1.15. Should he buy or sell futures contracts? How many contracts are needed to alter the beta?

10. On May 15 two-month Treasury bills are selling at a price of 98. July 15 Treasury bill futures are priced at 100.4. Cash available can earn 9 percent interest. What are the July futures contracts worth?

11. You contract to buy NYSE futures expiring in eight days for 166. The NYSE futures price for the following eight days is: 170, 168, 163, 164, 159, 156, 154, 160; initial margin = $5,500; maintenance margin = $2,000.

    Construct a table with day, settlement price, value of the contract, marking-to-market change, equity, and excess equity (loss). Fill in the table and show any margin calls. Assume that profits are kept in the account.

12. Weekly NYSE futures closing prices are as follows:

October 8	344.60
October 15	338.70
October 22	332.90
October 29	339.50
November 5	341.80

    On November 6 the following information is relevant:

NYSE Index	331.61
NYSE futures price	335.75
Treasury-bill yield	6.86%

Dividends on index stocks   3.24%
Days until futures expiration   79

a. Using the data above, calculate the fair futures price. Is arbitrage possible? Why?

b. Calculate the projected net profit of an arbitrage transaction.

13. A pension fund manager is considering using the S&P 500 Index as a means of investing some available funds. Based on the following information, advise this manager:

a. Whether an arbitrage opportunity exists by finding the fair futures price.

b. If an arbitrage opportunity exists, then:

   i. How should the transaction be carried out? (Short or long arbitrage?)

   ii. What is the net profit from this investment?

S&P 500 Index	343.69
Treasury-bill yield	7.62
Dividends on index stocks	4.20%
S&P 500 futures price	347.65
Days until futures expiration	75

14. A portfolio manager has outperformed the market for the last eight quarters of the most recent bull market. His portfolio has a beta of 1.6. He expects some volatility in the market for the next quarter or two and wishes to lower the portfolio's beta to .8. How many S&P 500 futures contracts are needed if the value of his portfolio is $10,000,000 and the S&P futures are at 525?

15. Suppose that the Treasury-bond futures price is 101–12. Which of the following four bonds is cheapest to deliver?

BOND	PRICE	CONVERSION FACTOR
1	125–05	1.2131
2	142–15	1.3792
3	115–31	1.1149
4	144–02	1.4026

C A S E

---■---

Orion Financial Management

Maria Gilbert is a principal in the firm of Orion Financial Management. For twenty years she was chief investment officer with Reliance Investments, the pension management arm of the Second National Bank of South Bend, Indiana. She left the bank in May 1995 in an attempt to turn her expertise into greater personal rewards.

    Two portfolios under management for medium-sized pension funds were on the top of her current agenda. The first portfolio was an index fund representing a cross section of the S&P 500 stocks. This portfolio had been established as a core

portfolio for the South Bend Firefighters, currently $10 million. The second portfolio was an actively managed fund for the Ryan County Public Employees Retirement Fund, which aggregated $2.75 million.

The firefighters portfolio was put in a cross section of S&P 500 stocks on December 23, 1995, when the S&P 500 Stock Index was at 500. One year later, on December 20, 1996, the S&P 500 Index closed at 595. On the same day the S&P 500 March/1997 futures contract closed at 600. The March/600 call on the S&P 500 March/1997 futures contract closed at 600. The March/600 call on the S&P 500 Index carried a premium of 18.75 points, and the March/600 put was at 8.50. The Ryan County fund was allocated as follows: cash equivalents, 9 percent; fixed-income securities, 36 percent; equities, 55 percent. Treasury-bond futures were priced at 95.

On December 20, 1996, Maria arrived at the office determined to adjust these two portfolios. However, she had mixed feelings about the stock market. On the one hand, she believed the market might continue its advance from an S&P 500 level of 595 to an index level of 640 during the next three months if corporate profits continued there upward surge. On the other hand, she worried that a downward correction could take the market to 545 if interest rates moved sharply higher as some were predicting. After pondering her options she decided to look more closely at alternative strategies for both funds, ignoring taxes and transaction costs for simplification of her task.

QUESTIONS

1. Suppose Gilbert thought the stock market would weaken and she wanted to lighten, but not eliminate, her equity position and increase the fixed income part of the Ryan portfolio. Indicate specific actions she could take in the futures markets to shift the allocation of the Ryan portfolio to zero cash, $1.6 million fixed-income, and $1.15 million equities.

2. Are the S&P 500 March stock index futures fairly priced on December 20? Explain. (Yields: Treasury-bills, 8 percent; S&P 500, 4 percent.)

3. Which of the following risk-management strategies would you recommend for the firefighters portfolio under the conditions in (a) and (b) below?
   a. Assume the odds of the market going up to 640 were 20 percent and the odds of the market falling to 545 were 80 percent.
   b. Assume the odds of the market going up to 640 were 60 percent and the odds of the market falling to 545 were 40 percent.
      i.   Do nothing.
      ii. Liquidate the portfolio.
      iii. Sell March futures.
      iv. Buy March/600 put.
      v.   Sell March futures and buy March/600 calls.
      vi. Sell March/600 call.

REFERENCES

FABOZZI, F. J., and G. M. KIPNIS, eds. *Stock Index Futures.* Homewood, Ill.: Dow Jones-Irwin, 1984.

FIGLEWSKI, S., and S. KON. "Portfolio Management with Stock Index Futures." *Financial Analysts Journal* (January–February 1982).

FINNERTY, J. E. and H. Y. PARK. "How To Profit from Program Trading." Journal of Portfolio Management, (Winter 1988).

GAY, G., R. KOLB, and R. CHIANG. "Interest Rate Hedging: An Empirical Test of Alternative Strategies." *Journal of Financial Research* (Fall 1983).

HANCOCK, G. D. "Futures Option Expirations and Volatility in the Stock Index Futures Market." *Journal of Futures Markets* (June 1991).

MILLER, MERTON H. "International Competitiveness of U. S. Futures Exchanges." *Journal of Applied Corporate Finance* (Winter 1991).

SAMORAJSKI, G. S., and B. D. PHELPS. "Using Treasury-Bond Futures to Enhance Total Returns." *Financial Analysts Journal* (January–February 1990).

SCARLATA, JODI G. "Institutional Developments in the Globalization of Securities and Futures Markets," *Review.* St. Louis: Federal Reserve Bank of St. Louis (January–February, 1992).

TECHNICAL ANALYSIS

Fundamentalists forecast stock prices on the basis of economic, industry, and company statistics. The principal decision variables ultimately take the form of earnings and dividends. The fundamentalist makes a judgment of the stock's value with a risk-return framework based upon earning power and the economic environment.

In this chapter we will examine an alternative approach to predicting stock price behavior. This approach is called *technical analysis*. Technical analysis is frequently used as a supplement to fundamental analysis rather than as a substitute for it. Thus, technical analysis can, and frequently does, confirm findings based on fundamental analysis.

The technician does not consider value in the sense in which the fundamentalist uses it. The technician believes the forces of supply and demand are reflected in patterns of *price* and *volume* of trading. By examination of these patterns, he predicts whether prices are moving higher or lower, and even by how much. In the narrowest sense, the technician believes that price fluctuations reflect logical and emotional forces. He further believes that price movements, whatever their cause, once in force persist for some period of time and can be detected.

Thus, technical analysis may be used for more than a supplement to fundamental analysis. Fundamental analysis allows the analyst to forecast holding-period yield and the riskiness of achieving that yield, but these figures alone do not necessarily prompt a buy or sell action. Technical analysis, however, may be useful in *timing* a buy or sell order—an order that may be implied by the forecasts of return and risk. For example, the technical analysis may reveal that a drop in price is warranted. Postponement of a purchase, then, if the technical analysis is correct, will raise the forecast holding period yield (HPY). Conversely, a sell order might be postponed because the charts reveal a rise in the price of the security in question.

The technician must (1) identify the trend, and (2) recognize when one trend comes to an end and prices start in the opposite direction. His central problem is to distinguish between reversals within a trend and real changes in the trend itself.

This problem of sorting out price changes is critical because prices do not change in a smooth, uninterrupted fashion.

The technician views price changes and their significance mainly through price and volume statistics. His bag of tools, or indicators, helps him measure price-volume, supply-demand relationships for the overall market as well as for individual stocks. Technicians seldom rely upon a single indicator, as no one indicator is infallible; they place reliance upon reinforcement provided by groups of indicators.

In this chapter we concentrate upon some of the major technical indicators employed to assess the direction of the general market and the direction of individual stocks.[1]

MARKET INDICATORS

The use of technical "indicators" to measure the direction of the overall market should precede any technical analysis of individual stocks because of the systematic influence of the general market on stock prices. In addition, some technicians feel that forecasting aggregates is more reliable because individual errors can be filtered out.

First, we will examine the seminal theory from which much of the substance of technical analysis has been developed—the Dow Theory—after which other key indicators of market activity will be examined in turn.

Dow Theory

Around the turn of the century, Charles H. Dow formulated a hypothesis that the stock market does not perform on a random basis but is influenced by three distinct cyclical trends that guide its general direction. By following these trends, he said, the general market direction can be predicted. Dow classified these cycles as primary, secondary, and minor trends. The primary trend is the long-range cycle that carries the entire market up or down. The secondary trend acts as a restraining force on the primary trend, tending to correct deviations from its general boundaries. Secondary trends usually last from several weeks to several months in length. The minor trends are the day-to-day fluctuations in the market. These have little analytic value because of their short duration and variations in amplitude. Primary and secondary trends are depicted in Figure 15–1.

The basic proposition in the Dow Theory is relatively simple. A bull market is in process when successive highs are reached after secondary corrections and when secondary upswings advance beyond previous secondary downswings. Such a process is illustrated in Figure 15–1. The theory also requires that the secondary

---

[1]An excellent source of much of the raw data for various indicators is found in the "Market Laboratory" section of *Barron's,* a weekly publication of Dow Jones.

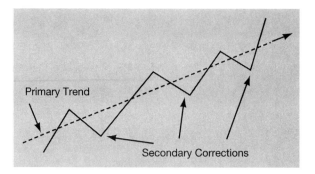

FIGURE 15–1   Representation of Dow Theory

downswing corrections will be of shorter duration than the secondary upswings. The reverse of these propositions would be true of a bear market.

The classical Dow Theory utilizes both the industrial average and the transportation average in determining the market position. When both averages are moving in the same direction, valid indicators of a continuing bull or bear market are implied.

Price Indicators

The two variables concerning groups of stocks or individual stocks that technicians watch with the most interest are the behavior of prices and the volume of trading contributing to and influenced by changing prices.

It was amply noted earlier that the change in a security's price is probably *the* most important component in the total rate of return resulting from holding a security. This fact has not escaped the technician any more than it has the fundamentalist. In examining the influence of the market on stock prices in general, technicians particularly note certain signals, or price indicators: price advances versus declines, new highs versus new lows, and the price patterns of the "most active" stocks.

ADVANCES AND DECLINES

Looking only at the popular stock averages such as the Dow Jones Industrial Average (DJIA) can often be misleading. A relatively few stocks may be moving ahead while the majority of stocks either are making no progress or are actually moving down. The average may be behaving contrary to the larger population of stocks.

The basic idea behind the measurement of advances and declines is to determine what the main body of stocks is really doing. Comparison of advances and declines is a means of measuring the dispersion, or breadth, of a general price rise or decline. The phrase often used is "breadth of the market."

Many measures could be used. The most common is to calculate the daily net difference between the number of New York Stock Exchange (NYSE) stocks that

advance and the number of those that decline. This net difference is added to the next day's difference, and so on, to form a continuous cumulative index. The index is plotted in line form and compared with the DJIA. For example:

	ADVANCES	DECLINES	BREADTH (CUMULATIVE ADVANCES LESS DECLINES)
Monday	1,000	400	+600
Tuesday	650	800	+450
Wednesday	500	1,100	−150
Thursday	900	700	+50
Friday	1,200	400	+850

The technician is more interested in change in breadth than in absolute level. Further, breadth is compared with a stock-market index, such as the DJIA. Normally, breadth and the DJIA will move in unison. The key signals occur when a divergence occurs between the two. When they diverge, the advance-decline line will show the truer direction of the market. The DJIA cannot move contrary to the market as a whole—at least, not for long. The longer the resistance, the greater the expected reversal. During a bull market, if breadth declines to new lows while the DJIA makes new highs, a peak in the averages is suggested. This peak will be followed by major downturn in stock prices generally. Breadth can also be used to detect recovery. The advance-decline line will begin rising as the DJIA is reaching new lows.

New Highs and New Lows

A supplementary measure to accompany breadth of the market is the high-low differential or index. The theory is that a rising market will generally be accompanied by an expanding number of stocks attaining new highs and a dwindling number of new lows. The reverse holds true for a declining market.

The number of NYSE stocks making new highs for the year minus the number making new lows is averaged for a five-day period. A moving average smooths out erratic daily fluctuations and exposes the trend. Such a high-low index would normally move with the market. Again, divergence from the market trend is a clue to future price movements.

The Most-Active List

Most major weekly market newspapers in the United States publish the twenty most active stocks for the week. By itself, this segment of the market is at first glance relatively useless because the makeup of the list changes from week to week. However, these issues taken as a whole represent only 1 percent of the total issues traded but account for almost 15 percent of the total volume. Viewed in this way, the list tends to have a recognizable pattern if certain dimensions are assigned.

The number of issues each week showing a net gain cannot exceed twenty, nor can they exceed twenty for a net loss. Because random variations often occur in the stock market, an additional time dimension of several weeks will tend to smooth an otherwise erratic curve. If three weeks of activity are added together to act as a stabilizer, then the upper and lower limits of the most-active list become +60 and −60.

The experience of the past decade has shown that the most-active indicator should approach −50 following a long and continuous decline that results in a selling climax, but in the case of an eroding decline, the indicator should move toward zero while the market continues to decline. In a bull market, the conditions are reversed, and oscillations around +35 are indications of strength in a rising market. A warning signal is flashed when the market continues to rise in the face of subsequent declines in the indicator.

Volume Indicators

Volume changes are believed by most technicians to be prerequisite to any change in price. Volume is a function of the demand for and supply of stocks and can signal turning points for the market as well as for individual stocks.

A Dow Theory tenet is that during bull markets, volume increases with price advances and decreases with price declines. In a major downward price trend, the reverse will hold true; volume will generally increase as prices decline and dwindle on price rallies. Further, volume generally falls in advance of major declines in the stock price averages and rises sharply during market bottoms. Thus, forecasting price changes requires examination of the trend of price changes as well as fluctuations in volume of transactions.

The financial press publishes daily data on upside and downside volume, and the technician can look closely at volume generated when the market was rising or falling during a given trading day. These data provide insight that is not available when net figures are utilized.

New York and American Exchanges Volume

The American Stock Exchange (AMEX) has long been identified as listing smaller, more fledgling companies than those listed on the NYSE. An estimated three-fourths of the shares traded on the AMEX are accounted for by the public, and three-fourths of the trading volume on the NYSE is institutional. Therefore, the AMEX is, rightly or not, viewed as a market for more speculative securities. Many technicians regard the relative volume on the NYSE and the AMEX as a measure or index of changes in the trend of prices.

Daily volume on each exchange is compared most often by dividing AMEX volume by NYSE volume. AMEX volume in excess of NYSE volume is rare, so the index would assume values between zero and 1.00. Values closer to 1.0 indicate that activity is high on the AMEX (more speculative stocks) relative to the NYSE (more investment-grade stocks). High percentage values in excess of .6 are thought to represent a zone of high speculation and an eventual change in trend from

bullish to bearish as speculative excesses bring about a collapse. Percentage values below .30 are considered healthy and representative of buying opportunities. Historically, when the index has gone above 60 percent, the market top was generally reached several months later.

SHORT SELLING

Around the twentieth of each month, the AMEX and NYSE make public the number of shares of key stocks that have been sold short. Recall that short selling refers to selling shares that are not owned. The seller has behaved in this way because he feels the stock will fall in price. He hopes to purchase the shares at a later date (cover his short position) below the selling price and reap a profit.

As a technical indicator, short selling is called *short interest.* The theory is that short sellers must eventually cover their positions. This buying activity increases the potential demand for stock. In effect, short interest has significance for the market as a whole, as well as for individual stocks.

Monthly short interest for the market can be related to average daily volume for the preceding month. Thus, monthly short interest divided by average daily volume gives a ratio. The ratio indicates how many days of trading it would take to use up total short interest. Historically, the ratio has varied between one-third of a day and four days.

In general, when the ratio is less than 1.0, the market is considered weak or weakening. It is common to say that the market is "overbought." A decline should follow sooner or later. The zone between 1.0 and 1.5 is considered a neutral indicator. Values above 1.5 indicate bullish territory with 2.0 and above highly favorable. This market is said to be "oversold." The most bullish effect would occur when the market is turning up and the short-interest ratio is high.

Data are now being made public regarding short selling by stock specialists. Specialists are permitted to use short selling as one of their tools to promote orderly markets in the stocks they specialize in. Increasing and high levels of specialist short selling tend to signal important market tops. Conversely, low levels of specialist short selling tend to signal market bottoms.

ODD-LOT TRADING

The small investor more often than not buys fewer than 100 shares of a given stock—an odd lot—and such buyers and sellers are called *odd lotters.* Many find reason to watch the buying and selling activities of the odd lotters very closely.

Odd lotters try to do the right thing most of the time; that is, they tend to buy stocks as the market retreats and sell stocks as the market advances. However, technicians feel that the odd lotter is inclined to do the wrong thing at critical turns in the market.

If we relate odd-lot purchases to odd-lot sales (purchase ÷ sales), we get an odd-lot index. An increase in the index suggests relatively more buying; a decrease indicates relatively more selling. During most of the market cycle, odd lotters are selling the advances and buying the declines. During advances, the odd-lot index is falling. However, at or near the market peak, the index begins to rise as odd lotters

sell proportionately less. The volume of odd-lot purchases increases noticeably just before a decline in the market. Similarly, during declines, the index is rising. Just before a rise in the market, the volume of odd-lot sales increases greatly and the index begins to fall.

ODD-LOT SHORT SALES.   The presumed lack of sophistication on the part of odd lotters is often further verified by looking at their activities in short selling. A ratio can be calculated by dividing odd-lot short sales by total odd-lot sales. This short sales/sales ratio is gauging the speculative activities of the man on the street, who, as a speculator, is presumed to be more wrong than the average odd lotter. Odd-lot short sellers tend to increase their short sales sharply near the bottom of a declining market. As soon as the market turns around, they tend to lose faith and reduce their short sales noticeably. An increasing ratio of short sales to sales suggests increasing bearishness; a falling ratio indicates decreasing bearishness.

Normally, a short-sale ratio of .5 percent suggests high optimism. A ratio in excess of 3 percent suggests high pessimism.

In Figure 15–2 we depict graphically a number of the indicators just discussed—namely, upside and downside volume, new highs and lows, short-interest ratio, and odd-lot short sales as a percentage of odd-lot sales. These graphs are presented with the DJIA for January 1982–October 1985. These are typical of data of this type that have been tracked for years by technicians.

Other Market Indicators

The number of indicators technicians use to predict changes in the trend of the overall market is almost limitless.[2] In the following paragraphs we will try to capture the essence of some other popular market indicators.

MUTUAL-FUND ACTIVITY

Mutual funds represent one of the most potent institutional forces in the market, and they are a source of abundant data that are readily available. The cash position of funds and their net subscriptions are followed closely by technicians.

Mutual funds keep cash to take advantage of favorable market opportunities and/or to provide for redemption of shares by holders. It is convenient to express mutual-fund cash as a percentage of net assets on a daily, monthly, or annual basis. In theory, a low cash ratio would indicate a reasonably fully invested position, with the implication that not much reserve buying power remains in the hands of funds as a group. Low ratios (on the order of 5 to 5½ percent) are frequently equated with market highs. At market bottoms, the cash ratio would be high to reflect heavy redemptions, among other things. Such a buildup of the cash ratio at market

---

[2]Many who are cynical about technical analysis cite elaborate efforts to tie market movements to sunspot activity (lunacy and speculation) or the length of women's skirts (hemline theory), and the use of various aspects of the occult, including tarot-card reading, palmistry, and so on.

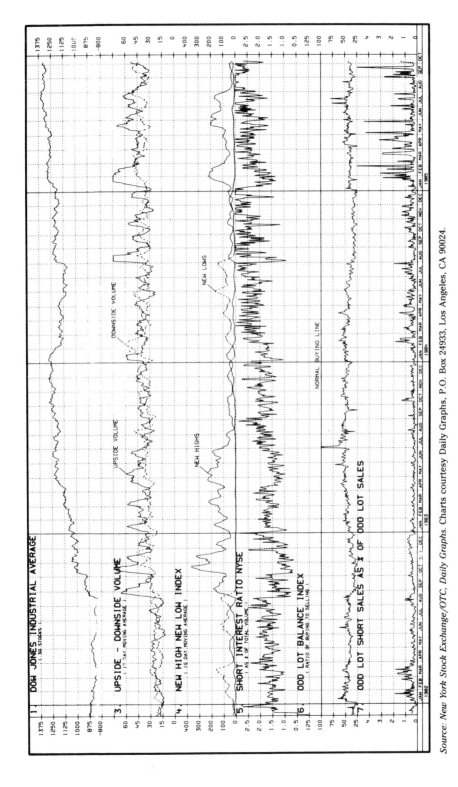

Source: New York Stock Exchange/OTC, Daily Graphs. Charts courtesy Daily Graphs, P.O. Box 24933, Los Angeles, CA 90024.

FIGURE 15–2   Various Indexes vs. the DJIA (*Source: New York Stock Exchange/OTC, Daily Graphs.* Charts courtesy Daily Graphs, P.O. Box 24933, Los Angeles, CA 90024.)

lows is an indication of potential purchasing power that can be injected into the market to propel it upward.

Another mutual-fund indicator that is monitored quite closely is net subscriptions (subscriptions to new shares, less redemptions of existing shares). Like the odd-lot statistics, this indicator measures public sentiment and the outlook for the stock market. The trend to more or less buying moves in tandem with the odd-lot purchase-to-sale ratio. The sales-redemption differential narrows considerably prior to market advances. In effect, market advances are preceded by a relative shift toward redemptions. Shifts toward relative buying (sales of new shares) tend to precede market declines.

Credit Balance Theory

Typically, investors receive credit balances in their accounts at their brokerage houses when they sell stock. At this point the investor has two choices: He can either have the credit balance forwarded to him or leave the credit balance in the account. However, these balances frequently earn no interest. Thus, the only reason for maintaining the credit balances in the account would be for purposes of reinvestment of these funds in the very near future.

Figures on these credit balances at brokerage houses are published regularly in the financial press and in such publications as the *Federal Reserve Bulletin.* Some feel that a build-up in these cash balances represents large reservoirs of potential buying power. In effect, investors are leaving the credit balances in their brokerage firm accounts because they anticipate a drop in prices and thus a buying opportunity. Conversely, a drop in credit balance suggests that prices will go up. Because an increase in prices was expected, investors have already used up their credit balances. However, technicians feel that investors in general, as their actions get reflected in credit balances, are usually wrong; that is, the investors are buying stocks when they should be selling them and selling stocks when they should be buying. As such, the credit balance theory is a contrary opinion theory.

In other words, technicians suggest that a wise investor will buy stocks as credit balances are rising and sell stocks as credit balances are dropping. In short, technicians say the wise investor should do the opposite of what the credit balances are doing.

Confidence Indicators

Two indicators of confidence have been popular with market analysts. One is based upon *Barron's* ratio of higher- to lower-grade bond yield. The other compares Standard & Poor's low-priced and high-grade common stocks.

Barron's indicator divides high-grade bond yields by the relatively higher yields of low-grade bonds. A rise in the index indicates a narrowing of the spread between high- and low-grade bonds. In a previous chapter we saw that narrowing yield spreads were indicative of boom times or rising stock markets; so a fall in the index would imply widening yield spreads and recessed conditions in the economy and markets. The assumption behind the value of the index is that "smart" money moves from high to low quality, or vice versa, in anticipation of major market

SUPER BOWL RESULTS AND STOCK MARKET ACTIVITY				
			PERCENT CHANGE FROM END OF PREVIOUS YEAR	
YEAR	WINNER	ORIGINAL CONFERENCE	DOW JONES INDUSTRIALS	STANDARD & POOR'S 500
1967	Green Bay Packers	NFC	15.2	20.1
1968	Green Bay Packers	NFC	4.3	7.7
1969	New York Jets	AFC	−15.2	−11.4
1970	Kansas City Chiefs	AFC	4.8	−0.1
1971	Baltimore Colts	NFC*	6.1	10.8
1972	Dallas Cowboys	NFC	14.6	15.8
1973	Miami Dolphins	AFC	−16.6	−17.5
1974	Miami Dolphins	AFC	−27.6	−29.6
1975	Pittsburgh Steelers	NFC*	38.3	31.5
1976	Pittsburgh Steelers	NFC*	17.9	19.1
1977	Oakland Raiders	AFC	−17.3	−11.5
1978	Dallas Cowboys	NFC	−3.1	1.1
1979	Pittsburgh Steelers	NFC*	4.2	12.3
1980	Pittsburgh Steelers	NFC*	14.9	25.8
1981	Oakland Raiders	AFC	−9.2	−9.7
1982	San Francisco 49ers	NFC	19.6	14.8
1983	Washington Redskins	NFC	20.3	17.3
1984	Los Angeles Raiders	AFC	−3.7	1.4
1985	San Francisco 49ers	NFC	27.7	26.3
1986	Chicago Bears	NFC	22.6	14.6
1987	N.Y. Giants	NFC	2.3	2.0
1988	Washington Redskins	NFC	11.8	12.4
1989	San Francisco 49ers	NFC	27.0	27.3
1990	San Francisco 49ers	NFC	−4.3	−6.6
1991	N.Y. Giants	NFC	20.3	26.3
1992	Washington Redskins	NFC	4.2	4.5

*Baltimore (now Indianapolis) and Pittsburgh are now members of the AFC.
AFC—American Football Conference.
NFC—National Football Conference.

shifts, and such a move causes yield spreads to change. To the extent that this is true, *Barron's* confidence index is a leading indicator of the economy and the stock market.

The S&P confidence indicator measures low-priced common stocks and high-grade common stocks. Speculative stocks are assumed to be closely identified with low-priced shares. Thus we have a low- and high-grade stock indicator much like *Barron's* low- and high-grade bond indicator. When the market is advancing, investors are willing to take greater risks and buy speculative (low-priced) stocks. During market declines, quality (in high-grade stocks) is sought. The index (low-

priced/high-grade) would fall prior to a market peak as confidence wanes and speculative stocks are changed for high-quality shares. A rise in the index would signal revival from a market bottom.

Forecasting Individual Stock Performance

After the technical analyst has forecast the probable future performance of the general market, he can turn his attention to individual stocks. Let us examine a few of the tools used for the technical analysis of individual common stocks.

As in forecasting the market, the technician believes that understanding historical price-volume information of individual securities is the key for determining their probable future performance. Technical analysts believe that history repeats itself, and thus, historical trends and patterns will be repeated through time. They seek to detect an evolving key trend or pattern in supply and demand conditions of the stock in question. The techniques that have evolved are aimed at detecting shifts in underlying supply and demand conditions as reflected in changes in volume and, consequently, prices. In this section we will discuss representative approaches in two broad categories of tools—those looking only at price, and those looking at price-volume relationships.

Price Analysis Approaches

Point-and-Figure Charting

Charting represents a key activity for the technical analyst. It provides visual assistance to him in detecting evolving and changing patterns of price behavior. The two oldest and most widely used charting procedures are point-and-figure charting and bar charting. These lie at the core of many technical schemes for individual stock analysis.

Perhaps the most baffling form of stock analysis, in the mind of the average investor, is the technique of point-and-figure charting.[3] The major features of this method of charting a security are that (1) it has no time dimension, (2) it disregards "small" changes in the stock price, and (3) it requires a stock to reverse direction a predetermined number of points before a change in direction is recorded on the chart.

A simple illustration will demonstrate the plotting technique quite easily. For stocks priced above 50 and below 100, the plotting increments are often one point, although the user may elect any increment he desires. All fractions are then discarded, so that $51^{7}/_{8}$ becomes 51. On a sheet of graph paper, the closing price of the stock being charted is recorded with an X. If the price at the close of the next trading day is within the plotting increment, no additional X can be en-

---

[3]One reason for this is the great number of variations on the basic point-and-figure approach. We present only one representative approach.

tered. (We are assuming that the chart only records closing-price information, to the exclusion of intraday activity.) Only when the stock price moves into another plotting increment are changes recorded. Therefore, a stock may move upward several points over a fairly long period with only a small amount of plotting. For example, if a stock moved from a price of 50 in small increments to a price of 53 over a three-month period, only four X's will have been made on the chart, as in Figure 15–3(a).

Obviously, if no additional parameters were assigned, only one vertical line of X's would develop. A *reversal spread* is used to prevent this. A reversal spread is the number of points (dollars) an issue must fall from its immediately previous high, or rise from its immediately previous low, to develop a new vertical column. When this occurs, a new column is started to the right. These reversal spreads are assigned according to the volatility of the issue. In the example, if the reversal spread were three points, and if the stock had gone from 50 to 60 without ever closing three points below the high for the column, the chart would look like Figure 15–3(b). However, if the stock developed a downtrend after reaching 60 and hit $56^1/_2$ on a close, a new column would be started, and all the points from 60 to 56 would be filled in, as in Figure 15–3(c). The stock is now in a downward cycle and will remain classified as such until a three-point reversal occurs, as in Figure 15–3(d), which shows that the stock moved from 40 to 43.

By ignoring the time element, we can see the forces of supply and demand at work in Figure 15–4(a), where the equilibrium price of the issue seems to be between 45 and 50. At any price above 50, the sellers move in, and at any price below 45, the buyers move in and clear the market. If the stock suddenly moves to 55, we are aware that this is outside the realm of the stock's normal trading range and some form of unusual activity is taking place.

Over the years, point-and-figure adherents have observed various formations that occur before major price movements. One such formation, for example, is the *triple top,* as illustrated in Figure 15–4(b). A triple top occurs when a stock reaches its third consecutive high at the same price level. A buy signal is given when the stock surpasses the third high. A time element should be noted somewhere on the chart for each high because the shorter the period from the first to the third high, the greater the underlying strength.[4]

Another key formation to point-and-figure chartists is the *congestion area.* A congestion area is formed on the chart by the lateral movement of X's. This comes about by a series of brief rallies and reversals, such as in Figure 15–4(a), that precludes the establishment of lengthy vertical columns. The width of the congestion area gives the technician some insight into the probable size and direction of a move by the stock to a "price target." Unfortunately, pinpointing when this target will be hit is difficult.[5]

---

[4]See Ernest J. Staby, *Stock Market Trading* (New York: Cornerstone Library, 1970), pp. 28–30.

[5]Daniel Seligman, "The Mystique of Point-and-Figure," *Fortune* 65, no. 3 (March 1962), pp. 113–15 ff. See also Robert A. Levy, "The Predictive Significance of Five Point Chart Patterns," *Journal of Business* (July 1971).

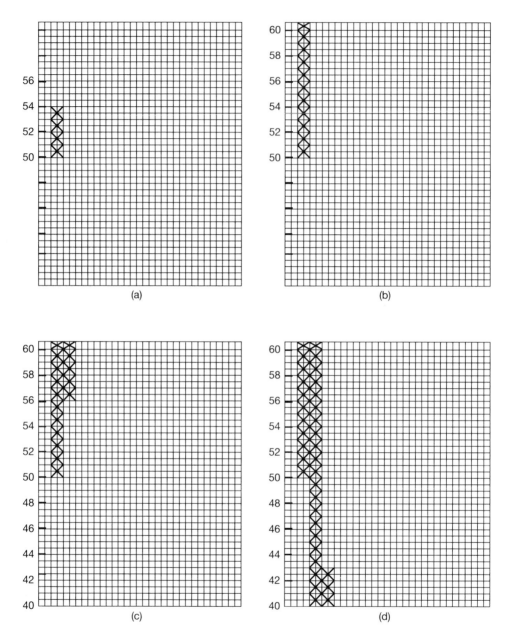

FIGURE 15–3   Sample Point-and-Figure Charts

A substantial number of patterns and corresponding rules have been developed by point-and-figure proponents over the years. These patterns can take considerable periods of time to evolve on the chart, particularly when large plotting increments (several points) and reversal spreads are used. To the extent that large

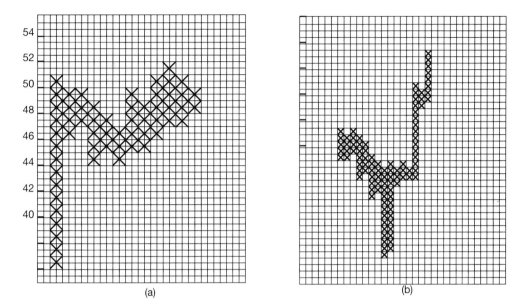

FIGURE 15–4   Sample Point-and-Figure Charts

numbers of investors adhere to the basic tenets of point-and-figure charting, the prophesies of the charts may very well be self-fulfilling.

BAR CHARTING

Point-and-figure charts have a measure scale only on the vertical axis (no time dimension). Bar charts contain measures on both axes—price on the vertical axis, and time on the horizontal axis. The horizontal axis can be marked off in any dimension the analyst wishes—days, weeks, or months. On bar charts, rather than just plotting a point on the graph at a point in time, the analyst plots a vertical line to represent the range of prices of the stock during the period. That is, if the analyst were plotting daily data, the top of the vertical line would represent the high price of the stock during the day, and the bottom of the line would represent the low price of the stock during the same day. A small horizontal line is drawn across the bar to denote the closing price at the end of the time period. Generally, bar charts contain, at the bottom, volume information for the same period that the price information covers. The *Wall Street Journal* publishes bar charts of the three Dow Jones averages—industrials, transportation, and utilities—each day.

Bar chartists, like point-and-figure chartists, have found key patterns to look for in determining the most probable price action of a stock. Typical patterns are illustrated in Figures 15–5 and 15–6. Figure 15–6 contains interpretations of certain of these patterns. These chart patterns are "classics" and have not changed in many years because they are formations that chartists look for in their charts.

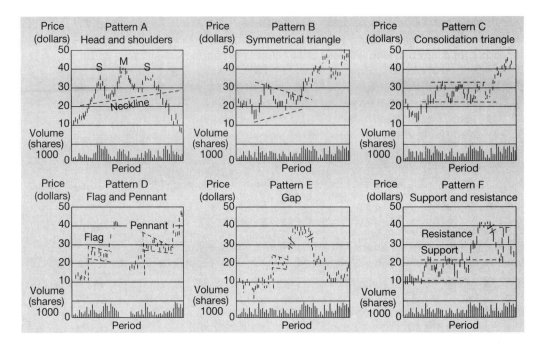

FIGURE 15–5 Typical Graphic Patterns Used in Technical Market Analysis (*Source:* Sidney M. Robbins, *Managing Securities* (Boston: Houghton Mifflin, 1954), p. 502.)

Figure 15–7 presents a classic bar chart for McDonald's from the Mansfield Stock Service. This service also provides bar charts of industry grouping. In Figure 15–8 is an explanation of the vast amount of information contained in the charts of this service.

THE 200-DAY MOVING AVERAGE

One of the most reliable and easily read technical indicators available to investors is the 200-day moving average of a security. The technique for computing the average is simple. The closing prices of the stock market observation are added up for the most recent 200 days it has been traded. This sum is divided by 200. The objective is to obtain a relatively simple and smooth curve for the issue. Random variations and erratic price changes tend to cancel out, and a general underlying trend becomes visible. For those who see this as a maze of adding-machine tape, the entire process for 744 major issues can be obtained each week from the Trendline Market Service.

In his book, Joseph E. Granville listed eight basic rules for using the 200-day moving average, in a chapter on "The Grand Strategy of Stock Trading":

1. If the 200-day average line flattens out following a previous decline, or is advancing, and the price of the stock penetrates that average line on the upside, this comprises a major buying signal.

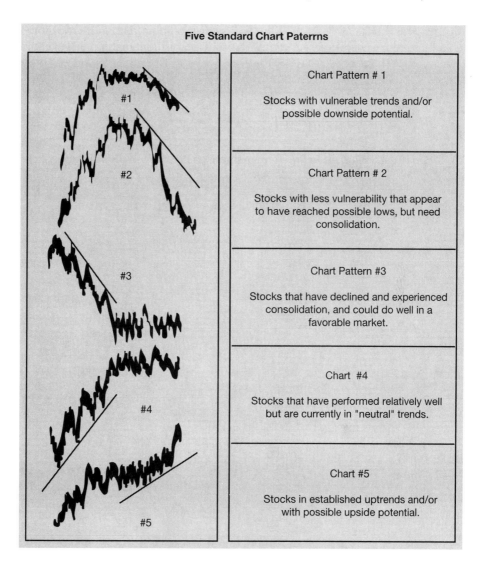

FIGURE 15–6   Five Standard Chart Patterns (*Source:* Yale Hirsch, *The 1971 Stock Trader's Almanac* (Old Tappan, N.J.: Hirsch Organization, 1970), p. 37.)

2. If the price of the stock falls below the 200-day moving average price while the average line is still rising, this is also considered to be a buying opportunity.

3. If the stock price is above the 200-day line and is declining toward that line, fails to go through and starts to turn up again, this is a buying signal.

4. If the stock price falls too fast under the declining 200-day average line, it is entitled to an advance back toward the average line and the stock can be bought for this short-term technical rise.

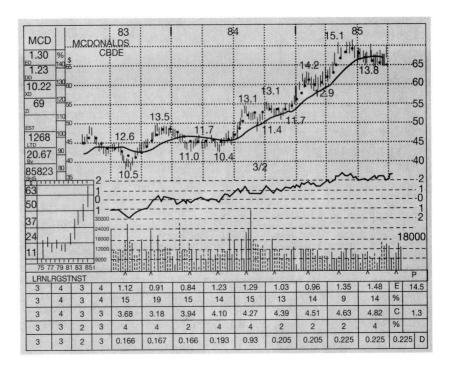

FIGURE 15–7   Bar Chart of McDonald's Corp. Stock (*Source:* McDonald's Corp., Mansfield Stock Chart Service, 26 Journal Square, Jersey City, NJ 07306.)

5. If the 200-day average line flattens out following a previous rise, or is declining, and the price of the stock penetrates that line on the downside, this comprises a major sell signal.

6. If the price of the stock rises above the 200-day moving average price line while the average line is still falling, this also is considered to be a selling opportunity.

7. If the stock price is below the 200-day line and is advancing toward that line, fails to go through and starts to turn down again, this is a selling signal.

8. If the stock price advances too fast above the advancing 200-day average line, it is entitled to a reaction back toward the average line and the stock can be sold for this short-term technical reaction.[6]

Obviously, these rules are only guidelines to assist the analyst in using the 200-day moving average as an indicator for individual securities. For the person who is trading in speculative issues, the technique gives signals based on trends or changing trends in the price of the security in question. See Figure 15–9 for an ex-

[6]Joseph E. Granville, *A Strategy of Daily Stock Market Timing for Maximum Profit* (Englewood Cliffs, N.J.: Prentice Hall, 1969), pp. 237–38.

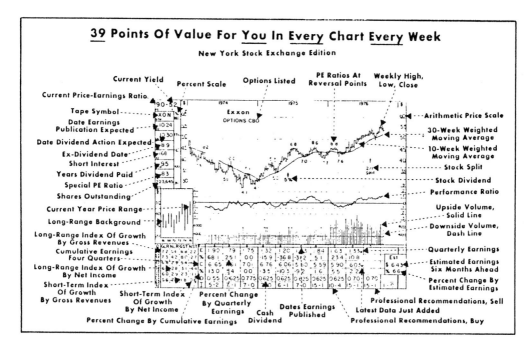

FIGURE 15–8   Information Contained in Mansfield Stock Service Charts (*Source:* Mansfield Stock Chart Service, 26 Journal Square, Jersey City, NJ 07306.)

ample of this type of chart. Here the smooth line represents the 200-day moving average.

RELATIVE STRENGTH

A more recent approach to technical analysis of price has been proposed by Robert Levy.[7] His method is called *relative-strength analysis.* A basic tenet of this technique is that certain securities perform better than other securities in a given market environment and that this behavior will remain relatively constant over time. Generally, this technique is used in conjunction with either (1) the stocks of individual companies or industries, or (2) portfolios consisting of stocks and bonds.

When the stock application is used, the analyst calculates ratios for the returns (over time) of the stock to those of its industry group, returns of the stock to those of the general market, and returns of the industry group to those of the general market.[8] These ratios are then plotted over time to see the relative strengths. Technicians using the relative-strength approach have observed that those firms and industries displaying greatest relative strength in good markets (bull) also

[7] Robert A. Levy, "Relative Strength as a Criterion for Investment Selection," *Journal of Finance* (December 1967), pp. 595–610.

[8] Both Moody's and Standard & Poor's services provide industry averages that can be used to calculate industry performance.

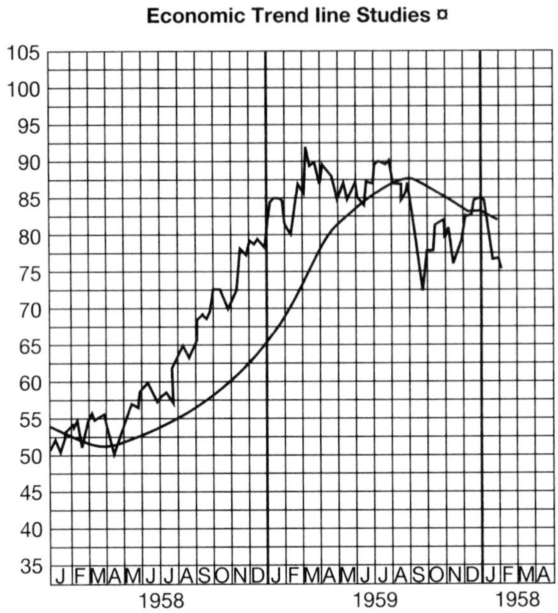

Economic Trend line Studies ¤

FIGURE 15–9   Sample 30-Week Moving-Average Stock Chart (*Source:* From the book *A Strategy of Daily Stock Market Timing for Maximum Profit,* by Joseph E. Granville, © 1960 by Prentice Hall, Inc. Published by Prentice Hall, Inc., Englewood Cliffs, N.J.)

show the greatest weakness in bad markets (bear). These "relatively strong" firms could well have high betas.

When the stock-bond approach is used, the analyst opts for a higher proportion of stocks in the portfolio (relative to bonds) as the market moves upward, and a higher proportion of bonds (relative to stocks) as the market moves upward, and a higher proportion of bonds (relative to stocks) as the market moves downward. In other words, he selects the security type with the most relative strength in the prevailing market. Levy has tested this procedure of switching between stocks and bonds and has concluded that the returns earned by a portfolio utilizing this technique outperform portfolios managed in a more naive manner—that is, by the "buy-and-hold strategy" of purchasing securities and then merely holding them regardless of any changes in the economic environment.[9]

Price-Volume Analysis Approaches

RESISTANCE-SUPPORT CHARTS

Earlier we discussed two well-known types of charts—point-and-figure and bar charts. There is a much newer variety of chart, whose avowed purpose is to detect resistance (areas of supply) as a stock's price goes up, and support (areas of de-

[9]Robert A. Levy, "Random Walks: Reality or Myth," *Financial Analysts Journal* (November–December 1967), pp. 69–77.

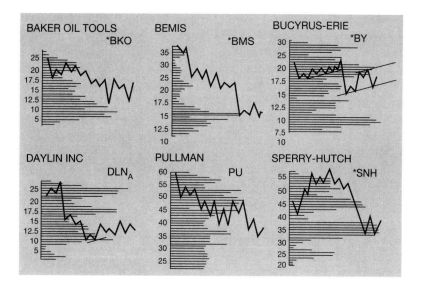

FIGURE 15–10   Sample Resistance-Support Charts (*Source:* Yale Hirsch, *The 1971 Stock Traders Almanac* (Old Tappan, N.J.: Hirsch Organization, 1970), p. 25.)

mand) as a stock goes down. The chart is constructed to show, in a series of horizontal lines, the levels at which the stock in question has traded in the past. The levels are determined regardless of the volume at which the stock traded, but rather at those levels at which the stock traded most often—the more often, the longer the horizontal line. The hypothesis is that popular levels (longer lines) encountered by the stock in an upward move present resistance; and conversely, popular levels (longer lines) encountered by the stock in a downward move provide support. A specimen of this chart form is shown in Figure 15–10.

PRICE-VOLUME BAR CHARTING

When we discussed the role of bar charting, we saw that the emphasis of technicians using this chart form was generally on price behavior; however, we noted that volume information is often included on bar charts. Chartists, following the seminal Dow Theory, believe that volume goes with the price trend—that a volume increase with an upward move in prices is good, and a volume increase with a downward move in prices is bad. Furthermore, if volume decreases during a price drop, this is good (a drying up of supply), and if volume decreases during a price rise, this is bad (a drying up of demand). These statements represent traditional technical folklore. It would be interesting to test the statistical validity of these views.

　　Ying has conducted an empirical study of price-volume relationships. His results were as follows:

1. A small volume is usually accompanied by a fall in price.
2. A large volume is usually accompanied by a rise in price.

3. A large increase in volume is usually accompanied by either a large rise in price or a large fall in price.

4. A large volume is usually followed by a rise in price.

5. If the volume has been decreasing consecutively for a period of five trading days, then the price will tend to fall over the next four trading days.

6. If the volume has been increasing consecutively for a period of five trading days, then the price will tend to rise over the next four trading days.[10]

Ying's conclusions seem to provide support for the traditionally held view, with one notable exception—number 5. That is, declining volume seems to be associated with price declines and thus would not be a bullish indicator.[11]

Computer-Aided Technical Analysis

With the increase of home-based computers with modems and the proliferation of stock-price quote services, have come numerous software packages so that the individual technical analyst can graph his own charts in the manner he prefers using the methods he follows for the companies or mutual funds he follows. Because so many services are now available, the cost of the software and time-usage charges have come down tremendously. *The Wall Street Journal* and *Investor's Business Daily* are filled with advertisements for these various services. Many services allow prices to be downloaded in a variety of ways, such as fifteen minute delayed process, daily closing, or weekly closing prices. The individual stock-price movements can be plotted on a personal computer against a relative strength line, a moving average line, or an index such as the S&P 500 Index. Data bases often contain daily high price, low price, closing prices, and volume in formation for thousands of stocks. Some companies provide the software, others provide the data base, still others provide the quote services.

Investor's Business Daily presents pages of statistical analysis of stocks on the NYSE, AMEX, and over-the-counter market as well as pages of graphs and charts on various indexes, commodities, and options every day the newspaper is published. Its daily stock listings contain among other items its own rank of stocks by earnings-growth rank, and relative share price strength together with percentage change in volume from normal trading patterns. Other statistical data, many of a technical sort such as accumulation-distribution raking, are provided on a rotating basis. Thus, an investor without the time or computer capabilities or facilities can have access to computer-screened data on thousands of stocks just by purchasing a

---

[10]Charles C. Ying, "Stock Market Prices and Volumes of Sales," *Econometrica* (July 1966), p. 676.

[11]We are aware of at least one trading system that refines the analysis even further. It looks at *each* transaction in the stock and weights the direction of price changes (upticks and downticks) between transactions by the number of round lots associated with the price change (trade).

newspaper. See Figure 15–11 for an illustration of certain tables from *Investor's Business Daily* and definitions of some of the terms.

OTHER TESTS, CONCLUSIONS, AND SUMMARY

A number of tests have been conducted to obtain statistically reliable estimates of the worth of various technical trading strategies. Many of these tests fall into a body of literature called the random-walk theory. These will be discussed in some detail in Chapter 17.

Here we will report in a general fashion their key conclusions.[12] First, with respect to tests of mechanical trading rules (procedures that are strictly followed regardless of economic circumstances) and price-volume relationships, the results have been inconclusive because of different findings of different researchers using different procedures and different samples. Attempts to reconcile these differences have been difficult. Tests of possible relationships between price and short interests have been more conclusive. Generally, no significant relationship between stock prices and short interests were found. Finally, tests of odd-lot and advance-decline theories have detected very tentative and unconvincing results regarding their validity. Thus, in summary, these tests have given less than overwhelming support to the various technical theories examined to date, while at the same time not supporting random walk unequivocally.[13] There are several reasons for this.

First, some have questioned whether the tests have been performed on technical theories as they are actually used in practice.[14] To the extent that the tests accurately reflect the practice, the results may have some meaning. To the extent that they do not, the results and their implications are of dubious value. Second, only selected phases of technical analysis have been rigorously tested, and then only one at a time. Yet untested technical procedures could prove to have greater usefulness than those already examined. Furthermore, technicians very infrequently use only one indicator at a time, but rather use several in conjunction with one another.[15] Thus, tools found lacking when tested one at a time may be useful when combined.

---

[12]This section draws heavily from a fine, nonmathematical review of tests of technical analysis by George F. Pinches, "The Random-Walk Hypothesis and Technical Analysis,' *Financial Analysts Journal* (March–April 1970), pp. 104–10.

[13]Technical analysis should be thought of as an adjunct to fundamental analysis, not as its replacement.

[14]It should be pointed out that the same technical theories are often applied differently by different technical analysts. Therefore the success of the strategy is often dependent on the analyst than the method alone.

[15]Commercial investment services exist that combine numerous technical indicators into a composite index or diffusion index. There are problems, however, such as which indicators to select, how to combine them, and then how to weight them in the index. Finally, the validity of the index needs to be tested.

60 NYSE Stocks With Greatest % Rise In Volume

Compared to stock's last 50 days avg. daily trading volume. Stocks over $15 and ½ pt. change. Stocks up in price listed first. Stocks up with EPS & Relative Strength 80 or more are **boldfaced.**

EPS Rnk	Rel. Str.	Acc. Dis	52-Week High	52-Week Low	Stock Name	Stock Symbol	Closing Price	Price Change	PE Ratio	Float (mil)	Volume (1000s)	% Change In Vol.
96	72	B	15⅜	8¾	Nutmeg Industries	NTM	17⅜	+ 2⅜	23	13	2,750	+4264
72	82	B	19⅞	11½	Park Electrochemicl	PKE	20½	+ ⅞	24	3.6	40	+1022
84	69	C	34¾	22¼	Loral Corporation o	LOR	35	+ 2¾	15	79	1,069	+451
1	55	.	16¼	15	Templeton China Fd	TCH	16⅞	+ ⅝	..	0.0	520	+360
66	47	B	30¾	24¼	Premier Industrial	PRE	28⅜	+ ½	27	32	109	+344
	80	B	29	17⅛	Taiwan Fund	TWN	28⅞	+ 1⅞	..	8.0	299	+258
92	**85**	**A**	**28⅞**	**16**	**Federal – mogul Cp o**	**FMO**	**29½**	**+ 1⅛**	**40**	**28**	**515**	**+257**
69	78	A	26¾	16½	Toro Co	TTC	25½	+ ½	21	10	88	+250
28	28	A	36⅜	21¼	Cyprus Amax Minrls o	CYM	26⅛	+ ⅞	9	47	1,511	+242
45	4	D	79½	19⅞	U S Surgical Corp o	USS	23	+ 2⅛	31	39	1,869	+221
82	58	D	43⅜	33¼	Donaldson Co	DCI	41¼	+ 1¼	19	12	55	+210
22	73	B	23⅞	17⅛	Harnischfeger Inds o	HPH	24⅝	+ 1	48	24	278	+207
82	69	A	26⅝	12⅛	Healthsouth Rehab o	HRC	21¾	+ 1⅞	17	29	609	+206
80	**89**	**.**	**22¾**	**12¼**	**China Tire Hldg Ltd**	**TIR**	**24½**	**+ 2⅛**	**7**	**6.1**	**275**	**+203**
45	53	B	70⅜	59¼	Norfolk Southern o	NSC	70⅞	+ 1⅝	19	140	478	+199
44	28	D	54	41½	F M C Corp o	FMC	45⅞	+ ¾	10	24	217	+190
69	71	B	21⅞	13⅝	Lafarge Corp o	LAF	22⅛	+ 1¾	..	22	411	+185
77	67	B	49⅛	32⅝	Owens-Corn Fibrgl o	OCF	47⅜	+ ⅝	24	43	328	+185
96	**88**	**A**	**28⅜**	**10½**	**Health Mgmt Asoc A**	**HMA**	**26⅞**	**+ 1⅜**	**25**	**20**	**242**	**+183**
72	92	A	28¼	11⅞	Medusa Corp	MSA	28⅞	+ 1⅝	32	15	149	+180
84	21	B	32	13½	Brilliance China	CBA	19⅜	+ 1¾	16	5.0	162	+171
78	96	.	43¾	18¼	Shanghai Petrochm	SHI	48⅛	+ 5¼	33	17	323	+168
75	91	A	23¼	12⅛	Pacific Scientific	PSX	23¾	+ ½	20	5.1	38	+165
67	63	B	55⅜	37½	Eaton Corp o	ETN	51⅝	+ ⅝	19	70	333	+156
69	45	.	19¾	17¾	Elsag Bailey Procss	EBY	19¾	+ ⅝	25	8.2	200	+139
17	86	B	24⅝	9⅞	Coeur D Alene Mines o	CDE	21½	+ ⅝	..	15	154	+138
18	56	A	55⅝	39⅛	Phelps Dodge o	PD	49¾	+ 1	17	70	1,006	+138
33	65	B	27⅜	17½	Freeprt McM Cp&Gld o	FCX	24¼	+ ⅝	90	199	727	+134
51	18	D	26	21¼	Ohio Edison Co o	OEC	21⅞	+ ½	12	153	378	+130
80	51	B	26⅝	17½	Manor Care Inc o	MNR	23¼	+ 1	20	37	289	+126
67	49	B	41	25¾	Bic Corp	BIC	32¾	+ ⅝	18	5.2	30	+122
	78	B	23¼	12⅝	Asia Pacific Fund o	APB	21⅝	+ 1⅛	..	11	190	+113
15	76	A	45⅝	24⅜	I M C Fertilizer Group o	IFL	42	+ 2¼	..	25	318	+103
92	25	B	26⅜	17⅛	Shawmut Natnl Corp o	SNC	21⅝	+ 1	20	88	741	+97
32	93	A	50	9⅝	U S G Corp o	USG	28⅞	+ 1⅛	2	27	176	+94
77	43	D	21	9¾	Pogo Producing Co o	PPP	15⅝	+ ¾	16	29	287	+90
18	62	A	63⅜	40⅝	I B M o	IBM	57⅜	+ 2⅛	..	565	4,881	+89
	88	B	30⅝	18⅛	Thai Fund Inc	TTF	31⅜	+ 1	..	10	92	+87
98	53	B	92½	71	Fund Amer Entrprise o	FFC	86	– 1⅝	7	7.4	931	+5158
22	47	B	38	28¾	Cleveland Cliffs Inc	CLF	33¾	– ⅞	24	12	1,418	+3230
15	55	B	37	17¾	Sequa Corp Cl B	SQAB	33	– 1	..	4.7	55	+1064
45	12	E	43	27	Rayonier Timberlnd	LOG	27¼	– 1	7	10	178	+426
81	15	D	33⅞	23	Circuit City Stores o	CC	21¼	– 1¾	17	92	2,519	+344
97	65	D	42	21⅝	Vornado Realty Trst	VNO	35⅝	– ⅞	26	14	64	+327
93	51	B	52¼	39½	Scana Corp	SCG	48⅝	– ⅝	13	46	274	+283
	90	A	22⅞	12¾	China Fund The	CHN	21⅝	– 1⅛	..	8.0	188	+248
64	28	B	64⅜	48⅜	Avon Products o	AVP	49¾	– 1½	15	71	1,025	+222
48	37	B	29⅞	23⅝	Eastern Utilties	EUA	26½	– ⅞	11	19	154	+215

FIGURE 15–11 Sample Listings from *Investor's Business Daily* (Source: *Investor's Business Daily*, December 14, 1993. Reprinted with permission.)

20 Most Active NYSE Stocks

(Average price of 20 most active = $32)

EPS Rnk	Rel Str.	Acc. Dis.	Stock Name	Closing Price	Chg.	Group Str.	Vol. (mil)	Vol. % Chg.
8	62	A	I B M	57⅜	+ 2⅛	E	4.88	+89
6	**72**	**B**	**Nutmeg Industries**	**17⅜**	**+ 2⅜**	**B**	**2.75**	**+4264**
2	21	B	Merck & Co	32⅞	− ⅛	B	2.71	−20
1	15	D	Circuit City Stores	21¼	− 1¾	A	2.52	+344
0	53	A	R J R Nabisco Hldgs	6½	+ ⅛	D	2.36	−38
4	69	A	Telefonos De Mex L	61½	+ ⅜	B	2.28	−37
6	55	D	Hanson PLC ADR	19⅝	....	C	2.25	−9
2	85	B	Chrysler Corp	56⅝	+ ½	B	2.25	+19
2	8	C	Limited Inc	18	....	C	2.14	+46
8	22	C	Occidental Pete	17⅜	− ⅝	E	2.11	+144
2	49	C	Global Marine Inc	3¾	....	E	1.94	+238
0	**88**	**A**	**National Medical Ent**	**13⅝**	**+ ½**	**A**	**1.87**	**+92**
5	4	D	U S Surgical Corp	23	+ 2⅛	B	1.87	+221
2	45	A	Glaxo Hldgs Plc	20¼	− ⅛	B	1.83	+42
9	95	D	E M C Corp Mass	16¼	+ ¾	A	1.78	+25
4	89	B	Amer Barrick Res	28⅜	+ ½	A	1.74	−1
2	86	A	General Motors Crp	56⅛	....	B	1.66	−37
3	39	A	Philip Morris Cos	55½	+ ⅝	D	1.61	−41
8	28	A	Cyprus Amax Minrls	26⅛	+ ⅞	B	1.51	+242
9	90	B	Paramount Comm	80⅜	− ¾	A	1.51	−21

20 Most % Up In Price

(Stocks Over $12)

EPS Rnk	Rel Str.	Stock Name	Closing Price	Net Up	Group Str.	Volume (100s)	Vol. % Change
96	**72**	**Nutmeg Industries**	**17⅜**	**+ 2⅜**	**B**	**2,749,6**	**+4264**
78	**96**	**Shanghai Petrochm**	**48⅛**	**+ 5¼**	**C**	**323,0**	**+168**
45	4	U S Surgical Corp	23	+ 2⅛	B	1,868,8	+221
84	21	Brilliance China	19⅜	+ 1¾	E	162,0	+171
80	**89**	**China Tire Hldg Ltd**	**24½**	**+ 2⅛**	**D**	**274,6**	**+203**
82	69	Healthsouth Rehab	21¾	+ 1⅞	A	608,9	+206
69	**71**	**Lafarge Corp**	**22⅛**	**+ 1¾**	**B**	**410,6**	**+185**
84	**69**	**Loral Corporation**	**35**	**+ 2¾**	**B**	**1,069,3**	**+451**
38	**84**	**Madeco S A ADS**	**24½**	**+ 1¾**	**B**	**36,4**	**+5**
	80	Taiwan Fund	28⅞	+ 1⅞	A	299,1	+258
12	49	Continuum Inc	20⅞	+ 1¼	A	74,7	+76
99	**90**	**EK Chor Chna Mtrcl**	**34½**	**+ 2**	**C**	**54,3**	**+6**
92	**75**	**Cummins Engine Co**	**54⅛**	**+ 3⅛**	**D**	**305,1**	**+25**
72	**92**	**Medusa Corp**	**28⅞**	**+ 1⅝**	**B**	**149,1**	**+180**
92	51	Getty Petroleum	13½	+ ¾	C	7,8	+66
93	82	Southwest Airlines	36	+ 2	C	1,090,2	+80
15	45	Conner Peripherals	13¾	+ ¾	A	1,163,2	+122
15	76	IMC Fertilizer Group	42	+ 2¼	B	317,8	+103
84	55	Living Centers Amer	23⅝	+ 1¼	A	21,6	−36
	83	Singapore Fund Inc	19	+ 1	A	94,5	+53

HOW TO READ OUR "INTELLIGENT" TABLES

We show vital news not found in The Wall Street Journal.

EPS Rank measures a company's earnings per share growth in the last 5 years and the stability of that growth. The % change in the last two quarters' earnings vs. same quarters a year earlier is combined and averaged with the 5-year record. Result is compared to all companies in the tables and ranked on a scale of 1 to 99, with 99 the highest. A 90 rank means the company produced earnings results in the top 10%. Companies with superior earnings records rank 80 or higher.

Rel Str (Relative Price Strength) measures daily each stock's relative price change over the last 12 months compared to all other stocks in the tables. Results are ranked 1 to 99. Stocks ranking below 70 indicate weaker or more laggard relative price performance.

The Accumulation-Distribution (Acc. Dis.) rating is derived by multiplying daily volume by change and direction in the stock price. "A" is strongest "E" weakest. Accumulation-Distribution should be used with other fundamental and technical factors to determine investment decisions.

52-Week High Low shows high and low stock price in last 52 weeks. NH or NL in place of price means new high or new low occurred that day. 52-week high is boldfaced if its closing price is within 10% of a new high in price.

Vol % Chg shows each company's trading volume for that day in terms of its % change above or below its average daily volume for the last 50 trading days. This news reveals if a stock's price change occurs on an abnormal volume increase or decrease. Plus 150 means a stock traded 150% more than normal. The number is boldfaced when it is +50% or more on +$10 stocks. **Vol 100s** gives the total shares traded for the day in hundreds (2 zeros omitted).

Grp Str (Industry Group Relative Strength) is shown Monday and compares group's stock-price performance over the past 6 months vs. 196 other groups. A=top 20%, B=top 40%, etc. with E=bottom 20%. Tuesday: **PE ratios** are shown; Wednesday: **Sponsorship Rank** averages the 3-year performance rank of all mutual funds owning the stock (A=best, E=worst); Thursday: **% Owned by Management** shows % of shares outstanding owned by management; Friday: **Dividend % yield** is shown every Friday. Letters at far right: (k) earnings due in next 4 weeks, (-) earnings report in today's *Investor's Business Daily,* (o) stock has listed options, (b) company is bankrupt, in receivership or reorganization. **Other letters:** (n) new issue; (l) liquidating; (un) units; (wi) when-issued; (wt) warrants; (x) ex-dividend, ex-rights or ex-distribution; (y) odd lots (actual number of shares) and ex-dividend or ex-rights; (z) odd lots (actual shares); (g) dividend or earnings in Canadian money; (e) dividends paid or declared in previous 12 months; (h) not subject to NASDAQ requirements. Tables include regional exchanges and institutional system trades.

FIGURE 15-11 *(continued)*

This has not yet been empirically investigated. Random-walk theorists, however, feel that they have gathered sufficient evidence to relegate technical analysis to a position comparable to reading a crystal ball.

QUESTIONS AND PROBLEMS

1. Explain the relationship of a basic law of economics and an underlying premise of technical analysis.

2. Dr. Knowitall of the psychology department at a large midwestern university claims he has a sound theoretical argument in favor of technical analysis. What do you think that argument is?

3. Assume that you are a statistician. Like every good statistician, you are extremely concerned with good sampling techniques. Comment on technical analysis from this point of view.

4. You are the top technical analyst in your firm, and your boss has turned to you for an answer to a difficult question. He wants to know which single indicator you think is the best and why you think so. What is your answer?

5. What is the alleged purpose of technical market indicators? Why is this important?

6. What is meant by breadth of the market? How is it measured?

7. Explain (a) the logic behind, and (b) the method of measuring, either *Barron's* confidence indicator or odd-lot trading.

8. If short selling indicates that the investor expects the price of the shorted security to decline, why does the technician become optimistic as the short interest goes up?

9. What is the basic premise of analysts who use the odd-lot trading index?

10. If a stock sells for 60 and moves in the following patterns over a ten-day period—60, 60¼, 60¾, 60½, 61, 61½, 63, 62¼, 61¾, 60½—how many X's would be plotted if the investor used point-and-figure charting with a one-point chart and a three-point reversal spread?

11. If the investor used bar charting and the data in Question 10, how many bars would there be in his chart? Why is this different from the number of X's in Question 10?

12. Compare and contrast bar charting and point-and-figure charting.

13. What general price-volume relationships do researchers use to predict the trend of the market?

14. What implications, if any, do Levy's findings using the relative-strength criterion have for a buy-and-hold strategy?

15. Suppose that the stock market has been declining. A technician is looking for signs of an upturn in the market. What sorts of reading should he or she be expecting from
   a. breadth of the market,
   b. volume of trading,
   c. odd-lot trading, and
   d. short selling?

16. Why do technicians feel that past price movements are useful in predicting future price movements?

17. Collect data on the DJIA for the past four months. Do you see any type of trend in the daily data? Why?

C A S E
∎

McDonald's Corp.

Ted Walsh has been intrigued for some time about technical analysis as an investment tool. During his graduate work as an MBA student at the University of Michigan he had been puzzled about the perennial attacks launched by efficient markets advocates against technical analysis in its many forms. Ted believes that stock prices move in trends, and that a trading system that keeps that in mind can be developed that can earn attractive returns.

Ted began to search for a technical tool that would require less judgment on the part of the user—one that had mechanical trigger points that would provide buy and sell signals. He became intrigued with a trading technique known as a filter rule. The basic procedure is as follows:

Use the first available price as a base price. If the price rises (falls) from the base price by the size of the filter or more, buy and hold (sell short) the stock until the price falls (rises) at least by the size of the filter from a subsequent high (low). When this price decrease (increase) occurs, liquidate the long position (cover the short position) and sell the stock short (assume a long position) until the price rises(falls) from a subsequent low (high) by the size of the filter or more. Repeat the process as often as indicated by the movement of the stock.

The following sequence of prices illustrated to him how to determine buy and sell points using a 1 percent filter rule: 13.38, 13.00, 13.75, 13.50, 14.38, 14.50, 14.75, 14.63, 14.75, 15.38, 15.88, 16.13, 15.88. Using the 1 percent filter he would short at the first 13.00 because the stock fell more than 1 percent from the base price of 13.38. He would cover the short and go long at 13.75 (stock moves up more than 1 percent). He liquidates his long position and goes short next at 15.88 (following 16.13) because after the 13.63 price the stock hits a subsequent high of 16.13, before falling 1 percent or more (to 15.88).

Ted was fortunate enough to have his college roommate, a registered representative with E. F. Hutton, get him stock price information for McDonald's Corp. (See Exhibit 1.)

EXHIBIT 1

Closing Bid Prices McDonald's Corp. Common Stock
September 1, 1984–August 15, 1985 (in Eighths of a Dollar)

	1984				1985							
	SEPT.	OCT.	NOV.	DEC.	JAN.	FEB.	MAR.	APR.	MAY	JUN.	JUL.	AUG.
1		49.3	52.7		HOL	57.4	61.7	59.5	59.3		69.3	66
2		49	53		51.1			59	59.5		69.7	66.1
3	HOL	49.1		51	51.6			58.2	60.1	67.1	69.4	
4	50.7	49.7		50.7	52	59.4	60.7	58.3		68.5	HOL	
5	51.3	49.5	52.7	50.3		60	61.5	HOL		68.6	69.5	66
6	50.7		53.5	50.6		59.1	60.6		60.4	69.5		65
7	50.3		53.3	50.6	52.5	60	58.5		61	69		65
8		49.6	52.6		53	61	59	59.1	60.6		69	65.3
9		49.5	52.1		54.1			59.1	61.7		68.3	65.2
10	50.1	49.6		50.6	54			60.2	62.5	68.7	67.6	
11	50	50.3		51.2	54.5	60.4	58.6	59.7		68.2	67.6	
12	50.1	51.6	52.6	52.4		59.6	59	59.7		67.1	67.3	65.1
13	51		52.1	52		60.7	58.4		63.2	66.1		65
14	51.3		51.7	52.2	55.4	61.2	59.1		63.7	66.7		64.4
15		53.2	51.6		55.4	60.1	59.6	60	63.5		67.6	64.4
16		53.3	51		55.6			59.7	63.7		67.6	64.3
17	51.3	53.6		52.1	54.6			60.2	64	67.3	68.2	
18	51	54.4		54.2	55.2	HOL	59.1	61		69.2	68	
19	51.4	55	50.5	53.3		59.2	60	60.7		68.6	68.5	
20	50.4		50.6	53		59.4	59.6		64.4	68.1		
21	50.4		51.2	53.2	56.2	59.3	59.5		64.4	67.3		
22		55	HOL		56.1	59.4	58.6	60.7	65.2		68.5	
23		53	53.3		57.4			61.1	66		67.4	
24	49.5	54.1		53.6	57.7		59.2	61.5	67	66.7	66.6	
25	49.3	54		HOL	58.1	59.7	59.2	63.2		66.7	65.4	
26	49.6	53.1	52.5	53.3		60.2	59.2	62.4		67.3	65.7	
27	49.6		53.2	53.3		59.5	60		HOL	67.5		
28	50.3		52.6	53.2	58.5	60.2	59.6		66.5	68.4		
29												
30		52.4	51.4		58.3			60.6	66.6		64.6	
31		52.4		51.5	57.1				66.6		65.6	

HOL—Holiday.
Blank spaces—Sat., Sun., and/or month-Ends.

QUESTIONS

1. Using a filter of 2 percent, calculate the dollar percentage gain or loss per transaction (ignore transaction costs). Estimate the mean percentage gain for the filter.

2. Assume a 2 percent commission cost to buy or sell shares. What is the mean percentage gain for the 2 percent filter, adjusted for transaction costs?

3. Is the 2 percent filter a profitable mechanical trading rule? Explain.

4. What are the advantages and disadvantages of the filter-rule approach?

REFERENCES

FOLGER, H., M. GRANITO, and L. SMITH. "A Theoretical Analysis of Real Estate Returns." *Journal of Finance* (July 1985), pp. 711–21.

KAPPLIN, S., and A. SCHWARTZ. "Investing in Real Estate Limited Partnerships." *American Association of Individual Investors Journal* (September 1986), pp. 8–12.

MARTIN, J., and J. PETTY. "An Analysis of the Performance of Publicly Traded Venture Capital Companies." *Journal of Financial and Quantitative Analysis* (September 1983), pp. 401–10.

PHALON, R. "Getting a Little Crowded: The Venture Capital Businesses Booming—A Mixed Blessing for Venture Capitalists." *Forbes* (February 15, 1982), pp. 51–52.

CHAPTER 16

EFFICIENT-MARKET THEORY

The primary aim of the text thus far has been to systematize the vast amount of publicly available information, both objective fact and subjective feeling, into a valuation framework so that one can reach a buy, sell, or hold decision. The methodology employed up until the preceding chapter is generally categorized as *fundamental analysis,* or *fundamentalism.* The more mystical approach discussed in Chapter 15 is called *technical analysis.* Our objective in this chapter is to review briefly these two approaches and then present yet a third theory to stock price behavior, one that had its origin in a voluminous body of literature generally lumped together under the label of the random-walk theory. In the process, we will explore this theory and explain the various statistical measures that have been employed to test its appropriateness or inappropriateness. Finally, we will discuss implications of random walk for both fundamental and technical analysis.

FUNDAMENTAL AND TECHNICAL ANALYSIS

Recall that in the fundamental approach, the security analyst or prospective investor is primarily interested in analyzing factors such as economic influences, industry factors, and pertinent company information such as product demand, earnings, dividends, and management, in order to calculate an intrinsic value for the firm's securities. He reaches an investment decision by comparing this value with the current market price of the security.

Technical analysts, or chartists, as they are commonly called, believe that they can discern patterns in price or volume movements, and that by observing and studying the past behavior patterns of given stocks, they can use this accumulated historical information to predict the future price movements in the security. Technical analysis, as we observed in the preceding chapter, comprises many different

subjective approaches, but all have one thing in common—a belief that these past movements are very useful in predicting future movements.[1]

In essence, the technician says that it is somewhat an exercise in futility to evaluate accurately a myriad of detailed information as the fundamentalist attempts to do. He chooses not to engage in this type of activity, but rather to allow others to do it for him. Thus, after numerous analysts and investors evaluate this mountain of knowledge, their undoubtedly diverse opinions will be manifested in the price and volume activity of the shares in question. As this occurs, the technician acts solely on the basis of that price and volume activity, without cluttering his mind with all the detail that he feels is superfluous to his analysis. He also believes that his price and volume analysis incorporates one factor that is not explicitly incorporated in the fundamentalist approach—namely, the psychology of the market.

Random Walk

Can a series of historical stock prices or rates of return be an aid in predicting future stock prices or rates of return? This, in effect, is the question posed by the random-walk theory.

The empirical evidence in the random-walk literature existed before the theory was established. That is to say, empirical results were discovered first, and then an attempt was made to develop a theory that could possibly explain the results. After these initial occurrences, more results and more theory were uncovered. This has led then to a diversity of theories, which are generically called the random-walk theory.

A good deal of confusion resulted from the diversity of the literature; and only recently has there been some clarification of the proliferation of empirical results and theories.[2] Our purpose here is to discuss briefly the substantive differences among these theories; however, in the rest of this chapter, we will not be concerned with these distinctions, but rather we will deal with an impressionistic stereotype that will represent the substance if not the detail of this random-walk model, perhaps more properly called the efficient-market model.

---

[1]For an excellent treatment of the bar-chart and the point-and-figure approaches to technical analysis, see Daniel Seligman's two excellent and somewhat cynical articles, "Playing the Market with Charts," *Fortune* 65, no. 2 (February 1962), p. 118; and "The Mystique of Point-and-Figure," *Fortune* 65, no. 3 (March 1962), p. 113.

[2]Much of the material in this section was adapted from Eugene F. Fama, "Efficient Capital Markets: A Review of Theory and Empirical Work," *Journal of Finance* 25, no. 2 (May 1970), pp. 383–417; and Eugene F. Fama, "Random Walks in Stock Market Prices," *Financial Analysts Journal* 21, no. 5 (September–October 1965), pp. 55–59.

THE EFFICIENT-MARKET HYPOTHESIS

It is advantageous to view the random-walk model or hypothesis as a special case of the more general efficient-market model or hypothesis. In fact, one might more readily understand the distinctions and variations of the various forms of the more general efficient-market hypothesis by viewing this hypothesis and its variations as lying on a continuum, with the so-called random-walk model at one end. In the following paragraphs we will briefly consider the three generally discussed forms of the efficient-market hypothesis—namely, the weak form, the semistrong form, and the strong form.

Weak Form

The *weak form* says that the current prices of stocks already fully reflect all the information that is contained in the historical sequence of prices. Therefore, there is no benefit—as far as forecasting the future is concerned—in examining the historical sequence of prices. This weak form of the efficient market hypothesis is popularly known as the random-walk theory. Clearly, if this weak form of the efficient market hypothesis is true, it is a *direct* repudiation of technical analysis. If there is no value in studying past prices and past price changes, there is no value in technical analysis. As we saw in the preceding chapter, however, technicians place considerable reliance on the charts of historical prices that they maintain even though the efficient-market hypothesis refutes this practice.

   In later sections of this chapter we will analyze statistical investigations of this weak form of the efficient-market hypothesis.

Semistrong Form

The *semistrong form* of the efficient-market hypothesis says that current prices of stocks not only reflect all informational content of historical prices but also reflect all *publicly available knowledge* about the corporations being studied. Furthermore, the semistrong form says that efforts by analysts and investors to acquire and analyze public information will not yield consistently superior returns to the analyst. Examples of the type of public information that will not be of value on a consistent basis to the analyst are corporate reports, corporate announcements, information relating to corporate dividend policy, forthcoming stock splits, and so forth.

   In effect, the semistrong form of the efficient market hypothesis maintains that as soon as information becomes publicly available, it is absorbed and reflected in stock prices. Even if this adjustment is not the correct one immediately, it will in a very short time be properly analyzed by the market. Thus the analyst would have great difficulty trying to profit using fundamental analysis. Furthermore, even while the correct adjustment is taking place, the analyst cannot obtain consistent superior returns. Why? Because the incorrect adjustments will not take place con-

sistently; that is, sometimes the adjustments will be overadjustments and sometimes they will be underadjustments. Therefore, an analyst will not be able to develop a trading strategy based on these quick adjustments to new publicly available information.

Tests of the semistrong form of the efficient-market hypothesis have tended (but not unanimously) to provide support for the hypothesis.[3] More on these tests will be discussed in a later section of the chapter.

Strong Form

To review briefly, we have seen that the weak form of the efficient-market hypothesis maintains that past prices and past price changes cannot be used to forecast future price changes and future prices. In the paragraphs that follow we will review many of the tests that have been conducted to test the *weak* form of the efficient-market hypothesis. We have examined the semistrong form of the efficient-market hypothesis, which says that publicly available information cannot be used to earn consistently superior investment returns. Several studies that tend to support the semistrong theory of the efficient-market hypothesis were cited. Finally, the *strong form* of the efficient-market hypothesis maintains that not only is publicly available information useless to the investor or analyst but *all information* is useless. Specifically, no information that is available, be it public or "inside," can be used to earn consistently superior investment returns.

The semistrong form of the efficient-market hypothesis could only be tested indirectly—namely, by testing what happened to prices on days surrounding announcements, of various types, such as earnings announcements, dividend announcements, and stock-split announcements. To test the strong form of efficient-market hypothesis, even more indirect methods must be used. For the strong form, as has already been mentioned, says that no type of information is useful. This implies that not even security analysts and portfolio managers who have access to information more quickly than the general investing public are able to use this information to earn superior returns. Therefore, many of the tests of the strong form of the efficient market hypothesis deal with tests of *mutual-fund performance*. Shortly, we will review some of the findings of these tests of mutual-fund performance and in Chapter 20 we will examine them in greater depth.

Tests of the trading of specialists on the floor of the stock exchanges and tests of the profitability of insider trading suggest that the possibility of excess profits ex-

---

[3]See, for example, Eugene F. Fama *et al.,* "The Adjustment of Stock Prices to New Information," *International Economic Review* 10, no. 1 (February 1969), pp. 1–21. Also see Myron S. Scholes, "The Market for Securities: Substitution vs. Price Pressure and the Effects of Information on Share Prices," *Journal of Business* 45, no. 2 (April 1972), pp. 179–211; Ray Ball and Phillip Brown, "An Empirical Evaluation of Accounting Income Numbers," *Journal of Accounting Research* 6 (Autumn 1968), pp. 159–78; and Ronald J. Jordan, "An Empirical Investigation of the Adjustment of Stock Prices to New Quarterly Earnings Information," *Journal of Financial and Quantitative Analysis* 7, no. 4 (September 1973), pp. 609–20.

ists for these two very special groups of investors who can use their special information to earn profits in excess of normal returns.[4]

The strict form of the efficient-market hypothesis states that two conditions are met: first, that successive price changes or changes in return are independent; and second, that these successive price changes or return changes are identically distributed—that is, these distributions will repeat themselves over time. In a practical sense, this seems to imply that in a random-walk world, stock prices will at any time fully reflect all publicly available information, and furthermore, that when new information becomes available, stock prices will instantaneously adjust to reflect it. The reader will note that the random-walk theorist is not interested in price or return levels, but rather in the changes between successive levels.[5]

The more general efficient-market model, when interpreted loosely, acknowledges that the markets may have some imperfections, such as transactions costs, information costs, and delays in getting pertinent information to all market participants; but it states that these potential sources of market inefficiency do not exist to such a degree that it is possible to develop trading systems whose expected profits or returns will be in excess of expected normal, equilibrium returns or profits. Generally, we define *equilibrium profits* as those that can be earned by following a simple buy-and-hold strategy rather than a more complex, mechanical system.[6] Thus, we see that the random-walk model represents a special, restrictive case of the efficient-market model.

The Efficient-Market Hypothesis and Mutual-Fund Performance

It has often been said that large investors such as mutual funds perform better in the market than the small investor does because they have access to better information. Therefore, it would be interesting to observe if mutual funds earned above-average returns, where these are defined as returns in excess of those that can be earned by a simple buy-and-hold strategy. The results of such an investigation would have interesting implications for the efficient-market hypothesis.

As we shall see in Chapter 20, researchers have found that mutual funds do not seem to be able to earn greater net returns (after sales expenses) than those

---

[4]See James H. Lorie and Victor Niederhoffer, "Predictive and Statistical Properties of Insider Trading," *Journal of Law and Economics* 11 (1968), pp. 35–53; and Scholes, "Market for Securities." It should be emphasized that these two examples of market inefficiencies represent very minor inefficiencies when compared with the market as a whole. See also Jeffrey Jaffe, "Special Information and Insider Trading," *Journal of Business* 47, no. 3 (July 1974), pp. 410–28; Joseph E. Finnerty, "Insiders and Market Efficiency," *Journal of Finance* 31, no. 4 (September 1976), pp. 1141–48; and Joseph E. Finnerty, "Insiders Activity and Inside Information: A Multivariate Analysis," *Journal of Financial and Quantitative Analysis* 11, no. 2 (June 1976), pp. 205–15.

[5]Often one will read in the random-walk literature of percentage changes in the prices or returns themselves.

[6]We will defer our discussion of such mechanical systems to a later section of this chapter.

that can be earned by investing randomly in a large group of securities and holding them. Furthermore, these studies indicate, mutual funds are not even able to earn *gross* returns (before sales expenses) superior to those of the naive buy-and-hold strategy. These results occur not only because of the difficulty in applying fundamental analysis in a consistently superior manner to a large number of securities in an efficient market but also because of portfolio overdiversification and its attendant problems—two of which are high bookkeeping and administrative costs to monitor the investments, and purchase of securities with less favorable risk-return characteristics. Therefore, it would seem that the mutual-fund studies lend some credence to the efficient-market hypothesis.

Empirical Tests of the Weak Form

Over the years an impressive literature has been developed describing empirical tests of random walk.[7] This research has been aimed at testing whether successive or lagged price changes are independent. In this section we will review briefly some of the major categories of statistical techniques that have been employed in this research, and we will summarize their major conclusions. These techniques generally fall into two categories: those that test for trends in stock prices and thus infer whether profitable trading systems could be developed and those that test such mechanical systems directly. Although certain of these studies were conducted many years ago, they are the basis upon which research on the efficient-market theory has been based, and are included here to provide the necessary conceptual basis for the theory and its evolution.

SIMULATION TESTS

Note Figures 16–1 and 16–2. These graphs were produced several years ago as part of an interesting experiment performed by Harry Roberts. The essence of this experiment was to examine the appearance of the actual level of the Dow Jones index expressed both in levels and in terms of weekly changes, and to compare these graphs with a simulated set of graphs.[8] A series of price changes was generated from random-number tables and then these changes were converted to graphs (on Figures 16–1, 16–2, and 16–3) depicting levels of the simulated Dow Jones index.

The reader will note the similarity between parts (a) and (b) of Figure 16–1, and also the similarity between Figures 16–2 and 16–3. Both figures reveal the "head-and-shoulders" pattern that is often referred to in the chartist literature. Because these very similar patterns were observed, between the actual and the simulated series, the inference is that the actual results may well be the result of random stock price movements.

[7]For an excellent collection of many of the early random-walk studies, see Paul H. Cootner, ed., *The Random Character of Stock Market Prices* (Cambridge, Mass.: MIT Press, 1967).

[8]Harry Roberts, "Stock Market Patterns and Financial Analysis: Methodological Suggestions," *Journal of Finance* (March 1959), pp. 1–10.

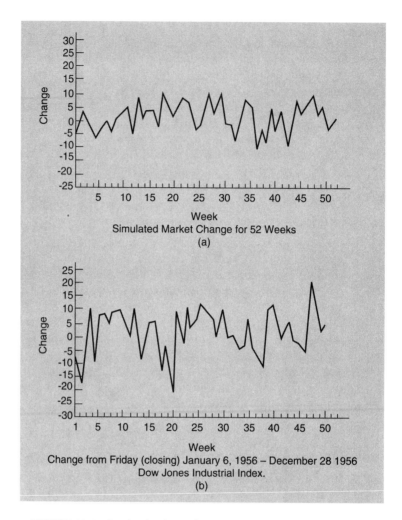

FIGURE 16–1   Simulated and Actual Market Changes (*Source:* Harry Roberts, "Stock Market Patterns and Financial Analysis: Methodological Suggestions," *Journal of Finance* (March 1959). Reprinted from *An Introduction to Risk and Return from Common Stocks* by Richard A. Brealey by permission of the MIT Press, Cambridge, Mass. Copyright 1969 by the Massachusetts Institute of Technology.)

SERIAL-CORRELATION TESTS

Because the random-walk theory is interested in testing for independence between successive price changes, correlation tests are particularly appropriate. These tests check to determine if price changes or proportionate price changes in some future period are related. For example, we are interested in seeing if price changes in a period $t + 1$ are correlated to price changes in the preceding period, period t. If in fact price changes are correlated, points plotted on a graph will tend to lie along a straight line. In Figure 16–4 we see such a relationship. Figure 16–4(a) implies that,

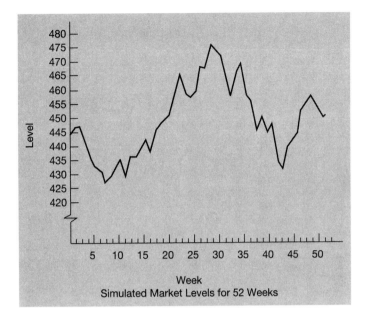

FIGURE 16–2   Simulated Market Levels

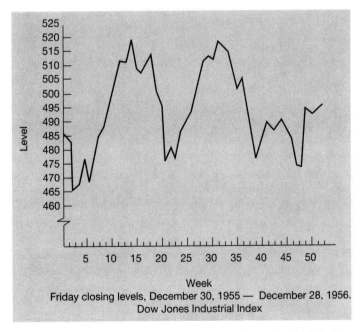

FIGURE 16–3   Actual Market Levels (*Source:* Harry Roberts, "Stock Market Patterns and Financial Analysis: Methodological Suggestions," *Journal of Finance* (March 1959). Reprinted from *An Introduction to Risk and Return from Common Stocks* by Richard A. Brealey by permission of the MIT Press, Cambridge, Mass. Copyright 1969 by the Massachusetts Institute of Technology.)

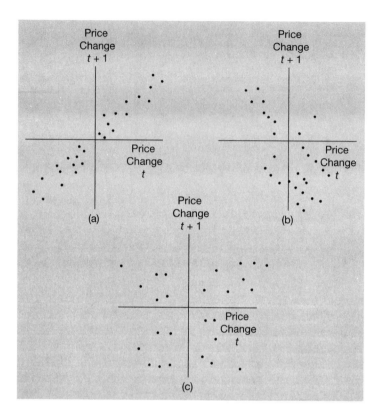

FIGURE 16–4   Scatter Diagrams to "Observe" Correlation

on average, a price rise in period *t* is followed by a price rise in period *t* + 1; Figure 16–4(b) implies that, on average, a price decline in period *t* + 1 follows a price rise in period *t;* the former, then, implies a correlation coefficient of close to + 1, the latter a correlation coefficient of close to −1. Figure 16–4(c), in which there does not appear any linear relationship in the scatter diagram, implies close to a zero correlation coefficient. In other words, the correlation coefficient can take on a value ranging from −1 to +1; a positive number indicates a direct correlation, a negative value implies an inverse relationship, and a value close to zero implies no relationship.

Table 16–1 reports the findings of one such test of serial correlation. As can be seen in this table, no large departure from zero was found in these particular serial and lagged serial correlation coefficients in daily prices of the Dow Jones stocks. Similar results have been found using series of commodity prices, other individual stocks' prices, and price indexes.

RUNS TESTS

There is a potential problem, however, when one uses a correlation coefficient to evaluate the possibility of independence in a particular series. This problem arises because correlation coefficients can be dominated by extreme values. That is, an

TABLE 16-1

Correlation Coefficients between Daily Price Changes and
Lagged Price Changes for Each of the Dow Jones Stocks

STOCKS	LAG (DAYS)									
	1	2	3	4	5	6	7	8	9	10
Allied Ch	.02	−.04	.01	−.00	.03	.00	−.02	−.03	−.02	−.01
Alcoa	.12	.04	−.01	.02	−.02	.01	.02	.01	−.00	−.03
Am Can	−.09	−.02	.03	−.07	−.02	−.01	.02	.03	−.05	−.04
Am T&T	−.04	−.10	.00	.03	.01	−.01	.00	.03	−.01	.01
Am Tob	.11	−.11	−.06	−.07	.01	−.01	.01	.05	.04	.04
Anacond	.07	−.06	−.05	−.00	.00	−.04	.01	.02	−.01	−.06
Beth Stl	.01	−.07	.01	.02	−.05	−.10	−.01	.00	−.00	−.02
Chrysler	.01	−.07	−.02	−.01	−.02	.01	.04	.06	−.04	.02
duPont	.01	−.03	.06	.03	−.00	−.05	.02	.01	−.03	.00
E Kodak	.03	.01	−.03	.01	−.02	.01	.01	.01	.01	.00
Gen Elect	.01	−.04	−.02	.03	−.00	.00	−.01	.01	−.00	.01
Gen Fds	.06	−.00	.05	.00	−.02	−.05	−.01	−.01	−.02	−.02
Gen Mot	−.00	−.06	−.04	−.01	−.04	.01	.02	.01	−.02	.01
Goodyr	−.12	.02	−.04	.04	−.00	−.00	.04	.01	−.02	.01
Int Harv	−.02	−.03	−.03	.04	−.05	−.02	−.00	.00	−.05	−.02
Int Nick	.10	−.03	−.02	.02	.03	.06	−.04	−.01	−.02	.03
Int Pap	.05	−.01	−.06	.05	.05	−.00	−.03	−.02	−.00	−.02
Johns Man	.01	−.04	−.03	−.02	−.03	−.08	.04	.02	−.04	.03
Owens Ill	−.02	−.08	−.05	.07	.09	−.04	.01	−.04	.07	−.04
Proct G	.10	−.01	−.01	.01	−.02	.02	.01	−.01	−.02	−.02
Sears Ro	.10	.03	.03	.03	.01	−.05	−.01	−.01	−.01	−.01
St Oil Cal	.03	−.03	−.05	−.03	−.05	−.03	−.01	.07	−.05	−.04
St Oil NJ	.01	−.12	.02	.01	−.05	−.02	−.02	−.03	−.07	.08
Swift Co	−.00	−.02	−.01	.01	.06	.01	−.04	.01	.01	.00
Texaco	.09	−.05	−.02	−.02	−.02	−.01	.03	.03	−.01	.01
Un Carbide	.11	−.01	.04	.05	−.04	−.03	.00	−.01	−.05	−.04
Unit Aire	.01	−.03	−.02	−.05	−.07	−.05	.05	.04	.02	−.02
US Steel	.04	−.07	.01	.01	−.01	−.02	.04	.04	−.02	−.04
Westg El	−.03	−.02	−.04	−.00	.00	−.05	−.02	.01	−.01	.01
Woolworth	.03	−.02	.02	.01	.01	−.04	−.01	.00	−.09	−.01
Averages	.03	−.04	−.01	.01	−.01	−.02	.00	.01	−.02	−.01

Source: R. A. Brealey, *An Introduction to Risk and Return from Common Stock* (Cambridge, Mass.: MIT Press, 1969), p. 13, adapted from Eugene F. Fama, "The Behavior of Stock Market Prices," *Journal of Business* 38 (January 1965), pp. 34–105.

extremely large or extremely low value or two in the series can unduly influence the results of the calculation used to determine the correlation coefficient. To overcome this possible shortcoming, some researchers have employed the runs test.

Runs tests ignore the absolute values of the numbers in the series and observe only their sign. The researchers then merely count the number of runs—consecutive sequences of signs—in the same direction. For example, the se-

quence $- - - + 0 +$ has four runs. Next, the actual number of runs observed is compared with the number that are to be expected from a series of randomly generated price changes. It has been found that when this is done, no significant differences are observed. These results further strengthen the random-walk hypothesis.

FILTER TESTS

The empirical tests of random walk we have examined thus far have been aimed at testing directly whether successive price or return changes are in fact independent—or in statistical terms, that their serial-correlation coefficients are not statistically significantly different from zero. If this is so, then an inference can be made that stock price changes appear to be random, and therefore developing successful mechanical trading systems would be extremely difficult. Now we will discuss briefly another set of tests that examine the random-walk hypothesis from a different, but more direct, approach. Categorized as filter tests, they have been developed as direct tests of specific mechanical trading strategies. In other words, no inferences about such strategies need be made, for the approach is to examine directly the validity of specific systems.

One such test is based on the premise that once a movement in price has surpassed a given percentage movement, the security's price will continue to move in the same direction. Thus the following rule, which is similar to the famous Dow Theory:

> If the daily closing price of a security moves up at least X%, buy the security until its price moves down at least X% from a subsequent high, at which time simultaneously sell and go short. The short position should be maintained until the price rises at least X% above a subsequent low, at which time cover and buy.[9]

As the reader has undoubtedly observed, the selection of a high filter will cut down his number of transactions and will lead to fewer false starts or signals, but it will also decrease his potential profit because he would have missed the initial portion of the move. Conversely, the selection of a smaller filter will ensure his sharing in the great bulk of the security's price movement, but he will have the disadvantage of performing many transactions, with their accompanying high costs, as well as often operating on false signals.

As we see in Table 16–2, only when the filter was at its smallest did this mechanical procedure outperform a simple buy-and-hold strategy, and even then, only before transactions costs were considered. Similar tests of various other trad-

[9]R. A. Brealey, *An Introduction to Risk and Return from Common Stocks* (Cambridge, Mass.: MIT Press, 1969), p. 25, adapted from Eugene F. Fama and Marshal E. Blume, "Filter Rules and Stock Market Trading," *Journal of Business* 39 (January 1966), pp. 226–41.

TABLE 16–2

Average Annual Rates of Return per Stock

VALUE OF X (%)	RETURN WITH TRADING STRATEGY (%)	RETURN WITH BUY-AND-HOLD STRATEGY (%)	TOTAL TRANSACTIONS WITH TRADING STRATEGY	RETURN WITH TRADING STRATEGY, AFTER COMMISSIONS (%)
0.5	11.5	10.4	12,514	−103.6
1.0	5.5	10.3	8,660	−74.9
2.0	0.2	10.3	4,784	−45.2
3.0	−1.7	10.3	2,994	−30.5
4.0	0.1	10.1	2,013	−19.5
5.0	−1.9	10.0	1,484	−16.6
6.0	1.3	9.7	1,071	−9.4
7.0	0.8	9.6	828	−7.4
8.0	1.7	9.6	653	−5.0
9.0	1.9	9.6	539	−3.6
10.0	3.0	9.3	435	−1.4
12.0	5.3	9.4	289	2.3
14.0	3.9	10.3	224	1.4
16.0	4.2	10.3	172	2.3
18.0	3.6	10.0	139	2.0
20.0	4.3	9.8	110	3.0

Source: R. A. Brealey, *An Introduction to Risk and Return from Common Stocks* (Cambridge, Mass.: MIT Press, 1969), adapted from Eugene F. Fama and Marshal E. Blume, "Filter Rules and Stock Market Trading," *Journal of Business* 39 (January 1966), pp. 226–41.

ing systems have yielded similar results, thus giving additional validity to the random-walk theory.

DISTRIBUTION PATTERNS

It is a rule of statistics that the sum or the distribution of random occurrences will conform to a normal distribution. Thus, if proportionate price changes are randomly generated events, then their distribution should be approximately normal. When such a test was conducted, only very slight deviations from normality were noted.[10] See Figure 16–5 for verification of this point. The differences, as can be seen, are, first, the appearance of a greater than normal number of extremely large and extremely small values; and second, a more peaked distribution—that is, a deficiency of medium-sized changes. This type of distribution is a member of the stable Paretian family. Generally, the small differences between these two distributions are overlooked in empirical work.

---

[10]Eugene F. Fama, "The Behavior of Stock Market Prices," *Journal of Business* 38 (January 1965), pp. 34–105.

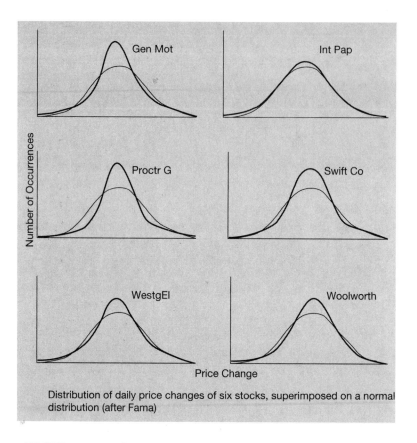

Distribution of daily price changes of six stocks, superimposed on a normal distribution (after Fama)

FIGURE 16–5   Distributions of Daily Price Changes of Six Stocks, Superimposed on a Normal Distribution (*Source:* Eugene F. Fama, "The Behavior of Stock Market Prices," *Journal of Business* 38 (January 1965), pp. 34–105. Reprinted from *An Introduction to Risk and Return from Common Stocks* by Richard A. Brealey, by permission of the MIT Press, Cambridge, Mass. Copyright 1969 by the Massachusetts Institute of Technology.)

REVERSAL EFFECT

Several recent studies report the tendency for poorly performing stocks of one time period (a week or month) to perform well in the subsequent time periods and for the best-performing stocks of one period to perform very poorly in the next period.[11] If this is true it should lead to a technical-based trading strategy, which is very simple to implement. Buy shares of the stocks that have recently done poorly and sell shares in those that have done well. This has been dubbed the *reversal effect*. Such an effect, if it persists after many investors have sought to exploit it, would contradict the efficient-market theory.

[11]Bruce Lehman, "Fads, Martingales and Market Efficiency," *Quarterly Journal of Economics* (February 1990) pp 1–28 and N. Jegadeesh, "Evidence of Predictable Behavior of Security Returns." *Journal of Finance* (September 1990), pp. 881–98.

EMPIRICAL TESTS OF THE SEMISTRONG FORM

As has already been stated, the semistrong form says that current stock prices will instantaneously reflect all publicly available information. The tests that will be summarized briefly in this section test whether in fact all publicly available information and news announcements, such as quarterly earnings reports, changes in accounting information, stocks splits, stock dividends, and the like, are quickly and adequately reflected in stock prices. Furthermore, these tests attempt to analyze if an analyst using such data when they become available to him can successfully use this information to obtain superior investment results. Fama, Fisher, Jensen, and Roll made a major contribution with their study of the semistrong-form hypothesis.[12] They tested the speed of the market's reaction to a firm's announcement of a stock split and the accompanying information with respect to a change in dividend policy. The authors concluded that the market was efficient with respect to its reaction to information on the stock split and also was efficient with respect to reacting to the informational content of stock splits vis-à-vis changes in dividend policy.

Ball and Brown conducted another test in this area by analyzing the stock market's ability to absorb the informational content of reported annual earnings per share information. In their study the authors examined stock price movements of companies that experienced "good" earnings reports as opposed to the stock price movements of companies that experienced "bad" earnings reports. A "good" earnings report was a reported earnings per share figure that was higher than the previously forecast earnings per share, and conversely a "bad" earnings report was a reported earnings per share figure that was lower than had been forecast previously. They found that those companies with "good" earnings reports experienced price increases in their stock and those with "bad" earnings reports experienced stock price declines. The interesting result was that about 85 percent of the informational content of the annual earnings announcement was reflected in stock price movements prior to the release of the actual annual earnings figure.[13]

Joy, Litzenberger, and McEnally conducted another stock price-earnings report test in this area. In their study the authors tested the impact of quarterly earnings announcements on the stock price adjustment mechanism. Some of their results somewhat contradicted the semistrong form of the efficient-market hypothesis. In some of their subtests, the authors found that favorable information contained in published quarterly earnings reports was not instantaneously reflected in stock prices.[14]

[12]Eugene F. Fama *et al.,* "The Adjustment of Stock Prices to New Information," *International Economic Review* 10, no. 1 (February 1969), pp. 1–21. A later study in this area finding strong support for the efficient-market theory was Frank K. Reilly and Eugene F. Drzycimski "Short-Run Profits from Stock Splits," *Financial Management* 10, no. 3 (Summer 1981), pp. 64–74.

[13]Ray Ball and Philip Brown, "An Empirical Evaluation of Accounting Income Numbers," *Journal of Accounting Research* 6 (Autumn 1968), pp. 159–78.

[14]O. Maurice Joy *et al.,* "The Adjustment of Stock Prices to Announcements of Unanticipated Changes in Quarterly Earnings," *Journal of Accounting Research* 15 (Autumn 1977), pp. 207–25.

Some students of the stock market believe that purchasing stock of corporations when they initially go public can provide excessive returns. This feeling is based on the hypothesis that underwriters tend to underprice securities when pricing an initial public offering (IPO) because of the underwriting risk they assume. The feeling is that if the issue is priced very conservatively, they will have no trouble in selling the issue out and recovering their investment. This has led some authors to test whether excessive returns excessive returns could be earned by purchasing a new issue at the offering price. An alternative approach to testing of the semistrong form of the efficient market hypothesis would be to test the returns of an investor who acquired the IPO shortly after it was initially offered and then held the security for various periods. The tests of purchasing new issues at the offering price showed that excessive returns could be earned if purchases were made at the offering price because of underpricing of the issues by the underwriters. However, the markets due tend to be efficient because this underpricing is compensated for by the market almost immediately after the new issue begins trading. The returns from purchasing after the offering appear to compensate the investor only for the additional risks inherent in such new issues. Therefore, these results generally support the semistrong form of the efficient-markets hypothesis.[15]

Another test that we will review of the semistrong form was a study conducted by Basu.[16] In his study, Basu tested for the informational content of the

[15]Roger G. Ibbotson and Jeffrey Jaffe, "Hot Issues Markets," *Journal of Finance* 30, no. 4 (September 1975), pp. 1027–42; Stanley Block and Marjorie Stanley, "The Financial Characteristics and Price Movement Patterns of Companies Approaching the Unseasoned Securities Market in the Late 1970s," *Financial Management* 9, no. 4 (Winter 1980), pp. 30–36; Roger G. Ibbotson, "Price Performance of Common Stock New Issues," *Journal of Financial Economics* 2, no. 3 (September 1975), pp. 235–72; Dennis E. Logue, "On the Pricing of Unseasoned New Issues, 1965–1969," *Journal of Financial and Quantitative Analysis* 8, no. 1 (January 1973), pp. 91–103; J. G. McDonald and A. K. Fisher, "New-Issue Stock Price Behavior," *Journal of Finance* 27, no. 1 (March 1972), pp. 91–102; Brian M. Neuberger and Carl T. Hammond, "A Study of Underwriters' Experience with Unseasoned New Issues," *Journal of Financial and Quantitative Analysis* 9, no. 2 (March 1974), pp. 165–77.

[16]S. Basu, "The Investment Performance of Common Stocks in Relation to Their Price-Earnings Ratios: A Test of the Efficient-Market Hypothesis," *Journal of Finance* 32 (June 1977), pp. 663–82. Later testing examined the effect of the size of the firm on risk-adjusted rates of return. These studies concluded that small firms outperformed larger firms. See, for example, Rolf W. Banz, "The Relationship between Return and Market Value of Common Stocks," *Journal of Financial Economics* 9 (March 1981), pp. 3–18; Marc R. Reinganum, "Misspecification of Capital Asset Pricing: Empirical Anomalies Based on Earnings Yield and Market Values," *Journal of Financial Economics* 9 (March 1981), pp. 19–46; Marc R. Reinganum, "Abnormal Returns in Small Firm Portfolios," *Financial Analysts Journal* 3 (March–April 1981), pp. 52–57; and Marc R. Reinganum, "Portfolio Strategies Based on Market Capitalization," *Journal of Portfolio Management* 9 (Winter 1983), pp. 29–36; Naie-fu Chen et al., "An Exploratory Investigation of the Firm Size Effect," *Journal of Financial Economics* 14 (1985), pp. 451–71; Rolf W. Banz, "Some Empirical Tests of the Theory of Arbitrage Pricing," *Journal of Finance* 38, no. 5 (1983), pp. 1393–1413; Hubert J. Dwyer, and Richard Lynn, *Are Small Companies All That They Are Supposed To Be?* (Westchester, N.Y.: Pace University Center for Applied Research, 1986), no. 60 (March 1986); Donald B. Keim, "Size Related Anomalies and Stock Return Seasonality," *Journal of Financial Economics* 12, (1983), pp. 13–32; Richard Roll, "A Possible Explanation of the Small Firm Effect," *Journal of Finance* 36, no. 4 (September 1981), pp. 879–88.

price-earnings multiple. He tested to see whether low P/E stocks tended to outperform stocks with high P/E ratios. If historical P/E ratios provided useful information to investors in obtaining superior stock market returns, this would be a refutation of the semistrong form of the efficient market hypothesis. Because if historical publicly available P/E information led an investor to buy a particular type of stock and this in turn led to abnormal returns, this would be a direct contradiction of the semistrong form. His results indicated that the low P/E portfolios experienced superior returns relative to the market and high P/E portfolios performed in an inferior manner relative to the overall market.

Other researchers tested a similar anomaly to the semistrong form of the efficient-markets hypothesis—namely, the size effect. These studies attempted to test whether smaller firms tended to experience larger returns than the larger firms experienced over the same time period. These studies indicated that small firms did provide the investor with significantly larger risk-adjusted returns than did the larger firms examined. However, other researchers have pointed out that this apparent anomaly results more from inappropriate risk measurements, the amount of attention analysts pay to the securities, volume of trading, frequency of trading, and transaction costs, rather than the size differential alone.

By way of summary, then, of the semistrong efficient tests we have reviewed here, the great majority provide strong empirical support for the hypothesis; however, there have been some notable exceptions to this support.[17] Most of the reported results demonstrate that stock prices do adjust rapidly to announcements of new information about stocks. Some of the studies indicate further that investors are typically unable to utilize this information to earn consistently above-average returns.

What the Random-Walk Model Says

Our generalization of the random-walk model, then, says that previous price changes or changes in return are useless in predicting future price or return changes. That is, if we attempt to predict future prices in absolute terms using only historical price-change information, we will not be successful.

Note that random walk says nothing more than that successive price changes are independent. This independence implies that prices at any time will on the average reflect the intrinsic value of the security. (Often one will find this intrinsic worth referred to as the present value of the stock's price, or its equilibrium value.) Furthermore, if a stock's price deviates from its intrinsic value because, among other things, different investors evaluate the available information differently or have different insights into future prospects of the firm, professional investors and astute nonprofessionals will seize upon the short-term or random deviations from the intrinsic value, and through their active buying and selling of the stock in question will force the price back to its equilibrium position.

[17]O. Maurice Joy and Charles P. Jones, "Earnings Reports and Market Efficiencies: An Analysis of Contrary Evidence," *Journal of Financial Research* 2, no. 1 (Spring 1979), pp. 51–63.

What the Random-Walk Model Does Not Say

It is unfortunate that so many misconceptions of the random-walk model exist. It is, in point of fact, a very simple statement.[18]

The random-walk model says nothing about relative price movements—that is, about selecting securities that may or may not perform better than other securities. It says nothing about decomposing price movements into such factors as *market, industry,* or *firm* factors. Certainly, it is entirely possible to detect trends in stock prices after one has removed the general market influences or other influences; however, this in no way would refute the random-walk model, for after these influences have been removed, we will in fact be dealing with relative prices and not with absolute prices, which lie at the heart of the random-walk hypothesis. Furthermore, these "trends" provide no basis for forecasting the future.

In addition, it should be reemphasized that the empirical results came first, to be followed by theory to explain the results; therefore, discussions about a competitive market, or instantaneous adjustments to new information, or knowledgeable market participants, or easy access to markets, are all in reality not part of the random-walk model, but rather possible explanations of the results we find when performing our empirical investigations.

Also, there seems to be a misunderstanding by many to the effect that believing in random walk means that one must also believe that analyzing stocks, and consequently stock prices, is a useless exercise, for if indeed stock prices are random, there is no reason for them to go up or down over any period of time. This is very wrong. The random-walk hypothesis is entirely consistent with an upward or downward movement in price, for as we shall see, the hypothesis supports fundamental analysis and certainly does not attack it.

Implications of Random Walk for Technical and Fundamental Analysis

The random-walk theory is inconsistent with technical analysis, or chartism.[19] Whereas random walk states that successive price changes are independent, the chartists claim that they are dependent—that is, that the historical price behavior of the stock will repeat itself into the future and that by studying this past behavior the chartist can in fact predict the future. Random walk, through the statistical testing discussed earlier in this chapter, directly opposes this line of reasoning and relegates technical analysis to a curious position of mysticism, seemingly completely unfounded on any substantive facts. The technicians, however, deny the findings of researchers in this area by saying that the statistical procedures employed in the literature of the past were too simple to detect complex, historical price relationships.

---

[18]Material in this section is in part adapted from C. W. J. Granger, "What the Random-Walk Model Does NOT Say," *Financial Analysts Journal* (May–June 1970), pp. 91–93.

[19]Specifically, random walk denies that a technical approach can be consistently successful over a long period of time.

The relationship between random walk and fundamental analysis is a bit more complex. First, random walk implies that short-run price changes are random about the true intrinsic value of the security. Thus, we can see that it is the day-to-day or week-to-week price changes, and consequently return changes, that are random, and not the price levels themselves. Consequently, it is entirely possible while believing in random walk to believe also in the existence of an upward or downward drift in prices of individual securities over a longer period. In other words, random walk says nothing about trends in the long run or how price levels are determined; it speaks only of the phenomenon of short-run price-change independence.

As a result, what the random-walk theory (particularly the semistrong form) really says to the fundamentalist operating in a random-walk world is that his fundamental analysis must be truly *exceptional* so that he can seize upon opportunities when security prices differ somewhat significantly from their intrinsic value. This means that the fundamentalist can be successful only in those instances when he either *possesses superior insight into the company's future prospects or possesses inside information.* It is clear even under random walk that such superior fundamental analysis will lead to superior profits for the astute security analyst or investor who projects his own data and does not merely rely on already publicly available historical data.

FUNCTIONS OF ASTUTE INVESTORS AND ANALYSTS IN A RANDOM-WALK MARKET

In a random-walk market, then, the functions of the analyst are (1) to determine the risk-return characteristics of stocks in the hope of occasionally coming across situations where his expectations differ markedly from those of the market as a whole, and (2) to make these risk-return combinations available to investors and investment counselors so they can construct portfolios with appropriate risk-return characteristics for their needs. The implications for the investor are (1) to plan on buying and holding the selected securities (with an emphasis on smaller firms—those with lesser total market values) until he sees adequate reason for revising his portfolio, and (2) under normal conditions, to buy a well-diversified portfolio whose returns are likely to parallel those of the market. The former implication arises because of the empirical findings discussed already, and the latter because of the difficulty of outperforming the market portfolio in an efficient market.

EMPIRICAL RESULTS OF TECHNICAL ANALYSIS

To date, little empirical work has been conducted in the area of technical analysis—certainly not nearly as much as has been done on random walk. What little has been done is not conclusive, nor are the results as consistent as those found in the random-walk literature. Most, if not all, chartist theories tested to date have yielded results that are not very reassuring to the chartist.

These negative chartist results can perhaps be defended. It is argued that the tests of various trading strategies that have been carried out thus far do not adequately simulate the behavior of the technical analysts that we meet in actual prac-

tice. The tests have been too simple, because they have been of one trading system or technical tool at a time, rather than testing various methods concurrently and then somehow weighing the results of the various tools and reaching a consensus.[20]

As for the empirical results of random walk, the chartists are not as concerned, for they state that either the tests employed are too simple or they are inappropriate. This latter reason refers to the point that most of the statistical methods employed in the random-walk literature assume that a linear relationship exists. If that assumption is inappropriate, then the methods and thus the results are also inappropriate.

SUMMARY

Three broad theories exist concerning stock price movements. The fundamentalists believe that by analyzing key economic and financial variables, they can estimate the intrinsic worth of the security and then determine what investment action to take. The technical or chartist school maintains that fundamental analysis is unnecessary; all that has to be done is to study historical price patterns and then decide how current price behavior fits into these. Because the technician believes that history repeats itself, he can then predict future movements in price based on the study of historical patterns. The random-walk school has demonstrated to its own satisfaction through empirical tests that successive price changes over short periods, such as a day, a week, or a month, are independent. To the extent that this independence exists, the random-walk theory directly contradicts technical analysis; and furthermore, to the extent that the stock markets are efficient in the dissemination of information and that they have informed market participants and the proper institutional setting, the random-walk school poses an important challenge to the fundamentalist camp as well.

If the markets are truly efficient, then the fundamentalist will be successful only when (1) he has inside information, or (2) he has *superior ability* to analyze publicly available information and gain insight into the *future* of the firm, and (3) he uses (1) and/or (2) to reach long-term buy-and-hold investment decisions.

The empirical evidence in support of the random-walk hypothesis rests primarily on statistical tests, such as runs tests, correlation analysis, and filter tests. The results have been almost unanimously in support of the random-walk hypothesis, the weak form of the efficient market hypothesis. The results of semistrong-form tests have been mixed.

The technician has done very little if anything to defend any of the chartist theories against the onslaught of random walk. All chartists have done is to claim that their various systems work. In the future, if their theories are to have widespread acceptance in the academic community, they will have to test and

---

[20]An excellent summary and review of the literature in this area can be found in George E. Pinches, "The Random-Walk Hypothesis and Technical Analysis," *Financial Analysts Journal* 26, no. 2 (March–April 1970), pp. 104–10.

demonstrate that their methods can consistently outperform a simple buy-and-hold strategy. The fundamentalist needs also to show that his efforts in analyzing securities are successful enough—that is, earn enough more profit than does a simplified strategy—to justify his expenditure of time and effort.

QUESTIONS AND PROBLEMS

1. Discuss briefly the essence of fundamental and of technical analysis.

2. How do technicians and random-walk advocates differ in their view of the stock market?

3. What is the connection between the efficient-market hypothesis and the studies of mutual-fund performance?

4. Explain the implications of the serial-correlation tests for
   a. the random-walk theory,
   b. technical analysis, and
   c. fundamental analysis.

5. What are the implications of filter tests for
   a. the random-walk theory,
   b. technical analysis, and
   c. fundamental analysis?

6. What sequence of events might bring about an "efficient market"?

7. Does the random-walk theory suggest that security price levels are random? Explain.

8. How is technical analysis generally regarded in the academic literature? Why? What do technical analysts have to say about this?

9. According to random-walk theorists, what does a chartist (technician) need to succeed in the stock market? A fundamentalist?

10. Mr. Elf Gnome is a well-known technical analyst (and authority on tarot). He shares an office with Randy Wok, MBA, who has recently joined the firm from Farout University. The market has been bearish for some time. Gnome is keenly watching his charts for a signal of a rally on the upside.
    a. Which *three* of the more *reliable* technical indicators might Gnome be watching closely? What *signal* would he expect to see from each that would suggest a reversal?
    b. Wok, amused by Gnome's antics, cried "Rubbish!" Why might he not trust Gnome's indicators? What might Gnome offer as a logical retort?

11. How can an investor identify an analyst with "superior" abilities?

12. If an investor does not possess "superior" abilities, what investment strategy might be advisable?

13. If a portfolio were managed by people with average abilities, what might be a reasonable strategy for them to employ?

14. What are some factors that should be considered by a portfolio manager even in an efficient market? Why would these be relevant to consider in advising a client?

15. If a firm consistently reports higher earnings per share, is this evidence of a problem with the efficient-markets hypothesis?

16. Must the return of all securities be equal if the stock market is efficient? Explain your answer.

17. Does the fact that small firms' risk-adjusted returns may outperform larger firms' risk-adjusted returns refute the semistrong form of the efficient-markets hypothesis? Explain your answer.

REFERENCES

BAESEL JEROME, GEORGE SHOWS, and EDWARD THORP. "Can Joe Granville Time the Market?" *Journal of Portfolio Management* 8, no. 3 (Spring 1982), p. 5.

BOHAN, JAMES. "Relative Strength: Further Positive Evidence." *Journal of Portfolio Management* 7, no. 1 (Fall 1981), p. 36.

BROWN, DAVID, and ROBERT H. JENNINGS. "On Technical Analysis." *Review of Financial Studies* 2 (1989), pp. 527–52.

COHEN, A. *How To Use the Three-Point Reversal Method of Point-and-Figure Stock Market Trading.* Larchmont, N.Y.: Chartcraft, 1980.

COOTNER, P.H. *The Random Character of Stock Prices.* Cambridge, Mass.: MIT Press, 1964.

DOLMAN, D. *The New Contrarian Investment Strategy,* New York: Random House, 1982.

LEHMAN, BRUCE. "Fads, Martingales and Market Efficiency." *Quarterly Journal of Economics* (February 1990), pp 1–28.

MALKIEL, BURTON G. *A Random Walk Down Wall Street.* New York: W. W. Norton 1990.

ZWEIG, M. *The ABC's of Market Forecasting: How To Use Barron's Market Laboratory Pages.* Princeton, N.J.: Dow Jones and Co., 1983.

CHAPTER 17

PORTFOLIO ANALYSIS

Individual securities, as we have seen, have risk-return characteristics of their own. Portfolios, which are combinations of securities, may or may not take on the aggregate characteristics of their individual parts.

Portfolio analysis considers the determination of future risk and return in holding various blends of individual securities. In this chapter we shall analyze the range of possible portfolios that can be constituted from a given set of securities. We will show how the "efficiency" of each such combination can be evaluated.

TRADITIONAL PORTFOLIO ANALYSIS

Traditional security analysis recognizes the key importance of risk and return to the investor. However, direct recognition of risk and return in portfolio analysis seems very much a "seat-of-the-pants" process in the traditional approaches, which rely heavily upon intuition and insight. The results of these rather subjective approaches to portfolio analysis have, no doubt, been highly successful in many instances. The problem is that the methods employed do not readily lend themselves to analysis by others.

Most traditional methods recognize return as some dividend receipt and price appreciation over a forward period. But the return for individual securities is not always over the same common holding period, nor are the rates of return necessarily time-adjusted. An analyst may well estimate future earnings and a P/E to derive future price. He will surely estimate the dividend. But he may not discount the values to determine the acceptability of the return in relation to the investor's requirements.

In any case, given an estimate of return, the analyst is likely to think of and express risk as the probable downside price expectation (either by itself or relative to upside appreciation possibilities). Each security ends up with some rough measure of likely return and potential downside risk for the future.

Portfolios, or combinations of securities, are thought of as helping to spread risk over many securities. This is good. However, the interrelationship between securities may be specified only broadly or nebulously. Auto stocks are, for example, recognized as risk-interrelated with tire stocks; utility stocks display defensive price movement relative to the market and cyclical stocks like steel; and so on.

This is not to say that traditional portfolio analysis is unsuccessful. It is to say that much of it might be more objectively specified in explicit terms.

WHY PORTFOLIOS?

You will recall that expected return from individual securities carries some degree of risk. *Risk* was defined as the standard deviation around the expected return.[1] In effect we equated a security's risk with the variability of its return. More dispersion or variability about a security's expected return meant the security was riskier than one with less dispersion.

The simple fact that securities carry differing degrees of expected risk leads most investors to the notion of holding more than one security at a time, in an attempt to spread risks by not putting all their eggs into one basket.[2] Diversification of one's holdings is intended to reduce risk in an economy in which every asset's returns are subject to some degree of uncertainty. Even the value of cash suffers from the inroads of inflation. Most investors hope that if they hold several assets, even if one goes bad, the others will provide some protection from an extreme loss.

Diversification

Efforts to spread and minimize risk take the form of diversification. The more traditional forms of diversification have concentrated upon holding a number of security types (stock, bonds) across industry lines (utility, mining, manufacturing groups). The reasons are related to inherent differences in bond and equity contracts, coupled with the notion that an investment in firms in dissimilar industries would most likely do better than in firms within the same industry. Holding one stock each from mining, utility, and manufacturing groups is superior to holding three mining stocks. Carried to its extreme, this approach leads to the conclusion that the best diversification comes through holding large numbers of securities scattered across industries. Many would feel that holding fifty such scattered stocks is five times more diversified than holding ten scattered stocks.

Most people would agree that a portfolio consisting of two stocks is probably less risky than one holding either stock alone. However, experts disagree with

---

[1]Standard deviation is a risk surrogate, not a synonym for risk. For a review of some aspects of risk, see Fred D. Arditti, "Risk and the Required Return on Equity," *Journal of Finance* (March 1967), pp. 19–36.

[2]Note that some advocate a concentration philosophy. This point of view stresses "putting all your eggs into one basket and keeping a sharp eye on the basket." See, for example, a classic, Gerald M. Loeb, *The Battle for Investment Survival* (New York: Simon and Schuster, 1965).

regard to the "right" kind of diversification and the "right" reason. The discussion that follows introduces and explores a formal, advanced notion of diversification conceived by the genius of Harry Markowitz.[3] Markowitz's approach to coming up with good portfolio possibilities has its roots in risk-return relationships. This is not at odds with traditional approaches in concept. The key differences lie in Markowitz's assumption that investor attitudes toward portfolios depend exclusively upon (1) expected return and risk, and (2) quantification of risk. And risk is, by proxy, the statistical notion of variance, or standard deviation of return. These simple assumptions are strong, and they are disputed by many traditionalists.[4]

EFFECTS OF COMBINING SECURITIES

Although holding two securities is probably less risky than holding either security alone, *is it possible to reduce the risk of a portfolio by incorporating into it a security whose risk is greater than that of any of the investments held initially?* For example, given two stocks, X and Y, with Y considerably more risky than X, a portfolio composed of some of X and some of Y may be less risky than a portfolio composed exclusively of the less risky asset, X.

Assume the following about stocks X and Y:

	STOCK X	STOCK Y
Return (%)	7 or 11	13 or 5
Probability	.5 each return	.5 each return
Expected return (%)	9*	9†
Variance (%)	4	16
Standard deviation (%)	2	4

*Expected return = (.5)(7) + (.5)(11) = 9
†Expected return = (.5)(13) + (.5)(5) = 9

Clearly, although X and Y have the same expected return, 9 percent, Y is riskier than X (standard deviation of 4 versus 2). Suppose that when X's return is high, Y's return is low, and vice versa. In other words, when the return on X is 11 percent, the return on Y is 5 percent; similarly, when the return on X is 7 percent, the return

[3]Harry M. Markowitz, *Portfolio Selection: Efficient Diversification of Investments* (New York: John Wiley, 1959). Competing portfolio models are found in Henry A. Latané, "Investment Criteria—A Three-Asset Portfolio Balance Model," *Review of Economics and Statistics* 45 (November 1963), pp. 427–30; and Jack Hirschleifer, "Investment Decision under Uncertainty: Application of the State-Preference Approach," *Quarterly Journal of Economics* 80 (May 1966), pp. 252–77.

[4]For a look at how practitioners view some aspects of the Markowitz approach, see Frank E. Block, "Elements of Portfolio Construction," *Financial Analysts Journal* (May–June 1969), pp. 123–29.

on Y is 13 percent. Question: Is a portfolio of some X and some Y in any way superior to an exclusive holding of X alone (has it less risk)?

Let us construct a portfolio consisting of two-thirds stock X and one-third stock Y. The average return of this portfolio can be thought of as the weighted-average return of each security in the portfolio; that is:

$$R_p = \sum_{i=1}^{N} X_i R_i \tag{17.1}$$

where:

R_p = expected return to portfolio
X_i = proportion of total portfolio invested in security i
R_i = expected return to security i
N = total number of securities in portfolio

Therefore,

$$R_p = (\tfrac{2}{3})(9) + (\tfrac{1}{3})(9) = 9$$

But what will be the range of fluctuation of the portfolio? In periods when X is better as an investment, we have $R_p = (\tfrac{2}{3})(11) + (\tfrac{1}{3})(5) = 9$; and similarly, when Y turns out to be more remunerative, $R_p = (\tfrac{2}{3})(7) + (\tfrac{1}{3})(13) = 9$. Thus, by putting part of the money into the riskier stock, Y, we are able to *reduce* risk considerably from what it would have been if we had confined our purchases to the less risky stock, X. If we held only stock X, our expected return would be 9 percent, which could in reality be as low as 7 percent in bad periods or as much as 11 percent in good periods. The standard deviation is equal to 2 percent. Holding a mixture of two-thirds X and one-third Y, our expected and experienced return will always be 9 percent, with a standard deviation of zero. We can hardly quarrel with achieving the same expected return for less risk. In this case we have been able to eliminate risk altogether.

The reduction of risk of a portfolio by blending into it a security whose risk is *greater than* that of any of the securities held initially suggests that deducing the riskiness of a portfolio simply by knowing the riskiness of individual securities is not possible. It is vital that we also know the *interactive risk* between securities!

The crucial point of how to achieve the proper proportions of X and Y in reducing the risk to zero will be taken up later. However, the general notion is clear. The risk of the portfolio is reduced by playing off one set of variations against another. Finding two securities each of which tends to perform well whenever the other does poorly makes more certain a reasonable return for the portfolio as a whole, even if one of its components happens to be quite risky.

This sort of hedging is possible whenever one can find two securities whose behavior is inversely related in the way stocks X and Y were in the illustration. Now we need to take a closer look at the matter of how securities may be correlated in terms of rate of return.

A Closer Look at Portfolio Risk

The risk involved in individual securities can be measured by standard deviation or variance. When two securities are combined, we need to consider their interactive risk, or *covariance*. If the rates of return of two securities move together, we say their interactive risk or covariance is positive. If rates of return are independent, covariance is zero. Inverse movement results in covariance that is negative. Mathematically, covariance is defined as

$$\text{cov}_{xy} = \frac{1}{N} \sum_{}^{N} [R_x - \overline{R}_x][R_y - \overline{R}_y]$$

where the probabilities are equal and

cov_{xy} = covariance between x and y
R_x = return on security x
R_y = return on security y
$\overline{R}_x$ = expected return to security x
$\overline{R}_y$ = expected return to security y
N = number of observations

Using our earlier example of stocks X and Y:

	RETURN	EXPECTED RETURN	DIFFERENCE
Stock X	7	9	−2
Stock Y	13	9	4
			Product −8
Stock X	11	9	2
Stock Y	5	9	−4
			Product −8

$$\text{cov} = \frac{1}{2}[(7 - 9)(13 - 9) + (11 - 9)(5 - 9)]$$

$$= \frac{1}{2}[(-8) + (-8)] = \frac{-16}{2} = -8$$

Instead of squaring the deviations of a single variable from its mean, we take two corresponding observations of the two stocks in question at the *same point in time,* determine the variation of each from its expected value, and multiply the two deviations together. If whenever x is below its average, so is y, then for those periods each deviation will be negative, and their product consequently will be positive. Hence we will end up with a covariance made up of an average of positive values, and its value will be large. Similarly, if one of the variables is relatively large whenever the other is small, one of the deviations will be positive and the other negative, and the covariance will be negative. This is true with our example above.

The *coefficient of correlation* is another measure designed to indicate the similarity or dissimilarity in the behavior of two variables. We define

$$r_{xy} = \frac{\text{cov}_{xy}}{\sigma_x \sigma_y}$$

where:

r_{xy} = coefficient of correlation of x and y
cov_{xy} = covariance between x and y
σ_x = standard deviation of x
σ_y = standard deviation of y

The coefficient of correlation is, essentially, the covariance taken not as an absolute value but relative to the standard deviations of the individual securities (variables). It indicates, in effect, how much x and y vary together as a proportion of their combined individual variations, measured by $\sigma_x \sigma_y$. In our example, the coefficient of correlation is

$$r_{xy} = -8/[(2)(4)] = -8/8 = -1.0$$

If the coefficient of correlation between two securities is -1.0, then a perfect negative correlation exists (r_{xy} cannot be less than -1.0). If the correlation coefficient is zero, then returns are said to be independent of one another. If the returns on two securities are perfectly correlated, the correlation coefficient will be $+1.0$, and perfect positive correlation is said to exist (r_{xy} cannot exceed $+1.0$).

Thus, correlation between two securities depends upon (1) the covariance between the two securities, and (2) the standard deviation of each security.

Portfolio Effect in the Two-Security Case

We have shown the effect of diversification on reducing risk. The key was not that two stocks provided twice as much diversification as one, but that by investing in securities with negative or low covariance among themselves, we could reduce the risk. Markowitz's efficient diversification involves combining securities with less than positive correlation in order to reduce risk in the portfolio without sacrificing any of the portfolio's return. In general, the lower the correlation of securities in the portfolio, the less risky the portfolio will be. This is true regardless of how risky the stocks of the portfolio are when analyzed in isolation. It is not enough to invest in *many* securities; it is necessary to have the *right* securities.

Let us conclude our two-security example in order to make some valid generalizations. Then we can see what three-security and larger portfolios might be like. In considering a two-security portfolio, portfolio risk can be defined more formally now as:

$$\sigma_p = \sqrt{X_x^2 \sigma_x^2 + X_y^2 \sigma_y^2 + 2X_x X_y (r_{xy} \sigma_x \sigma_y)} \qquad \text{(17.2)}$$

where:

σ_p = portfolio standard deviation
X_x = percentage of total portfolio value in stock X
X_y = percentage of total portfolio value in stock Y
σ_x = standard deviation of stock X
σ_y = standard deviation of stock Y
r_{xy} = correlation coefficient of X and Y

Note: $r_{xy}\sigma_x\sigma_y$ = cov$_{xy}$.

Thus, we now have the standard deviation of a portfolio of two securities. We are able to see that portfolio risk (σ_p is sensitive to (1) the proportions of funds devoted to each stock, (2) the standard deviation of each stock, and (3) the covariance between the two stocks. If the stocks are independent of each other, the correlation coefficient is zero ($r_{xy} = 0$). In this case, the last term in Equation 17.2 is zero. Second, if r_{xy} is greater than zero, the standard deviation of the portfolio is greater than if $r_{xy} = 0$. Third, if r_{xy} is less than zero, the covariance term is negative, and portfolio standard deviation is less than it would be if r_{xy} were greater than or equal to zero. Risk can be totally eliminated only if the third term is equal to the sum of the first two terms. This occurs only if first, $r_{xy} = -1.0$, and second, the percentage of the portfolio in stock X is set equal to $X_x = \sigma_y/(\sigma_x + \sigma_y)$.

To clarify these general statements, let us return to our earlier example of stocks X and Y. In our example, remember that:

	STOCK X	STOCK Y
Expected return (%)	9	9
Standard deviation (%)	2	4

We calculated the covariance between the two stocks and found it to be -8. The coefficient of correlation was -1.0. The two securities were perfectly negatively correlated.

CHANGING PROPORTIONS OF X AND Y

What happens to portfolio risk as we change the total portfolio value invested in X and Y? Using Equation 17.2, we get:

STOCK X (%)	STOCK Y (%)	PORTFOLIO STANDARD DEVIATION
100	0	2.0
80	20	0.8
66	34	0.0
20	80	2.8
0	100	4.0

Notice that portfolio risk can be brought down to zero by the skillful balancing of the proportions of the portfolio to each security. The preconditions were $r_{xy} = -1.0$ and $X_x = \sigma_y/(\sigma_x + \sigma_y)$, or $4/(2 + 4) = .666$.

CHANGING THE COEFFICIENT OF CORRELATION

What would be the effect using $x = \frac{2}{3}$ and $y = \frac{1}{3}$ if the correlation coefficient between stocks X and Y had been other than -1.0? Using Equation 17.2 and various values for r_{xy}, we have:

r_{xy}	PORTFOLIO STANDARD DEVIATION
-0.5	1.34*
0.0	1.9
$+0.5$	2.3
$+1.0$	2.658

$$*\sigma_p = \sqrt{(.666)^2(2)^2 + (.334)^2 + (2)(.666)(.334)(-.5)(2)(4)}$$
$$= \sqrt{1.777 + 1.777 - (.444)(4)} = \sqrt{1.777} = 1.34$$

If no diversification effect had occurred, then the total risk of the two securities would have been the weighted sum of their individual standard deviations:

$$\text{Total undiversified risk} = (.666)(2) + (.334)(4) = 2.658$$

Because the undiversified risk is equal to the portfolio risk of perfectly positively correlated securities ($r_{xy} = +1.0$), we can see that favorable portfolio effects occur only when securities are not perfectly positively correlated. The risk in a portfolio is less than the sum of the risks of the individual securities taken separately whenever the returns of the individual securities are not perfectly positively correlated; also, the smaller the correlation between the securities, the greater the benefits of diversification. A negative correlation would be even better.

In general, some combination of two stocks (portfolios) will provide a smaller standard deviation of return than either security taken alone, as long as the correlation coefficient is less than the ratio of the smaller standard deviation to the larger standard deviation:

$$r_{xy} < \frac{\sigma_x}{\sigma_y}$$

Using the two stocks in our example:

$$-1.00 < \frac{2}{4}$$

$$-1.00 < +.50$$

If the two stocks had the same standard deviations as before but a coefficient of correlation of, for example, +.70, there would have been no portfolio effect because +.70 is not less than +.50.

GRAPHIC ILLUSTRATION OF PORTFOLIO EFFECTS

The various cases where the correlation between two securities ranges from −1.0 to +1.0 are shown in Figure 17–1. Return is shown on the vertical axis and risk is measured on the horizontal axis. Points A and B represent pure holdings (100 percent) of securities A and B. The intermediate points along the line segment AB represent portfolios containing various combinations of the two securities. The line segment identified as $r_{ab} = + 1.0$ is a straight line. This line shows the inability of a portfolio of perfectly positively correlated securities to serve as a means to reduce variability or risk. Point A along this line segment has no points to its left; that is, there is no portfolio composed of a mix of our perfectly correlated securities A and B that has a lower standard deviation than the standard deviation of A. Neither A nor B can help offset the risk of the other. The wise investor who wished to minimize risk would put all his eggs into the safer basket, stock A.

The segment labeled $r_{ab} = 0$ is a hyperbola. Its leftmost point will not reach the vertical axis. There is no portfolio where $\sigma_p = 0$. There is, however, an inflection just above point A that we shall explain in a moment.

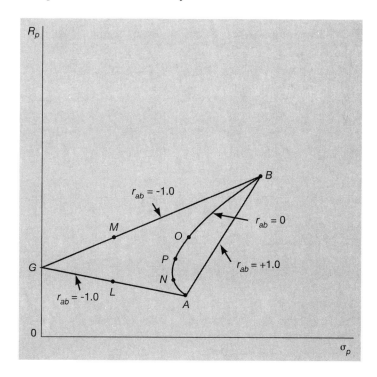

FIGURE 17–1   Portfolios of Two Securities with Differing Correlation of Returns

The line segment labeled $r_{ab} = -1.0$ is compatible with the numerical example we have been using. This line shows that with perfect inverse correlation, portfolio risk can be reduced to zero. Notice points L and M along the line segment AGB, or $r_{ab} = -1.0$. Point M provides a higher return than point L, while both have equal risk. Portfolio L is clearly inferior to portfolio M. All portfolios along the segment GLA are clearly inferior to portfolios along the segment GMB. Similarly, along the line segment APB, or $r_{ab} = 0$, segment BOP contains portfolios that are superior to those along segment PNA.

Markowitz would say that all portfolios along all line segments are "*feasible,*" but some are more "*efficient*" than others.

The Three-Security Case

In Figure 17–2 we depict the graphics surrounding a three-security portfolio problem. Points A, B, and C each represent 100 percent invested in each of the stocks A, B, and C. The locus AB represents all portfolios composed of some proportions of A and B, the locus AC represents all portfolios composed of A and C, and so on. The general shape of the lines AB, AC, and BC suggests that these security pairs have correlation coefficients less than $+ 1.0$.

What about portfolios containing some proportions of all three securities? Point G can be considered some combination of A and B. The locus CG is then a

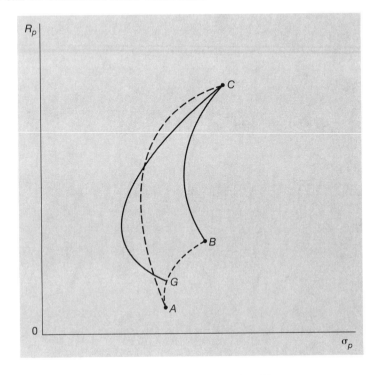

FIGURE 17–2   Three-Security Portfolios

three-security line. The number of such line segments representing three-security mixtures can be seen from Figure 17–3, where any point inside the shaded area will represent some three-security portfolio. Whereas the two-security locus is generally a curve, a three-security locus will normally be an entire region in the R_p, σ_p diagram.

Consider for a moment three portfolio points within the R_p, σ_p diagram in Figure 17–3. Call the portfolios $P1$, $P2$, and $P3$. If we stop to think for a moment, the number of three-security portfolios is enormous—much larger than the number of two-security portfolios. Faced with the order of magnitude of portfolio possibilities, we need some shortcut to cull out the bulk of possibilities that are clearly nonoptimal. Looking at portfolios $P1$ and $P2$, we might observe the fact that because $P2$ lies to the left of and below $P1$, $P2$ is probably more appealing to the conservative investor, and $P1$ appeals to those willing to gamble a bit more. Would a rational investor select $P3$? We think not because it involves a lower return than $P2$ but has the same risk. Thus, we say that a portfolio is *inefficient,* or dominated, if some other portfolio lies directly above it (or directly to the left of it) in the risk-return space.

In general, an efficient portfolio has either (1) more return than any other portfolio with the same risk or (2) less risk than any other portfolio with the same return. In Figure 17–3 the boundary of the region identified as the curve LC dominates all other portfolios in the region. Portfolios along the segment AL represent inefficient portfolios because they show increased risk for lower return. Each point

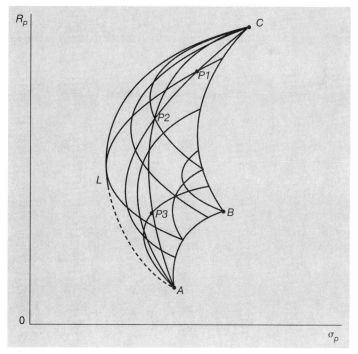

FIGURE 17–3   Region of Portfolio Points with Three Securities

on the segment *AL* is dominated by a more efficient portfolio directly above it on segment *LC*.

The actual determination of risk and return on various three-security portfolios such as *P*1, *P*2, and *P*3 requires that we extend our earlier formulas for two-asset portfolios.

RISK-RETURN IN A THREE-SECURITY PORTFOLIO

The three-security case uses the same formulation for expected portfolio return indicated earlier in Equation 17.1:

$$R_p = \sum_{i=1}^{N} X_i R_i$$

The portfolio standard deviation depends as before upon the standard deviations of return for its components, their correlation coefficients, and the proportions invested.

$$\sigma_p^2 = \sum_{i=1}^{N} \sum_{j=1}^{N} X_i X_j r_{ij} \sigma_i \sigma_j \tag{17.3}$$

σ_p^2 = expected portfolio variance

$\sqrt{\sigma_p^2}$ = portfolio standard deviation

X_i = proportion of total portfolio invested in security i

X_j = proportion of total portfolio invested in security j

r_{ij} = coefficient of correlation between securities i and j

σ_i = standard deviation of security i

σ_j = standard deviation of security j

N = total number of securities in the portfolio

$\sum_{i=1}^{N} \sum_{j=1}^{N}$ = double summation sign means N^2 numbers are to be added together. Each number is obtained by substituting one of the possible pairs of values for i and j into the expression.

For $N = 2$:

$$\sigma_p^2 = X_1 X_1 r_{1.1} \sigma_1 \sigma_1 + X_1 X_2 r_{1.2} \sigma_1 \sigma_2 + X_2 X_1 r_{2.1} \sigma_2 \sigma_1 + X_2 X_2 r_{2.2} \sigma_2 \sigma_2$$

The first and last terms can be simplified. Clearly, the return on a security is perfectly (positively) correlated with itself. Thus, $r_{1.1} = 1$, as does $r_{2.2} = 1$. Because $r_{2.1} = r_{2.1}$, the second and third terms can be combined. The result is:

$$\sigma_p^2 = X_1^2 \sigma_1^2 + X_2^2 \sigma_2^2 + 2 X_1 X_2 r_{1.2} \sigma_1 \sigma_2$$

Because $r_{ij} \sigma_i \sigma_j = \text{cov}_{ij}$, we can simplify further to:

$$\sigma_p^2 = \sum_{i=1}^{N} \sum_{j=1}^{N} X_i X_j \text{cov}_{ij} \tag{17.3a}$$

EXAMPLE.   Consider the following three securities and the relevant data on each:

	STOCK 1	STOCK 2	STOCK 3
Expected return	10	12	8
Standard deviation	10	15	5
Correlation coefficients:			
Stocks 1, 2 = .3			
2, 3 = .4			
1, 3 = .5			

Question: What are portfolio risk and return if the following proportions are assigned to each stock? Stock 1 = .2, stock 2 = .4, and stock 3 = .4.

The portfolio return would be as per Equation 17.1:

$$R_p = \sum_{i=1}^{N} X_i R_i$$

or

$$R_p = (.2)(10) + (.4)(12) + (.4)(8) = 10$$

Using the formula for portfolio risk (Equation 17.3a) and expanding it for $N = 3$, we get:

$$\sigma_p^2 = X_1^2\sigma_1^2 + X_2^2\sigma_2^2 + X_3^2\sigma_3^2 + 2X_1X_2r_{1,2}\sigma_1\sigma_2 + 2X_2X_3r_{2,3}\sigma_2\sigma_3 + 2X_1X_3r_{1,3}\sigma_1\sigma_3$$

Substituting the appropriate values, we have

$$\sigma_p^2 = (.2)^2(10)^2 + (.4)^2(15)^2 + (.4)^2(5)^2 + (2)(.2)(.4)(.3)(10)(15)$$

$$+ (2)(.4)(.4)(.4)(15)(5) + (2)(.2)(.4)(.5)(10)(5)$$

$$= 4 + 36 + 4 + 7.20 + 9.6 + 4$$

$$= 64.8$$

$$\sigma_p = 8.0$$

What we have just done, through a process that is somewhat arduous (particularly without a calculator), is to calculate return and risk on a portfolio consisting of certain proportions of stocks 1, 2, and 3. This portfolio is simply one of many three-security combinations that would comprise our risk-return space or diagram. Although we found that a portfolio consisting of 20 percent of stock 1 and 40 percent each of stocks 2 and 3 had an expected return of 10 percent and a standard deviation of return of 8.0, is it possible that a portfolio of different weights lies (1) directly above or (2) directly to the left of our example portfolio? Remember, if another portfolio met conditions (1) or (2) relative to our example portfolio, it would dominate, or be more efficient.

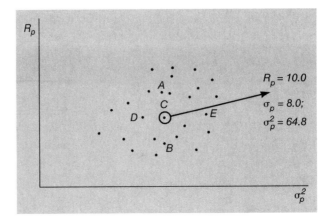

FIGURE 17–4   Feasible Portfolios in a Risk-Return Space

Tracing Out the Efficiency Locus

Figure 17–4 is intended to enunciate the dilemma of determining efficient portfolios. Our example three-security portfolio is identified among a mass of feasible portfolios in the risk-return diagram. We can see that it is inefficient because other portfolios (1) exceed its return at the same level of risk (e.g., portfolio A), and (2) have lower risk for the same level of return (e.g., portfolio D).

Harry Markowitz devised an ingenious computational model designed to trace out the efficiency locus and to identify the portfolios that comprise it. In other words, he produced a scheme whereby large numbers of feasible portfolios could be ignored completely where they were dominated by more efficient portfolios.

In the calculations, Markowitz used the techniques of quadratic programming.[5] He assumed that one could deal with N securities or fewer. Using the expected return and risk for each security under consideration and covariance estimates for each pair of securities, he is able to calculate risk and return for any portfolio comprising of some or all of these securities. In particular, for any specific value of expected return, using the programming calculation he determines the least-risk portfolio. With another value of expected return, a similar procedure again yields the minimum-risk combination.

In Figure 17–5 we depict the process. For return level R_i, the programming calculation indicates that point L_i is the least-risk portfolio at that level of return. Because no portfolio points lie to the left of L_i, it is the most efficient portfolio at that level of return. The locus of points from A to B is the result of the tracing process. We have our efficiency locus, or so-called *efficient frontier*. The line AB di-

---

[5]A graphic approach to the solution of the efficient frontier can be found in J. F. Weston and W. Beranek, "Programming Investment Portfolio Construction," *Analysts Journal* (May 1955), pp. 51-55.

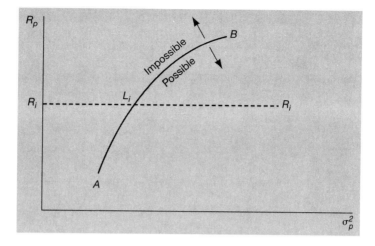

FIGURE 17–5 Schematic Showing Markowitz Efficiency Calculation

vides the space between portfolios that are "possible" and those that cannot be attained ("impossible").

All portfolios that can be created from the available list of candidate securities are referred to as feasible (possible) portfolios. However, only those portfolios that provide the highest return for a given level of risk or the lowest risk for a given level of return are referred to as efficient portfolios.

The N-Security Case

Most real-world portfolio-analysis problems involve portfolios larger than three stocks, chosen from a universe of securities that itself is quite large. In dealing with two-stock portfolios drawn from a modest universe of three-stock candidates, the number of possible portfolio combinations is not overwhelming. Neglecting the proportions devoted to each security, the possible two-stock combinations from stocks D, E, and F are DE, DF, and EF. Now let us gauge the changes brought about by attempting to draw two-stock portfolios from an expanded universe of five candidates, D, E, F, G, and H. The possible combinations are DE, DF, DG, DH, EF, EG, EH, FG, FH, and GH. The mere addition of two new stock candidates causes the number of possible portfolios to increase from three to ten. In general, the number of possibilities increases far more rapidly than does the number of stocks to be considered. Mathematical analysis and the computer go a long way toward culling the bulk of possible portfolios on the grounds that they are clearly nonoptimal. The time required to calculate and discriminate by hand ten-stock portfolios, with varying percentages devoted to each security taken from the almost two thousand stocks on the New York Stock Exchange (NYSE) alone boggles the mind!

The movement from three- to N-security portfolios not only highlights the enormity of the calculation problem and the assistance provided by the Markowitz algorithm, it also points up the expansion of the data bits required for fundamental analysis. The inputs to the portfolio analysis of a set of N securities are (1) N expected returns, (2) N variances of return, and (3) $(N^2 - N)/2$ covariances. Thus, the Markowitz calculation requires a total of $[N(N + 3)/2]$ separate pieces of information before efficient portfolios can be calculated and identified. To use the Markowitz technique for portfolios of the following size, we need the corresponding pieces of information (estimates):

NUMBER OF SECURITIES	BITS OF INFORMATION
10	65
50	1,325
100	5,150*
1,000	501,500

*$[100(100 + 3)/2]$

Clearly, the Markowitz model is extremely demanding in its data needs and computational requirements. Moreover, in the real world of investments, securities analysts typically do not think in terms of some of the Markowitz input requirements. For example, an analyst responsible for following airline stocks makes it his business to know the expected return and risk on individual stocks he follows (e.g., United, Delta, USAir, etc.). However, the Markowitz model requires correlation inputs for each security relative to each other security in the universe utilized. Our airline analyst would need to keep track of the correlation between each airline stock and each of, say, 100 other stocks (e.g., United Airlines and IBM). The investment world does not operate this way. Now we can see the operational necessity to simplify this process to use a common "index" for looking at the correlation of each stock rather than the correlation of each stock to all other stocks.

MARKOWITZ RISK-RETURN OPTIMIZATION: AN EXAMPLE

One example of the optimization approach can be illustrated using a broad group of asset classes. The return, standard deviation, and correlation numbers are shown in Tables 17–1 and 17–2.

Figure 17–6 shows an array of portfolios. The lower line (stock-bond frontier) is the risk-return mix for all possible combinations of stocks and bonds (domestic and foreign) in a portfolio. The full-asset frontier reflects the return and risk combinations available from all investment-grade assets. Clearly, the full-asset frontier offers more return per unit of risk than the limited stock-bond frontier. Furthermore, the full-asset frontier gives a wider range of risk-return options. Together these are powerful arguments for taking a global view to investing.

TABLE 17–1

Illustrative Long-Term Expectations: Optimization Inputs

	EXPECTED RETURN %	RISK %
Large capitalization stocks	12.20	16.50
Small capitalization stocks	13.85	22.00
International stocks	12.60	20.50
Venture capital	19.50	40.00
Domestic bonds	8.70	8.50
International dollar bonds	8.65	8.00
Nondollar bonds	8.65	11.00
Real estate	10.50	14.00
Treasury bills	6.50	

TABLE 17–2

Long-Term Forecasts of Correlations between Asset Classes

	1	2	3	4	5	6	7	8	9
1. Large capitalization equity	1.00								
2. Small capitalization equity	.85	1.00							
3. International equity	.55	.55	1.00						
4. Venture capital	.40	.45	.55	1.00					
5. Domestic bonds	.45	.40	.30	.15	1.00				
6. International dollar bonds	.45	.40	.35	.20	.90	1.00			
7. Nondollar fixed income	.15	.25	.75	.40	.40	.40	1.00		
8. Real estate	.50	.55	.50	.45	.30	.35	.30	1.00	
9. Cash equivalents	.00	.00	.00	.00	.00	.00	.00	.00	1.00

The Sharpe Index Model

William Sharpe, who among others has tried to simplify the process of data inputs, data tabulation, and reaching a solution, has developed a simplified variant of the Markowitz model that reduces substantially its data and computational requirements.[6]

First, simplified models assume that fluctuations in the value of a stock relative to that of another do not depend primarily upon the characteristics of those two securities alone. The two securities are more apt to reflect a broader influence that might be described as general business conditions. Relationship between securities occur only through their individual relationships with some index or indexes of business activity. The reduction in the number of covariance estimates needed eases considerably the job of security-analysis and portfolio-analysis computation.

[6]W. F. Sharpe, "A Simplified Model for Portfolio Analysis," *Management Science* 9 (January 1963), pp. 277–93.

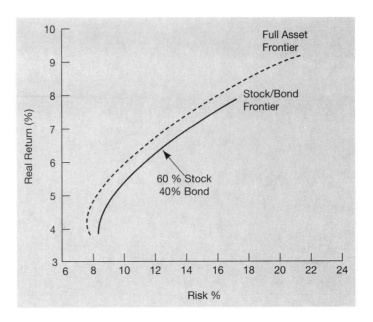

FIGURE 17–6   Attainable Efficient Frontiers (Return less assumed 5 percent inflation rate.)

Thus the covariance data requirement reduces from $(N^2 - N)/2$ under the Markowitz technique to only N measures of each security as it relates to the index. In other words:

NUMBER OF SECURITIES	MARKOWITZ COVARIANCES	SHARPE INDEX COEFFICIENTS
10	45	10
50	1,225	50
100	4,950	100
1,000	499,500	1,000
2,000	1,999,000	2,000

However, some additional inputs are required using Sharpe's technique, too. Estimates are required of the expected return and variance of one or more indexes of economic activity. The indexes to which the returns of each security are correlated are likely to be some securities-market proxy, such as the Dow Jones Industrial Average (DJIA) or the Standard & Poor's 500 Stock Index. The use of economic indexes such as gross national product and the consumer price index was found by Smith to lead to poor estimates of covariances between securities.[7] Overall, then,

[7]Keith V. Smith, "Stock Price and Economic Indexes for Generating Efficient Portfolios," *Journal of Business* 42 (July 1969), pp. 326–36.

the Sharpe technique requires $3N + 2$ separate bits of information, as opposed to the Markowitz requirement of $[N(N + 3)]/2$.

Sharpe's single-index model has been compared with multiple-index models for reliability in approximating the full covariance efficient frontier of Markowitz. The more indexes that are used, the closer one gets to the Markowitz model (where every security is, in effect, an index). The result of multiple-index models can be loss of simplicity and computational savings inherent in these shortcut procedures. The research evidence suggests that index models using stock price indexes are preferable to those using economic indexes in approximating the full covariance frontier. However, the relative superiority of single versus multiple index models is not clearly resolved in the literature.[8]

RISK-RETURN AND THE SHARPE MODEL

Sharpe suggested that a satisfactory simplification would be to abandon the covariances of each security with each other security and to substitute information on the relationship of each security to the market. In his terms, it is possible to consider the return for each security to be represented by the following equation:

$$R_i = \alpha_i + \beta_i I + e_i$$

where:

R_i = expected return on security i
α_i = intercept of a straight line or alpha coefficient
β_i = slope of straight line or beta coefficient
I = expected return on index (market)
e_i = error term with a mean of zero and a standard deviation which is a constant

In other words, the return on any stock depends upon some constant (α), plus some coefficient (β), times the value of a stock index (I), plus a random component (e). Let us look at a hypothetical stock and examine the historical relationship between the stock's return and the returns of the market (index).

See Figure 20-7 for the historical relationship between the return on a hypothetical security and the return on the DJIA. If we mathematically "fit" a line to the small number of observations, we get an equation for the line of the form $y = \alpha + \beta x$. In this case the equation turns out to be $y = 8.5 - .05x$.

The equation $y = \alpha + \beta x$. has two terms or coefficients that have become commonplace in the modern jargon of investment management. The α, or intercept, term is called by its Greek name *alpha*. The β, or slope, term is referred to as the *beta coefficient*. The alpha value is really the value of y in the equation when

[8]See K. J. Cohen and J. A. Pogue, "An Empirical Evaluation of Alternative Selection Models," *Journal of Business* 40, no. 2 (April 1967), pp. 166–93; and B. A. Wallingford, "A Survey and Comparison of Portfolio Selection Models," *Journal of Finance and Quantitative Analysis* (June 1967), pp. 85–106.

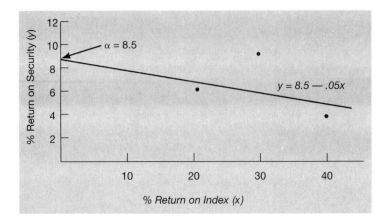

FIGURE 17–7   Security Returns Correlated with *DJIA*

the value of x is zero. Thus, for our hypothetical stock, when the return on the DJIA is zero the stock has an expected return of 8.5 percent [$y = 8.5 - .05(0)$]. The beta coefficient is the slope of the regression line and as such it is a measure of the sensitivity of the stock's return to movements in the market's return. A beta of +1.0 suggests that, ignoring the alpha coefficient, a 1 percent return on the DJIA is matched by a 1 percent return on the stock. A beta of 2.5 would suggest great responsiveness on the part of the stock to changes in the DJIA. A 5 percent return on the index, ignoring the alpha coefficient, leads to an expected return on the stock of 12.5 percent (2.5 times 5 percent). While the alpha term is not to be ignored, we shall see a bit later the important role played by the beta term or beta coefficient.

The Sharpe index method permits us to *estimate* a security's return then by utilizing the values of α and β for the security and an estimate of the value of the index. Assume the return on the index (I) for the year ahead is expected to be 25 percent. Using our calculated values of $\alpha = 8.5$ and $\beta = -.05$ and the estimate of the index of $I = 25$, the return for the stock is estimated as:

$$R_i = 8.5 - .05(25)$$

$$R_i = 8.5 - 1.25$$

$$R_i = 7.25$$

The expected return on the security in question will be 7.25 percent if the return on the index is 25 percent, and if α and B are stable coefficients.

For portfolios, we need merely take the weighted average of the estimated returns for each security in the portfolio. The weights will be the proportions of the portfolio devoted to each security. For each security, we will require α and B estimates. One estimate of the index (I) is needed. Thus:

$$R_p = \sum_{i=1}^{N} X_i(\alpha_i + \beta_i I)$$ **(17.4)**

where all terms are as explained earlier, except that R_p is the expected portfolio return, X_i is the proportion of the portfolio devoted to stock i, and N is the total number of stocks.

The notion of security and portfolio *risk* in the Sharpe model is a bit less clear on the surface than are return calculations. The plotted returns and some key statistical relationships are shown below.[9]

YEAR	SECURITY RETURN (%)	INDEX RETURN (%)
1	6	20
2	5	40
3	10	30
Average	= 7	30
Variance from average	= 4.7	66.7
Correlation coefficient	= −.189	
Coefficient of determination	= .0357	

Notice that when the index return goes up (down), the security's return generally goes down (up). Note changes in return from years 1 to 2 and 2 to 3. This reverse behavior accounts for our negative correlation coefficient (r).

The *coefficient of determination* (r^2) tells us the percentage of the variance of the security's return that is explained by the variation of return on the index (or market). Only about 3.5 percent of the variance of the security's return is explained by the index; some 96.5 percent is not. In other words, of the total variance in the return on the security (4.7), the following is true:

Explained by index = 4.7 × .0357 = .17

Not explained by index = 4.7 × .9643 = 4.53

Sharpe noted that the variance explained by the index could be referred to as the *systematic risk*. The unexplained variance is called the residual variance, or *unsystematic risk*.

Sharpe suggests that systematic risk for an individual security can be seen as:

[9]It should be noted that such a small number of observations makes results prone to considerable error. The modest number of observations is simply an illustrative convenience. The negative beta coefficient is not typical for stocks in general.

$$\text{Systematic risk} = \beta^2 \times (\text{Variance of index})$$

$$= \beta^2 \sigma_I^2$$

$$= (-.05)^2(66.7)$$

$$= (.0025)(66.7)$$

$$= .17$$

$$\text{Unsystematic risk} = (\text{Total variance of security return}) - (\text{Systematic risk})$$

$$= e^2$$

$$= 4.7 - .17$$

$$= 4.53$$

Then:

$$\text{Total risk} = \beta^2 \sigma_I^2 + e^2$$

$$= .17 + 4.53$$

$$= 4.7$$

And portfolio variance is

$$\sigma_p^2 = \left[\left(\sum_{i=1}^{N} X_i \beta_i \right)^2 \sigma_I^2 \right] + \left[\sum_{i=1}^{N} X_i^2 e_i^2 \right] \tag{17.5}$$

where all symbols are as before, plus:

σ_p^2 = variance of portfolio return
σ_I^2 = expected variance of index
e_i^2 = variation in security's return not caused by its relationship to the index

PORTFOLIO ANALYSIS: AN EXPANDED EXAMPLE

We shall use an example to show how efficient portfolios might be constructed using the ideas of Sharpe. What follows is concerned with generating the efficient frontier. In Chapters 18 and 20 we will extend the example to include selection of a "best" portfolio and the monitoring of performance over subsequent time periods.

Listed in Table 17–3 are seventeen common stocks. Let us assume that these stocks have emerged from the security-analysis stage as candidates for portfolios. A uniform holding period was used in estimating risk and return for each stock. Specifically, each stock was examined as a possible holding for a one-year period. Our task here is to discover the efficient combinations of these stocks.

TABLE 17–3

Stock-Selection Candidates

COMPANY	DESCRIPTION
Aetna Life and Casualty	Largest all-line insurance company in the United States.
Citicorp	Owns Citibank, the second largest commercial bank in the United States.
High Voltage Engineering Co.	Manufactures plastic insulation products, electrical connectors and switches, builders' instruments, electron processing systems, and scientific equipment.
K Mart	The second largest retail store chain in the United States.
McDermott	Provides the oil industry with offshore oil development and production facilities.
McDonald's Corp.	World's largest chain of fast-food restaurants.
Nucor Corp.	Steel fabricator.
Pargas	One of the largest distributors of liquified petroleum gas on the east and west coasts.
Pitney Bowes, Inc.	World's largest manufacturer of postage meters and related mailing equipment.
Quaker Oats	Major worldwide producer of brand-name packaged foods.
Raytheon Co.	Produces a wide range of electronic and computer equipment.
Southwest Forest Products Co.	Produces newsprint.
Texaco	One of the largest integrated oil companies in the United States.
USAir	The nation's fourth largest airline company.
United States Shoe	Manufactures, imports, wholesales, and retails footwear for men.
United States Steel	Steel manufacturer and producer of cement, chemicals, and oilfield equipment.
Wisconsin Gas Co.	The largest distributor of natural gas in Wisconsin.

Data Needed for Each Stock

Under the Markowitz system of portfolio analysis, we need three bits of information for each stock: (1) expected return for the holding period, (2) expected risk for the holding period, and (3) expected covariance for each pair of stocks. The Sharpe simplification would require (1) and (2), and for (3), covariance estimates for each stock relative to the market (index).[10] In addition, for the Sharpe model we need to estimate the return and variance on the index for the holding period.

---

[10]Markowitz data requirements for seventeen stocks would be 170, and Sharpe 53.

TABLE 17–4

Alpha, Beta, and Residual Variance for Seventeen Stocks (vs. S&P 500 Index)

	ALPHA (%)	BETA	EXPECTED RETURN (%)*	RESIDUAL VARIANCE (%)
Aetna Life and Casualty	0.17	0.93	10.4	45.15
Citicorp	−0.59	1.26	13.3	29.48
High Voltage Engineering	1.27	1.50	17.8	150.30
K Mart	−0.28	1.17	12.6	45.42
McDermott	1.02	1.05	12.5	114.06
McDonald's Corp.	0.85	1.36	15.8	43.29
Nucor Corp.	2.48	1.37	17.5	132.25
Pargas	0.47	0.86	9.9	82.08
Pitney Bowes, Inc.	1.55	1.07	13.3	66.58
Quaker Oats	−0.16	0.97	10.5	86.49
Raytheon Co.	2.52	1.17	15.4	51.98
Southwest Forest Products Co.	0.76	0.87	10.3	59.28
Texaco	−0.28	0.91	9.7	22.27
USAir	1.47	1.73	20.5	196.28
United States Shoe	1.63	1.09	13.6	94.09
United States Steel	0.64	0.98	11.4	48.86
Wisconsin Gas Co.	0.28	0.87	9.8	17.64

*Assuming a return on the index (market) of 11 percent.

For each of the stocks listed in Table 17–3, the regression coefficients (α, β) and the residual variance (e^2) were calculated from historical data. Monthly rates of return on each stock were regressed against the Standard & Poor's 500 Stock Index monthly rates of return for a five-year period.[11] Results are shown in Table 17–4.

The most crucial input before beginning to generate efficient portfolios was an estimate of the return and risk on the S&P Index for the holding period (one year ahead). The return on the S&P was estimated by projecting an estimated level of the index one year ahead plus expected dividends on the index. The return was estimated at 11 percent, with a risk (variance) of 26.37 percent.

These two estimates, return and risk on the S&P, serve as the focal point for estimating return and risk for each stock and, therefore, portfolios of stocks. Recall that, using the Sharpe method, return and risk estimates for portfolios are built by using the α, β, and e^2 estimates for portfolios for individual stocks applied to the projected return-risk variables for the index. Let us examine what the return-risk values would be for a one-stock portfolio, using USAir data and Equations 17.4 and 17.5 for portfolio return and portfolio risk:

[11]It is customary to calculate alpha and beta using monthly data for the most recent five-year period. Some analysts use quarterly data.

$$R_p = \sum_{i=1}^{N} X_i(\alpha_i + \beta_i I)$$

$$= 1.00\,[1.47 + (1.73)(11)]$$

$$R_p = 20.5$$

$$\sigma_p^2 = \left(\sum_{i=1}^{N} X_i\beta_i\right)^2 \sigma_I^2 + \sum_{i=1}^{N} (X_i^2 e_i^2)$$

$$= \beta_i^2 \sigma_I^2 + e_i^2 \text{ (since } X_i = 1.00)$$

$$= (2.99)(26.37) + (196.28)$$

$$= 78.84 + 196.28$$

$$= 275.12$$

$$\sigma_p = 16.6$$

Generating the Efficient Frontier

Using the required inputs, the Sharpe model and a computer, a series of "corner" portfolios was generated rather than an infinite number of points along the efficient frontier. The traceout of the efficient frontier connecting corner portfolios is shown in Figure 17–8. Table 17–5 shows the stocks and relative proportions invested at several corner portfolios.

Corner portfolios are portfolios calculated where a security either enters or leaves the portfolio. Corner portfolio 1 is a one-stock portfolio. It contains the stock with the greatest return (and risk) from the set—in this case, USAir. Notice in Table 17–5 that the return of 20.5 percent (.205) and the standard deviation or risk of 16.6 percent (.1659) for corner portfolio 1 (USAir) correspond to the earlier calculations shown to arrive at these figures.[12] The computer program proceeds down the efficient frontier finding the corner portfolios. Corner portfolio 2 is introduced with the appearance of a second stock, High Voltage Engineering. Typically, the number of stocks increases as we move down the frontier until we reach the last corner portfolio—the one that provides the minimum attainable risk (variance) and the lowest return. To understand better what is happening between any two successive corner portfolios, examine numbers 8 and 9. Between these two, Pitney Bowes stock makes its initial appearance.

The actual number of stocks entering into any given efficient portfolio is largely determined by boundaries, if any, set on the maximum and/or minimum percentage that can be devoted to any one security from the total portfolio. If these percentages (weights) are free to take on any values, the efficient frontier may con-

---

[12]The reader is invited to prove the expected return and standard deviation for corner portfolio 2, using Equations 17.4 and 17.5.

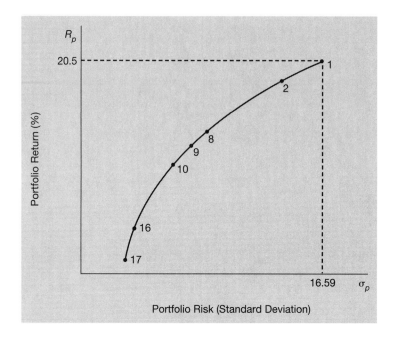

FIGURE 17–8   Efficient Frontier Connecting "Corner" Portfolios

tain one- or two-security portfolios at the low or high extremes. Setting maximum (upper-bound) constraints assures a certain minimum number of stocks held. The efficient frontier in Figure 17–8 had no constraints placed upon weights.

A method for constructing optimum portfolios using simple ranking devices will be illustrated in Chapter 18.

"ADEQUATE" DIVERSIFICATION

Many traditional approaches to diversification stress that the more securities one holds in a portfolio, the better. Markowitz-type diversification stresses not the number of securities but the right kinds; the right kinds of securities are those that exhibit less than perfect positive correlation.

An unfortunate fact is that nearly all securities are positively correlated with each other and the market. King noted that about half the variance in a typical stock results from elements that affect the whole market (systematic risk).[13] The upshot of this is that risk cannot be reduced to zero in portfolios of any size. The

[13]B. F. King, "Market and Industry Factors in Stock Price Behavior," *Journal of Business* 39, no. 1 (January 1966), pp. 139–90.

TABLE 17–5

Selected Corner Portfolios

SECURITY	CORNER PORTFOLIO NUMBER					
	1	2	8	9	13	17
Aetna Life and Casualty						.055
Citicorp					.018	
High Voltage. Engineering Co		.060	.139	.113	.074	.026
K Mart					.015	.020
McDermott					.040	.037
McDonald's Corp.			.228	.221	.178	.074
Nucor Corp.			.180	.153	.110	.053
Pargas						.041
Pitney Bowes, Inc.				.061	.106	.082
Quaker Oats						.019
Raytheon Co.			.257	.262	.236	.146
Southwest Forest Products Co.					.022	.068
Texaco						.065
USAir	1.00	.940	.178	.134	.075	.020
United States Shoe			.018	.056	.081	.060
United States Steel					.044	.072
Wisconsin Gas Co.						.163
Expected return (%)	20.5	20.3	17.0	16.54	15.4	12.8
Expected standard deviation (%)	16.6	15.9	8.4	7.90	7.2	5.9

one-half of total risk that is not related to market forces (unsystematic) can be reduced by proper diversification, but once unsystematic risk is reduced or eliminated, we are left with systematic risk, which no one can escape (other than by not buying securities).

Thus, beyond some finite number of securities, adding more is expensive in time and money spent to search them out and monitor their performance; and this cost is not balanced by any benefits in the form of additional reduction of risk! Evans and Archer's work suggest that unsystematic risk can be reduced naively by holding as few as ten to fifteen stocks.[14] (In fact, risk can be increased by duplicating within industries.) This results from simply allowing unsystematic risk on these stocks to average out to near zero. With Markowitz-type diversification, risk can technically be reduced below the systematic level if securities can be found whose rates of return have low enough correlations. Negative correlations are ideal.

[14]John L. Evans and S. H. Archer, "Diversification and the Reduction of Dispersion: An Empirical Analysis," *Journal of Finance* (December 1968), pp. 761–69.

SUMMARY

Investors are concerned not only with expected return on their investments but also their riskiness. However, knowing the riskiness of individual securities does not make it possible to deduce the riskiness of a portfolio of those securities. Using the ideas of Markowitz and others, we learned that portfolios are packages of securities that are constructed by knowing the return and risk on individual securities and also the *interactive* risk that exists *between* securities.

Our discussion in this chapter proceeded logically from the construction of feasible portfolios of two securities to bigger portfolios from a large universe of securities. We noted that some portfolios dominate others in that they provide either (1) the same return but lower risk, or (2) the same risk but higher return. These criteria distinguish portfolios that are feasible (possible) from those that are more "efficient."

The growing complexities of considering interactive risk in large populations of security candidates call for shortcuts in method. The ideas of Sharpe in simplifying the portfolio-analysis process were introduced. Finally, seventeen candidate stocks for analysis were packaged into feasible and efficient portfolios, using the Sharpe methodology and a computer.

QUESTIONS

1. Write out the Markowitz expressions for expected return and standard deviation for the case of four securities.

2. Distinguish between a *feasible* and an *efficient* portfolio. Is an inefficient portfolio ever a feasible portfolio?

3. How many inputs are needed for a portfolio analysis involving sixty securities if covariances are computed using
    a. the Markowitz technique, and
    b. the Sharpe index method?

4. Refer to the stock example in Table 17–4.
    a. Which stock would most likely be selected by an aggressive investor wishing to hold a single security and expecting the S&P 500 return next year to be .20.
    b. The last column in Table 17–4 shows the unexplained variance (risk) for each of the seventeen candidate stocks. What significance, if any, is there to stocks with the largest unexplained variances (e^2)?
    c. Which stock would a defensive investor place all his money in if he wanted to minimize his risk when the S&P 500 was expected to decline 10 percent?

5. Stock N has a standard deviation of .15 and stock O has a standard deviation of .20. Can the standard deviation in a portfolio containing these two securities be reduced? Why or why not?

6. Suppose two stocks have a correlation of +1.0. Can a portfolio of these two stocks reduce risk? Explain.

7. Refer to Table 17–2. Which pair of assets would give the most risk-reducing potential? The least?

8. What does the coefficient of determination tell us that its sister statistic, the correlation coefficient, does not tell us?

9. What is a *corner portfolio?* What is its role in creating an efficient frontier?

10. In what ways does the Sharpe system for generating efficient portfolios differ from the Markowitz system?

PROBLEMS

1. Stocks R and S display the following returns over the past two years:

YEAR	STOCK R RETURN (%)	STOCK S RETURN (%)
19 × 3	10	12
19 × 4	16	18

   a. What is the expected return on a portfolio made up of 40 percent R and 60 percent S?
   b. What is the standard deviation of each stock?
   c. What is the covariance of stocks R and S?
   d. Determine the correlation coefficient of stocks R and S.
   e. What is the portfolio risk of a portfolio made up of 40 percent R and 60 percent S?

2. Consider a third security, T, along with stocks R and S in Problem 1. Its return over the past two years was: 19×3, 16 percent; 19×4, 10 percent. Would this security provide any advantages in combination with stock R? With stock S? With stocks R and S together?

3. Stocks Y and Z display the following parameters:

	STOCK Y	STOCK Z
Expected return	15	20
Expected variance	9	16
Covariance yz = +8		

Does an investor gain any advantage in holding some of Y and some of Z? Why?

4. Shown below are the returns on Xerox and the S&P 500 Stock Index for a five-year period.

YEAR	RETURN ON XEROX	RETURN ON S&P 500
1	.29	(.10)
2	.31	.24
3	.10	.11
4	.06	(.08)
5	(.07)	.03

   a. Plot the returns on Xerox versus the S&P 500 on a graph.
   b. Calculate the regression equation for the returns you have plotted (i.e., alpha, beta, and residual variance), and draw the line for this equation on your graph.
   c. Indicate (i) total variance for Xerox, and (ii) the proportions that are explained and not explained by the S&P 500.

5. The return on Xerox for year 6 was .177. The S&P 500 return was .14. Would the return on Xerox for year 6 be suggested by your regression equation in 4b? Why or why not?

6. Show that the portfolio return and standard deviation for corner portfolio 2 in Table 17–5 are 20.3 and 15.9, respectively.

7. Stock L has a standard deviation of 5 and stock M has a standard deviation of 15. The coefficient of correlation of the returns of stocks L and M is +.40. Can a portfolio of these two stocks be produced that has a smaller standard deviation of return than either security taken alone? Why or why not?

8. Following are data for several stocks. The data result from correlating returns on these stocks versus returns on a market index:

STOCK	A	B	e2
MNO	−.05	+1.6	.04
PQR	+.08	−0.3	.00
LUV	.00	+1.1	.10

   a. Which single stock would you prefer to own from a risk-return viewpoint if the market index were expected to have a return of +.10 and a variance of return of .10?
   b. What does the e2 value for PQR imply? The a value for LUV?

9. Examine Table 17–5. Suppose you had $250,000 to invest and you chose corner portfolio 8. What stocks would you pick and what amounts would be invested in each?

10. The following data is offered on two stocks:

STOCK	EXPECTED RETURN	STANDARD DEVIATION
W	.15	.30
X	.10	.20

The correlation between the two stocks is +1.0

Determine the expected return and risk on the following combinations of these two stocks:

	% STOCK W	% STOCK X
a.	70	30
c.	50	50
d.	30	70
e.	10	90

11. Refer to Tables 17–1 and 17–2. What is the expected return and risk on a portfolio consisting of equal amounts of venture capital and domestic bonds?

12. Stock Z has the following statistics: variance = .20, beta = 1.2, alpha = .02, correlation with market index = .4, variance of market index = .15.
a. What is the coefficient of determination for this stock?
b. What is the unsystematic risk for this stock?

REFERENCES

FARRELL, J. I., JR. *Guide to Portfolio Management.* New York: McGraw-Hill, 1983.

HAGIN, R. *Modern Portfolio Theory.* Homewood, Ill.: Dow Jones-Irwin, 1979.

HARRINGTON, D. R. *Modern Portfolio Theory.* 2d ed. Englewood Cliffs, N.J.: Prentice Hall, 1987.

MARKOWITZ, H. M. *Portfolio Selection: Diversification of Investments.* New York: John Wiley, 1959.

MARKOWITZ, H. M. "Individual versus Institutional Investing." *Financial Services Review* 1 (1991).

MOSSIN, J. "Equilibrium in a Capital Asset Market." *Econometrica,* (October 1966).

SHARPE, W. F. "Capital Asset Prices: A Theory of Market Equilibrium under Conditions of Risk." *Journal of Finance* (September 1964).

SHARPE, W. F. *Portfolio Theory and Capital Markets.* New York: McGraw-Hill, 1970.

STATMAN, M. "How Many Stocks Make a Diversified Portfolio?" *Journal of Financial and Quantitative Analysis* (September 1987).

CHAPTER 18

PORTFOLIO SELECTION

In this chapter we are concerned with the question, How should an investor go about selecting the one best portfolio to meet his needs? Or, more explicitly, how should an investor go about selecting securities to purchase and deciding how many dollars to invest in each?

First, we will examine modern selection techniques suggested by the work of Markowitz and others. Next, we will explore the more traditional means employed to provide investment counsel and portfolio selection, such as is preeminent among portfolio managers currently.

RISK AND INVESTOR PREFERENCES

Our examination of the theory behind Markowitz-type diversification revealed the substance behind the determination of an efficient frontier, or locus of portfolio opportunities. The issue now is, How should investors (analysts) choose a "best" option on the efficient frontier?

Our central vehicle for attacking this problem is the satisfaction an investor receives from investment opportunities. Our assumption has been that risk-return measures on portfolios are the main determinants of an investor's attitude toward them. We need to look closely at the manner in which risk affects preference.

Utility functions, or indifference curves, are normally used to represent someone's preferences. Let us invent a set of preferences or indifference curves for a hypothetical investor, as displayed in Figure 18–1. For the moment, we will make no pretense that this indifference "map" depicts any real investor any of us may know. This investor has indifference curves that are parallel to one another and linear. The higher a curve, the more desirable the situations lying along it. Each curve carries equal satisfaction along its length. We have labeled the indifference (utility) curves from 1 to 6 in order of increasing desirability. The investor's problem is to find the feasible portfolio tangent to the best attainable (highest) indifference

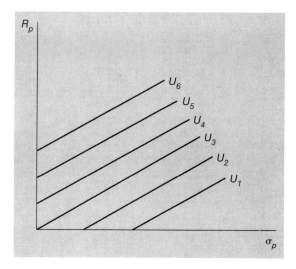

FIGURE 18–1   Indifference Map for Hypothetical Investor

curve (line). If we combine the efficient frontier with the family of indifference curves, as in Figure 18–2, we can see how the investor might solve his problem. Point *B* is his "best" portfolio because (1) it is efficient, and (2) at that point, the frontier will be tangent to the indifference curve (line).

Because most investors would be expected to seek more return for additional risk assumed, utility or indifference curves (lines) are positively sloped. See Figure 18–3 for a set of indifference curves (lines) for a risk lover. His indifference curves are negative sloping and convex toward the origin. With the risk averter, the lower

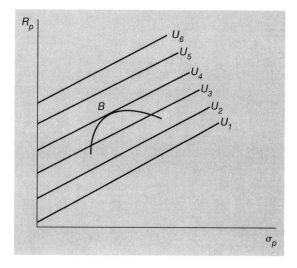

FIGURE 18–2   Indifference Map and Efficient Frontier for Hypothetical Investor

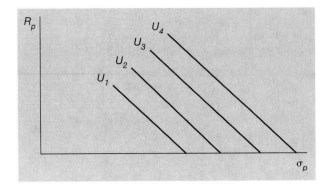

FIGURE 18–3   Risk-Lover Indifference Curves

the σ_p of his portfolio, the happier, he is; the risk lover is happier the higher the level of σ_p.[1]

The degree of slope associated with indifference curves will indicate the degree of risk aversion for the investor in question. A sort of aggressive versus conservative risk preference is shown in Figures 18–4 and 18–5. The conservative investor (Figure 18–4) requires large increases in return for assuming small increases in risk; the more aggressive investor will accept smaller increases in return

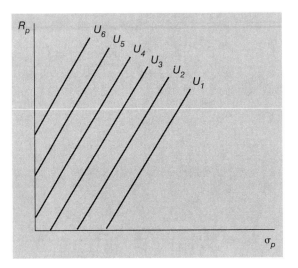

FIGURE 18–4   Risk-Fearing Investor's Indifference Curves

[1]If an efficient frontier were drawn on Figure 18–3, the only point of tangency with the risk lover's indifference curves would be at the upper-right point of the frontier. This point contains one security and follows the risk lover's maxim of putting all one's eggs into a single basket.

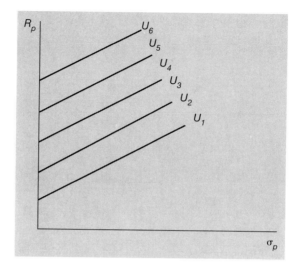

FIGURE 18–5   Less-Risk-Fearing Investor's Indifference Curves

for large increases in risk. Both dislike risk, but they trade off risk and return in different degrees.

Although differences may occur in the slope of indifference curves, they are assumed to be positive sloping for most rational investors. A more important question is whether indifference curves are curves and not straight lines as depicted so far.

Does different utility accrue to given increments of return? For example, the utility received from $100,000 may or may not be worth twice that received from $50,000. In effect, in Figure 18–6 we can see three different slopes to an indifference or utility curve (line). Curve *A* depicts increasing marginal utility, curve *B* constant utility, and curve *C* diminishing marginal utility. While constant marginal utility (straight line) would suggest that, say, doubling return doubles utility (satisfaction), increasing marginal utility means that increasingly larger satisfaction is to be found from the same increase in return. Increasing marginal utility would suggest the case of the inveterate gambler who is, in fact, a risk lover. Curve *C*, diminishing marginal utility, is probably identified with the way most investors behave. In sum, constant marginal utility of return means that an investor is risk-neutral; decreasing marginal utility means that he is risk-averse; increasing marginal utility suggests that he likes risk.

Selecting the "Best" Portfolio

Establishing efficient portfolios (minimum risk for a given expected return) comprising broad classes of assets (e.g., stocks, bonds, real estate) lends itself to the mean-variance methodology suggested by Markowitz. Determining efficient port-

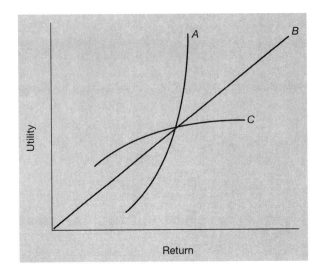

FIGURE 18–6   Various Marginal-Utility Curves

folios within an asset class (e.g., stocks) can be achieved with the single index (beta) model proposed by Sharpe.

The following pages will help us to understand how to select the best portfolio from an available set using both the Markowitz and the Sharpe techniques. It is imperative to remember that the outcomes are sensitive, as always, to the validity of the inputs. There is an old saw in computer science that says "Garbage-in, garbage-out" (GIGO, for short).

Simple Markowitz Portfolio Optimization[2]

It is possible to develop a fairly simple decision rule for selecting an optimal portfolio for an investor that can take both risk and return into account. This is called a risk-adjusted return. For simplicity, it can be termed the *utility* of the portfolio for the investor in question. Utility is the expected return of the portfolio minus a risk penalty. This risk penalty depends on portfolio risk and the investor's risk tolerance.

THE RISK PENALTY

The more risk one must bear, the more undesirable is an additional unit of risk. Theoretically, and as a computational convenience, it can be assumed that twice the risk is four times as undesirable. The risk penalty is as follows:

[2]This section draws heavily upon William Sharpe, "Practical Aspects of Portfolio Optimization," in *Improving the Investment Decision Process* (Charlottesville, VA.: Institute of Chartered Financial Analysts/Dow Jones-Irwin, 1984).

THE PSYCHOLOGY OF RISK AVERSION

There are a number of studies in the field of behavioral psychology that strongly suggest why investing is uncomfortable. Findings reveal that value is often the product of investors' stress and anxiety caused by framing investments as probable losses.

Work in this field encompasses two broad areas. The first is called *prospect theory,* which reveals how people react to judgments about uncertain events when the probability of events is defined. The other area is called *heuristics* ("to find out"). Studies in this area investigate how people process information about the future to try to establish a range of possibilities for likely events. The remarkable insights that emerge from this work are that both of these cognitive processes—i.e., establishing a sense of the probability of future events and reacting to them—reveal systematic biases or distortions.

It's no surprise that stock market investing, dominated by our orientation toward future events, is emotional and therefore subject to cognitive biases. The psychology of the stock market is based on how investors form judgments about uncertain future events and how they react to these judgments.

One of the most important findings of prospect theory is that people do not react consistently when faced with risk. Instead, they exhibit certain systematic biases. Let's explore a series of examples to illustrate.

We offer you the following choice problem: You have two options. The first is to accept $3,000 right now—with 100 percent certainty—or accept the possibility of receiving $4,000—with an 80 percent probability of success. Which offer would you accept?

Behavioral psychologists pose this choice problem and find respondents chose $3,000 with 100 percent certainty. In fact, this finding is not in itself remarkable. It conforms to traditional feelings about investment risk aversion: When seeking gains, people require more gain to compensate for an increase of risk.

Of course, there is a reason for choosing the second option. The expected value of the first choice is $3,000; yet the expected value for the second choice is $3,200 (4,000 × .8). As it turns out, the extra expected return of $200 does not carry the day with most respondents, who exhibit risk-averse tendencies when seeking gains.

Let's change the frame of the problem and see what you would choose. You can take a $3,000 loss—with total certainty—or you can have a $4,000 loss with 80 percent probability. Which will you choose?

In studies conducted with similar problems, the majority of people would take the greater loss with 80 percent probability. Upon reflection, this is a remarkable result because it violates the very risk-averse tendencies that we saw earlier. In general, investors seek risk to avoid a certain loss yet avoid risk when seeking gains.

The disproportionality of people's tolerance for losses, as compared to the pleasure of gains, can lead to inefficiencies in the stock market. With great frequency, investors find reasons to become intensely afraid of various sectors of the economy, particularly industry groups and specific companies. The prices of "troubled" stocks (electric utilities with nuclear plants, cigarette companies, polluters) present opportunities for the investor who can "stomach" the discomfort caused by the possibility of probable loss. Put it this way: Excess return inherent in these stocks is being paid to you by the seller to relieve him of the stress of ownership—the stress being generated by the perceived possibility of substantial loss.

Investors also tend to overpay for the prospect of big rewards (oil find, new drug, hit movie) while systematically overvaluing potential calamities.

$$\text{Risk penalty} = \frac{\text{Risk squared}}{\text{Risk tolerance}}$$

Risk squared is the variance of return of the portfolio. Risk tolerance is a number from 0 through 100. The size of the risk tolerance number reflects the investor's willingness to bear more risk for more return. Low (high) tolerance indicates low (high) willingness. Risk penalty is less as tolerance is increased.

For example, if a portfolio's expected return is 13 percent, variance of return (risk squared) is 225 percent, and the investor's risk tolerance is 50, the risk penalty is 4.5 percent:

$$\text{Risk penalty} = \frac{225\%}{50} = 4.5\%$$

Because utility is expected return minus the risk penalty, we have:

$$\text{Utility} = 13 - 4.5 = 8.5\%$$

The optimal (best) portfolio for an investor would be the one from the opportunity set (efficient frontier) that maximizes utility.

Illustration of Process

The reader is encouraged to refer to Tables 17–1 and 17–2, which provided the necessary inputs using nine asset classes to generate efficient portfolios.

Table 18–1 uses only six asset classes for convenience of illustration. Various allocations are shown with resulting risk, return, and utility data. A risk tolerance

TABLE 18–1

Risk, Return, and Utility for Various Mixes of Asset Classes

	PORTFOLIO				
	A	B	C	D	E
Real estate			25.0%		16.7%
U.S. fixed income	50.0%	33.3%	25.0%	20.0%	16.7%
International fixed income				20.0%	16.7%
U.S. equities		33.3%	25.0%	20.0%	16.7%
Intl. equities				20.0%	16.7%
Cash equivalents	50.0%	33.4%	25.0%	20.0%	16.7%
Total	100.0%	100.0%	100.0%	100.0%	100.0%
	PORTFOLIO PARAMETERS				
Expected return	7.60%	9.13%	9.48%	9.73%	9.85%
Expected variance	0.19%	0.52%	0.61%	0.74%	0.75%
Standard deviation	4.32%	7.24%	7.79%	8.59%	8.67%
Risk tolerance	50.00%	50.00%	50.00%	50.00%	50.00%
Risk penalty	0.37%	1.05%	1.21%	1.47%	1.50%
Utility	7.23%	8.08%	8.26%	8.26%	8.35%

TABLE 18–2

Utility of Various Portfolios with a
Risk Tolerance of 30 Percent Applied

| | PORTFOLIO | | | | |
PORTFOLIO PARAMETERS	A	B	C	D	E
Expected return	7.60%	9.13%	9.48%	9.73%	9.85%
Expected variance	0.19%	0.52%	0.61%	0.74%	0.75%
Standard deviation	4.32%	7.24%	7.79%	8.59%	8.67%
Risk tolerance	30.00%	30.00%	30.00%	30.00%	30.00%
Risk penalty	0.62%	1.75%	2.02%	2.46%	2.50%
Utility	6.98%	7.38%	7.45%	7.27%	7.35%

of 50 suggests that the optimum portfolio is E because its utility of 8.35 percent is the highest. Table 18–2 alters the risk tolerance to 30. This suggests that the "best" portfolio is portfolio C.

Using risk-return data for various asset classes over the period 1926–81, Sharpe has shown the composition of optimal portfolios for investors with risk tolerance from 10 to 100. For example, someone with a risk tolerance of 100 would hold a passive portfolio of roughly 20 percent corporate bonds, 35 percent real estate, 40 percent equities, and about 5 percent cash equivalents. See Figure 18–7.

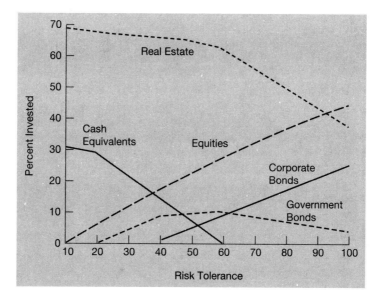

FIGURE 18–7   Composition of Optimal Portfolios for Investors with
Different Risk Tolerances

SIMPLE SHARPE PORTFOLIO OPTIMIZATION

The construction of an optimal portfolio[3] is simplified if a single number measures the desirability of including a stock in the optimal portfolio. If we accept the single-index model (Sharpe), such a number exists. In this case, the desirability of any stock is directly related to its *excess return-to-beta ratio*:

$$\frac{R_i - R_F}{\beta_i}$$

where:

R_i = expected return on stock i

R_F = return on a riskless asset

β_i = expected change in the rate of return on stock i associated with a 1 percent change in the market return

If stocks are ranked by excess return to beta (from highest to lowest), the ranking represents the desirability of any stock's inclusion in a portfolio. The number of stocks selected depends on a unique cutoff rate such that all stocks with higher ratios of $(R_i - R_F)/\beta_i$ will be included and all stocks with lower ratios excluded.

To determine which stocks are included in the optimum portfolio, the following steps are necessary:

1. Calculate the excess return-to-beta ratio for each stock under review and the rank from highest to lowest.

2. The optimum portfolio consists of investing in all stocks for which $(R_i - R_F)/\beta_i$ is greater than a particular cutoff point C*.

Ranking Securities

Tables 18–3 and 18–4 represent an example of this procedure. Table 18–3 contains the data necessary to determine an optimal portfolio. It is the normal output generated from a single index model, plus the ratio of excess return to beta. There are ten securities in the tables. They are already ranked. Selecting the optimal portfolio involves the comparison of $(R_i - R_F)/\beta_i$ with C*. For the moment, assume that C* = 5.45. Examining Table 18–3 shows that for securities 1 to 5, $(R_i - R_F)/\beta_i$ is

---

[3]This analysis draws upon E. J. Elton, M. J. Gruber, and M. W. Padberg, "Optimum Portfolios from Simple Ranking Devices," *Journal of Portfolio Management* (Spring 1978), pp. 15–19. Another simplified asset mix model is developed in Y. Benari, "An Asset Allocation Paradigm," *Journal of Portfolio Management* (Winter 1988).

TABLE 18–3

Data Needed To Find Optimal Portfolio ($R_F = 5\%$)

(1) SECURITY NO., i	(2) MEAN RETURN, R_i	(3) EXCESS RETURN, $R_i - R_F$	(4) BETA, B_i	(5) UNSYSTEMATIC RISK, σ_{ei}^2	(6) EXCESS RETURN- TO-BETA, $(R_i - R_F)/B_i$
1	15.0	10.0	1.0	50	10.0
2	17.0	12.0	1.5	40	8.0
3	12.0	7.0	1.0	20	7.0
4	17.0	12.0	2.0	10	6.0
5	11.0	6.0	1.0	40	6.0
6	11.0	6.0	1.5	30	4.0
7	11.0	6.0	2.0	40	3.0
8	7.0	2.0	.8	16	2.5
9	7.0	2.0	1.0	20	2.0
10	5.6	.6	.6	6	1.0

greater than C^*, while for security 6 it is less than C^*. Hence, an optimal portfolio consists of securities 1 to 5.

Establishing a Cutoff Rate

All securities whose excess return-to-risk ratio are above the cutoff rate are selected and all whose ratios are below are rejected. The value of C^* is computed from the characteristics of all of the securities that belong in the optimum portfolio. To determine C^* it is necessary to calculate its value as if different numbers of securities were in the optimum portfolio. Suppose C_i is a candidate for C^*. The value of C_i is calculated when i securities are assumed to belong to the optimal portfolio.

TABLE 18–4

Calculations for Determining Cutoff Rate with $\sigma_m^2 = 10$

(1) SECURITY NO.	(2) $\dfrac{(R_i - R_F)}{B_i}$	(3) $\dfrac{(R_i - R_F)B_i}{\sigma_{ei}^2}$	(4) $\dfrac{B_i^2}{\sigma_{ei}^2}$	(5) $\displaystyle\sum_{i=1}^{j} \dfrac{(R_i - R_F)B_i}{\sigma_{ei}^2}$	(6) $\displaystyle\sum_{i=1}^{j} \dfrac{B_i^2}{\Sigma_{ei}^2}$	(7) C
1	10	2/10	2/100	2/10	2/100	1.67
2	8	4.5/10	5.625/100	6.5/10	7.625/100	3.69
3	7	3.5/10	5/100	10/10	12.625/100	4.42
4	6	24/10	40/100	34/10	52.625/100	5.43
5	6	1.5/10	2.5/100	35.5/10	55.125/100	5.45
6	4	3/10	7.5/100	38.5/10	62.625/100	5.30
7	3	3/10	10/100	41.5/10	72.625/100	5.02
8	2.5	1/10	4/100	42.5/10	76.625/100	4.91
9	2.0	1/10	5/100	43.5/10	81.625/100	4.75
10	1.0	.6/10	6/100	44.1/10	87.625/100	4.52

Because securities are ranked from highest excess return to beta to lowest, we know that if a particular security belongs in the optimal portfolio, all higher-ranked securities also belong in the optimal portfolio. We proceed to calculate values of a variable C_i as if the first-ranked security were in the optimal portfolio ($i = 1$), then the first- and second-ranked securities were in the optimal portfolio ($i = 2$), and so on. These C_i are candidates for C^*. We have found the optimum C_i, that is, C^*, when all securities used in the calculation of C_i have excess returns to beta above C_i and all securities not used to calculate C_i have excess return to betas below C_i. For example, in column (7) of Table 18-4 we see the C_i for which all securities used in the calculation i [rows (1) through (5) in the table] have a ratio of excess return to beta above C_i and all securities not used in the calculation of C_i [rows (6) through (10) in the table] have an excess return-to-beta ratio below C_i. C_5 serves the role of a cutoff rate in the way a cutoff rate was defined earlier. In particular, C_5 is the only C_i that when used as a cutoff rate selects only the stocks used to construct it. There will always be one and only one C_i with this property and it is C^*.

Finding the Cutoff Rate C*

For a portfolio of i stocks, C_i is given by:

$$C_i = \frac{\sigma_m^2 \sum_{i=1}^{i} \frac{(R_i - R_F)\beta_i}{\sigma_{ei}^2}}{1 + \sigma_m^2 \sum_{i=1}^{i} \frac{\beta_i^2}{\sigma_{ei}^2}}$$

where:

σ_m^2 = variance in the market index

σ_{ei}^2 = variance of a stock's movement that is not associated with the movement of the market index; this is the stock's unsystematic risk

The value of C_i for the first security in our list is thus:

EXPRESSION	CALCULATION	DATA LOCATION TABLE
$\dfrac{(R_i - R_F)\beta_i}{\sigma_{ei}^2}$	$\dfrac{(15 - 5)1}{50} = \dfrac{2}{10}$	Column (3)
$\sum_{i=1}^{1} \dfrac{(R_i - R_F)\beta_i}{\sigma_{ei}^2}$	Same as above (since $i = 1$)	Column (5)
$\dfrac{\beta_i^2}{\sigma_{ei}^2}$	$\dfrac{(1)^2}{50} = \dfrac{2}{100}$	Column (4) [cumulated in column (6)]

Putting all this information together yields:

$$C_i = \frac{10\left(\dfrac{2}{10}\right)}{1 + 10\left(\dfrac{2}{100}\right)} = 1.67$$

For security 2 ($i = 2$) column (3) is:

$$\frac{(17 - 5)1.5}{40} = \frac{4.5}{10}$$

Now column (5) is the sum of column (3) for security 1 and security 2 or:

$$\frac{2}{10} + \frac{4.5}{10} = \frac{6.5}{10}$$

Column (4) is:

$$\frac{(1.5)^2}{40} = \frac{5.625}{100}$$

Column (6) is the sum of column (4) for security 1 and 2, or:

$$\frac{2}{100} + \frac{5.625}{100} = \frac{7.625}{100}$$

and C_2 is:

$$C_2 = \frac{\sigma_m^2 \,[\text{column (5)}]}{1 + \sigma_m^2[\text{column (6)}]} = \frac{10\left(\dfrac{6.5}{10}\right)}{1 + 10\left(\dfrac{7.625}{100}\right)} = 3.69$$

Proceeding in the same fashion, we can find all the C_i's.

Arriving at the Optimal Portfolio

Once we know which securities are to be included in the optimum portfolio, we must calculate the percent invested in each security. The percentage invested in each security is:

$$X_i^0 = \frac{Z_i}{\sum\limits_{j=1}^{N} Z_j}$$

where:

$$Z_i = \frac{\beta_i}{\sigma_{ei}^2} \left(\frac{R_i - R_F}{\beta_i} - C^* \right)$$

The second expression determines the relative investment in each security, and the first expression simply scales the weights on each security so that they sum to 1 (ensure full investment). The residual variance on each security σ_{ei}^2 plays an important role in determining how much to invest in each security. Applying this formula to our example, we have:

$$Z_1 = \frac{2}{100}(10 - 5.45) = .091$$

$$Z_2 = \frac{3.75}{100}(8 - 5.45) = .095625$$

$$Z_3 = \frac{5}{100}(7 - 5.45) = .0775$$

$$Z_4 = \frac{20}{100}(6 - 5.45) = .110$$

$$Z_5 = \frac{2.5}{100}(6 - 5.45) = .01375$$

$$\sum_{i=1}^{5} Z_i = .387875$$

Dividing each Z_i by the sum of the Z_i, we would invest 23.5 percent of our funds in security 1, 24.6 percent in security 2, 20 percent in security 3, 28.4 percent in security 4, and 3.5 percent in security 5.

The characteristics of a stock that make it desirable can be determined before the calculations of an optimal portfolio is begun. The desirability of any stock is solely a function of its excess return-to-beta ratio.

Consideration of New Securities

The techniques discussed also simplify the problem of revising portfolios as new securities enter the decision universe.

In our example, C^* was equal to 5.45; thus, if a new security is suggested that has an excess return-to-risk ratio of less than C^* (5.45), we would know that it could not enter into the optimum portfolio. The existence of a cutoff rate is extremely useful because most new securities candidates that have an excess return-to-beta ratio above 5.45 would have to be included in the optimal portfolio.

The impact of a new security on which securities are included in the optimal portfolio is easy to figure. For example, consider a security with an excess return of

TABLE 18–5

SECURITY	$\dfrac{(R_i - R_f)B_i}{\sigma_{ei}^2}$ EX RTN. × BETA/ RES. VAR	$\dfrac{B_i^2}{\sigma_{ei}^2}$ BETA SQD./ RES. VAR.	$\sum\limits_{i=1}^{j} \dfrac{(R_i - R_f)B_i}{\sigma_{ei}^2}$ EX. RTN. × BETA/ RES. VAR.	$\sum\limits_{i=1}^{j} \dfrac{B_i^2}{\sigma_{ei}^2}$ BETA SQD./ RES. VAR.	C CUTOFF VALUE	Z VALUE
USAir	0.119	0.01525	0.119	0.01525	2.24	0.021
Nucor	0.109	0.01419	0.228	0.02944	3.39	0.024
High Voltage	0.107	0.01497	0.336	0.04441	4.08	0.018
Raytheon	0.189	0.02634	0.525	0.07075	4.83	0.040
McDonald's	0.277	0.04273	0.801	0.11347	5.29	0.034
U.S. Shoe	0.077	0.01263	0.878	0.12610	5.35	0.008
Pitney Bowes	0.102	0.01720	0.980	0.14329	5.41	0.008
Citicorp	0.268	0.05385	1.248	0.19715	5.31	
McDermott	0.051	0.00967	1.299	0.20681	5.31	
K Mart	0.144	0.03014	1.443	0.23695	5.25	
U.S. Steel	0.089	0.01966	1.532	0.25661	5.20	
Quaker Oats	0.000	0.01088	1.532	0.26749	5.01	
Aetna	0.000	0.01916	1.532	0.28664	4.72	
Southwest	0.000	0.01277	1.532	0.29941	4.54	
Pargas	0.000	0.00901	1.532	0.30842	4.42	
Wisconsin	0.000	0.04291	1.532	0.35133	3.93	
Texaco	0.000	0.03718	1.532	0.38852	3.59	

9, a beta of 1, and a residual risk of 10. Then, initially assuming that this security should be added to the previously optimum portfolio, we obtain a cutoff rate of 5.37. Because this is larger than the excess return-to-beta ratio for any security previously excluded from the portfolio, the optimum portfolio consists of the old portfolio with the addition of the new security. It is possible that the old portfolio will not remain optimal. The change may involve a change in one or two of the securities whose excess return-to-beta ratio is near the cutoff rate.

Portfolio Selection Example

In Table 18–5 we demonstrate the application of this selection system with the list of candidate stocks introduced in Chapter 17. Notice that the cutoff rate is 5.41 and includes seven stocks in the portfolio. The largest holding is Raytheon and the smallest is U.S. Shoe. The portfolio mix is shown in Figure 18–8.

The risk-free rate here is 7 percent, and the expected return on the market is 11 percent. The expected variance of return on the market is 26 percent.

The sum of all the Z values greater than zero is .153. Consequently, the portion of the total portfolio dedicated to each stock with a positive Z value is: $Z/.153$. For example, Nucor would be 15.7% of the portfolio ($.024/.153$).

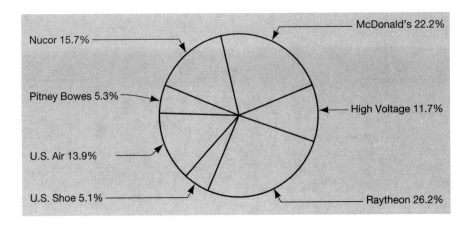

FIGURE 18–8   Stock Portfolio Composition

Significance of Beta in the Portfolio

Sharpe notes that proper diversification and the holding of a sufficient number of securities can reduce the unsystematic component of portfolio risk to zero by averaging out the unsystematic risk of individual stocks. What is left is systematic risk which, because it is determined by the market (index), cannot be eliminated through portfolio balancing. Thus, the Sharpe model attaches considerable significance to systematic risk and its most important measure, the beta coefficient (β).

According to the model, the risk contribution to a portfolio of an individual stock can be measured by the stock's beta coefficient. The market index will have a beta coefficient of + 1.0. A stock with a beta of, for example, + 2.0 indicates that it contributes far more risk to a portfolio than a stock with, say, a beta of + .05. Stocks with negative betas are to be coveted because they help reduce risk beyond the unsystematic level.

Because efficient portfolios eliminate unsystematic risk, the riskiness of such portfolios is determined exclusively by market movements. Risk in an efficient portfolio is measured by the portfolio beta. See Table 18–6 for the beta coefficients of each stock in the portfolio that was chosen from the efficient frontier. The beta for the portfolio is simply the weighted average of the betas of the component securities. Our optimal portfolio has a beta of 1.35, which suggests that it has a sensitivity above the + 1.0 attributed to the market. If this portfolio is properly diversified (proper number of stocks and elimination of unsystematic risk), it should move up or down about one-third more than the market. Such a high beta suggests an aggressive portfolio. If the market moves up over the holding period, our portfolio will be expected to advance substantially. However, a market decline should find this portfolio falling considerably in value.

SOCIALLY RESPONSIBLE INVESTING

Some investors have decided that their personal portfolios should more closely reflect their social views. This has been referred to as socially responsible investing. At a time when many institutional investors are selling stock in companies that deal in tobacco products or pollute the environment, a growing number of individuals have also been putting their money where their ethical values are. Estimates suggest that in 1992 individuals had intrusted more than $10 billion with managers using social and political investment criteria.

To some critics, avoiding a company to protest apartheid, industrial pollution, or a lack of women in positions of authority is akin to throwing money away. They feel that when you make noneconomic choices you get noneconomic results. That's spelled "less profit." By restricting your investments in any way, you cannot be better off they contend. When you limit the number of opportunities, you limit some of the potential for return. Proponents counter by suggesting that the loss isn't necessarily great because the universe of potential investments is huge even if one eliminates some companies. With small personal portfolios, which by their nature are limited in breadth, does it really matter?

The real problem say critics is not return, but market risk. Restricted portfolios tend to eliminate large multinational corporations, and replace them with smaller firms whose stock is more volatile. Investments with low market risk typically fall less rapidly than more volatile investments in a down market and rise less sharply in a bull market.

The greater risk should actually improve return over long periods of time because active stocks tend to gain more than they lose. But for the risk-averse investor, the greater volatility of smaller capitalization companies may be something to avoid.

Proponents of social investing have little doubt on the wisdom of their approach. They set their own ethical standards to avoid tobacco companies, nuclear utilities or weapons makers without sacrificing return. Some say concern about a company's social responsibility can actually improve return by helping investors avoid potential problems. A company that will be spending millions to clean up its pollutions or on product liability suits could get damaged severely.

Beta in Stock Selection

It is easy to see the central role played by the beta coefficient in the determination of expected return and risk for stocks as well as portfolios.

Some analysts have proposed using beta coefficients to approach the problem of stock selection. In this approach, the outlook for the market is assessed. Portfolios are constructed by optimizing beta coefficients in line with the market outlook. For example, if the market is expected to advance in the future, portfolios would be constructed containing stocks with beta coefficients that give maximum return. Such stocks would also carry high risks when the beta coefficients are large. A beta of + 1.0 would indicate a stock with "average" volatility relative to the market. A beta of + 2.0 would mean that if the market return was forecast as 10 percent, the stock would have an estimated return of 20 percent (excluding the value of alpha).

TABLE 18–6

Stock Portfolio for One-Year Holding Period

COMPANY	(1) BETA	(2) PORTFOLIO PROPORTION (%)	(1) × (2) WEIGHTED BETA
High Voltage Engineering Co.	1.50	11.7	.175
McDonald's Corp.	1.36	22.2	.302
Nucor Corp.	1.37	15.7	.215
Pitney Bowes, Inc.	1.07	5.3	.056
Raytheon Co.	1.17	26.2	.306
USAir Corp.	1.73	13.9	.240
United States Shoe	1.09	5.1	.055
		100.0	1.35

If the outlook suggests a market decline, stocks with large positive beta coefficients might be sold short. Stocks with negative betas would provide resistance to the market downtrend. Suppose the forecast is for a 10 percent decline in the market. A stock with a beta of + 2.0 would provide a negative return of 20 percent if held long. If the stock is sold short, a gain of 20 percent is suggested. If the 10 percent market decline is forecast, a stock with a beta of − 1.0 would provide a return of +10 percent [− 1.0 × − .10]. Unfortunately, stocks with negative betas are scarce.

These approaches to stock selection are valid under two key assumptions. First, it is necessary to forecast the timing and direction of market moves with reasonable accuracy. Second, the historical measure of beta must persist at roughly similar levels during the forecast period.

Under the first assumption, the continuous tailoring of portfolio volatility in order to capitalize on anticipated market moves can operate *against* the investment-return objectives of the portfolio. This is especially the case if the timing and direction of the forecast market moves are not consistently correct.

The second assumption is equally important. Whereas the variability of market returns is able to explain roughly 75 to 95 percent of the variability of the returns of most portfolios, owing to the averaging effects that are achieved by diversification, the market is able to explain only 15 to 65 percent of the volatility of most individual securities. As a result, the statistical significance of the estimated coefficients is suspect in the case of some common stocks. Moreover, questions have been raised on the stability of these coefficients during short- to intermediate-term periods, and this is the time horizon of interest to most portfolio managers.

PREDICTING BETA

Care must be exercised in interpreting a historical beta. It cannot be assumed that beta is fixed over time. Quite the contrary, there is reason to expect that beta does change. Historical betas should not obscure the fact that although they are useful

when interpreting past performance, prediction requires betas that are forward-looking estimates.

Much of the mystery surrounding beta can be avoided by remembering that beta does not describe a causal relationship. A certain level of market return does not result in a certain level of security return. Instead, both market and security returns depend on a third variable—the economy. Economic events cause systematic changes in both security and market index prices.

Properly viewed, beta reflects the fact that both market and security returns depend on common events. Thus, the most logical way to forecast beta is to quantify the relationship between market and security returns and these factors. What, for example, is the relationship between changes in the expected rate of inflation and the returns of both individual securities and the market? Compared to the market, which securities are sensitive to inflation and which are not?

Most of the risk and return in a portfolio is linked to the market. In turn, the market component of risk and return for a security is derived from the economic events that affect many stocks. It follows that considerable benefits can be derived from an extension of fundamental security analysis that is concerned with the relationship between a security's return and economywide events—so-called *fundamental betas*.

Barr Rosenberg has developed a way of predicting fundamental betas through *relative response coefficients*. Basically, a relative response coefficient is the ratio of the expected response of a security to the expected response of the market if both the security and the market are affected by the same event. For example, if the event is inflation, those stocks that react to inflation in the same way as the market will have a high relative response coefficient for this event. Similarly, stocks that are not as sensitive to inflation as the market will have a low relative response coefficient for inflation.

Assume that we wish to study the impact of future energy and inflation developments on the market and on two stocks. There is an equal likelihood that future events in each of these areas will turn out to have favorable, unchanged, or unfavorable implications. This situation, plus the relative response that each event-outcome combination is expected to elicit, are depicted in Table 18–7. Stock

TABLE 18–7

Contributions to Return for Hypothetical Event-Outcome Sequences

EVENT	OUTCOME	PERCENTAGE CONTRIBUTION TO RETURN		
		MARKET	STOCK T	STOCK U
Energy	Favorable	+3	+2	+6
	Unchanged	0	0	0
	Unfavorable	−3	−2	−6
Inflation	Favorable	+2	+4	0
	Unchanged	0	0	0
	Unfavorable	−2	−4	0

T is expected to respond two-thirds as much as the market to an energy-related event, whereas stock U is anticipated to react twice as strongly as the market. To an inflation event, stock T is expected to respond twice as much as the market, whereas stock U is not expected to show any reaction to inflation events.

The relationships portrayed in Table 18–7 can be used to contrast the expected values and variances of returns on securities with those of the market when both are affected by the same macroeconomic events. In this illustration, the expected (average) impact of these two events on market return is zero, and the variance is 30 percent.[4] The variance of future market returns can be separated into the variances generated by each of the two events. In this illustration, energy uncertainties cause 24 percentage points of the variance in market returns. Similarly, the variance caused by inflation uncertainty amounts to 6 percent.

In general terms, a security's beta is determined by:

1. the proportional contributions of various categories of economic events to market variance; and

2. the relative response of security returns to these same events—the relative response coefficients.

More specifically, the beta for any security is the weighted average of its relative response coefficients, each weighted by the proportion of total variance in market returns due to that event.

In the example in Table 18–7, energy is the greatest source of uncertainty (variance). Thus, in the calculation of beta, energy uncertainty receives proportionately more emphasis. In terms of response to the two economic events, stock U is expected to be volatile in a changing energy situation. It is not surprising, therefore, that the betas for stocks T and U are .9 and 1.1, respectively.

The importance of the foregoing discussion of the composition of beta is that a security's beta will change when:

1. the variance contributed by the various categories of economic events changes, and

2. the response coefficients change.

Also, to the degree that these changes can be predicted or explained, beta can be predicted or explained.

An accurate prediction of beta is the most important element in predicting the future behavior of a portfolio. That is, in the portfolio context, the relevant risk

---

[4]To assist the reader who wishes to pursue this subject in more detail, the numerical example used here is identical to that used by Rosenberg. The procedure used to calculate this variance (as well as other information) is found in B. Rosenberg and J. Guy, "Prediction of Systematic Risk from Investment Fundamentals," *Financial Analysts Journal* 32, no. 3 (May–June 1976), pp. 60–72, and no. 4 (July–August 1976), pp. 62–70.

of a security lies in its impact on the risk of a portfolio. Further, the risk of a well-diversified portfolio is almost exclusively linked to the sensitivity of its component securities to future market moves. For this purpose, backward-looking betas are inappropriate.

Instead, it is necessary to (1) consider the sources of such future moves, (2) project the security's reaction to such sources, and (3) assign probabilities to the likelihood of each possible occurrence. This process, in turn, requires a thorough understanding of (1) the economics of the relevant industry, (2) both operating leverage and financial leverage of the company, and (3) other fundamental factors with meaningful relative response coefficients.

Rosenberg's fundamentally derived betas have been shown to be more accurate than historically derived estimates. Six risk indexes are based on current fundamental characteristics of each company and are measures of the following: (1) market variability, (2) earnings variability, (3) low valuation and unsuccess, (4) immaturity and smallness, (5) growth orientation, and (6) financial risk. Rosenberg has found that, in the past, stock returns have tended to be related to these factors, and forecasts of beta are improved by adjusting them through appropriate weightings of these factors. To calculate fundamentally based predictions of beta and residual risk, Rosenberg uses the following six indexes of risk.

1. *Market variability.* Measures the impact of certain factors on the relationship between the market variability of returns and security returns.

2. *Earnings variability.* Measures the variability of earnings. Earnings variability contributes to risk.

3. *Low valuation and "unsuccess."* Designed to measure the variability of returns (risk) inherent in consistently low-market-valuation stocks with dismal operating records.

4. *Immaturity and smallness.* Differentiates between the older and larger firms—which have accumulated substantial fixed assets and have a more secure economic position and a lower degree of risk—and the small, younger, and riskier firms.

5. *Growth orientation.* Measures the risk associated with the so-called high-multiple (P/E) stocks.

6. *Financial structure.* Measures financial risk by incorporating leverage (long-term debt and equity as a percentage of book value), coverage of fixed charges, the ratio of debt to total assets, liquidity, and net monetary debt. In general, the more highly leveraged a financial structure, the greater is the risk to the common stockholders.

Because stock returns are now specified relative to this more detailed multifactor model, the system can provide a more precise measurement of the risk characteristics of a portfolio. Instead of simply separating systematic risk from

unsystematic or residual risk, we can now split residual risk into what is called specific risk and extramarket covariance.

Specific risk is the uncertainty in the return that arises from events that are specific to the firm. Specific risk is unrelated to events that affect other firms and is sometimes referred to as the "unique" or "independent" risk of the company.

Extramarket covariance is the remaining component of residual risk. It is manifested as a tendency of related assets to move together in a way that is independent of the market as a whole. The term *covariance* refers to the tendency of stock prices to move together, or "covary." The term *extramarket* means that these comovements are not related to the movements of the market as a whole. Extramarket covariance can be thought of as the middle ground between systematic and specific risk. Systematic risk affects all firms. Specific risk affects only one firm. Extramarket covariance impacts a homogeneous group of firms, such as those belonging to a certain industry or those with large capitalizations.

For individual stocks specific risk is most important, accounting for about 50 percent of the total risk, with the remainder about equally divided between systematic risk and extramarket covariance. For a well-diversified portfolio, systematic risk is likely to be 80 to 90 percent of the total risk.

For portfolios with concentrations of stocks in certain industry groups, or classes of stocks such as interest-sensitive stocks, extramarket covariance is very important. Thus, the construction of prudent, well-reasoned portfolios requires the prediction of all three aspects of risk: systematic, specific, and extramarket. It is noteworthy in this regard that the Rosenberg prediction scheme derives estimates of both market returns and extramarket covariances from a single underlying model.

TRADITIONAL PORTFOLIO SELECTION

Traditionally, portfolio selection has been viewed as an art form, perhaps even a craft. Portfolio people are builders. Much of their work has its roots in a kind of life-cycle, interior-decorator approach.[5]

Security-portfolio selection must be preceded by attention to financial planning. Needs must be analyzed and provision made for such things as emergency savings, adequate insurance, and home ownership. For many people, basic living expenses, savings, insurance, and shelter costs absorb most, if not all, income and resources. For these people, direct securities investing may never be a practical reality. Others frequently plunge into the securities markets before paying proper attention to financial planning prerequisites. The question of appropriate portfolio selection would presume that an investor had his financial house in order first.

[5]An early look at some practical aspects of selection can be found in K. V. Smith, "The Major Asset Mix Problem for the Individual Investor," *Journal of Contemporary Business* (Winter 1974).

A step-by-step traditional approach to portfolio building recognizes several basic tenets.[6] First, investors prefer large to smaller returns from securities. Second, the way to achieve this goal is to take more risk. Third, the ability to achieve higher returns is dependent upon (1) the investor's judgment of risk, and (2) his ability to assume specific risks. Spreading money among many securities can reduce risk.

As components of risk, the theory recognizes specific types of risk and non-risk factors bearing upon return—namely, interest-rate risk, purchasing-power risk, financial risks (including business, financial, and market risk), and nonrisk variables such as taxation and marketability. Portfolios are presumably constructed by employing securities associated with varying degrees of risk and non-risk factors.

The financial interior-decorator approach would follow a general sequence of steps. First, an investor must determine the minimum income necessary to avoid hardship under the most adverse economic conditions. Family and economic factors are the principal ingredients in the projection of nonsecurity income and expenses. Economic factors take into account the family balance sheet (assets and debts) and income statement (income and expenses). Family factors affect income and expenses through such variables as the number of dependents and their ages and health. Income-expense differentials establish the minimum income required from investments.

Second, the larger the principal in relation to the minimum investment income required, the greater the risk of loss of income that can be tolerated. Of course, one must plan for changes in principal available, changes in income from other sources, and changes in minimum expenses. Take two contrasting situations. In both, the principal amount is $100,000 and future expenses are forecast at $20,000 per year. Salary income is $18,000 in one case and only $8,000 in the other. In the former situation, the income "gap" is $2,000; the latter case has a gap of $12,000. A portfolio of $100,000 would have to yield 2 percent in the first case ($2,000/$100,000), and 12 percent ($12,000/$100,000) in the second. If good-quality bonds yield 8 percent, in the first example only $25,000 of principal is needed to provide the required income. This means that $75,000 can be invested at greater risk. The latter case requires (1) increasing outside income, and/or (2) reducing expenses, and/or (3) using some of the principal (assuming that additional principal is not forthcoming). Thus, the future budgeting of nonsecurity income and expenses tells us the *degree of risk of principal or income the portfolio can tolerate.* Quality bonds and common stocks with generous, stable yields provide income with minimum risk to principal. The greater price volatility associated with stocks in general over bonds can be tolerated when required portfolio income is not substantial relative to principal available.

Third, the more nearly investment income generated at current rates of yield on high-grade bonds meets the minimum investment-income requirements projected on an inflation basis, the greater is the ability to risk loss of purchasing

---

[6]Harry Sauvain, *Investment Management* (Englewood Cliffs, N.J.: Prentice Hall, 1973).

power of investment income. It is necessary to see that nonsecurity income (such as salary) and expenses may rise at different rates as price-level changes occur. If expenses rise more rapidly than nonsecurity income, income from fixed-income securities will make the investor vulnerable to rises in the price level. This would suggest a need for some defense against inflation, in the form of securities that provide larger dollar income at a higher price level. More relative emphasis might be placed upon convertible securities that can be purchased at modest premiums over investment and conversion value. The greater the need for inflation protection, the more the emphasis moves to straight common-stock commitments.

Overall, in this decision-making process, an investor would be assessing the kinds of risk and degree of each type that he can tolerate. In addition, the importance of nonrisk factors such as marketability and taxation would be assessed after the risk factors. The fundamental risk factors bear upon income and principal in constant (price-level-adjusted) dollars. Financial risk can be minimized by commitments to top-quality bonds. These securities, however, offer poor resistance to inflation. Stocks provide better inflation protection than bonds but are more vulnerable to financial risk. Good-quality convertibles may bridge the financial-risk-purchasing-power-risk dilemma. The problems associated with interest-rate risk suggest that maturity is of major concern. Short-term fixed-income securities offer greatest risk to income; long-term fixed-income securities offer greatest risk to principal.

What we emerge with from this approach is a series of *compromises* on risk and nonrisk factors after an investor has assessed the major risk categories he or she is trying to minimize. The final answer will be in terms of relative portfolio weights assigned to classes of securities—that is, bonds (quality, maturity), stocks (income, cyclical, growth), and hybrids (convertibles). The specific securities chosen will be the more attractive in each class as judged by security analysis. Not uncommonly, the dollar amounts devoted to each security or class of securities will be a simple equal allotment.

Defining Investment Objectives[7]

Establishing portfolios for individuals is the most diverse of investment situations. Every investor has a different set of circumstances, needs, and opportunities. Considerations that shape and modify investment strategies and objectives are extremely wide.[8]

Portfolios differ widely in their requirements, time horizons, risk thresholds, and cash flows. The objective of portfolio management is to reconcile these variables in such a manner as to minimize risk and maximize return, but the goal and

---

[7]Donald L. Tuttle and John L. Maginn, *Determinants of Portfolio Policy* (Charlottesville, Va.: Institute of Chartered Financial Analysts, 1982).

[8]Our discussion emphasizes personal portfolio selection. Institutional portfolios are addressed along similar lines. Basic security types are dictated very much by laws and regulations in addition to the debt-to-equity ratios and the term structure of liabilities.

the process of reconciling the variables is the same regardless of who owns the assets in question.

All portfolios share one objective: to provide the largest pool of assets from which the owner can finance expenditures now or at some future date. Because the future is uncertain, however, we can never know precisely what the value of assets will be over time, and we know even less about what their purchasing power will be. The degree of risk that we take should, therefore, vary in each case, based upon the *time horizon* within which we have to work and the likelihood that the portfolio will enjoy a net cash inflow or will be subject to cash withdrawals. The latter is a matter of *liquidity*. The art of portfolio management consists of nothing more than selecting securities that fit within the time and cash flow constraints of the investor; the application of this process to differing portfolios is only a variation on a constant theme.

Traditionally investors differentiate among four goals: current income, growth in current income, capital appreciation, and preservation of capital. If viewed rationally, however, all investors should want to achieve all four of these goals; obviously, no one wants to lose money, while everyone wants to have as much as possible. The problem is that most of the time circumstances deny us the opportunity to achieve all four goals simultaneously. The search for capital gains inevitably involves risk of loss of capital; assured income is seldom available with opportunities for capital gains—high income is frequently associated with high risk. Therefore, when the time horizon is short or when investors have to face cash withdrawals from the portfolio, they lean toward assets with the greatest certainty of income and capital value. As the time horizon stretches out into the future, and when investors are adding to rather than withdrawing principal, they can live more comfortably with uncertainty.[9]

LIFE-CYCLE APPROACH

The return and risk possibilities are virtually unconstrained for individuals, a unique investing situation. Why? Because, assuming a minimum wealth or income position, essentially all possible asset categories and all investment strategies are open to the individual investing directly for his own account.

That is, the individual has available the entire risk spectrum of investable assets ranging from essentially risk-free assets such as short-term government fixed-income securities to the riskiest assets such as common-stock option contracts and commodities futures contracts.

In addition, the individual can choose from among the entire spectrum of investment strategies. Unlike other investors, he can establish either long or short positions in securities. And he can opt for a variety of different leverage positions; that is, the individual can invest all of his net worth in a portfolio of risky assets or

---

[9]W. G. Droms, ed., *Asset Allocation for the Individual Investor* (Charlottesville, Va.: Institute of Chartered Financial Analysts, 1987).

part of net worth in risky assets and part in safe assets, or all in risky assets plus borrowing on margin and investing that borrowed money in risky assets.

Individuals' risk and return preferences are often portrayed in terms of stages of their "life cycle." That is, individuals are described by the stage of their lifetime or career where they are currently located.

The first stage is the early career stage. Assets are typically much less than liabilities, especially when the latter include a large home mortgage and other debts from credit purchases. The individual's assets are typically nondiversified, with house equity the largest asset held, and inaccessible, in the form of employer pension contributions. Priorities include savings for liquidity purposes, life insurance for death protection and, only third, investments. But because the individual has a very long time horizon with a potentially growing stream of discretionary income, he can undertake high-return, high-risk capital-gain-oriented investments.

The midcareer individual is in the second stage. Assets equal or exceed liabilities, savings and life insurance programs are well under way, a basic investment program has been established, and home equity and potential pension benefits are substantial. At the same time, while the time horizon is still relatively long, it is not so long that capital preservation is unimportant. The investor can continue to undertake high-risk, high-return investments and reap the growth and capital gain benefits therefrom, but may wish to reduce the overall risk exposure involved.

The final phase is late career or nearing retirement, where the individual's time horizon has diminished and income needs—in terms of size and stability—have risen. Assets significantly exceed liabilities; savings, pension, and life insurance programs are complete; and the house mortgage has been repaid. Income is reduced to investment returns, Social Security, and other pension payments. The investor's portfolio is typically shifted to significantly lower-return, lower-risk assets with large dividend or interest payment components and relatively secure asset values because inflationary economic conditions may require the sale of assets to make up income shortfall.

Investment Constraints

LIQUIDITY

Just as was true of investment objectives, the constraints imposed on individual investors are subject to wide variance. That is true of liquidity needs that are highly individualistic, and hence, highly variable across individuals.

Some individuals use their investment accounts as combinations of checking and savings accounts. For these individuals, an adequate amount of funds should be kept in a liquidity reserve as large as the largest cash drain net of cash inflows that is budgeted. This reserve is usually easy to program. It should be invested in exceptionally high-quality, short-maturity debt issues such as a money-market fund or the types of issues—Treasury bills, commercial paper, certificates of deposit, and bankers acceptances—in which these funds are invested.

Furthermore, if the assets held have poor marketability, such as residential real estate or stock in a closely held business, liquidity needs should be estimated especially carefully and funded generously.

TIME HORIZON

Almost as important as risk and return in investment decision making is time horizon. This is the investment planning period for individuals. It is highly variable from individual to individual.

As indicated in the discussion of life cycles, individuals who are early in their life cycle have a long horizon, one which can absorb and smooth out the ups and downs of risky combinations of assets like common stock portfolios. These individuals can build portfolios of riskier assets and can use more risky investment strategies.

Later in life individuals have a much shorter horizon and should therefore tend toward less volatile portfolios, typically consisting of more bonds than stocks, with the former of higher quality and shorter duration (maturity/coupon combination) and the latter of higher quality and lower volatility.

TAX CONSIDERATIONS

Individuals are subject to a wide range of marginal tax rates. Our discussion in Chapter 2 noted that taxes were an important modifier of portfolio strategy. High-bracket investors should consider investing the fixed-income portion of their portfolio in a diversified group of municipal bonds if their taxable equivalent expected return exceeds that of taxable issues of equal risk. These same investors no doubt will look to investing the equity portion of their portfolios in a diversified group of stocks with large capital gains components relative to dividend income for a given level of risk.

CONSIDERING RISK

Our discussions of risk have emphasized the fact that, for most investment decisions, the major uncertainty is the probable volatility in the price of the asset and, in particular, its volatility relative to the prices of all similar types of assets.

Because most people obviously want to make as much money as possible, the determining question in structuring a portfolio is the consequences of loss. This seems far more important than the chance of loss. Even if the chance of loss is small (such as the probability of dying at age thirty), the consequences can be so serious that the individual must either avoid the risk altogether or must insure against it if he is unable to avoid it.

This is why the retired investor is conventionally viewed as an investor unable to take much risk. Because he typically has neither the life expectancy nor the earning power outside his portfolio to provide the opportunity to recoup losses, any diminution in his capital or income may immediately impact upon his standard of living. His opposite, the aggressive businessperson, on the other hand, has sufficient earning power to sustain his living standard and also many years to recoup his

losses. At an even further extreme, the consequences would be virtually minimal for a young man who will inherit millions from aging parents.

We might ask the same questions about the consequences of gain. To what extent would an increase in capital or income significantly improve the living standard of the investor? A retiree with less than $100,000 to invest might lead an entirely different life if it were $200,000, while a multimillionaire (and his heirs) might live precisely the same whether his assets never changed in value or whether they doubled.

The consequences of loss or gain seldom fit in such a way that the risk exposure of the portfolio is easy to determine. This is often a subjective decision; some people never feel rich enough, while others would rather take a chance of going broke next year. The authors know of a seventy-five-year-old who asked his broker to place most of his wealth in the options market. He was tired of being besieged by inflation. Here is a classic case of presumed risk aversion gone awry. Additionally, we know a millionaire whose broker tried to get him into the options market. This august gentleman reminded his broker, "Remember, you don't have to make me rich—I am rich!" This presumed risk seeker also did not fit the mold.

Identifying Objectives and Constraints

A brief example will serve to illustrate the process of identifying investment objectives, constraints, and developing an investment policy statement.

John Simpson is a twenty-seven-year-old attorney employed by a large firm since graduating from law school two years ago. Anne, his twenty-six-year-old wife, is employed as a psychologist for the local school district. They are childless now but may have children in a few years.

John and Anne have accumulated $10,000 in savings and recently inherited $50,000 in cash. They believe they can save at least $5,000 yearly. They are in a 28 percent income tax bracket currently and both have excellent career opportunities. They are eager to develop a financial plan and understand that it will need to be periodically adjusted as their circumstances change.

INVESTMENT OBJECTIVE

Their investment objective is to maximize total return with above-average risk. They can concentrate on building capital and can assume above-average risk because both are successfully employed, have recently inherited $50,000, and are able to save on an annually.

INVESTMENT CONSTRAINTS

1. Liquidity: Needs are minimal.
2. Time horizon: Long-term; both are young and there is no apparent need for change in plans for the foreseeable future.
3. Tax considerations: Currently in low to medium tax bracket.

4. Unique needs and circumstances:
   a. Age: Both young; early in investor life cycle.
   b. Family circumstances: More than adequate income, recent inheritance, no apparent unusual financial responsibilities.
   c. Sources and amount of income: Both are employed in successful career opportunities with ability to save part of their income.
   d. Wealth: Recent inheritance of $50,000 with the likelihood of savings and growth of assets increasing over the years to come.
5. Legal constraint: None.

INVESTMENT POLICY STATEMENT

They should maximize growth of total return with above-average risk and minimal liquidity needs, all in the context of a long time horizon. Diversification should stress its positive role as a growth-of-capital enhancement technique. No income needs or other constraints require special attention.

Investment Objectives and Asset Mixes

In Table 18–8 we list primary, secondary, and tertiary investment objectives for investors and a guideline of appropriate asset mixes (debt and equity securities) that should meet these objectives. The four objectives are current income, growth of income, appreciation, and stability of principal. Note that certain combinations of objectives are not shown; these tend to be mutually inconsistent or even unacceptable. For example, if stability of principal is the primary objective of the portfolio, it is unacceptable to have either growth of income or appreciation as a secondary goal. Stability of principal suggests that short-term debt instruments be held. These instruments offer neither growth of income nor meaningful appreciation potential. Similarly, a primary objective of growth of income is not compatible with a secondary goal of stability of principal.

An Example of Traditional Portfolio Selection[10]

Following is an illustration of traditional portfolio construction. The case illustrated has many different ingredients that provide some interesting challenges.

BACKGROUND

P. V. Wise, CFA, a portfolio manager at Investment Associates, is preparing for a meeting with Mary Atkins to discuss her portfolio. Wise has just learned that Atkins has been diagnosed as having a terminal illness and is not expected to live

---

[10]This example is adapted from Chartered Financial Analysts Examinations with permission of the Institute of Chartered Financial Analysts (ICFA).

TABLE 18–8

Investment Objectives and Asset Mixes

PRIMARY OBJECTIVE	SECONDARY OBJECTIVE	ASSET MIX	NOTES
Stability of principal Current income	Current income Stability of principal	Short-term debt portfolio Fixed-income portfolio	Minimum maturities necessary to achieve required income flow.
	Growth of income	40–60% debt 40–60% equities	Stability of principal third. Within the debt portfolio the portion invested short-term will depend on the need for stability of principal relative to stability of income.
	Growth of income	50–65% equities 35–50% debt	Appreciation third. Fixed income is to secure needed level and stability of income. Maturity of debt is not constrained by a need for stability of principal.
Growth of income	Current income	60–100% equities 0–40% debt	Appreciation should be third and debt portion could be tax-exempt issues. Stability is fourth goal.
	Appreciation	75–100% equities 0–25% debt	Current income should be third; stability is fourth goal.
Appreciation	Growth of income	0–10% debt 90–100% equities	

for more than nine months. Wise expects this news to affect the investment of her portfolio and notes that her investment policy statement should be updated.

Mary Atkins, age sixty-six, became a client of Investment Associates five years ago upon the death of her husband, Charles Atkins. Atkins had owned a successful newspaper business, which he sold two years before his death to Merit Enterprises, a publishing and broadcasting conglomerate, in exchange for shares of Merit common stock. Atkins had believed that Merit had a bright future and requested that the stock be retained, if possible. Although Mary Atkins had consented to sell some Merit shares to provide better portfolio diversification, the remaining Merit holding still represents a large percentage of her portfolio's total value.

The Atkins portfolio has a market value of $2 million. Recent sales of Merit stock generated a $50,000 capital gain. The portfolio currently produces $118,200

of annual income, more than half of which is exempt from federal income taxes. Mary Atkins also receives substantial income from a life annuity purchased before her husband's death. This income level allows Mary Atkins to live comfortably, although her income has not kept pace with inflation during the past five years. Fortunately, she is covered adequately by medical insurance.

The Atkinses had no children. Their wills provide that the assets remaining after Mary Atkins's death be used to create the Atkins Endowment Fund for the benefit of Good Samaritan Hospital. Because her life expectancy is less than one year, Mary Atkins wants to make sure that her financial affairs are in order. She looks forward to the meeting with Investment Associates, expecting that they can devise a portfolio that satisfies her immediate financial needs, as well as the future needs of the Good Samaritan Hospital.

Good Samaritan is a 180-bed, nonprofit hospital with an annual operating budget of $12.5 million. Until five years ago, the hospital's operating revenues were sufficient to meet operating expenses and even to generate an occasional small surplus. More recently, however, rising costs and declining occupancy rates are causing Good Samaritan to incur operating deficits averaging $350,000 annually.

As a result, the hospital's Board of Governors decided to increase the endowment's current investment income objective from 5 to 6 percent of total assets in order to reduce the size of the deficit.

The market value of Good Samaritan's existing endowment assets is $7.5 million. The portfolio generates approximately $375,000 of income annually, up from less than $200,000 five years ago. This increased income resulted from higher interest rates and a shift in asset mix toward more bonds. The new 6 percent requirement will raise investment income to approximately $450,000 yearly.

The hospital has not received any significant additions to its endowment assets in the past five years.

Wise has reviewed Atkins's original, five-year-old investment policy statement (Exhibit 1) and the current portfolio (Exhibit 2) in preparation for the meeting with Mary Atkins. He has constructed a new investment policy statement and recommendation for specific investment actions to be taken in the near future.

Because Mary Atkins is now expected to live no more than nine months, investment policy for her portfolio should begin to look beyond the current circumstances to the probable creation of the Atkins Endowment Fund. The first part of this case illustrates the unique investment considerations of endowment funds in contrast with those appropriate for a wealthy individual investor. The second part deals with the fundamentals of investing for endowments. The third part provides an opportunity to modify an investment strategy for different economic and capital market expectations.

INVESTMENT POLICY

Investment policy for Mary Atkins's portfolio must express her investment objectives and consider all relevant constraints on the achievement of the portfolio. The return requirements, risk tolerance, time horizon, and legal and regulatory considerations will not change significantly.

EXHIBIT 1

Original Investment Policy Statement for Mary Atkins

Objectives

Return Requirements: Mary Atkins requires a minimum of $50,000 after-tax investment income annually. Future investment income growth should attempt to keep pace with inflation. Given the fact that the assets will go to a charitable remainderman eventually, capital growth is also needed.

Risk Tolerance: Mary Atkins can assume modest risk to achieve income growth, provided that her minimum income need (adjusted for future inflation) is met. If the size of the fund builds over time, somewhat increased risk could be incurred to facilitate growth of capital.

Constraints

Liquidity: Because death taxes have been provided for and the assets will go to an endowment at her death, liquidity needs are low, except for any related to investment considerations.

Time Horizon: Mary Atkins's shorter-than-average personal time horizon is not an important investment consideration because her wealth will go to an endowment fund, which has an infinite time horizon, on her death.

Laws and Regulations: Because this is a personal portfolio, regulatory and legal constraints are not significant investment factors.

Tax Considerations: Mary Atkins is in the highest income tax bracket and would benefit from appropriate tax-advantaged investments.

Policy

The following guidelines were developed and approved following agreement between Investment Associates and Mary Atkins on the above objectives and constraints:

Asset Allocation:
50 to 70%—Domestic stocks and issues convertible into domestic stocks.
20 to 50%—Fixed-income investments, principally tax-exempt.
  0 to 20%—Short-term reserves, principally tax-exempt.

Diversification: With the exception of Merit Enterprises, individual common stock (and common stock equivalent) holdings should not exceed $50,000 at cost or $100,000 at market. Individual fixed-income holdings should not exceed $100,000 at cost or $150,000 at market.

Quality Criteria: All convertible securities and debt instruments must be rated no less than BBB as defined by Standard & Poor's, or its equivalent as defined by other rating agencies. All domestic stocks must have a history of at least five years of continuous dividend payment.

EXHIBIT 2

Investment Portfolio of Mrs. Atkins

		RECENT PRICE	MARKET VALUE	COST BASIS	ANNUAL INCOME
Shares	***Domestic Stocks***				
20,220	Merit Enterprises	$39	$788,600	$475,000	$24,800
1,000	Caterpillar Tractor	32	32,000	50,000	500
1,000	General Electric	58	58,000	50,000	2,000
500	IBM	122	61,000	38,000	2,200
2,000	Penn Power & Light	24	48,000	40,000	5,000
1,000	Standard Oil of Indiana	57	57,000	49,000	3,000
1,300	Weyerhauser	28	36,400	49,000	1,700
			$1,081,000	$751,000	$39,200
Par Value	***Convertible Issues***				
$50,000	John Deere 9% bonds due 2008	98	$49,000	$50,000	$4,500
$50,000	American Medical 13% bonds due 2001	140	70,000	50,000	6,500
			$119,000	$100,000	$11,000
Par Value	***Municipal Bonds***				
$100,000	Albuquerque, N.M., School Bonds 6.6% due 6/15/91	92	$92,000	$100,000	$6,600
$100,000	Cincinnati, Ohio, GO 10% due 12/1/92	101	101,000	100,000	10,000
$100,000	Illinois State GO 8.6% due 10/1/95	101	101,000	100,000	8,600
$100,000	Lynchburg, Va., GO 7.5% due 6/1/91	93	93,000	100,000	7,500
$100,000	Oregon State GO 8.2% due 2/1/91	89	89,000	100,000	8,200
$100,000	Sacramento, Calif., Util. Rev. Bonds 11.0% due 5/1/94	108	108,000	100,000	11,000
$100,000	Sheboygan, Wisc., GO 10.20% due 4/1/91	106	106,000	100,000	10,200
			$690,000	$700,000	$62,100
Market Value	***Short-Term Reserves***				
$110,000	Tax-exempt money market fund	1	$ 110,000	$ 110,000	$ 5,900
	Total portfolio		$2,000,000	$1,661,000	$118,200

OBJECTIVES

RETURN REQUIREMENTS.   Mary Atkins requires a minimum of $50,000 after-tax investment income annually. Future investment income growth should attempt to keep pace with inflation. Given the fact that the assets will go to a charitable remainderman at Mary Atkins's death, capital growth is also needed. The hospital is currently targeting a 6 percent income return, which is consistent with Mrs. Atkins' own income objective.

RISK TOLERANCE.   Mary Atkins can afford to take moderate risk to achieve income growth with some capital appreciation, given that her $50,000 minimum income need, adjusted for future inflation, is met. If the fund becomes large enough, somewhat increased risk could be incurred to facilitate growth of capital.

CONSTRAINTS

LIQUIDITY.   The liquidity constraint should perhaps be changed from "low" to "moderate" to reflect greater uncertainty during the next year. Mary Atkins may have heavy medical expenses; furthermore, she may live longer than is currently expected but remain in poor health. Also, after her death, the presence of cash reserves may facilitate reinvestment for the endowment's purposes. Thus, somewhat greater consideration could be given to liquidity.

TIME HORIZON.   Mary Atkins's shorter-than-average time horizon is not an important investment consideration because her wealth will go to an endowment fund, which has an infinite time horizon, on her death.

LAWS AND REGULATIONS.   Endowment funds are subject to state regulatory and legal constraints. These constraints do not conflict with prudent investment of Mary Atkins's portfolio while she is alive.

TAXES.   The most important area of change concerns taxes. Mary Atkins is in the maximum tax bracket for income and capital gains, whereas the endowment fund operates free of taxes. Therefore, tax policy for the portfolio should emphasize favorable tax benefits in the short term and postpone actions having unfavorable tax consequences. The analyst should seek agreement on taking capital losses to offset the $50,000 gain already realized on earlier sales of the Merit stock and on deferring further capital gains until the tax-exempt endowment fund receives the assets. Sales to take losses would also create the cash that would increase liquidity.

UNIQUE PREFERENCES AND CIRCUMSTANCES.   The investment of the Atkins portfolio must reflect the objectives and constraints of the Good Samaritan Hospital—the beneficiary of the assets upon Mary Atkins's death—when they do not conflict with those of Mary Atkins. The major constraint for her is the tax consequences.

ASSET ALLOCATION

The policy statement concerning asset allocation does not require immediate change in asset allocation ranges but should no longer specify that fixed-income and short-term investments be "principally tax-exempt."

SPECIFIC INVESTMENT ACTIONS

Several specific investment actions should be taken with regard to the Atkins portfolio. Mary Atkins should agree to sell her Caterpillar Tractor and Weyerhauser stocks, as well as the three municipal bonds that are selling significantly below cost. The capital losses generated from these sales would more than offset the $50,000 gain in Merit stock already taken this year. (The Deere convertible bonds have a slight loss, but the transaction costs would outweigh the small loss realized.) A desirable action to preserve the preexisting asset proportions would be to reinvest the common stock proceeds into new common stock holdings and the bond proceeds into new bonds, depending on capital market expectations. A modest increase in short-term reserves is indicated for a portion of the fixed-income money. Such reserves should be kept in tax-exempt issues, but longer maturities could be put into taxable bonds, because these can later be held in the endowment fund, which is not subject to federal taxation; their presence would have only minor adverse tax consequences for Mary Atkins in the short run.

SUMMARY

This chapter considered both modern and traditional approaches to portfolio selection. A simple technique was introduced for constructing optimal portfolios based upon the basic ideas of Markowitz and others. In addition, this chapter expanded on the significance of beta in stock and portfolio selection.

The chapter concluded with an examination of the basic principles of traditional portfolio selection applicable to the portfolios of individuals. An example showed how these principles could be utilized to construct a hypothetical portfolio.

QUESTIONS

1. Using the notion of corner points and the efficient frontier developed in Chapter 17, show on a risk-return diagram that the "best" portfolio (corner point) for a risk-lover would be corner point 1 in Figure 17–8.

2. How is the cutoff rate determined in the portfolio ranking system introduced in this chapter? What is the interpretation of this cutoff point in economic terms?

3. The candidate stocks in the sample problem in the chapter led to a "best" portfolio shown in Table 18–6.
   a. Why do you suppose that McDonald's and Raytheon account for almost half the total portfolio?
   b. How would we go about assessing the trade-off between transaction-cost savings and changes in portfolio return and risk by making Pitney Bowes and U.S. Shoe an even 6 percent each of the portfolio?

4. Why is the highest indifference curve (line) rather than the lowest the most important in selecting a portfolio for an investor?

5 Distinguish the risk-return attitude (trade-off) of a risk lover from that of someone who is risk-averse. Would you characterize yourself as a risk-lover or a risk-averse individual?

6. Explain the meaning of a risk penalty. What risk tolerance number would an extremely risk-averse investor use in determining her utility?

7. How is excess return-to-beta ratio used in portfolio optimization?

8. Dr. Paul Renard believes the market will rise about 10 percent in the next two months. He has told you that his list of stock picks includes those stocks with the highest betas. Is this a wise strategy? Explain.

9. What is a relative response coefficient? How is it used in portfolio analysis?

10. What are Rosenberg's six indexes of risk that he uses in predicting a stock's beta?

PROBLEMS

1. In what ways is corner portfolio 17 better for a risk-averse person than the placement of all funds in the least-risk stock, Wisconsin Gas Co. (see Table 17–5)?

2. What is the optimum portfolio in choosing among the following securities and assuming $R_f = 5$ percent and $\sigma_m^2 = 10$ percent?

SECURITY	EXPECTED RETURN	BETA	σ_{ei}^2
A	15	1.0	30
B	12	1.5	20
C	11	2.0	40
D	8	.8	10
E	9	1.0	20
F	14	1.5	10

3. Refer to the following diagram.
   a. Which portfolios shown are "feasible" (possible)?
   b. Which portfolio would a risk-lover choose? Why?

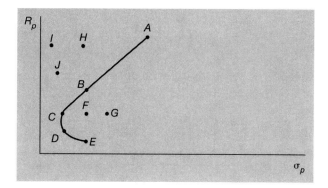

c. Which portfolio(s) would an irrational investor choose? Why?

d. Which portfolios shown are "efficient"? Why?

4. Describe the manner in which raising the return on a riskless asset (R_f) would alter the selection of the optimal portfolio in Question 2 above. (No calculations are required.)

5. The "best" stock portfolio can be discovered as that corner portfolio that maximizes $\theta = (R_p - R_f)/\sigma_p$ where R_p = expected return on the portfolio; σ_p is the expected standard deviation on the portfolio; R_f = risk-free rate.

   a. Show that corner point 9 provides a higher value for sigma than corner point 8 in Table 17-5.

   b. Determine the riskless rate at which sigma is the same for corner points 8 and 9.

6. Use the numbers in Table 18–1 to choose the "best" portfolio for someone with a risk tolerance of 70 percent?

7. You are attempting to construct an optimum portfolio. Over your holding period you have forecast an expected return on the market of 13.5 percent with a market variance of 25 percent. The Treasury security rate available is 7 percent (risk-free). The following securities are under review:

STOCK	ALPHA	BETA	RESIDUAL VARIANCE
Boeing	3.72	.99	9.35
Bristol-Myers	0.60	1.27	5.92
Browning-Ferris	0.41	.96	9.79
Emerson Electric	−0.22	1.21	5.36
Mountain States Telephone	0.45	.75	4.52

What is the optimum portfolio?

8. A widow in her seventies and in good health comes to you for advice about her investments. Her husband left her a portfolio that consists mostly of low-yielding "growth" stocks that are now at prices that approximate their adjusted cost. She has found that the income available is not nearly enough to help her maintain a comfortable standard of living. She needs $25,000 income

before taxes from her investments. The current market value of the portfolio is $400,000, and its current yield is 2.3 percent. Because she will need this higher income for perhaps the next ten years, you have suggested that she place at least half of the portfolio in high-yielding straight corporate bonds.

a. List the assumptions you made regarding the investment environment and the widow's situation in order to consider the immediate investment of one-half of the portfolio in bonds is a *prudent* decision.

b. Describe the types of investments you would select for the remainder of the portfolio that is not invested in high-yielding straight corporate bonds.

9. Alonzo Reilly is a successful business executive who retired at age fifty-eight after thirty years of service to a privately owned firm. He is married and has three adult children who are self-supporting. At the time of his retirement, the Reillys owned their own home, had savings of $50,000 in bank deposits, and owned miscellaneous good-quality stocks and bonds. Reilly is entitled to a yearly taxable pension of $30,000. Upon retirement, he liquidated shares he had acquired in his company over twenty-five years through a stock purchase plan. The proceeds were $170,000 after taxes. Reilly requires an annual pretax income of $45,000–$50,000 to maintain his present living standard. The following table indicates various categories of securities available in the market, together with assumed yields. Based upon these opportunities, three portfolios have been constructed for Reilly. Indicate the portfolio from the accompanying table that best meets the needs of the Reillys as you perceive them to be. Provide a brief list of substantive reasons to support this portfolio mix.

CATEGORY OF SECURITY	ASSUMED CURRENT YIELDS*	PORTFOLIO 1	PORTFOLIO 2	PORTFOLIO 3
Money-market securities	9.5%	$10,000		$10,000
U.S. government bonds:				
Short-term	9.00			$20,000
Intermediate-term	9.50		$20,000	$30,000
Long-term	10.00			$50,000
Long-term corporate bonds:				
AAA rated	9.25			$50,000
AA rated	9.40			
A rated	9.60		$30,000	
BBB rated	10.00		$20,000	
Municipal bonds	6.00	$80,000	$20,000	
Preferred stocks	9.00			$20,000
Transportation stocks	5.00			
Utility stocks	9.00	$10,000	$30,000	$20,000
Financial stocks	5.50	$10,000	$20,000	
Industrial stocks	5.00	$110,000	$80,000	$20,000
Total		$220,000	$220,000	$220,000
Current yield ($)		$12,700	$15,780	$19,825

*Dividend/market price or interest/market price.

10. The following questions relate to the Sharpe and Markowitz methodology. Suppose we had the following data on four stocks:

STOCK	MARKOWITZ EXPECTED RETURN	ALPHA	VARIANCE			CORRELATION MATRIX*				
			SYSTEMATIC	UNSYS-TEMATIC		A	B	C	D	MARKET
A	17%	−.06	5%	4%	A	1	.4	.7	.2	.74
B	13	.10	2	6	B		1	.6	.5	.50
C	9	.00	3	1	C			1	.9	.87
D	7	−.14	3	2	D				1	.78

*For example, correlation of returns between B and C is .6; between B and Market, .50.

    a. Markowitz would argue that a portfolio consisting of equal dollar investments in stocks A, B, C, and D should provide an expected return of 11.5 percent and an expected risk (standard deviation of return) of 2.52 percent. Do you agree or disagree? Why?

    b. Suppose the market is expected to have a return over a forward period of 12 percent with a return variance of 6 percent. Calculate the expected return and risk for a portfolio consisting of equal portions of stocks A and C.

11. Refer to the case of Mary Atkins in the text. Assume the situation has changed.

    Before Wise was able to take any of the investment actions identified for discussion at the pending meeting, Mary Atkins died and title to the assets passed to the hospital's Board of Governors. The board announced that it would select a manager for the Atkins Endowment Fund from among four firms with experience in managing endowment portfolios. It would leave the portfolio with Investment Associates temporarily, but it requested that major purchases or sales be deferred until the manager decision has been made and an appropriate investment policy has been adopted.

    Investment Associates is one of the four firms under consideration. Wise now has the task of preparing for a presentation to the board of Good Samaritan Hospital. Wanting an expression of investment philosophy for endowment funds, the board requested that each firm address the following issues in its presentation:

    a. Prepare an Investment Policy statement for the Atkins Endowment Fund, taking into account all relevant objectives and constraints.

    b. What immediate changes, if any, would you recommend for the Atkins portfolio pending the selection of a new portfolio manager?

    c. Assume that your firm is selected as the new manager for the fund. Disregarding Good Samaritan's other endowment assets and basing your answer on the economic and capital market expectations supplied by the Board of Governors (Exhibit A1), what specific actions would you take?

EXHIBIT A1

Good Samaritan Hospital Board of Governors
Twelve-Month Forecast

ECONOMIC EXPECTATIONS

	FORECAST	RANGE
Real GNP	3.5%	3.0 to 4.0%
Inflation	4.7	4.0 to 5.5

CAPITAL MARKET EXPECTATIONS

	CURRENT ANNUAL YIELD LEVEL	EXPECTED ANNUAL RETURN	STANDARD DEVIATION OF RETURN
Domestic stocks	4.2%	22.5%	25.2%
Domestic bonds	11.7	19.4	18.4
Cash equivalents	9.0	8.6	2.2

12. Jack O'Keefe is human resources manager for WasteCo, a medium-sized waste-management company. The company pension program allows employees to place retirement contributions in a number of mutual funds. Three employees have asked O'Keefe to prepare investment guidelines for each of them. Prepare a statement of investment objectives and constraints for each of the employees listed below.

a. Anne Marie Costello, assistant director, accounting. Anne Marie is thirty-two, single, and in very good health. She is planning to buy a $60,000 home ($51,000 mortgaged) and a car. Her salary is $28,000 and she has accumulated $20,000 in a plan investment account.

b. Babu Sikha, assistant vice president, public relations. Babu is fifty-nine (will retire in three years), is married, and has no children. His wife is employed in executive position at local bank. They own a $135,000 house (mortgage paid off last year), have $50,000 in an IRA currently invested in a fund buying small company stocks holding $90,000 in bank CDs, and a $100,000 portfolio of growth stocks. Both of the Sikha's are in excellent health and without major debts. Babu's salary is $60,000 and he has accumulated $160,000 in his plan investment account.

c. Natale Vaughn, plant manager, is sixty-four. She intends to retire in eight months. Natale is married and has no children. Her husband retired two years ago. The Vaughns own a $150,000 house outright, and have $100,000 in an IRA (invested in a short-term bond fund), $100,000 in bank CDs, and a $125,000 portfolio of top-name common stocks. There are no family

health problems and no major debts. Vaughn's salary is $70,000 and she has accumulated $225,000 in her plan investment account.

C A S E

QuanTech Partners

QuanTech Partners is an investment management firm headquartered in Denver with regional offices in Salt Lake, Albuquerque, and Phoenix. QuanTech's primary activity is to provide portfolio management services to individuals with a net worth of $15 million or more. The firm also performs related custodial and performance monitoring services. Annual fees run from 1 to 2 percent of the market value of a portfolio depending upon services rendered.

Since its founding in 1985, the firm has enjoyed amazing growth. Starting with just $15 million, it now oversees assets well in excess of $550 million. The firm's staff consists of a small group of financial analysts, information systems personnel, and regional portfolio managers. The small labor force is augmented by a state-of-the-art computer system and the application of the discipline of sophisticated model building and quantitative techniques. The root of the construction and selection of optimum portfolios is the basic model developed by Nobel Laureat Dr. William Sharpe.

Jason Cate, a Ft. Collins businessman, rose rapidly to success and fortune by developing and marketing a highly succcessful line of computer software for children's games. Cate is an extraordinary software designer and a brillant entrepreneur. He visited the Denver office of QuanTech Partners in October 1995 to discuss the placement of $6 million in the hands of the firm for investment purposes. Cate had successful apartment holdings throughout Colorado and New Mexico in addition to the equity in his software business. He had recently liquidated his stock investments in an account with Dewey and Reiss, a Dallas brokerage firm. The portfolio had performed poorly, providing him with an annual rate of return of 7.3 percent over the past three years.

Cate had heard of the success QuanTech had enjoyed for its clients using sophisticated mathematical models and had decided that his investments could certainly perform no worse than they had in the hands of Dewey and Reiss. He asked QuanTech for a simple demonstration of how they created portfolios for clients. The regional portfolio manager, Janet Merck, prepared a list of stocks with the essential ingredients used by the firm in the selection of efficient combinations of candidate stocks. (See Exhibit 1.) She felt that these stocks would provide a useful base for demonstrating the process to Cate.

QUESTION

Construct an optimum portfolio.

EXHIBIT 1

List of Candidate Stocks

SECURITY	ALPHA	BETA	UNSYSTEMATIC RISK
Merck	0.20	1.11	8.90
Reebok	0.00	1.20	10.70
Tootsie Roll	0.60	1.08	9.81
Walt Disney	0.60	1.05	5.25
Ryan Homes	0.30	1.10	12.65
Kellogg	1.30	0.90	4.32
Boise Cascade	−0.10	1.12	6.23
Coors	−0.30	1.15	7.00
Wal Mart	−0.20	1.10	5.33
PepsiCo	0.30	1.00	4.24
Bank of America	0.80	0.90	6.00
Microsoft	0.40	0.95	9.70
American Brands	0.55	0.80	4.08
Houston Gas	1.20	0.70	10.55
IBM	−0.20	0.85	7.55
Rochester Telephone	0.40	0.75	4.5
El Paso Electric	0.30	0.75	6.26
Amway	1.00	0.60	8.9
Risk-free rate	6.00		
Market return	12.00		
Market variance	25.00		

C A S E

The Conaways

Roger Conaway was recently disabled as a result of an uninsured fall while repairing a light fixture in his apartment. Both he and his wife Phyllis are age fifty-six. Roger spent twenty years employed by a family-owned trucking firm as its credit manager. Phyllis is unable to work because of a permanent disability. The couple live in an apartment in Worcester, Massachusetts.

Roger will still be able to take care of all the household chores that his wife cannot. Also, their eight-year-old Honda will be sold because neither can now drive. Travel, mainly to doctors and the nearby hospital, will be done via public transportation, by taxi, or with help from friends and neighbors. Conaway's firm will continue to maintain medical insurance for him and his wife until both attain age sixty-five, when Medicare will be in effect. The only insurance in place is Roger's $25,000 ordinary life policy (cash surrender value: $900). Social Security payments of $6,600 and an early retirement company pension of $10,400 will begin

EXHIBIT 1

Portfolio of Roger and Phyllis Conaway,
as of November 20, 1993

COMMON SHARES	ISSUER/DESCRIPTION	PER SHARE COST
200	Exxon	$64.00
75	Wal Mart	$30.00
70	Baltimore Gas Preferred B	$74.00
300	Kellogg	$60.00
100	Southwest Airlines	$33.00
300	Balanced mutual fund	$19.00*

Total Equities

BONDS (PAR)		MATURITY DATE	COUPON	COST (% PAR)
$6,000	Boise Cascade Convertible	2016	7.00%	95.0%
$10,000	Bethlehem Steel	2005	8.45%	96.5%
$10,000	Nabisco	2007	7.75%	100.0%
$10,000	U.S. Treasury	2010	0.00%	33.0%
$40,000	General Host	2002	11.50%	107.5%
$10,000	AT&T	2000	6.00%	100.0%
$50,000	State of Minnesota	2008	4.00%	100.0% [†]

Total Fixed Income

RESERVES			
$1,200	Checking account	0.00%	$1,200
$29,000	Passbook savings	6.00%	$29,000
			$30,200

Total cash and equivalents

REAL ESTATE	Florida real estate	$9,500 [‡]

*Current market value, $19.50, and pays a $0.60 dividend.
[†]Current market price is 100.
[‡]Purchased ten years ago; market value is $12,000.

immediately (both amounts are after taxes). Conaway feels he and his wife can adjust their life style but will need $30,000, after-tax, annually.

Conaway and his wife have accumulated a portfolio of securities over the past twenty years through savings and funds provided from the estate of Marge's mother, who died several years ago. Exhibit 1 details their current holdings.

Current market data are as follows:

BONDS	UTILITIES	INDUSTRIALS
Aaa	10.43%	9.54%
Aa	10.57	9.88
A	10.83	10.46

TREASURIES		DIVIDEND YIELDS	
3-5 years	8.18		
5	8.37	S&P 500	3.64%
10	8.30	Utilities	7.00
Longer	9.10		

QUESTIONS

1. Identify and describe an appropriate set of investment objectives and investment constraints for the Conaway's and write a comprehensive investment policy statement based on these objectives and constraints.

2. Does the present portfolio fulfill their objectives? Why or why not?

3. State and explain your asset allocation recommendations for the Conaway's based on your policy statement from Question 1.

4. Identify current holdings you would eliminate from the portfolio and justify your action in each case.

C A S E

George and Emily Allen*

Harvey Bowles recently joined Perennial Trust Co., a firm specializing in financial management for wealthy families. Bowles's first assignment is the Allen family, a new client who came to Perennial upon the death of Charles A. Allen. Bowles soon will be meeting with the late Allen's widow, Emily Allen, and son, George Allen. To familiarize himself with the Allen's situation, he read the following memorandum prepared by Perennial's new business officer:

Emily Allen, age eighty-four, lives simply on the income from a trust created by her husband, the Charles A. Allen Trust for Emily Allen. The current status of this trust is shown in Exhibit 1. Emily Allen is the trust's only income beneficiary; on her death, the assets go to her son, George, free of taxes (which were paid at Charles A. Allen's death). Mrs. Allen contributes her excess income to various charities, and occasionally makes gifts to George and members of his family. She

---

*This case is an abridgement of a problem that appeared in the Chartered Financial Analyst Examination II series. It is reprinted with the permission of the Association for Investment Management and Research, Charlottesville, Va.

EXHIBIT 1

Investment Assets of Charles A. Allen Trust for Emily Allen

	COST	MARKET VALUE	AFTER-TAX YIELDS
Short-term reserves (tax-exempt)	$ 3,000,000	$ 3,000,000	4%
Growth stocks	500,000	1,000,000	1%
Cyclical stocks	1,000,000	1,000,000	2%
Defensive stocks	3,000,000	4,000,000	2%
Tax-exempt bonds	4,000,000	4,500,000	7%
Equity real estate*	1,000,000	2,000,000	6%
Total	$12,500,000	$15,500,000	

*Exclusive of personal residence.

feels George is somewhat irresponsible, although a good son, father, and husband. Emily Allen lived through the Great Depression, is not comfortable in the current financial environment, and has often said, "We saw great companies and great fortunes destroyed. We were terrified, we suffered great hardship, yet my husband was able to build our fortune by investing wisely over the years." The Allen Trust's only investment restriction is a requirement that George Allen be consulted, as a courtesy, before any investment action is taken.

George Allen, age fifty-four, is married and has three sons, one in prep school and two in college. Allen is not employed, but volunteers his services to a variety of civic and charitable organizations. Neither he nor his wife, a homemaker, seem to be financially sophisticated, although Allen is a strong believer in free investment markets and free enterprise. He feels that "smart investors can double their money every five years" and looks forward to financing businesses for his sons as they graduate from college. Their lifestyle and family needs require an annual income of $100,000. This now is derived from investment income and occasional gifts from his mother. Mr. Allen's *current* investment portfolio is shown in Exhibit 2.

EXHIBIT 2

Investment Assets of George Allen

	COST	MARKET VALUE	AFTER-TAX YIELDS
Money-market checking	$ 50,000	$ 50,000	3%
Growth stocks	150,000	300,000	1%
Cyclical stocks	200,000	250,000	2%
Defensive stocks	300,000	400,000	2%
Venture capital fund	100,000	100,000	0%
Tax-exempt bonds	300,000	400,000	7%
Equity real estate*	200,000	300,000	6%
Total	$1,300,000	$1,800,000	

*Exclusive of personal residence.

EXHIBIT 3

Perennial Trust Co. Three- to Five-Year Expected *Annual Investment Returns*

CONTINUED PROSPERITY (60% PROBABILITY)	EXPECTED ANNUAL TOTAL RETURN	EXPECTED TOTAL RETURN RANGE	EXPECTED INCOME COMPONENT OF TOTAL RETURN
Short-term reserves (tax-exempt)	5%	4–6%	5%
Stocks (S&P 500 Index)	14%	0–28%	4%
Tax-exempt bonds	7%	2–12%	7%
Equity real estate	9%	6–12%	6%
HIGH-INFLATION SCENARIO (20% PROBABILITY)			
Short-term reserves (tax-exempt)	9%	6–12%	9%
Stocks (S&P 500 Index)	16%	−6–38%	5%
Tax-exempt bonds	2%	−8–12%	7%
Equity real estate	14%	9–19%	6%
DEFLATION/DEPRESSION SCENARIO (20% PROBABILITY)			
Short-term reserves (tax-exempt)	2%	0–4%	2%
Stocks (S&P 500 Index)	−5%	−20–10%	2%
Tax-exempt bonds	15%	10–20%	7%
Equity real estate	−3%	−10–5%	3%

Before his meeting with the Allens, Bowles reviews Perennial's latest investment return projections. His firm believes that continued prosperity is the most likely outlook for the next three to five years, but is mindful of the possibility of two disturbing alternatives: first, a return to high inflation, or, second, a drift into deflation/depression. Exhibit 3 presents the details of Perennial's projections.

QUESTIONS

1. Treating the Allen family as an entity, create an investment policy statement to fit their combined situation.

2. Based on your answer to Question 1, recommend and justify a new asset-allocation strategy for *each* of the existing Allen portfolios. Your allocation must total 100 percent for each portfolio.

3. Assume that Emily Allen dies suddenly. Revise your allocation strategy for George Allen. Your allocation must total 100 percent.

REFERENCES

BENARI, Y. "An Asset Allocation Paradigm." *Journal of Portfolio Management* (Winter 1988).

BLACK, F. "The Investment Policy Spectrum." *Financial Analysts Journal* (January–February 1976).

DROMS, W. G., ed. Asset Allocation for the Individual Investor. Charlottesville, Va.: Institute of Chartered Financial Analysts, 1987.

ELTON, E. J., M. J. GRUBER, and M. W. PADBERG. "Optimum Portfolios from Simple Ranking Devices." *Journal of Portfolio Management* (Spring 1978).

JOEHNK, M. D., ed. *Asset Allocation for Institutional Portfolios.* Charlottesville, Va.: Institute of Chartered Financial Analysts, 1987.

MARKOWITZ, H. M. "Individual versus Institutional Investing." *Financial Services Review* 1 (1991).

MAGINN, J. L., and D. L. TUTTLE, eds. Managing Investment Portfolios: A Dynamic Process. 2d ed. Sponsored by the Association of Investment Management and Research. Boston: Warren, Gorham and Lamont, 1990.

ROSENBERG, B., and J. GUY. "Prediction of Systematic Risk from Investment Fundamentals." *Financial Analysts Journal* (May–June 1976).

SMITH, K. V. "The Major Asset Mix Problem for the Individual Investor." *Journal of Contemporary Business* (Winter 1974).

CHAPTER 19

CAPITAL MARKET
THEORY

W̲e presented the fundamental principles of portfolio management in Chapters 17 and 18. Here we use these principles to discuss capital market theory and the capital asset pricing model.

In a few words, capital-market theory is concerned with how asset pricing should occur if investors behaved as Markowitz suggested. The capital asset pricing model uses the results of capital market theory to derive the relationship between the expected returns and systematic risk of individual securities and portfolios.

CAPITAL-MARKET THEORY

Assumptions Underlying Capital Market Theory

Capital market theory is a major extension of the portfolio theory of Markowitz.[1] *Portfolio theory* is really a description of how rational investors should build efficient portfolios. *Capital market theory* tells us how assets should be priced in the capital markets if, indeed, everyone behaved in the way portfolio theory suggests. The *capital asset pricing model* (CAPM) is a relationship explaining how assets should be priced in the capital markets.

The real world is complex, to be sure. To understand it and build models of how it works, we need to sweep away those complexities we think have only a minor effect on its behavior. Most of the complexities that have to be removed in the stock market concern institutional frictions. These include such things as commissions, taxation, short-selling rules, and margin requirements, to name a few.

The specific assumptions underlying capital market theory are:

---

[1]The development of capital market theory is traceable largely to William Sharpe, "Capital Asset Prices: A Theory of Market Equilibrium under Conditions of Risk," *Journal of Finance* (September 1964), pp. 425–42.

1. Investors make decisions based solely upon risk-and-return assessments. These judgments take the form of expected values and standard deviation measures.

2. The purchase or sale of a security can be undertaken in infinitely divisible units. We can buy $1 of McDonald's stock.

3. Investors can short sell any amount of shares without limit.

4. Purchases and sales by a single investor cannot affect prices. This means that there is perfect competition where investors in total determine prices by their actions. Otherwise, monopoly power could influence prices (returns).

5. There are no transaction costs. Where there are transaction costs, returns would be sensitive to whether the investor owned a security before the decision period.

6. The purchase or sale of securities is done in the absence of personal income taxes. This means that we are indifferent to the form in which the return is received (dividends or capital gains).

7. The investor can borrow or lend any amount of funds desired at an identical riskless rate (e.g., the Treasury bill rate).

8. Investors share identical expectations with regard to the relevant decision period, the necessary decision inputs, their form and size. Thus investors are presumed to have identical planning horizons and to have identical expectations regarding expected returns, variances of expected returns, and covariances of all pairs of securities. Otherwise, there would be a family of efficient frontiers because of differences in expectations.

This might seem to many as creating a kind of "toy world" fabricated to satisfy the whims of eccentric academics. Many of the assumptions no doubt seem objectionable. However, despite the strict assumptions, the model we will view does a very good job of describing prices in the capital markets. Reality is not materially distorted by making these assumptions.

The Capital Asset Pricing Model

Recall that portfolio theory implied that each investor faced an efficient frontier. In general, the efficient frontier will differ among investors because of differences in expectations. When we introduce riskless borrowing and lending some significant changes are involved. Lending is best thought of as an investment in a riskless security. This security might be a savings account, Treasury bills, or even high-grade commercial paper. Borrowing can be thought of as the use of margin. Borrowing and lending options transform the efficient frontier into a straight line. See Figure 19–1 for the standard efficient frontier $ABCD$. Assume that an investor can lend at the rate of $R_F = .05$, which represents the rate on U.S. Treasury bills. Hence the point R_F represents a risk-free investment ($R_F = .05$; $\sigma_p = 0$). The investor could place all or part of his funds in this riskless asset. If he placed part of his

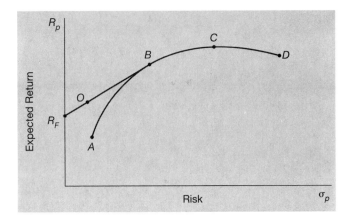

FIGURE 19–1   Efficient Frontier with Introduction of Lending

funds in the risk-free asset and part in one of the portfolios of risky securities along the efficient frontier, what would happen? He could generate portfolios along the straight-line segment $R_F B$.

Let us examine the properties of a given portfolio along the straight-line segment $R_F B$. Consider point B on the original efficient frontier $ABCD$ where, say, R_p = .10 and σ_σ = .06. If we placed one-half of available funds in the riskless asset and one-half in the risky portfolio, B, the resulting combined risk-return measures for the mixed portfolio, O, can be found from Equations 19.1 and 19.2:

$$R_p = XR_M + (1 - X)R_F \tag{19.1}$$

where:

$$
\begin{aligned}
R_p &= \text{expected return on portfolio} \\
X &= \text{percentage of funds invested in risky portfolio} \\
(1 - X) &= \text{percentage of funds invested in riskless asset} \\
R_M &= \text{expected return on risky portfolio} \\
R_F &= \text{expected return on riskless asset}
\end{aligned}
$$

and:

$$\sigma_p = X\sigma_M \tag{19.2}$$

where:

$$
\begin{aligned}
\sigma_p &= \text{expected standard deviation of the portfolio} \\
X &= \text{percentage of funds invested in risky portfolio} \\
\sigma_M &= \text{expected standard deviation on risky portfolio}
\end{aligned}
$$

For our example, the risk-return measures for portfolio M are:

$$R_p = (\tfrac{1}{2})(.10) + (\tfrac{1}{2})(.05) = .075$$

$$\sigma_p = (\tfrac{1}{2})(.06) + (\tfrac{1}{2})(.00) = .03$$

The result indicates that our return and risk have been reduced. All points between R_F and B can be similarly determined using Equations 19.1 and 19.2. As stated, the locus of these points will be a straight line.

Introduction of the possibility of borrowing funds will change the shape of our efficient frontier in Equation 19.1 to the right of point B. In borrowing, we consider the possibilities associated with total funds invested being enlarged through trading on the equity.

Consider three cases. If we assume that X is the percentage of investment wealth or equity placed in the risky portfolio, then where $X = 1$, investment wealth is totally committed to the risky portfolio. Where $X < 1$, only a fraction of X is placed in the risky portfolio, and the remainder is lent at the rate R_F. The third case, $X > 1$, signifies that the investor is borrowing rather than lending. It may be easier to visualize this by rewriting Equation 19.1 as follows:

$$R_p = XR_M - (X - 1)R_F \tag{19.3}$$

where all terms are as in Equation 19.1 and the term R_F is the borrowing rate. For simplicity, the borrowing rate and lending rate are assumed to be equal or 5 percent. The first component of Equation 19.3 is the gross return made possible because the borrowed funds, as well as the original wealth or equity, are invested in the risky portfolio. The second term refers to the cost of borrowing on a percentage basis. For example, $X = 1.25$ would indicate that the investor borrows an amount equal to 25 percent of his investment wealth. This is equivalent to a margin requirement of 80 percent ($X = 1/$margin requirement). His *net* return on his investment wealth would become:

$$R_p = (1.25)(.10) - (0.25)(.05) = .1125$$

The associated risk would become:

$$\sigma_p = X\sigma_p = (1.25)(.06) = .075$$

Hence, the levered portfolio provides increased return with increased risk.

The introduction of borrowing and lending has given us an efficient frontier that is a straight line throughout. In Figure 19–2 we show the new efficient frontier. Point M now represents the optimal combination of risky securities. The existence of this combination simplifies our problem of portfolio selection. The investor need only decide how much to borrow or lend. No other investments or combination of investments available is as efficient as point M. The decision to purchase M is the investment decision. The decision to buy some riskless asset (lend) or to borrow (leverage the portfolio) is the financing decision.

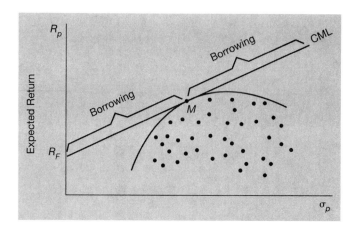

FIGURE 19–2   Capital Market Line Assuming Lending and Borrowing
at the Risk-Free Rate

These conditions give rise to what has been referred to as the *separation theorem*. The theorem implies that all investors, conservative or aggressive, should hold the same mix of stocks from the efficient set. They should use borrowing or lending to attain their preferred risk class.[2] This conclusion flies in the face of more traditional notions of selection of portfolios. Traditional portfolio-building rules would construct certain types of portfolios for conservative clients and others for investors who are more daring. *This analysis suggests that both types of investors should hold identically risky portfolios. Desired risk levels are then achieved through combining portfolio* M *with lending and borrowing.*

If all investors face similar expectations and the same lending and borrowing rate, they will face a diagram such as that in Figure 19–3 and, furthermore, all of the diagrams will be identical. The portfolio of assets held by any investor will be identical to the portfolio of risky assets held by any other investor. If all investors hold the same risky portfolio, then, in equilibrium, it must be the market portfolio *(M)*. The market portfolio is a portfolio comprised of all risky assets. Each asset will be held in the proportion that the market value of the asset represents to the total market value of all risky assets. For example, if Exxon represents 2 percent of all risky assets, then the market portfolio contains 2 percent Exxon stock and each investor will take 2 percent of the money that will be invested in risky assets and place it in Exxon stock. This is the key: All investors will hold combinations of only two portfolios, the market portfolio and a riskless security.

The straight line depicted in Figure 19–3 is referred to as the *capital market line* (CML). All investors will end up with portfolios somewhere along the CML and all efficient portfolios would lie along the CML. However, not all securities or portfolios lie along the CML. From the derivation of the efficient frontier we know that all portfolios, except those that are efficient, lie below the CML.

[2]W. F. Sharpe, *Portfolio Theory and Capital Markets* (New York: McGraw-Hill, 1970), p. 70.

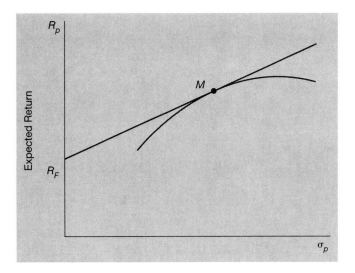

FIGURE 19–3   Efficient Frontier with Borrowing and Lending

Observing the CML tells us something about the market price of risk. The equation of the CML (connecting the riskless asset with a risky portfolio) is:

$$Re = \frac{R_F + R_M - R_F}{\sigma_M}\, \sigma_e$$

where the subscript e denotes an efficient portfolio.

The term $(R_M - R_F)/\sigma_M$ can be thought of as the extra return that can be gained by increasing the level of risk (standard deviation) on an efficient portfolio by one unit. The entire second term on the right side of the equation is thus the market price of risk times the amount of risk in the portfolio. The expression R_F is the price of time; that is, it is the price paid for delaying consumption for one period. The expected return on an efficient portfolio is:

(Price of time) + (Price of risk)(Amount of risk)

Although this equation sets the return on an efficient portfolio, we need to go beyond to deal with returns on nonefficient portfolios or on individual securities.

Security Market Line

For well-diversified portfolios, nonsystematic risk tends to go to zero, and the only relevant risk is systematic risk measured by beta. Because we assume that investors are concerned only with expected return and risk, the only dimensions of a security that need be of concern are expected return and beta.

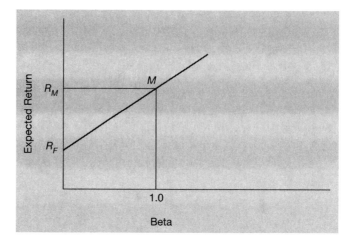

FIGURE 19–4 The Security Market Line

We have seen that all investments and all portfolios of investments lie along a straight line in the return-to-beta space. To determine this line we need only connect the intercept (beta of zero, or riskless security) and the market portfolio (beta of one and return of R_M). These two points identify the straight line shown in Figure 19–4. The equation of a straight line is:

$$R_i = \alpha + b\beta_i$$

The first point on the line is the riskless asset with a beta of zero, so:

$$R_F = \alpha + b(0)$$
$$R_F = \alpha$$

The second point on the line is the market portfolio with a beta of 1. Thus,

$$R_M = \alpha + b(1)$$
$$R_M - \alpha = b$$
$$(R_M - R_F) = b$$

Combining the two results gives us:

$$R_i = R_F + \beta_i (R_M - R_F)$$

This is a key relationship. It is called the *security market line* (SML). It describes the expected return for all assets and portfolios of assets, efficient or not. The difference between the expected return on any two assets can be related simply to

their difference in beta. The higher beta is for any security, the higher must be its expected return. The relationship between beta and expected return is linear.

Recall that in Chapter 3 we said that the risk of any stock could be divided into systematic and unsystematic risk. Beta is an index of systematic risk. This equation suggests that systematic risk is the only important ingredient in determining expected returns. Unsystematic risk is of no consequence. It is not total variance of returns that affects returns, only that part of the variance in returns that cannot be eliminated by diversification.

RELAXING SOME ASSUMPTIONS
OF THE CAPITAL ASSET PRICING MODEL

The assumptions underlying the CAPM were set out earlier. In this section, we discuss the impact of relaxing some of these assumptions. One of the key assumptions was that investors could borrow and lend any amount of money at the risk-free rate. We can reasonably assume that investors have the ability to lend as much as they want at the risk-free rate (buy Treasury bills). However, the proposition that investors can borrow unlimited amounts of money at a cost identical to the risk-free rate is not so easy to defend. First, the prime rate of interest one pays to borrow from a local bank exceeds the Treasury bill rate (borrowing rate exceeds lending rate). Second, the Federal Reserve Board has set the maximum amount that an investor can borrow against securities at 50 percent of their market value.

The first effect, the fact that the borrowing rate exceeds the lending rate is depicted in Figure 19–5. The segment R_f–F represents the opportunities available from some combination of investing in risk-free securities and portfolio F on the efficient frontier. We cannot extend this line beyond portfolio F because it is assumed that you cannot borrow at the risk-free rate to acquire further units of portfolio F. If you borrow at R_b, it is possible to find the point of tangency at point K. This suggests that you can borrow at R_b and invest in portfolio K to extend the line to G. Thus, the capital market line is made up of the line segment R_f–F, a curve segment F–K, and another line segment K–G.

The borrowing portfolios are not as profitable as when we borrowed at R_F. When investors possess different expectations about risk and return, each faces a unique capital market line. These lines, when added for all investors, would be a set of lines whose breadth was determined by the divergence of expectations. The possession of similar information would cause the band to be narrow.

The rates of return used in our Markowitz model were all before taxes. The CAPM assumed we live in a world without taxes. Moreover, investors did not face differential rates related to source of income (dividends versus capital gains). Certainly tax rates differ between individual and institutional investors. For nontaxable institutions (e.g., pension funds) the CAPM does not have to be modified. Alternatively, if investors face high taxes, this has a major impact.

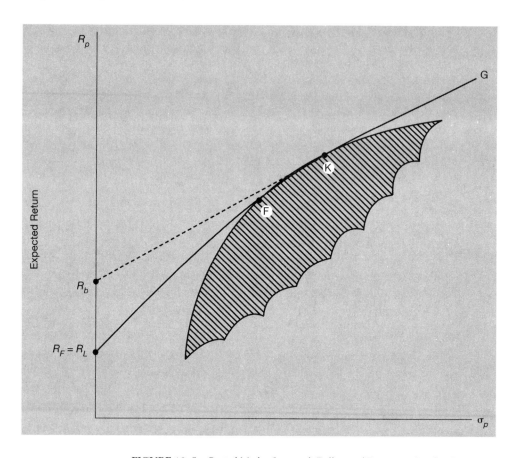

FIGURE 19–5   Capital Market Line with Differential Borrowing-Lending Rates

TESTING THE CAPITAL ASSET PRICING MODEL

The CAPM was developed on the basis of a set of unrealistic assumptions. Because the assumptions are not correct in their entirety, the SML equation might not represent an accurate description of how investors behave and how rates of return are established in the market. Consider the possibility that large numbers of investors may not fully diversified and have not eliminated all diversifiable risk from their portfolios. This would suggest that beta is not be an adequate measure of risk and the SML would not explain how required returns are established. For this and other reasons the CAPM may not be completely valid, and the SML will not produce accurate estimates of R_i. Therefore, the CAPM must be tested empirically and validated before it can be used with any real confidence. We next attempt to give some of the results of significant work on the question of validity.

Stability of Beta Coefficients

According to the CAPM, the beta that should be used to estimate a stock's market risk reflects investors' estimates of the stock's future volatility in relation to that of the market. Clearly, we do not know now how a stock will be related to the market in the future, nor do we know how the average investor views this expected future relative volatility. All we know is past volatility, which we can use to calculate historical betas. If historical betas are stable over time, then investors could use past betas as estimates of future volatility. Stability suggests that if beta were calculated by using data from the period of, say, 1990 to 1994, then approximately the same beta should be found for 1995–99.

Investigators have studied the question of beta stability. They have calculated betas for individual securities and portfolios of securities for a range of time spans. Their first conclusion is that the betas of individual stocks are unstable, that suggests that past betas for individual securities are not good estimators of their future risk. Their second conclusion is that betas of portfolios are reasonably stable. In other words, past portfolio betas are good estimators of future portfolio volatility. In effect, the errors in the estimates of beta for individual securities tend to offset one another when combined in a portfolio.

Testing the Capital Asset Pricing Model Based on the Slope of the Security Market Line

As noted, the CAPM tells us that a linear relationship exists between a security's required rate of return and its beta. Further, when the SML is graphed, the vertical axis intercept should be R_f, and the required rate of return for a stock (or portfolio) with $B = 1.0$ should be R_m, the required rate of return on the market. Researchers have attempted to test the validity of the model by calculating betas and realized rates of return, plotting these values in graphs, and then observing whether the intercept is equal to R_f, the regression line is linear, and the line passes through the point $B = 1.0$. Also, most of the studies actually analyze portfolios rather than individual securities because security betas are so unstable.

Before discussing the results of the tests, it is critical to recognize that although the CAPM is an ex ante, or forward-looking model, the data used to test it are entirely historical. The realized rates of return over past holding periods are not necessarily equal to expected rates of return with which the model should deal. Also historical betas may or may not reflect either current of expected future risk. This lack of ex ante data makes testing the true CAPM extremely difficult. Some key results of these studies are notable.

First, the evidence generally shows a significant positive relationship between realized returns and systematic risk. However, the slope of the relationship is usually less than that predicted by the CAPM. Second, the relationship between risk and return appears to be linear. There is no evidence of significant curvature in the risk-return relationship. Third, tests that attempt to assess the relative im-

portance of market and company-specific risk do not yield definitive results. The CAPM theory implies that company-specific risk is not relevant, yet both kinds of risk appear to be positively related to security returns; that is, higher returns are required to compensate for diversifiable as well as nondiversifiable risk. Fourth, some research questions whether testing the CAPM is even conceptually possible. It has been demonstrated that the linear relationship that prior research observed resulted from the mathematical properties of the models being tested. Could it be that a finding of linearity proved nothing whatever about the validity of the CAPM? This conclusion does not disprove the CAPM theory, but it does show that proving that investors behave in accordance with the theory is impossible. Last, if the CAPM were completely valid, it should apply to all financial assets. However, when bonds, for example, are introduced into the analysis, they do not plot on the SML.

Is the Capital Asset Pricing Model Salvageable?

The CAPM is appealing in its elegance and logic. When you look at the math the theory becomes most appealing. However, doubts begin to arise when one examines the assumptions more closely and these doubts are as much reinforced by the empirical tests. The models focus on market rather than total risk is clearly a useful way of thinking about the riskiness of assets in general. Thus, as a conceptual model the CAPM is of truly fundamental importance. Although the CAPM is enticing with it precision of numbers we do not know precisely how to measure any of the inputs required to implement the CAPM. These inputs should all be ex ante, yet we only have ex post data available. Historical data for Rm and betas vary greatly depending on the time period studied and the methods used to estimate them. The estimates used in the CAPM are subject to potentially large errors.

Because the CAPM represents the way people who want to maximize returns while minimizing risk ought to behave, assuming they can get all the necessary data, the model is definitely here to stay. Attempts will continue to improve the model and to make it more useful.

ARBITRAGE PRICING THEORY

The CAPM asserts that only a single number—a security's beta against the market—is required to measure risk. At the core of arbitrage pricing theory (APT) is the recognition that several systematic factors affect security returns.[3]

The returns on an individual stock will depend upon a variety of anticipated and unanticipated events. Anticipated events will be incorporated by investors into their expectations of returns on individual stocks and thus will be incorporated into market prices. Generally, however, most of the return ultimately realized will re-

---

[3]Stephen Ross, "The Arbitrage Theory of Capital Asset Pricing," *Journal of Economic Theory,* 13 (December 1976), pp. 341–60.

sult from unanticipated events. Of course, change itself is anticipated, and investors know that the most unlikely occurrence of all would be the exact realization of the most probable future scenario. But even though we realize that some unforeseen events will occur, we do not know their direction or their magnitude. What we can know is the sensitivity of returns to these events.

Systematic factors are the major sources of risk in portfolio returns. Actual portfolio returns depend upon the same set of common factors, but this does not mean that all portfolios perform identically. Different portfolios have different sensitivities to these factors.

Because the systematic factors are primary sources of risk, it follows that they are the principal determinants of the expected, as well as the actual, returns on portfolios. The actual return, R, on any security or portfolio may be broken down into three constituent parts, as follows:

$$R = E + bf + e \qquad \textbf{(19.4)}$$

where:

E = expected return on the security
b = security's sensitivity to change in the systematic factor
f = the actual return on the systematic factor
e = returns on the unsystematic, idiosyncratic factors

Equation 19.4 merely states that the actual return equals the expected return, plus factor sensitivity times factor movement, plus residual risk.

Empirical work suggests that a three- or four-factor model adequately captures the influence of systematic factors on stock-market returns. Equation 19.4 may thus be expanded to:

$$R = E + (b1)(f1) + (b2)(f2) + (b3)(f3)$$
$$+ (b4)(f4) + e$$

Each of the four middle terms in this equation is the product of the returns on a particular economic factor and the given stock's sensitivity to that factor. Suppose $f3$ is associated with labor productivity. As labor productivity unexpectedly increases, $f3$ is positive, and firms with high $b3$ would find their returns very high. The subtler rationale and higher mathematics of APT are left for development elsewhere.

What are these factors? They are the underlying economic forces that are the primary influences on the stock market. Research suggests that the most important factors are unanticipated inflation, changes in the expected level of industrial production, unanticipated shifts in risk premiums, and unanticipated movements in the shape of the term structure of interest rates.

The biggest problems in APT are factor identification and separating unanticipated from anticipated factor movements in the measurement of sensitivities.

Any one stock is so influenced by idiosyncratic forces that determines the precise relationship between its return and a given factor is very difficult. Far more critical is the measurement of the b's. The b's measure the sensitivity of returns to unanticipated movements in the factors. By just looking at how a given stock relates to, say, movements in the money supply, we would be including the influence of both anticipated and unanticipated changes, when only the latter are relevant.

Empirical testing of the APT is still in its infancy, and concrete results proving the APT or disproving the CAPM do not exist. For these reasons it is useful to regard CAPM and APT as different variants of the true equilibrium pricing model. Both are, therefore, useful in supplying intuition into the way security prices and equilibrium returns are established.[4]

SUMMARY

In this chapter we saw how capital market theory, building upon the fundamentals of risk diversification through portfolio management, establishes a linear relationship between the expected return and total risk on all efficient portfolios. Such portfolios include only those composed of varying percentages of a risk-free asset and the market portfolio. From here we turned to the CAPM that uses the results of capital market theory to derive a linear relationship between the expected return and systematic risk on all assets.

QUESTIONS

1. Point out the differences between the efficient frontier under capital market theory and under the Markowitz approach.

2. What does it mean to assume that all investors have homogeneous expectations? Why is this assumption necessary to capital market theory?

3. What is the relationship between borrowing and lending rates in the "real" world? How does this real world relationship affect the shape of the CML and the identification of the optimal portfolio?

4. What is the SML? Explain the rationale behind it.

5. Capital market theory and the CAPM are based on certain specific assumptions, and the CAPM suggests rather specific things about asset pricing.
   a. What are the basic assumptions underlying capital market theory?
   b. What happens to the CML and the choice of an optimal portfolio if the borrowing rate is allowed to exceed the lending rate?

[4]Readers seeking a less mathematical approach to the APT should see D. H. Bower, R. S. Bower, and D. E. Logue, "A Primer on Arbitrage Pricing Theory," *Midland Corporate Finance Journal* (Fall 1984).

   c. What assets lie on both the SML and the CML? What assets should never lie on the CML?

   d. What specifically should a "true believer" in the CAPM do with his money if he seeks to hold a portfolio with a beta of 1.25?

6. In the empirical testing of CAPM, what are two major questions that must be addressed?

7. Draw a diagram showing the theoretical SML and what it appears to look like based upon empirical testing.

8. Do beta coefficients appear to be stable over time for individual stocks? For portfolios?

9. Why in the perfect world of the CAPM are the investment decision and the financing decision separate?

10. Suppose you expected inflation to move from 4 to 6 percent. What would this do to the SML?

PROBLEMS

1. The following data are available to you as a portfolio manager:

SECURITY	EXPECTED RETURN	BETA	STANDARD DEVIATION
Blue	.32	1.70	.50
White	.30	1.40	.35
Red	.25	1.10	.40
Grey	.22	.95	.24
Black	.20	1.05	.28
Brown	.14	.70	.18
NYSE stock index	.12	1.00	.20
Treasury bills	.08	0	0

   a. Draw the SML. Plot each stock on your graph.

   b. In terms of an SML, which of the securities listed above are undervalued? Why?

2. Assume that a portfolio in Problem 1 is constructed using equal portions of the six stocks listed.

   a. What are the expected return and risk on such a portfolio?

   b. What would the expected return and risk be if this portfolio were margined at 40 percent with the cost of borrowing at 8 percent?

3. Assume the assets below are correctly priced according to the SML. Derive the SML. What is the expected return on an asset with a beta of 2?

$$R_1 = 6\% \qquad\qquad B_1 = 0.5$$
$$R_2 = 12\% \qquad\qquad B_2 = 1.5$$

4. Assume the SML is given as $R_i = 0.04 + 0.08B$ and the estimated betas on two stocks are $B_x = 0.5$ and $B_y = 2.0$. What must the expected return on each of the two securities be in order for one to feel that they are a good purchase?

5. Draw the SML for the following conditions: $R_f = .08$, $R_m = .12$.

6. Calculate the expected return on the following stocks if $R_f = .05$ and $R_m = .11$

STOCK	BETA
1	−.80
2	.03
3	.44
4	.76
5	1.10
6	1.75

REFERENCES

BOWER, D. H., R. S. BOWER, and D. E. LOGUE. "A Primer on Arbitrage Pricing Theory." Midland Corporate Finance Journal (Fall 1984).

BREALEY, RICHARD A. "Portfolio Theory Versus Portfolio Practice." *Journal of Portfolio Management* (Summer 1990).

CHEN, F. N., R. ROLL, and S. ROSS. "Economic Forces and the Stock Market." *Journal of Business* (July 1986).

COGGIN, T. D., and J. E. HUNTER. "A Meta-Analysis of Pricing 'Risk' Factors in APT." *Journal of Portfolio Management* (Fall 1987).

HARRINGTON, D. R. *Modern Portfolio Theory.* 2d ed. Englewood Cliffs, N.J.: Prentice Hall, 1987.

MOSSIN, J. "Equilibrium in a Capital Asset Market." *Econometrica* (October 1966).

MULLINS, D. "Does the Capital Asset Pricing Model Work?" *Harvard Business Review* (January–February 1982).

ROSS, S. A. "The Arbitrage Theory of Capital Asset Pricing." *Journal of Economic Theory* (December 1976).

ROLL, R. and S. A. ROSS. "An Empirical Investigation of the Arbitrage Pricing Theory." *Journal of Finance* (December 1980).

SHANKEN, J. "Multivariate Proxies and Asset Pricing Relationships." *Journal of Financial Economics* (March 1987).

SHARPE, W. F. *Portfolio Theory and Capital Markets.* New York: McGraw-Hill, 1970.

_____ "Factor "Factor Models, CAPMs, and the APT." *Journal of Portfolio Management* (Fall 1984).

MANAGED PORTFOLIOS AND PERFORMANCE MEASUREMENTS

I n this chapter we will discuss various types of managed portfolios, looking at broad categories as well as at differences among portfolios in each category. To do this, we will need to specify measures of portfolio performance. These will include the relative merits of return criteria and risk criteria, the adherence of the portfolio's management to publicly stated investment objectives, or some combination of these factors. Finally, we will examine sources of information on various types of managed portfolios.

CLASSIFICATION OF MANAGED PORTFOLIOS

Investment Companies

CLOSED-END COMPANIES

A *closed-end investment company* is so named because its basic capitalization is limited, or "closed." That is, these firms sell shares much as a regular industrial company does. Closed-end firms can also use leverage by selling senior securities—bonds and preferred stocks. Instead of using proceeds from the stock sale to purchase land, equipment, and inventory, the closed-end investment company uses the proceeds to purchase securities of other firms.

The closed-end company differs from the open-end company in how its shares are traded after the initial offering.[1] The closed-end companies' shares are traded on organized exchanges, like those of any other company. Thus, when an investor buys shares in a closed-end investment company, he must generally buy them from another person. The buyer pays the nominal commission on such a purchase.

---

[1]When the close-end company desires to raise more capital, it can do so just as any other company can, through the sale of additional shares.

The shares of a closed-end company can sell above or below the net asset value of the shares. *Net asset value* is the total market value of the fund's portfolio minus any liabilities, divided by the total number of shares outstanding. Reasons that closed-end investment companies sell at a discount are the investor's attitude concerning the abilities of the fund's management, lack of sales effort (brokers earn less commission on closed-end fund shares than on open-end fund shares), the riskiness of the fund itself, or the riskiness associated with the lack of marketability of the fund's shares because of a thin float (that is, a small number of shares outstanding).[2] Nonetheless, when these funds sell at unusually large discounts (relative to their historical discounts), they can present interesting investment opportunities.

DUAL FUNDS

The *dual fund* is a special type of closed-end investment company. As its name implies, it has two types of stock: income shares and capital shares. When the investor purchases shares in a dual fund, he specifies which class of stock he wants. The holders of the capital shares receive all the capital gains earned on all the shares of the fund. The holders of the income shares receive all the interest and dividends earned on all the shares of the fund. Thus, it can be seen that the investments of the dual fund's managers are divided into securities that promise a sizable dividend return and securities that promise substantial capital appreciation. The income investor enjoys leverage to the extent that he receives income on all the shares owned by the fund, and conversely the capital investor enjoys leverage to the extent that he receives capital gains on all the shares owned by the fund.

Potential problems can arise if management is unable to balance its investments properly. That is, if too large a share of the portfolio is invested in stocks with large capital gain potential, there is likely to be too little dividend income earned. Conversely, as too large a share of the portfolio is invested in high-dividend-yielding securities, there is likely to be little capital appreciation.[3]

OPEN-END COMPANIES

The *open-end investment company,* more commonly referred to as a *mutual fund,* is characterized by the continual selling and redeeming of its shares. In other words, the mutual fund does not have a fixed capitalization. It sells its shares to the investing public whenever it can at their net asset value per share, and it stands ready to repurchase these shares directly from the investment public for

[2]For an interesting discussion of closed-end investment company discounts, see Eugene J. Pratt, "Myths Associated with Closed-End Investment Company Discounts," *Financial Analysts Journal* (July–August 1966), pp. 79–82.

[3]See John P. Shelton, Eugene F. Brigham, and Alfred E. Hofflander, Jr., "An Evaluation and Appraisal of Dual Funds," *Financial Analysts Journal* (May–June 1967), pp. 131–39; and James A. Gentry and John R. Pike, "Dual Funds Revisited," *Financial Analysts Journal* (March–April 1968), pp. 149–57.

their net asset value per share. In the case of a "no-load" mutual fund, the investment company sells its shares by mail to the investor. Because no salesperson is involved, there is no sales commission (load). In the case of a "load" fund, the shares are sold by a salesperson. His entire selling commission (load) is added to the net asset value, and a portion of the investor's equity is removed as the "load" at the beginning of the contract to purchase shares. This process is called *front-end loading,* and thus the name *load fund.* The load charge or commission is generally about 6 percent of the sale price. Exit fees, or *back-end loading,* are also available.

In addition, both the closed-end and open-end funds charge a management fee to defray the costs of operating the portfolios—including such expenses as brokerage fees, transfer costs, bookkeeping expenses, and analysts' salaries. In the case of a load fund, a share with a net asset value of $10 would cost $10.60 if the load fee were 6 percent. If this fund were a no-load, the cost would be only the $10 net asset value. In the newspaper listings of mutual-fund shares, therefore, the bid-ask prices are equal for the no-load shares; the load funds have higher ask prices.

Types of Mutual Funds

Mutual funds state specific investment objectives in their prospectuses. For example, the main types of objectives are growth, balanced income, and industry-specialized funds. *Growth funds* typically possess diversified portfolios of common stocks in the hope of achieving large capital gains for their shareholders. The *balanced fund* generally holds a portfolio of diversified common stocks, preferred stocks, and bonds with the hope of achieving capital gains and dividend and interest income, while at the same time conserving the principal. *Income funds* concentrate heavily on high-interest and high-dividend-yielding securities. Bond funds vary also in the average duration of its holdings. Portfolios with low durations are significantly less sensitive to changes in interest rates than those with high durations. The *industry-specialized mutual fund* obviously specializes in investing in portfolios of selected industries; such a fund appeals to investors who are extremely optimistic about the prospects for these few industries and are willing to assume the risks associated with such a concentration of their investment dollars. Families of funds have developed that allow investors to switch from a fund with one objective to a fund (in the same family) with a different objective for a modest fee. An investor might be motivated to do this as the stock market and interest rates go through various phases.

The Mutual Fund Phenomenon

The mutual-fund industry has exploded. The first fund was started in 1924. Since then the number of funds has proliferated to the point that currently well in excess of 4,000 publicly trade funds with assets of more than $1.5 trillion exist. Investors

became attracted to the market and mutual funds because they represented a sensible, efficient vehicle for individual investors to participate in the market. Funds of all types were created (some were discussed in the previous paragraphs) and funds with different cost and expense characteristics were also created (they will be discussed shortly).

The individual investor can in effect employ a team of investment professionals to manage the investors money under the direction of a portfolio or fund manager. These individuals work full-time on studying the markets, market trends, and individual stocks. They have access to for more dates thus an individual could possibly assemble—even if he had the time and the ability to use the data meaningfully. The mutual fund also allows the investor to purchase a very diversified portfolio of securities for a small investment—often as little as $500 or $1,000. It is impossible to purchase a diversified portfolio of individual securities for such a modest initial investment outside of a mutual fund. The fund will hold the investor's shares, handle all the paperwork, and provide much of the needed record keeping. Because of the size of the trades of a mutual fund, the investment company achieves savings on transaction costs, such as brokerage commissions over those the individual investor would have to pay.

Management Companies

Often the management company that runs a fund handles several funds. When this occurs the group of funds is referred to as a family of funds. Thus, within the family of funds the investment company can offer a variety of funds by investment objective, such as aggressive growth, large capitalization growth, balanced, fixed-income, and so on, or by cost structure.

A fee or sales charge is often assessed when a fund is purchased. When this occurs, the fund is referred to as a *front-end* local fund. When the fee is assessed upon redemption of the shares in a mutual fund, the fund is referred to as a *back-end* local fund. Often the "exit" fee is reduced as the investor's holding period increases. For example, the fund may charge a 6 percent load if the fund is held less than a year, but 5 percent if held for two years, and the percentage would decrease in this example 1 percent per year the shares are held. This encourages the investor to leave the funds under the control of the management company for a longer time. Funds also charge *operating expenses.* These include investment advisory fees and administrative expenses. These are usually discussed in terms of a percentage of assets under management, Some funds also charge *services fees.* These fees cover the fund's advertising, distribution, and marketing expenses, and are also a form of commissions paid to brokers called *trail commissions.* These fees are assessed annually, whereas the *back-end* and *front-end* loads are onetime charges.

The investor should carefully consider the nature and extent of fees that the various mutual funds he is considering assess. These fees vary widely among the funds and can significantly impact performance over time. The fees are disclosed in the fund's *prospectus* as are many other facts about the funds, its investment philosophy, and management style.

All investment companies are in business to make money. The investor needs to realize that a no-load fund (which does not charge a front-end load) still has expenses that the investor must pay. Thus, the investor must match the performance objectives of the fund and the way it charges for its services with his own objectives and time horizon for investing in order to make a prudent investment selection.

MONEY-MARKET FUNDS

In the early 1980s high yields prevailed in U.S. government securities, particularly in issues of short-term maturities, and there was uncertainty about the stock market. In addition to government securities of short-term duration, similar high returns prevailed in other types of short-term issues known as *money-market instruments*. Frequently, large dollar amounts are required as minimum purchases for these types of issues. For example, the minimum dollar amount of U.S. Treasury bills that can be purchased is $10,000. Therefore, because of these high yields and because of the often large initial investment required, substantial interest developed in mutual funds that invested entirely in such issues.

These money-market funds represent still another variety of open-end company that the mutual-fund industry has brought to the investor's attention. The industry has continually been on the lookout for new types of funds to market.

MUNICIPAL BOND FUNDS

Municipal bond funds invest in a portfolio consisting entirely of tax-exempt bonds. Therefore, the earnings that are passed on to the investor are totally tax-free to the investor. Prior to 1976, because of the existing tax laws in the United States, these municipal bond funds took the form of so-called *unit trusts*. These unit trusts do not make continuous offerings as do the open-end funds. The units can either be purchased as new funds are formed or they can be purchased in the over-the-counter market after the initial offering of these units is completed. Normally, these units sell on issuance at $1,000 per unit plus accrued interest. The interest on these units is usually paid monthly. The portfolio comprising the unit trust is fixed; that is, it is purchased before the units are sold to the public.

The Tax Reform Act of 1976 changed the previous tax law and allowed an open-end type of company such as a municipal-bond to pass its income on to the shareholder in a tax-free manner. This permitted municipal bond funds that are set up as regular open-end companies to come into existence. The only difference between the municipal-bond fund and the traditional stock open-end company is the portfolio composition. Namely, the portfolio of the municipal-bond is comprised totally of tax-exempt municipal bonds. Statistics on these unit trusts are not included in industry totals of the mutual-fund industry because the unit trusts are considered different from the normal managed investment company. Statistics on the traditional managed investment companies are given later in this chapter.

INDEX FUNDS

Partly because of the overall poor performance of managed funds and the market in general during the late 1960s and early 1970s, and because of a growing awareness of the efficient-market hypothesis and the random-walk theory as outlined in Chapter 16, a new type of fund has become increasingly popular. This new type of fund is called an *index fund.* An index fund consists of a portfolio designed to reflect the composition of some broad-based market index. It does so by holding securities in the same proportion as the index itself. Frequently these index funds are constructed along the line of the S&P 500 Index—that is, the portfolio of the index fund is constructed in exactly the same proportion with respect to dollars involved as the S&P 500 Index. Therefore, by definition, the index fund is constructed to have a beta of 1.0 with respect to the S&P 500 Index if that is the index being emulated. In fact, an ideal index fund would be one holding all available common stocks in exact proportion to their outstanding market value. However, such an ideal fund would actually be impossible to construct and manage. Therefore, one hopes an S&P 500 Index fund will be a good surrogate for this ideal type of fund.[4]

Two other main reasons contribute to the growing interest in index funds. First, the expenses involved in administering index funds are considerably lower than those involved in handling a truly managed portfolio because the construction of the index-fund portfolio is entirely based upon maintaining proportions of the index being followed. As such, considerably lower transaction costs are involved because fewer purchases and sales of securities would take place. Furthermore, there would be much less need for expensive batteries of security analysts and portfolio managers. Thus, the overall administrative expenses would also be reduced. Second, with the passage of the new pension reform law, the investment trust laws surrounding the liability of portfolio managers of pension funds have changed with regard to the risk and return of the portfolio they manage. A discussion of the main changes as they affect portfolio managers is the subject of our next section.

Pension Fund Management and Employee Retirement Income Security Act

A *pension fund* is a plan whereby an employer puts aside funds to provide for periodic payments to employees after they retire. Pension-fund assets represent an extremely large and fast-growing pool of institutional capital.

In 1974 the federal government passed the Employee Retirement Income Security Act (ERISA). This act has had many far-reaching ramifications. Here we are primarily concerned with the impact on pension-fund institutional managers. Many

---

[4]Walker R. Good, Robert Ferguson, and Jack Treynor, "Investor's Guide to the Index Fund Controversy," *Financial Analysts Journal* (November–December 1976), pp. 27–36.

critics have stated that this complex piece of legislation will greatly influence the behavior of institutional portfolio managers and especially pension-fund managers. This act created a federal standard for the legal fiduciary responsibility of the pension-fund manager. It expressly states that the fiduciary must act with care, skill, prudence, and diligence under the circumstances then prevailing that a prudent man acting in a like capacity and familiar with such matters would use in the conduct of an enterprise of a like character and with like aims. The act goes on to say that the fiduciary will be personally liable to make good to the plan any losses resulting from the breach of these responsibilities. The courts have ruled thus far that the fiduciary must produce a reasonable income and must preserve the capital of the fund. In fact, the preservation of capital is the key responsibility. It seems logical, therefore, that an index fund might well be sought after by pension-fund managers in order to escape liability under ERISA. This is because the pension-fund manager might argue that his fund did as well as or no worse than the market as a whole performed over the period in question.

Trust Agreement

Commercial banks frequently offer their services as trustees for the management of an individual's portfolio. The fee charged for this service is generally a percentage of the size of the fund, decreasing with the size of the portfolio.

Generally, the trustee (or trustees) exercises complete discretion over the investments of the fund in a very conservative manner. Complete discretion means that the trustee selects which stocks to buy, at what prices, and the quantity he thinks appropriate, on his own, without consulting the person whose money he is managing. The legal statutes generally apply a Prudent man rule to judge whether proper management has occurred.

A special type of trust that has become popular is the common trust. Common trusts are essentially similar to mutual funds, except that the minimum investment in a common trust is substantially higher than that required in a mutual fund. In a common trust administered by a bank, the monies of a number of investors are commingled and are used to purchase a diversified portfolio of securities. A basic advantage of the common trust is that a more personal relationship exists between the bank and the investor. Furthermore, a common trust is an alternative available to smaller investors because it requires less cost and principal investment than the usual trust arrangement does.

Professional Investment Counsel

The investor who uses a professional investment counsel hires the services of either a bank or an outside investment consultant to advise him on his investment policy. Typically, the investor discusses his objectives with the counsel, and as a result the

investment counselor suggests alternative investment possibilities to the client. (In some cases, the counselor may even have total discretion.) The range of services can vary considerably under this type of arrangement, and consequently, so do the costs; however, the minimum cost of such a personal service is so high as to preclude this investment route for the typical small investor.

ALLEGED ADVANTAGES OF MANAGED PORTFOLIOS

Frequently, investors feel insecure in managing their own investments, because they consider themselves inadequate to perform this delicate task successfully. Often the investor feels he lacks the education, background, time, foresight, resources, and temperament to carry out the proper handling of his portfolio. When this occurs, the logical step is to hire a professional portfolio manager. Most often the source chosen takes the form of a mutual fund or open-end investment company.

The main reasons for selecting an open-end investment company involve the management, diversification, and liquidity aspects of this organization form. Managers trained in the ways of security analysis devote full time to the carrying out of the fund's investment objectives as specified in its prospectus. This permits a constant monitoring of the securities comprising the portfolio. Furthermore, large amounts of money entrusted to the fund enable it to be diversified in investments across industry and security types (that is, common stocks with various prospects, preferred stocks, and bonds) to an extent not possibly achieved by the average investor. Furthermore, these institutions are able to obtain lower brokerage commissions than an individual small investor. This diversification evolves as a result of stated objectives of the fund. The rapid explosion of mutual-fund investing can be seen in Table 20–1. In Table 20–2 we see the split-up in the many types of mutual funds available at the end of 1992. The investor can shop for a fund whose objectives are most in line with his own.

Finally, open-end companies represent a liquid type of investment; that is, shares can be readily converted into cash, because the company stands ready to redeem its outstanding shares. A New York Stock Exchange (NYSE) study released during 1985 revealed that 47 million Americans owned stock investments, and the tendency was for the stock investments to be indirect through investments in mutual funds rather than direct through the selection of individual company shares by the investor. For a discussion of the growing interest in overseas funds see the accompanying box.

Let us examine the record to determine if these alleged advantages have in fact accrued to investors. Because most of the theory surrounding performance measurement, as well as the actual empirical work that has been conducted, has been connected with mutual funds, we will place our emphasis in this area. However, it should be noted that the notion of performance measurement is not something applicable only to open-end investment companies. Performance evaluation is necessary in *all* kinds of portfolios, whether individually or professionally managed.

TABLE 20–1

Growth of Mutual Funds*
($000 Omitted)

YEAR	TOTAL NET ASSETS	GROSS SALES	REDEMPTIONS	NET SALES	REDEMPTION RATE	SHAREHOLDER ACCOUNTS	NUMBER OF FUNDS
1992	$1,054,815,400	$362,478,100	$165,674,900	$196,803,200	17.8%	50,000,000e	2,993
1991	807,000,000	234,454,000	115,414,300	119,039,700	16.9%	45,030,062	2,612
1990	570,743,600	149,512,500	98,250,000	51,261,600	17.5%	39,614,000	2,362
1989	553,861,700	125,711,000	91,655,500	34,055,500	17.9%	36,968,300	2,253
1988	472,296,600	95,292,900	92,474,100	2,818,600	20.0%	36,013,000	2,111
1987	453,842,400	190,628,000	116,224,300	74,403,700	26.5%	36,971,000	1,781
1986	424,792,000	212,847,900	67,012,700	148,835,200	19.8%	29,790,200	1,356
1985	251,695,100	114,313,500	33,763,300	80,550,200	17.4%	19,845,600	1,071
1984	137,126,200	45,856,800	20,030,100	25,826,700	16.0%	14,424,000	820
1983	113,600,000	40,300,000	14,700,000	25,600,000	15.4%	12,065,000	653
1982	76,800,000	15,738,300	7,571,800	8,166,500	11.6%	8,190,300	539
1981	55,207,000	9,710,400	7,469,600	2,240,800	13.2%	7,175,500	486
1980	58,399,621	9,993,744	8,199,983	1,793,761	15.2%	7,325,000	548
1979	49,297,059	7,465,400	8,379,500	(914,000)†	17.8%	7,482,200	446
1978	44,979,675	6,705,299	7,232,420	(527,121)†	16.1%	8,190,551	444
1977	45,049,151	6,399,655	6,026,041	373,614	13.0%	8,515,079	427
1976	47,537,486	4,330,240	6,801,163	(2,470,923)†	15.2%	8,879,413	404
1975	42,178,683	3,307,213	2,686,343	(379,130)†	9.7%	9,712,513	390
1974	34,061,746	3,091,473	3,380,923	(289,450)	8.4%	9,970,439	416
1973	46,518,535	5,359,288	5,651,064	(1,291,766)†	10.6%	10,330,862	421
1972	59,830,646	4,892,502	6,562,876	(1,670,374)†	11.4%	10,635,287	410
1971	55,045,328	5,147,186	4,750,222	396,964	9.3%	10,900,952	392
1970	47,618,100	4,625,802	2,987,572	1,638,230	6.2%	10,690,312	356
1969	48,290,733	6,718,283	3,838,682	3,056,637	7.3%	10,391,534	269
1968	52,677,188	6,819,763	3,661,646	2,981,081	7.9%	9,080,168	240
1967	44,701,302	4,669,575	2,744,197	1,925,378	6.9%	7,904,132	204
1966	34,829,353	4,671,842	2,005,079	2,666,763	5.7%	7,701,656	182
1965	35,220,243	4,358,144	1,962,432	2,395,712	6.1%	6,709,343	170

TABLE 20–1

(continued)

YEAR	TOTAL NET ASSETS	GROSS SALES	REDEMPTIONS	NET SALES	REDEMPTION RATE	SHAREHOLDER ACCOUNTS	NUMBER OF FUNDS
1964	29,116,254	3,402,978	1,874,094	1,528,884	6.9%	6,301,908	159
1963	25,214,436	2,459,105	1,505,335	953,770	6.3%	6,151,935	165
1962	21,270,735	2,699,049	1,122,695	1,576,354	5.1%	5,910,455	169
1961	22,788,812	2,950,860	1,160,357	1,790,503	5.8%	5,319,201	170
1960	17,025,684	2,097,246	841,815	1,255,431	5.1%	4,897,600	161
1959	15,817,962	2,279,982	785,627	1,494,355	5.4%	4,276,077	155
1958	13,242,388	1,619,768	511,263	1,108,505	4.7%	3,630,096	151
1957	8,714,143	1,390,557	406,716	983,841	4.6%	3,110,392	143
1956	9,046,431	1,346,738	432,750	913,988	5.1%	2,518,049	135
1955	7,837,524	1,207,458	442,550	764,908	6.4%	2,085,325	125
1954	6,109,390	862,817	399,702	463,115	7.8%	1,703,846	115
1953	4,146,061	672,005	238,778	433,227	5.9%	1,537,250	110
1952	3,931,407	782,902	196,022	586,880	5.6%	1,359,000	110
1951	3,129,629	674,610	321,550	353,060	11.4%	1,110,432	103
1950	2,530,563	518,811	280,728	238,083	12.5%	938,651	98
1949	1,973,547	385,536	107,587	277,939	6.2%	842,198	91
1948	1,505,762	273,787	127,171	146,616	8.7%	722,118	87
1947	1,409,165	266,924	88,732	178,192	6.5%	672,654	80
1946	1,311,108	370,353	143,612	226,741	11.1%	580,221	74
1945	1,284,185	292,359	109,978	182,381	10.2%	497,875	73
1944	882,191	169,228	70,815	98,413	9.2%	421,675	68
1943	653,653	116,062	51,221	64,841	8.9%	341,435	68
1942	486,850	73,140	25,440	47,700	5.6%	312,609	68
1941	401,611	53,312	45,024	8,288	10.6%	293,251	68
1940	447,959	‡	‡	‡	‡	296,056	68

*Data pertains to conventional fund members of the Investment Company Institute; money market funds not included. Institute "gross sales" figures include the proceeds of initial fund underwritings prior to 1970.

†Net redemptions.

‡Not available.

TABLE 20–2

Classification of Mutual Funds by Type

TYPE OF FUND	NO. OF FUNDS	COMBINED ASSETS
Asset Allocation	30	8,202.9
Balanced	61	24,066.7
Corporate Bond	195	61,087.3
Corporate High Yield	76	32,394.2
Energy/Natural Resources	16	1,510.7
Equity Income	64	22,332.6
Financial Services	9	1,583.3
Flexible Income	54	30,391.4
Gold and Precious Metals	32	2,172.5
Government Mortgage-Backed	74	51,254.7
Government Securities	202	104,780.7
Growth and Current Income	207	135,809.3
Health Care	11	5,131.2
International Bond	70	25,274.2
International Equity	165	41,430.7
Long-Term Growth	363	127,304.5
Maximum Capital Gain	97	57,779.6
Municipal Bond	185	89,076.3
Municipal High Yield	29	21,997.8
Municipal Single State	376	84,214.4
Other	29	1,472.4
Small Company Growth	65	22,907.2
Technology	16	2,976.7
Utilities	27	16,110.3
Taxable Money Market	365	362,500.0
Tax-Free Money Market	178	76,600.0

Based on December 31, 1992, Assets

Taxable Fixed Income 19.5%

Tax-Free Fixed Income 13.8%

Partial Equity 4.4%

Money Market 25.7%

Equity 31.1%

Tax-Free Money Market 5.4%

OVERSEAS FUNDS REMAIN ATTRACTIVE IN '94 BUT INVESTORS SHOULD UNDERSTAND THE PLUG COULD BE PULLED

By Doug Rogers
Investor's Business Daily

American investors have fallen in love with overseas markets, sending a record $23.55 billion abroad in international and global funds this year alone.

Many have been rewarded with handsome returns. Most sectors of international and global mutual funds are up 20% to 40% this year. That doubtless has been responsible for a further opening of the tap.

Monthly purchases, which have been in the low hundreds of millions of dollars through last year, have jumped to the multibillion-dollar dollar level in the second half of this year.

T. Rowe Price International Stock Fund has jumped to $3.7 billion in assets from $1.9 billion, for example. **Franklin International Fund's** assets have leapt to $240 million from $15 million at the end of last year.

"We think the flows overseas will continue because investors are learning that the U.S. isn't the only—or even the best—game in town," said Don Kreuger, a Templeton portfolio manager who runs two Franklin-Templeton Group funds.

He notes that Hong Kong's market, which is up almost 240% form its year-end 1990 level, according to Micropal Inc. figures, is still selling at price-earnings levels two-thirds or three-fourths of U.S. stocks, while the Hong Kong economy is growing at twice the U.S. rate.

Effect On U.S. Market

Some attribute the rush overseas to recent weakness in the U.S. market. "The line of causality is that by the beginning of this year, many people thought U.S. stocks were overvalued and U.S. interest rates could fall no further," said Christian Wignall, chief investment officer at San Francisco-based GT Global Financial Services.

"And as foreign stocks had underperformed the U.S. market for the previous four years, the relative attractiveness seemed to tip in favor of foreign stocks."

Others say U.S. investors wouldn't venture overseas to such a great extent without being confident of the domestic market. "The big inflows to overseas markets were a result of increased confidence in the domestic market and the terrific returns overseas," said Avi Nachmany, analyst at New York-based research firm Strategic Insight.

During the bear market of 1987, purchases of overseas funds decreased more than those of domestic funds, Nachmany notes. "Basically, the concept is, if you don't know what to do, you don't want to send your money far away where there is a higher degree of uncertainty," he said. "Even when there might be some opportunities elsewhere, you just come closer to home."

Kreuger, portfolio manager of **Franklin International Equity** (up 21% year-to-date) and **Franklin Pacific Growth** (up 43%) funds, says the rush overseas doesn't seem to be impinging on the U.S. market, in which the Dow Jones industrial average set a new high only three weeks ago.

"For the month of October, 14% of assets went to global or international funds, but the U.S. market still hit new highs," he said. "So there is enough liquidity to continue to reach new highs."

Kreuger surmises that investors accustomed to the volatility of the Nasdaq market, which is about 2.7% off its high set in mid-October, might feel at home in overseas markets.

Effects Of A U.S. Bear Market

Most agree that a U.S. bear market could lead to a stampede out of such lofty emerging markets as Malaysia and Singapore and even more-developed Hong Kong, possibly trampling shareholders of funds that retain their exposure to various markets, come what may.

U.S. flows overseas are not significant in the world market, but because they have been concentrated in particular stocks in smaller markets, its effect has been magnified, Wignall point out.

"If in 1994 U.S. interest rates rise, and more people realize the economy is very

strong, then it would have a detrimental effect on foreign markets, particularly some of the more thinly traded ones," Wignall said.

Higher deposit rates and corporate growth in the U.S. could cause American investors to bring their money home, he argues. "I think the big surprise for the U.S. investor will be the sheer strength of the U.S. economy," Wingall said.

He's looking for headlines to be boasting of an economy booming at 4% to 4.5% real growth early next year amid falling unemployment and further productivity gains with little or no inflation.

Americans are increasingly buying into industry and academic gospel to diversify overseas. With that they may be becoming more committed to global investing. Strategic Insight's Nachmany says. But he believes that a sharp correction in the domestic market could still spur Americans to reel in their investments.

Kreuger allows that the effect of a U.S. bear market on emerging markets will be a new experience for many portfolio managers and retail investors alike. "During the last bear market, we didn't have a lot of individual investors overseas," he said. "But they are the marginal investors now, providing a lot of liquidity. If they sell, they could drive overseas markets down."

Overall, managers agree that international funds offer a good way to diversify a portfolio to reduce market risk, but many caution that investors should limit their exposure to these markets to the extent they are comfortable with expected volatility.

Source: Investor's Business Daily, Reprinted with permission.

MANAGEMENT-PERFORMANCE EVALUATION

We are interested in discovering if the management of a mutual fund is performing well; that is, has management done better through its selective buying and selling of securities than would have been achieved through merely "buying the market"—picking a large number of securities randomly and holding them throughout the period?

One of the most popular ways of measuring management's performance is by comparing the yields of the managed portfolio with the market or with a random portfolio. The portfolio-yield formula parallels the holding-period-yield formula for stocks that was presented in Chapter 3 and is:

$$\frac{NAV_t + D_t}{NAV_{t-1}} - 1 \qquad\qquad \textbf{(20.1)}$$

where:

NAV_t = per-share net asset value at the end of year t
D_t = the total of all distributions—both income and capital gains—per share during year t
NAV_{t-1} = per-share net asset value at the end of the previous year

TABLE 20–3

Year-by-Year Ranking of Individual Fund Returns

FUND	RETURN ON NET	1951	1952	1953	1954	1955	1956	1957	1958	1959	1960
Keystone Lower Price	18.7	29	1	38	5	3	8	35	1	1	36
T. Rowe Price Growth	18.7	1	33	2	8	14	15	2	25	7	4
Dreyfus	18.4	37	37	14	3	7	11	3	2	3	7
Television Electronic	18.4	21	4	9	2	33	20	16	2	4	20
National Investors Corp.	18.0	3	35	4	19	27	4	5	5	8	1
De Vegh Mutual Fund	17.7	32	4	1	8	14	4	8	15	23	36
Growth Industries	17.0	7	34	14	17	9	9	20	5	6	11
Massachusetts Investors Growth	16.9	5	36	31	11	9	1	23	4	9	4
Franklin Custodian	16.5	26	2	4	13	33	20	16	5	9	4
Investment Co. of America	16.0	21	15	14	11	17	15	23	15	15	15
Chemical Fund Inc.	15.6	1	39	14	27	3	33	1	27	4	23
Founders Mutual	15.6	21	13	25	8	2	20	16	11	13	28
Investment Trust of Boston	15.6	6	3	25	3	14	26	31	20	29	20
American Mutual	15.5	14	13	4	22	14	13	16	25	25	4
Keystone Growth	15.3	29	15	25	1	1	1	39	11	13	38
Keystone High	15.2	10	7	3	27	23	36	5	27	25	11
Aberdeen Fund	15.1	32	23	9	25	9	7	10	27	7	30
Massachusetts Investors Trust	14.8	8	9	14	16	9	15	20	18	32	28
NYSE Market Average*	14.7										
Texas Fund, Inc.	14.6	3	15	9	32	23	26	5	27	37	7
Eaton & Howard Stock	14.4	14	9	4	17	20	15	13	37	29	17
Guardian Mutual	14.4	21	26	25	34	31	29	13	20	15	2
Scudder, Stevens, Clark	14.3	14	23	14	19	27	15	29	9	15	30
Investors Stock Fund	14.2	8	28	21	22	27	20	23	5	29	23
Fidelity Fund, Inc.	14.1	21	26	25	34	31	29	13	20	15	23
Fundamental Investment	13.8	14	15	31	16	9	11	31	18	25	30
Century Shares	13.5	14	28	35	25	3	20	23	31	34	2
Bullock Fund Ltd.	13.5	29	9	21	19	14	9	20	34	34	20
Financial Industries	13.0	26	15	31	13	19	29	34	20	9	35
Group Common Stock	13.0	38	8	25	27	27	33	8	20	34	17
Incorporated Investors	12.9	14	13	37	6	3	13	37	11	18	39
Equity Fund	12.9	14	27	21	32	31	33	13	31	18	23
Selected American Shares	12.8	21	15	21	31	23	20	23	15	32	30
Dividend Shares	12.7	32	7	14	34	20	32	4	37	37	11
General Capital Corp.	12.4	10	28	9	38	35	39	23	34	13	23
Wisconsin Fund	12.3	32	26	4	37	35	38	10	34	18	7
International Resources	12.3	10	37	39	22	35	1	37	39	1	11
Delaware Fund	12.1	36	23	25	27	39	26	29	9	23	30
Hamilton Fund	11.9	38	28	9	34	35	36	10	31	18	17
Colonial Energy	10.9	10	15	35	39	20	4	36	20	39	10

*The NYSE market average represents what a tax-exempt investor could have expected to earn by randomly picking (for example, with a dart) a large number of stocks listed on the NYSE and holding them ten years while reinvesting the dividends. The data were published by L. Fisher and J. Lorie, "Rates of Return on Investments in Common Stock," *Journal of Business* (January 1964), pp. 1–21. *Source:* Eugene F. Fama. "The Behavior of Stock Market Prices," *Journal of Business,* January 1965 (Chicago: University of Chicago Press, January 1965), p. 93.

Thus, if $NAV_t = \$11$, $D_t = \$1$, and $NAV_{t-1} = \$10$, the yield will be:

$$\frac{11 + 1}{10} - 1 = \frac{12}{10} - 1 = 1.2 - 1 = .2, \text{ or } 20\%$$

The two yields (managed portfolio and unmanaged portfolio) calculated by Equation 20.1 are then compared. The portfolio with the highest one-year holding-period yield is by this criterion deemed the better portfolio.[5]

This evaluation implies something about the management of the various portfolios under examination. In Table 20–3, we see the returns on a sample of thirty-nine mutual funds during 1951–60. It is of interest that fewer than half these sample funds were able to earn returns in excess of the 14.7 percent earned by the market (as measured by the NYSE market average). In addition, note how inconsistent the funds' relative rankings were from year to year. However, merely measuring and comparing the returns on a managed and unmanaged portfolio is not enough.

First, if the managed portfolio did better than the unmanaged portfolio, the investor in the mutual fund should not rejoice too soon. He had to pay a management fee as well as suffer a reduction in equity equal to the loading charge (in the case of a load fund). So he must determine if the excess return is sufficient to cover these added expenses he has incurred by purchasing a mutual fund rather than purchasing a diversified portfolio on his own and paying the commissions (assuming he has this option). Second, the investor must determine the relative riskiness of the portfolio under analysis. The managed portfolio could have achieved higher returns than the market or the unmanaged portfolio by taking on considerably more risky investments. It is not surprising under such circumstances for higher returns to occur, for higher returns *should* go along with higher risks. Only after the relative risks of the portfolios have been considered is a comparison of returns meaningful.

Sharpe's Performance Measure for Portfolios

William Sharpe has attempted to get a summary measure of portfolio performance.[6] His measure properly adjusts performance for risk. The Sharpe Index is given by:

$$S_t = \frac{\bar{r}_t - r^*}{\sigma_t} \tag{20.2}$$

---

[5]This is the general formula used by the Arthur Wiesenberger Services, New York. Representative reproductions from this excellent investment service will be presented in a later section of this chapter.

[6]William F. Sharpe, "Mutual Fund Performance," *Journal of Business, Supplement on Security Prices* (January 1966), pp. 119–38.

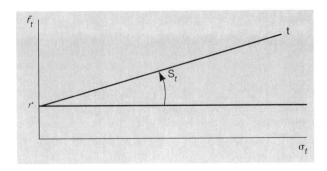

FIGURE 20–1   Graphical Representation of the Sharpe Index, S_t

where:

S_t = Sharpe Index
$\bar{r}_t$ = average return on portfolio t
r^* = riskless rate of interest
σ_t = standard deviation (risk) of the returns of portfolio t

Thus, the Sharpe Index measures the risk premiums of the portfolio (where the risk premium is the excess return required by investors for the assumption of risk) relative to the *total* amount of risk in the portfolio.

Graphically, the index, S_t, measures the slope of the line emanating from the riskless rate outward to the portfolio in question. (See Figure 20–1). Thus, the Sharpe Index summarizes the risk and return of a portfolio in a single measure that categorizes the performance of the fund on a risk-adjusted basis. The larger the S_t, the better the portfolio has performed. For example, assume that portfolio A has an average return of 10 percent with a standard deviation of 2 percent, and portfolio B has an $\bar{r}_B$ of 12 percent and σ_B of 4 percent. Further assume that $r^* = 5$ percent. Then the Sharpe Index (by Equation 20.2) for A equals:

$$\frac{.10 - .05}{.02} = 2.5$$

and for B:

$$\frac{.12 - .05}{.04} = 1.75$$

Thus, A ranked as the better portfolio because its index is higher (2.5 > 1.75), despite the fact that portfolio B had a higher return (12% > 10%). The Sharpe Index and the Treynor Index, which we are about to discuss, have yielded very similar results in actual empirical tests.[7]

[7]*Ibid.*, p. 129.

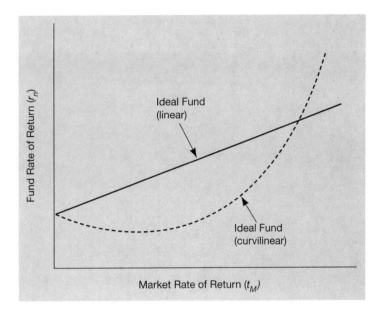

FIGURE 20–2   Treynor's Characteristic Line of an Ideal Fund

Treynor's Performance Measure for Portfolios

A key to understanding Treynor's portfolio-performance measure is the concept of a characteristic line.[8] In Figure 20–2 we see the graphical representation of a characteristic line of an ideal mutual fund.[9] More accurately, this linear representation is an approximation of what is probably more frequently a curvilinear relationship. This curvilinear representation is the dashed line in Figure 20–2. If a line were added to this graph that intersected the origin at a 45° angle, it would represent a portfolio return that was equivalent to the return of the market portfolio. The ideal fund lies above and to the left of the imaginary 45° line. Its return is at all times superior to the one earned on the market portfolio. When the market portfolio earns a low or negative return, the ideal portfolio still earns a positive return; and when the market portfolio earns a positive return, the ideal fund earns an even higher return. To put it more succinctly, the *characteristic line* relates the market return to a specific portfolio return without any direct adjustment for risk. This line can be "fitted" via a least-squares regression such as that involving a single index of a market portfolio. The Sharpe model we discussed in Chapter 17 was a single-index idea.

[8]Jack L. Treynor, "How to Rate Management of Investment Funds," *Harvard Business Review* (January–February 1965), pp. 63–75.

[9]This discussion parallels a comment on Treynor's paper that appears in Kalman J. Cohen and Frederick S. Hammer, *Analytical Methods in Banking* (Homewood, Ill.: Richard D. Irwin, 1966), pp. 374–78.

The slope of the characteristic line is the beta coefficient, a measure of the portfolio's systematic risk. Some people view systematic risk as a type of volatility measure. Thus, by comparing the slopes of characteristic lines, the investor gets an indication of the fund's volatility. The steeper the line, the more systematic risk or volatility the fund possesses. Treynor has proposed incorporating these various concepts into a single index to measure portfolio performance more accurately. This index is given by the following equation:

$$T_n = \frac{\bar{r}_n - r^*}{\beta_n} \tag{20.3}$$

where:

T_n = Treynor Index
$\bar{r}_n$ = average return on portfolio n
r^* = riskless rate of interest
β_n = beta coefficient of portfolio n

Thus, the Treynor Index measures the risk premium of the portfolio, where risk premium equals the difference between the return of the portfolio and the riskless rate. This risk premium is related to the amount of *systematic* risk assumed in the portfolio. So the Treynor Index sums up the risk and return of a portfolio in a single number, while categorizing the performance of the portfolio. Graphically, the index measures the slope of the line emanating outward from the riskless rate to the portfolio under consideration. This is shown in Figure 20–3.

Note the differences in the axes of Figures 20–1 and 20–3. For example, if we assume the same two hypothetical portfolios, A and B, from the previous section, and furthermore assume that the beta coefficients are .5 and 1.0, then the Treynor Index (by Equation 20.3) for A equals:

$$\frac{.10 - .05}{.5} = .10$$

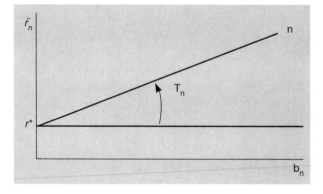

FIGURE 20–3   Graphical Representation of the Treynor Index, T_n

and for B:

$$\frac{.12 - .05}{1.0} = .07$$

Again, portfolio A performed better than B. Both the Sharpe and Treynor Indexes ranked A higher than B despite B's higher return.

Jensen's Performance Measure for Portfolios

The Treynor and Sharpe Indexes provide measures for ranking the *relative perfor-mances* of various portfolios, on a risk-adjusted basis. Jensen attempts to construct a measure of *absolute performance* on a risk-adjusted basis—that is, a definite stan-dard against which performances of various funds can be measured.[10] This standard is based on measuring the "portfolio manager's *predictive ability*—that is, his abil-ity to earn returns through successful prediction of security prices which are higher than those which we would expect *given* the level of riskiness of his portfolio."[11] In other words, we are attempting to determine if more than expected returns are being earned for the portfolio's riskiness.

A simplified version of his basic model is given by:

$$\overline{R}_{jt} - R_{Ft} = \alpha_j + \beta_j (\overline{R}_{Mt} - R_{Ft}) \tag{20.4}$$

where:

$\overline{R}_{jt}$ = average return on portfolio j for period t
R_{Ft} = riskless rate of interest for period t
α_j = intercept that measures the forecasting ability of the portfolio manager
β_j = a measure of systematic risk
$\overline{R}_{Mt}$ = average return of a market portfolio for period t

The reader should note the similarity between this model and the basic Sharpe and Treynor models. An implication of forms of the Sharpe and Treynor models is that the intercept of the line is at the origin. In the Jensen model, the intercept can be at any point, *including* the origin. For example, in Figure 20–4, the upper line repre-sents a case of superior management performance. In fact, α_j = a positive value represents the average superior extra return accruing to that particular portfolio because of superior management talent. The line α_j = 0 indicates neutral perfor-mance by management; that is, management has done as well as an unmanaged market portfolio or a large, randomly selected portfolio managed with a naive buy-

---

[10]The discussion in this section closely parallels the development found in Michael C. Jensen, "The Performance of Mutual Funds in the Period 1945–1964," *Journal of Finance* (May 1968), pp. 389–416.
[11]*Ibid.*, p. 389.

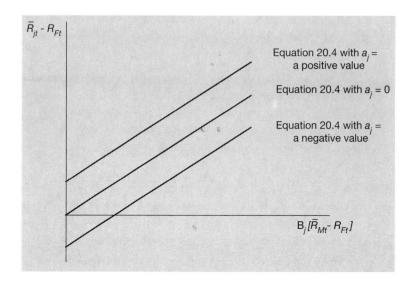

FIGURE 20–4   Graphical Representations of Jensen's Measure of
Management Ability

and-hold strategy. The lower line, α_j = a negative value, indicates inferior management performance, because management did not do as well as an unmanaged portfolio of equal systematic risk. This situation could arise in part because portfolio returns were not sufficient to offset the expenses incurred in the selection and managing process.

The intercept may be interpreted in this fashion by examining Equation 20.4. This occurs because if the portfolio manager is performing in a superior fashion, his intercept will have a positive value because it will indicate that his portfolio is consistently overperforming the overall market. This would happen if he either had superior ability in selecting undervalued securities or had superior ability in recognizing turning points in the market. Conversely, if the intercept were negative, it would indicate that the manager consistently underperformed the overall market. That is, the risk-adjusted returns of his portfolio were consistently lower than the risk-adjusted returns of the market over the same period of time. In Figure 20–5 we show an application of the Jensen approach that has been reported by a major Wall Street brokerage firm.[12]

Other Observations on Performance Measures

Up to this point in our discussion we have discussed only three different approaches to measuring portfolio performance, which all utilize a risk-adjusted return measurement. However, it should be observed that prior to the development

[12]G. Gordon Biggar, Jr., *Risk-Adjusted Portfolio Performance: Its Investment Implications* (New York: Smith, Barney, 1971).

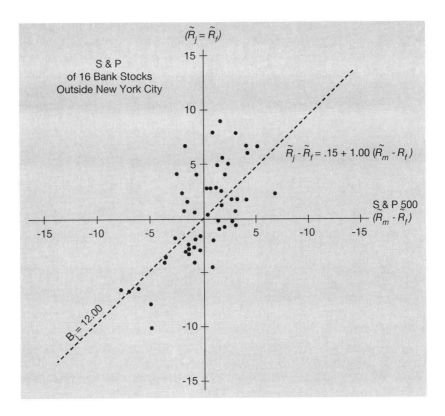

FIGURE 20–5   Application of the Jensen Approach Conducted by Smith, Barney*
(*Source:* G. Gordon Biggar, Jr., *Risk-Adjusted Portfolio Performance: Its Investment Implications* (New York: Smith, Barney, 1971), p. 20.)

*Scatter diagram comparing the volatility of monthly investment returns (less the return on Treasury bills R_f) of the S&P Bank Stock Index of 16 bank stocks outside New York City (vertical axis) and the S&P 500 Stock Index (horizontal axis) during the period January 1967–September 1971. The slope (B_j) of the dashed line measures the degree of volatility of the S&P Bank Stock Index in relation to that of the S&P 500 Stock Index.

of these measures, portfolio managers' performance was measured essentially by observing the rates of return they were able to earn over time. It was necessary for them to demonstrate that their rates of return equaled or exceeded the returns of an unmanaged portfolio—that is, either a portfolio constructed by random choice or a portfolio that represented the returns of the market as a whole and then was held for the duration of the test period. Another possible measurement of portfolio performance is to check if the manager was successful in obtaining a beta for the invested portfolio that was consistent with the objectives of the investor for his individual portfolio. That is, was the level of risk assumed by the portfolio manager consistent with the level of risk that the investor wished to assume? Another factor to consider in portfolio management is to evaluate the portfolio manager's ability to completely diversify away unsystematic risk. Because this nonmarket risk can be completely diversified away in a properly constructed portfolio, an efficient market

will pay only for the market or systematic risk. In fact, several of the performance measurement techniques discussed earlier in this chapter incorporate this belief. Several studies subsequent to those already reported have criticized these models because some felt they introduced various types of bias into the results. However, no clear-cut resolution of the problems has been reached, and we feel that some combination of the models already discussed will yield effective portfolio performance measurement techniques.

EMPIRICAL TESTS OF MUTUAL-FUND PERFORMANCE

We have thus far examined various proposals that have been put forward for mutual-fund performance evaluation. In this section we will examine the results of a number of key empirical tests that have been conducted to answer questions such as, "Can mutual funds do better for me than I can do by myself?" "Are the management and selling fees that mutual funds charge worth the price?" and "Do managed funds adhere to their stated investment objectives?"

We have already seen in Table 20–3 that the answer to the first question above is negative; that is, mutual funds contained in this particular sample did not, on the average, outperform the returns that could be earned by following a naive strategy over the sample period. Because of the growing importance of investment companies in the United States, the Securities and Exchange Commission (SEC) engaged the Wharton School of Finance and Commerce to conduct a study of mutual funds.[13] The investigation found no relationship between the performance of the mutual funds studied and the management fees and sales charges that these funds levied. "The fact that the analysis does not reveal a significant relation between management fees and performance indicates, in other words, that investors cannot assume the existence of higher management fees implies that superior management ability is thereby being purchased by the funds."[14] The study reached a similar conclusion with regard to sales charges.[15]

Jensen concluded that the funds in his study "were *on average* not able to predict security prices well enough to outperform a buy-the-market-and-hold policy, but also that there is very little evidence that any *individual* fund was able to do significantly better than that which we expected from mere random chance." The reader can observe this by noting the preponderance of negative alphas in Figure 20–6. Here we see the frequency distribution of the alphas. These are the intercept values by which Jensen measures the ability of professional fund management. It

---

[13]Irwin Friend, et al., *A Study of Mutual Funds,* prepared for the SEC by the Wharton School of Finance and Commerce, Report of the Committee on Interstate and Foreign Commerce, 87th Cong., 2d sess., August 28, 1962.

[14]Friend et al., "Summary and Conclusions," *ibid.,* as reprinted in Hsiu-Kwang Wu and Alan J. Zakon, *Elements of Investments* (New York: Holt, Rinehart and Winston, 1965), p. 384.

[15]This latter conclusion would seem to imply that the investor might be better advised to invest in a no-load fund than in a load fund.

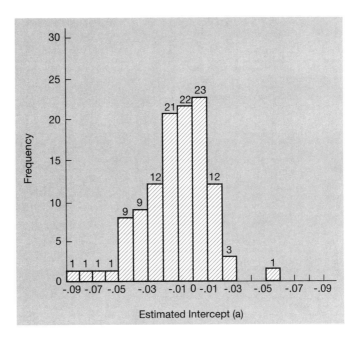

FIGURE 20–6   Frequency Distribution of Estimated Intercepts (*Source:* Michael C. Jensen, "The Performance of Mutual Funds in the Period 1945–1964," *Journal of Finance* (May 1968), pp. 389–416)

should be noted that this distribution is skewed to the left. This indicates the preponderance of alphas less than zero—an indication of negative management worth.[16] Sharpe reached a similar conclusion by comparing the Sharpe Index, the ratio of risk premium to risk, of a number of mutual funds with that of the Dow Jones Industrial Average (DJIA).[17] Perhaps these findings are in part responsible for the growing popularity of funds, such as the Stagecoach Fund, that are constructed in the same proportions as some market index, such as the S&P 500 (an index fund). These funds would perform as well as the market.

The SEC as part of its Institutional Investor Study found some evidence that, in its sample, mutual funds outperformed the market by very small amounts. The SEC study was carried out on a risk-adjusted basis. However, a perhaps more enlightening finding of this same study was that there was no consistency with respect to which funds provided the investor with superior performance. Specifically, during the five-year period 1960–64 the least volatile funds in the sample tended to provide the strongest performance, while during the five-year period 1965–69 the more volatile funds in the sample provided the best performance. Thus the mutual

[16]Jensen found that the funds earned (net of expenses) "about 1.1 percent less per year (compounded continuously) than they should have earned given their level of systematic risk." Jensen, "Performance of Mutual Funds," p. 405.

[17]Sharpe, "Mutual Fund Performance," p. 125.

TABLE 20–4

Comparative Portfolio Performance

QUARTER	S&P 500 STOCK INDEX	PERCENT-AGE OF RETURN	"BEST" PORTFOLIO	PERCENT-AGE OF RETURN
1	98.35	—	100.0	—
2	106.94	8.7	130.1	30.1
3	111.39	4.2	153.1	17.6
4	103.42	−7.2	119.3	−22.0
5	111.32	7.6	132.8	11.2
6	111.83	0.4	138.8	4.5
7	114.77	2.6	139.9	0.7
8	114.07	−0.6	136.6	−2.3
Average		2.24%		5.68%
σ		4.92		15.23
Beta		1.00		2.83

funds in this study demonstrated a considerable lack of consistency in terms of which type of funds provided regular, superior performance.[18]

In general, empirical investigations have found that fund managers are able to assess properly the risks and potential returns associated with alternative investment opportunities and have thus been able to meet their investment objectives fairly well.[19]

EXTENDED EXAMPLE OF PERFORMANCE MEASUREMENT

In Chapters 17 and 18 we introduced a group of stocks from which feasible portfolios were generated. A single "best" portfolio was chosen for holding, unmanaged, for a forward period. Table 20–4 is a listing of the subsequent results for the portfolio, and the S&P 500 Stock Index, a representation of the market portfolio. The data represent the standing of both portfolios at the end of eight subsequent quarters (two years).

The quarterly returns on the two portfolios suggest that the "best" portfolio had an average quarterly return of 5.68 percent; the S&P Index showed an average return of 2.24 percent. At first blush it appears that the "best" portfolio outperformed the "market" by a difference of 3.44 percent per quarter. Let us see how

---

[18]*Institutional Investors Study Report of the Securities and Exchange Commission* (Washington, D.C.: Government Printing Office, 1971), Vol. II.

[19]However, the actual volatility of the portfolio proved to be a better appraisal of the funds' ultimate performance than did the words of management as expressed in their prospectuses. See Irwin Friend, Marshall Blume, and Jean Crockett, *Mutual Funds and Other Institutional Investors* (New York: McGraw-Hill, 1970), p. 150; and Donald E. Farrar, *The Investment Decision under Uncertainty* (Englewood Cliffs, N.J.: Prentice Hall, 1962), p. 73.

these portfolios rank using the Sharpe, Treynor, and Jensen approaches to portfolio evaluation.

The reader should note that our calculation of returns uses only price changes. Dividends are not taken into consideration. The Treasury bill rate (r^*) on a quarterly return basis averaged 1.75 percent over the performance evaluation period.

Sharpe Model

The only inputs needed for the Sharpe model are:

$$r_t = \text{average return on the "best" portfolio}$$

$$r_m = \text{average return on the market portfolio}$$

$$\sigma_t = \text{standard deviation of returns on the "best" portfolio}$$

$$\sigma_m = \text{standard deviation of returns on the market portfolio}$$

For this particular example, the input values can be extracted from Table 20–4. Simply substituting these values into the model we have:

$$S_t = \frac{5.68 - 1.75}{15.23} = .26$$

$$S_m = \frac{2.24 - 1.75}{4.92} = .10$$

The higher reading for the "best" portfolio suggests that it achieved superior excess return-to-risk relative to the market portfolio.

Treynor Model

The Treynor model and that of Sharpe differ only in that Treynor replaces the standard deviation in the denominator with beta. The beta value of the market is, of course, 1.00. The beta coefficient for the "best" portfolio is calculated by performing a simple regression procedure using the returns on the "best" portfolio as the dependent variable and the returns on the market portfolio as the independent variable. This results in a beta for the "best" portfolio of 2.83. The Treynor results are:

$$T_n = \frac{5.68 - 1.75}{2.83} = 1.39$$

$$T_m + \frac{2.24 - 1.75}{1.00} = 0.49$$

Again, the "best" portfolio outranks the market portfolio.

Jensen Model

The implementation of the Jensen model requires that we regress the quarterly differences between portfolio returns and the Treasury bill rate for the "best" portfolio. This gives us the return earned on the portfolio in excess of the risk-free rate. The equation that results for the "best" portfolio is:

$$(r_i - r^*) = 2.55 + 2.83 \, (r_m - r^*)$$

where alpha is equal to 2.55 and beta is 2.83.

The alpha coefficient is the key. This 2.55 percent represents a measure of the bonus performance owing to superior portfolio management.

The equation for the security market line in Chapter 17 is helpful here as a more direct approach to an answer. The equation was:

$$R_i = R_F + \beta_i(R_M - R_F)$$

Using the data at hand we have:

$$R_i = 1.75 + 2.83 \, (2.24 - 1.75)$$

$$= 3.13$$

This is the *expected* return from the portfolio, given the risk-free rate, the portfolio beta, and the return on the market portfolio. Because the actual return on the "best" portfolio was 5.68 percent, the excess earned over the expected return is 2.55 percent (5.68 − 3.13). This is also our alpha from before.

MUTUAL FUNDS AS AN INVESTMENT

Before we leave the subject of mutual funds, several closing remarks are in order. The fact that many of the studies just cited concluded that mutual funds have not performed very admirably does not lead to the seemingly obvious conclusion that mutual funds represent a bad investment outlet. What the studies concluded were that, *on average,* mutual funds included in the various samples did not perform better than a market portfolio or a large randomly selected portfolio bought and held by the investor; however, exceptions to these summary conclusions were found in all cases.[20] Therefore, profitable investment opportunities existed in both the load and no-load areas. Furthermore, it is *impossible* for many investors to assemble a large, diversified portfolio of the kind that seems to do better than or as well as the

---

[20]It is interesting to note that the mediocre performance of mutual funds in general was apparently accomplished with considerably varying portfolios. For an interesting discussion of this, see Lawrence J. Marks, "In Defense of Performance," *Financial Analysts Journal* (November–December 1962), pp. 135–37.

managed portfolios, because of capital limitations and higher commissions that must be paid. Indeed, mutual funds may represent the only opportunity many investors have for investing in an intelligent, diversified fashion in the securities of U.S. corporations.[21]

SOURCES OF INVESTMENT-COMPANY INFORMATION

One of the sources of investment-company information available to the investor is Wiesenberger's *Investment Companies,* issued annually. On Figure 20–7 is typical of the pages that capsulize information about individual funds. As can be seen, the summary contains a history of the fund, statement of objectives, something about its portfolio composition, key statistical data, and the result of a hypothetical $10,000 investment in the fund over a ten-year period. (The information is explained in the margin notes.)

Morningstar through its *Morningstar Mutual Funds* service publishes, in loose-leaf fashion, a vast amount of information on individual funds. This information is also available for direct use in the investor's personal computer. A portion of the information on the funds is updated every other week. An example of a typical sheet from Morningstar is shown in Figure 20–8. The fund is discussed, much historical information is given and analyzed, and the top portfolio holdings are listed. In addition, the service ranks the fund for return, risk, and overall rating.

Forbes, an investment magazine published twice a month, annually rates the performance of investment companies. Its system attempts to incorporate in a summary measure both return and risk considerations. Basically, the approach used is to compare the fund's performance with that of the general market during periods of rising and falling markets. Funds that consistently perform exceptionally well when compared with the market in up markets receive an A+ rating; those that do not do as well receive ratings down to a possible low of D−. In a similar fashion, *Forbes* compares the relative performance of individual funds with the market portfolio in declining markets. Thus each fund receives two ratings—one in up markets, and one in down markets.

From these ratings, the investor gets a rough indication of the potential risks of investing in a given fund, both when investment conditions are favorable and when they are unfavorable. Furthermore, an investor can choose a fund whose performance is in line with his risk preferences. For example, the investor who is very risk-averse will prefer a fund that has performed consistently well in both kinds of markets (probably betas of one or less). On the other hand, a less risk-averse person or a more aggressive investor might prefer a fund that has done exceptionally well in up markets, even if it means assuming exceptional risk if a down market occurs (betas greater than one). Needless to say, it is an ideal portfolio whose performance excels in both rising and falling markets.

---

[21]The reader will recall the advantages of proper Markowitz diversification, as explained in Chapter 17. In addition, it should be pointed out that mutual funds may in fact overdiversify, as noted in Chapter 18.

The annual *Investment Companies Yearbook* is the oldest, largest and most complete fund publication in the industry. Widely regarded as the *"bible"* of the mutual fund industry, the *Yearbook* is used by many firms to train new management candidates. The *Yearbook* provides detailed year-end profiles and summary statistics on over 4,500 funds, including open-end funds, variable annuities and closed-end funds — making it the single most comprehensive source of fund information available anywhere.

The fund's background and basic investment objectives and policies.

General information on the fund's administration and operations.

A full 11-year statistical summary showing changes and trends in assets, portfolio characteristics, expenses and performance.

A risk-to-reward 'scatter graph' shows how the fund compares to its peers and the broader market on a risk-adjusted basis. The vertical axis plot performance (3-year annualized total return) and the horizontal axis plots risk (standard deviation). The fund's position is denoted with a triangle. All other funds in the same investment category are plotted as single dots. The point of intersection of the dashed line represents the plot point of the S&P 500 (for equity funds) or the Lehman Bros. Gov't/Corporate Index (for bond funds). In general the upper left quadrant (high return, low risk) is most desirable, while the lower right (high risk, low return) is least desirable.

CDA Rating

Portfolio characteristics show the fund's 10 largest holdings, the sector breakdown of the portfolio, the average P/E and the market capitalization of the fund.

Shareholder information includes basic information about investing in the fund.

Performance and risk statistics as of the calendar year-end for both the fund and its investment objective category.

Total return performance of a hypothetical $10,000 investment made 10 years ago (or at the fund's inception for funds less than 10 years old) at the current sales charge. Both the staring value and the current value of the original investment are shown at the bottom. The average performance for the objective category is also graphed for comparative purposes.

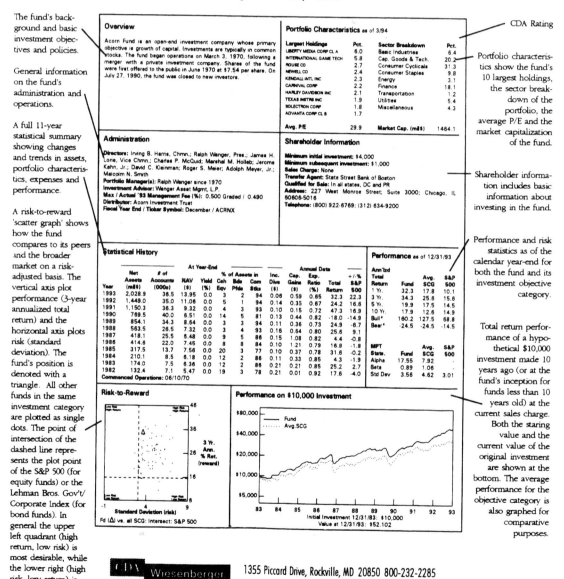

Overview

Acorn Fund is an open-end investment company whose primary objective is growth of capital. Investments are typically in common stocks. The fund began operations on March 3, 1970, following a merger with a private investment company. Shares of the fund were first offered to the public in June 1970 at $7.54 per share. On July 27, 1990, the fund was closed to new investors.

Portfolio Characteristics as of 3/94

Largest Holdings	Pct.	Sector Breakdown	Pct.
LIBERTY MEDIA CORP CL A	6.0	Basic Industries	6.4
INTERNATIONAL GAME TECH	5.8	Cap. Goods & Tech.	20.2
ROUSE CO	2.7	Consumer Cyclicals	31.3
NEWELL CO	2.4	Consumer Staples	9.8
KENDALL INTL INC	2.3	Energy	3.1
CARNIVAL CORP	2.2	Finance	18.1
HARLEY DAVIDSON INC	2.1	Transportation	1.2
TEXAS INSTRS INC	1.9	Utilities	5.4
SOLECTRON CORP	1.8	Miscellaneous	4.3
ADVANTA CORP CL B	1.7		

Avg. P/E 29.9   **Market Cap. (mil$)** 1464.1

Administration

Directors: Irving B. Harris, Chmn.; Ralph Wanger, Pres.; James H. Lorie, Vice Chmn.; Charles P. McQuid; Marshal M. Holleb; Jerome Kahn, Jr.; David C. Kleinman; Roger S. Meier; Adolph Meyer, Jr.; Malcolm N. Smith
Portfolio Manager(s): Ralph Wanger since 1970
Investment Advisor: Wanger Asset Mgmt. L.P.
Max / Actual '93 Management Fee (%): 0.500 Graded / 0.490
Distributor: Acorn Investment Trust
Fiscal Year End / Ticker Symbol: December / ACRNX

Shareholder Information

Minimum initial investment: $4,000
Minimum subsequent investment: $1,000
Sales Charge: None
Transfer Agent: State Street Bank of Boston
Qualified for Sale: In all states, DC and PR
Address: 227 West Monroe Street; Suite 3000; Chicago, IL 60606-5016
Telephone: (800) 922-6769; (312) 634-9200

Statistical History

	Net Assets (mil$)	# of Accounts (000s)	At Year-End NAV ($)	Yield (%)	Cash Equ (%)	% of Assets in Bds Pfds	Com Stks	Inc. Divs ($)	Annual Data Cap. Gains ($)	Exp. Ratio (%)	Total Return	+/-% S&P 500
1993	2,028.9	38.5	13.95	0.0	3	2	94	0.06	0.59	0.65	32.3	22.3
1992	1,449.0	35.0	11.08	0.0	5	1	94	0.14	0.35	0.67	24.2	16.6
1991	1,150.3	36.3	9.32	0.0	4	3	93	0.10	0.15	0.72	47.3	16.9
1990	769.5	40.0	6.51	0.0	14	5	81	0.13	0.44	0.82	-18.0	-14.9
1989	854.1	34.3	8.64	0.0	3	3	94	0.11	0.36	0.73	24.9	-6.7
1988	563.5	26.5	7.32	0.0	3	4	93	0.16	0.64	0.80	25.5	9.1
1987	418.1	25.5	6.48	0.0	9	5	86	0.15	1.08	0.82	4.4	-0.8
1986	414.6	22.0	7.45	0.0	8	8	84	0.10	1.21	0.79	16.8	-1.8
1985	317.5	13.7	6.18	0.0	12	2	86	0.14	0.35	0.78	31.6	-0.2
1984	210.1	8.5	6.36	0.0	20	3	77	0.10	0.33	0.85	4.3	-1.9
1983	174.0	7.5	5.47	0.0	12	2	86	0.21	0.21	0.85	25.2	2.7
1982	132.4	7.1		0.0	19	3	78	0.21	0.01	0.92	17.6	-4.0

Commenced Operations: 06/10/70

Performance as of 12/31/93

Ann'lzd Total Return	Fund	Avg. SCG	S&P 500
1 Yr.	32.3	17.8	10.1
3 Yr.	34.3	25.6	15.6
5 Yr.	19.9	17.5	14.5
10 Yr.	17.9	12.6	14.9
Bull*	160.2	127.5	68.8
Bear*	-24.5	-24.5	-14.5

MPT Stats.	Fund	Avg. SCG	S&P 500
Alpha	17.55	7.92	
Beta	0.89	1.06	
Std Dev	3.56	4.62	3.01

Risk-to-Reward

Fd (Δ) vs. all SCG: Intersect: S&P 500

Performance on $10,000 Investment

Initial Investment 12/31/83: $10,000
Value at 12/31/93: $52,102

FIGURE 20–7 Acorn Fund (*Source:* © 1992 CDA Investment Technologies, 1355 Piccard Drive, Rockville, MD 20850, 800-232-2285.)

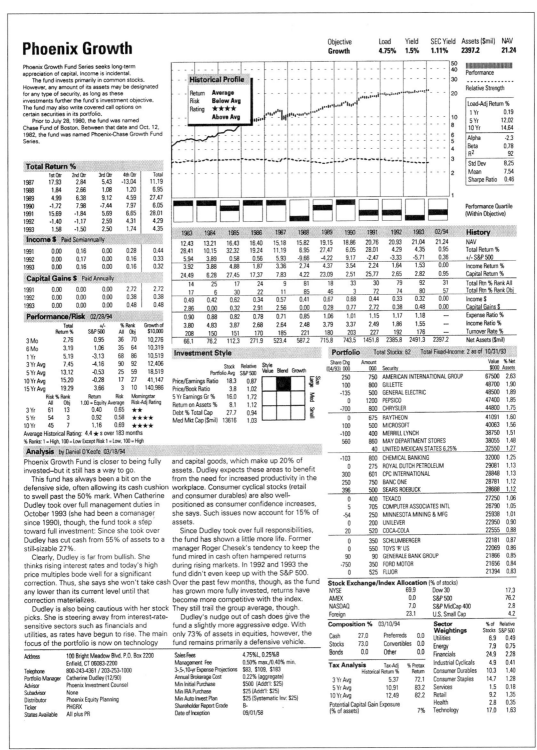

FIGURE 20-8 Sample *Morningstar* Page (*Source: Morningstar Mutual Funds*, 1993.
Reprinted with permission, Morningstar, Inc.)

Money magazine also regularly evaluates various funds. See Figure 20–9 for an example of the kinds of information typically included.

SUMMARY

In this chapter we have examined a number of alternative types of managed portfolios available to the investor. These have included closed-end investment companies, open-end investment companies or mutual funds, dual funds, money market funds, municipal bond unit trusts and funds, index funds, pension funds, ERISA, trust agreements, common trusts, and professional investment counsel. We discussed the characteristics of these alternative investment opportunities, as well as the alleged advantages of such professionally managed portfolios. We analyzed a number of alternative measures of performance evaluation, including the Sharpe, Treynor, and Jensen approaches. Then we reported the results in the summary fashion of a number of key empirical studies of mutual-fund performance. Finally, we concluded with a survey of key sources of information on investment companies.

QUESTIONS AND PROBLEMS

1. Distinguish between closed-end and open-end investment companies.
2. What are the alleged advantages of professionally supervised portfolios? Have empirical tests offered support for these contentions?
3. How can one measure the holding-period yield on a market portfolio?
4. Many people advocate mutual funds for small investors. They suggest that the best strategy for small investors is to buy shares in a good mutual fund and put them away. What do you think of this advice?
5. What is the essential difference between the Sharpe and Treynor Indexes of portfolio performance? Which do you think is preferable? Why?
6. How can the elements of the Sharpe Index be calculated?
7. What is a characteristic line? How can it be determined?
8. What is the meaning of the alpha value in the Jensen model?
9. What are the implications, if any, of the results of studies of mutual-fund performance for the random-walk theory?
10. Why may Sharpe's and Treynor's measures of performance give conflicting performance rankings?
11. Management Capital, Inc. (MCI), manages four mutual funds of American Investors Group (AIG). The funds are balanced, investment growth, fixed income, and variable growth. The data below include annual total return for each fund followed by key statistical measures. The average return on riskless securities during the measurement period was 5 percent per annum.

Twenty Great Funds That Deliver Year After Year

Each of the funds below—half with sales loads, half without—passed the initial selection criteria outlined in the main story by outperforming its category average in 1991 and by finishing in the top 40% of its type over the past three or five years. In addition, each outgunned its group average in at least three of the past five calendar years. Remember, though, that the aggressive funds on the list, however consistent they are compared with their peers, may still be too jumpy for your tastes. So before buying, examine the fund's year-by-year returns and investment approach.

FUND	TYPE	MONEY RISK-ADJUSTED GRADE	% COMPOUND ANNUAL GAIN TO JAN. 1, 1992/QUINTILE			YEARS FUND OUTPERFORMED CATEGORY AVERAGE SINCE 1986	% MAXIMUM INITIAL SALES LOAD	TELEPHONE
			ONE YEAR	THREE YEARS	FIVE YEARS			
GROWTH								
Berger One Hundred	Gro	A	88.8/1	38.3/1	25.5/1	Four	None	800-333-1001
Twentieth Century Ultra	Max	A	86.5/1	40.8/1	27.6/1	Four	None	800-345-2021
Hartwell Emerging Growth	SCG	A	72.5/1	34.9/1	24.9/1	Five	4.75	800-343-2898
AIM Constellation	Max	A	70.4/1	31.2/1	22.0/1	Five	5.50	800-347-1919
INDEX II	Gro	A	58.7/1	31.6/1	24.5/1	Five	5.50	800-443-9975
Alger Small Capitalization	SCG	A	55.3/1	39.8/1	25.9/1	Four	None†	800-992-3863
Janus Fund	Max	A	42.8/1	27.5/1	20.3/1	Five	None	800-525-8983
Delaware Delcap I	Max	A	42.3/2	22.5/1	20.5/1	Five	4.75	800-523-4640
TOTAL RETURN								
Monetta Fund	G&I	A	55.9/1	26.0/1	20.1/1	Four	None	800-666-3882
Selected American	G&I	B	46.3/1	19.1/1	15.6/1	Four	None	800-553-5533
Financial Industrial Income	Eql	A	46.2/1	24.8/1	18.7/1	Four	None	800-525-8085
Kidder Peabody Equity Income	Eql	B	46.0/1	24.3/1	15.1/1	Four	5.75	212-656-1731
Cigna Value	G&I	A	43.5/1	24.3/1	19.7/1	Five	5.00	800-572-4462
CGM Mutual	Bal	B	40.9/1	20.1/1	15.2/1	Four	None	800-345-4048
AIM Charter	G&I	A	37.8/1	27.2/1	18.8/1	Four	5.50	800-347-1919
IDS Equity Plan	G&I	B	32.4/2	18.3/2	14.4/1	Four	5.00	800-328-8300
INTERNATIONAL/GLOBAL								
Oppenheimer Global	Glo	A	27.4/2	19.6/1	15.2/1	Four	5.75	800-525-7048
Harbor International	Intl	—	21.5/1	14.5/1	19.9/1*	Four	None	800-422-1050
Templeton Foreign	Intl	A	18.3/1	14.4/1	17.9/1	Five	8.50	800-237-0738
Scudder Global	Glo	B	17.2/3	14.7/1	13.1/2	Three	None	800-225-2470

*Four-year return; fund not in existence for full five-year period
†Fund may impose back-end load.

FIGURE 20–9 *Money* Magazine's Ranking of Mutual Funds (*Source: Lipper Analytical Services as reported by Money,* February 1992. Reprinted with permission.)

	BALANCED	INVESTMENT GROWTH	FIXED INCOME	VARIABLE GROWTH	DJIA
19X9	−.085	−.117	−.001	.141	−.116
19X8	.028	.032	.056	.035	.077
19X7	.100	.201	.030	.255	.190
19X6	−.093	−.117	−.014	−.101	−.156
19X5	.032	.083	.032	.153	.142
19X4	.096	.123	.045	.113	.187
19X3	.118	.142	.066	.134	.206
19X2	−.072	−.139	.054	−.170	−.076
19X1	.166	.235	.071	.240	.224
Return	.0282	.0403	.0373	.0798	.0654
Variance	.009	.020	.001	.021	.023
Beta	.6207	.9127	.1379	.6991	
Rho	.65	.94	.96	.82	

a. Rank the performance of these portfolios using the Sharpe and Treynor techniques.

b. Consider the Jensen method of ranking portfolios relative to the market. What is the overall performance of each fund relative to the market?

c. Which funds had the most unsystematic risk during the evaluation period? Explain.

12. Suppose that seven portfolios experienced the following results during a ten-year period:

PORTFOLIO	AVERAGE ANNUAL RETURN (%)	STANDARD DEVIATION (%)	CORRELATION WITH THE MARKET
A	15.6	27.0	.81
B	11.8	18.0	.55
C	8.3	15.2	.38
D	19.0	21.2	.75
E	−6.0	4.0	.45
F	23.5	19.3	.63
G	12.1	8.2	.98
Market	13.0	12.0	
Treasury bills	6.0		

a. Rank these portfolios using (i) Sharpe's method, and (ii) Treynor's method.

b. Compare the rankings in part (a) and explain the reasons behind any differences noted.

c. Did any portfolios outperform the market? Why or why not?

13. Under what circumstances might an investor want to switch from an aggressive growth common-stock fund to a money market fund within a family of mutual funds?

14. If you were going to invest for a long period, say a minimum of fifteen years, would you prefer a front-end load fund or a no-load with a high 12b-1 fee? Assume in all other respects the funds are identical. Explain your answer.

C A S E

■

The Parallax Fund

Scott Dunaway is a professional financial planner. His business involves advising clients on comprehensive financial programs including budgeting, tax matters, and investments. Frequently he advises clients on investment vehicles simply by recommending consideration of mutual funds. These are often appropriate for someone who wants to achieve professional management and diversification at a relatively low cost.

The Parallax Fund has recently been brought to his attention by the fund's sponsors, who have attempted to sell the merits of the fund to financial advisers such as Dunaway. In order to carry out a responsible examination, Dunaway has gathered financial information on Parallax as well as several other funds he knows well from past experience.

Exhibit 1 contains comparative annual rates of return on the Parallax Fund, the S&P 500 Stock Index, and U.S. Treasury bills for 1968–82. In Exhibit 2 we present data on five other investment companies for the same period.

EXHIBIT 1

Annual Rates of Return Parallax Fund, S&P 500 Stock Index, U.S. Treasury Bills, 1968–82

YEAR	PARALLAX	S&P 500	TREASURY BILLS
1968	17.1	10.8	5.4
1969	−14.6	−8.5	6.7
1970	1.7	3.5	6.5
1971	8.0	14.1	4.3
1972	11.5	18.7	4.1
1973	−5.8	−14.5	7.0
1974	−15.6	−26.0	7.9
1975	38.5	36.9	5.8
1976	33.2	23.6	5.0
1977	−7.0	−7.2	5.3
1978	2.9	7.4	6.2
1979	27.4	18.2	10.0
1980	23.0	31.5	11.4
1981	−0.6	−4.9	14.1
1982	21.4	20.4	10.7

EXHIBIT 2

Performance Data for Five Investment Companies, 1968–82

	RETURN	STANDARD DEVIATION OF RETURN	BETA	R^2
Classic Fund	1.95	20.03	.983	.819
Foresight Fund	11.57	18.33	.971	.881
Oxford Fund	8.41	22.92	1.169	.816
Epsilon Fund	9.05	24.04	1.226	.816
Tree Top Fund	7.86	15.46	.666	.582

QUESTIONS

1. Calculate the necessary ingredients for the Parallax Fund that are needed for evaluating its performance, using the Sharpe, Treynor, and Jensen performance evaluation techniques.

2. Rank Parallax along with the other five funds in Exhibit 2 according to the Sharpe, Treynor, and Jensen techniques. How do you reconcile any conflicts in rankings?

REFERENCES

BREALEY, RICHARD A. "Portfolio Theory versus Portfolio Practice." *Journal of Portfolio Management* (Summer 1990), pp. 6–10.

CANGETOEG. J., M. LEIBOVITZ, and S. KOGELMAN. "Duration Targeting and the Management of Multiperiod Returns." *Financial Analysts Journal* (September–October 1990), pp. 35–45.

CHANG, E., and W. LEVELLEN. "Market Timing and Mutual Fund Investment Performance." *Journal of Business* (January 1984).

SHANKY, H. "An Update on Mutual Funds: Better Grades." *Journal of Portfolio Management* (Winter 1982), pp. 29–34.

SHILLING, D. G. "Market Timing: Better Than a Buy-and-Hold Strategy." *Financial Analysts Journal* (March–April 1992) pp. 46–50.

VEIT, T., and J. CHENEY. "Are Mutual Funds Market Timers?" *Journal of Portfolio Management* (Winter 1982).

INDEX